C000056919

Collins World Atlas

MINI EDITION

Collins

COLLINS WORLD ATLAS
MINI EDITION

Collins
An imprint of HarperCollins Publishers
Westerhill Road, Bishopbriggs,
Glasgow
G64 2QT

First Published as Collins Mini Atlas of the World 1999
Second edition 2004
Third Edition 2007
Fourth Edition 2009

Fifth Edition 2013
Reprinted 2013

Copyright © HarperCollins Publishers 2012
Maps © Collins Bartholomew Ltd 2012

Printed in Hong Kong

British Library Cataloguing in Publication Data.
A catalogue record for this book is available from the British Library.

ISBN 978-0-00-749228-2
imp 002

All mapping in this atlas is generated from Collins Bartholomew™
digital databases. Collins Bartholomew™, the UK's leading
independent geographical information supplier, can provide a digital,
custom, and premium mapping service to a variety of markets.
For further information:
Tel: +44 (0) 208 307 4515
e-mail: collinsbartholomew@harpercollins.co.uk
or visit our website at: www.collinsbartholomew.com

Follow us on Twitter @collinsmaps

Pages	Title	Scale

GEOGRAPHICAL INFORMATION

Pages	Title	Scale
6–19	**COUNTRIES of the WORLD**	
20–21	**OCEANIA** Physical Features	
22–23	**ASIA** Physical Features	
24–25	**EUROPE** Physical Features	
26–27	**AFRICA** Physical Features	
28–29	**NORTH AMERICA** Physical Features	
30–31	**SOUTH AMERICA** Physical Features	
32–33	**OCEANS and POLES** Physical Features	
34–35	**CLIMATE**	
36–37	**LAND COVER**	
38–39	**POPULATION**	
40–41	**URBANIZATION**	
42–43	**SYMBOLS and ABBREVIATIONS**	

WORLD

Pages	Title	Scale
44–45	**WORLD** Physical Features	1:170 000 000
46–47	**WORLD** Countries	1:170 000 000

OCEANIA

Pages	Title	Scale
48–49	OCEANIA	1:70 000 000
50–51	**AUSTRALIA**	1:25 000 000
52–53	**AUSTRALIA** Southeast	1:10 000 000
54	**NEW ZEALAND**	1:10 000 000

ANTARCTICA

Pages	Title	Scale
55	ANTARCTICA	1:60 000 000

ASIA

Pages	Title	Scale
56–57	ASIA	1:70 000 000
58–59	**SOUTHEAST ASIA**	1:30 000 000
60–61	**MALAYSIA and INDONESIA** West	1:15 000 000
62–63	**CONTINENTAL SOUTHEAST ASIA**	1:15 000 000
64	**PHILIPPINES**	1:15 000 000

CONTENTS

Pages	Title	Scale
65	**NORTH KOREA AND SOUTH KOREA**	1:9 000 000
66–67	**JAPAN**	1:10 000 000
68–69	**CHINA AND MONGOLIA**	1:30 000 000
70–71	**CHINA** Central	1:15 000 000
72–73	**SOUTH ASIA**	1:20 000 000
74–75	**PAKISTAN, INDIA AND BANGLADESH**	1:15 000 000
76–77	**CENTRAL ASIA**	1:20 000 000
78–79	**ARABIAN PENINSULA**	1:15 000 000
80–81	**EAST MEDITERRANEAN**	1:15 000 000
82–83	**RUSSIAN FEDERATION**	1:42 000 000
84–85	EUROPE	1:40 000 000
86–87	**EUROPEAN RUSSIAN FEDERATION**	1:20 000 000
88–89	**NORTHEAST EUROPE**	1:8 000 000
90–91	**UKRAINE AND MOLDOVA**	1:8 000 000
92–93	**SCANDINAVIA AND ICELAND**	1:10 000 000
94–95	**BRITISH ISLES**	1:8 000 000
96	**SCOTLAND**	1:4 000 000
97	**IRELAND**	1:4 000 000
98–99	**ENGLAND AND WALES**	1:4 000 000
100–101	**NORTHWEST EUROPE**	1:4 000 000
102–103	**CENTRAL EUROPE**	1:8 000 000
104–105	**FRANCE AND SWITZERLAND**	1:8 000 000
106–107	**SPAIN AND PORTUGAL**	1:8 000 000
108–109	**ITALY AND THE BALKANS**	1:8 000 000
110–111	**GREECE, ROMANIA AND BULGARIA**	1:8 000 000
112–113	AFRICA	1:60 000 000
114–115	**NORTHWEST AFRICA**	1:26 000 000

CONTENTS

Pages	Title	Scale
116–117	**NORTHEAST AFRICA**	1:26 000 000
118–119	**CENTRAL AFRICA**	1:20 000 000
120–121	**SOUTHERN AFRICA**	1:20 000 000
122–123	**REPUBLIC of SOUTH AFRICA**	1:10 000 000
124–125	NORTH AMERICA	1:70 000 000
126–127	**CANADA**	1:30 000 000
128–129	**CANADA** West	1:15 000 000
130–131	**CANADA** East	1:15 000 000
132–133	**UNITED STATES OF AMERICA**	1:25 000 000
134–135	**USA** West	1:11 000 000
136–137	**USA** North Central	1:11 000 000
138–139	**USA** South Central	1:11 000 000
140–141	**USA** Northeast	1:11 000 000
142–143	**USA** Southeast	1:11 000 000
144–145	**MEXICO**	1:15 000 000
146–147	**CARIBBEAN**	1:20 000 000
148–149	SOUTH AMERICA	1:70 000 000
150–151	**SOUTH AMERICA** North	1:25 000 000
152–153	**SOUTH AMERICA** South	1:25 000 000
154–155	**BRAZIL** Southeast	1:10 000 000
	OCEANS	
156–157	**PACIFIC OCEAN**	1:120 000 000
158	**ATLANTIC OCEAN**	1:120 000 000
159	**INDIAN OCEAN**	1:120 000 000
160	**ARCTIC OCEAN**	1:60 000 000
161–256	INDEX	

AFGHANISTAN
Islamic State of Afghanistan
Capital Kābul

Area sq km	652 225	**Currency**	Afghani
Area sq miles	251 825	**Languages**	Dari, Pashto
Population	32 358 000		(Pashtu), Uzbek,
			Turkmen

ALBANIA
Republic of Albania
Capital Tirana (Tiranë)

Area sq km	28 748	**Currency**	Lek
Area sq miles	11 100	**Languages**	Albanian, Greek
Population	3 216 000		

ALGERIA
People's Democratic Republic of Algeria
Capital Algiers (Alger)

Area sq km	2 381 741	**Currency**	Algerian dinar
Area sq miles	919 595	**Languages**	Arabic, French,
Population	35 980 000		Berber

ANDORRA
Principality of Andorra
Capital Andorra la Vella

Area sq km	465	**Currency**	Euro
Area sq miles	180	**Languages**	Catalan, Spanish,
Population	86 000		French

ANGOLA
Republic of Angola
Capital Luanda

Area sq km	1 246 700	**Currency**	Kwanza
Area sq miles	481 354	**Languages**	Portuguese,
Population	19 618 000		Bantu, local lang.

ANTIGUA AND BARBUDA
Capital St John's

Area sq km	442	**Currency**	East Caribbean
Area sq miles	171		dollar
Population	90 000	**Languages**	English, creole

ARGENTINA
Argentine Republic
Capital Buenos Aires

Area sq km	2 766 889	**Currency**	Argentinian peso
Area sq miles	1 068 302	**Languages**	Spanish, Italian,
Population	40 765 000		Amerindian lang.

ARMENIA
Republic of Armenia
Capital Yerevan (Erevan)

Area sq km	29 800	**Currency**	Dram
Area sq miles	11 506	**Languages**	Armenian, Yezidi
Population	3 100 000		

AUSTRALIA
Commonwealth of Australia
Capital Canberra

Area sq km	7 692 024	**Currency**	Australian dolla
Area sq miles	2 969 907	**Languages**	English, Italian
Population	22 606 000		Greek

AUSTRIA
Republic of Austria
Capital Vienna (Wien)

Area sq km	83 855	**Currency**	Euro
Area sq miles	32 377	**Languages**	German,
Population	8 413 000		Croatian, Turki

AZERBAIJAN
Republic of Azerbaijan
Capital Baku (Bakı)

Area sq km	86 600	**Currency**	Azerbaijani ma
Area sq miles	33 436	**Languages**	Azeri, Armenian
Population	9 306 000		Russian, Lezgia

THE BAHAMAS
Commonwealth of The Bahamas
Capital Nassau

Area sq km	13 939	**Currency**	Bahamian dolla
Area sq miles	5 382	**Languages**	English, creole
Population	347 000		

BAHRAIN
Kingdom of Bahrain
Capital Manama (Al Manāmah)

Area sq km	691	**Currency**	Bahraini dinar
Area sq miles	267	**Languages**	Arabic, English
Population	1 324 000		

BANGLADESH
People's Republic of Bangladesh
Capital Dhaka (Dacca)

Area sq km	143 998	**Currency**	Taka
Area sq miles	55 598	**Languages**	Bengali, Englisł
Population	150 494 000		

BARBADOS
Capital Bridgetown

Area sq km	430	**Currency**	Barbados dolla
Area sq miles	166	**Languages**	English, creole
Population	274 000		

BELARUS
Republic of Belarus
Capital Minsk

Area sq km	207 600	**Currency**	Belarus rouble
Area sq miles	80 155	**Languages**	Belorussian,
Population	9 559 000		Russian

BELGIUM
Kingdom of Belgium
Capital Brussels (Bruxelles)

Area sq km	30 520	**Currency**	Euro
Area sq miles	11 784	**Languages**	Dutch (Flemish),
Population	10 754 000		French (Walloon),
			German

BELIZE
Capital Belmopan

Area sq km	22 965	**Currency**	Belize dollar
Area sq miles	8 867	**Languages**	English, Spanish,
Population	318 000		Mayan, creole

BENIN
Republic of Benin
Capital Porto-Novo

Area sq km	112 620	**Currency**	CFA franc*
Area sq miles	43 483	**Languages**	French, Fon,
Population	9 100 000		Yoruba, Adja,
			local lang.

BHUTAN
Kingdom of Bhutan
Capital Thimphu

Area sq km	46 620	**Currency**	Ngultrum,
Area sq miles	18 000		Indian rupee
Population	738 000	**Languages**	Dzongkha,
			Nepali, Assamese

BOLIVIA
Plurinational State of Bolivia
Capital La Paz/Sucre

Area sq km	1 098 581	**Currency**	Boliviano
Area sq miles	424 164	**Languages**	
Population	10 088 000		Spanish, Quechua,
			Aymara

BOSNIA-HERZEGOVINA
Republic of Bosnia and Herzegovina
Capital Sarajevo

Area sq km	51 130	**Currency**	Marka
Area sq miles	19 741	**Languages**	Bosnian, Serbian,
Population	3 752 000		Croatian

BOTSWANA
Republic of Botswana
Capital Gaborone

Area sq km	581 370	**Currency**	Pula
Area sq miles	224 468	**Languages**	English, Setswana,
Population	2 031 000		Shona, local lang.

BRAZIL
Federative Republic of Brazil
Capital Brasília

Area sq km	8 514 879	**Currency**	Real
Area sq miles	3 287 613	**Languages**	Portuguese
Population	196 655 000		

BRUNEI
State of Brunei Darussalam
Capital Bandar Seri Begawan

Area sq km	5 765	**Currency**	Brunei dollar
Area sq miles	2 226	**Languages**	Malay, English,
Population	406 000		Chinese

BULGARIA
Republic of Bulgaria
Capital Sofia (Sofiya)

Area sq km	110 994	**Currency**	Lev
Area sq miles	42 855	**Languages**	Bulgarian,
Population	7 446 000		Turkish, Romany,
			Macedonian

BURKINA FASO
Democratic Republic of Burkina Faso
Capital Ouagadougou

Area sq km	274 200	**Currency**	CFA franc*
Area sq miles	105 869	**Languages**	French, Moore
Population	16 968 000		(Mossi), Fulani,
			local lang.

BURUNDI
Republic of Burundi
Capital Bujumbura

Area sq km	27 835	**Currency**	Burundian franc
Area sq miles	10 747	**Languages**	Kirundi (Hutu,
Population	8 575 000		Tutsi), French

CAMBODIA
Kingdom of Cambodia
Capital Phnom Penh

Area sq km	181 035	**Currency**	Riel
Area sq miles	69 884	**Languages**	Khmer,
Population	14 305 000		Vietnamese

CAMEROON
Republic of Cameroon
Capital Yaoundé

Area sq km	475 442	**Currency**	CFA franc*
Area sq miles	183 569	**Languages**	French, English,
Population	20 030 000		Fang, Bamileke,
			local lang.

CANADA
Capital Ottawa

Area sq km	9 984 670	**Currency**	Canadian dollar
Area sq miles	3 855 103	**Languages**	English, French
Population	34 350 000		

CAPE VERDE
Republic of Cape Verde
Capital Praia

Area sq km	4 033	**Currency**	Cape Verde
Area sq miles	1 557		escudo
Population	501 000	**Languages**	Portuguese, creole

CENTRAL AFRICAN REPUBLIC
Capital Bangui

Area sq km	622 436	**Currency**	CFA franc*
Area sq miles	240 324	**Languages**	French, Sango,
Population	4 487 000		Banda, Baya,
			local lang.

CHAD
Republic of Chad
Capital Ndjamena

Area sq km	1 284 000	**Currency**	CFA franc*
Area sq miles	495 755	**Languages**	Arabic, French,
Population	11 525 000		Sara, local lang.

CHILE
Republic of Chile
Capital Santiago

Area sq km	756 945	**Currency**	Chilean peso
Area sq miles	292 258	**Languages**	Spanish,
Population	17 270 000		Amerindian lang.

CHINA
People's Republic of China
Capital Beijing (Peking)

Area sq km	9 584 492	**Currency**	Yuan, HK dollar,
Area sq miles	3 700 593		Macao pataca
Population	1 332 079 000	**Languages**	Mandarin
			(Putonghua),
			Hsiang,Cantonese,
			Wu, regional lang.

COLOMBIA
Republic of Colombia
Capital Bogotá

Area sq km	1 141 748	**Currency**	Colombian pe...
Area sq miles	440 831	**Languages**	Spanish,
Population	46 927 000		Amerindian la...

COMOROS
United Republic of the Comoros
Capital Moroni

Area sq km	1 862	**Currency**	Comoros franc
Area sq miles	719	**Languages**	Shikomor
Population	754 000		(Comorian),
			French, Arabic

CONGO
Republic of the Congo
Capital Brazzaville

Area sq km	342 000	**Currency**	CFA franc*
Area sq miles	132 047	**Languages**	French, Kongo...
Population	4 140 000		Monokutuba,
			local lang.

CONGO, DEMOCRATIC REPUBLIC OF THE
Capital Kinshasa

Area sq km	2 345 410	**Currency**	Congolese fran...
Area sq miles	905 568	**Languages**	French, Linga...
Population	67 758 000		Swahili, Kongo
			local lang.

COSTA RICA
Republic of Costa Rica
Capital San José

Area sq km	51 100	**Currency**	Costa Rican co...
Area sq miles	19 730	**Languages**	Spanish
Population	4 727 000		

CÔTE D'IVOIRE (IVORY COAST)
Republic of Côte d'Ivoire
Capital Yamoussoukro

Area sq km	322 463	**Currency**	CFA franc*
Area sq miles	124 504	**Languages**	French, creole,
Population	20 153 000		Akan, local lan...

CROATIA
Republic of Croatia
Capital Zagreb

Area sq km	56 538	**Currency**	Kuna
Area sq miles	21 829	**Languages**	Croatian, Serb...
Population	4 396 000		

CUBA
Republic of Cuba
Capital Havana (La Habana)

Area sq km	110 860	**Currency**	Cuban peso
Area sq miles	42 803	**Languages**	Spanish
Population	11 254 000		

CYPRUS
Republic of Cyprus
Capital Nicosia (Lefkosia)

Area sq km	9 251	**Currency**	Euro
Area sq miles	3 572	**Languages**	Greek, Turkish,
Population	1 117 000		English

CZECH REPUBLIC
Capital Prague (Praha)

Area sq km	78 864	**Currency**	Czech koruna
Area sq miles	30 450	**Languages**	Czech, Moravian,
Population	10 534 000		Slovakian

DENMARK
Kingdom of Denmark
Capital Copenhagen (København)

Area sq km	43 075	**Currency**	Danish krone
Area sq miles	16 631	**Languages**	Danish
Population	5 573 000		

DJIBOUTI
Republic of Djibouti
Capital Djibouti

Area sq km	23 200	**Currency**	Djibouti franc
Area sq miles	8 958	**Languages**	Somali, Afar,
Population	906 000		French, Arabic

DOMINICA
Commonwealth of Dominica
Capital Roseau

Area sq km	750	**Currency**	East Caribbean
Area sq miles	290		dollar
Population	68 000	**Languages**	English, creole

DOMINICAN REPUBLIC
Capital Santo Domingo

Area sq km	48 442	**Currency**	Dominican peso
Area sq miles	18 704	**Languages**	Spanish, creole
Population	10 056 000		

EAST TIMOR (Timor-Leste)
Democratic Republic of Timor-Leste
Capital Dili

Area sq km	14 874	**Currency**	US dollar
Area sq miles	5 743	**Languages**	Portuguese, Tetun,
Population	1 154 000		English

ECUADOR
Republic of Ecuador
Capital Quito

Area sq km	272 045	**Currency**	US dollar
Area sq miles	105 037	**Languages**	Spanish, Quechua,
Population	14 666 000		Amerindian lang.

EGYPT
Arab Republic of Egypt
Capital Cairo (Al Qāhirah)

Area sq km	1 000 250	**Currency**	Egyptian pound
Area sq miles	386 199	**Languages**	Arabic
Population	82 537 000		

EL SALVADOR
Republic of El Salvador
Capital San Salvador

Area sq km	21 041	**Currency**	El Salvador colón,
Area sq miles	8 124		US dollar
Population	6 227 000	**Languages**	Spanish

EQUATORIAL GUINEA
Republic of Equatorial Guinea
Capital Malabo

Area sq km	28 051	**Currency**	CFA franc*
Area sq miles	10 831	**Languages**	Spanish, French,
Population	720 000		Fang

ERITREA
State of Eritrea
Capital Asmara

Area sq km	117 400	**Currency**	Nakfa
Area sq miles	45 328	**Languages**	Tigrinya, Tigre
Population	5 415 000		

ESTONIA
Republic of Estonia
Capital Tallinn

Area sq km	45 200	**Currency**	Euro
Area sq miles	17 452	**Languages**	Estonian, Russian
Population	1 341 000		

ETHIOPIA
Federal Democratic Republic of Ethiopia
Capital Addis Ababa (Ādīs Ābeba)

Area sq km	1 133 880
Area sq miles	437 794
Population	84 734 000

Currency Birr
Languages Oromo, Amharic, Tigrinya, local lang.

FIJI
Republic of Fiji
Capital Suva

Area sq km	18 330
Area sq miles	7 077
Population	868 000

Currency Fiji dollar
Languages English, Fijian, Hindi

FINLAND
Republic of Finland
Capital Helsinki (Helsingfors)

Area sq km	338 145
Area sq miles	130 559
Population	5 385 000

Currency Euro
Languages Finnish, Swedish

FRANCE
French Republic
Capital Paris

Area sq km	543 965
Area sq miles	210 026
Population	63 126 000

Currency Euro
Languages French, Arabic

GABON
Gabonese Republic
Capital Libreville

Area sq km	267 667
Area sq miles	103 347
Population	1 534 000

Currency CFA franc*
Languages French, Fang, local lang.

THE GAMBIA
Republic of The Gambia
Capital Banjul

Area sq km	11 295
Area sq miles	4 361
Population	1 776 000

Currency Dalasi
Languages English, Malinke, Fulani, Wolof

Gaza
Semi-autonomous region
Capital Gaza

Area sq km	363
Area sq miles	140
Population	1 535 120

Currency Israeli shekel
Languages Arabic

GEORGIA
Republic of Georgia
Capital Tbilisi

Area sq km	69 700
Area sq miles	26 911
Population	4 329 000

Currency Lari
Languages Georgian, Russ Armenian, Aze Ossetian, Abkh

GERMANY
Federal Republic of Germany
Capital Berlin

Area sq km	357 022
Area sq miles	137 849
Population	82 163 000

Currency Euro
Languages German, Turkis

GHANA
Republic of Ghana
Capital Accra

Area sq km	238 537
Area sq miles	92 100
Population	24 966 000

Currency Cedi
Languages English, Hausa, Akan, local lang

GREECE
Hellenic Republic
Capital Athens (Athina)

Area sq km	131 957
Area sq miles	50 949
Population	11 390 000

Currency Euro
Languages Greek

GRENADA
Capital St George's

Area sq km	378
Area sq miles	146
Population	105 000

Currency East Caribbean dollar
Languages English, creole

GUATEMALA
Republic of Guatemala
Capital Guatemala City

Area sq km	108 890
Area sq miles	42 043
Population	14 757 000

Currency Quetzal, US dol.
Languages Spanish, Mayan lang.

GUINEA
Republic of Guinea
Capital Conakry

Area sq km	245 857
Area sq miles	94 926
Population	10 222 000

Currency Guinea franc
Languages French, Fulani, Malinke, local lang.

GUINEA-BISSAU
Republic of Guinea-Bissau
Capital Bissau

Area sq km	36 125	**Currency** CFA franc*
Area sq miles	13 948	**Languages** Portuguese,
Population	1 547 000	crioulo, local lang.

GUYANA
Co-operative Republic of Guyana
Capital Georgetown

Area sq km	214 969	**Currency** Guyana dollar
Area sq miles	83 000	**Languages** English, creole,
Population	756 000	Amerindian lang.

HAITI
Republic of Haiti
Capital Port-au-Prince

Area sq km	27 750	**Currency** Gourde
Area sq miles	10 714	**Languages** French, creole
Population	10 124 000	

HONDURAS
Republic of Honduras
Capital Tegucigalpa

Area sq km	112 088	**Currency** Lempira
Area sq miles	43 277	**Languages** Spanish,
Population	7 755 000	Amerindian lang.

HUNGARY
Capital Budapest

Area sq km	93 030	**Currency** Forint
Area sq miles	35 919	**Languages** Hungarian
Population	9 966 000	

ICELAND
Republic of Iceland
Capital Reykjavík

Area sq km	102 820	**Currency** Icelandic króna
Area sq miles	39 699	**Languages** Icelandic
Population	324 000	

INDIA
Republic of India
Capital New Delhi

Area sq km	3 064 898	**Currency** Indian rupee
Area sq miles	1 183 364	**Languages** Hindi, English,
Population	1 241 492 000	many regional lang.

INDONESIA
Republic of Indonesia
Capital Jakarta

Area sq km	1 919 445	**Currency** Rupiah
Area sq miles	741 102	**Languages** Indonesian,
Population	242 326 000	local lang.

IRAN
Islamic Republic of Iran
Capital Tehrān

Area sq km	1 648 000	**Currency** Iranian rial
Area sq miles	636 296	**Languages** Farsi, Azeri,
Population	74 799 000	Kurdish, regional lang.

IRAQ
Republic of Iraq
Capital Baghdād

Area sq km	438 317	**Currency** Iraqi dinar
Area sq miles	169 235	**Languages** Arabic, Kurdish,
Population	32 665 000	Turkmen

IRELAND
Capital Dublin (Baile Átha Cliath)

Area sq km	70 282	**Currency** Euro
Area sq miles	27 136	**Languages** English, Irish
Population	4 526 000	

ISRAEL
State of Israel
Capital Jerusalem* (Yerushalayim) (El Quds)

Area sq km	20 770	**Currency** Shekel
Area sq miles	8 019	**Languages** Hebrew, Arabic
Population	7 562 000	

* De facto capital. Disputed.

ITALY
Italian Republic
Capital Rome (Roma)

Area sq km	301 245	**Currency** Euro
Area sq miles	116 311	**Languages** Italian
Population	60 789 000	

JAMAICA
Capital Kingston

Area sq km	10 991	**Currency** Jamaican dollar
Area sq miles	4 244	**Languages** English, creole
Population	2 751 000	

JAPAN
Capital Tōkyō

Area sq km	377 727	Currency Yen
Area sq miles	145 841	Languages Japanese
Population	126 497 000	

JORDAN
Hashemite Kingdom of Jordan
Capital 'Ammān

Area sq km	89 206	Currency Jordanian dinar
Area sq miles	34 443	Languages Arabic
Population	6 330 000	

KAZAKHSTAN
Republic of Kazakhstan
Capital Astana (Akmola)

Area sq km	2 717 300	Currency Tenge
Area sq miles	1 049 155	Languages Kazakh, Russian, Ukrainian, German, Uzbek, Tatar
Population	16 207 000	

KENYA
Republic of Kenya
Capital Nairobi

Area sq km	582 646	Currency Kenyan shilling
Area sq miles	224 961	Languages Swahili, English, local lang.
Population	41 610 000	

KIRIBATI
Republic of Kiribati
Capital Bairiki

Area sq km	717	Currency Australian dollar
Area sq miles	277	Languages Gilbertese, English
Population	101 000	

KOSOVO
Republic of Kosovo
Capital Prishtinë (Priština)

Area sq km	10 908	Currency Euro
Area sq miles	4 212	Languages Albanian, Serbian
Population	2 180 686	

KUWAIT
State of Kuwait
Capital Kuwait (Al Kuwayt)

Area sq km	17 818	Currency Kuwaiti dinar
Area sq miles	6 880	Languages Arabic
Population	2 818 000	

KYRGYZSTAN
Kyrgyz Republic
Capital Bishkek (Frunze)

Area sq km	198 500	Currency Kyrgyz som
Area sq miles	76 641	Languages Kyrgyz, Russian, Uzbek
Population	5 393 000	

LAOS
Lao People's Democratic Republic
Capital Vientiane (Viangchan)

Area sq km	236 800	Currency Kip
Area sq miles	91 429	Languages Lao, local lang.
Population	6 288 000	

LATVIA
Republic of Latvia
Capital Rīga

Area sq km	64 589	Currency Lats
Area sq miles	24 938	Languages Latvian, Russian
Population	2 243 000	

LEBANON
Republic of Lebanon
Capital Beirut (Beyrouth)

Area sq km	10 452	Currency Lebanese poun
Area sq miles	4 036	Languages Arabic, Armenia French
Population	4 259 000	

LESOTHO
Kingdom of Lesotho
Capital Maseru

Area sq km	30 355	Currency Loti, S. African rand
Area sq miles	11 720	Languages Sesotho, English Zulu
Population	2 194 000	

LIBERIA
Republic of Liberia
Capital Monrovia

Area sq km	111 369	Currency Liberian dollar
Area sq miles	43 000	Languages English, creole, local lang.
Population	4 129 000	

LIBYA
Capital Tripoli (Ṭarābulus)

Area sq km	1 759 540	Currency Libyan dinar
Area sq miles	679 362	Languages Arabic, Berber
Population	6 423 000	

LIECHTENSTEIN
Principality of Liechtenstein
Capital Vaduz

Area sq km	160	Currency Swiss franc
Area sq miles	62	Languages German
Population	36 000	

LITHUANIA
Republic of Lithuania
Capital Vilnius

Area sq km	65 200	**Currency**	Litas
Area sq miles	25 174	**Languages**	Lithuanian,
Population	3 307 000		Russian, Polish

LUXEMBOURG
Grand Duchy of Luxembourg
Capital Luxembourg

Area sq km	2 586	**Currency**	Euro
Area sq miles	998	**Languages**	Letzeburgish,
Population	516 000		German, French

MACEDONIA (F.Y.R.O.M.)
Republic of Macedonia
Capital Skopje

Area sq km	25 713	**Currency**	Macedonian denar
Area sq miles	9 928	**Languages**	Macedonian,
Population	2 064 000		Albanian, Turkish

MADAGASCAR
Republic of Madagascar
Capital Antananarivo

Area sq km	587 041	**Currency**	Malagasy franc
Area sq miles	226 658		Malagasy ariary
Population	21 315 000	**Languages**	Malagasy, French

MALAWI
Republic of Malawi
Capital Lilongwe

Area sq km	118 484	**Currency**	Malawian kwacha
Area sq miles	45 747	**Languages**	Chichewa,
Population	15 381 000		English, local lang.

MALAYSIA
Federation of Malaysia
Capital Kuala Lumpur/Putrajaya

Area sq km	332 965	**Currency**	Ringgit
Area sq miles	128 559	**Languages**	Malay, English,
Population	28 859 000		Chinese, Tamil,
			local lang.

MALDIVES
Republic of the Maldives
Capital Male

Area sq km	298	**Currency**	Rufiyaa
Area sq miles	115	**Languages**	Divehi
Population	320 000		(Maldivian)

MALI
Republic of Mali
Capital Bamako

Area sq km	1 240 140	**Currency**	CFA franc*
Area sq miles	478 821	**Languages**	French, Bambara,
Population	15 840 000		local lang.

MALTA
Republic of Malta
Capital Valletta

Area sq km	316	**Currency**	Euro
Area sq miles	122	**Languages**	Maltese, English
Population	418 000		

MARSHALL ISLANDS
Republic of the Marshall Islands
Capital Delap-Uliga-Djarrit

Area sq km	181	**Currency**	US dollar
Area sq miles	70	**Languages**	English,
Population	55 000		Marshallese

MAURITANIA
Islamic Arab and African Rep. of Mauritania
Capital Nouakchott

Area sq km	1 030 700	**Currency**	Ouguiya
Area sq miles	397 955	**Languages**	Arabic, French,
Population	3 542 000		local lang.

MAURITIUS
Republic of Mauritius
Capital Port Louis

Area sq km	2 040	**Currency**	Mauritius rupee
Area sq miles	788	**Languages**	English, creole,
Population	1 307 000		Hindi, Bhojpurī,
			French

MEXICO
United Mexican States
Capital Mexico City

Area sq km	1 972 545	**Currency**	Mexican peso
Area sq miles	761 604	**Languages**	Spanish,
Population	114 793 000		Amerindian lang.

MICRONESIA, FEDERATED STATES OF
Capital Palikir

Area sq km	701	**Currency**	US dollar
Area sq miles	271	**Languages**	English, Chuukese,
Population	112 000		Pohnpeian,
			local lang.

MOLDOVA
Republic of Moldova
Capital Chișinău (Kishinev)

Area sq km	33 700	**Currency**	Moldovan leu
Area sq miles	13 012	**Languages**	Romanian,
Population	3 545 000		Ukrainian,
			Gagauz, Russian

MONACO
Principality of Monaco
Capital Monaco-Ville

Area sq km	2	**Currency**	Euro
Area sq miles	1	**Languages**	French,
Population	35 000		Monégasque,
			Italian

MONGOLIA
Capital Ulan Bator (Ulaanbaatar)

Area sq km	1 565 000	**Currency**	Tugrik (tögrög)
Area sq miles	604 250	**Languages**	Khalka
Population	2 800 000		(Mongolian),
			Kazakh,
			local lang.

MONTENEGRO
Republic of Montenegro
Capital Podgorica

Area sq km	13 812	**Currency**	Euro
Area sq miles	5 333	**Languages**	Serbian
Population	632 000		(Montenegrin),
			Albanian

MOROCCO
Kingdom of Morocco
Capital Rabat

Area sq km	446 550	**Currency**	Moroccan dirham
Area sq miles	172 414	**Languages**	Arabic, Berber,
Population	32 273 000		French

MOZAMBIQUE
Republic of Mozambique
Capital Maputo

Area sq km	799 380	**Currency**	Metical
Area sq miles	308 642	**Languages**	Portuguese,
Population	23 930 000		Makua, Tsonga,
			local lang.

MYANMAR (Burma)
Republic of the Union of Myanmar
Capital Nay Pyi Taw

Area sq km	676 577	**Currency**	Kyat
Area sq miles	261 228	**Languages**	Burmese, Shan,
Population	48 337 000		Karen, local lang.

NAMIBIA
Republic of Namibia
Capital Windhoek

Area sq km	824 292	**Currency**	Namibian doll
Area sq miles	318 261	**Languages**	English, Afrika
Population	2 324 000		German, Ovan
			local lang.

NAURU
Republic of Nauru
Capital Yaren

Area sq km	21	**Currency**	Australian doll
Area sq miles	8	**Languages**	Nauruan, Engl
Population	10 000		

NEPAL
Federal Democratic Republic of Nepal
Capital Kathmandu

Area sq km	147 181	**Currency**	Nepalese rupee
Area sq miles	56 827	**Languages**	Nepali, Maithi
Population	30 486 000		Bhojpuri, Engl
			local lang.

NETHERLANDS
Kingdom of the Netherlands
Capital Amsterdam/The Hague ('s-Graven

Area sq km	41 526	**Currency**	Euro
Area sq miles	16 033	**Languages**	Dutch, Frisian
Population	16 665 000		

NEW ZEALAND
Capital Wellington

Area sq km	270 534	**Currency**	New Zealand
Area sq miles	104 454		dollar
Population	4 415 000	**Languages**	English, Maori

NICARAGUA
Republic of Nicaragua
Capital Managua

Area sq km	130 000	**Currency**	Córdoba
Area sq miles	50 193	**Languages**	Spanish,
Population	5 870 000		Amerindian lar

NIGER
Republic of Niger
Capital Niamey

Area sq km	1 267 000	**Currency**	CFA franc*
Area sq miles	489 191	**Languages**	French, Hausa,
Population	16 069 000		Fulani, local lar

NIGERIA
Federal Republic of Nigeria
Capital Abuja

Area sq km	923 768	**Currency**	Naira
Area sq miles	356 669	**Languages**	English, Hausa, Yoruba, Ibo, Fulani, local lang.
Population	162 471 000		

NORTH KOREA
Democratic People's Republic of Korea
Capital P'yŏngyang

Area sq km	120 538	**Currency**	North Korean won
Area sq miles	46 540	**Languages**	Korean
Population	24 451 000		

NORWAY
Kingdom of Norway
Capital Oslo

Area sq km	323 878	**Currency**	Norwegian krone
Area sq miles	125 050	**Languages**	Norwegian
Population	4 925 000		

OMAN
Sultanate of Oman
Capital Muscat (Masqat)

Area sq km	309 500	**Currency**	Omani riyal
Area sq miles	119 499	**Languages**	Arabic, Baluchi, Indian lang.
Population	2 846 000		

PAKISTAN
Islamic Republic of Pakistan
Capital Islamabad

Area sq km	803 940	**Currency**	Pakistani rupee
Area sq miles	310 403	**Languages**	Urdu, Punjabi, Sindhi, Pashto (Pashtu), English, Balochi
Population	176 745 000		

PALAU
Republic of Palau
Capital Melekeok (Ngerulmud)

Area sq km	497	**Currency**	US dollar
Area sq miles	192	**Languages**	Palauan, English
Population	21 000		

PANAMA
Republic of Panama
Capital Panama City

Area sq km	77 082	**Currency**	Balboa
Area sq miles	29 762	**Languages**	Spanish, English, Amerindian lang.
Population	3 571 000		

PAPUA NEW GUINEA
Independent State of Papua New Guinea
Capital Port Moresby

Area sq km	462 840	**Currency**	Kina
Area sq miles	178 704	**Languages**	English, Tok Pisin (creole), local lang.
Population	7 014 000		

PARAGUAY
Republic of Paraguay
Capital Asunción

Area sq km	406 752	**Currency**	Guaraní
Area sq miles	157 048	**Languages**	Spanish, Guaraní
Population	6 568 000		

PERU
Republic of Peru
Capital Lima

Area sq km	1 285 216	**Currency**	Nuevo sol
Area sq miles	496 225	**Languages**	Spanish, Quechua, Aymara
Population	29 400 000		

PHILIPPINES
Republic of the Philippines
Capital Manila

Area sq km	300 000	**Currency**	Philippine peso
Area sq miles	115 831	**Languages**	English, Filipino, Tagalog, Cebuano, local lang.
Population	94 852 000		

POLAND
Polish Republic
Capital Warsaw (Warszawa)

Area sq km	312 683	**Currency**	Złoty
Area sq miles	120 728	**Languages**	Polish, German
Population	38 299 000		

PORTUGAL
Portuguese Republic
Capital Lisbon (Lisboa)

Area sq km	88 940	**Currency**	Euro
Area sq miles	34 340	**Languages**	Portuguese
Population	10 690 000		

QATAR
State of Qatar
Capital Doha (Ad Dawḥah)

Area sq km	11 437	**Currency**	Qatari riyal
Area sq miles	4 416	**Languages**	Arabic
Population	1 870 000		

ROMANIA
Capital Bucharest (Bucureşti)

Area sq km	237 500	**Currency**	Romanian leu
Area sq miles	91 699	**Languages**	Romanian,
Population	21 436 000		Hungarian

RUSSIAN FEDERATION
Capital Moscow (Moskva)

Area sq km	17 075 400	**Currency**	Russian rouble
Area sq miles	6 592 849	**Languages**	Russian, Tatar,
Population	142 836 000		Ukrainian,
			local lang.

RWANDA
Republic of Rwanda
Capital Kigali

Area sq km	26 338	**Currency**	Rwandan franc
Area sq miles	10 169	**Languages**	Kinyarwanda,
Population	10 943 000		French, English

ST KITTS AND NEVIS
Federation of St Kitts and Nevis
Capital Basseterre

Area sq km	261	**Currency**	East Caribbean
Area sq miles	101		dollar
Population	53 000	**Languages**	English, creole

ST LUCIA
Capital Castries

Area sq km	616	**Currency**	East Caribbean
Area sq miles	238		dollar
Population	176 000	**Languages**	English, creole

ST VINCENT AND THE GRENADINES
Capital Kingstown

Area sq km	389	**Currency**	East Caribbean
Area sq miles	150		dollar
Population	109 000	**Languages**	English, creole

SAMOA
Independent State of Samoa
Capital Apia

Area sq km	2 831	**Currency**	Tala
Area sq miles	1 093	**Languages**	Samoan, English
Population	184 000		

SAN MARINO
Republic of San Marino
Capital San Marino

Area sq km	61	**Currency**	Euro
Area sq miles	24	**Languages**	Italian
Population	32 000		

SÃO TOMÉ AND PRÍNCIPE
Democratic Rep. of São Tomé and Prínc
Capital São Tomé

Area sq km	964	**Currency**	Dobra
Area sq miles	372	**Languages**	Portuguese, creo
Population	169 000		

SAUDI ARABIA
Kingdom of Saudi Arabia
Capital Riyadh (Ar Riyāḍ)

Area sq km	2 200 000	**Currency**	Saudi Arabian
Area sq miles	849 425		riyal
Population	28 083 000	**Languages**	Arabic

SENEGAL
Republic of Senegal
Capital Dakar

Area sq km	196 720	**Currency**	CFA franc*
Area sq miles	75 954	**Languages**	French, Wolof,
Population	12 768 000		Fulani, local lan

SERBIA
Republic of Serbia
Capital Belgrade (Beograd)

Area sq km	77 453	**Currency**	Serbian dinar,
Area sq miles	29 904	**Languages**	Serbian,
Population	7 306 677		Hungarian

SEYCHELLES
Republic of Seychelles
Capital Victoria

Area sq km	455	**Currency**	Seychelles rupe
Area sq miles	176	**Languages**	English, French
Population	87 000		creole

SIERRA LEONE
Republic of Sierra Leone
Capital Freetown

Area sq km	71 740	**Currency**	Leone
Area sq miles	27 699	**Languages**	English, creole,
Population	5 997 000		Mende, Temne,
			local lang.

SINGAPORE
Republic of Singapore
Capital Singapore

Area sq km	639	**Currency**	Singapore dolla
Area sq miles	247	**Languages**	Chinese, Englis
Population	5 188 000		Malay, Tamil

SLOVAKIA
Slovak Republic
Capital Bratislava

Area sq km	49 035	**Currency** Euro
Area sq miles	18 933	**Languages** Slovak,
Population	5 472 000	Hungarian, Czech

SLOVENIA
Republic of Slovenia
Capital Ljubljana

Area sq km	20 251	**Currency** Euro
Area sq miles	7 819	**Languages** Slovene, Croatian,
Population	2 035 000	Serbian

SOLOMON ISLANDS
Capital Honiara

Area sq km	28 370	**Currency** Solomon Islands
Area sq miles	10 954	dollar
Population	552 000	**Languages** English, creole,
		local lang.

SOMALIA
Somali Republic
Capital Mogadishu (Muqdisho)

Area sq km	637 657	**Currency** Somali shilling
Area sq miles	246 201	**Languages** Somali, Arabic
Population	9 557 000	

SOUTH AFRICA, REPUBLIC OF
Capital Pretoria (Tshwane)/Cape Town

Area sq km	1 219 090	**Currency** Rand
Area sq miles	470 693	**Languages** Afrikaans,
Population	50 460 000	English, nine
		official local lang.

SOUTH KOREA
Republic of Korea
Capital Seoul (Sŏul)

Area sq km	99 274	**Currency** South Korean
Area sq miles	38 330	won
Population	48 391 000	**Languages** Korean

SOUTH SUDAN
Republic of South Sudan
Capital Juba

Area sq km	644 329	**Currency** South Sudan
Area sq miles	248 775	pound
Population	8 260 490	**Languages** English, Arabic,
		Dinka, Nuer,
		local lang.

SPAIN
Kingdom of Spain
Capital Madrid

Area sq km	504 782	**Currency** Euro
Area sq miles	194 897	**Languages** Spanish (Castilian),
Population	46 455 000	Catalan, Galician,
		Basque

SRI LANKA
Democratic Socialist Republic of Sri Lanka
Capital Sri Jayewardenepura Kotte

Area sq km	65 610	**Currency** Sri Lankan rupee
Area sq miles	25 332	**Languages** Sinhalese,
Population	21 045 000	Tamil, English

SUDAN
Republic of the Sudan
Capital Khartoum

Area sq km	1 861 484	**Currency** Sudanese pound
Area sq miles	718 725	(Sudani)
Population	36 371 510	**Languages** Arabic, Dinka,
		Nubian, Beja,
		Nuer, local lang.

SURINAME
Republic of Suriname
Capital Paramaribo

Area sq km	163 820	**Currency** Suriname guilder
Area sq miles	63 251	**Languages** Dutch,
Population	529 000	Surinamese,
		English, Hindi

SWAZILAND
Kingdom of Swaziland
Capital Mbabane

Area sq km	17 364	**Currency** Emalangeni,
Area sq miles	6 704	South African
Population	1 203 000	rand
		Languages Swazi, English

SWEDEN
Kingdom of Sweden
Capital Stockholm

Area sq km	449 964	**Currency** Swedish krona
Area sq miles	173 732	**Languages** Swedish
Population	9 441 000	

SWITZERLAND
Swiss Confederation
Capital Bern (Berne)

Area sq km	41 293	**Currency** Swiss franc
Area sq miles	15 943	**Languages** German, French,
Population	7 702 000	Italian, Romansch

SYRIA
Syrian Arab Republic
Capital Damascus (Dimashq)

Area sq km	185 180	**Currency**	Syrian pound
Area sq miles	71 498	**Languages**	Arabic, Kurdish,
Population	20 766 000		Armenian

TAIWAN
Republic of China
Capital Taibei

Area sq km	36 179	**Currency**	Taiwan dollar
Area sq miles	13 969	**Languages**	Mandarin
Population	23 164 000		(Putonghua), Min,
			Hakka, local lang.

The People's Republic of China claims Taiwan as its 23rd province.

TAJIKISTAN
Republic of Tajikistan
Capital Dushanbe

Area sq km	143 100	**Currency**	Somoni
Area sq miles	55 251	**Languages**	Tajik, Uzbek,
Population	6 977 000		Russian

TANZANIA
United Republic of Tanzania
Capital Dodoma

Area sq km	945 087	**Currency**	Tanzanian shilling
Area sq miles	364 900	**Languages**	Swahili, English,
Population	46 218 000		Nyamwezi,
			local lang.

THAILAND
Kingdom of Thailand
Capital Bangkok (Krung Thep)

Area sq km	513 115	**Currency**	Baht
Area sq miles	198 115	**Languages**	Thai, Lao,
Population	69 519 000		Chinese, Malay,
			Mon-Khmer lang.

TOGO
Republic of Togo
Capital Lomé

Area sq km	56 785	**Currency**	CFA franc*
Area sq miles	21 925	**Languages**	French, Ewe,
Population	6 155 000		Kabre, local lang.

TONGA
Kingdom of Tonga
Capital Nuku'alofa

Area sq km	748	**Currency**	Pa'anga
Area sq miles	289	**Languages**	Tongan, English
Population	105 000		

TRINIDAD AND TOBAGO
Republic of Trinidad and Tobago
Capital Port of Spain

Area sq km	5 130	**Currency**	Trinidad and
Area sq miles	1 981		Tobago dollar
Population	1 346 000	**Languages**	English, creole,
			Hindi

TUNISIA
Republic of Tunisia
Capital Tunis

Area sq km	164 150	**Currency**	Tunisian dinar
Area sq miles	63 379	**Languages**	Arabic, French
Population	10 594 000		

TURKEY
Republic of Turkey
Capital Ankara

Area sq km	779 452	**Currency**	Lira
Area sq miles	300 948	**Languages**	Turkish, Kurdish
Population	73 640 000		

TURKMENISTAN
Republic of Turkmenistan
Capital Aşgabat (Ashkhabad)

Area sq km	488 100	**Currency**	Turkmen manat
Area sq miles	188 456	**Languages**	Turkmen, Uzbek,
Population	5 105 000		Russian

TUVALU
Capital Vaiaku

Area sq km	25	**Currency**	Australian dollar
Area sq miles	10	**Languages**	Tuvaluan, English
Population	10 000		

UGANDA
Republic of Uganda
Capital Kampala

Area sq km	241 038	**Currency**	Ugandan shilling
Area sq miles	93 065	**Languages**	English, Swahili,
Population	34 509 000		Luganda,
			local lang.

UKRAINE
Capital Kiev (Kyiv)

Area sq km	603 700	**Currency**	Hryvnia
Area sq miles	233 090	**Languages**	Ukrainian,
Population	45 190 000		Russian

UNITED ARAB EMIRATES
Federation of Emirates
Capital Abu Dhabi (Abū Ȥaby)

Area sq km	77 700	**Currency**	UAE dirham
Area sq miles	30 000	**Languages**	Arabic, English
Population	7 891 000		

UNITED KINGDOM
United Kingdom of Great Britain and
Northern Ireland
Capital London

Area sq km	243 609	**Currency**	Pound sterling
Area sq miles	94 058	**Languages**	English, Welsh,
Population	62 417 000		Gaelic

UNITED STATES OF AMERICA
Capital Washington D.C.

Area sq km	9 826 635	**Currency**	US dollar
Area sq miles	3 794 085	**Languages**	English, Spanish
Population	313 085 000		

URUGUAY
Oriental Republic of Uruguay
Capital Montevideo

Area sq km	176 215	**Currency**	Uruguayan peso
Area sq miles	68 037	**Languages**	Spanish
Population	3 380 000		

UZBEKISTAN
Republic of Uzbekistan
Capital Tashkent

Area sq km	447 400	**Currency**	Uzbek som
Area sq miles	172 742	**Languages**	Uzbek, Russian,
Population	27 760 000		Tajik, Kazakh

VANUATU
Republic of Vanuatu
Capital Port Vila

Area sq km	12 190	**Currency**	Vatu
Area sq miles	4 707	**Languages**	English,
Population	246 000		Bislama (creole),
			French

VATICAN CITY
Vatican City State or Holy See
Capital Vatican City

Area sq km	0.5	**Currency**	Euro
Area sq miles	0.2	**Languages**	Italian
Population	800		

VENEZUELA
Bolivarian Republic of Venezuela
Capital Caracas

Area sq km	912 050	**Currency**	Bolívar fuerte
Area sq miles	352 144	**Languages**	Spanish,
Population	29 437 000		Amerindian lang.

VIETNAM
Socialist Republic of Vietnam
Capital Ha Nôi (Hanoi)

Area sq km	329 565	**Currency**	Dong
Area sq miles	127 246	**Languages**	Vietnamese, Thai,
Population	88 792 000		Khmer, Chinese,
			local lang.

West Bank
Disputed territory

Area sq km	5 860	**Currency**	Jordanian dinar,
Area sq miles	2 263		Israeli shekel
Population	2 513 283	**Languages**	Arabic, Hebrew

Western Sahara
Disputed territory (Morocco)
Capital Laâyoune

Area sq km	266 000	**Currency**	Moroccan dirham
Area sq miles	102 703	**Languages**	Arabic
Population	548 000		

YEMEN
Republic of Yemen
Capital Șan'ā'

Area sq km	527 968	**Currency**	Yemeni riyal
Area sq miles	203 850	**Languages**	Arabic
Population	24 800 000		

ZAMBIA
Republic of Zambia
Capital Lusaka

Area sq km	752 614	**Currency**	Zambian kwacha
Area sq miles	290 586	**Languages**	English, Bemba,
Population	13 475 000		Nyanja, Tonga,
			local lang.

ZIMBABWE
Republic of Zimbabwe
Capital Harare

Area sq km	390 759	**Currency**	Zimbabwean
Area sq miles	150 873		dollar (suspended)
Population	12 754 000	**Languages**	English, Shona,
			Ndebele

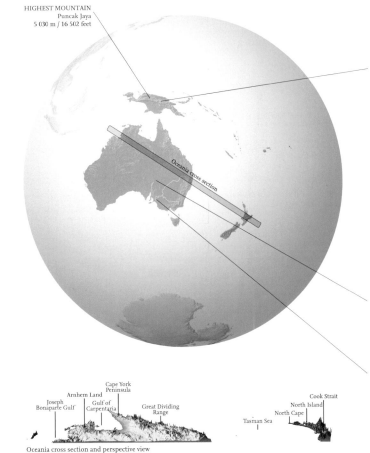

Total Land Area 8 844 516 sq km / 3 414 868 sq miles
(includes New Guinea and Pacific Island nations)

HIGHEST MOUNTAIN
Puncak Jaya
5 030 m / 16 502 feet

Oceania cross section

Oceania cross section and perspective view

Joseph
Bonaparte Gulf

Arnhem Land

Gulf of
Carpentaria

Cape York
Peninsula

Great Dividing
Range

Tasman Sea

North Cape

North Island

Cook Strait

HIGHEST MOUNTAINS	metres	feet	Map page
Puncak Jaya, Indonesia	5 030	16 502	59 D3
Puncak Trikora, Indonesia	4 730	15 518	59 D3
Puncak Mandala, Indonesia	4 700	15 420	59 D3
Puncak Yamin, Indonesia	4 595	15 075	—
Mt Wilhelm, Papua New Guinea	4 509	14 793	59 D3
Mt Kubor, Papua New Guinea	4 359	14 301	—

LARGEST ISLAND
New Guinea
808 510 sq km /
312 166 sq miles

LARGEST ISLANDS	sq km	sq miles	Map page
New Guinea	808 510	312 166	59 D3
South Island, New Zealand	151 215	58 384	54 B2
North Island, New Zealand	115 777	44 701	54 B1
Tasmania	67 800	26 178	51 D4

LONGEST RIVERS	km	miles	Map page
Murray-Darling	3 672	2 282	52 B2
Darling	2 844	1 767	52 B2
Murray	2 375	1 476	52 B3
Murrumbidgee	1 485	923	52 B2
Lachlan	1 339	832	53 C2
Cooper Creek	1 113	692	52 B1

LARGEST LAKES	sq km	sq miles	Map page
Lake Eyre	0–8 900	0–3 436	52 A1
Lake Torrens	0–5 780	0–2 232	52 A1

LARGEST LAKE AND LOWEST POINT
Lake Eyre
0–8 900 sq km / 0–3 436 sq miles
16 m / 53 feet below sea level

LONGEST RIVER AND
LARGEST DRAINAGE BASIN
Murray-Darling
3 672 km / 2 282 miles
1 058 000 sq km / 409 000 sq miles

Total Land Area 45 036 492 sq km / 17 388 589 sq miles

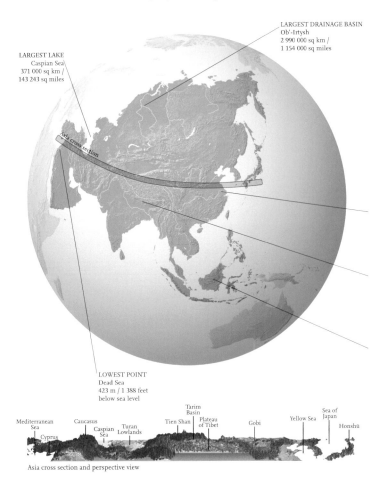

LARGEST DRAINAGE BASIN
Ob'-Irtysh
2 990 000 sq km /
1 154 000 sq miles

LARGEST LAKE
Caspian Sea
371 000 sq km /
143 243 sq miles

LOWEST POINT
Dead Sea
423 m / 1 388 feet
below sea level

Mediterranean Sea | Cyprus | Caucasus | Caspian Sea | Turan Lowlands | Tien Shan | Tarim Basin | Plateau of Tibet | Gobi | Yellow Sea | Sea of Japan | Honshū

Asia cross section and perspective view

HIGHEST MOUNTAINS	metres	feet	Map page
Mt Everest (Sagarmatha/ Qomolangma Feng), China/Nepal	8 848	29 028	75 C2
K2 (Qogir Feng), China/Pakistan	8 611	28 251	74 B1
Kangchenjunga, India/Nepal	8 586	28 169	75 C2
Lhotse, China/Nepal	8 516	27 939	—
Makalu, China/Nepal	8 463	27 765	—
Cho Oyu, China/Nepal	8 201	26 906	—

LARGEST ISLANDS	sq km	sq miles	Map page
Borneo	745 561	287 861	61 C1
Sumatra (Sumatera)	473 606	182 859	60 A1
Honshū	227 414	87 805	67 B3
Celebes (Sulawesi)	189 216	73 056	58 C3
Java (Jawa)	132 188	51 038	61 B2
Luzon	104 690	40 421	64 B1

LONGEST RIVER
Yangtze (Chang Jiang)
6 380 km /
3 965 miles

LONGEST RIVERS	km	miles	Map page
Yangtze (Chang Jiang)	6 380	3 965	70 C2
Ob'-Irtysh	5 568	3 460	86 F2
Yenisey-Angara-Selenga	5 550	3 449	83 H3
Yellow (Huang He)	5 464	3 395	70 B2
Irtysh	4 440	2 759	86 F2
Mekong	4 425	2 750	63 B2

HIGHEST MOUNTAIN
Mt Everest
8 848 m / 29 028 feet

LARGEST LAKES	sq km	sq miles	Map page
Caspian Sea	371 000	143 243	81 C1
Lake Baikal (Ozero Baykal)	30 500	11 776	69 D1
Lake Balkhash (Ozero Balkash)	17 400	6 718	77 D2
Aral Sea (Aral'skoye More)	17 158	6 625	76 B2
Ysyk-Köl	6 200	2 394	77 D2

LARGEST ISLAND
Borneo
745 561 sq km /
287 861 sq miles

Total Land Area 9 908 599 sq km / 3 825 710 sq miles

LARGEST ISLAND
Great Britain
218 476 sq km /
84 354 sq miles

Europe cross section

HIGHEST MOUNTAIN
El'brus
5 642 m / 18 510 feet

Europe cross section and perspective view

Cordillera
Cantabrica

Land's
End

Bay of
Biscay

Pyrenees

Massif
Central

Alps

Adriatic Sea

Carpathian
Mountains

Black Sea

Crimea

Sea
of Azov

Caucasus

HIGHEST MOUNTAINS	metres	feet	Map pages
El'brus, Russian Federation	5 642	18 510	87 D4
Gora Dykh-Tau, Russian Federation	5 204	17 073	—
Shkhara, Georgia/Russian Federation	5 201	17 063	—
Kazbek, Georgia/Russian Federation	5 047	16 558	76 A2
Mont Blanc, France/Italy	4 810	15 781	105 D2
Dufourspitze, Italy/Switzerland	4 634	15 203	—

LARGEST ISLANDS	sq km	sq miles	Map pages
Great Britain	218 476	84 354	95 C3
Iceland	102 820	39 699	92 A3
Ireland	83 045	32 064	97 C2
Ostrov Severnyy (part of Novaya Zemlya)	47 079	18 177	86 E1
Spitsbergen	37 814	14 600	82 C1

LONGEST RIVER AND
LARGEST DRAINAGE BASIN
Volga
3 688 km / 2 292 miles
1 380 000 sq km / 533 000 sq miles

LONGEST RIVERS	km	miles	Map pages
Volga	3 688	2 292	89 F2
Danube	2 850	1 771	110 A1
Dnieper	2 285	1 420	91 C2
Kama	2 028	1 260	86 E3
Don	1 931	1 200	89 E3
Pechora	1 802	1 120	86 E2

LARGEST LAKE AND LOWEST POINT
Caspian Sea
371 000 sq km / 143 243 sq miles
28m / 92 feet below sea level

LARGEST LAKES	sq km	sq miles	Map pages
Caspian Sea	371 000	143 243	81 C1
Lake Ladoga (Ladozhskoye Ozero)	18 390	7 100	86 C2
Lake Onega (Onezhskoye Ozero)	9 600	3 707	86 C2
Vänern	5 585	2 156	93 F4
Rybinskoye Vodokhranilishche	5 180	2 000	89 E2

Total Land Area 30 343 578 sq km / 11 715 655 sq miles

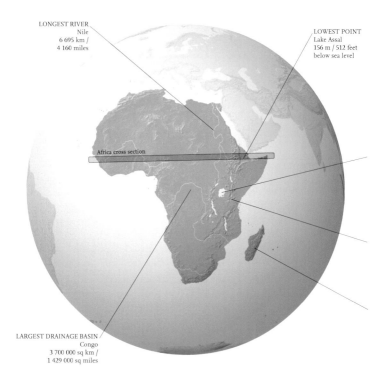

LONGEST RIVER
Nile
6 695 km /
4 160 miles

LOWEST POINT
Lake Assal
156 m / 512 feet
below sea level

Africa cross section

LARGEST DRAINAGE BASIN
Congo
3 700 000 sq km /
1 429 000 sq miles

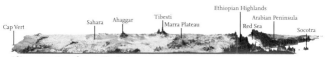

Cap Vert   Sahara   Ahaggar   Tibesti   Marra Plateau   Ethiopian Highlands   Arabian Peninsula   Red Sea   Socotra

Africa cross section and perspective view

HIGHEST MOUNTAINS	metres	feet	Map page
Kilimanjaro, Tanzania	5 892	19 330	119 D3
Mt Kenya (Kirinyaga), Kenya	5 199	17 057	119 D3
Margherita Peak, Democratic Republic of the Congo/Uganda	5 110	16 765	119 C2
Meru, Tanzania	4 565	14 977	119 D3
Ras Dejen, Ethiopia	4 533	14 872	117 B3
Mt Karisimbi, Rwanda	4 510	14 796	—

LARGEST ISLANDS	sq km	sq miles	Map page
Madagascar	587 040	226 656	121 D3

LONGEST RIVERS	km	miles	Map page
Nile	6 695	4 160	116 B1
Congo	4 667	2 900	118 B3
Niger	4 184	2 600	115 C4
Zambezi	2 736	1 700	120 C2
Webi Shabeelle	2 490	1 547	117 C4
Ubangi	2 250	1 398	118 B3

LARGEST LAKES	sq km	sq miles	Map page
Lake Victoria	68 870	26 591	52 B2
Lake Tanganyika	32 600	12 587	119 C3
Lake Nyasa (Lake Malawi)	29 500	11 390	121 C1
Lake Volta	8 482	3 275	114 C4
Lake Turkana	6 500	2 510	119 D2
Lake Albert	5 600	2 162	119 D2

LARGEST LAKE
Lake Victoria
68 870 sq km /
26 591 sq miles

HIGHEST MOUNTAIN
Kilimanjaro
5 892 m / 19 330 feet

LARGEST ISLAND
Madagascar
587 040 sq km /
226 656 sq miles

Total Land Area 24 680 331 sq km / 9 529 076 sq miles
(including Hawaiian Islands)

HIGHEST MOUNTAIN
Mt McKinley
6 194 m / 20 321 feet

LARGEST ISLAND
Greenland
2 175 600 sq km /
839 999 sq miles

North America cross section

LOWEST POINT
Death Valley
86 m / 282 feet
below sea level

Coast Ranges · Rocky Mountains · Great Plains · Lake Michigan · Lake Huron · Lake Erie · Chesapeake Bay · Appalachian Mountains · Long Island · Cape Cod · Nova Scotia

North America cross section and perspective view

HIGHEST MOUNTAINS	metres	feet	Map page
Mt McKinley, USA	6 194	20 321	124 F2
Mt Logan, Canada	5 959	19 550	126 B2
Pico de Orizaba, Mexico	5 610	18 405	145 C3
Mt St Elias, USA	5 489	18 008	126 B2
Volcán Popocatépetl, Mexico	5 452	17 887	145 C3
Mt Foraker, USA	5 303	17 398	—

LARGEST LAKE
Lake Superior
82 100 sq km /
31 699 sq miles

LARGEST ISLANDS	sq km	sq miles	Map page
Greenland	2 175 600	839 999	127 I2
Baffin Island	507 451	195 927	127 G2
Victoria Island	217 291	83 896	126 D2
Ellesmere Island	196 236	75 767	127 F1
Cuba	110 860	42 803	146 B2
Newfoundland	108 860	42 031	131 E2
Hispaniola	76 192	29 418	147 C2

LONGEST RIVERS	km	miles	Map page
Mississippi-Missouri	5 969	3 709	133 D3
Mackenzie-Peace-Finlay	4 241	2 635	126 C2
Missouri	4 086	2 539	137 E3
Mississippi	3 765	2 340	142 C3
Yukon	3 185	1 979	126 A2
St Lawrence	3 058	1 900	131 D2

LONGEST RIVER AND
LARGEST DRAINAGE BASIN
Mississippi-Missouri
5 969 km / 3 709 miles
3 250 000 sq km / 1 255 000
sq miles

LARGEST LAKES	sq km	sq miles	Map page
Lake Superior	82 100	31 699	140 B1
Lake Huron	59 600	23 012	140 C2
Lake Michigan	57 800	22 317	140 B2
Great Bear Lake	31 328	12 096	126 C2
Great Slave Lake	28 568	11 030	128 C1
Lake Erie	25 700	9 923	140 C2
Lake Winnipeg	24 387	9 416	129 E2
Lake Ontario	18 960	7 320	141 D2

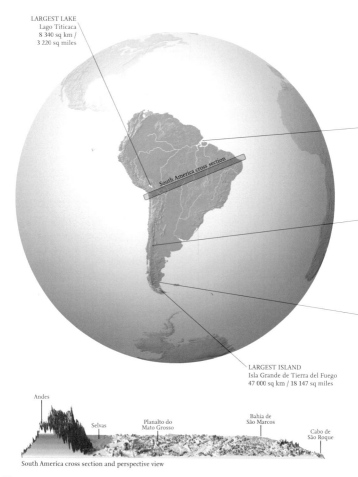

Total Land Area 17 815 420 sq km / 6 878 534 sq miles

LARGEST LAKE
Lago Titicaca
8 340 sq km /
3 220 sq miles

South America cross section

LARGEST ISLAND
Isla Grande de Tierra del Fuego
47 000 sq km / 18 147 sq miles

Andes

Selvas

Planalto do
Mato Grosso

Bahia de
São Marcos

Cabo de
São Roque

South America cross section and perspective view

HIGHEST MOUNTAINS	metres	feet	Map page
Cerro Aconcagua, Argentina	6 959	22 831	153 B4
Nevado Ojos del Salado, Argentina/Chile	6 908	22 664	152 B3
Cerro Bonete, Argentina	6 872	22 546	—
Cerro Pissis, Argentina	6 858	22 500	—
Cerro Tupungato, Argentina/Chile	6 800	22 309	—
Cerro Mercedario, Argentina	6 770	22 211	—

LARGEST ISLANDS	sq km	sq miles	Map page
Isla Grande de Tierra del Fuego	47 000	18 147	153 B6
Isla de Chiloé	8 394	3 241	153 A5
East Falkland	6 760	2 610	153 C6
West Falkland	5 413	2 090	153 B6

LONGEST RIVER AND
LARGEST DRAINAGE BASIN
Amazon
8 516 km / 4 049 miles
7 050 000 sq km / 2 722 000 sq miles

LONGEST RIVERS	km	miles	Map page
Amazon (Amazonas)	6 516	4 049	150 C1
Río de la Plata-Paraná	4 500	2 796	153 C4
Purus	3 218	2 000	150 B2
Madeira	3 200	1 988	150 C2
São Francisco	2 900	1 802	151 E3
Tocantins	2 750	1 709	151 D2

HIGHEST MOUNTAIN
Cerro Aconcagua
6 959 m / 22 831 feet

LARGEST LAKES	sq km	sq miles	Map page
Lake Titicaca	8 340	3 220	152 B2

LOWEST POINT
Laguna del Carbón
105 m / 345 feet below sea level

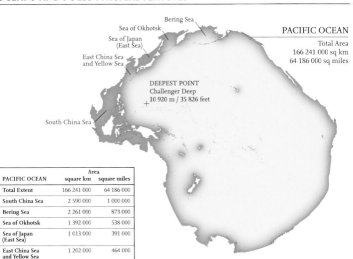

Bering Sea

Sea of Okhotsk

Sea of Japan
(East Sea)

East China Sea
and Yellow Sea

PACIFIC OCEAN

Total Area
166 241 000 sq km
64 186 000 sq miles

DEEPEST POINT
Challenger Deep
10 920 m / 35 826 feet

South China Sea

PACIFIC OCEAN	Area	
	square km	square miles
Total Extent	166 241 000	64 186 000
South China Sea	2 590 000	1 000 000
Bering Sea	2 261 000	873 000
Sea of Okhotsk	1 392 000	538 000
Sea of Japan (East Sea)	1 013 000	391 000
East China Sea and Yellow Sea	1 202 000	464 000

ANTARCTICA

Total Land Area 12 093 000 sq km /
4 669 107 sq miles (excluding ice shelves)

HIGHEST MOUNTAIN
Vinson Massif
4 897 m / 16 066 feet

HIGHEST MOUNTAINS	Height	
	metres	feet
Vinson Massif	4 897	16 066
Mt Tyree	4 852	15 918
Mt Kirkpatrick	4 528	14 855
Mt Markham	4 351	14 275
Mt Jackson	4 190	13 747
Mt Sidley	4 181	13 717

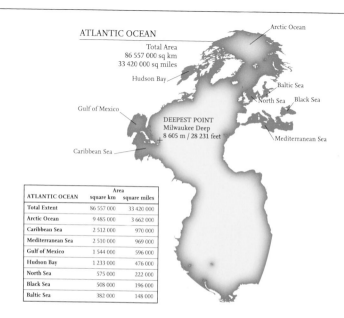

ATLANTIC OCEAN

Total Area
86 557 000 sq km
33 420 000 sq miles

Arctic Ocean

Hudson Bay

Baltic Sea

North Sea   Black Sea

Gulf of Mexico

DEEPEST POINT
Milwaukee Deep
8 605 m / 28 231 feet

Mediterranean Sea

Caribbean Sea

ATLANTIC OCEAN	Area	
	square km	square miles
Total Extent	86 557 000	33 420 000
Arctic Ocean	9 485 000	3 662 000
Caribbean Sea	2 512 000	970 000
Mediterranean Sea	2 510 000	969 000
Gulf of Mexico	1 544 000	596 000
Hudson Bay	1 233 000	476 000
North Sea	575 000	222 000
Black Sea	508 000	196 000
Baltic Sea	382 000	148 000

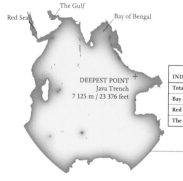

The Gulf

Red Sea   Bay of Bengal

DEEPEST POINT
Java Trench
7 125 m / 23 376 feet

INDIAN OCEAN	Area	
	square km	square miles
Total Extent	73 427 000	28 350 000
Bay of Bengal	2 172 000	839 000
Red Sea	453 000	175 000
The Gulf	238 000	92 000

INDIAN OCEAN

Total Area
73 427 000 sq km
28 350 000 sq miles

MAJOR CLIMATIC REGIONS AND SUB-TYPES

Köppen classification system
Winkel Tripel Projection
scale 1:200 000 000

• Weather extreme location

WORLD WEATHER EXTREMES

	Location
Highest shade temperature	56.7°C / 134°F Furnace Creek, Death Valley, California, USA (10 July 1913)
Hottest place – Annual mean	34.4°C / 93.9°F Dalol, Ethiopia
Driest place – Annual mean	0.1 mm / 0.004 inches Atacama Desert, Chile
Most sunshine – Annual mean	90% Yuma, Arizona, USA (over 4 000 hours)
Least sunshine	Nil for 182 days each year, South Pole
Lowest screen temperature	-89.2°C / -128.6°F Vostok Station, Antarctica (21 July 1983)
Coldest place – Annual mean	-56.6°C / -69.9°F Plateau Station, Antarctica
Wettest place – Annual mean	11 873 mm / 467.4 inches Meghalaya, India
Highest surface wind speed	
- High altitude	372 km per hour/231 miles per hour Mount Washington, New Hampshire, USA, (12 April 1934)
- Low altitude	408 km per hour/254 miles per hour Barrow Island, Australia (10 April 1996)
- Tornado	512 km per hour / 318 miles per hour in a tornado, Oklahoma City, Oklahoma, USA (3 May 1999)
Greatest snowfall	31 102 mm / 1 224.5 inches Mount Rainier, USA (19 February 1971 – 18 February 1972)

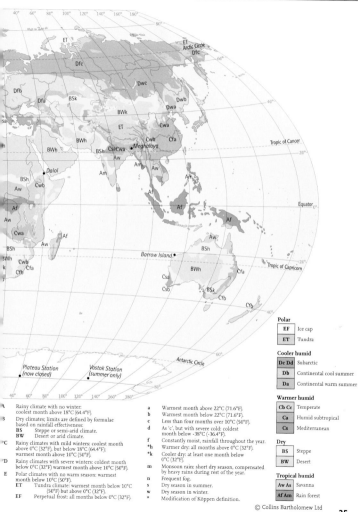

A Rainy climate with no winter:
coolest month above 18°C (64.4°F).

B Dry climates; limits are defined by formulae
based on rainfall effectiveness:
BS   Steppe or semi-arid climate.
BW Desert or arid climate.

*C Rainy climates with mild winters: coolest month
above 0°C (32°F), but below 18°C (64.4°F);
warmest month above 10°C (50°F).

*D Rainy climates with severe winters: coldest month
below 0°C (32°F) warmest month above 10°C (50°F).

E Polar climates; no warm season: warmest
month below 10°C (50°F).
ET Tundra climate: warmest month below 10°C
(50°F) but above 0°C (32°F).
EF Perpetual frost: all months below 0°C (32°F).

a   Warmest month above 22°C (71.6°F).
b   Warmest month below 22°C (71.6°F).
c   Less than four months over 10°C (50°F).
d   As 'c', but with severe cold: coldest
month below -38°C (-36.4°F).
f   Constantly moist, rainfall throughout the year.
*h Warmer dry: all months above 0°C (32°F).
*k Cooler dry: at least one month below
0°C (32°F).
m Monsoon rain: short dry season, compensated
by heavy rains during rest of the year.
n Frequent fog.
s   Dry season in summer.
w Dry season in winter.
*   Modification of Köppen definition.

Polar

| EF | Ice cap |
| ET | Tundra |

Cooler humid

Dc Dd	Subarctic
Db	Continental cool summer
Da	Continental warm summer

Warmer humid

Cb Cc	Temperate
Ca	Humid subtropical
Cs	Mediterranean

Dry

| BS | Steppe |
| BW | Desert |

Tropical humid

| Aw As | Savanna |
| Af Am | Rain forest |

© Collins Bartholomew Ltd

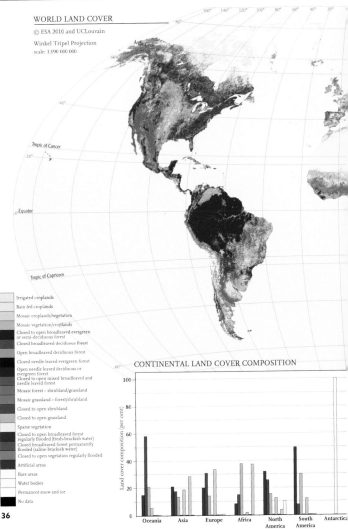

WORLD LAND COVER

© ESA 2010 and UCLouvain

Winkel Tripel Projection
scale: 1:190 000 000

Legend:

- Irrigated croplands
- Rain fed croplands
- Mosaic croplands/vegetation
- Mosaic vegetation/croplands
- Closed to open broadleaved evergreen or semi-deciduous forest
- Closed broadleaved deciduous forest
- Open broadleaved deciduous forest
- Closed needle leaved evergreen forest
- Open needle leaved deciduous or evergreen forest
- Closed to open mixed broadleaved and needle leaved forest
- Mosaic forest – shrubland/grassland
- Mosaic grassland – forest/shrubland
- Closed to open shrubland
- Closed to open grassland
- Sparse vegetation
- Closed to open broadleaved forest regularly flooded (fresh-brackish water)
- Closed broadleaved forest permanently flooded (saline-brackish water)
- Closed to open vegetation regularly flooded
- Artificial areas
- Bare areas
- Water bodies
- Permanent snow and ice
- No data

CONTINENTAL LAND COVER COMPOSITION

Land cover composition (per cent)

Oceania — Asia — Europe — Africa — North America — South America — Antarctica

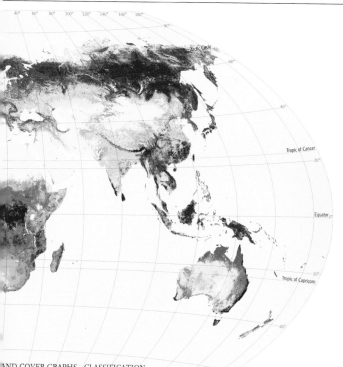

AND COVER GRAPHS - CLASSIFICATION

Class description	Map classes
Forest/Woodland	Evergreen needleleaf forest
	Evergreen broadleaf forest
	Deciduous needleleaf forest
	Deciduous broadleaf forest
	Mixed forest
Shrubland	Closed shrublands
	Open shrublands
Grass/Savanna	Woody savannas
	Savannas
	Grasslands
Wetland	Permanent wetlands
Crops/Mosaic	Croplands
	Cropland/Natural vegetation mosaic
Urban	Urban and built-up
Snow/Ice	Snow and Ice
Barren	Barren or sparsely vegetated

GLOBAL LAND COVER COMPOSITION

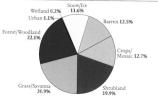

Snow/Ice 11.6%
Wetland 0.2%
Urban 0.1%
Forest/Woodland 22.1%
Barren 12.5%
Crops/Mosaic 12.7%
Grass/Savanna 26.9%
Shrubland 19.9%

WORLD POPULATION DISTRIBUTION

Population Density
Winkel Tripel Projection
scale 1:190 000 000

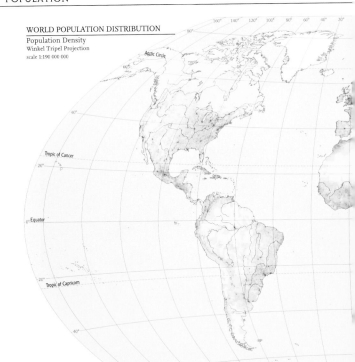

KEY POPULATION STATISTICS FOR MAJOR REGIONS

	Population 2011 (millions)	Growth (per cent)	Infant mortality rate	Total fertility rate	Life expectancy (years)
World	6 974	1.1	42	2.45	69
More developed regions[1]	1 240	0.3	6	1.7	78
Less developed regions[2]	5 774	1.3	46	2.6	67
Africa	1 046	2.3	71	4.4	55
Asia	4 207	1.0	37	2.2	70
Europe[3]	739	0.1	6	1.6	77
Latin America and the Caribbean[4]	597	1.1	19	2.2	75
North America	348	0.9	6	2.0	79
Oceania	37	1.5	19	2.5	78

1. Europe, North America, Australia, New Zealand and Japan.
2. Africa, Asia (excluding Japan), Latin America and the Caribbean and Oceania (excluding Australia and New Zealand).
3. Includes Russian Federation.
4. South America, Central America (including Mexico) and all Caribbean Islands.

Except for population (2011) the data are annual averages projected for the period 2010–2015.

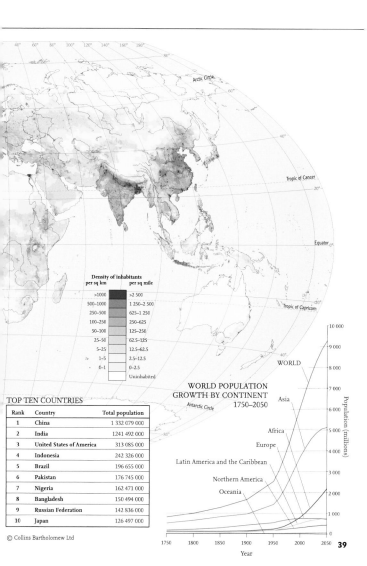

Density of inhabitants

per sq km	per sq mile
>1000	>2 500
500–1000	1 250–2 500
250–500	625–1 250
100–250	250–625
50–100	125–250
25–50	62.5–125
5–25	12.5–62.5
1–5	2.5–12.5
0–1	0–2.5
	Uninhabited

TOP TEN COUNTRIES

Rank	Country	Total population
1	China	1 332 079 000
2	India	1 241 492 000
3	United States of America	313 085 000
4	Indonesia	242 326 000
5	Brazil	196 655 000
6	Pakistan	176 745 000
7	Nigeria	162 471 000
8	Bangladesh	150 494 000
9	Russian Federation	142 836 000
10	Japan	126 497 000

WORLD POPULATION GROWTH BY CONTINENT 1750–2050

WORLD
Asia
Africa
Europe
Latin America and the Caribbean
Northern America
Oceania

Population (millions)

THE WORLD'S MAJOR CITIES

Urban agglomerations with over
1 million inhabitants.
Winkel Tripel Projection
scale 1:190 000 000

LEVEL OF URBANIZATION BY MAJOR REGION 1970–2030

Urban population as a percentage of total population

	1970	2010	2030
World	36.1	50.5	59.0
More developed regions[1]	64.7	75.2	80.9
Less developed regions[2]	25.3	45.1	55.0
Africa	23.6	40.0	49.9
Asia	22.7	42.2	52.8
Europe[3]	62.8	72.8	78.4
Latin America and the Caribbean[4]	57.1	79.6	84.9
Northern America	73.8	82.1	86.7
Oceania	70.8	70.2	71.4

1. Europe, North America, Australia,
New Zealand and Japan.

2. Africa, Asia (excluding Japan), Latin
America and the Caribbean, and
Oceania (excluding Australia and
New Zealand).

3. Includes Russian Federation.

4. South America, Central America
(including Mexico) and all Caribbean
Islands.

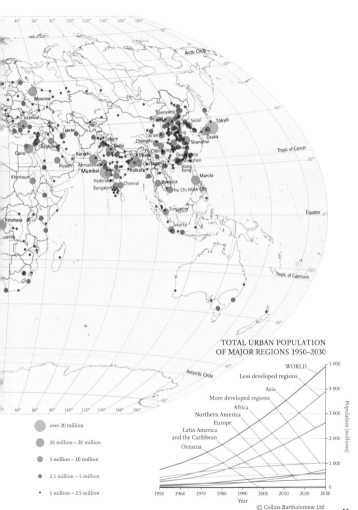

TOTAL URBAN POPULATION
OF MAJOR REGIONS 1950–2030

WORLD
Less developed regions
Asia
More developed regions
Africa
Northern America
Europe
Latin America
and the Caribbean
Oceania

Population (millions)

5 000
4 000
3 000
2 000
1 000
0

1950 1960 1970 1980 1990 2000 2010 2020 2030
Year

© Collins Bartholomew Ltd

over 20 million

10 million – 20 million

5 million – 10 million

2.5 million – 5 million

1 million – 2.5 million

Moscow
Istanbul
Tehran
Baghdad
Cairo
Khartoum
Riyadh
Kinshasa
uanda
Shenyang
Beijing
Seoul
Tōkyō
Lahore
Delhi
Xi'an
Chengdu
Zhengzhou
Ōsaka
Karachi
Chongqing
Wuhan
Shanghai
Ahmadabad
Dhaka
Guangzhou
Mumbai
Pune
Chittagong
Shenzhen
Hyderabad
Kolkata
Hong
Kong
Bangalore
Chennai
Bangkok
Manila
Ho Chi Minh City
Singapore
Jakarta

SYMBOLS

Map symbols used on the map pages are explained here. The status of nations and their boundaries are shown in this atlas as they are in reality at time of going to press, as far as can be ascertained. Where international boundaries are subject of disputes the aim is to take a strictly neutral viewpoint, based on advice from expert consultants. Settlements are classified in terms of both population and administrative significance. The abbreviations listed are those used in place names on the map pages and within the index.

BOUNDARIES

International boundary

Disputed international boundary or alignment unconfirmed

Undefined international boundary in the sea.
All land within this boundary is part of state or territory named.

Disputed territory boundary

Administrative boundary
Shown for selected countries only.

Ceasefire line or other boundary described on the map

TRANSPORT

Motorway

Main road

Track

Main railway

Canal

Main airport

LAND AND WATER FEATURES

Lake

Impermanent lake

Salt lake or lagoon

Impermanent salt lake

Dry salt lake or salt pan

River

Impermanent river

Ice cap / Glacier

123   Pass
      height in metres

123   Summit
△   height in metres

∴   Site of special interest

Wall

CITIES AND TOWNS

Population	National Capital	Administrative Capital Shown for selected countries only	Other City or Town
over 10 million	**BEIJING** ▣	**São Paulo** ◉	**New York** ◉
5 to 10 million	**PARIS** ▣	**St Petersburg** ◉	**Chicago** ◉
1 to 5 million	**KUWAIT** ☐	**Sydney** ○	**Seattle** ○
500 000 to 1 million	**BANGUI** ☐	**Winnipeg** ○	**Jeddah** ○
100 000 to 500 000	WELLINGTON ☐	Edinburgh ○	Apucarana ○
50 000 to 100 000	PORT OF SPAIN ▫	Bismarck ○	Invercargill ○
under 50 000	MALABO ▫	Charlottetown ○	Ceres ○

STYLES OF LETTERING

Cities and towns are explained separately

		Physical features	
Country	**FRANCE**	Island	*Gran Canaria*
Overseas Territory/Dependency	**Guadeloupe**	Lake	*Lake Erie*
Disputed Territory	WESTERN SAHARA	Mountain	*Mt Blanc*
Administrative name Shown for selected countries only.	**SCOTLAND**	River	*Thames*
Area name	PATAGONIA	Region	*LAPPLAND*

CONTINENTAL MAPS

BOUNDARIES

——— International boundary

------ Disputed international boundary

•••••••• Ceasefire line

CITIES AND TOWNS

National capital	Other city or town
Kuwait □	Seattle ○

ABBREVIATIONS

Arch.	Archipelago				
B.	Bay				
	Bahia, Baía	Portuguese	bay		
	Bahía	Spanish	bay		
	Baie	French	bay		
C.	Cape				
	Cabo	Portuguese, Spanish	cape, headland		
	Cap	French	cape, headland		
Co	Cerro	Spanish	hill, peak, summit		
E.	East, Eastern				
Est.	Estrecho	Spanish	strait		
Gt	Great				
I.	Island, Isle				
	Ilha	Portuguese	island		
	Islas	Spanish	island		
Is	Islands, Isles				
	Islas	Spanish	islands		
Khr.	Khrebet	Russian	mountain range		
L.	Lake				
	Loch	(Scotland)	lake		
	Lough	(Ireland)	lake		
	Lac	French	lake		
	Lago	Portuguese, Spanish	lake		
M.	Mys	Russian	cape, point		
Mt	Mount				
	Mont	French	hill, mountain		
Mt.	Mountain				

Mts	Mountains			
	Monts	French	hills, mountains	
N.	North, Northern			
O.	Ostrov	Russian	island	
Pt	Point			
Pta	Punta	Italian, Spanish	cape, point	
R.	River			
	Rio	Portuguese	river	
	Río	Spanish	river	
	Rivière	French	river	
Ra.	Range			
S.	South, Southern			
	Salar, Salina, Salinas	Spanish	saltpan, saltpans	
Sa	Serra	Portuguese	mountain range	
	Sierra	Spanish	mountain range	
Sd	Sound			
S.E.	Southeast, Southeastern			
St	Saint			
	Sankt	German	saint	
	Sint	Dutch	saint	
Sta	Santa	Italian, Portuguese, Spanish	saint	
Ste	Sainte	French	saint	
Str.	Strait			
W.	West, Western			
	Wadi, Wādī	Arabic	watercourse	

Winkel Tripel Projection

1:170 000 000

MILES 0   1000   2000   3000

ARCTIC OCEAN

40° 80° 120° 160°

80°

Arctic Circle

Central Siberian Plateau

West Siberian Plain

Yenisey

Severnaya

Ob'

Sea of Okhotsk

Bering Sea

Ural Mountains

Irtysh

Lake Baikal

Amur

EUROPE

Volga

Aral Sea

Gobi

40°

Danube Black Sea El'brus 5642 △

Caspian Sea

Tien Shan

Sea of Japan

EUROPE

Kunlun Shan

Honshū

Mediterranean Sea

Zagros Mts.

Himalaya

Mt. Everest 8848 △

Yangtze

East China Sea

PACIFIC

Nile

Indus

Tropic of Cancer

20°

Red Sea

Arabian Peninsula

Arabian Sea

Deccan

Bay of Bengal

Mekong

South China Sea

Philippines

Challenger Deep 10920 ●

Mariana Trench

OCEAN

AFRICA

Ethiopian Highlands

Sri Lanka

Micronesia

Maldives

Sumatra

Borneo

Puncak Jaya 5030 △

New Guinea

Melanesia

Equator

Congo Basin

Great Rift Valley

Lake Victoria Kilimanjaro 5892 △

Seychelles

INDIAN

Java

Celebes

Arafura Sea

Zambezi

Madagascar

OCEAN

AUSTRALIA

Coral Sea

Kalahari Desert

Great Victoria Desert

Darling

Great Dividing Range

Tropic of Capricorn

20°

Cape of Good Hope

Great Australian Bight

Tasman Sea

New Zealand

Îles Kerguélen

Tasmania

40°

Davis Sea

60°

Antarctic Circle

Ross Sea

80°

ANTARCTICA

40° 80° 120° 160°

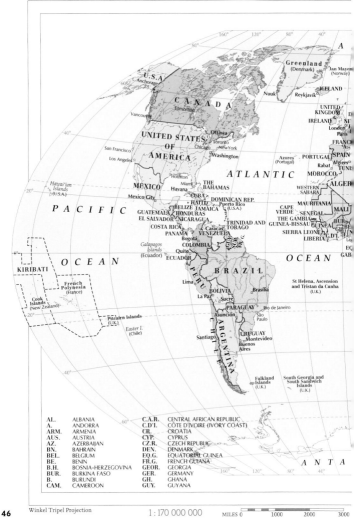

		C.A.R.	CENTRAL AFRICAN REPUBLIC
AL.	ALBANIA	C.D'I.	CÔTE D'IVOIRE (IVORY COAST)
A.	ANDORRA	CR.	CROATIA
ARM.	ARMENIA	CYP.	CYPRUS
AUS.	AUSTRIA	CZ.R.	CZECH REPUBLIC
AZ.	AZERBAIJAN	DEN.	DENMARK
BN.	BAHRAIN	EQ.G.	EQUATORIAL GUINEA
BEL.	BELGIUM	FR.G.	FRENCH GUIANA
BE.	BENIN	GEOR.	GEORGIA
B.H.	BOSNIA-HERZEGOVINA	GER.	GERMANY
BUR.	BURKINA FASO	GH.	GHANA
B.	BURUNDI	GUY.	GUYANA
CAM.	CAMEROON		

1 : 170 000 000   MILES 0   1000   2000   3000

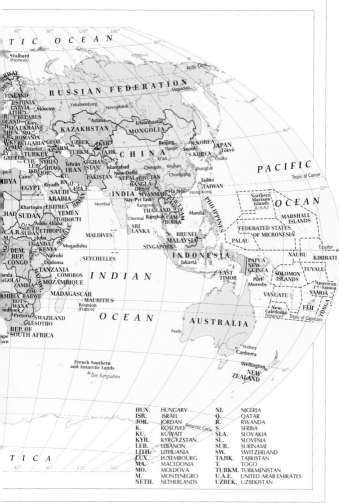

HUN.	HUNGARY	NI.	NIGERIA
ISR.	ISRAEL	Q.	QATAR
JOR.	JORDAN	R.	RWANDA
K.	KOSOVO	S.	SERBIA
KU.	KUWAIT	SLA.	SLOVAKIA
KYR.	KYRGYZSTAN	SL.	SLOVENIA
LEB.	LEBANON	SUR.	SURINAME
LITH.	LITHUANIA	SW.	SWITZERLAND
LUX.	LUXEMBOURG	TAJIK.	TAJIKISTAN
MA.	MACEDONIA	T.	TOGO
MO.	MOLDOVA	TURKM.	TURKMENISTAN
M.	MONTENEGRO	U.A.E.	UNITED ARAB EMIRATES
NETH.	NETHERLANDS	UZBEK.	UZBEKISTAN

0   1000   2000   3000   4000   5000 KILOMETRES

© Collins Bartholomew Ltd

Tropic of Cancer

B 120° C 135° D 150° E 165° F

1

Wake Island
(U.S.A.)

Pagan Northern
Mariana Islands
(U.S.A.)

15°

Saipan Capitol Hill
Guam Hagåtña
(U.S.A.)

MARSHALL
ISLANDS

Yap *Gaferut*
Chuuk Pohnpei Palikir

Caroline Islands

Delap-Uliga-
Djarrit
Majuro

2

FEDERATED STATES
OF MICRONESIA

Kosrae

*Gilbert
Islands* *Tarau*
Bairiki

Equator

ASIA

Yaren
NAURU

Kingsmill
Group

TU

New Ireland
Mount Bismarck
New Wilhelm Sea Rabaul
Guinea 4509 New
PAPUA Britain Bougainville I.
NEW Solomon
GUINEA Sea
Port
Moresby

SOLOMON ISLANDS

Malaita
Honiara

Guadalcanal *Santa Cruz
Islands*

R

FI

3

*Arafura
Sea*

Torres Strait

Gulf of
Carpentaria

Darwin

Timor Sea

Cairns

Coral Sea
Islands Territory
(Australia)

VANUATU
Espiritu Santo *Banks
Islands*

Malakula Éfaté
Coral Port Vila

New Sea Iles
Caledonia Loyauté
(France)

Vit

Cape Lévêque

15°

Townsville

Nouméa

INDIAN
OCEAN

Broome

*Lake
Argyle*

AUSTRALIA

North West
Cape

Uluru Alice Springs
867

Brisbane

*Norfolk
Island
(Australia)*

Tropic of Capricorn

Lake Eyre

*Lord Howe
Island
(Australia)*

North Cape

4

*Lake
Torrens*

Darling

Canberra
Sydney

Auckland

North
Island

Kalgoorlie

Great
Australian Bight

Murray Mount
Kosciuszko
2229

Tasman

Perth

Adelaide

Kangaroo
Island

Melbourne

Wellington

Sea

Bass Strait

Christchurch

30°

Cape Leeuwin

Tasmania

Hobart

*South
Island*

Aoraki
3754

Stewart Island

*Auckland Islands
(N.Z.)*

5

*Campbell Island
(N.Z.)*

*Macquarie Island
(Australia)*

90° A 45° 105° B 120° Longitude 135° east of Greenwich 150° E 165°

1 : 72 000 000

MILES 0 500 1000

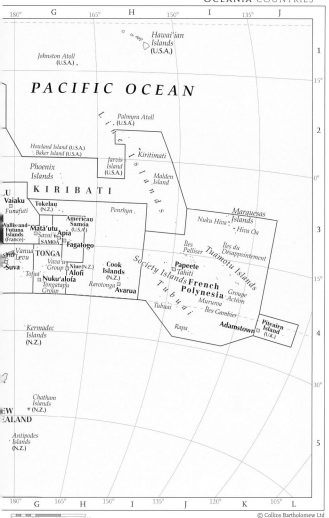

180°   G   165°   H   150°   I   135°   J

1

Hawai'ian Islands (U.S.A.)

15°

Johnston Atoll (U.S.A.)

PACIFIC OCEAN

2

Palmyra Atoll (U.S.A.)

Line Islands

Kiritimati

Howland Island (U.S.A.)
Baker Island (U.S.A.)

Jarvis Island (U.S.A.)

0°

Phoenix Islands

K I R I B A T I

Malden Island

Marquesas Islands

Nuku Hiva · Hiva Oa

LU
Vaiaku
Funafuti

Tokelau (N.Z.)

Penrhyn

Îles du Désappointement

3

Wallis-and-Futuna Islands (France)

American Samoa (U.S.A.)

Matā'utu · Savai'i · Apia

SAMOA

Fagatogo

Îles Palliser

Tuamotu Islands

Vanua Levu

TONGA

Vava'u Group

Niue (N.Z.)

Alofi

Cook Islands (N.Z.)

Society Islands

Papeete

Tahiti

Suva

Tofua

Nuku'alofa

Tongatapu Group

Rarotonga

Avarua

French Polynesia

Groupe Acteon

15°

Tubuai

Mururoa

Îles Gambier

Kermadec Islands (N.Z.)

Tubuai

Rapa

Adamstown

Pitcairn Island (U.K.)

4

30°

Chatham Islands (N.Z.)

EW
ALAND

Antipodes Islands (N.Z.)

5

180°   G   165°   H   150°   I   135°   J   120°   K   105°   L

0   500   1000   1500 KILOMETRES

© Collins Bartholomew Ltd

49

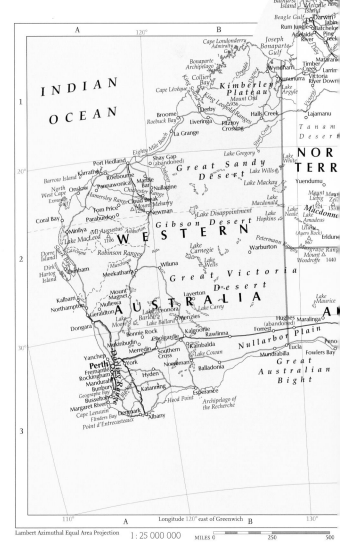

Lambert Azimuthal Equal Area Projection   1 : 25 000 000   MILES 0   250   500

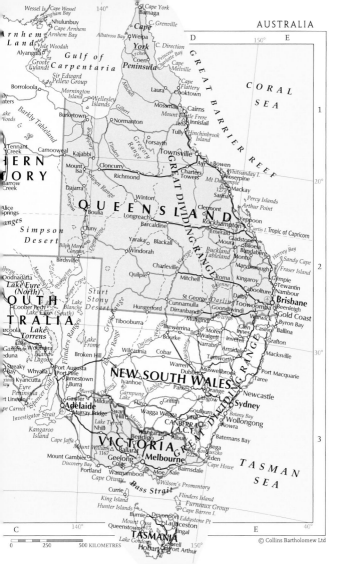

Gulf of Carpentaria

Cape York Peninsula

CORAL SEA

GREAT BARRIER REEF

QUEENSLAND

NORTHERN TERRITORY

Simpson Desert

Sturt Stony Desert

SOUTH AUSTRALIA

NEW SOUTH WALES

VICTORIA

TASMAN SEA

Bass Strait

TASMANIA

Wessel Is Cape Wessel
Ngham Bay
Nhulunbuy
Cape Arnhem
Arnhem Bay
Albatross Bay Weipa
Alyangula Isle Woodah
Borroloola Groote
Eylandt
ly Sir Edward
aters Pellew Group
Mornington
Island Wellesley
Islands Gilbert
Burketown Normanton
Tennant Forsayth
Creek Camooweal Kajabbi Tully
Mount Cloncurry Townsville
Isa Richmond Charters Ayr Bowen
Towers Whitsunday I.
Dajarra Mackay
Winton Clermont
Boulia Longreach Rockhampton
Barcaldine Yeppoon
Cluny Emerald Gladstone
Yaraka Blackall Moura Bundaberg
Windorah Monto Maryborough
Birdsville Charleville Mitchell Roma Gympie
Quilpie Nambour
Oodnadatta St George Dalby Brisbane
Coober Pedy Cunnamulla Toowoomba Gold Coast
Hungerford Goondiwindi Warwick
Tibooburra Brewarrina Moree Casino
Bourke Walgett Grafton
Wilcannia Cobar Narrabri Armidale Macksville
Broken Hill Warren Tamworth Port Macquarie
Iyanhoe Dubbo Muswellbrook
Port Augusta Griffith Parkes Newcastle
Adelaide Wagga Wagga Sydney
Mildura Yass Wollongong
CANBERRA
Bendigo Albury Nowra
Ballarat Geelong Melbourne Bairnsdale
Mount Gambier Colac Sale Eden
Portland Warrnambool Wilson's Promontory
King Island
Burnie Devonport
Queenstown Launceston
Hobart Port Arthur

© Collins Bartholomew Ltd   51

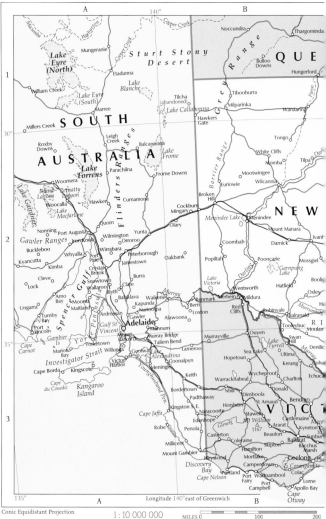

Conic Equidistant Projection   1 : 10 000 000   MILES 0   100   200

0   100   200   300 KILOMETRES

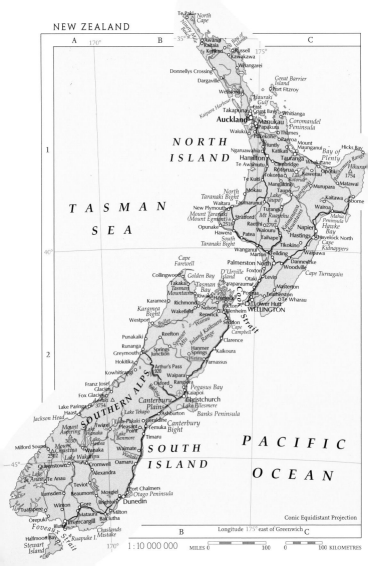

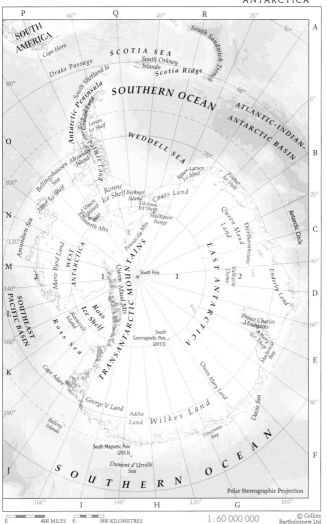

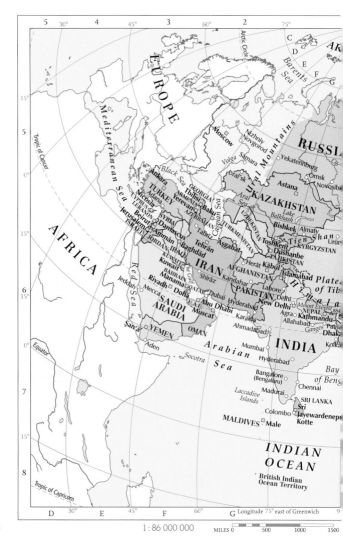

EUROPE

Arctic Circle

C
Barents
Sea
E
F
G

Tropic of Cancer

Mediterranean Sea

Moscow
Nizhniy
Novgorod
Yekaterinburg

RUSSI
Ob

Volga
Samara
Ural'sk
Omsk
Novosib

Black Sea
Ankara
GEORGIA
Tbilisi
Yerevan
ARMENIA
Baku
KAZAKHSTAN
Astana

TURKEY
Adana
Nicosia
CYPRUS
LEBANON
SYRIA
Damascus
AZERBAIJAN
Tabrīz
Aral
Sea
UZBEKISTAN
Lake
Balkhash
Bishkek
Almaty
Tien Shan
Urür

AFRICA
Beirut
ISRAEL
Jerusalem
Amman
JORDAN
IRAQ
Baghdād
Tehrān
TURKMENISTAN
Aşgabat
Toshkent
TAJIKISTAN
Dushanbe
KYRGYZSTAN

KUWAIT
Kuwait
IRAN
Herāt
Kabul
Islamabad
Plate
of Tib

Red Sea
Jeddah
Mecca
BAHRAIN
Manama
QATAR
Doha
Riyadh
U.A.E.
Abu Dhabi
Muscat
Dubai
Shīrāz
Kandahar
AFGHANISTAN
Lahore
PAKISTAN
New Delhi
Delhi
Hyderabad
Karachi
Mount Everest 884
NEPAL
Agra
Kathmandu
Allahabad
Himala
Patna
Ganges
Dhak

SAUDI
ARABIA
Şan'ā'
YEMEN
OMAN
Ahmadabad
Kolka

Aden
Arabian
Sea

Equator
Socotra
Mumbai
Hyderabad
INDIA

Bangalore
(Bengaluru)
Chennai
Bay
of Beng

Laccadive
Islands
Madurai
SRI LANKA
Sri
Jayewardenepu
Kotte
Colombo

MALDIVES
Male

INDIAN
OCEAN

British Indian
Ocean Territory

Tropic of Capricorn

D   30°   E   45°   F   60°   G Longitude 75° east of Greenwich   9

56

1 : 86 000 000

MILES 0   500   1000   1500

© Collins Bartholomew Ltd

0   1000   2000 KILOMETRES

Pyinmana, Taung-ngu, Louangphabang, Nam Đinh, Gulf of Tongking, Xuwen, Haikou, Luzo, Batan Islands, Strai
Chiang Rai, Chiang Mai, Phayao, Nan, Phonsavan, Thanh Hoa, Chenghai, Wencheng, Qionghai, Babuyan Islands
Lampang, Phrae, Uttaradit, VIENTIANE (Viangchan), Vinh, Ha Tinh, Dongfang, Wanning, Laoag, City, Tugu
Mawlamyaing, Phitsanulok, Khon Kaen, Savannakhet, Đông, Hội, Hainan Dao (China), Vigan, Bontoc, Lu.
Ye (Yai), Lop Buri, Tak, THAILAND, Ubon, Salavan, Huế, Đa Nẵng, San Fernando, Dagupan
Tavoy, Ayutthaya, Nakhon Ratchasima, Ratchathani, Pakxé, Quang Ngai, Quezon City, MANILA
BANGKOK (Krung Thep), Pattaya, Surin, CAMBODIA, Quy Nhon, Lucena, Batangas
Myeik (Mergui), Palaw, Chanthaburi, Bătdâmbâng, Buôn Mê Thuột, Nha Trang, Mindoro, Calamian Group, Roml
Tenasserim, Prachuap Khiri Khan, Kâmpóng Spœ, Takêv, PHNOM PENH, Biên, Đà Lạt, Puerto Princesa, Taytay, Neg
Ranong, Chumphon, Sihanoukville, Long Xuyên, Phan Thiết, Palawan, Sulu Sea
Takua Pa, Nakhon Si Thammarat, Rach Gia, Ca Mau, Cần, Ho Chi Minh City (Saigon), Mouths of the Mekong, Brooke's Point
Phuket, Krabi, Phatthalung, Mui Ca Mau, Bac Liêu, SOUTH CHINA SEA, Balabac Strait, Kudat, Banggi, Zamboar
Hat Yai, Songkhla, Yala, Kota Bharu, Kota Kinabalu, Gunung Kinabalu, Sandakan, Isab
Banda Aceh, Sigli, Bireun, Langsa, Alor Star, Sungai Petani, Pasir Putih, MALAYSIA, BANDAR SERI BEGAWAN, BRUNEI, SABAH, Lahad Datu, Semporna, Tawau, Archipe
Pangkalansusu, George Town, Taiping, Kuala Terengganu, Natuna Besar, Kepulauan Anambas, Igan, Miri, Tarakan, C
Medan, Ipoh, Kuala Lipis, Bintulu, Mukah, Tarakan, Tanjungselor, Semenan
Simeulue, Tebingtinggi, KUALA LUMPUR, PUTRAJAYA, Kepulauan Natuna, Likuta, Kuching, Sibu, SARAWAK, Tanjungredeb, Moutong, Dongga
Sibolga, Pematangsiantar, Melaka, Muar, Keluang, Sambas, Seria, Sri Aman, Sangkulirang, Tomi, Palu, Teli
Gunungsitoli, Rantauprapat, Duri, SINGAPORE, Kepulauan Riau, Singkawang, Lubok Antu, Samarinda, CELEBES (SULAWESI), Poso
Minas, Johor Bahru, Kepulauan Tambelan, Pontianak, Mempawah, BORNEO, Balikpapan, Parepare, Makale
Pakanbaru, Bukittinggi, Pulau-pulau Batu, Sijunjung, Kepulauan Lingga, Belinyu, Ketapang, Sukadana, Sampit, Amuntal, Kotabaru, Watampone, Ko
Padang, Jambi, G. Kerinci 3805, Pangkalpinang, Bangka, Pulau Karimata, Kendawangan, Pangkalanbun, Banjarmasin, Martapura, Makassar, Bontosunggu, Ben
Sijunjung, Sekayu, Pangkalan, Sungailiat, Belitung, Tanahpameran, Kep. Bonerate
Bengkulu, Lahat, Palembang, Manggar, Muarabungo, Laut Jawa (Java Sea), Tg Selatan, Laut, Selat Makassar (Macassar Strait), Kep. Tanahjampea
G. Dempo 3159, Bintuhan, Toboali, INDONESIA, Madura, Kangean, Laut Bali (Bali Sea), Laut Flores (Fl
Enggano, Krui, Bandar Lampung, JAKARTA, Cirebon, Semarang, Kepulauan Kangean, Mataram, Dompu, Raba, Simbawa
Sukabumi, Bandung, Surakarta, Surabaya, Jember, Denpasar, Bima, Sumba
Cilacap, Cilacap, Malang, Selat Lombok, Waikabubak, Wang
Tk Palabuhanratu, JAVA (JAWA), Lesser Sunda Island, Sumba
Greater Sunda Islands, Christmas I. (Australia), Selat Sunda, Waingapu, Tim
INDIAN OCEAN

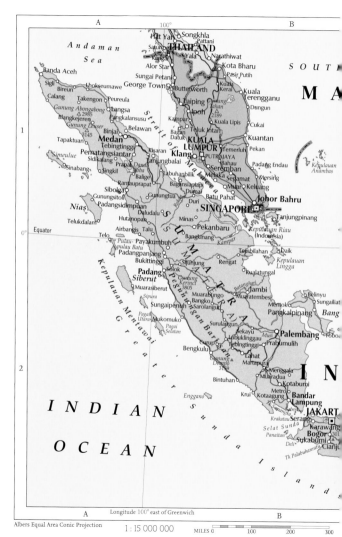

Albers Equal Area Conic Projection · 1 : 15 000 000 · MILES 0 100 200 300

Kudat   *Banggi*   S U L U
SEA
Kota Belud
Gunung
Kinabalu
Kota   4095   Sandakan
Kinabalu   Ranau
Beaufort   SABAH   Lamag   Lahad
Labuan   Kuamut   Datu
BANDAR SERI   Pensiangan   Semporna
BEGAWAN   Tumbdao
BRUNEI   CELEBES   1
Kuala Belait   Lutong   Lumbis   Tawau
Miri   Seria   Kubuang   Tarakan
SEA
Long   Tanjungselor
Bintulu   Pakan
Igan Mukah   Belaga   Tanjungredeb
Sarikei   Sibu   Kanut   Sepinang
Liku   Saratok   Kapit   Datadian
Sematan   Debak   Sangkulirang
Kuching   Kota   2988   Sambaliung
Sambas   Samarahan   Sri Aman   Longiram   Bontang
Pemangkat   Senani   Lubok   Muaralaung   Samarinda
gkawang   Antu   Putusibau   *Mahakam*
mbelan   Bengkayang   Semitau   Tenggarong
mpawah   gabang   Sanggau   Sintang   Balikpapan
Pontianak   Nangahpinoh   Muaratewe   Babana
Balaiberkuak   Pegunungan Schwaner   Bukit
Telukbatang   Rantaupanjang   Barito   Tanahgrogot   Gandadiwata
Sukadana   Nangatayap   Palangkaraya   Amuntai   Polewali
Ketapang   Sukaraja   Sampit   Kandangan   Majene
Kendawangan   Pangkalanbuun   Kualapembuang   Martapura   Kotabaru
njungpandan   Sukaraja   Banjarmasin   Pagatan
Manggar   Tanjung   Laut
elitung   Puting   Tanjung
Selatan

B O R N E O
S A R A W A K
KALIMANTAN

Natuna Besar
Panarik
*Kepulauan
Natuna*

CHINA SEA
LAYSIA

*Selat Makassar
(Macassar Strait)*

D O N E S I A   2
L A U T   J A W A
(J A V A   S E A)   *Kepulauan
Laut Kecil*
*Pulau-pulau
Karimunjawa*
Kemujan   *Bawean*   Sabalana
*Tanjung
Bugel*   *Kepulauan
Kangean*
wakarta   *Tanjung
Indramayu*   Tuban   Bangkalan   *Madura*
ebon   Tegal Pekalongan   Pati   Sumenep   *Laut Bali
(Bali Sea)*   *Kepulauan
Tengah*
andung   Kudus   *Selat Madura*
Garut   Semarang   Surabaya   Situbondo
mis   Temanggung   Surakarta   Jombang   Pasuruan   Banyuwangi   *Sumbawa*
Cilacap   Kebumen   Madiun   G. Rauns   Raba
Yogyakarta   *Malang*   Singaraja   Alas   Dompu
J A V A   Lumajang   Jember   Gilimanuk   Mataram   Sumbawabesar
(J A W A)   *Barung*   *Bali*   Praya   Taliwang
Denpasar   Lombok

© Collins Bartholomew Ltd

0   250   500 KILOMETRES

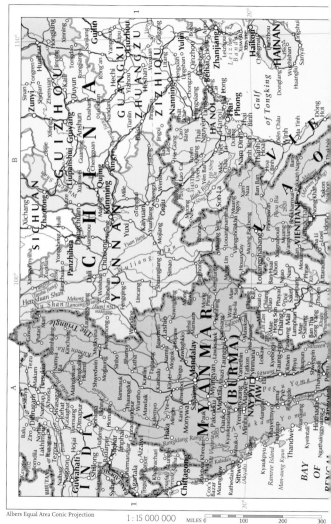

Albers Equal Area Conic Projection   1 : 15 000 000   MILES 0   100   200   300

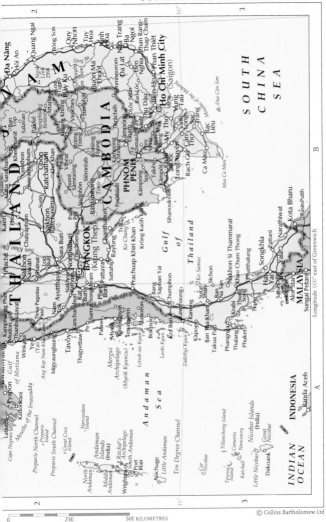

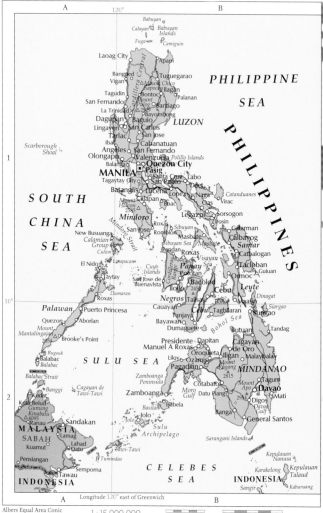

Albers Equal Area Conic Projection

Longitude 120° east of Greenwich

1 : 15 000 000   MILES 0 — 100   0 — 250 KILOMETRES

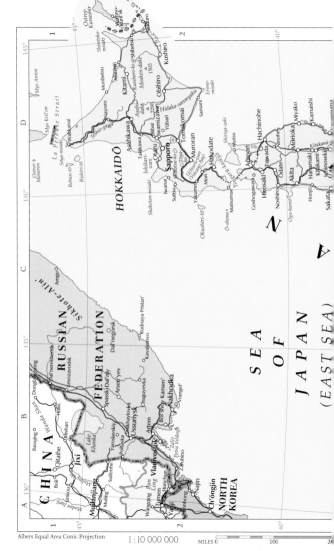

Albers Equal Area Conic Projection

1 : 10 000 000

MILES 0   100   200

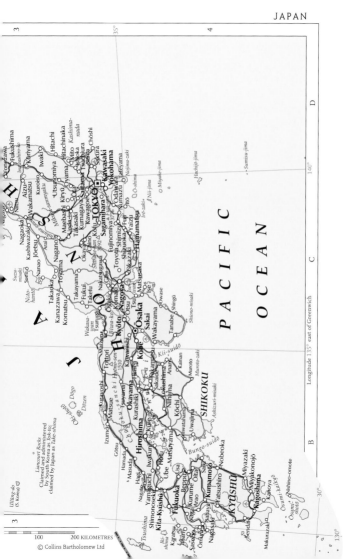

3

35°

D

4

Yonezawa
Fukushima
Koriyama
Iwaki
Nihonmatsu
Hitachinaka
Hitachi
Kashima-nada
Aizu
Kuroiso
Mito
Kashima
Chōshi
Utsunomiya
Tsuchiura
Maebashi
Kiryū
Kumagaya
Saitama
TOKYO
Kawasaki
Yokohama
Takasaki
Kawagoe
Nagano
Ōta
Chino
Odawara
Katsuura
Nagaoka
Sagamihara
Nojima-zaki
Kashiwazaki
Jōetsu
Nakatsugawa
Fuji
Atami
Numazu
Tateyama
Suzu-misaki
Noto-hantō
Toyama
Takayama
Nakatsugawa
Toyota
Shimizu
Shizuoka
Hamamatsu
Yaizu
Inō-zaki
O-shima
Niijima-jima
Miyake-jima
Hachijō-jima
Sumisu-jima
Takaoka
Kanazawa
Komatsu
Fukui
Takefu
Gifu
Ōgaki
Nagoya
Ōtsu
Ise
Owase
Owase
Shingū
Shimo-misaki
Wakasa-wan
Maizuru
Tottori
Kurayoshi
Matsue
Tsuyama
Himeji
Kōbe
Ōsaka
Kyōto
Sakai
Wakayama
Tanabe
Kii-suidō
Kainan
Murotozaki
Muroto-zaki
Izumo
Yonago
Okayama
Kurashiki
Nishinomiya
Anan
Takamatsu
Sakaide
Naruto
Tokushima
Ashizuri-misaki
Gōtsu
Hamada
Masuda
Hiroshima
Iwakuni
Tokuyama
Kure
Matsuyama
Niihama
Kōchi
Uwajima
Kawanoe
Bungo-suidō
Ōzu
Hagi
Yamaguchi
Ube
Shimonoseki
Nagato
Kita-Kyūshū
Fukuoka
Beppu
Ōita
Saiki
Nobeoka
Karatsu
Imari
Saga
Kurume
Nagasaki
Ōmuta
Kumamoto
Yatsushiro
Hitoyoshi
Miyazaki
Miyakonojō
Kagoshima
Kanoya
Sendai
Makurazaki
Ōsumi-shotō
Nishino-omote
Tsushima
Izuhara
Gotō-rettō

P A C I F I C

O C E A N

Longitude 135° east of Greenwich

B

C

30°

130°

100   200 KILOMETRES

© Collins Bartholomew Ltd

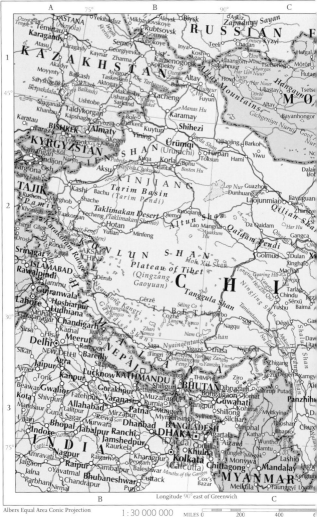

TAIWAN: The People's Republic of China claims Taiwan as its 23rd province.

PACIFIC OCEAN

EAST CHINA SEA

Sea of Japan (East Sea)

Yellow Sea

Tropic of Cancer

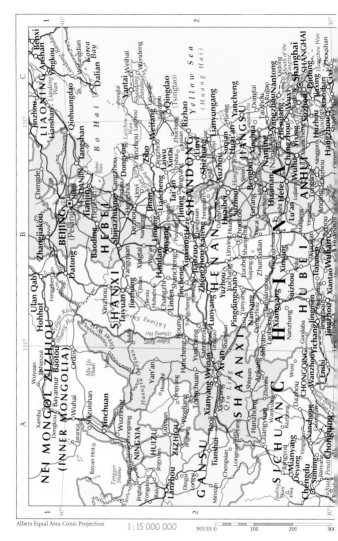

Albers Equal Area Conic Projection

1 : 15 000 000

MILES 0   100   200   300

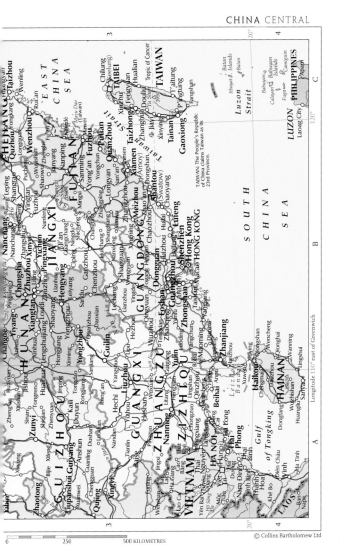

TAIWAN: The People's Republic
of China claims Taiwan as its
23rd Province.

Longitude 110° east of Greenwich

© Collins Bartholomew Ltd

0   250   500 KILOMETRES

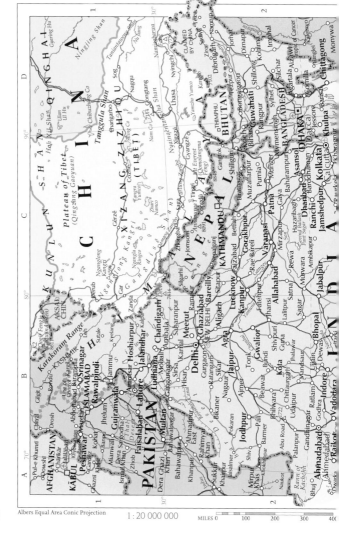

Albers Equal Area Conic Projection

1 : 20 000 000

MILES 0   100   200   300   400

MYANMAR
(BURMA)

Sittwe

Mauñgdaw

akan Yoma

Ramree

Kyaukpyu

Cape Negrais

Kyeintali

Thandwe

B A Y

O F

B E N G A L

North Andaman

Andaman Islands
(India)

Middle Andaman

Little Andaman

Port Blair South
Andaman

Ten Degree Channel

Nicobar Islands
(India)

INDIAN OCEAN

Veraval

Dīu

Gulf of Khambat

Daman

Dhule

Nandurbar

Jalgaon

Akola

Chandrapur

Raipur

Mahānadi

Cuttack

Bhubaneshwar

Puri

Nagpur

Bhandara

Aurangabad

Qalna

Yavatmal

Bhatapuri

Nirmal

Nanded

Bhadrāchalam

Bissamcuttak

Ravaagada

Srikakulam

Bhanjanagar

Titlagarh

Brahmapur

Nashik

Kalyan

Ahmadnagar
(Ahmednagar)

Parbhani

Nizāmābad

Karīmnagar

Warangal

Rajahmundry

Kākināda

Mouths of the Godāvari

Navi Mumbai

Puñe
(Poona)

Pandharpur

Gulbarga
(Kalburgi)

Secunderabad

Hyderabad

khammam

Eluru

Vijayawada

Mumbai
(Bombay)

Srivardhan

Chiplun

Sangli

Solapur

Bijapur

Raichur

Mahbubnagar

Kurnool

Nandyal

Guntūr

Ongole

Mouths of the Krishna

Ratnagiri

Kolhāpur

Miraj

Mahbub

Bhima

Decan

Nalgonda

Kāvali

Kolhāpur

Panaji

Madgaon

Belgaum

Dharwad

Hubli-Dharwad

Bhadrāvati

Chitradurga

Anantapur

Cuddapah
(Kadapa)

Nellore

Goa

Karwar

Shimoga
(Shivamogga)

Davangere

Tumkūr
(Tumakuru)

Tirupati

Kāñchipuram

Kārāikāl

ARABIAN

SEA

Mangalore

Kasaragod

Udupi

Hassan

Bangalore
(Bengaluru)

Mysore
(Mysuru)

Salem

Tiruppattūr

Tiruchchirāppalli

Puducherry
(Pondicherry)

Cuddalore

Chennai
(Madras)

Kannur
(Cannanore)

Kozhikode
(Calicut)

Coimbatore

Erode

Tiruppūr

Dindigul

Thanjāvur

Amindivi
Islands

Kalpeni

Andrott

Kavaratti

Lakshadweep
(Laccadive)
Islands
(India)

Thrissur

Kochi
(Cochin)

Ernakulam

Madurai

Rajapalaiyam

Kollam
(Quilon)

Nagercoil

Alappuzha

Kāraikkudi

Tuticorin
(Thoothukudi)

Thiruvananthapuram

Gulf
of Mannar

Mannar

Jaffna

Medawachchiya

Trincomalee

Batticaloa

SRI LANKA

Anuradhapura

Kurunegala

Kandy

Negombo

SRI JAYEWARDENEPURA
KOTTE

Colombo

Ratnapura

Galle

Matara · Dondra Head

Hambantota

Palk
Strait

Rāmeswaram

Tirunelveli

MALDIVES

Thiladhunmathi

Minicoy

Kalpeni

Nine Degree Channel

Eight Degree Channel

0   200   400   600 KILOMETRES

Albers Equal Area Conic Projection

1 : 15 000 000

MILES 0   100   200   300

© Collins Bartholomew Ltd

0   250   500 KILOMETRES

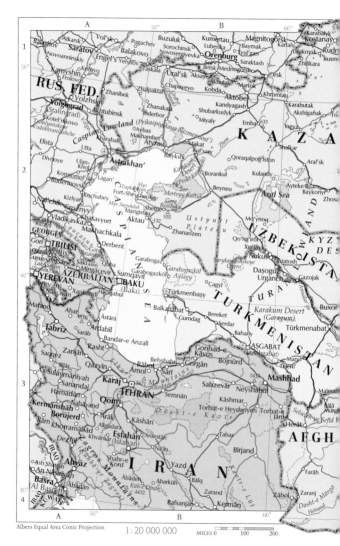

Albers Equal Area Conic Projection

1 : 20 000 000

MILES 0   100   200

Longitude 70° east of Greenwich

© Collins Bartholomew Ltd

0   200   400   600 KILOMETRES

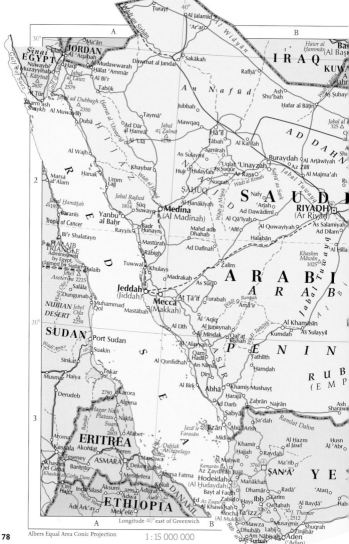

Longitude 40° east of Greenwich

78   Albers Equal Area Conic Projection   1 : 15 000 000

© Collins
Bartholomew Ltd

MILES 0 100 200 0 250 500 KILOMETRES

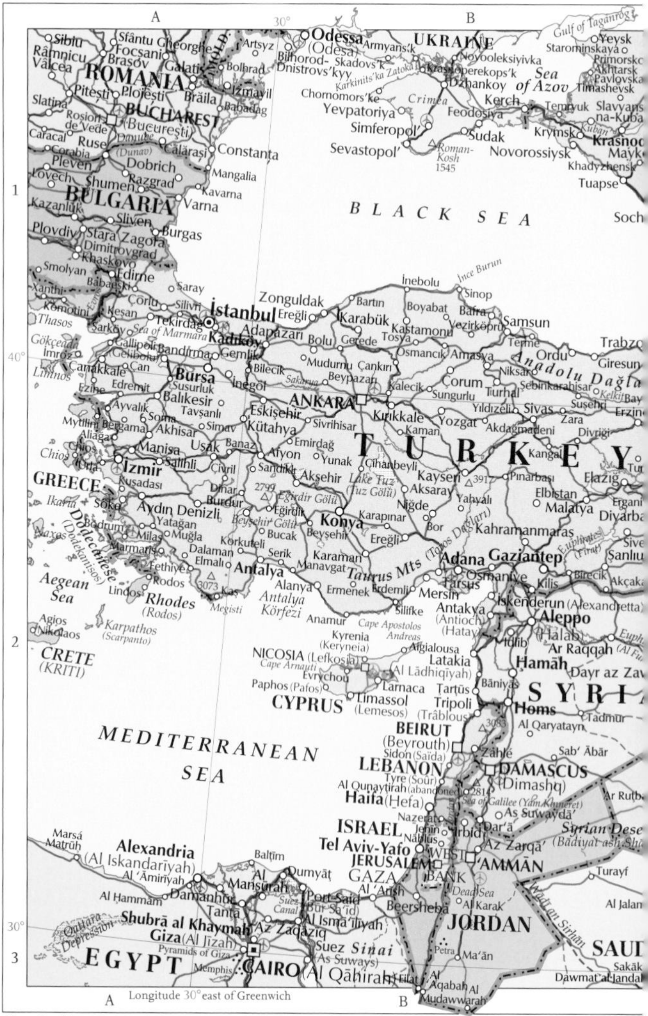

Albers Equal Area Conic Projection

1 : 15 000 000

MILES 0 100 200 300

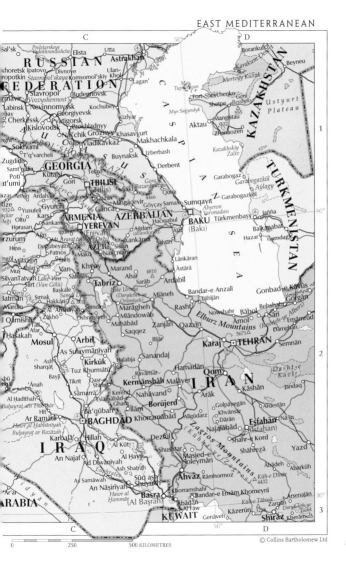

© Collins Bartholomew Ltd

0   250   500 KILOMETRES

Conic Equidistant Projection

1 : 42 000 000

MILES 0   250   500   750

0   500   1000   1500 KILOMETRES

83

A B C D E F G

60° 50° 40° 30° 20° 10° 0° 10°

2

Arctic Circle

60°

Jan Mayen
(Norway)

ICELAND
Reykjavík

Norwegian
Sea

3

ATLANTIC

Tórshavn
Faroe
Islands
(Denmark)

Bergen

OCEAN

50°

Oslo

Glasgow Edinburgh

Aalborg

DENMARK

AL.	ALBANIA
B.H.	BOSNIA-HERZEGOVINA
CR.	CROATIA
CZ.R.	CZECH REPUBLIC
HUN.	HUNGARY
K.	KOSOVO
LIE.	LIECHTENSTEIN
LUX.	LUXEMBOURG
M.	MACEDONIA
MO.	MONTENEGRO
NETH.	NETHERLANDS
SER.	SERBIA
SW.	SWITZERLAND

IRELAND
Belfast
Dublin
Birmingham

North
Sea

UNITED
KINGDOM
Manchester
NETH.
The Hague

Copenhagen

Hambu
Berli

Amsterdam

Cardiff
London Brussels
English Channel BELGIUM
Channel Islands
(U.K.)
Paris
Nantes Orléans

Essen
GERMAN
Frankfurt
am Main
Luxembourg
Dun-R
Strasbourg
Bern Zürich
Geneva
LIE.
SW.
Vaduz
Munic

40°

Bay of
Biscay

Bordeaux

Lyon
Turin
Milan

PO

Ljublja

SAN
MAH

Azores
(Portugal)

Ponta
Delgada

Oporto

Andorra
la Vella
Marseille

Madrid

MONACO

Vatican City

Corsica

ANDORRA

Rome

5

Lisbon

Tagus

SPAIN

Barcelona
Palma
de Mallorca

Valencia
Balearic
Islands

Sardinia
Tyrrhe
Sea

Napl

Seville

Cartagena

M e d i t e

Palermo

r

30°

Madeira
(Portugal)

Cádiz

Gibraltar
(U.K.)

6

AFRICA

Valle
MAL

D E F G

20° 10° 0° 10°

Longitude 10° west of Greenwich

1 : 39 000 000   MILES 0   250   500   750

0   500   1000 KILOMETRES

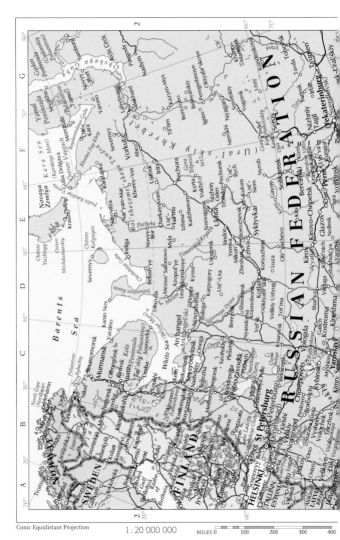

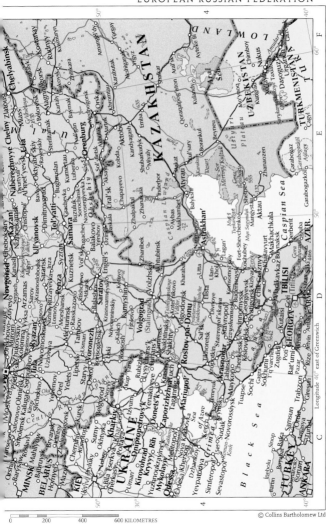

Conic Equidistant Projection   1 : 8 000 000   MILES 0   50   100   150

Longitude 25° east of Greenwich

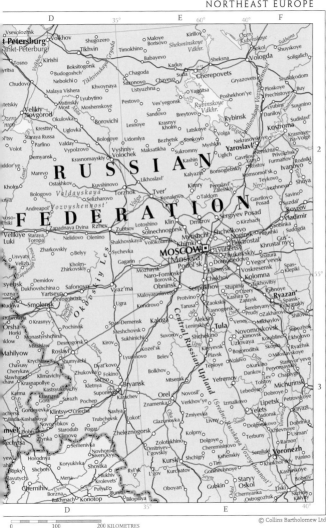

Conic Equidistant Projection

Longitude 25° east of Greenwich

1 : 8 000 000

MILES 0   50   100   150

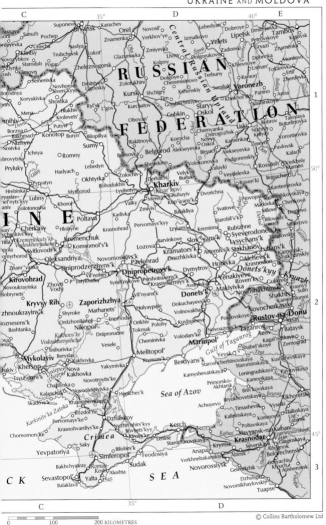

© Collins Bartholomew Ltd

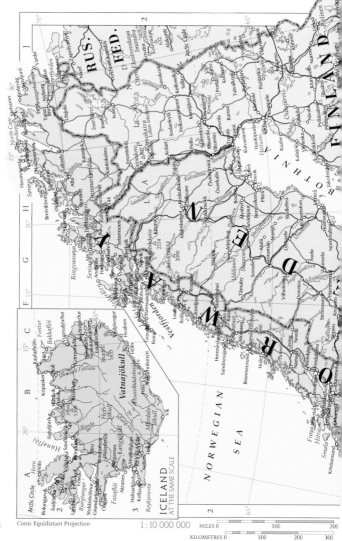

ICELAND
AT THE SAME SCALE

Conic Equidistant Projection

1 : 10 000 000   MILES 0 · · · · 100 · · · · 200

KILOMETRES 0 · · · 100 · · · 200 · · · 300

RUS. FED.

FINLAND

GULF OF BOTHNIA

NORWEGIAN SEA

North Cape

Arctic Circle

Vatnajökull

REYKJAVÍK

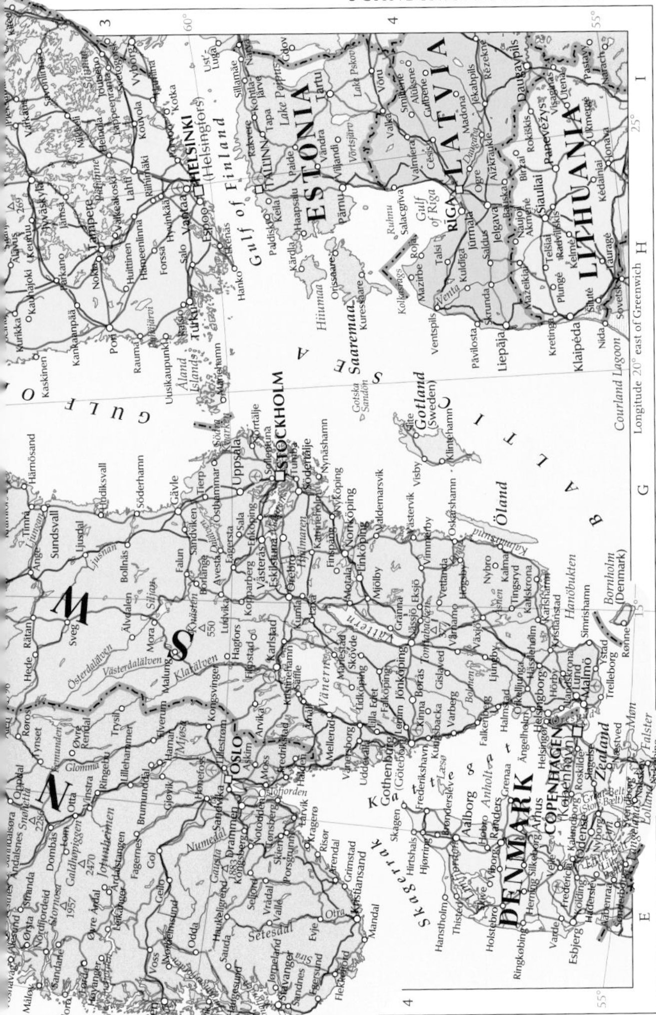

DENMARK

COPENHAGEN
København

STOCKHOLM

HELSINKI
Helsingfors

OSLO

ESTONIA

TALLINN

LATVIA

RIGA

LITHUANIA

Gulf of Finland

Gulf of Riga

BALTIC SEA

GULF

Gotland (Sweden)

Öland

Saaremaa

Hiiumaa

Bornholm (Denmark)

Skagerrak

Kattegat

Gothenburg (Göteborg)

Bergen

Stavanger

Kristiansand

Ålborg

Århus

Odense

Esbjerg

Sundsvall

Härnösand

Gävle

Uppsala

Västerås

Turku

Tampere

Vyborg (Vipuri)

Lahti

Pärnu

Tartu

Jelgava

Šiauliai

Panevėžys

Klaipėda

Liepāja

Ventspils

Visby

Kalmar

Karlskrona

Malmö

Lund

Helsingborg

Trelleborg

Falster

Lolland

Norrköping

Linköping

Jönköping

Borås

Halmstad

Falun

Östersund

Hjörring

Frederikshavn

Longitude 20° east of Greenwich

Courland Lagoon

© Collins Bartholomew Ltd

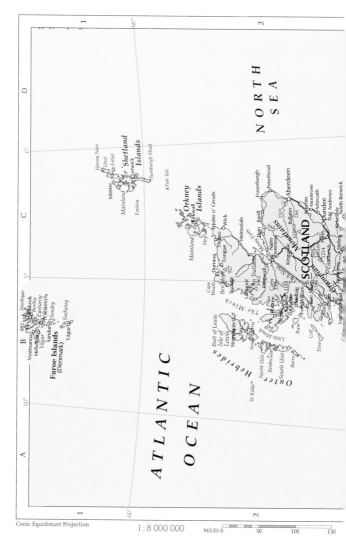

ATLANTIC
OCEAN

NORTH
SEA

SCOTLAND

Grampian Mountains

Faroe Islands
(Denmark)

Nordoyar
882
Vestmanna
Mykines
Bordoy
Eysturoy
Vagar
TÓRSHAVN
Sandoy
Vágur
Suduroy

Shetland
Islands

Herma Ness
Unst
Fetlar
Isbister
Lerwick
Mainland
Foula
Sumburgh Head

Fair Isle

Orkney
Islands

Mainland
Kirkwall
John o' Groats
Hoy
Wick
Thurso
Helmsdale

Cape
Wrath
Durness
Ben Hope
927
Scourie
Tongue

Butt of Lewis
Isle of Lewis
Lewis
Stornoway
Harris
North Uist
Benbecula
South Uist
Barra

Outer Hebrides

St Kilda

The Minch

Little Minch

Rum
Coll
Tiree

Ullapool
Carn
Eighe
1182
Ben Nevis
1344

Loch Ness
Inverness
Nairn
Elgin
Banff
Fraserhead
Peterhead
Aberdeen

Dee
Don
Ballater
Brechin
Montrose
Arbroath
Dundee
St Andrews

Kingussie
Schiehallion
1083
Tay
Perth
Stirling
Dunfermline
North Berwick

The Trossachs

Mull
Oban
Mallaig
Arisaig

Loch Lomond

Colonsay

Conic Equidistant Projection

1 : 8 000 000

MILES 0   50   100   150

0   100   200 KILOMETRES

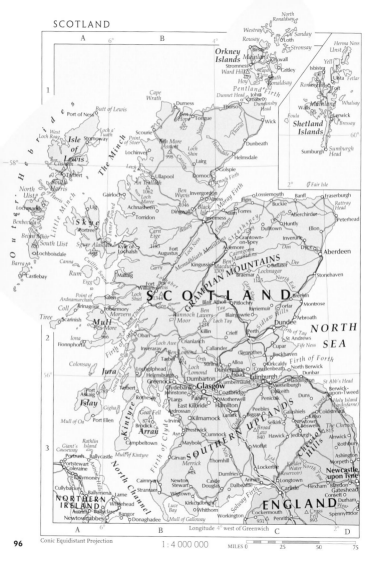

Conic Equidistant Projection

1 : 4 000 000

MILES 0   25   50   75

© Collins Bartholomew Ltd

Longitude 8° west of Greenwich

1 : 4 000 000

0   50   100 KILOMETRES

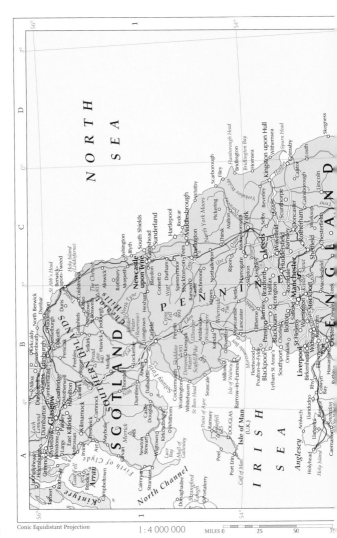

Conic Equidistant Projection

1 : 4 000 000

MILES 0   25   50   75

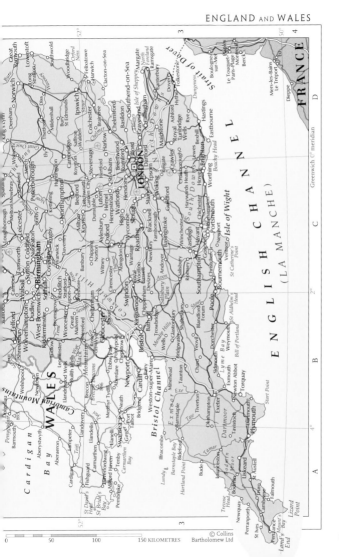

© Collins
Bartholomew Ltd

0   50   100   150 KILOMETRES

NORTH SEA

East Frisian Islands

West Frisian Islands
(Waddeneilanden)

NETHERLANDS
AMSTERDAM

THE HAGUE
('S-Gravenhage)
(Den Haag)

Rotterdam

BELGIUM

BRUSSELS
Bruxelles

Cologne

Düsseldorf

Essen
Dortmund

MÜNSTERLAN

Aachen

LUXEMBOURG

FRANCE

Conic Equidistant Projection

Longitude 6° east of Greenwich

1 : 4 000 000

MILES 0   25   50   75

1 : 8 000 000

MILES 0   50   100

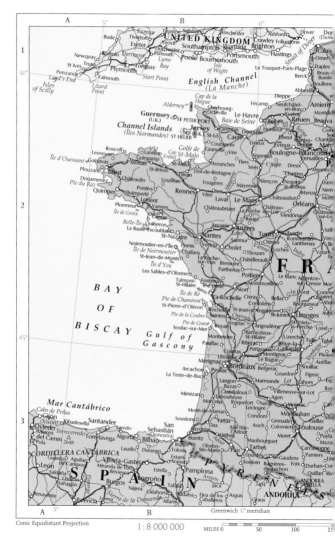

Map of southwest United Kingdom, northwest France, and northern Spain, showing the English Channel (La Manche), Bay of Biscay, and Gulf of Gascony.

Labels include:

United Kingdom: Bude, Tiverton, Exmoor, Taunton, Salisbury, Winchester, Ashford, Dover, Tivington, Exeter, Dorchester, Dartmoor, Exmouth, Southampton, Worthing, Crawley, Brighton, Folkestone, Hastings, Newquay, Bodmin, Lyme Bay, Poole, Bournemouth, Portsmouth, St Ives, Truro, Torquay, Isle of Wight, Penzance, Plymouth, Falmouth, Start Point, Land's End, Lizard Point, Isles of Scilly

France: Cherbourg-Octeville, Cap de la Hague, Le Havre, Baie de Seine, Fécamp, Neufchâtel-en-Bray, Dieppe, Amiens, Rouen, Beauvais, Calais, Le Touquet-Paris-Plage, Berck, Abbeville, Doullens, Guernsey (U.K.), ST PETER PORT, Jersey (U.K.), ST HELIER, Channel Islands (Îles Normandes), Roscoff, Lannion, Cap Fréhel, St-Malo, Golfe de St-Malo, Granville, Coutances, Caen, Lisieux, Évreux, Honfleur, Deauville, Carentan, St-Lô, Bayeux, Boulogne-Billancourt, Versailles, Chartres, Dreux, L'Aigle, Argentan, Sées, Alençon, Nogent-le-Rotrou, Orléans, Vendôme, Châteaudun, Blois, Île d'Ouessant, Lesneven, Guipavas, Plouzané, Brest, Châteaulin, Douarnenez, Quimper, Pte du Raz, Quimperlé, Ploemeur, Lorient, Île de Groix, Belle-Île, Quiberon, La Baule-Escoublac, St-Nazaire, Morlaix, Guingamp, St-Brieuc, Dinan, Dol-de-Bretagne, Fougères, Vitré, Laval, Mayenne, Le Mans, La Flèche, Château-du-Loir, Tours, Amboise, Romorantin-Lanthenay, Vannes, Redon, Nantes, Ancenis, Angers, Saumur, Cholet, Chinon, Loches, Châtellerault, Poitiers, Thouars, Bressuire, Parthenay, Niort, La Rochelle, Île de Ré, Île d'Oléron, Rochefort, St-Jean-d'Angély, Cognac, Saintes, Royan, Soulac-sur-Mer, Angoulême, Limoges, St-Junien, St-Yrieix-la-Perche, Uzerche, Tulle, Brive-la-Gaillarde, Périgueux, Ribérac, Libourne, Bergerac, Bordeaux, Pessac, Mérignac, Arcachon, La Teste-de-Buch, Langon, Bazas, Marmande, Agen, Villeneuve-sur-Lot, Cahors, Montauban, Toulouse, Auch, Tarbes, Lourdes, Bagnères-de-Luchon, Foix, Pamiers, Carcassonne, Bayonne, Biarritz, St-Jean-de-Luz, Dax, Mont-de-Marsan, Pau, Oloron-Ste-Marie, PYRÉNÉES, ANDORRA, ANDORRA LA VELLA

Spain: Mar Cantábrico, Cabo de Peñas, Gijón (Xixón), Avilés, Oviedo, Mieres del Camín, Ribadesella, Torrelavega, Santander, Laredo, Bilbao, San Sebastián (Donostia), Irun, Vitoria-Gasteiz, Durango, Laudio, CORDILLERA CANTÁBRICA, León, Burgos, Logroño, Pamplona, Jaca, SPAIN

Water bodies: English Channel (La Manche), BAY OF BISCAY, Gulf of Gascony, Mar Cantábrico

Conic Equidistant Projection   1 : 8 000 000   MILES 0   50   100   15[0]

0   100   200 KILOMETRES

Conic Equidistant Projection

1 : 8 000 000

MILES 0   50   100   15

A   10°   B   5°

Gulf
Gasco

*Cabo
Ortegal*
Ortigueira○ Cervo
Mar Cantábrico
Ferrol○ ○Viveiro   Luarca Avilés *Cabo de Peñas*   Santander
A Coruña○ ○Vilalba   Ribadeo○ Gijón
Betanzos○   Cangas Salas○ Oviedo○ Ribadesella Toredo Bilbao
Cape Finisterre Santiago○ ○Ordes Lugo○   del Narcea○ Mieres○ Torrecerredo Torrelavega Laudio
(Cabo Fisterra) de Compostela Melide○ Sarria Peña del Camin○ △2648   Vitoria-Gaste
Muros○   ○Estrada   Becerreá Ubiña ○Pola   CORDILLERA CANTÁBRICA Miranda de Ebro
Vilagarcia de Arousa○   △2417   Guardo Briviesca Burgos
Pontevedra○ Ourense○ Monforte○ Ponferrada○ Astorga○ León de Campoo Aguilar Osorno○ Lerma Sierra de la
Marin○ de Lemos ○Barco Truchas○   Saldaña Palencia Aranda
Vigo○ A Cañiza○   Xinxo○ *Sierra de* Benavente○   Medina Valladolid de Duero Ayllón○
Tui○ Fondevila○ de Limia la Cabrera Zamora○ de Rioseco Cuéllar Cerezo de
Verín○   Macedo○ Valladolid   Abajo○ Medi
Viana do Castelo○   Chaves○ de Cavaleiros○ Mirandela○ ○Toro Tordesillas○ Segovia Sigüer
Braga○ Vila Real○ Fermoselle○ Medina Arévalo○ de Cuadarrama Guadalaj
Póvoa de Varzim○ Guimarães○ Torre de Moncorvo○ del Campo Peñaranda Ávila Alcalá de △E
Oporto○   Ledesma○ de Bracamonte○ Henares B
Vila Nova de Gaia○ (Porto) São João○ Lamego○ Meda○ Lumbrales○   SPAIN MADRID
Ovar○ da Madeira Duero   Salamanca○ Fuenlabrada○ Toledo○
Aveiro○ Viseu○ ○Águeda Vilar○ Ciudad Rodrigo○ de Gredos   Ocaña○ Tarancón
Ílhavo○   Formoso○ Guarda○ Navalmoral○ Talavera○ Montes de Toledo
Mealhada○   Torre Sabugal○ Plasencia○ de la Mata de la Reina Embalse Madridejos○
Coimbra○ PORTUGAL △1993 Fundão○ Coria○ Sierra de Pedro Cáceres○ de Cíjara   Alcázar de Socue
Figueira○ ○Lousã Sierra da Estrela Castelo○   Navalvillar○ San Juan
da Foz   Branco○   de Pela○   Villarrob
Pombal○   Abrantes○ Trujillo○ Miajadas○ Ciudad
Marinha○ ○Tomar Ponte○ Portalegre○   Navalvillar○ Real○ Daimiel○ Manzan
Grande Torres○ de Sor   Campo Maior○ Don Villanbo Almadén○ Valdepen
Batalha○ Caldas da Rainha○ Novas○   Elvas○ Benito de la Serena○ Villanuev
Peniche○ ○Entroncamento Coruche○   Estremoz○ Cabeza del Buey○ Puertollano○ de los Infan
Torres Vedras○ Santarém○   Mérida○ Badajoz○   Hinojosa Pozoblanco○
Vila Franca de Xira○   Ponte○   Olivenza○   del Duque○
Amadora○   Redondo○ Almendralejo○ Peñarroya-Pueblonuevo○
Cascais○ LISBON   Zafra○   SIERRA MORENA Andújar Linares
Almada○ (Lisboa) Alcácer do Sal○ Torrão○ Amareleja○ Fregenal○   Azuaga○ Córdoba○ Úbeda
Cabo Espichel   Grândola○ Barragem de Alqueva de la Sierra○ Constantina○   Jaén○ Baeza○
Baía de Setúbal Sines○ Aljustrel○ Beja○ Serpa○   Palma del Río○ Montilla○ Martos○
Cabo de   Castro○   Valverde○ Lora○ Puente○ Lucena○ Alcaudete○
Sines Odemira○ Almodôvar○ Verde○ del Camino○ del Río○ Genil○ Alcalá la Real○ Baz
Aljezur○   Mértola○   Écija○ Osuna○ Antequera○ Granada○ Guadix○
Cabo de São Vicente Portimão○ *Algarve* Tavira○ Ayamonte○ Huelva○ Marchena○   Vélez- Nevad
Lagos○ ○Albufeira○ Olhão○ Faro○   Sevilla○   Loja○ Málaga Mulha
Sagres○   *Cabo de*   Almonte○ Utrera○   Málaga○ △3482
Santa María Lebrija○ Arcos○ Ronda○   Motril○
Golfo   Sanlúcar○ de la Frontera○ Torremolinos○ Almuñécar○ Adra
de Cádiz de Barrameda○ Jerez de la○ Marbella○ *Costa del Sol* Almr
Cádiz○ Frontera○   Estepona○ Alboran
San○   Algeciras○ Gibraltar (U.K.) Sea
Fernando○ Vejer de la Frontera○   *Europa Point*
Cabo de Trafalgar Strait of Gibraltar Ceuta
MOROCCO Tangier○ (Spain) *Cabo Negro*
Asilah○ Tánger○   Tetouan○

10°   B   5°

© Collins Bartholomew Ltd

0   100   200 KILOMETRES

Conic Equidistant Projection

1 : 8 000 000

Longitude 10° east of Greenwich

MILES 0   50   100   150

© Collins Bartholomew Ltd

0   100   200 KILOMETRES

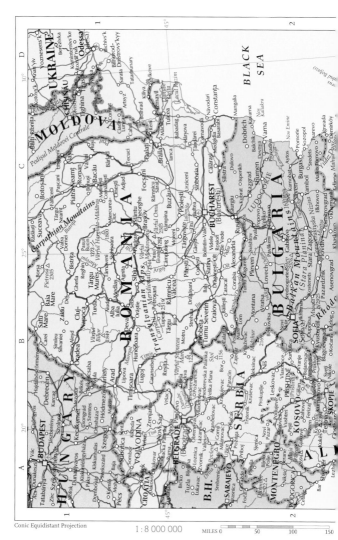

Conic Equidistant Projection

1 : 8 000 000

MILES 0   50   100   150

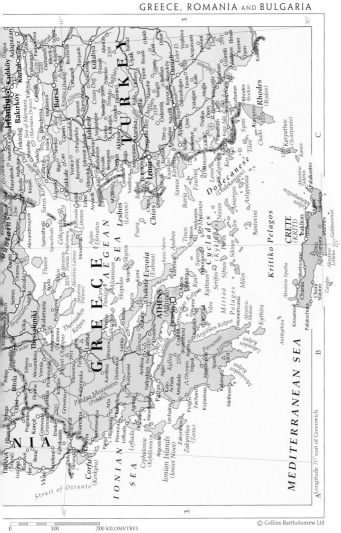

MEDITERRANEAN SEA

© Collins Bartholomew Ltd

0   100   200 KILOMETRES

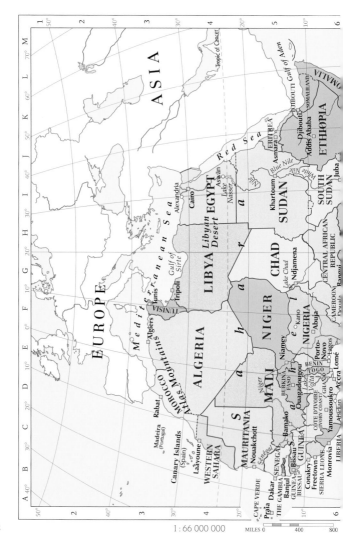

1 : 66 000 000   MILES 0   400   800

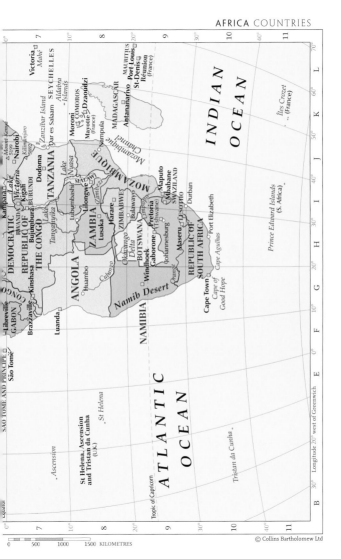

© Collins Bartholomew Ltd

Lambert Azimuthal
Equal Area Projection

A B

20° A 10°

SPAIN
Cartager
Gibraltar (U.K.) Málaga Almería
Tangier Mostaganem
Strait Gibraltar Ceuta (Spain) Oran
(Tanger) Tetouan Melilla Sidi B
Kenitra Ksar el Kebir Oujda Spain Abbé
RABAT Larache Taza Tlemcen
Casablanca Meknes Fès (Fez) Plat
El Jadida MOROCCO

1

A T L A N T I C
O C E A N

Madeira
(Portugal)
FUNCHAL

Safi Settat Beni
Essaouira Mellal Haut Atlas (High Atlas)
Marrakech Tizi △ 167 Rachida Bechar Grand Er
Toubkal Ouarzazate Abadla Occiden
Taroudant Anti-Atlas Beni El Hom
Agadir Hamada du Drâa Abbès
Tiznit Sidi Ifni Ksabi Timimo

30°

SANTA
CRUZ DE Lanzarote Guelmim
La Palma TENERIFE Gran Fuerteventura ALG
La Gomera Canaria El Eglab Adrar Sbaa
El Hierro LAS PALMAS Reggane In Sal
Canary Islands DE GRAN LAÂYOUNE Sebkha
(Islas Canarias) CANARIA Es Semara Chenachane Mekerr
(Spain) Boujdour Sebkha
Matti

2

Galtat Aïn
Zemmour Ben Tili
WESTERN Bir Chegga E R G C H E C H
Ad Dakhla Mogrein
Tropic of Cancer SAHARA El Hammâmi Taoudenni
Administered S OURÂNE
by Morocco Zouérat Taneazrouft
Tichla Fdérik
Choûm

20°

Nouâdhibou
Akjoujt Atâr Araouane M A L I
Nouâmghâr
NOUAKCHOTT Adrar
MAURITANIA des
Ifôghas
Tidjikja Tichit Kidal
St-Louis Rosso Boutilimit Magta Tenzah Anéfis
Dagana Lahjar QualâtaTenagia Qualâta Gourma-
Louga Aleg HÔD Néma Rharous Bourem
DAKAR Linguère Kaédi Kiffa 'Ayoûn el Gao Ménaka
Atroûs TRIGUI Gundam Ansongo
Mbour Bakel Sélibabi Yélimané Bassikounou Niger Timbuktu H
Kaolack Matam Kayes Nioro Faguibine Hombori
SENEGAL Diéma Lac Niangay Djibo NIAME
BANJUL Kolokani Ségou Djenné Tougan Tillabéri
THE GAMBIA Kita BAMAKO Koro Bandiagara Gorom
Ziguinchor Kolda Kéniéba Satadougou Koutiala Koudougou Gorom
GUINEA Mali Siguiri Sikasso BURKINA FASO
BISSAU Tambacounda Kankan Kouroussa Bougouni Bobo OUAGADOUGOU NIAME
Arquipélago Boké Dabola Mandiana Dioulasso Mango BEN
dos Bijagós Labé Dinguiraye Banfora Tenkodogo
CONAKRY Kindia Siguiri Fada-N'Gourma
FREETOWN Forécariah Faranah Odienné Korhogo Bolgatanga
SIERRA Kenema Nzérékoré Man CÔTE D'IVOIRE GHANA
LEONE Zorzor Danané Bouaké Yamoussoukro Tamale
Robertsport Gbanga IVORY COAST Kumasi
MONROVIA YAMOUSSOUKRO Bouaflé Sunyani
LIBERIA Buchanan Gagnoa Abidjan LOMÉ
Greenville Divo ACCRA
Harper San-Pédro Tabou Sassandra Cape Coast Big h
G U L F O F G U I N E A of Ben

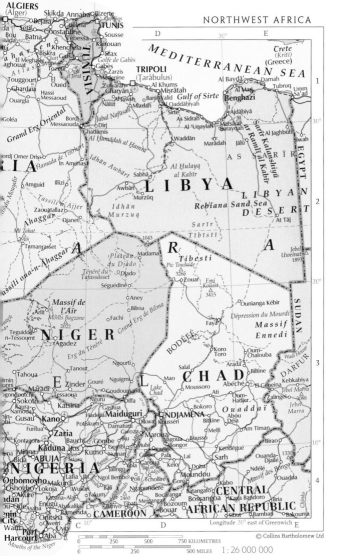

ALGIERS
(Alger)
Skikda Annaba
Bejaïa Guelma Bizerte
Sétif Constantine TUNIS
Batna Tébessa Sousse
Khenchela
Biskra Gafsa Kairouan
El Meghaïer Sfax
Touggourt Tozeur Golfe de Gabès
Chott el Jerid Gabès
El Oued Médenine
Ghardaïa Hassi Zuwārah
Messaoud Gharyān
Ouargla Bordj Ghadāmis

TRIPOLI
(Ṭarābulus)
Al Khums Misrātah
Al Hawsh Banī Walīd
Nālūt Mizdah
Al Qaddāhiyah
Sirte
Al Fuqahā
MEDITERRANEAN SEA

Crete
(Kriti)
(Greece)

Al Baydā' Darnah
Al Marj Tubruq Umm
Benghazi Sa'ad
Ajdābiyā

Sarīr
Al Jaghbūb
Maradah Jālū Siwah

Grand Erg Oriental
Hamada de Tinhert
Ghadāmis
Al Ḥamādah al Ḥamrā'
Jabal Nafūsah
Dirj
Waddān

Omer Driss
In Amenas
Idhān Awbārī
Sabhā Al Ḥulayq
al Kabir
Awbārī
Murzūq
Rebiana Sand Sea

LIBYA
L I B Y A N

D E S E R T

At Tāj

Tassili n'Ajjer
Zaouatallaz
Djanet

Idhān
Murzūq

Sarīr Tibastī

Amguid
Illizi

EGYPT

Ahaggar
Mt Tahat
2918
Tamanrasset

Tassili oua-n-Ahaggar

A
H
A
G
G
A
R

1043
Plateau
du Djado
Madama
Djado
Séguédine

Tibesti
Pic Toussidé
3260
Zouar

Jebel
Uweinat
1893

Emi
Koussi
3415

SUDAN

Arlit
Ténéré du
Tafassâsset
Aney
Bilma
Fachi

Ounianga Kébir

Dépression du Mourdi

Massif
Ennedi

Massif de
l'Aïr
Mons Bagzane
2022
Agadez

Teguidda
n-Tessoumt
Tahoua

NIGER
Erg du Ténéré

Faya

BODÉLÉ

DARFUR

Koro
Toro

Wadi Howar

Arada

Kebkabiya

Tanout
Ngourti
Salal
Biltine
El Geneina

Zinder
Gouré
Nguigmi
Mao
Moussoro
Abéché

Tessaoua
Nguru
Lake
Chad
Ati
Oum-
Hadjer
Ouaddaï
Zalingei

Maradi
Sokoto
Katsina
Gashua
Diffa
Bokoro
Abou
Deïa
Jebel
Marra
3088
Jebel
Marra

Gusau
Funtua
Hadejia
Damaturu
Dikwa
Kousséri
Massakory
Bitkine
Am Timan

Kano
Maiduguri
NDJAMENA
Melfi

Zaria
Potiskum
Maroua
Magoua
Boussou
Kaduna
Bauchi
Gombe
Biu
Mubi
Gombi
Bongor
Kendégué

CHAD

Birao
1330

ABUJA
Jos
Numan
Guider
Pala
Laï
Sarh
Ouanda-
Djallé
Ouadda

Minna
Bida
Kontagora
Lafia
Jalingo
Ngol Bembo
Garoua
Kélo
Doba
Ndélé

NIGERIA
Makurdi
Wukari
Poli
Ngaoundéré
Bocaranga
Bossangoa
Bambari
Bria
Bakouma

Ogbomosho
Lokoja
Katsina-Ala
Takum
Bali
Tibati
Meïganga
Bouar
Kabo
Bozoum
Kaga Bandoro

Bamenda

CENTRAL

Akure
Enugu
Abakaliki
2460
Banyo
Bouar
Bangassou
Sibut
Bamban
Bakouma

Onitsha
Owerri
CAMEROON
AFRICAN REPUBLIC

Port
Harcourt
Aba
Uyo

Mouths of the Niger

C 10°
D
Longitude 20° east of Greenwich
E

© Collins Bartholomew Ltd

0   250   500   750 KILOMETRES
0   250   500 MILES
1 : 26 000 000

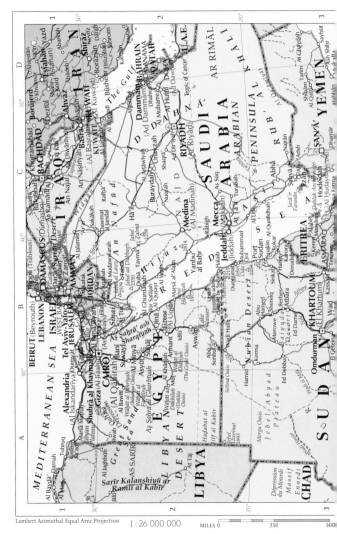

Lambert Azimuthal Equal Area Projection   1 : 26 000 000   MILES 0   250   500

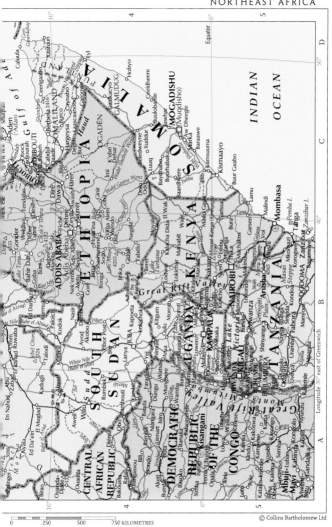

© Collins Bartholomew Ltd

0   250   500   750 KILOMETRES

118   Lambert Azimuthal Equal Area Projection   1 : 20 000 000   MILES 0   100   200   300   400

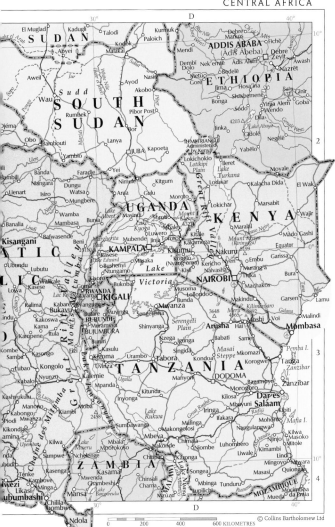

0   200   400   600 KILOMETRES

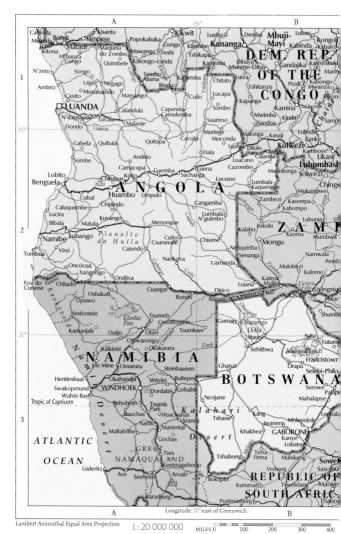

Lambert Azimuthal Equal Area Projection   1 : 20 000 000   MILES 0   100   200   300   400

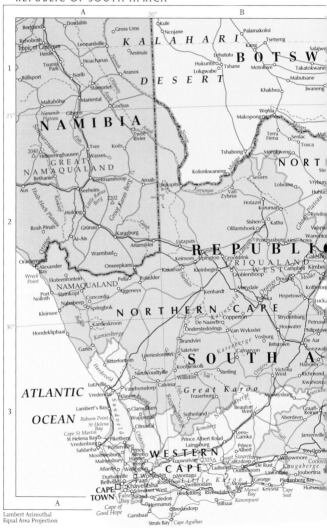

Lambert Azimuthal
Equal Area Projection

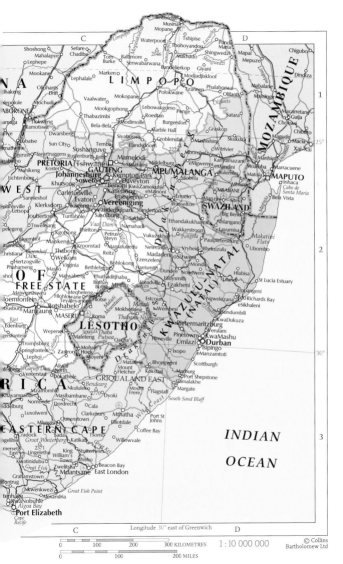

INDIAN

OCEAN

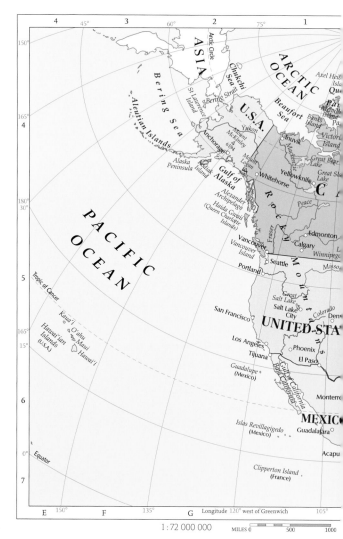

4   45°   3   60°   2   75°   1

150°

ASIA

Arctic Circle

ARCTIC OCEAN

Axel Heil
Isla
Que

Par
Melvil
Island
Pa

Bering Sea

Chukchi
Sea

Beaufort
Sea

Banks
Island

Bering Strait

St Lawrence
Island

U.S.A.

Inuvik

Mackenzie

Victoria
Island

165°
4

Anchorage

Yukon

Mount
McKinley
6194

Mount
Logan
5959

Yellowknife

Great Bear
Lake

Great Sla
Lake

C

Aleutian Islands

Alaska
Peninsula

Kodiak
Island

Gulf of
Alaska

Whitehorse

Rocky

Peace

180°
30°

PACIFIC

Alexander
Archipelago

Haida Gwaii
(Queen
Charlotte
Islands)

Fraser

Edmonton

L

Calgary

Winnipeg

OCEAN

Vancouver

Vancouver
Island

Seattle

Mou

Misso

Portland

5

Tropic of Cancer

Great
Salt Lake

n t

San Francisco

Salt Lake
City

Colorado

Den

165°
15°

Kaua'i   O'ahu

Hawaiian
Islands
(U.S.A.)

Maui

Hawai'i

Los Angeles

Tijuana

UNITED STA

Phoenix

El Paso

Guadalupe
(Mexico)

Gulf of California

6

Monter

Islas Revillagigedo
(Mexico)

MEXIC

Guadalajara

0°

Equator

Clipperton Island
(France)

Acapu

7

E   150°   F   135°   G   Longitude 120° west of Greenwich   105°

1 : 72 000 000   MILES 0   500   1000

1   75°   2   60°   3   45°   4

Greenland Sea

Ellesmere Island

Elizabeth Islands

Devon Island

Baffin Bay

Baffin Island

Greenland

Nuuk

Denmark Strait

Davis Strait

Foxe Basin

Southampton Island

Hudson Strait

Cape Farewell

0°

4

15°

CA NA DA

Labrador Sea

Hudson Bay

Belcher Islands

Nelson

James Bay

Île d'Anticosti

Newfoundland

St John's

St-Pierre

30°

Lake Winnipeg

Lake Nipigon

Gulf of St Lawrence

St Pierre and Miquelon (France)

Thunder Bay

Québec

Montréal

Halifax

Portland

Cape Sable

Ottawa

Toronto

Azores

Great Lakes

Minneapolis

Detroit

Cleveland

Boston

New York

Washington

5

30°

Chicago

Pittsburgh

Philadelphia

Columbus

St Louis

Kansas

Memphis

S OF AMERICA

Cape Hatteras

Bermuda (U.K.)

AT LA N T I C

O C E A N

15°

Dallas

Atlanta

Houston

New Orleans

Jacksonville

Orlando

THE BAHAMAS

Nassau

Turks and Caicos Islands (U.K.)

Virgin Islands (U.S.A)

Virgin Islands (U.K.)

6

Gulf of Mexico

Miami

Havana

CUBA

Santo Domingo

San Juan

ST KITTS AND NEVIS

ANTIGUA AND BARBUDA

Cayman Islands (U.K.)

Kingston HAITI

Puerto Rico (U.S.A)

Guadeloupe (France)

DOMINICA

ico City

Mérida

Yucatán

Veracruz

Pico de Orizaba

JAMAICA

DOMINICAN REPUBLIC

Port-au-Prince

Martinique (France)

ST LUCIA

BARBADOS

Caribbean Sea

GRENADA

ST VINCENT AND THE GRENADINES

0°

BELIZE

Belmopan

GUATEMALA

HONDURAS

Tegucigalpa

Aruba (Neth.)

TRINIDAD AND TOBAGO

emala City

San Salvador

EL SALVADOR

NICARAGUA

Managua

Lake Nicaragua

Canal de Panamá

7

San José

COSTA RICA

Panama City

PANAMA

S O U T H   A M E R I C A

90°   J   75°   K   60°   L   45°

EUROPE

0   500   1000   1500 KILOMETRES

© Collins Bartholomew Ltd

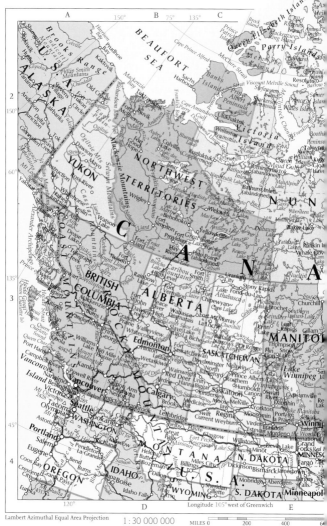

Lambert Azimuthal Equal Area Projection   1 : 30 000 000   MILES 0   200   400   60

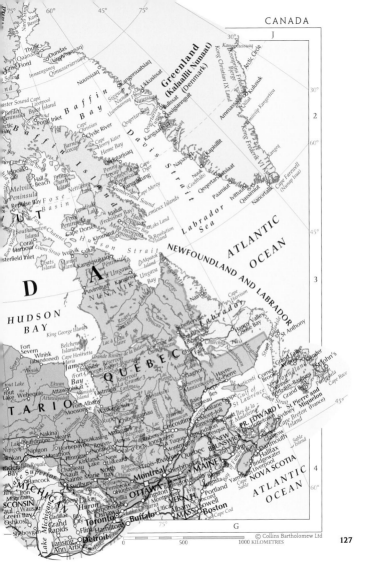

© Collins Bartholomew Ltd

128   Lambert Azimuthal Equal Area Projection   1 : 15 000 000   MILES 0   100   200   300

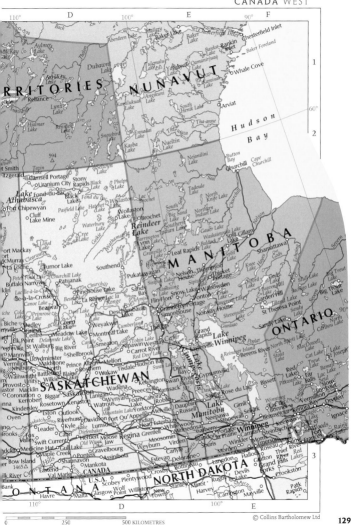

© Collins Bartholomew Ltd

0   250   500 KILOMETRES

A · 90° · B · 80° · C

MANITOBA

Hudson Bay

NUNAVUT

James Bay

ONTARIO

QU

Lake Superior

CANADA
U.S.

MICHIGAN

WISCONSIN

Lake Huron

OTTAWA

Lake Ontario

Montréal

Toronto

NEW

Milwaukee

Chicago

Lake Michigan

INDIANA

Detroit

Lake Erie

OHIO

YORK

B · Longitude 80° west of Greenwich · C

Lambert Azimuthal Equal Area Projection   1 : 15 000 000   MILES 0   100   200   300

Tasiujaq   Kangiqsualujjuaq   Koroc   Hebron
Kangiqsualujjuaq   Cod Island
Nutsuliang (Fort Chimo)   Kosoak   Rivière   George   ATLANTIC
Thévenet   Fraser   Nain
Méton   OCEAN
Ghakonateau   Kasserine   Voisey's Bay
Cambrien   Matuashish
Lac   Utsasdik Inlet
Lac   Lac Cuers   Davis Inlet
Lannin   (abandoned)   Cape Harrison   1
Mopedale
Lac Gotchois   Hopedale
Makkovik
Caniapiscau   Nipishish   Rigolet   Sandwich Bay
Réservoir de   Schefferville   Lake   Groswater Bay   Cartwright
caniapiscau   Menihek   Esker   Smallwood   North West River
forge   Lac   Churchill   Reservoir   Lake Melville   Mealy Mountains   Port Hope
Grande 4   Bermen   Falls   Happy Valley-Goose Bay   Alexis   Simpson
E C   Opiscoteo   Labrador   Churchill   Minipi Lake
Fermont   Ashuanipi   Red Bay   Belle Isle
Lac   Joseph   St-Barbe   Cook's Harbour
Naococane   St-Anthony   Roddickton
Gagnon   Petit Lac   Port aux   Grey Islands
Réservoir   Manouagan   Choix   Horse Islands
Lac Plétipi   Réservoir   Blanc-Sablon
Manicouagan   St-Augustin   Twillingate   Notre Dame Bay   Fogo
Lac   Lac   La Tabatière   Springdale   Grand   Bonavista
Manouane   Berté   Harrington   Windsor   Bay
Réservoir   Harbour   Deer Lake   Gander   Bonavista
Outardes Quatre   Lac   Mingan   Havre-St-Pierre   Natashquan   Newfoundland   Porth
Lac Péribonka   Chute   Sept-Îles   Corner Brook   Round   Clarenville   Cove
odes-Passes   eau Brûlé   Baie-   Port-Menier   Île d'Anticosti   Stephenville   Lake   Terrenceville   Pouch
Réservoir   Comeau   Mt Jacques   Gaspé   Gulf of St Lawrence   Channel-Port-   Burgeo   Cove
manicouagan   Hauterive   Cartier   (Golfe du St-Laurent)   aux Basques   St John's
Ichinav   Betsiamites   des-Monts   1268   Harbour Breton   Bay Bulls
stashi   Forestville   Ste-Anne-   Grand Bank   Placentia
Aima   des-Monts   Matane   Pén. de Gaspésie   St Pierre and   Burin   Bay
Chicoutimi   Rimouski   Grande-Rivière   Miquelon   Trepassey
onquière   Trois-   Amqui   Cabot Strait   (France) ST-PIERRE   Cape Race
St-Siméon   Pistoles   Iles de la
Rivière-du-Loup   St Quentin   Bathurst   Havre-Aubert   Madeleine
St-Paul   Edmundston   Caraquet   Cape Breton
ontmagny   Grand Falls   Miramichi   PRINCE EDWARD   Island
ECE   Presque Isle   Nepisiguit   Tracadie   ISLAND   Chéticamp   Glace Bay
Thetford   Caribou   Woodstock   Minto   Summerside   Souris   Sydney
Mines   St-George   Kahibdi   Bouctouche   Charlottetown   Inverness   d'Or Lake
mmondville   Asbestos   Fredericton   NEW   Riverview   Moncton   Amherst   New Glasgow   Port   Lake
res   Millinocket   BRUNSWICK   Sackville   Glasgow   Hawkesbury
rookeook   Mégantic   Gander   Sussex   Truro   Antigonish
chelbu   Bingham   Dover-Foxcroft   Saint   Wolfville   Sherbrooke
awoon   Skowhegan   Bangor   John   NOVA SCOTIA
Groveton   MAINE   Machias   Dartmouth
sbury   Waterville   Bucksport   Bay of Fundy   Halifax
ers   Augusta   Ellsworth   Digby   Bridgewater   Sable Island
Jeffer   Lewiston   Bar   Lunenburg
.H. Conway   Brunswick   Harbor   Yarmouth   Liverpool   ATLANTIC
Laconia   Portland   Cape   Shelburne
iester   Middleford   Sable   OCEAN   2
Portsmouth
Manchester
nua   Portsmouth
ridge   Lowell
Boston
Quincy   Massachusetts Bay
Worcester   Cape Cod

0   250   500 KILOMETRES

© Collins Bartholomew Ltd

Lambert Azimuthal Equal Area Projection   1 : 25 000 000   MILES 0   250   5

133

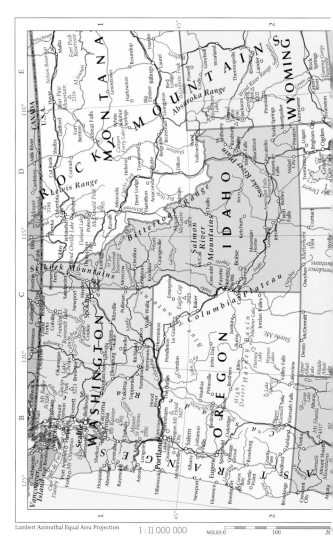

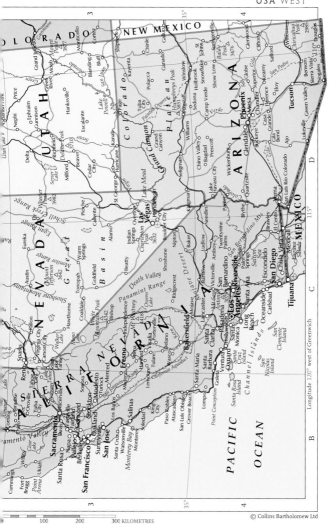

100   200   300 KILOMETRES

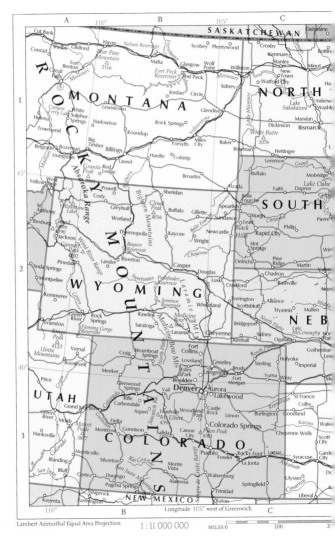

Lambert Azimuthal Equal Area Projection   1 : 11 000 000   MILES 0   100   2

© Collins Bartholomew Ltd

0   100   200   300 KILOMETRES

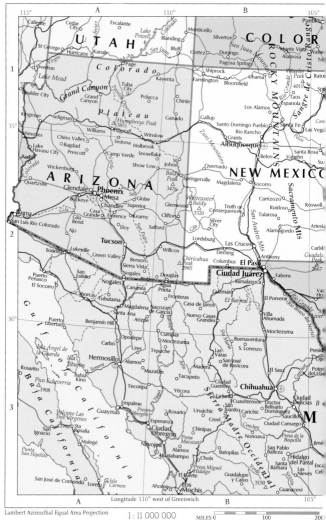

Lambert Azimuthal Equal Area Projection   1 : 11 000 000   MILES 0   100   200

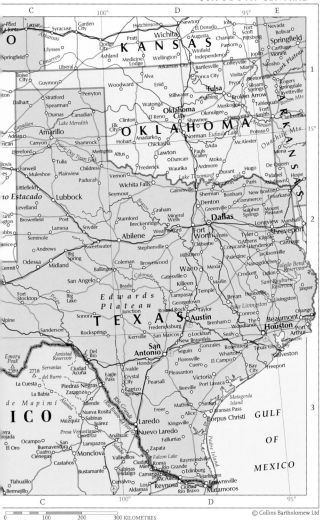

0   100   200   300 KILOMETRES

Lambert Azimuthal Equal Area Projection 1 : 11 000 000 MILES 0 100 200

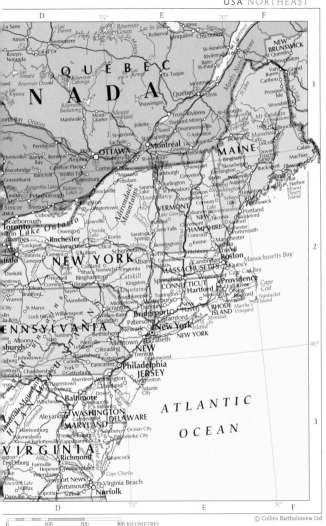

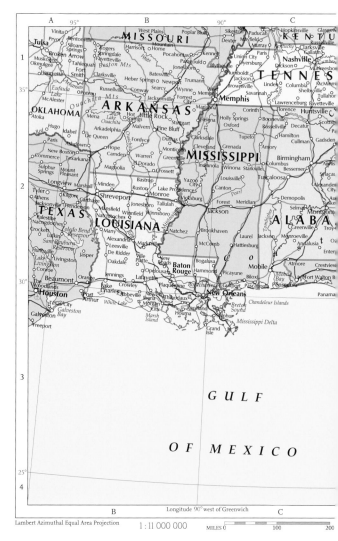

Lambert Azimuthal Equal Area Projection   1 : 11 000 000   MILES 0   100   200

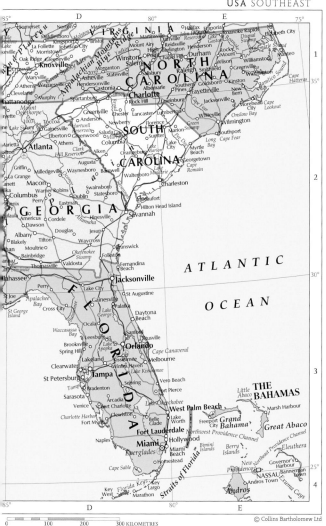

ATLANTIC

OCEAN

300 KILOMETRES

© Collins Bartholomew Ltd

143

Lambert Azimuthal Equal Area Projection   1 : 15 000 000   MILES 0   100   200   300

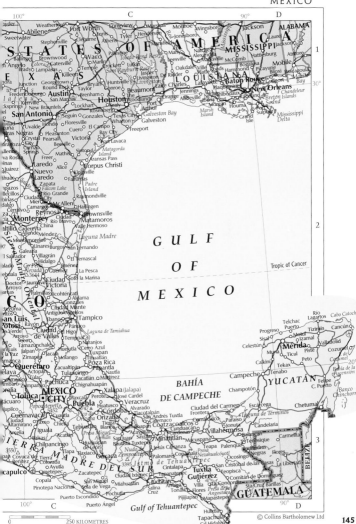

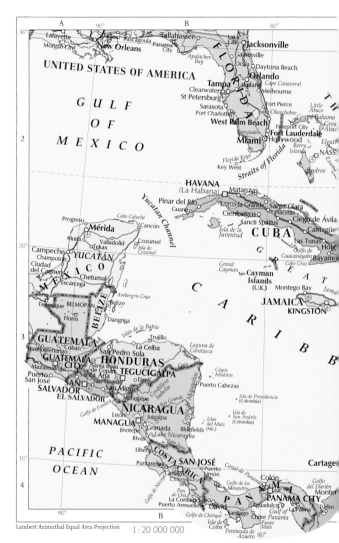

Map of the Gulf of Mexico, Central America and the Caribbean

United States of America

Lafayette · Biloxi · Pascagoula · Tallahassee · Lake City · Jacksonville
Morgan City · New Orleans · Panama City · Gainesville
Apalachee Bay · Ocala · Daytona Beach

UNITED STATES OF AMERICA

Tampa · Lakeland · Orlando
Clearwater · FLORIDA · Melbourne
St Petersburg · Cape Canaveral
Sarasota · Fort Pierce
Port Charlotte · Lake Okeechobee · Freeport City · Grand Bahama · Great Abaco
West Palm Beach · Little Abaco
Everglades · Fort Lauderdale
Miami · Hollywood · Berry Islands · Eleuthera
NASS
Florida Keys · Straits of Florida · Andros
Key West

GULF OF MEXICO

HAVANA (La Habana) · Matanzas
Pinar del Río · Sagua la Grande · Santa Clara · Placetas · Ciego de Ávila
Guane · Cienfuegos · Sancti Spíritus · CUBA · Camagüey
Isla de la Juventud · Las Tunas · Holguín
Golfo de Guacanayabo · Bayamo

Progreso · Cabo Catoche · Cancún
Muna · Mérida · GREAT
Valladolid · Cozumel
Campeche · Tekax · Isla de Cozumel
Champotón · YUCATÁN · Grand Cayman · Cayman Islands (U.K.) · Montego Bay · JAMAICA · KINGSTON
Ciudad del Carmen · M E X I C O · Chetumal
Escárcega · Ambergris Caye · CARIBB
Palenque · Belize
Tenosique · BELMOPAN · Belize
Flores · Dangriga · Islas de la Bahía · Trujillo
Coban · GUATEMALA · La Ceiba · Laguna de Caratasca
Huehuetenango · San Pedro Sula · HONDURAS · Coco
GUATEMALA CITY · Santa Rosa de Copán · Cayos Miskitos
Mazatenango · Santa Ana · TEGUCIGALPA · Danlí · Puerto Cabezas
Puerto SAN · San Miguel · Río Grande
San José · SALVADOR · Matagalpa · Cordillera Isabelia · Isla de Providencia (Colombia)
EL SALVADOR · NICARAGUA
Golfo de Fonseca · León · Juigalpa · Isla de San Andrés (Colombia)
MANAGUA · Bluefields · Islas del Maíz (Nic.)
Jinotepe · Granada · Lake Nicaragua
Rivas · San Juan

PACIFIC OCEAN

Liberia · COSTA · SAN JOSÉ · Cartagena
Puntarenas · RICA · Puerto Limón · Canal de Panamá · Colón · Golfo del Darién
Cartago · Golfo de los Mosquitos · Monter
Chirripó · 3819 · Aguadulce · PANAMA CITY
Pen. de Osa · La Concepción · David · P A N A M Á · Turbo
Puerto Armuelles · Santiago · Chitré · Gulf of Panama
Golfo de Chiriquí · Punta Mala
Isla de Coiba · Península de Azuero

Lambert Azimuthal Equal Area Projection   1 : 20 000 000

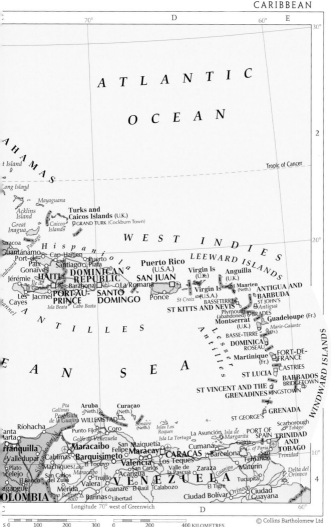

ATLANTIC

OCEAN

Tropic of Cancer

WEST INDIES

LEEWARD ISLANDS

Hispaniola

BAHAMAS

Acklins Island
Great Inagua
Mayaguana
Long Island

Turks and Caicos Islands (U.K.)
⊡ GRAND TURK (Cockburn Town)
Caicos Islands

Baracoa
Guantánamo
Cap-Haïtien
Paix
Santiago
Puerto Plata
Gonaïves
Jérémie
Île de la Gonâve
Barahona
Les Cayes
Jacmel
Isla Beata
Cabo Beata

HAITI
DOMINICAN REPUBLIC
PORT-AU-PRINCE
SANTO DOMINGO
La Romana
Ponce

Puerto Rico (U.S.A.)
SAN JUAN
St Croix

Virgin Is (U.K.)
Virgin Is (U.S.A.)

Anguilla (U.K.)
St Maarten (Neth.)
BASSETERRE
ST JOHN'S
St Antigua

ANTIGUA AND BARBUDA

ST KITTS AND NEVIS
Plymouth (abandoned)
Montserrat (U.K.)
BRADES

Guadeloupe (Fr.)
BASSE-TERRE
Marie-Galante (Fr.)

DOMINICA
ROSEAU

Martinique (Fr.)
FORT-DE-FRANCE

ST LUCIA
CASTRIES

BARBADOS
BRIDGETOWN

ST VINCENT AND THE GRENADINES
KINGSTOWN

ST GEORGE'S
GRENADA

Lesser Antilles

WINDWARD ISLANDS

CARIBBEAN SEA

Pta Gallinas
Peninsula de la Guajira
Aruba (Neth.)
Curaçao (Neth.)
WILLEMSTAD
Bonaire (Neth.)
Punto Fijo
Coro
Golfo de Venezuela
Islas Los Roques
Isla La Tortuga
La Asunción
Isla de Margarita

Scarborough
Tobago
PORT OF SPAIN
TRINIDAD AND TOBAGO
Trinidad
Güiria
G. of Paria

Ríohacha
Santa Marta
ranquilla
Valledupar
Cabimas
Machiques
San Carlos del Zulia
El Banco
agangué
El Plato
celejo
COLOMBIA

Maracaibo
Lake Maracaibo
Barquisimeto
San Felipe
Acarigua
Trujillo
Mérida
Valera
Guanare
Barinas
Libertad

Valencia
Maracay
Los Teques
San Fernando
El Baúl
Calabozo

CARACAS
Barcelona
Valle de la Pascua
Zaraza
Cumaná
San Maiquetía

Maturín
El Tigre
Tucupita
Delta del Orinoco

Guanipa
Ciudad Bolívar
Ciudad Guayana

VENEZUELA

Orinoco

Longitude 70° west of Greenwich

S 0   100   200   300   0   200   400 KILOMETRES

© Collins Bartholomew Ltd

148

1 : 50 000 000

MILES 0   500   1000

Lambert Azimuthal Equal Area Projection   1 : 25 000 000   MILES 0   250   500

C   50°   D   40° E

ATLANTIC

OCEAN

10°

EORGETOWN
New
Amsterdam
Nieuw   PARAMARIBO
Nickerie   St-Laurent-du-Maroni
Professor van
Blommestein Me   Kourou
URINAME   CAYENNE
French   Chapoque
Pontoetoe   **Guiana**   1

Serra Tumucumaque   Lourenço   Calçoene
Santana   *Ilha de Maracá*
Amapá

Arere   Porto   Cabo
Santana   *Norguarinho*   Mouths of the Amazon
Mazagão   Chaves   *Baía de Marajó*   Equator   0°
riximina   Óbidos   Almeirim   *Ilha de Marajó*
acara   Monte   Breves   **Belém**   Bragança
ucurituba   Alegre   Portel   Cametá   Viseu   2
Santarém   Castanhal
Altamira   Pinheiro   Curuçá   São Luís   Camocim
Tucuruí   Viana   Parnaíba
Represa de   Itapecuru-   Luziliândia   **Fortaleza**
Itaituba   *Tucuruí*   Jacundá   Mirim   Piripiri   Caucaia
Maracanã   Grajaú   Codó   Tianguá   Maior   Caninde   Aracati
areacanga   Marabá   Bacabal   Timon   Sobral   Quixadá   Macau Touros
Imperatriz   Barra   Caxias   Teresina   Taua   **Mossoró**   *Ponta do Calçanhar*
Manuelzinho   São   Tocantinópolis   do Corda   Pres. Dutra   Palmeiras   Iguatu   Sousa   **Natal**
Félix   Araguaína   Porto Franco   *Açude Boa*   Floriano   Picos   Crato   **João**
A   R   A   Z   I   L   Conceição   Balsas   *Esperança*   Oeiras   Juazeiro   Campina   **Pessoa**
do Araguaia   Carolina   Jerumenha   do Norte   Grande   Jaboatão
Serra   Santa Maria   Uruçuí   São Raimundo Nonato   Floresta   Garanhuns   Olinda
do Cachimbo   das Barreiras   Pedro   Canto do Buriti   Paulistana   Garanhuns   **Recife**
erra Gaúchos Óbidos   Afonso   Caracol   Petrolina   *Serra da Fraincana*   **Maceió**
Porto   **Palmas**   *Barragem de*   Juazeiro   Arapiraca
Artur   Porto   *Sobradinho*   Senhor do Bonfim   Paulo   Monte Santo
amantino   Nacional   Xique-   Jacobina   Aracaju
Dianópolis   Corrente   Xique   Irecê   Serrinha   Estância
Serra   São Félix   Barreiras   Ibotirama   Feira de   Alagoinhas
do Roncador   Natividade   Santana   Bom Jesus   Santana   **Salvador**
Ilha do   da Lapa   Sto Antônio   Jequié   Ubaitaba
acres   *Bananal*   Porangatu   Correntina   Itaberaba   de Jesus   Ilhéus
Cuiabá   Barra do   Cavalcante   Posse   Januária   Brumado   Guanambi   Itabuna   Una
Garças   Uruaçu   Niquelândia   Formosa   Vitória da   Itapetinga
Rondonópolis   Goiás   **BRASÍLIA**   Arinos   Montes Claros   Conquista   Porto Seguro
berto   Alto Garças   Iporá   Anápolis   Unaí   Salinas   Almenara
abel   Itiquira   *Serra do*   **Goiânia**   Paracatu   Jequitaí   Teófilo   Alcobaça
Coxim   *Caiapó*   Vianópolis   Otoni
Taquari   Rio Verde   Jataí   Itumbiara   Araguari   Patos
Rio Verde de Mato Grosso   de Minas

C   50°   D   40° E

0   250   500   750 KILOMETRES

© Collins Bartholomew Ltd   **151**

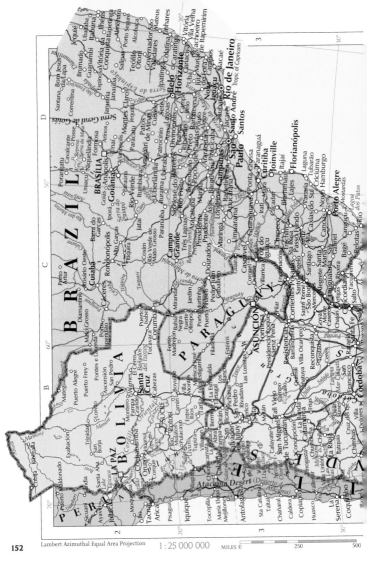

Lambert Azimuthal Equal Area Projection   1 : 25 000 000   MILES 0   250   500

ATLANTIC

OCEAN

URUGUAY

MONTEVIDEO

BUENOS AIRES
Lomas de Zamora La Plata

Mar del Plata

Pinamar

Necochea

ARGENTINA

Falkland Islands
(U.K.)
STANLEY
West
Falkland
East
Falkland

Bahía Blanca

Golfo San Matías
Península
Valdés

Comodoro Rivadavia

Golfo
San
Jorge

PATAGONIA

Puerto Santa Cruz
Río Gallegos

Río Grande

SANTIAGO

Valparaíso

Concepción

Valdivia

Osorno
Puerto
Montt

0   250   500   750 KILOMETRES

154   Lambert Azimuthal Equal Area Projection   1 : 10 000 000   MILES 0   100   200

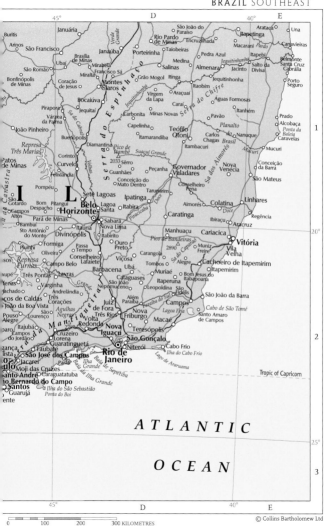

ATLANTIC

OCEAN

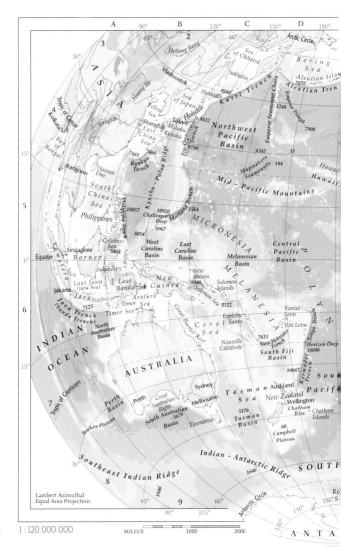

A 90° B 120° C 150° D 180°

2

3

Arctic Circle

45°

30°

Heilong Jiang

Sea of Okhotsk

Bering Sea

A S I A

Vladivostok

Sakhalin

Aleutian Islands

Tropic of Cancer

Huang He

60°

Hokkaidō

9550

Kuril Trench

Aleutian Trench

Emperor Seamount Chain

1240

7822

Emperor Trough

7900

4 Kolkata

Yellow Sea

Yangtze

Sea of Japan

Honshū

8412

Shanghai

Tokyo

East China Sea

Kyūshū

Northwest Pacific Basin

Bay of Bengal

15°

Rangoon

Hainan Dao

7181

7460

Ryukyu Trench

Izu-Ogasawara Trench

9780

6345

18

Hawaii

Mapmakers Seamounts

104

Hawaii

South China Sea

Kyushu – Palau Ridge

Mariana Trench

Mid - Pacific Mountains

5

Philippines

10057

Philippine Trench

10920

Challenger Deep

8967

1564

M I C R O N E S I A

Central Pacific Basin

Equator

Singapore

8054

Celebes Sea

5484

West Caroline Basin

East Caroline Basin

Melanesian Basin

P

O

L

Y

N

0°

Borneo

Sulawesi

Laut Jawa (Java Sea)

Laut Banda

7288

New Guinea

New Britain

5940

Solomon Islands

M E L A N E S I A

Jakarta

Java

Sumatra

Arafura Sea

Solomon Trench

8322

Vanua Levu

Viti Levu

6

Java Trench (Sunda Trench)

Timor Sea

7125

North Australian Basin

Great Barrier Reef

Coral Sea

Espíritu Santo

7633

New Hebrides Trench

Nouvelle Calédonie

South Fiji Basin

Horizon Deep

10800

Tonga Trench

I N D I A N

15°

AUSTRALIA

10047

Kermadec Trench

S o u

P a c i f i

O C E A N

Tropic of Capricorn

7

Broken Plateau

Perth Basin

Perth

Great Australian Bight

Sydney

Melbourne

South Australian Basin

5670

T a s m a n Sea

Auckland

New Zealand

Wellington

Chatham Rise

Chatham Islands

Tasmania

5176

Tasman Basin

60

Campbell Plateau

Southeast Indian Ridge

8

1340

Indian - Antarctic Ridge

1646

S O U T H

Lambert Azimuthal
Equal Area Projection

45°

9

90°

60°

105°

Antarctic Circle

150°

180° S

120°

Ro

A N T A

MILES 0   1000   2000

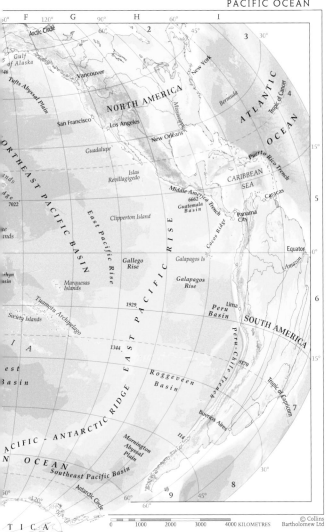

F 120° G 90° H 60° 2 45° 30° 3

Arctic Circle

Gulf of Alaska

Vancouver

Tufts Abyssal Plain

NORTH AMERICA

New York

San Francisco

Los Angeles

New Orleans

Mississippi

Bermuda

Tropic of Cancer

ATLANTIC

4

OCEAN

15°

Guadalupe

Islas Revillagigedo

Middle America Trench

6662

Guatemala Basin

CARIBBEAN SEA

Puerto Rico Trench

Caracas

5

NORTHEAST PACIFIC BASIN

7022

Clipperton Island

East Pacific Rise

Cocos Ridge

Panama City

Gallego Rise

Galapagos Is

Equator

0°

Amazon

rhyn asin

Marquesas Islands

EAST PACIFIC RISE

Galapagos Rise

Lima

Peru Basin

6

Tuamotu Archipelago

1929

SOUTH AMERICA

Society Islands

I A

1344

Peru-Chile Trench

15°

est

Basin

Roggeveen Basin

8170

Tropic of Capricorn

7

PACIFIC - ANTARCTIC RIDGE

Mornington Abyssal Plain

Buenos Aires

114

N OCEAN

Southeast Pacific Basin

30°

Antarctic Circle

60°

120°

60°

60°

45°

8

9

T I C A

0 1000 2000 3000 4000 KILOMETRES

© Collins Bartholomew Ltd

157

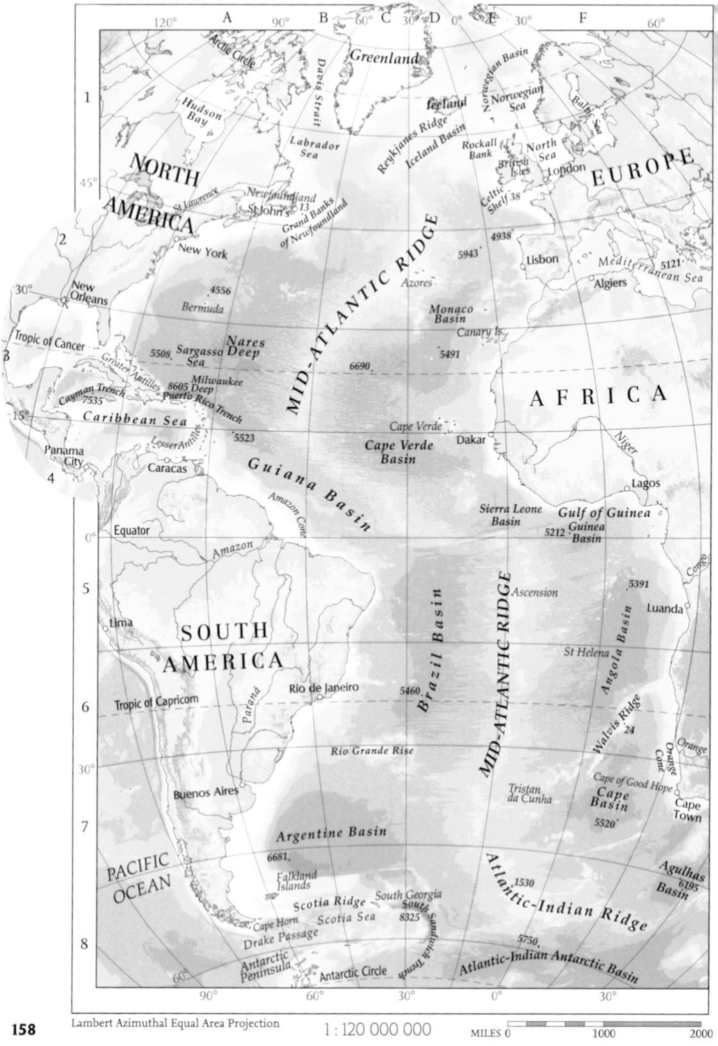

120° A 90° B 60° C 30° D E 30° F 60°

Arctic Circle
Davis Strait
Greenland
Iceland
Norwegian Basin
Norwegian Sea
Baltic Sea
1
Hudson Bay
Labrador Sea
Reykjanes Ridge
Iceland Basin
Rockall Bank
North Sea
British Isles
London
EUROPE

NORTH AMERICA
St Lawrence
Newfoundland
St John's 13
Grand Banks of Newfoundland
Celtic Shelf 38
4938
Lisbon
Mediterranean Sea
5121
45°
New York
5943
Azores
Algiers

New Orleans
4556
Bermuda
Monaco Basin
Canary Is.
2
Tropic of Cancer
Nares Deep
Sargasso Sea
5508
5491
AFRICA
Greater Antilles
Cayman Trench 7535
13
Milwaukee
8605 Deep
Puerto Rico Trench
6690
3
15°
Caribbean Sea
Lesser Antilles
5523
Cape Verde
Cape Verde Basin
Dakar

Panama City
Caracas
Guiana Basin
Niger
Lagos
4
Amazon Cone
Sierra Leone Basin
Gulf of Guinea
Guinea Basin
5212
Congo
Equator
Amazon
0°

Lima
SOUTH AMERICA
Ascension
5391
Luanda
5
Brazil Basin
St Helena
Angola Basin
MID-ATLANTIC RIDGE

Paraná
Rio de Janeiro
5460
6
Tropic of Capricorn
Walvis Ridge 24
Orange Cone
30°
Buenos Aires
Rio Grande Rise
Tristan da Cunha
Cape of Good Hope
Cape Basin
5520
Cape Town
Agulhas Basin 6195
7
PACIFIC OCEAN
Argentine Basin
6681
1530
Falkland Islands
Atlantic-Indian Ridge
Scotia Ridge
South Georgia
South Sandwich Trench
8325
5750
Atlantic-Indian Antarctic Basin
8
Cape Horn
Drake Passage
Scotia Sea
Antarctic Peninsula
Antarctic Circle
90° 60° 30° 0° 30°

MID-ATLANTIC RIDGE

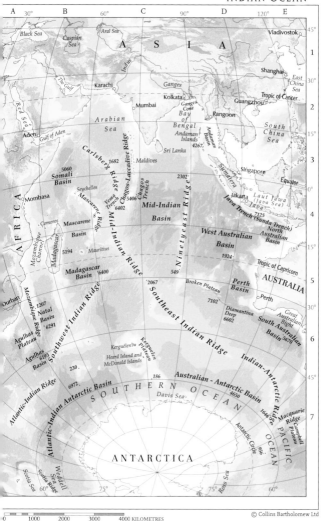

A 30° B 60° C 90° D 120° E

Black Sea
Caspian Sea
Aral Sea
Vladivostok
45°
A S I A
1
Indus
The Gulf
Karachi
Ganges
Shanghai
East China Sea
30°
Tropic of Cancer
Kolkata
Guangzhou
Mumbai
Ganges Cone
Bay of Bengal
Rangoon
2
Arabian Sea
Andaman Islands
4267
South China Sea
Aden
Gulf of Aden
15°
Sri Lanka
Somali Basin
Carlsberg Ridge
1682
Chagos-Laccadive Ridge
Maldives
2302
Sumatra
Singapore
3
5060
Seychelles
Vema Trench
6402
Chagos Trench
5406
Mid-Indian Ridge
7125
Equator
Mombasa
Mascarene Ridge
Mid-Indian Basin
Nineteast Ridge
Jakarta
Laut Jawa (Java Sea)
Java Trench (Sunda Trench)
North Australian Basin
0°
A F R I C A
Comoros
Mascarene Basin
West Australian Basin
4
5194
Mauritius
15°
Madagascar
1924
Tropic of Capricorn
Mozambique Channel
Madagascar Basin
6400
549
Broken Plateau
Perth Basin
AUSTRALIA
Durban
1207
Natal Basin
6291
2067
7102
Diamantina Deep
6602
Perth
Great Australian Bight
30°
5
Agulhas Plateau
6195
Agulhas Basin
Southwest Indian Ridge
Mozambique Ridge
South Australian Basin
5670
230
Kerguélen Plateau
Kerguelen Plateau
Indian-Antarctic Ridge
45°
6
Atlantic-Indian Ridge
Heard Island and McDonald Islands
6972
Atlantic-Indian Antarctic Basin
186
Australian-Antarctic Basin
4650
Davis Sea
956
Macquarie Ridge
Campbell Plateau
1648
P A C I F I C
S O U T H E R N   O C E A N
O C E A N
7
Scotia Sea
Weddell Sea
Scotia Ridge
Antarctic Circle
Ross Sea
75°
75°
60°
A N T A R C T I C A

0   1000   2000   3000   4000 KILOMETRES

© Collins Bartholomew Ltd

159

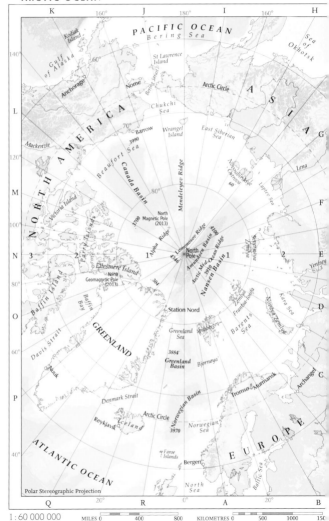

1 : 60 000 000   MILES 0   400   800   KILOMETRES 0   500   1000   150

INTRODUCTION TO THE INDEX

he index includes all names shown on the
naps in the Atlas of the World. Names are
eferenced by page number and by a grid
eference. The grid reference correlates to
ne alphanumeric values which appear within
ach map frame. Each entry also includes the
ountry or geographical area in which the
eature is located. Entries relating to names
ppearing on insets are indicated by a small
ox symbol: □, followed by a grid reference if
he inset has its own alphanumeric values.

Jame forms are as they appear on the maps,
vith additional alternative names or name
orms included as cross-references which
efer the user to the entry for the map form
f the name. Names beginning with Mc or
1ac are alphabetized exactly as they appear.
he terms Saint, Sainte, etc., are abbreviated
o St, Ste, etc., but alphabetized as if in the
ull form.

Names of physical features beginning with
generic, geographical terms are permuted –
the descriptive term is placed after the main
part of the name. For example, Lake Superior
is indexed as Superior, Lake; Mount Everest
as Everest, Mount. This policy is applied to
all languages.

Entries, other than those for towns and cities,
include a descriptor indicating the type of
geographical feature. Descriptors are not
included where the type of feature is implicit
in the name itself.

Administrative divisions are included to
differentiate entries of the same name and
feature type within the one country. In such
cases, duplicate names are alphabetized in
order of administrative division. Additional
qualifiers are also included for names within
selected geographical areas.

NDEX ABBREVIATIONS

dmin. div.	administrative division	g.	gulf	reg.	region
afgh.	Afghanistan	Ger.	Germany	Rep.	Republic
alg.	Algeria	Guat.	Guatemala	Rus. Fed.	Russian Federation
arg.	Argentina	hd	headland	S.	South
austr.	Australia	Hond.	Honduras	Switz.	Switzerland
ut. reg.	autonomous region	imp. l.	impermanent lake	Tajik.	Tajikistan
ut. rep.	autonomous republic	Indon.	Indonesia	Tanz.	Tanzania
azer.	Azerbaijan	isth.	isthmus	terr.	territory
3angl.	Bangladesh	Kazakh.	Kazakhstan	Thai.	Thailand
3ol.	Bolivia	Kyrg.	Kyrgyzstan	Trin. and Tob.	Trinidad and Tobago
3os.-Herz.	Bosnia Herzegovina	lag.	lagoon		
3ulg.	Bulgaria	Lith.	Lithuania	Turkm.	Turkmenistan
Can.	Canada	Lux.	Luxembourg	U.A.E.	United Arab Emirates
.A.R.	Central African Republic	Madag.	Madagascar	U.K.	United Kingdom
²ol.	Colombia	Maur.	Mauritania	Ukr.	Ukraine
zech Rep.	Czech Republic	Mex.	Mexico	Uru.	Uruguay
)em. Rep.	Democratic	Moz.	Mozambique	U.S.A.	United States of America
Congo	Republic of the Congo	mun.	municipality		
lepr.	depression	N.	North	Uzbek.	Uzbekistan
les.	desert	Neth.	Netherlands	val.	valley
)om. Rep.	Dominican Republic	Nic.	Nicaragua	Venez.	Venezuela
		N.Z.	New Zealand		
esc.	escarpment	Pak.	Pakistan		
est.	estuary	Para.	Paraguay		
ith.	Ethiopia	Phil.	Philippines		
ˇin.	Finland	plat.	plateau		
or.	forest	P.N.G.	Papua New Guinea		
		Pol.	Poland		
		Port.	Portugal		
		prov.	province		

100 Mile House

1

128 B2 100 Mile House Can.

A

93 E4 Aabenraa Denmark
100 C2 Aachen Ger.
93 E4 Aalborg Denmark
100 B2 Aalst Belgium
100 B2 Aarschot Belgium
68 C2 Aba China
115 C4 Aba Nigeria
81 C2 Ābādān Iran
81 D2 Ābādeh Iran
114 B1 Abadla Alg.
115 C4 Abakaliki Nigeria
83 H3 Abakan Rus. Fed.
150 A3 Abancay Peru
81 D2 Abarkūh Iran
66 D2 Abashiri Japan
117 B4 Abaya, Lake Eth.
       Ābaya Wenz r. Eth./Sudan see
       Blue Nile
82 G3 Abaza Rus. Fed.
108 A2 Abbasanta Sardegna Italy
104 C1 Abbeville France
142 B3 Abbeville U.S.A.
55 O2 Abbot Ice Shelf Antarctica
74 B1 Abbottabad Pak.
115 E3 Abéché Chad
114 B4 Abengourou Côte d'Ivoire
114 C4 Abeokuta Nigeria
99 A2 Aberaeron U.K.
96 C2 Aberchirder U.K.
99 B3 Aberdare U.K.
99 A3 Aberdaron U.K.
122 B3 Aberdeen S. Africa
96 C2 Aberdeen U.K.
141 D3 Aberdeen MD U.S.A.
137 D1 Aberdeen SD U.S.A.
134 B1 Aberdeen WA U.S.A.
129 E1 Aberdeen Lake Can.
134 B2 Abert, Lake U.S.A.
99 A2 Aberystwyth U.K.
86 F2 Abez' Rus. Fed.
78 B3 Abha Saudi Arabia
       Abiad, Bahr el r. Sudan/
       Uganda see White Nile
114 B4 Abidjan Côte d'Ivoire
137 D3 Abilene KS U.S.A.
139 D2 Abilene TX U.S.A.
99 C3 Abingdon U.K.
91 D3 Abinsk Rus. Fed.
130 B2 Abitibi, Lake Can.
       Abo Fin. see Turku
74 B2 Abohar India
114 C4 Abomey Benin
60 A1 Abongabong, Gunung mt.
       Indon.
118 B2 Abong Mbang Cameroon
64 A2 Aborlan Phil.
115 D3 Abou Déia Chad
106 B2 Abrantes Port.
152 B3 Abra Pampa Arg.
136 A2 Absaroka Range mts U.S.A.
81 C1 Abşeron Yarımadası pen. Azer.
78 B3 Abū 'Arīsh Saudi Arabia
79 C2 Abu Dhabi U.A.E.
116 B3 Abu Hamed Sudan
115 C4 Abuja Nigeria
81 C2 Abū Kamāl Syria
152 B1 Abuná r. Bol./Brazil
150 B2 Abuná Brazil
74 B2 Abu Road India
116 B2 Abū Sunbul Egypt
117 A3 Abu Zabad Sudan
       Abū Ẓaby U.A.E. see Abu Dhabi
117 A4 Abyei Sudan
145 B2 Acambaro Mex.
106 B1 A Cañiza Spain
144 B2 Acaponeta Mex.
145 C3 Acapulco Mex.
151 D2 Acará Brazil
150 B1 Acarigua Venez.
145 C3 Acatlán Mex.
145 C3 Acayucan Mex.
114 B4 Accra Ghana
98 B2 Accrington U.K.
74 B2 Achalpur India
97 A2 Achill Island Ireland
101 D1 Achim Ger.
96 B2 Achnasheen U.K.
91 D2 Achuyevo Rus. Fed.
111 C3 Acipayam Turkey
109 C3 Acireale Sicilia Italy
147 C2 Acklins Island Bahamas
153 B4 Aconcagua, Cerro mt. Arg.
106 B1 A Coruña Spain
108 A2 Acqui Terme Italy
145 C2 Acuponeta Mex.
139 D2 Ada U.S.A.
79 C2 Adam Oman
49 J4 Adamstown Pitcairn Is
       'Adan Yemen see Aden
80 B2 Adana Turkey
111 D2 Adapazarı Turkey
       Adapazarı Turkey see
       Adapazarı
108 A1 Adda r. Italy
78 B2 Ad Dafinah Saudi Arabia
78 B2 Ad Dahnā' des. Saudi Arabia
78 B2 Ad Dahnā' des. Saudi Arabia
114 A2 Ad Dakhla Western Sahara
       Ad Dammam Saudi Arabia see
       Dammam
78 A2 Ad Dār al Ḥamrā'
       Saudi Arabia
78 B3 Ad Darb Saudi Arabia
78 B2 Ad Dawādimī Saudi Arabia
       Ad Dawḥah Qatar see Doha
78 B2 Ad Dilam Saudi Arabia
116 B2 Ad Dir'iyah Saudi Arabia
117 B4 Addis Ababa Eth.
81 C2 Ad Dīwānīyah Iraq
52 A2 Adelaide Austr.
50 C1 Adelaide River Austr.
101 D2 Adelebsen Ger.
55 J2 Adélie Land Antarctica
78 B3 Aden Yemen
117 C3 Aden, Gulf of Somalia/Yemen
100 C2 Adenau Ger.
79 C2 Adh Dhayd U.A.E.
59 C3 Adi i. Indon.
78 A3 Ādī Ārk'ay Eth.
116 B3 Adigrat Eth.
75 B3 Adilabad India
141 D2 Adirondack Mountains U.S.A.
       Ādīs Ābeba Eth. see Addis Ababa
117 B4 Ādīs Alem Eth.
110 C1 Adjud Romania
50 B1 Admiralty Gulf Austr.
128 A2 Admiralty Island U.S.A.
147 B3 Adour r. France
106 C2 Adra Spain
114 B2 Adrar Alg.
140 C2 Adrian MI U.S.A.
139 C1 Adrian TX U.S.A.
108 B2 Adriatic Sea Europe
116 B3 Ādwa Eth.
83 K2 Adycha r. Rus. Fed.
91 D3 Adygeysk Rus. Fed.
114 B4 Adzopé Côte d'Ivoire
111 B3 Aegean Sea Greece/Turkey
101 D1 Aerzen Ger.
106 B1 A Estrada Spain
116 B3 Afabet Eritrea
76 C3 Afghanistan country Asia
78 B2 'Afīf Saudi Arabia
80 B2 Afyon Turkey
115 C3 Agadez Niger
114 B1 Agadir Morocco
74 B2 Agar India
75 D2 Agartala India
81 C2 Ağdam (abandoned) Azer.
105 C3 Agde France
104 C3 Agen France
122 A2 Aggeneys S. Africa
111 B3 Agia Varvara Greece
111 B3 Agios Dimitrios Greece
111 C3 Agios Efstratios i. Greece
111 C3 Agios Nikolaos Greece
110 B1 Agnita Romania
75 B2 Agra India
81 C2 Ağrı Turkey
       Ağrı Dağı mt. Turkey see
       Ararat, Mount
108 B3 Agrigento Sicilia Italy
111 B3 Agrinio Greece
109 B2 Agropoli Italy
154 B2 Água Clara Brazil
146 B4 Aguadulce Panama
144 B2 Aguanaval r. Mex.
144 B1 Agua Prieta Mex.
144 B2 Aguascalientes Mex.
155 C1 Águas Formosas Brazil
106 B1 Águeda Port.
106 C1 Aguilar de Campoo Spain
107 C2 Águilas Spain
144 B2 Aguililla Mex.
122 B3 Agulhas, Cape S. Africa
155 D2 Agulhas Negras mt. Brazil
111 C2 Ağva Turkey
115 C2 Ahaggar plat. Alg.
115 C2 Ahaggar, Tassili oua-n-
       plat. Alg.
81 C2 Ahar Iran
100 C1 Ahaus Ger.
81 C2 Ahlat Turkey
100 C2 Ahlen Ger.
74 B2 Ahmadabad India
73 B3 Ahmadnagar India
74 B2 Ahmadpur East Pak.
74 B1 Ahmadpur Sial Pak.
       Ahmadabad India see
       Ahmadabad
       Ahmadnagar India see
       Ahmadnagar
144 B2 Ahome Mex.
79 C2 Ahram Iran
101 E1 Ahrensburg Ger.
104 C2 Ahun France
81 C2 Ahvāz Iran
122 A2 Ai-Ais Namibia
80 B2 Aigialousa Cyprus
111 B3 Aigio Greece
143 D2 Aiken U.S.A.
97 B1 Ailt an Chorráin Ireland
155 D1 Aimorés Brazil
155 D1 Aimorés, Serra dos hills Brazil
114 B2 'Aïn Ben Tili Maur.
107 D2 Aïn Defla Alg.
114 B1 Aïn Sefra Alg.
136 D2 Ainsworth U.S.A.
       Aintab Turkey see Gaziantep

107 D2 Aïn Taya Alg.
115 A2 Aïn Tédélès Alg.
115 C3 Aïr, Massif de l' mts Niger
26 A1 Airbangis Indon.
128 C2 Airdrie Can.
59 B3 Aire-sur-l'Adour France
101 E3 Aisch r. Ger.
128 A1 Aishihik Lake Can.
100 A1 Aisne r. France
59 D3 Aitape P.N.G.
110 B1 Aiud Romania
105 D3 Aix-en-Provence France
105 D3 Aix-les-Bains France
62 A1 Aizawl India
88 C2 Aizkraukle Latvia
67 C3 Aizu-Wakamatsu Japan
105 C3 Ajaccio Corse France
115 E1 Ajdābiyā Libya
74 B2 Ajmer India
138 A2 Ajo U.S.A.
77 D2 Akadyr Kazakh.
87 E3 Akbulak Rus. Fed.
80 B2 Akçakale Turkey
80 B2 Akdağmadeni Turkey
88 A2 Åkersberga Sweden
118 C2 Aketi Dem. Rep. Congo
81 D4 Akhalkalaki Georgia
79 C2 Akhdar, Jabal mts Oman
80 A1 Akhisar Turkey
81 D4 Akhtubinsk Rus. Fed.
130 B1 Akimiski Island Can.
66 D3 Akita Japan
114 A3 Akjoujt Maur.
77 D1 Akkol' Kazakh.
88 B2 Akmenrags pt Latvia
Akmola Kazakh. see Astana
117 B4 Akobo S. Sudan
74 B2 Akola India
78 A3 Akordat Eritrea
127 G2 Akpatok Island Can.
92 □A3 Akranes Iceland
140 C2 Akron U.S.A.
75 B1 Aksai Chin terr. Asia
80 B2 Aksaray Turkey
76 B1 Aksay Kazakh.
91 D2 Aksay Rus. Fed.
80 B2 Akşehir Turkey
76 C2 Akshiganak Kazakh.
77 E2 Aksu China
74 A3 Āksum Eth.
76 B2 Aktau Kazakh.
76 B1 Aktobe Kazakh.
77 D2 Aktogay Kazakh.
88 C3 Aktsyabrski Belarus
115 C4 Akure Nigeria
92 □B2 Akureyri Iceland
142 C2 Alabama r. U.S.A.
142 C2 Alabama state U.S.A.
111 C3 Alaçatı Turkey
81 C1 Alagir Rus. Fed.
151 E3 Alagoinhas Brazil
107 C1 Alagón Spain
79 B2 Al Aḩmadī Kuwait
77 E2 Alakol', Ozero salt l. Kazakh.
92 J2 Alakurtti Rus. Fed.
78 B3 Al 'Alayyah Saudi Arabia
80 B2 Al 'Amādīyah Iraq
80 A2 Al 'Amirīyah Egypt
135 C3 Alamo U.S.A.
138 B2 Alamogordo U.S.A.
144 A2 Alamos Sonora Mex.
144 A2 Alamos Sonora Mex.
144 B2 Alamos r. Mex.
136 B3 Alamosa U.S.A.
93 G3 Åland Islands Fin.

80 B2 Alanya Turkey
73 B4 Alappuzha India
80 B3 Al 'Aqabah Jordan
78 B2 Al 'Aqiq Saudi Arabia
107 C2 Alarcón, Embalse de resr Spain
80 B2 Al 'Arīsh Egypt
78 B2 Al Arṭāwīyah Saudi Arabia
61 C2 Alas Indon.
111 C3 Alaşehir Turkey
128 A2 Alaska state U.S.A.
124 F3 Alaska, Gulf of U.S.A.
81 C1 Alāt Azer.
87 D3 Alatyr' Rus. Fed.
150 A2 Alausí Ecuador
93 H3 Alavus Fin.
52 B2 Alawoona Austr.
108 A2 Alba Italy
107 C2 Albacete Spain
110 B1 Alba Iulia Romania
109 C2 Albania country Europe
50 A3 Albany Austr.
130 B1 Albany r. Can.
143 D2 Albany GA U.S.A.
141 E2 Albany NY U.S.A.
134 B2 Albany OR U.S.A.
Al Başrah Iraq see Basra
51 D1 Albatross Bay Austr.
116 A2 Al Bawiti Egypt
115 E1 Al Bayḑā' Libya
78 B3 Al Bayḑā' Yemen
143 D1 Albemarle U.S.A.
143 E1 Albemarle Sound sea chan. U.S.A.
108 A2 Albenga Italy
51 C2 Alberga watercourse Austr.
119 D2 Albert, Lake Dem. Rep. Congo/Uganda
128 C2 Alberta prov. Can.
100 B2 Albert Kanaal canal Belgium
137 E2 Albert Lea U.S.A.
104 C3 Albi France
78 A2 Al Bi'r Saudi Arabia
78 B3 Al Birk Saudi Arabia
78 B2 Al Biyāḑh reg. Saudi Arabia
106 C2 Alboran Sea Europe
Alborz, Reshteh-ye mts Iran see Elburz Mountains
106 B2 Albufeira Port.
138 B1 Albuquerque U.S.A.
79 C2 Al Buraymī Oman
53 C3 Albury Austr.
106 B2 Alcácer do Sal Port.
106 C1 Alcalá de Henares Spain
106 C2 Alcalá la Real Spain
108 B3 Alcamo Sicilia Italy
107 C1 Alcañiz Spain
106 B2 Alcántara Spain
106 C2 Alcaraz Spain
106 C2 Alcaraz, Sierra de mts Spain
106 C2 Alcaudete Spain
106 C2 Alcázar de San Juan Spain
91 D2 Alchevs'k Ukr.
155 E1 Alcobaça Brazil
107 C2 Alcoy-Alcoi Spain
107 D2 Alcúdia Spain
145 C2 Aldama Mex.
83 J3 Aldan Rus. Fed.
83 J2 Aldan r. Rus. Fed.
95 C4 Alderney i. Channel Is
114 A3 Aleg Maur.
155 D2 Alegre Brazil
152 C3 Alegrete Brazil
83 K3 Aleksandrovsk-Sakhalinskiy Rus. Fed.
91 D1 Alekseyevka Belgorodskaya Oblast' Rus. Fed.

91 D1 Alekseyevka Belgorodskaya Oblast' Rus. Fed.
89 E3 Aleksin Rus. Fed.
109 D2 Aleksinac Serbia
118 B3 Alèmbé Gabon
155 D2 Além Paraíba Brazil
93 F3 Ålen Norway
104 C2 Alençon France
92 □C2 Aleppo Syria
150 A3 Alerta Peru
128 B2 Alert Bay Can.
105 C3 Alès France
110 B1 Aleşd Romania
108 A2 Alessandria Italy
93 E3 Ålesund Norway
124 C3 Aleutian Islands U.S.A.
83 L3 Alevina, Mys c. Rus. Fed.
128 A2 Alexander Archipelago is U.S.A.
122 A2 Alexander Bay S. Africa
142 C2 Alexander City U.S.A.
55 O2 Alexander Island Antarctica
53 C3 Alexandra Austr.
54 A3 Alexandra N.Z.
111 B2 Alexandreia Greece
Alexandretta Turkey see İskenderun
116 A1 Alexandria Egypt
110 C2 Alexandria Romania
123 C3 Alexandria S. Africa
142 B2 Alexandria LA U.S.A.
137 D1 Alexandria MN U.S.A.
141 D3 Alexandria VA U.S.A.
52 A3 Alexandrina, Lake Austr.
111 C2 Alexandroupoli Greece
131 E1 Alexis r. Can.
128 B2 Alexis Creek Can.
77 E1 Aleysk Rus. Fed.
107 C1 Alfaro Spain
81 C3 Al Fāw Iraq
101 D2 Alfeld (Leine) Ger.
155 C2 Alfenas Brazil
Al Fujayrah U.A.E. see Fujairah
Al Furāt r. Iraq/Syria see Euphrates
106 B2 Algeciras Spain
107 C2 Algemesí Spain
78 A3 Algena Eritrea
Alger Alg. see Algiers
114 C2 Algeria country Africa
79 C3 Al Ghaydah Yemen
108 A2 Alghero Sardegna Italy
78 B2 Al Ghurdaqah Egypt
79 B2 Al Ghwaybiyah Saudi Arabia
115 C1 Algiers Alg.
123 C3 Algoa Bay S. Africa
137 E2 Algona U.S.A.
106 C1 Algorta Spain
81 C2 Al Ḩadīthah Iraq
79 C2 Al Hajar al Gharbī mts Oman
107 C2 Alhama de Murcia Spain
80 A2 Al Ḩammām Egypt
78 B2 Al Ḩanākīyah Saudi Arabia
81 C2 Al Ḩasakah Syria
81 C2 Al Ḩayy Iraq
78 B3 Al Ḩazm al Jawf Yemen
79 C3 Al Ḩibāk des. Saudi Arabia
78 B2 Al Ḩillah Saudi Arabia
79 B2 Al Ḩinnāh Saudi Arabia
Al Ḩudaydah Yemen see Hodeidah
79 B2 Al Ḩufūf Saudi Arabia
115 D2 Al Ḩulayq al Kabīr hills Libya
79 C2 'Alīābād Iran
111 C3 Aliağa Turkey
111 B2 Aliakmonas r. Greece

Alicante

107 C2 Alicante Spain
139 D3 Alice U.S.A.
109 C3 Alice, Punta pt Italy
51 C2 Alice Springs Austr.
75 B2 Aligarh India
81 C2 Aligūdarz Iran
69 E1 Alihe China
118 B3 Alima r. Congo
111 C3 Aliova r. Turkey
117 C3 Ali Sabieh Djibouti
Al Iskandariyah Egypt see Alexandria
116 B1 Al Ismā'īlīyah Egypt
123 C3 Aliwal North S. Africa
115 E2 Al Jaghbūb Libya
78 B2 Al Jahrah Kuwait
79 B1 Al Jalamīd Saudi Arabia
115 D1 Al Jawsh Libya
106 B2 Aljezur Port.
Al Jīzah Egypt see Giza
79 B2 Al Jubayl Saudi Arabia
79 C2 Al Jumaylīyah Qatar
78 B2 Al Junaynah Saudi Arabia
106 B2 Aljustrel Port.
78 B2 Al Kahfah Saudi Arabia
79 C2 Al Kāmil Oman
80 B2 Al Karak Jordan
79 C2 Al Khābūrah Oman
78 B2 Al Khamāsin Saudi Arabia
116 B2 Al Khārijah Egypt
79 C2 Al Khaṣab Oman
78 B3 Al Khawkhah Yemen
79 C2 Al Khawr Qatar
115 D1 Al Khums Libya
79 B2 Al Khunn Saudi Arabia
79 C2 Al Kir'ānah Qatar
100 B1 Alkmaar Neth.
81 C2 Al Kūt Iraq
Al Kuwayt Kuwait see Kuwait
Al Lādhiqīyah Syria see Latakia
75 C2 Allahabad India
83 K2 Allakh-Yun' Rus. Fed.
141 D2 Allegheny r. U.S.A.
140 C3 Allegheny Mountains U.S.A.
97 B1 Allen, Lough l. Ireland
145 D2 Allende Coahuila Mex.
145 B2 Allende Nuevo León Mex.
141 D2 Allentown U.S.A.
101 D1 Aller r. Ger.
136 C2 Alliance NE U.S.A.
140 C2 Alliance OH U.S.A.
78 B2 Al Līth Saudi Arabia
96 C2 Alloa U.K.
131 C2 Alma Can.
Alma-Ata Kazakh. see Almaty
106 B2 Almada Port.
106 C2 Almadén Spain
Al Madinah Saudi Arabia see Medina
116 B1 Al Mafraq Jordan
78 B3 Al Maḥwīt Yemen
78 B2 Al Majma'ah Saudi Arabia
135 B2 Almanor, Lake U.S.A.
107 C2 Almansa Spain
80 B2 Al Manṣūrah Egypt
79 C2 Al Manṣūrah U.A.E.
115 E1 Al Marj Libya
77 D2 Almaty Kazakh.
106 C1 Almazán Spain
151 C2 Almeirim Brazil
100 C1 Almelo Neth.
155 D1 Almenara Brazil
106 B1 Almendra, Embalse de resr Spain
106 B2 Almendralejo Spain
106 C2 Almería Spain

106 C2 Almería, Golfo de b. Spain
87 E3 Al'met'yevsk Rus. Fed.
78 B2 Al Mindak Saudi Arabia
116 B2 Al Minyā Egypt
79 B2 Al Mish'āb Saudi Arabia
106 B2 Almodóvar Port.
106 B2 Almonte Spain
75 B2 Almora India
79 B2 Al Mubarrez Saudi Arabia
79 C2 Al Muḍaibī Oman
80 B3 Al Mudawwarah Jordan
Al Mukallā Yemen see Mukalla
Al Mukhā Yemen see Mocha
106 C2 Almuñécar Spain
78 A2 Al Muwaylih Saudi Arabia
111 B3 Almyros Greece
96 B2 Alness U.K.
98 C1 Alnwick U.K.
49 G4 Alofi Niue
111 B3 Alonnisos i. Greece
59 C3 Alor i. Indon.
59 C3 Alor, Kepulauan is Indon.
60 B1 Alor Star Malaysia
Alost Belgium see Aalst
86 C2 Alozero (abandoned) Rus. Fed.
140 C1 Alpena U.S.A.
139 C2 Alpine U.S.A.
105 D2 Alps mts Europe
79 B3 Al Qa'āmīyāt reg. Saudi Arabia
115 D1 Al Qaddāḥīyah Libya
Al Qāhirah Egypt see Cairo
78 B2 Al Qā'īyah Saudi Arabia
81 C2 Al Qāmishlī Syria
80 B2 Al Qaryatayn Syria
79 B3 Al Qaṭn Yemen
Alqueva, Barragem de resr Port.
80 B2 Al Qunayṭirah (abandoned) Syria
78 B3 Al Qunfidhah Saudi Arabia
116 B2 Al Quşayr Egypt
78 B2 Al Quwayyah Saudi Arabia
101 D2 Alsfeld Ger.
92 H2 Alta Norway
92 H2 Altaelva r. Norway
68 B1 Altai Mountains Asia
143 D2 Altamaha r. U.S.A.
151 C2 Altamira Brazil
109 C2 Altamura Italy
68 B1 Altay China
68 C1 Altay Mongolia
105 D2 Altdorf Switz.
107 C2 Altea Spain
101 F2 Altenburg Ger.
100 C2 Altenkirchen (Westerwald) Ger.
111 C3 Altınoluk Turkey
111 D3 Altıntaş Turkey
152 B2 Altiplano plain Bol.
154 B1 Alto Araguaia Brazil
154 B1 Alto Garças Brazil
121 C2 Alto Molócuè Moz.
129 E3 Altona U.S.A.
141 D2 Altoona U.S.A.
154 B1 Alto Sucuriú Brazil
154 B1 Alto Taquari Brazil
102 C2 Altötting Ger.
68 B2 Altun Shan mts China
134 B2 Alturas U.S.A.
139 D2 Altus U.S.A.
88 C2 Alūksne Latvia
78 A2 Al 'Ulā Saudi Arabia
115 D1 Al 'Uqaylah Libya
Al Uqsur Egypt see Luxor
91 C3 Alushta Ukr.
139 D1 Alva U.S.A.

145 C3 Alvarado Mex.
93 F3 Älvdalen Sweden
93 F3 Älvdalen val. Sweden
92 H2 Älvsbyn Sweden
78 A2 Al Wajh Saudi Arabia
74 B2 Alwar India
81 C2 Al Widyān plat. Iraq/Saudi Arabia
Alxa Youqi China see Ehen Hudag
Alxa Zuoqi China see Bayan Ho
51 C1 Alyangula Austr.
88 B3 Alytus Lith.
135 C3 Alzada U.S.A.
100 D3 Alzey Ger.
50 C2 Amadeus, Lake imp. l. Austr.
127 G2 Amadjuak Lake Can.
106 B2 Amadora Port.
78 B2 Amā'ir Saudi Arabia
93 F4 Åmål Sweden
111 B3 Amaliada Greece
59 D3 Amamapare Indon.
154 A2 Amambaí Brazil
154 B2 Amambaí r. Brazil
69 E3 Amami-Ō-shima i. Japan
69 E3 Amami-shotō is Japan
77 C1 Amankel'dy Kazakh.
109 C3 Amantea Italy
151 C1 Amapá Brazil
151 D2 Amareleja Port.
139 C1 Amarillo U.S.A.
108 B2 Amaro, Monte mt. Italy
80 B1 Amasya Turkey
150 C1 Amazon r. S. America
151 D1 Amazon, Mouths of the Brazil
Amazonas r. S. America see Amazon
74 B1 Ambala India
121 □D3 Ambanja Madag.
150 A2 Ambato Ecuador
121 □D3 Ambato Boeny Madag.
121 □D3 Ambato Finandrahana Madag.
121 □D2 Ambatolampy Madag.
121 □D2 Ambatondrazaka Madag.
101 E3 Amberg Ger.
146 B3 Ambergris Caye i. Belize
75 C2 Ambikapur India
121 □D2 Ambilobe Madag.
98 B1 Ambleside U.K.
121 □D3 Amboasary Madag.
121 □D3 Ambohimahasoa Madag.
59 C3 Ambon Indon.
59 C3 Ambon i. Indon.
121 □D3 Ambositra Madag.
121 □D3 Ambovombe Madag.
135 C3 Amboy U.S.A.
120 A1 Ambriz Angola
144 B2 Amealco Mex.
144 B2 Ameca Mex.
100 B1 Ameland i. Neth.
134 D2 American Falls U.S.A.
134 D2 American Falls Reservoir U.S.A.
135 D2 American Fork U.S.A.
49 G3 American Samoa terr. S. Pacific Ocean
143 D2 Americus U.S.A.
100 B1 Amersfoort Neth.
55 F2 Amery Ice Shelf Antarctica
137 E2 Ames U.S.A.
111 B3 Amfissa Greece
83 J2 Amga Rus. Fed.
66 B1 Amgu Rus. Fed.
115 C2 Amguid Alg.
83 K3 Amgun' r. Rus. Fed.
131 D2 Amherst Can.
104 C2 Amiens France

73 B3 **Amindivi Islands** India
122 A1 **Aminuis** Namibia
74 A2 **Amir Chah** Pak.
129 D2 **Amisk Lake** Can.
139 C3 **Amistad Reservoir** Mex./U.S.A.
98 C2 **Amlwch** U.K.
80 B2 **'Ammān** Jordan
127 I2 **Ammassalik** Greenland
78 B3 **Am Näbiyah** Yemen
82 B3 **Amol** Iran
111 C3 **Amorgos** i. Greece
142 C2 **Amory** U.S.A.
130 C2 **Amos** Can.
 Amoy China see **Xiamen**
155 C4 **Amparo** Brazil
107 D1 **Amposta** Spain
75 B2 **Amravati** India
74 B1 **Amritsar** India
100 B1 **Amstelveen** Neth.
100 B1 **Amsterdam** Neth.
103 C2 **Amstetten** Austria
115 E3 **Am Timan** Chad
76 B2 **Amudar'ya** r. Asia
126 E1 **Amund Ringnes Island** Can.
126 C2 **Amundsen Gulf** Can.
55 M2 **Amundsen Sea** Antarctica
61 C2 **Amuntai** Indon.
 Amur r. China see
 Heilong Jiang
78 A3 **'Amur, Wadi** watercourse
 Sudan
83 I2 **Anabar** r. Rus. Fed.
83 I2 **Anabarskiy Zaliv** b. Rus. Fed.
134 D1 **Anaconda** U.S.A.
139 D1 **Anadarko** U.S.A.
80 B1 **Anadolu Dağları** mts Turkey
83 M2 **Anadyr'** r. Rus. Fed.
81 C2 **'Ānah** Iraq
145 B2 **Anáhuac** Mex.
60 B1 **Anambas, Kepulauan** is Indon.
137 E2 **Anamosa** U.S.A.
80 B2 **Anamur** Turkey
67 B4 **Anan** Japan
73 B3 **Anantapur** India
74 B1 **Anantnag** India
90 B2 **Anan'yiv** Ukr.
91 D3 **Anapa** Rus. Fed.
154 C1 **Anápolis** Brazil
152 B3 **Añatuya** Arg.
97 B1 **An Baile Thiar** Ireland
65 B2 **Anbyon** N. Korea
104 B2 **Ancenis** France
108 B2 **Ancona** Italy
153 A5 **Ancud** Chile
 Anda China see **Daqing**
97 A2 **An Daingean** Ireland
93 E3 **Åndalsnes** Norway
142 C2 **Andalusia** U.S.A.
73 D3 **Andaman Islands** India
63 A3 **Andaman Sea** Indian Ocean
121 □D2 **Andapa** Madag.
100 B1 **Andelst** Neth.
92 G2 **Andenes** Norway
100 B2 **Andenne** Belgium
100 B2 **Anderlecht** Belgium
126 C2 **Anderson** r. Can.
134 B2 **Anderson** AK U.S.A.
140 B2 **Anderson** IN U.S.A.
143 D2 **Anderson** SC U.S.A.
148 D3 **Andes** mts S. America
77 D2 **Andijon** Uzbek.
121 □D2 **Andilamena** Madag.
121 □D2 **Andilanatoby** Madag.
121 □D2 **Andoany** Madag.
 Andong China see **Dandong**
65 B2 **Andong** S. Korea
107 D1 **Andorra** country Europe

107 D1 **Andorra la Vella** Andorra
99 C3 **Andover** U.K.
154 B2 **Andradina** Brazil
89 D2 **Andreapol'** Rus. Fed.
155 D2 **Andrelândia** Brazil
139 C2 **Andrews** U.S.A.
109 C2 **Andria** Italy
121 □D3 **Androka** Madag.
146 C2 **Andros** i. Bahamas
111 B3 **Andros** i. Greece
143 E4 **Andros Town** Bahamas
73 B3 **Andrott** i. India
90 B1 **Andrushivka** Ukr.
92 G2 **Andselv** Norway
106 C2 **Andújar** Spain
120 A2 **Andulo** Angola
114 C3 **Anéfis** Mali
115 D3 **Aney** Niger
83 H3 **Angara** r. Rus. Fed.
69 C1 **Angarsk** Rus. Fed.
93 G3 **Ånge** Sweden
144 A2 **Ángel de la Guarda, Isla** i. Mex.
64 B1 **Angeles** Phil.
150 B1 **Angel Falls** Venez.
93 F4 **Ängelholm** Sweden
92 G3 **Ångermanälven** r. Sweden
104 B2 **Angers** France
129 E1 **Angikuni Lake** Can.
98 A2 **Anglesey** i. U.K.
121 C2 **Angoche** Moz.
79 C2 **Angohrän** Iran
120 A2 **Angola** country Africa
140 C2 **Angola** U.S.A.
128 A2 **Angoon** U.S.A.
104 C2 **Angoulême** France
77 D2 **Angren** Uzbek.
147 D3 **Anguilla** terr. West Indies
75 C2 **Angul** India
93 F4 **Anholt** i. Denmark
71 B3 **Anhua** China
70 B2 **Anhui** prov. China
154 B1 **Anhumas** Brazil
154 C1 **Anicuns** Brazil
66 D1 **Aniva, Mys** c. Rus. Fed.
65 B2 **Anju** N. Korea
70 A2 **Ankang** China
80 B2 **Ankara** Turkey
70 B2 **Anlu** China
91 E1 **Anna** Rus. Fed.
115 C1 **Annaba** Alg.
101 F2 **Annaberg-Buchholtz** Ger.
78 B2 **An Nafüd** des. Saudi Arabia
81 C2 **An Najaf** Iraq
96 C3 **Annan** U.K.
141 D3 **Annapolis** U.S.A.
75 C2 **Annapurna I** mt. Nepal
140 C2 **Ann Arbor** U.S.A.
150 B1 **Anna Regina** Guyana
81 C2 **An Näşirïyah** Iraq
105 D2 **Annecy** France
78 B3 **An Nimäş** Saudi Arabia
62 B1 **Anning** China
142 C2 **Anniston** U.S.A.
105 C2 **Annonay** France
79 B2 **An Nu'ayrïyah** Saudi Arabia
121 □D2 **Anorontany, Tanjona** hd
 Madag.
71 B3 **Anpu** China
70 B2 **Anqing** China
102 C2 **Ansbach** Ger.
70 C1 **Anshan** China
71 A3 **Anshun** China
114 C3 **Ansongo** Mali
150 A3 **Antabamba** Peru
80 B2 **Antakya** Turkey
121 □E2 **Antalaha** Madag.
80 B2 **Antalya** Turkey

80 B2 **Antalya Körfezi** g. Turkey
121 □D2 **Antananarivo** Madag.
55 Q3 **Antarctic Peninsula** Antarctica
96 B2 **An Teallach** mt. U.K.
106 C2 **Antequera** Spain
138 B2 **Anthony** U.S.A.
114 B2 **Anti-Atlas** mts Morocco
105 D3 **Antibes** France
131 D2 **Anticosti, Île d'** i. Can.
131 D2 **Antigonish** Can.
147 D3 **Antigua** i. Antigua
147 D3 **Antigua and Barbuda** country
 West Indies
145 C2 **Antiguo-Morelos** Mex.
111 B3 **Antikythira** i. Greece
 Antioch Turkey see **Antakya**
49 F6 **Antipodes Islands** N.Z.
152 A3 **Antofagasta** Chile
154 C3 **Antonina** Brazil
97 C1 **Antrim** U.K.
97 C1 **Antrim Hills** U.K.
121 □D2 **Antsalova** Madag.
121 □D2 **Antsirabe** Madag.
121 □D2 **Antsiranana** Madag.
121 □D2 **Antsohihy** Madag.
 Antwerp Belgium see
 Antwerpen
100 B2 **Antwerpen** Belgium
 An Uaimh Ireland see **Navan**
74 B2 **Anupgarh** India
73 C4 **Anuradhapura** Sri Lanka
51 C3 **Anxious Bay** Austr.
70 B2 **Anyang** China
65 B2 **Anyang** S. Korea
108 B2 **Anzio** Italy
66 D2 **Aomori** Japan
54 B2 **Aoraki** mt. N.Z.
108 A1 **Aosta** Italy
143 D3 **Apalachee Bay** U.S.A.
150 B2 **Apaporis** r. Col.
154 B2 **Aparecida do Tabuado** Brazil
64 B1 **Aparri** Phil.
86 C2 **Apatity** Rus. Fed.
144 B3 **Apatzingán** Mex.
100 B1 **Apeldoorn** Neth.
100 C1 **Apen** Ger.
108 A2 **Apennines** mts Italy
49 G3 **Apia** Samoa
154 C2 **Apiaí** Brazil
64 B2 **Apo, Mount** vol. Phil.
101 E2 **Apolda** Ger.
52 B3 **Apollo Bay** Austr.
143 D3 **Apopka, Lake** U.S.A.
154 B1 **Aporé** r. Brazil
80 B2 **Apostolos Andreas, Cape** Cyprus
133 E3 **Appalachian Mountains** U.S.A.
53 C2 **Appin** Austr.
140 B2 **Appleton** U.S.A.
108 B2 **Aprilia** Italy
91 D3 **Apsheronsk** Rus. Fed.
154 B2 **Apucarana** Brazil
154 B2 **Apucarana, Serra da** hills
 Brazil
78 A2 **Aqaba, Gulf of** Asia
154 A1 **Aquidauana** r. Brazil
75 C2 **Ara** India
117 A4 **Arab, Bahr el** watercourse
 Sudan
 Arabian Gulf Asia see **The Gulf**
78 B2 **Arabian Peninsula** Asia
56 G5 **Arabian Sea** Indian Ocean
151 E3 **Aracaju** Brazil
151 F2 **Aracati** Brazil
154 B2 **Araçatuba** Brazil
155 D1 **Aracruz** Brazil

Araçuaí

155 D1 Araçuaí Brazil
110 B1 Arad Romania
115 E3 Arada Chad
156 C6 Arafura Sea Austr./Indon.
154 B1 Aragarças Brazil
107 C1 Aragón r. Spain
151 D2 Araguaia r. Brazil
151 E2 Araguaína Brazil
154 C1 Araguari Brazil
67 C3 Arai Japan
115 C2 Arak Alg.
81 C2 Arāk Iran
62 A1 Arakan Yoma mts Myanmar
81 C1 Arak's r. Armenia
76 C2 Aral Sea salt l. Kazakh./Uzbek.
76 C2 Aral'sk Kazakh.
Aral'skoye More salt l. Kazakh./Uzbek. see Aral Sea
106 C1 Aranda de Duero Spain
109 D2 Aranđelovac Serbia
97 B2 Aran Islands Ireland
106 C1 Aranjuez Spain
122 A1 Aranos Namibia
139 D3 Aransas Pass U.S.A.
67 B4 Arao Japan
114 B3 Araouane Mali
151 E2 Arapiraca Brazil
154 B3 Arapongas Brazil
154 C3 Araquari Brazil
78 B1 'Ar'ar Saudi Arabia
154 C2 Araraquara Brazil
151 E2 Araras Brazil
154 B3 Araras, Serra das mts Brazil
52 B3 Ararat Austr.
81 C2 Ararat, Mount Turkey
155 D2 Araruama, Lago de lag. Brazil
155 E1 Arataca Brazil
Aratürük China see Yiwu
81 C2 Arauca Col.
154 C1 Araxá Brazil
81 C2 Arbīl Iraq
96 C2 Arbroath U.K.
Arbū-ye Shamālī, Dasht-e des. Afgh.
104 B3 Arcachon France
143 D3 Arcadia U.S.A.
134 B2 Arcata U.S.A.
145 B3 Arcelia Mex.
86 D2 Archangel Rus. Fed.
51 D1 Archer r. Austr.
134 D2 Arco U.S.A.
106 B2 Arcos de la Frontera Spain
127 F2 Arctic Bay Can.
160 Arctic Ocean World
126 C2 Arctic Red r. Can.
81 C2 Ardabīl Iran
81 C1 Ardahan Turkey
93 E3 Årdalstangen Norway
100 B3 Ardennes plat. Belgium
81 D2 Ardestān Iran
53 C2 Ardlethan Austr.
139 D2 Ardmore U.S.A.
96 A2 Ardnamurchan, Point of U.K.
52 A2 Ardrossan Austr.
96 B3 Ardrossan U.K.
135 B3 Arena, Point U.S.A.
93 E4 Arendal Norway
101 E1 Arendsee (Altmark) Ger.
150 A3 Arequipa Peru
151 C2 Arere Brazil
106 C1 Arévalo Spain
108 B2 Arezzo Italy
104 B3 Argentan France
153 B4 Argentina country S. America
153 B6 Argentino, Lago l. Arg.
104 C2 Argenton-sur-Creuse France
110 C2 Argeş r. Romania

74 A1 Arghandāb Rōd r. Afgh.
111 B3 Argolikos Kolpos b. Greece
111 B3 Argos Greece
111 B3 Argostoli Greece
107 C1 Arguis Spain
69 E1 Argun' r. China/Rus. Fed.
50 B1 Argyle, Lake Austr.
93 F4 Århus Denmark
122 A2 Ariamsvlei Namibia
152 A2 Arica Chile
96 A2 Arinagour U.K.
155 C1 Arinos Brazil
150 C3 Aripuanã Brazil
150 B2 Aripuanã r. Brazil
150 B2 Ariquemes Brazil
154 B1 Arinhã r. Brazil
138 A2 Arizona state U.S.A.
144 A1 Arizpe Mex.
78 B2 'Arjah Saudi Arabia
92 G2 Arjeplog Sweden
142 B2 Arkadelphia U.S.A.
77 C1 Arkalyk Kazakh.
142 B2 Arkansas r. U.S.A.
142 B1 Arkansas state U.S.A.
137 D3 Arkansas City U.S.A.
Arkhangel'sk Rus. Fed. see Archangel
97 C2 Arklow Ireland
102 C1 Arkona, Kap c. Ger.
82 G1 Arkticheskogo Instituta, Ostrova is Rus. Fed.
105 C3 Arles France
115 C3 Arlit Niger
100 B3 Arlon Belgium
97 C1 Armagh U.K.
116 B2 Armant Egypt
81 C1 Armavir Rus. Fed.
81 C1 Armenia country Asia
150 A1 Armenia Col.
144 B3 Armeria Mex.
53 D2 Armidale Austr.
130 B1 Armstrong Can.
80 B1 Armyans'k Ukr.
80 B2 Arnauti, Cape Cyprus
100 B2 Arnhem Neth.
51 C1 Arnhem, Cape Austr.
51 C1 Arnhem Bay Austr.
51 C1 Arnhem Land reg. Austr.
108 B2 Arno r. Italy
52 A2 Arno Bay Austr.
130 C2 Arnprior Can.
100 D2 Arnsberg Ger.
101 E2 Arnstadt Ger.
122 A2 Aroab Namibia
101 D2 Arolsen Ger.
78 A3 Aroma Sudan
108 A1 Arona Italy
144 B2 Aros r. Mex.
81 C2 Ar Ramādī Iraq
96 B3 Arran i. U.K.
97 B1 Arranmore Island Ireland
80 B2 Ar Raqqah Syria
104 C1 Arras France
78 B2 Ar Rass Saudi Arabia
145 C3 Arriagá Mex.
79 C2 Ar Rimāl reg. Saudi Arabia
Ar Riyāḍ Saudi Arabia see Riyadh
145 C2 Arroyo Seco Mex.
79 C2 Ar Rustāq Oman
80 C2 Ar Ruṭbah Iraq
81 D3 Arsenjān Iran
66 B2 Arsen'yev Rus. Fed.
111 B3 Arta Greece
144 B3 Arteaga Mex.
66 B2 Artem Rus. Fed.
91 D2 Artemivs'k Ukr.

104 C2 Artenay France
138 C2 Artesia U.S.A.
51 E2 Arthur Point Austr.
54 B2 Arthur's Pass N.Z.
152 C4 Artigas Uru.
129 D1 Artillery Lake Can.
90 B2 Artsyz Ukr.
77 D3 Artux China
81 C1 Artvin Turkey
59 C3 Aru, Kepulauan is Indon.
119 D2 Arua Uganda
147 D3 Aruba terr. West Indies
119 D3 Arusha Tanz.
69 C1 Arvayheer Mongolia
129 E1 Arviat Can.
92 G2 Arvidsjaur Sweden
93 F4 Arvika Sweden
87 D3 Arzamas Rus. Fed.
107 C2 Arzew Alg.
100 C2 Arzfeld Ger.
101 F2 Aš Czech Rep.
115 C4 Asaba Nigeria
74 B1 Asadābād Afgh.
66 D2 Asahi-dake vol. Japan
66 D2 Asahikawa Japan
78 B3 Āsalē l. Eth.
123 D1 Asansol India
131 C2 Asbestos Can.
152 B2 Ascea Italy
113 D7 Ascension i. S. Atlantic Ocean
145 D3 Ascensión, Bahía de la b. Mex.
100 D3 Aschaffenburg Ger.
100 C2 Ascheberg Ger.
101 E2 Aschersleben Ger.
108 B2 Ascoli Piceno Italy
92 G3 Åsele Sweden
110 B2 Asenovgrad Bulg.
76 B3 Aşgabat Turkm.
50 A2 Ashburton watercourse Austr.
54 B2 Ashburton N.Z.
142 B2 Ashdown U.S.A.
143 D1 Asheville U.S.A.
53 D1 Ashford Austr.
99 D3 Ashford U.K.
Ashgabat Turkm. see Aşgabat
98 C1 Ashington U.K.
67 B4 Ashizuri-misaki pt Japan
136 D3 Ashland KS U.S.A.
140 C3 Ashland KY U.S.A.
140 C2 Ashland OH U.S.A.
134 B2 Ashland OR U.S.A.
140 A1 Ashland WI U.S.A.
88 C3 Ashmyany Belarus
78 B3 Ash Sharawrah Saudi Arabia
Ash Shāriqah U.A.E. see Sharjah
81 C2 Ash Sharqāṭ Iraq
81 C2 Ash Shaṭrah Iraq
79 B3 Ash Shiḥr Yemen
79 C2 Ash Shināş Oman
78 B2 Ash Shu'bah Saudi Arabia
78 B2 Ash Shumlūl Saudi Arabia
140 C2 Ashtabula U.S.A.
131 D1 Ashuanipi Lake Can.
106 B2 Asilah Morocco
108 A2 Asinara, Golfo dell' b. Sardegna Italy
82 G3 Asino Rus. Fed.
88 C3 Asipovichy Belarus
78 B2 'Asīr reg. Saudi Arabia
93 F4 Askim Norway
116 B3 Askiz Rus. Fed.
116 B3 Asmara Eritrea
93 F4 Åsnes l. Sweden
116 B2 Asoteriba, Jebel mt. Sudan

103 D2 **Aspang-Markt** Austria
136 B3 **Aspen** U.S.A.
54 A2 **Aspiring, Mount** N.Z.
117 C3 **Assab** Eritrea
Aş Şaḩrā' al Gharbīyah *des.*
Egypt *see* **Western Desert**
Aş Şaḩrā' ash Sharqīyah *des.*
Egypt *see* **Eastern Desert**
78 B2 **As Salamiyah** Saudi Arabia
81 C2 **As Samāwah** Iraq
79 C2 **Aş Şanam** *reg.* Saudi Arabia
115 E2 **As Sarir** *reg.* Libya
100 C1 **Assen** Neth.
100 B2 **Assesse** Belgium
115 D1 **As Sidrah** Libya
129 D3 **Assiniboia** Can.
128 C2 **Assiniboine, Mount** Can.
154 B2 **Assis** Brazil
78 B2 **Aş Şubayḩiyah** Kuwait
81 C2 **As Sulaymānīyah** Iraq
78 B2 **As Sulaymi** Saudi Arabia
78 B2 **As Sulayyil** Saudi Arabia
78 B2 **As Süq** Saudi Arabia
80 B2 **As Suwaydā'** Syria
79 C2 **As Suwayq** Oman
As Suways Egypt *see* **Suez**
111 B3 **Astakos** Greece
77 D1 **Astana** Kazakh.
81 C2 **Āstārā** Iran
108 A2 **Asti** Italy
74 B1 **Astor** Pak.
106 B1 **Astorga** Spain
134 B1 **Astoria** U.S.A.
87 D4 **Astrakhan'** Rus. Fed.
88 C3 **Astravyets** Belarus
111 C3 **Astypalaia** *i.* Greece
152 C3 **Asunción** Para.
116 B2 **Aswān** Egypt
116 B2 **Asyūţ** Egypt

152 B3 **Atacama, Desierto de** *des.*
Chile *see* **Atacama Desert**
152 B3 **Atacama, Salar de** *salt flat*
Chile
152 B3 **Atacama Desert** *des.* Chile
114 C4 **Atakpamé** Togo
111 B3 **Atalanti** Greece
150 A3 **Atalaya** Peru
77 C3 **Atamyrat** Turkm.
78 B3 **'Aţaq** Yemen
114 A2 **Atâr** Maur.
135 B3 **Atascadero** U.S.A.
77 D2 **Atasu** Kazakh.
111 C3 **Atavyros** *mt.* Greece
116 B3 **Atbara** Sudan
116 B3 **Atbara** *r.* Sudan
77 C1 **Atbasar** Kazakh.
137 D3 **Atchison** U.S.A.
108 B2 **Aterno** *r.* Italy
108 B2 **Atessa** Italy
94 A1 **Ath** Belgium
128 C2 **Athabasca** Can.
129 C2 **Athabasca** *r.* Can.
129 D2 **Athabasca, Lake** Can.
111 B3 **Athens** Greece
143 D2 **Athens** GA U.S.A.
140 C3 **Athens** OH U.S.A.
143 D1 **Athens** TN U.S.A.
139 D2 **Athens** TX U.S.A.
Athina Greece *see* **Athens**
97 C2 **Athlone** Ireland
111 B3 **Athos** *mt.* Greece
97 C2 **Athy** Ireland
115 D3 **Ati** Chad
130 A2 **Atikokan** Can.
87 D3 **Atkarsk** Rus. Fed.
143 D2 **Atlanta** U.S.A.
137 D2 **Atlantic** U.S.A.

141 E3 **Atlantic City** U.S.A.
158 **Atlantic Ocean** World
122 A3 **Atlantis** S. Africa
114 B1 **Atlas Mountains** Africa
114 C1 **Atlas Saharien** *mts* Alg.
128 B2 **Atlin** Can.
128 A2 **Atlin Lake** Can.
142 C2 **Atmore** U.S.A.
139 D2 **Atoka** U.S.A.
75 C2 **Atrai** *r.* India
78 B2 **Aţ Ţā'if** Saudi Arabia
115 E2 **At Tāj** Libya
63 B2 **Attapu** Laos
130 B1 **Attawapiskat** Can.
130 B1 **Attawapiskat** *r.* Can.
130 B1 **Attawapiskat Lake** Can.
100 C2 **Attendorn** Ger.
116 B2 **Aţ Ţür** Egypt
78 B3 **At Turbah** Yemen
76 B2 **Atyrau** Kazakh.
105 C3 **Aubenas** France
126 C2 **Aubry Lake** Can.
142 C2 **Auburn** AL U.S.A.
135 B3 **Auburn** CA U.S.A.
137 D2 **Auburn** NE U.S.A.
141 D2 **Auburn** NY U.S.A.
104 C2 **Aubusson** France
104 C3 **Auch** France
54 B1 **Auckland** N.Z.
48 F6 **Auckland Islands** *is* N.Z.
101 F2 **Aue** Ger.
102 C2 **Augsburg** Ger.
109 C3 **Augusta** *Sicilia* Italy
143 D2 **Augusta** GA U.S.A.
137 D3 **Augusta** KS U.S.A.
141 F2 **Augusta** ME U.S.A.
50 A2 **Augustus, Mount** Austr.
100 A2 **Aulnoye-Aymeries** France
62 A2 **Aunglan** Myanmar
122 B2 **Auob** *watercourse* Namibia/
S. Africa
74 B3 **Aurangabad** India
100 C1 **Aurich** Ger.
154 B1 **Aurilândia** Brazil
104 C3 **Aurillac** France
136 C3 **Aurora** CO U.S.A.
140 B2 **Aurora** IL U.S.A.
137 D2 **Aurora** NE U.S.A.
122 A2 **Aus** Namibia
137 E2 **Austin** MN U.S.A.
135 C3 **Austin** NV U.S.A.
139 D2 **Austin** TX U.S.A.
50 A2 **Australia** *country* Oceania
159 D7 **Australian-Antarctic Basin**
Southern Ocean
53 C3 **Australian Capital Territory**
admin. div. Austr.
102 C2 **Austria** *country* Europe
144 B3 **Autlán** Mex.
105 C2 **Autun** France
105 C2 **Auxerre** France
105 D2 **Auxonne** France
104 C2 **Avallon** France
131 E2 **Avalon Peninsula** Can.
154 C2 **Avaré** Brazil
49 H4 **Avarua** Cook Is
91 D2 **Avdiyivka** Ukr.
106 B1 **Aveiro** Port.
109 B2 **Avellino** Italy
100 A2 **Avesnes-sur-Helpe** France
93 G3 **Avesta** Sweden
108 B2 **Avezzano** Italy
96 C2 **Aviemore** U.K.
109 C2 **Avigliano** Italy
105 C3 **Avignon** France
106 C1 **Ávila** Spain
106 B1 **Avilés** Spain

109 C3 **Avola** *Sicilia* Italy
99 B2 **Avon** *r.* England U.K.
99 C3 **Avon** *r.* England U.K.
104 B2 **Avranches** France
54 B1 **Awanui** N.Z.
117 C4 **Awash** Eth.
117 C3 **Awash** *r.* Eth.
115 D2 **Awbārī** Libya
115 D2 **Awbārī, Idhān** *des.* Libya
117 C4 **Aw Dheegle** Somalia
96 B2 **Awe, Loch** *l.* U.K.
84 B1 **Awel, S.** Sudan
126 E1 **Axel Heiberg Island** Can.
114 B4 **Axim** Ghana
150 A3 **Ayacucho** Peru
77 E2 **Ayagoz** Kazakh.
68 B2 **Ayakkum Hu** *salt l.* China
106 B2 **Ayamonte** Spain
83 K3 **Ayan** Rus. Fed.
150 A3 **Ayaviri** Peru
76 A2 **Aybas** Kazakh.
91 D2 **Aydar** *r.* Ukr.
77 C2 **Aydarko'l ko'li** *l.* Uzbek.
111 C3 **Aydın** Turkey
Ayers Rock *h.* Austr. *see* **Uluru**
99 C3 **Aylesbury** U.K.
106 C1 **Ayllón** Spain
129 D1 **Aylmer Lake** Can.
117 B4 **Ayod** S. Sudan
83 M2 **Ayon, Ostrov** *i.* Rus. Fed.
114 B3 **'Ayoûn el 'Atroûs** Maur.
51 D1 **Ayr** Austr.
96 B3 **Ayr** U.K.
98 A1 **Ayre, Point of** Isle of Man
76 C2 **Ayteke Bi** Kazakh.
110 C2 **Aytos** Bulg.
145 C3 **Ayutla** Mex.
63 B2 **Ayutthaya** Thai.
111 C3 **Ayvacık** Turkey
111 C3 **Ayvalık** Turkey
114 C3 **Azaouagh, Vallée de**
watercourse Mali/Niger
77 C2 **Azat, Gory** *h.* Kazakh.
Azbine *mts* Niger *see*
Aïr, Massif de l'
81 C1 **Azerbaijan** *country* Asia
77 C1 **Azhibeksor, Ozero** *salt l.*
Kazakh.
86 B2 **Azopol'ye** Rus. Fed.
84 D5 **Azores** *aut. reg.* Port.
91 D2 **Azov** Rus. Fed.
91 D2 **Azov, Sea of** Rus. Fed./Ukr.
Azraq, Bahr el *r.* Eth./Sudan
see **Blue Nile**
106 B2 **Azuaga** Spain
146 B4 **Azuero, Península de** *pen.*
Panama
153 B4 **Azul** Arg.
80 B2 **Az Zaqāziq** Egypt
80 B2 **Az Zarqā'** Jordan
78 B3 **Az Zaydīyah** Yemen
114 C2 **Azzel Matti, Sebkha** *salt pan*
Alg.
78 B2 **Az Zilfī** Saudi Arabia
78 B3 **Az Zuqur** *i.* Yemen

B

63 B2 **Ba, Sông** *r.* Vietnam
117 C4 **Baardheere** Somalia
77 C3 **Bābā, Koh-e** *mts* Afgh.
110 C2 **Babadag** Romania
111 C2 **Babaeski** Turkey
117 C3 **Bāb al Mandab** *str.* Africa/Asia
61 C2 **Babana** Indon.

Babar

59 C3 Babar *i.* Indon.
119 D3 Babati Tanz.
89 E2 Babayevo Rus. Fed.
128 B2 Babine *r.* Can.
128 B2 Babine Lake Can.
59 C3 Babo Indon.
81 D2 Bābol Iran
122 A3 Baboon Point S. Africa
88 C3 Babruysk Belarus
64 B1 Babuyan *i.* Phil.
64 B1 Babuyan Islands Phil.
151 D2 Bacabal Brazil
59 C3 Bacan *i.* Indon.
110 C1 Bacău Romania
52 B3 Bacchus Marsh Austr.
77 D3 Bachu China
129 E1 Back *r.* Can.
109 C1 Bačka Palanka Serbia
63 B3 Bac Liêu Vietnam
64 B1 Bacolod Phil.
130 C1 Bacqueville, Lac *l.* Can.
106 B2 Badajoz Spain
62 A1 Badarpur India
101 E2 Bad Berka Ger.
101 D2 Bad Berleburg Ger.
101 E1 Bad Bevensen Ger.
100 C2 Bad Ems Ger.
103 D2 Baden Austria
102 B2 Baden-Baden Ger.
101 E2 Bad Harzburg Ger.
101 D2 Bad Hersfeld Ger.
102 C2 Bad Hofgastein Austria
101 D2 Bad Homburg vor der Höhe Ger.
74 A2 Badin Pak.
    Bādiyat ash Shām *des.* Asia *see* Syrian Desert
101 E2 Bad Kissingen Ger.
100 C3 Bad Kreuznach Ger.
101 E2 Bad Lauterberg im Harz Ger.
101 D2 Bad Lippspringe Ger.
101 D3 Bad Mergentheim Ger.
101 D2 Bad Nauheim Ger.
100 C2 Bad Neuenahr-Ahrweiler Ger.
101 E2 Bad Neustadt an der Saale Ger.
101 E1 Bad Oldesloe Ger.
101 D2 Bad Pyrmont Ger.
78 A2 Badr Ḥunayn Saudi Arabia
101 D1 Bad Salzuflen Ger.
101 E2 Bad Salzungen Ger.
102 C1 Bad Schwartau Ger.
101 E1 Bad Segeberg Ger.
100 C3 Bad Sobernheim Ger.
73 C4 Badulla Sri Lanka
100 D1 Bad Zwischenahn Ger.
106 C2 Baeza Spain
114 A3 Bafatá Guinea-Bissau
160 C2 Baffin Bay *sea* Can./Greenland
127 G2 Baffin Island Can.
118 B2 Bafia Cameroon
114 A3 Bafing *r.* Africa
114 A3 Bafoulabé Mali
118 B2 Bafoussam Cameroon
76 B3 Bāfq Iran
80 B1 Bafra Turkey
79 C2 Bāft Iran
119 C2 Bafwasende Dem. Rep. Congo
119 D3 Bagamoyo Tanz.
60 B1 Bagan Datuk Malaysia
120 B2 Bagani Namibia
60 B1 Bagansiapiapi Indon.
138 A2 Bagdad U.S.A.
152 C4 Bagé Brazil
97 C2 Bagenalstown Ireland
81 C2 Baghdād Iraq
77 C3 Baghlān Afgh.
104 C3 Bagnères-de-Luchon France

88 B3 Bagrationovsk Rus. Fed.
    Bagrax China *see* Bohu
64 B1 Baguio Phil.
115 C3 Bagzane, Monts *mts* Niger
79 D2 Bāhā Kālāt Iran
    Bahamas *country* West Indies *see* The Bahamas
146 C2 Bahamas, The *country* West Indies
75 C2 Baharampur India
    Bahariya Oasis Egypt *see* Bahrīyah, Wāḥāt al
76 B3 Baharly Turkm.
60 B1 Bahau Malaysia
72 B2 Bahawalnagar Pak.
74 B2 Bahawalpur Pak.
153 B4 Bahía Blanca Arg.
144 A2 Bahía Kino Mex.
152 C3 Bahía Negra Para.
144 A2 Bahía Tortugas Mex.
117 B3 Bahir Dar Eth.
75 C2 Bahraich India
79 C2 Bahrain *country* Asia
116 A2 Bahrīyah, Wāḥāt al *oasis* Egypt
110 B1 Baia Mare Romania
69 E1 Baicheng China
131 D2 Baie-Comeau Can.
    Baie-du-Poste Can. *see* Mistissini
131 C2 Baie-St-Paul Can.
65 B1 Baihe China
69 D1 Baikal, Lake Rus. Fed.
110 B2 Băileşti Romania
68 C2 Baima China
143 D2 Bainbridge U.S.A.
48 F2 Bairiki Kiribati
    Bairin Youqi China *see* Daban
53 C3 Bairnsdale Austr.
71 A3 Baise China
65 B1 Baishan *Jilin* China
65 B1 Baitou Shan *mt.* China/N. Korea
70 A2 Baiyin China
116 B3 Baiyuda Desert Sudan
103 D2 Baja Hungary
144 A1 Baja California *pen.* Mex.
78 B3 Bājil Yemen
114 A3 Bakel Senegal
135 C3 Baker CA U.S.A.
136 C1 Baker MT U.S.A.
134 C2 Baker OR U.S.A.
134 B1 Baker, Mount *vol.* U.S.A.
129 E1 Baker Foreland *hd* Can.
49 G2 Baker Island N. Pacific Ocean
129 E1 Baker Lake Can.
129 E1 Baker Lake Can.
135 C3 Bakersfield U.S.A.
91 C3 Bakhchysaray Ukr.
91 C1 Bakhmach Ukr.
    Bākhtarān Iran *see* Kermānshāh
    Baki Azer. *see* Baku
111 C2 Bakırköy Turkey
92 □C2 Bakkaflói *b.* Iceland
118 C2 Bakouma C.A.R.
81 C1 Baku Azer.
64 A2 Balabac Phil.
64 A2 Balabac *i.* Phil.
64 A2 Balabac Strait Malaysia/Phil.
61 C2 Balaiberkuak Indon.
52 A2 Balaklava Austr.
91 C3 Balaklava Ukr.
91 D2 Balakliya Ukr.
87 D3 Balakovo Rus. Fed.
76 C3 Bālā Murghāb Afgh.
145 C3 Balancán Mex.

111 C3 Balan Dağı *h.* Turkey
64 B3 Balanga Phil.
75 C2 Balangir India
87 D3 Balashov Rus. Fed.
103 D2 Balaton, Lake Hungary
103 D2 Balatonboglár Hungary
150 C2 Balbina, Represa de *resr* Brazil
97 C2 Balbriggan Ireland
52 A2 Balcanoona Austr.
110 C2 Balchik Bulg.
54 A3 Balclutha N.Z.
129 E2 Baldock Lake Can.
129 C2 Baldy Mountain *h.* Can.
138 B2 Baldy Peak U.S.A.
    Baleares, Islas *is* Spain *see* Balearic Islands
107 D2 Balearic Islands *is* Spain
155 E1 Baleia, Ponta da *pt* Brazil
130 C1 Baleine, Grande Rivière de la *r.* Can.
131 D1 Baleine, Rivière à la *r.* Can.
75 C2 Baleshwar India
108 A2 Balestrieri, Punta *mt.* Sardegna Italy
61 C2 Bali *i.* Indon.
115 C4 Bali Nigeria
60 A1 Balige Indon.
75 C2 Baliguda India
111 C3 Balıkesir Turkey
61 C2 Balikpapan Indon.
59 D3 Balimo P.N.G.
102 B2 Balingen Ger.
    Bali Sea Indon. *see* Laut Bali
76 B3 Balkanabat Turkm.
110 B2 Balkan Mountains Bulg./S.M.
77 D2 Balkash Kazakh.
77 D2 Balkhash, Lake Kazakh.
    Balkhash, Ozero *l.* Kazakh. *see* Balkhash, Lake
50 B3 Balladonia Austr.
97 B1 Ballaghaderreen Ireland
92 G2 Ballangen Norway
52 B3 Ballarat Austr.
50 B2 Ballard, Lake *imp. l.* Austr.
96 C2 Ballater U.K.
114 B3 Ballé Mali
53 D1 Ballina Austr.
97 B1 Ballina Ireland
97 B2 Ballinasloe Ireland
139 D2 Ballinger U.S.A.
97 B2 Ballinrobe Ireland
97 C1 Ballycastle Ireland
97 C1 Ballycastle U.K.
97 C1 Ballyclare U.K.
97 C1 Ballymena U.K.
97 C1 Ballymoney U.K.
97 D1 Ballynahinch U.K.
97 B1 Ballyshannon Ireland
95 B2 Ballyvoy U.K.
51 C2 Balonne *r.* Austr.
74 B2 Balotra India
72 B2 Balrampur India
52 B2 Balranald Austr.
110 B2 Balş Romania
151 D2 Balsas Brazil
145 C3 Balsas Mex.
90 B2 Balta Ukr.
90 B2 Bălţi Moldova
93 G4 Baltic Sea *g.* Europe
80 B2 Balţīm Egypt
123 C1 Baltimore S. Africa
141 D3 Baltimore U.S.A.
88 A3 Baltiysk Rus. Fed.
62 A1 Balu India
88 C2 Balvi Latvia
77 D2 Balykchy Kyrg.
87 E4 Balykshi Kazakh.

79	C2	Bam Iran
51	D1	Bamaga Austr.
130	A1	Bamaji Lake Can.
114	B3	Bamako Mali
118	C2	Bambari C.A.R.
101	E3	Bamberg Ger.
119	C2	Bambili Dem. Rep. Congo
119	C2	Bambouti C.A.R.
155	C2	Bambuí Brazil
118	B2	Bamenda Cameroon
74	A1	Bāmyān Afgh.
119	C2	Banalia Dem. Rep. Congo
151	C3	Bananal, Ilha do i. Brazil
74	B2	Banas r. India
111	C3	Banaz Turkey
62	B2	Ban Ban Laos
97	C1	Banbridge U.K.
99	C2	Banbury U.K.
130	C2	Bancroft Can.
119	C2	Banda Dem. Rep. Congo
75	C2	Banda India
59	C3	Banda, Kepulauan is Indon.
59	C3	Banda, Laut sea Indon.
60	A1	Banda Aceh Indon.
79	C2	Bandar-e ʻAbbās Iran
81	C2	Bandar-e Anzalī Iran
79	C2	Bandar-e Chārak Iran
81	C2	Bandar-e Emām Khomeynī Iran
79	C2	Bandar-e Lengeh Iran
79	C2	Bandar-e Maqām Iran
60	B2	Bandar Lampung Indon.
61	C1	Bandar Seri Begawan Brunei
		Banda Sea Indon. see Banda, Laut
155	D2	Bandeiras, Pico de mt. Brazil
123	C1	Bandelierkop S. Africa
144	B2	Banderas, Bahía de b. Mex.
114	B3	Bandiagara Mali
111	C2	Bandırma Turkey
97	B3	Bandon Ireland
118	B3	Bandundu Dem. Rep. Congo
61	B2	Bandung Indon.
128	C2	Banff Can.
96	C2	Banff U.K.
114	B3	Banfora Burkina Faso
64	B2	Banga Phil.
73	B3	Bangalore India
118	C2	Bangassou C.A.R.
59	C3	Banggai Indon.
59	C3	Banggai, Kepulauan is Indon.
61	C1	Banggi i. Sabah Malaysia
60	B2	Bangka i. Indon.
61	C2	Bangkalan Indon.
60	B1	Bangkinang Indon.
60	B2	Bangko Indon.
63	B2	Bangkok Thai.
75	C2	Bangladesh country Asia
63	B2	Ba Ngoi Vietnam
97	D1	Bangor Northern Ireland U.K.
98	A2	Bangor Wales U.K.
141	F2	Bangor U.S.A.
63	A2	Bang Saphan Yai Thai.
64	B1	Bangued Phil.
118	B2	Bangui C.A.R.
121	B2	Bangweulu, Lake Zambia
62	B2	Ban Huai Khon Thai.
116	B2	Banī Suwayf Egypt
115	D1	Banī Walīd Libya
80	B2	Bāniyās Syria
109	C2	Banja Luka Bos.-Herz.
61	C2	Banjarmasin Indon.
114	A3	Banjul Gambia
128	A2	Banks Island B.C. Can.
126	C2	Banks Island N.W.T. Can.
48	F3	Banks Islands Vanuatu
129	E1	Banks Lake Can.
54	B2	Banks Peninsula N.Z.
75	C2	Bankura India
62	A1	Banmauk Myanmar
62	B2	Ban Mouang Laos
97	C1	Bann r. U.K.
62	B2	Ban Napè Laos
63	A3	Ban Na San Thai.
143	E4	Bannerman Town Bahamas
74	B1	Bannu Pak.
74	B2	Banswara India
63	A3	Ban Tha Kham Thai.
62	A2	Ban Tha Song Yang Thai.
63	B2	Ban Tôp Laos
97	B3	Bantry Ireland
97	B3	Bantry Bay Ireland
118	B2	Banyo Cameroon
107	D1	Banyoles Spain
61	C2	Banyuwangi Indon.
		Bao'an China see Shenzhen
69	D2	Baochang China
70	B2	Baoding China
70	A2	Baoji China
62	B1	Bao Lac Vietnam
63	B2	Bao Lôc Vietnam
66	B1	Baoqing China
62	A1	Baoshan China
70	B1	Baotou China
81	C2	Ba'qūbah Iraq
109	C2	Bar Montenegro
117	C4	Baraawe Somalia
147	C2	Baracoa Cuba
53	C2	Baradine Austr.
78	A3	Barahona Dom. Rep.
116	B3	Baraka watercourse Eritrea/Sudan
61	C1	Baram r. Sarawak Malaysia
72	B1	Baramulla India
74	B1	Baramulla India
88	C3	Baranavichy Belarus
78	A2	Baranis Egypt
90	B1	Baranivka Ukr.
128	A2	Baranof Island U.S.A.
59	C3	Barat Daya, Kepulauan is Indon.
155	D2	Barbacena Brazil
147	E3	Barbados country West Indies
107	D1	Barbastro Spain
104	B2	Barbezieux-St-Hilaire France
51	D2	Barcaldine Austr.
107	D1	Barcelona Spain
150	B1	Barcelona Venez.
105	D3	Barcelonnette France
150	B2	Barcelos Brazil
		Barco Creek watercourse Austr. see Cooper Creek
103	D2	Barcs Hungary
75	C2	Barddhaman India
103	D2	Bardejov Slovakia
79	C2	Bardsīr Iran
75	B2	Bareilly India
160	B2	Barents Sea Arctic Ocean
78	A3	Barentu Eritrea
75	C2	Barh India
141	F2	Bar Harbor U.S.A.
109	C2	Bari Italy
74	B1	Barī Kōṭ Afgh.
150	A1	Barinas Venez.
75	C2	Baripada India
75	D2	Barisal Bangl.
60	B2	Barisan, Pegunungan mts Indon.
61	C2	Barito r. Indon.
79	C2	Barkā Oman
88	C2	Barkava Latvia
51	C1	Barkly Tableland reg. Austr.
68	C2	Barkol China
110	C1	Bârlad Romania
105	D2	Bar-le-Duc France
50	A2	Barlee, Lake imp. l. Austr.
109	C2	Barletta Italy
53	C2	Barmedman Austr.
74	B2	Barmer India
99	A2	Barmouth U.K.
101	D1	Barnstedt Ger.
98	C1	Barnard Castle U.K.
53	B2	Barnato Austr.
82	G3	Barnaul Rus. Fed.
127	G2	Barnes Icecap Can.
100	B1	Barneveld Neth.
98	C2	Barnsley U.K.
99	A3	Barnstaple U.K.
99	A3	Barnstaple Bay U.K.
143	D2	Barnwell U.S.A.
		Baroda India see Vadodara
150	B1	Barquisimeto Venez.
96	A1	Barra i. U.K.
53	D2	Barraba Austr.
151	D2	Barra do Corda Brazil
154	B1	Barra do Garças Brazil
150	D2	Barra do São Manuel Brazil
150	A3	Barranca Lima Peru
150	A2	Barranca Loreto Peru
152	C3	Barranqueras Arg.
150	A1	Barranquilla Col.
151	D3	Barreiras Brazil
130	C2	Barrie Can.
128	B2	Barrière Can.
52	B2	Barrier Range hills Austr.
53	D2	Barrington, Mount Austr.
129	D2	Barrington Lake Can.
53	C1	Barringun Austr.
97	C2	Barrow r. Ireland
51	C2	Barrow Creek Austr.
98	B1	Barrow-in-Furness U.K.
50	A2	Barrow Island Austr.
126	E2	Barrow Strait Can.
99	B3	Barry U.K.
130	C2	Barrys Bay Can.
74	B2	Barsalpur India
135	C4	Barstow U.S.A.
105	C2	Bar-sur-Aube France
80	B1	Bartın Turkey
51	D1	Bartle Frere, Mount Austr.
139	D1	Bartlesville U.S.A.
103	E1	Bartoszyce Pol.
61	C2	Barung i. Indon.
69	D1	Baruun-Urt Mongolia
91	D2	Barvinkove Ukr.
53	C2	Barwon r. Austr.
88	C3	Barysaw Belarus
110	C2	Basarabi Romania
105	D2	Basel Switz.
91	C2	Bashtanka Ukr.
64	B2	Basilan i. Phil.
99	D3	Basildon U.K.
99	C3	Basingstoke U.K.
81	C2	Başkale Turkey
130	C2	Baskatong, Réservoir resr Can.
		Basle Switz. see Basel
118	C2	Basoko Dem. Rep. Congo
81	C2	Basra Iraq
128	C2	Bassano Can.
114	C4	Bassar Togo
63	A2	Bassein Myanmar
147	D3	Basse-Terre Guadeloupe
147	D3	Basseterre St Kitts and Nevis
114	B3	Bassikounou Maur.
51	D3	Bass Strait Austr.
79	C2	Bastak Iran
101	E2	Bastheim Ger.
75	C2	Basti India
105	D3	Bastia Corse France
100	B2	Bastogne Belgium

Bastrop

142 B2 Bastrop U.S.A.
Basuo China *see* Dongfang
118 A2 Bata Equat. Guinea
83 J2 Batagay Rus. Fed.
154 B2 Bataguassu Brazil
106 B2 Batalha Port.
71 C3 Batan *i.* Pak.
118 B2 Batangafo C.A.R.
64 B1 Batangas Phil.
60 B2 Batanghari *r.* Indon.
71 C3 Batan Islands Phil.
141 D2 Batavia U.S.A.
91 D2 Bataysk Rus. Fed.
130 B2 Batchawana Mountain *h.* Can.
50 C1 Batchelor Austr.
63 B2 Bătdâmbâng Cambodia
53 D3 Batemans Bay Austr.
142 B1 Batesville U.S.A.
89 D2 Batetskiy Rus. Fed.
99 A1 Bath U.K.
74 B1 Bathinda India
53 C2 Bathurst Austr.
131 D2 Bathurst Can.
126 D2 Bathurst Inlet Can.
126 D2 Bathurst Inlet (abandoned) Can.
50 C1 Bathurst Island Austr.
126 E1 Bathurst Island Can.
78 B1 Bāţin, Wādī al *watercourse* Asia
81 C2 Batman Turkey
115 C1 Batna Alg.
142 B2 Baton Rouge U.S.A.
144 B3 Batopilas Mex.
118 B2 Batouri Cameroon
154 B1 Batovi Brazil
92 I1 Bātsfjord Norway
73 C4 Batticaloa Sri Lanka
109 B2 Battipaglia Italy
129 D2 Battle *r.* Can.
140 B2 Battle Creek U.S.A.
135 C2 Battle Mountain U.S.A.
74 B1 Battura Glacier Pak.
117 B4 Batu *mt.* Eth.
60 A2 Batu, Pulau-pulau *is* Indon.
81 C1 Bat'umi Georgia
60 B1 Batu Pahat Malaysia
59 C3 Baubau Indon.
115 C3 Bauchi Nigeria
104 B2 Baugé France
154 B2 Baume-les-Dames France
154 C2 Baurú Brazil
154 B1 Baús Brazil
88 B2 Bauska Latvia
102 C1 Bautzen Ger.
144 B2 Bavispe *r.* Mex.
87 E3 Bavly Rus. Fed.
62 A1 Bawdwin Myanmar
61 A1 Bawean *i.* Indon.
114 B3 Bawku Ghana
146 C2 Bayamo Cuba
Bayan Gol China *see* Dengkou
68 C1 Bayanhongor Mongolia
70 A2 Bayan Hot China
70 A1 Bayannuur China
69 D2 Bayan Shutu China
69 D1 Bayan-Uul Mongolia
64 B2 Bayawan Phil.
80 C1 Bayburt Turkey
140 C2 Bay City *MI* U.S.A.
139 D3 Bay City *TX* U.S.A.
86 F2 Baydaratskaya Guba Rus. Fed.
117 C4 Baydhabo Somalia
81 C2 Bayji Iraq
Baykal, Ozero *l.* Rus. Fed. *see* Baikal, Lake
83 I3 Baykal'skiy Khrebet *mts* Rus. Fed.

76 C2 Baykonyr Kazakh.
87 E3 Baymak Rus. Fed.
64 B1 Bayombong Phil.
104 B3 Bayonne France
101 E3 Bayramiç Turkey
101 E3 Bayreuth Ger.
78 B3 Bayt al Faqīh Yemen
106 C2 Baza Spain
106 C2 Baza, Sierra de *mts* Spain
74 A1 Bāzārak Afgh.
76 A2 Bazardyuzyu, Gora *mt.* Azer./ Rus. Fed.
104 B3 Bazas France
74 A2 Bazdar Pak.
70 A2 Bazhong China
79 D2 Bazmān Iran
79 D2 Bazmān, Kūh-e *mt.* Iran
121 □D2 Bé, Nosy *i.* Madag.
99 D3 Beachy Head U.K.
123 C3 Beacon Bay S. Africa
50 B1 Beagle Gulf Austr.
121 □D2 Bealanana Madag.
97 B1 Béal an Mhuirthead Ireland
130 B2 Beardmore Can.
Bear Island Arctic Ocean *see* Bjørnøya
134 E1 Bear Paw Mountain U.S.A.
147 C3 Beata, Cabo *c.* Dom. Rep.
147 C3 Beata, Isla *i.* Dom. Rep.
137 D2 Beatrice U.S.A.
135 C3 Beatty U.S.A.
53 D1 Beaudesert Austr.
52 B3 Beaufort Austr.
61 C1 Beaufort *Sabah* Malaysia
143 D2 Beaufort U.S.A.
160 L2 Beaufort Sea Can./U.S.A.
122 B3 Beaufort West S. Africa
96 B2 Beauly *r.* U.K.
100 B2 Beaumont Belgium
54 A3 Beaumont N.Z.
139 E2 Beaumont U.S.A.
105 C2 Beaune France
100 B2 Beauraing Belgium
129 E2 Beauséjour Can.
104 C2 Beauvais France
129 D2 Beauval Can.
129 D2 Beaver *r.* Can.
135 D3 Beaver U.S.A.
140 B2 Beaver Creek Can.
140 B2 Beaver Dam U.S.A.
129 E2 Beaver Hill Lake Can.
140 B1 Beaver Island U.S.A.
128 C2 Beaverlodge Can.
74 B2 Beawar India
154 C2 Bebedouro Brazil
101 D2 Bebra Ger.
106 B1 Becerreá Spain
114 B1 Béchar Alg.
140 C3 Beckley U.S.A.
117 B4 Bedelē Eth.
99 C2 Bedford U.K.
140 B3 Bedford U.S.A.
100 C1 Bedum Neth.
53 D2 Beechroft Peninsula Austr.
101 F1 Beelitz Ger.
51 D1 Beenleigh Austr.
80 B2 Beersheba Israel
139 D3 Beeville U.S.A.
53 C3 Bega Austr.
107 D1 Begur, Cap de *c.* Spain
128 C1 Behchokò Can.
81 D2 Behshahr Iran
69 E1 Bei'an China
71 A3 Beihai China
70 B2 Beijing China
100 C1 Beilen Neth.
96 A2 Beinn Mhòr *h.* U.K.

121 C2 Beira Moz.
80 B2 Beirut Lebanon
123 C1 Beitbridge Zimbabwe
106 B2 Beja Port.
115 C1 Béja Alg.
106 B1 Béjar Spain
74 A2 Bejī *r.* Pak.
103 E2 Békés Hungary
103 E2 Békéscsaba Hungary
121 □D3 Bekily Madag.
74 A2 Bela Pak.
123 C1 Bela-Bela S. Africa
118 B2 Bélabo Cameroon
109 D2 Bela Crkva Serbia
61 C1 Belaga *Sarawak* Malaysia
88 C3 Belarus *country* Europe
Belau *country* N. Pacific Ocean *see* Palau
123 D2 Bela Vista Moz.
60 A1 Belawan Indon.
83 M2 Belaya *r.* Rus. Fed.
103 D1 Bełchatów Pol.
130 C1 Belcher Islands Can.
117 C4 Beledweyne Somalia
151 D2 Belém Brazil
138 B2 Belen U.S.A.
89 E3 Belev Rus. Fed.
97 D1 Belfast U.K.
141 F2 Belfast U.S.A.
105 D2 Belfort France
73 B3 Belgaum India
100 B2 Belgium *country* Europe
91 D1 Belgorod Rus. Fed.
109 D2 Belgrade Serbia
134 D1 Belgrade U.S.A.
60 B2 Belinyu Indon.
61 B2 Belitung *i.* Indon.
146 B3 Belize Belize
146 B3 Belize *country* Central America
83 K1 Bel'kovskiy, Ostrov *i.* Rus. Fed.
128 B2 Bella Bella Can.
104 C2 Bellac France
128 B2 Bella Coola Can.
53 C1 Bellata Austr.
136 C2 Belle Fourche U.S.A.
136 C2 Belle Fourche *r.* U.S.A.
143 D3 Belle Glade U.S.A.
104 B2 Belle-Île *i.* France
131 E1 Belle Isle *i.* Can.
131 E1 Belle Isle, Strait of Can.
130 C2 Belleville Can.
137 D3 Belleville *IL* U.S.A.
137 D3 Belleville *KS* U.S.A.
134 B1 Bellevue U.S.A.
134 B1 Bellingham U.S.A.
55 O2 Bellingshausen Sea Antarctica
105 D2 Bellinzona Switz.
108 B1 Belluno Italy
122 A3 Bellville S. Africa
155 E1 Belmonte Brazil
146 B3 Belmopan Belize
69 E1 Belogorsk Rus. Fed.
121 □D3 Beloha Madag.
155 D1 Belo Horizonte Brazil
140 B2 Beloit U.S.A.
86 C2 Belomorsk Rus. Fed.
91 D3 Belorechensk Rus. Fed.
87 E3 Beloretsk Rus. Fed.
Belorussia *country* Europe *see* Belarus
86 F2 Beloyarskiy Rus. Fed.
86 C2 Beloye, Ozero *l.* Rus. Fed.
Beloye More *sea* Rus. Fed. *see* White Sea
86 C2 Belozersk Rus. Fed.
77 E2 Belukha, Gora *mt.* Kazakh./ Rus. Fed.

86 D2 Belush'ye Rus. Fed.
89 D2 Belyy Rus. Fed.
82 F2 Belyy, Ostrov i. Rus. Fed.
101 F1 Belzig Ger.
137 I1 Bemidji U.S.A.
118 C3 Bena Dibele Dem. Rep. Congo
53 C3 Benalla Austr.
106 B1 Benavente Spain
96 A2 Benbecula i. U.K.
134 B2 Bend U.S.A.
123 C3 Bendearg mt. S. Africa
52 B3 Bendigo Austr.
121 C2 Bene Moz.
102 C2 Benešov Czech Rep.
109 B2 Benevento Italy
159 C2 Bengal, Bay of sea Indian Ocean
Bengaluru India see Bangalore
70 B2 Bengbu China
115 E1 Benghazi Libya
61 B1 Bengkayang Indon.
60 B2 Bengkulu Indon.
120 A2 Benguela Angola
84 B2 Ben Hope h. U.K.
152 B2 Beni r. Bol.
119 C2 Beni Dem. Rep. Congo
114 B1 Beni Abbès Alg.
107 C2 Benidorm Spain
114 B1 Beni Mellal Morocco
114 C3 Benin country Africa
114 C4 Benin, Bight of g. Africa
115 C4 Benin City Nigeria
153 C4 Benito Juárez Arg.
150 B2 Benjamin Constant Brazil
144 A1 Benjamin Hill Mex.
59 C3 Benjina Indon.
96 B2 Ben Lawers mt. U.K.
96 B2 Ben Lomond h. U.K.
96 C2 Ben Macdui mt. U.K.
96 A2 Ben More h. U.K.
54 B2 Benmore, Lake N.Z.
96 B1 Ben More Assynt h. U.K.
128 A2 Bennett Can.
83 K1 Bennetta, Ostrov i. Rus. Fed.
96 B1 Ben Nevis mt. U.K.
141 E2 Bennington U.S.A.
123 C3 Benoni S. Africa
101 D3 Bensheim Ger.
138 A2 Benson U.S.A.
58 C3 Benteng Indon.
140 B2 Benton Harbor U.S.A.
142 B1 Bentonville U.S.A.
115 C4 Benue r. Nigeria
97 B1 Benwee Head Ireland
96 B2 Ben Wyvis mt. U.K.
70 C1 Benxi China
Beograd Serbia see Belgrade
75 C2 Beohari India
67 B4 Beppu Japan
109 C2 Berane Montenegro
109 C2 Berat Albania
59 C3 Berau, Teluk b. Indon.
116 B3 Berber Sudan
117 C3 Berbera Somalia
118 B2 Berbérati C.A.R.
104 C1 Berck France
91 D2 Berdyans'k Ukr.
90 B2 Berdychiv Ukr.
90 A2 Berehove Ukr.
59 D3 Bereina P.N.G.
76 B3 Bereket Turkm.
129 E2 Berens River Can.
90 A2 Berezhany Ukr.
90 C2 Berezivka Ukr.
90 B1 Berezne Ukr.
86 D2 Bereznik Rus. Fed.
86 E3 Berezniki Rus. Fed.

86 F2 Berezovo Rus. Fed.
107 D1 Berga Spain
111 C3 Bergama Turkey
108 A1 Bergamo Italy
102 C1 Bergen Mecklenburg-Vorpommern Ger.
101 D1 Bergen Niedersachsen Ger.
93 E3 Bergen Norway
100 B2 Bergen op Zoom Neth.
104 C3 Bergerac France
100 C2 Bergheim (Erft) Ger.
100 C2 Bergisch Gladbach Ger.
122 A1 Bergland Namibia
92 H2 Bergsviken Sweden
83 M3 Beringa, Ostrov i. Rus. Fed.
100 B2 Beringen Belgium
156 C2 Bering Sea N. Pacific Ocean
83 N2 Bering Strait Rus. Fed./U.S.A.
135 B3 Berkeley U.S.A.
100 B1 Berkhout Neth.
55 Q2 Berkner Island Antarctica
110 B2 Berkovitsa Bulg.
92 I1 Berlevåg Norway
101 F1 Berlin Ger.
141 E2 Berlin U.S.A.
101 E2 Berlingerode Ger.
53 D3 Bermagui Austr.
144 B2 Bermejillo Mex.
152 B3 Bermejo Bol.
131 D1 Bermen, Lac l. Can.
125 K4 Bermuda terr. N. Atlantic Ocean
105 D2 Bern Switz.
101 E2 Bernburg (Saale) Ger.
127 F2 Bernier Bay Can.
100 C3 Bernkastel-Kues Ger.
121 □D3 Beroroha Madag.
52 B2 Berri Austr.
107 D2 Berrouaghia Alg.
146 C2 Berry Islands Bahamas
100 C1 Bersenbrück Ger.
90 B2 Bershad' Ukr.
131 D1 Berté, Lac l. Can.
118 B2 Bertoua Cameroon
150 B2 Beruri Brazil
98 B1 Berwick-upon-Tweed U.K.
91 C2 Beryslav Ukr.
121 □D2 Besalampy Madag.
105 D2 Besançon France
129 D2 Besnard Lake Can.
142 C2 Bessemer U.S.A.
76 B2 Besshoky, Gora h. Kazakh.
106 B1 Betanzos Spain
118 B2 Bétaré Oya Cameroon
122 A2 Bethanie Namibia
123 C3 Bethlehem S. Africa
141 D2 Bethlehem U.S.A.
121 □D3 Betioky Madag.
77 D2 Betpakdala plain Kazakh.
121 □D3 Betroka Madag.
121 □D2 Betsiamites r. Madag.
137 E2 Bettendorf U.S.A.
75 C2 Bettiah India
75 B2 Betul India
75 B2 Betwa r. India
98 B2 Bews-y-coed U.K.
98 C2 Beverley U.K.
101 D2 Beverungen Ger.
100 B1 Beverwijk Neth.
99 D3 Bexhill U.K.
111 C3 Beykoz Turkey
114 B4 Beyla Guinea
76 B2 Beyneu Kazakh.
80 B1 Beypazarı Turkey
Beyrouth Lebanon see Beirut
80 B2 Beyşehir Turkey

80 B2 Beyşehir Gölü l. Turkey
91 D2 Beysug r. Rus. Fed.
88 C2 Bezhanitsy Rus. Fed.
89 E2 Bezhetsk Rus. Fed.
105 C3 Béziers France
75 C2 Bhadrak India
73 B3 Bhadravati India
75 C2 Bhagalpur India
74 A2 Bhairi Hol mt. Pak.
74 B1 Bhakkar Pak.
62 A1 Bhamo Myanmar
75 C3 Bhanjanagar India
74 B2 Bharatpur India
74 B2 Bharuch India
75 C3 Bhavnagar India
75 C3 Bhawanipatna India
123 D2 Bhekuzulu S. Africa
74 B2 Bhilwara India
73 B3 Bhima r. India
123 C3 Bhisho S. Africa
74 B2 Bhiwani India
123 C3 Bhongweni S. Africa
74 B2 Bhopal India
75 C2 Bhubaneshwar India
74 A2 Bhuj India
74 B2 Bhusawal India
75 D2 Bhutan country Asia
62 B2 Bia, Phou mt. Laos
59 C3 Biak Indon.
59 D3 Biak i. Indon.
103 E1 Biała Podlaska Pol.
103 D1 Białogard Pol.
103 E1 Białystok Pol.
109 C3 Bianco Italy
104 B3 Biarritz France
105 D2 Biasca Switz.
66 D2 Bibai Japan
120 A2 Bibala Angola
102 B2 Biberach an der Riß Ger.
115 C4 Bida Nigeria
141 E2 Biddeford U.S.A.
99 A3 Bideford U.K.
101 D2 Biedenkopf Ger.
105 D2 Biel Switz.
101 D1 Bielefeld Ger.
108 A1 Biella Italy
103 D1 Bielsko-Biała Pol.
63 B2 Biên Hoa Vietnam
130 C1 Bienville, Lac l. Can.
100 B3 Bièvre Belgium
118 B3 Bifoun Gabon
111 C2 Biga Turkey
123 D2 Big Bend Swaziland
129 D2 Biggar Can.
96 C3 Biggar U.K.
134 D1 Big Hole r. U.S.A.
136 B1 Bighorn r. U.S.A.
136 B2 Bighorn Mountains U.S.A.
139 C2 Big Lake U.S.A.
140 B2 Big Rapids U.S.A.
138 B2 Big River Can.
129 E2 Big Sand Lake Can.
137 D2 Big Sioux r. U.S.A.
139 C2 Big Spring U.S.A.
134 E1 Big Timber U.S.A.
130 B1 Big Trout Lake Can.
130 A1 Big Trout Lake Can.
109 C2 Bihać Bos.-Herz.
75 C2 Bihar Sharif India
110 B1 Bihor, Vârful mt. Romania
114 A3 Bijagós, Arquipélago dos is Guinea-Bissau
81 C2 Bijār Iran
109 C2 Bijeljina Bos.-Herz.
109 C2 Bijelo Polje Montenegro
71 A3 Bijie China
74 B2 Bikaner India

69 E1 Bikin Rus. Fed.
118 B3 Bikoro Dem. Rep. Congo
79 C2 Bilād Banī Bū ʿAlī Oman
75 C2 Bilaspur India
90 C2 Bila Tserkva Ukr.
63 A2 Bilauktaung Range mts Myanmar/Thai.
106 E1 Bilbao Spain
111 C2 Bilecik Turkey
103 E1 Biłgoraj Pol.
90 C2 Bilhorod-Dnistrovs'kyy Ukr.
119 C2 Bili Dem. Rep. Congo
83 M2 Bilibino Rus. Fed.
134 E1 Billings Rus. Fed.
99 B3 Bill of Portland hd U.K.
115 D3 Bilma Niger
115 D3 Bilma, Grand Erg de des. Niger
51 E2 Biloela Austr.
91 C2 Bilohirs'k Ukr.
90 B1 Bilohir"ya Ukr.
91 C1 Bilopillya Ukr.
91 D2 Bilovods'k Ukr.
142 C2 Biloxi U.S.A.
51 C2 Bilpa Morea Claypan salt flat Austr.
101 E2 Bilshausen Ger.
115 E3 Biltine Chad
90 C2 Bilyayivka Ukr.
143 E3 Bimini Islands Bahamas
75 B2 Bina-Etawa India
59 C3 Binaija, Gunung mt. Indon.
118 B3 Bindu Dem. Rep. Congo
121 C2 Bindura Zimbabwe
107 D1 Binéfar Spain
53 D1 Bingara Austr.
100 C3 Bingen am Rhein Ger.
141 F1 Bingham U.S.A.
141 D2 Binghamton U.S.A.
81 C2 Bingöl Turkey
60 A1 Binjai Indon.
60 B2 Bintuhan Indon.
61 C1 Bintulu Sarawak Malaysia
70 B2 Binzhou China
109 C2 Biograd na Moru Croatia
118 A2 Bioko i. Equat. Guinea
118 C1 Birao C.A.R.
75 C2 Biratnagar Nepal
128 C2 Birch Mountains Can.
51 C2 Birdsville Austr.
80 B2 Birecik Turkey
60 A1 Bireun Indon.
75 C2 Birganj Nepal
154 B2 Birigüi Brazil
76 B3 Birjand Iran
98 B2 Birkenhead U.K.
99 C2 Birmingham U.K.
142 C2 Birmingham U.S.A.
114 A2 Bîr Mogreïn Maur.
115 C3 Birnin-Kebbi Nigeria
115 C3 Birnin Konni Niger
69 E1 Birobidzhan Rus. Fed.
97 C2 Birr Ireland
96 C1 Birsay U.K.
78 A2 Bi'r Shalatayn Egypt
91 D1 Biryuch Rus. Fed.
88 B2 Biržai Lith.
75 B2 Bisalpur India
138 B2 Bisbee U.S.A.
104 A2 Biscay, Bay of sea France/Spain
102 C2 Bischofshofen Austria
130 B2 Biscotasi Lake Can.
77 D2 Bishkek Kyrg.
135 C3 Bishop U.S.A.
69 E1 Bishui China
150 B1 Bisinaca Col.
115 C1 Biskra Alg.

136 C1 Bismarck U.S.A.
48 D3 Bismarck Sea sea P.N.G.
107 D2 Bissa, Djebel mt. Alg.
114 A3 Bissau Guinea-Bissau
129 E2 Bissett Can.
128 C2 Bistcho Lake Can.
110 B1 Bistriţa Romania
110 C1 Bistriţa r. Romania
100 C3 Bitburg Ger.
105 D2 Bitche France
115 D3 Bitkine Chad
109 D2 Bitola Macedonia
109 C2 Bitonto Italy
122 A3 Bitterfontein S. Africa
134 D1 Bitterroot r. U.S.A.
134 C1 Bitterroot Range mts U.S.A.
91 D1 Bityug r. Rus. Fed.
115 C4 Biu Nigeria
67 C3 Biwa-ko l. Japan
68 B1 Biysk Rus. Fed.
115 C1 Bizerte Tunisia
92 □A2 Bjargtangar hd Iceland
92 G2 Bjästa Sweden
92 G2 Bjerkvik Norway
82 C2 Bjørnøya i. Arctic Ocean
114 B3 Bla Mali
137 E3 Black r. U.S.A.
51 D2 Blackall Austr.
98 B2 Blackburn U.K.
134 D2 Blackfoot U.S.A.
102 B2 Black Forest mts Ger.
136 C2 Black Hills U.S.A.
96 B2 Black Isle pen. U.K.
129 D2 Black Lake Can.
129 D2 Black Lake Can.
99 B3 Black Mountains hills U.K.
98 B2 Blackpool U.K.
62 B1 Black River r. Vietnam
140 A2 Black River Falls U.S.A.
140 C3 Blacksburg U.S.A.
80 B1 Black Sea Asia/Europe
97 A1 Blacksod Bay Ireland
97 C2 Blackstairs Mountains hills Ireland
114 B4 Black Volta r. Africa
97 C2 Blackwater r. Ireland
128 B1 Blackwater Lake Can.
50 A3 Blackwood r. Austr.
76 A2 Blagodarnyy Rus. Fed.
110 B2 Blagoevgrad Bulg.
69 E1 Blagoveshchensk Rus. Fed.
129 D2 Blaine Lake Can.
137 D2 Blair U.S.A.
96 C2 Blair Atholl U.K.
96 C2 Blairgowrie U.K.
143 D2 Blakely U.S.A.
105 D2 Blanc, Mont mt. France/Italy
153 B4 Blanca, Bahía b. Arg.
52 A1 Blanche, Lake imp. l. Austr.
152 B2 Blanco r. Bol.
131 E1 Blanc-Sablon Can.
92 □A2 Blanda r. Iceland
99 B3 Blandford Forum U.K.
135 E3 Blanding U.S.A.
107 D1 Blanes Spain
60 A1 Blangkejeren Indon.
100 C2 Blankenheim Ger.
100 C2 Blankenrath Ger.
103 D2 Blansko Czech Rep.
121 C2 Blantyre Malawi
98 C1 Blaydon U.K.
53 C2 Blayney Austr.
54 B2 Blenheim N.Z.
115 C1 Blida Alg.
130 B2 Blind River Can.
123 C2 Bloemfontein S. Africa
123 C2 Bloemhof S. Africa

123 C2 Bloemhof Dam S. Africa
92 □A2 Blönduós Iceland
97 C1 Bloody Foreland pt Ireland
138 B1 Bloomfield U.S.A.
140 B2 Bloomington Il. U.S.A.
140 B3 Bloomington IN U.S.A.
140 C3 Bluefield U.S.A.
146 B3 Bluefields Nic.
53 C2 Blue Mountains Austr.
134 C1 Blue Mountains U.S.A.
116 B3 Blue Nile r. Eth./Sudan
126 D2 Bluenose Lake Can.
140 C3 Blue Ridge mts U.S.A.
97 B1 Blue Stack Mountains hills Ireland
54 A3 Bluff N.Z.
135 E3 Bluff U.S.A.
152 D3 Blumenau Brazil
52 A2 Blyth Austr.
98 C1 Blyth U.K.
135 D4 Blythe U.S.A.
142 C1 Blytheville U.S.A.
114 A4 Bo Sierra Leone
64 B1 Boac Phil.
151 D2 Boa Esperança, Açude resr Brazil
150 B1 Boa Vista Brazil
53 C2 Bobadah Austr.
71 B3 Bobai China
121 □D2 Bobaomby, Tanjona c. Madag.
114 B3 Bobo-Dioulasso Burkina Faso
89 F3 Bobrov Rus. Fed.
91 C1 Bobrovytsya Ukr.
91 C2 Bobrynets' Ukr.
121 □D3 Boby mt. Madag.
150 B2 Boca do Acre Brazil
155 D1 Bocaiúva Brazil
118 B2 Bocaranga C.A.R.
103 E2 Bochnia Pol.
100 C2 Bocholt Ger.
100 C2 Bochum Ger.
101 E1 Bockenem Ger.
118 B2 Boda C.A.R.
83 I3 Bodaybo Rus. Fed.
115 D3 Bodélé reg. Chad
92 H2 Boden Sweden
99 A3 Bodmin U.K.
99 A3 Bodmin Moor moorland U.K.
92 F2 Bodø Norway
111 C3 Bodrum Turkey
118 C3 Boende Dem. Rep. Congo
142 C2 Bogalusa U.S.A.
114 B3 Bogandé Burkina Faso
68 B2 Bogda Shan mts China
53 D1 Boggabilla Austr.
97 B2 Boggeragh Mountains hills Ireland
100 B3 Bogny-sur-Meuse France
97 C2 Bog of Allen reg. Ireland
53 C3 Bogong, Mount Austr.
60 B2 Bogor Indon.
89 E3 Bogoroditsk Rus. Fed.
150 A1 Bogotá Col.
82 G3 Bogotol Rus. Fed.
83 H3 Boguchany Rus. Fed.
91 D2 Boguchar Rus. Fed.
70 B2 Bo Hai g. China
100 A3 Bohain-en-Vermandois France
70 B2 Bohai Wan b. China
123 C2 Bohlokong S. Africa
102 C2 Böhmer Wald mts Ger.
91 D1 Bohodukhiv Ukr.
64 B2 Bohol i. Phil.
64 B2 Bohol Sea Phil.
68 B2 Bohu China
155 C2 Boi, Ponta do pt Brazil

154 B1 Bois r. Brazil
126 C2 Bois, Lac des l. Can.
134 C2 Boise U.S.A.
139 C1 Boise City U.S.A.
123 C2 Boitumelong S. Africa
101 E1 Boizenburg Ger.
76 B3 Bojnúrd Iran
114 C2 Bokatola Dem. Rep. Congo
114 A3 Boké Guinea
118 C3 Bokele Dem. Rep. Congo
93 E4 Boknafjorden sea chan. Norway
115 D3 Bokoro Chad
63 A2 Bokpyin Myanmar
89 D2 Boksitogorsk Rus. Fed.
122 B2 Bokspits Botswana
114 A3 Bolama Guinea-Bissau
63 B2 Bolavén, Phouphiang plat. Laos
104 C2 Bolbec France
77 E2 Bole China
118 B3 Boleko Dem. Rep. Congo
114 B3 Bolgatanga Ghana
90 B2 Bolhrad Ukr.
76 B4 Boli China
62 B2 Bolikhamxai Laos
110 C2 Bolintin-Vale Romania
137 E3 Bolívar U.S.A.
150 A1 Bolívar, Pico mt. Venez.
152 B2 Bolivia country S. America
89 E3 Bolkhov Rus. Fed.
105 C3 Bollène France
93 G3 Bollnäs Sweden
53 C1 Bollon Austr.
101 E2 Bollstedt Ger.
93 F4 Bolmen l. Sweden
118 B3 Bolobo Dem. Rep. Congo
108 B2 Bologna Italy
89 D2 Bologovo Rus. Fed.
89 D2 Bologoye Rus. Fed.
118 B2 Bolomba Dem. Rep. Congo
83 H1 Bol'shevik, Ostrov i. Rus. Fed.
    Bol'shezemel'skaya Tundra
    lowland Rus. Fed.
66 B2 Bol'shoy Kamen' Rus. Fed.
    Bol'shoy Kavkaz mts
    Asia/Europe see Caucasus
83 K2 Bol'shoy Lyakhovskiy, Ostrov
    i. Rus. Fed.
100 B1 Bolsward Neth.
98 B2 Bolton U.K.
92 □A2 Bolungarvík Iceland
108 B1 Bolzano Italy
118 B3 Boma Dem. Rep. Congo
53 D2 Bomaderry Austr.
53 C3 Bombala Austr.
    Bombay India see Mumbai
155 D3 Bom Despacho Brazil
75 D2 Bomdila India
151 D3 Bom Jesus da Lapa Brazil
155 D2 Bom Jesus do Itabapoana
    Brazil
115 D1 Bon, Cap c. Tunisia
147 D3 Bonaire mun. West Indies
50 B1 Bonaparte Archipelago is
    Austr.
131 E2 Bonavista Can.
131 E2 Bonavista Bay Can.
118 C2 Bondo Dem. Rep. Congo
114 B4 Bondoukou Côte d'Ivoire
58 C3 Bonerate, Kepulauan is Indon.
155 C1 Bonfinópolis de Minas Brazil
117 B4 Bonga Eth.
75 D2 Bongaigaon India
118 C2 Bongandanga Dem. Rep.
    Congo
118 C2 Bongo, Massif des mts C.A.R.
115 D3 Bongor Chad

114 B4 Bongouanou Côte d'Ivoire
63 B2 Bông Sơn Vietnam
139 D2 Bonham U.S.A.
105 D3 Bonifacio Corse France
108 A2 Bonifacio, Strait of
    France/Italy
101 D2 Bonn Ger.
134 C1 Bonners Ferry U.S.A.
50 A3 Bonnie Rock Austr.
129 C2 Bonnyville Can.
108 A2 Bonorva Sardegna Italy
61 C1 Bontang Indon.
64 B1 Bontoc Phil.
58 B3 Bontosunggu Indon.
123 C3 Bontrug S. Africa
52 B2 Booligal Austr.
53 C1 Boomi Austr.
53 D1 Boonah Austr.
137 E2 Boone U.S.A.
142 C1 Booneville U.S.A.
137 E3 Boonville U.S.A.
53 C2 Boorowa Austr.
126 F2 Boothia, Gulf of Can.
126 E2 Boothia Peninsula Can.
100 C2 Boppard Ger.
144 B2 Boquilla, Presa de la resr Mex.
109 D2 Bor Serbia
117 B4 Bor S. Sudan
80 B2 Bor Turkey
121 □E2 Boraha, Nosy i. Madag.
76 B2 Borankul Kazakh.
93 F4 Borås Sweden
79 C2 Borāzjān Iran
150 A2 Borba Brazil
104 B3 Bordeaux France
127 F2 Borden Peninsula Can.
52 B3 Bordertown Austr.
107 D2 Bordj Bou Arréridj Alg.
107 D2 Bordj Bounaama Alg.
115 C1 Bordj Messaouda Alg.
115 C2 Bordj Omer Driss Alg.
94 B1 Borðoy i. Faroe Is
92 □A3 Borgarnes Iceland
108 A1 Borgosesia Italy
87 D3 Borisoglebsk Rus. Fed.
87 D2 Borisoglebskiy Rus. Fed.
91 D1 Borisovka Rus. Fed.
100 C2 Borken Ger.
92 G2 Borkenes Norway
100 C1 Borkum Ger.
100 C1 Borkum i. Ger.
93 G3 Borlänge Sweden
101 F2 Borna Ger.
    Borneo i. Asia
93 F4 Bornholm i. Denmark
111 C3 Bornova Turkey
90 B1 Borodyanka Ukr.
89 D2 Borovichi Rus. Fed.
89 E2 Borovsk Rus. Fed.
51 C1 Borroloola Austr.
110 B1 Borşa Romania
90 B2 Borshchiv Ukr.
69 D1 Borshchovochnyy Khrebet
    mts Rus. Fed.
101 E1 Börßum Ger.
    Bortala China see Bole
81 C2 Borüjerd Iran
90 A2 Boryslav Ukr.
91 C1 Boryspil' Ukr.
91 C1 Borzna Ukr.
69 D1 Borzya Rus. Fed.
109 C1 Bosanska Dubica Bos.-Herz.
109 C1 Bosanska Gradiška Bos.-Herz.
109 C2 Bosanska Krupa Bos.-Herz.
109 C2 Bosanski Novi Bos.-Herz.
109 C2 Bosansko Grahovo Bos.-Herz.
123 C3 Boshof S. Africa

109 C2 Bosnia-Herzegovina country
    Europe
118 B2 Bosobolo Dem. Rep. Congo
110 C2 Bosporus str. Turkey
118 B2 Bossangoa C.A.R.
118 B2 Bossembélé C.A.R.
68 B2 Bosten Hu l. China
98 C2 Boston U.K.
141 E2 Boston U.S.A.
142 B1 Boston Mountains U.S.A.
53 D2 Botany Bay Austr.
110 B2 Botev mt. Bulg.
93 G3 Bothnia, Gulf of Fin./Sweden
110 C1 Botoşani Romania
123 C2 Botshabelo S. Africa
120 B3 Botswana country Africa
109 C3 Botte Donato, Monte mt. Italy
136 C1 Bottineau U.S.A.
100 C2 Bottrop Ger.
154 C2 Botucatu Brazil
114 B4 Bouaké Côte d'Ivoire
118 B2 Bouar C.A.R.
114 B1 Bou Arfa Morocco
131 D2 Bouctouche Can.
107 C2 Bougaa Alg.
114 B3 Bougouni Mali
100 B3 Bouillon Belgium
107 D2 Bouira Alg.
114 A2 Boujdour Western Sahara
136 B2 Boulder U.S.A.
135 D3 Boulder City U.S.A.
51 C2 Boulia Austr.
104 C2 Boulogne-Billancourt France
99 D3 Boulogne-sur-Mer France
118 B3 Boumango Gabon
118 B2 Boumba r. Cameroon
107 D2 Boumerdes Alg.
114 B4 Bouna Côte d'Ivoire
114 B4 Boundiali Côte d'Ivoire
134 D2 Bountiful U.S.A.
114 B3 Bourem Mali
104 C2 Bourganeuf France
105 D2 Bourg-en-Bresse France
104 C2 Bourges France
53 C2 Bourke Austr.
99 C3 Bournemouth U.K.
115 C1 Bou Saâda Alg.
115 D3 Bousso Chad
114 A3 Boutilimit Maur.
129 C3 Bow r. Can.
51 C2 Bowen Austr.
129 C3 Bow Island Can.
140 B3 Bowling Green KY U.S.A.
140 C2 Bowling Green OH U.S.A.
136 C1 Bowman U.S.A.
101 D3 Boxberg Ger.
100 B2 Boxtel Neth.
80 B1 Boyabat Turkey
97 B2 Boyle Ireland
97 C2 Boyne r. Ireland
136 B2 Boysen Reservoir U.S.A.
152 B3 Boyuibe Bol.
111 C3 Bozburun Turkey
111 C3 Bozcaada i. Turkey
111 C3 Bozdağ mt. Turkey
111 C3 Boz Dağları mts Turkey
111 C3 Bozdoğan Turkey
134 D1 Bozeman U.S.A.
118 B2 Bozoum C.A.R.
111 D3 Bozüyük Turkey
109 C2 Brač i. Croatia
130 C2 Bracebridge Can.
99 C3 Bracknell U.K.
109 C2 Bradano r. Italy
143 D3 Bradenton U.S.A.
98 C2 Bradford U.K.
141 D2 Bradford U.S.A.

Brady

139 D2 Brady U.S.A.
96 C2 Braemar U.K.
106 B1 Braga Port.
151 D2 Bragança Brazil
106 B1 Bragança Port.
155 C2 Bragança Paulista Brazil
89 D3 Brahin Belarus
73 C3 Brahmapur India
62 A1 Brahmaputra r. China/India
110 C1 Brăila Romania
137 E1 Brainerd U.S.A.
99 D3 Braintree U.K.
100 B2 Braives Belgium
101 D1 Brake (Unterweser) Ger.
100 D1 Bramsche Ger.
88 D2 Branco r. Brazil
101 F1 Brandenburg Ger.
129 E3 Brandon Can.
97 A2 Brandon Mountain h. Ireland
122 B3 Brandvlei S. Africa
103 D1 Braniewo Pol.
130 B2 Brantford Can.
131 D2 Bras d'Or Lake Can.
155 D1 Brasil, Planalto do plat. Brazil
154 C1 Brasilândia Brazil
154 C1 Brasília Brazil
155 D1 Brasília de Minas Brazil
88 C2 Braslaw Belarus
110 C1 Braşov Romania
103 D2 Bratislava Slovakia
83 H3 Bratsk Rus. Fed.
102 C2 Braunau am Inn Austria
101 E1 Braunschweig Ger.
92 □A2 Brautarholt Iceland
Bravo del Norte, Río r.
Mex./U.S.A. see Rio Grande
135 C4 Brawley U.S.A.
97 D2 Bray Ireland
150 C2 Brazil country S. America
139 D3 Brazos r. U.S.A.
118 B3 Brazzaville Congo
109 C2 Brčko Bos.-Herz.
96 C2 Brechin U.K.
100 B2 Brecht Belgium
138 C2 Breckenridge U.S.A.
103 D2 Břeclav Czech Rep.
99 B3 Brecon U.K.
99 B3 Brecon Beacons reg. U.K.
100 B2 Breda Neth.
122 B3 Bredasdorp S. Africa
102 B2 Bregenz Austria
92 H1 Breivikbotn Norway
92 E3 Brekstad Norway
101 D1 Bremen Ger.
101 D1 Bremerhaven Ger.
134 B1 Bremerton U.S.A.
101 D1 Bremervörde Ger.
139 D2 Brenham U.S.A.
108 B1 Brennero Italy
102 C2 Brenner Pass Austria/Italy
99 D3 Brentwood U.K.
108 B1 Brescia Italy
108 B1 Bressanone Italy
96 □ Bressay i. U.K.
104 B2 Bressuire France
88 B3 Brest Belarus
104 B2 Brest France
142 C3 Breton Sound b. U.S.A.
151 C2 Breves Brazil
53 C1 Brewarrina Austr.
134 C1 Brewster U.S.A.
89 E2 Breytovo Rus. Fed.
109 C1 Brezovo Polje plain Croatia
118 C2 Bria C.A.R.
105 D3 Briançon France
90 B2 Briceni Moldova
99 B3 Bridgend U.K.

141 E2 Bridgeport CT U.S.A.
136 C2 Bridgeport NE U.S.A.
147 E3 Bridgetown Barbados
131 D2 Bridgewater Can.
99 B3 Bridgwater U.K.
98 C1 Bridlington U.K.
98 C1 Bridlington Bay U.K.
105 D2 Brig Switz.
134 D2 Brigham City U.S.A.
54 B3 Brighton N.Z.
99 C3 Brighton U.K.
105 D3 Brignoles France
101 D2 Brilon Ger.
109 C2 Brindisi Italy
91 D2 Brin'kovskaya Rus. Fed.
53 D1 Brisbane Austr.
99 B3 Bristol U.K.
143 D1 Bristol U.S.A.
99 A3 Bristol Channel est. U.K.
128 B2 British Columbia prov. Can.
56 G7 British Indian Ocean
Territory terr. Indian Ocean
95 B2 British Isles is Europe
123 C2 Brits S. Africa
122 B3 Britstown S. Africa
104 C2 Brive-la-Gaillarde France
106 C1 Briviesca Spain
103 D2 Brno Czech Rep.
143 D2 Broad r. U.S.A.
130 C1 Broadback r. Can.
96 C3 Broad Law h. U.K.
136 B1 Broadus U.S.A.
129 D2 Brochet Can.
129 D2 Brochet, Lac l. Can.
131 D2 Brochet, Lac au l. Can.
101 E1 Bröckel Ger.
126 D1 Brock Island Can.
130 C2 Brockville Can.
127 F2 Brodeur Peninsula Can.
96 B3 Brodick U.K.
103 D1 Brodnica Pol.
90 B1 Brody Ukr.
139 D1 Broken Arrow U.S.A.
137 D2 Broken Bow U.S.A.
52 B2 Broken Hill Austr.
99 B2 Bromsgrove U.K.
93 E4 Brønderslev Denmark
92 F2 Brønnøysund Norway
64 A2 Brooke's Point Phil.
142 B2 Brookhaven U.S.A.
134 B2 Brookings OR U.S.A.
137 D2 Brookings SD U.S.A.
129 C2 Brooks Can.
126 B2 Brooks Range mts U.S.A.
143 D3 Brooksville U.S.A.
96 B2 Broom, Loch inlet U.K.
50 B1 Broome Austr.
134 B2 Brothers U.S.A.
Broughton Island Can. see
Qikiqtarjuaq
90 C1 Brovary Ukr.
139 C2 Brownfield U.S.A.
128 C3 Browning U.S.A.
142 C1 Brownsville TN U.S.A.
139 D3 Brownsville TX U.S.A.
139 D2 Brownwood U.S.A.
92 □A2 Brú Iceland
104 C2 Bruay-la-Bussière France
140 B1 Bruce Crossing U.S.A.
103 D2 Bruck an der Mur Austria
Bruges Belgium see Brugge
100 A2 Brugge Belgium
128 C2 Brûlé Can.
151 D3 Brumado Brazil
93 F3 Brumunddal Norway
61 C1 Brunei country Asia
102 C2 Brunico Italy

101 D1 Brunsbüttel Ger.
143 D2 Brunswick GA U.S.A.
141 F2 Brunswick ME U.S.A.
53 D1 Brunswick Heads Austr.
136 C2 Brush U.S.A.
100 B2 Brussels Belgium
Bruxelles Belgium see
Brussels
139 D2 Bryan U.S.A.
89 D3 Bryansk Rus. Fed.
91 D2 Bryukhovetskaya Rus. Fed.
103 D1 Brzeg Pol.
114 A3 Buba Guinea-Bissau
80 B2 Bucak Turkey
150 A1 Bucaramanga Col.
53 C3 Buchan Austr.
114 A4 Buchanan Liberia
110 C2 Bucharest Romania
101 D1 Bucholz in der Nordheide Ger.
110 C1 Bucin, Pasul pass Romania
101 D1 Bückeburg Ger.
138 A2 Buckeye U.S.A.
96 C2 Buckhaven U.K.
96 C2 Buckie U.K.
51 C1 Buckingham Bay Austr.
51 D2 Buckland Tableland reg. Austr.
52 A2 Buckleboo Austr.
141 F2 Bucksport U.S.A.
București Romania see
Bucharest
89 D3 Buda-Kashalyova Belarus
103 D2 Budapest Hungary
75 B2 Budaun India
108 A2 Buddusò Sardegna Italy
99 A3 Bude U.K.
87 D4 Budennovsk Rus. Fed.
89 D2 Budogoshch' Rus. Fed.
108 A2 Budoni Sardegna Italy
118 A2 Buea Cameroon
144 B2 Buenaventura Mex.
106 C1 Buendia, Embalse de resr Spain
155 C1 Buenópolis Brazil
153 C4 Buenos Aires Arg.
153 A5 Buenos Aires, Lago l. Arg./Chile
141 D2 Buffalo NY U.S.A.
136 C1 Buffalo SD U.S.A.
136 B2 Buffalo WY U.S.A.
129 D2 Buffalo Narrows Can.
122 A2 Buffels watercourse S. Africa
110 C2 Buftea Romania
103 E1 Bug r. Pol.
61 C2 Bugel, Tanjung pt Indon.
109 C2 Bugojno Bos.-Herz.
64 A2 Bugsuk i. Phil.
87 E3 Buguruslan Rus. Fed.
110 C1 Buhuşi Romania
99 B2 Builth Wells U.K.
69 D1 Buir Nur l. Mongolia
120 A3 Buitepos Namibia
109 D2 Bujanovac Serbia
119 C3 Bujumbura Burundi
69 D1 Bukachacha Rus. Fed.
119 C3 Bukavu Dem. Rep. Congo
60 B2 Bukittinggi Indon.
119 D3 Bukoba Tanz.
53 D2 Bulahdelah Austr.
121 B3 Bulawayo Zimbabwe
111 C3 Buldan Turkey
123 D2 Bulembu Swaziland
69 C1 Bulgan Mongolia
110 C2 Bulgaria country Europe
54 B2 Buller r. N.Z.
52 B1 Bulloo Downs Austr.
122 A1 Büllsport Namibia
58 C3 Bulukumba Indon.
118 B3 Bulungu Dem. Rep. Congo
118 C2 Bumba Dem. Rep. Congo

62 A1 **Bumhkang** Myanmar
118 B3 **Buna** Dem. Rep. Congo
50 A3 **Bunbury** Austr.
97 C1 **Buncrana** Ireland
119 D3 **Bunda** Tanz.
51 E2 **Bundaberg** Austr.
51 D2 **Bundarra** Austr.
74 B2 **Bundi** India
67 B4 **Bundoran** Ireland
53 C3 **Bungendore** Austr.
67 B4 **Bungo-suidō** *sea chan.* Japan
119 C3 **Bunia** Dem. Rep. Congo
118 C3 **Bunianga** Dem. Rep. Congo
119 D3 **Bura** Kenya
78 B2 **Buraydah** Saudi Arabia
100 D2 **Burbach** Ger.
117 C4 **Burco** Somalia
100 B1 **Burdaard** Neth.
80 D2 **Burdur** Turkey
117 B3 **Burē** Eth.
99 D2 **Bure** *r.* U.K.
74 B1 **Burewala** Pak.
101 C2 **Burgas** Bulg.
101 E1 **Burg bei Magdeburg** Ger.
101 E1 **Burgdorf** *Niedersachsen* Ger.
101 E1 **Burgdorf** *Niedersachsen* Ger.
131 C2 **Burgeo** Can.
123 D1 **Burgersfort** S. Africa
100 A2 **Burgh-Haamstede** Neth.
145 C2 **Burgos** Merc.
106 C1 **Burgos** Spain
111 C3 **Burhaniye** Turkey
74 B2 **Burhanpur** India
101 D1 **Burhave (Butjadingen)** Ger.
131 E2 **Burin** Can.
151 D2 **Buriti Bravo** Brazil
155 C1 **Buritis** Brazil
51 C1 **Burketown** Austr.
114 B3 **Burkina Faso** *country* Africa
134 D2 **Burley** U.S.A.
136 C3 **Burlington** CO U.S.A.
137 E1 **Burlington** IA U.S.A.
143 E1 **Burlington** NC U.S.A.
141 E2 **Burlington** VT U.S.A.
       Burma *country* Asia *see*
       Myanmar
134 B2 **Burney** U.S.A.
51 D4 **Burnie** Austr.
98 B2 **Burnley** U.K.
134 C2 **Burns** U.S.A.
128 B2 **Burns Lake** Can.
77 E2 **Burqin** China
52 A2 **Burra** Austr.
109 D2 **Burrel** Albania
97 B2 **Burren** *reg.* Ireland
53 C2 **Burrendong, Lake** *resr* Austr.
53 C2 **Burren Junction** Austr.
107 C2 **Burriana** Spain
53 C2 **Burrinjuck Reservoir** Austr.
144 B2 **Burro, Serranías del** *mts* Mex.
111 C2 **Bursa** Turkey
116 B2 **Bür Safājah** Egypt
       Bür Sa'īd Egypt *see* **Port Said**
130 C1 **Burton, Lac** *l.* Can.
99 C2 **Burton upon Trent** U.K.
59 C3 **Buru** *i.* Indon.
119 C3 **Burundi** *country* Africa
119 C3 **Bururi** Burundi
91 C1 **Buryn'** Ukr.
99 D2 **Bury St Edmunds** U.K.
118 C3 **Busanga** Dem. Rep. Congo
79 C2 **Büshehr** Iran
119 D3 **Bushenyi** Uganda
118 C3 **Businga** Dem. Rep. Congo
50 A3 **Busselton** Austr.
139 C3 **Bustamante** Mex.

118 C2 **Buta** Dem. Rep. Congo
119 C3 **Butare** Rwanda
123 C2 **Buthe-Buthe** Lesotho
140 D2 **Butler** U.S.A.
59 C3 **Buton** *i.* Indon.
134 D1 **Butte** U.S.A.
60 B1 **Butterworth** Malaysia
96 A1 **Butt of Lewis** *hd* U.K.
64 B2 **Button Bay** Can.
64 B2 **Butuan** Phil.
91 E1 **Buturlinovka** Rus. Fed.
75 C2 **Butwal** Nepal
101 D2 **Butzbach** Ger.
117 C4 **Buulobarde** Somalia
117 C5 **Buur Gaabo** Somalia
117 C4 **Buurhabaka** Somalia
76 C3 **Buxoro** Uzbek.
101 D1 **Buxtehude** Ger.
89 F2 **Buy** Rus. Fed.
87 D4 **Buynaksk** Rus. Fed.
111 C3 **Büyükmenderes** *r.* Turkey
110 C1 **Buzău** Romania
121 C2 **Búzi** Moz.
87 E3 **Buzuluk** Rus. Fed.
110 C2 **Byala** Bulg.
88 C3 **Byalynichy** Belarus
88 D3 **Byarezina** *r.* Belarus
88 B3 **Byaroza** Belarus
103 D1 **Bydgoszcz** Pol.
88 C3 **Byerazino** Belarus
88 C2 **Byeshankovichy** Belarus
89 D3 **Bykhaw** Belarus
127 F2 **Bylot Island** Can.
53 C3 **Byrock** Austr.
53 D1 **Byron Bay** Austr.
83 J2 **Bytantay** *r.* Rus. Fed.
103 D1 **Bytom** Pol.
103 D1 **Bytów** Pol.

C

154 B2 **Caarapó** Brazil
64 B1 **Cabanatuan** Phil.
117 C3 **Cabdul Qaadir** Somalia
106 B2 **Cabeza del Buey** Spain
152 B2 **Cabezas** Bol.
150 A1 **Cabimas** Venez.
120 A1 **Cabinda** Angola
118 B3 **Cabinda** *prov.* Angola
155 D2 **Cabo Frio** Brazil
155 D2 **Cabo Frio, Ilha do** *i.* Brazil
130 C2 **Cabonga, Réservoir** *resr* Can.
51 E2 **Caboolture** Austr.
150 A2 **Cabo Pantoja** Peru
144 A1 **Caborca** Mex.
144 B2 **Cabo San Lucas** Mex.
64 B1 **Cabot Strait** Can.
155 D1 **Cabral, Serra do** *mts* Brazil
107 D2 **Cabrera, Illa de** *i.* Spain
106 B1 **Cabrera, Sierra de la** *mts* Spain
129 D2 **Cabri** Can.
107 C2 **Cabriel** *r.* Spain
151 D2 **Caçador** Brazil
109 D2 **Čačak** Serbia
108 A2 **Caccia, Capo** *c.* *Sardegna* Italy
151 E1 **Cáceres** Brazil
106 B2 **Cáceres** Spain
128 B2 **Cache Creek** Can.
114 A3 **Cacheu** Guinea-Bissau
151 E2 **Cachimbo, Serra do** *hills* Brazil
154 B1 **Cachoeira Alta** Brazil
155 D2 **Cachoeiro de Itapemirim**
       Brazil
114 A3 **Cacine** Guinea-Bissau
120 A2 **Cacolo** Angola

154 B2 **Caçu** Brazil
103 D2 **Čadca** Slovakia
101 D1 **Cadenberge** Ger.
145 C2 **Cadereyta** Mex.
140 B2 **Cadillac** U.S.A.
106 B2 **Cádiz** Spain
106 B2 **Cádiz, Golfo de** *g.* Spain
128 C2 **Cadotte Lake** Can.
104 B2 **Caen** France
98 A2 **Caernarfon** U.K.
98 A2 **Caernarfon Bay** U.K.
152 B3 **Cafayate** Arg.
64 B2 **Cagayan de Oro** Phil.
64 A2 **Cagayan de Tawi-Tawi** *i.* Phil.
108 B2 **Cagli** Italy
108 A3 **Cagliari** *Sardegna* Italy
108 A3 **Cagliari, Golfo di** *b.* *Sardegna*
       Italy
76 B2 **Çagyl** Turkm.
97 B3 **Caha Mountains** *hills* Ireland
120 B2 **Caianda** Angola
97 A3 **Cahermore** Ireland
97 C2 **Cahir** Ireland
97 A3 **Cahirsiveen** Ireland
97 C2 **Cahore Point** Ireland
104 C3 **Cahors** France
90 B2 **Cahul** Moldova
121 C2 **Caia** Moz.
151 C3 **Caiabis, Serra dos** *hills* Brazil
120 B2 **Caianda** Angola
154 B1 **Caiapó, Serra do** *mts* Brazil
154 B1 **Caiapônia** Brazil
147 C2 **Caicos Islands** Turks and
       Caicos Is
96 C2 **Cairngorm Mountains** U.K.
98 A1 **Cairnryan** U.K.
51 D1 **Cairns** Austr.
116 B1 **Cairo** Egypt
98 C2 **Caistor** U.K.
120 A2 **Caiundo** Angola
150 A2 **Cajamarca** Peru
109 C2 **Čakovec** Croatia
123 C3 **Cala** S. Africa
150 B1 **Calabozo** Venez.
110 B2 **Calafat** Romania
153 A6 **Calafate** Arg.
107 C1 **Calahorra** Spain
104 C1 **Calais** France
141 F1 **Calais** U.S.A.
152 B3 **Calama** Chile
64 A1 **Calamian Group** *is* Phil.
107 C1 **Calamocha** Spain
120 A1 **Calandula** Angola
60 A1 **Calang** Indon.
64 B1 **Calapan** Phil.
110 C2 **Călărași** Romania
107 C1 **Calatayud** Spain
64 B1 **Calayan** *i.* Phil.
64 B1 **Calbayog** Phil.
151 E2 **Calcanhar, Ponta do** *pt* Brazil
151 C1 **Calçoene** Brazil
       Calcutta India *see* **Kolkata**
106 B2 **Caldas da Rainha** Port.
154 C1 **Caldas Novas** Brazil
152 A3 **Caldera** Chile
134 C2 **Caldwell** U.S.A.
123 C3 **Caledon** *r.* Lesotho/S. Africa
122 A3 **Caledon** S. Africa
153 B5 **Caleta Olivia** Arg.
98 A1 **Calf of Man** *i.* Isle of Man
128 C2 **Calgary** Can.
150 A1 **Cali** Col.
       Calicut India *see* **Kozhikode**
135 D3 **Caliente** U.S.A.
135 B2 **California** *state* U.S.A.
144 A1 **California, Gulf of** Mex.
135 B3 **California Aqueduct** *canal*
       U.S.A.

Calitzdorp

122 B3 Calitzdorp S. Africa
145 C2 Calkini Mex.
52 B1 Callabonna, Lake imp. l. Austr.
96 B2 Callander U.K.
150 A3 Callao Peru
108 B3 Caltagirone Sicilia Italy
108 B3 Caltanissetta Sicilia Italy
120 A2 Caluquembe Angola
117 D3 Caluula Somalia
105 C3 Calvi Corse France
107 D2 Calvià Spain
144 B2 Calvillo Mex.
122 A3 Calvinia S. Africa
109 C2 Calvo, Monte mt. Italy
144 B2 Camacho Mex.
120 A2 Camacupa Angola
146 C2 Camagüey Cuba
150 A3 Camana Peru
154 B1 Camapuã Brazil
145 C2 Camargo Mex.
63 B3 Ca Mau Vietnam
63 B3 Ca Mau, Mui c. Vietnam
63 B2 Cambodia country Asia
99 A3 Camborne U.K.
105 C1 Cambrai France
99 B2 Cambrian Mountains hills U.K.
54 C1 Cambridge N.Z.
99 D2 Cambridge U.K.
141 E2 Cambridge MA U.S.A.
141 D3 Cambridge MD U.S.A.
137 E1 Cambridge MN U.S.A.
140 C2 Cambridge OH U.S.A.
131 D1 Cambrien, Lac l. Can.
53 D2 Camden Austr.
142 B2 Camden AR U.S.A.
141 F2 Camden ME U.S.A.
118 B2 Cameroon country Africa
118 B2 Cameroon Highlands slope Cameroun/Nigeria
151 D2 Cametá Brazil
64 B1 Camiguin i. Phil.
152 B3 Camiri Bol.
151 D2 Camocim Brazil
51 C1 Camooweal Austr.
63 A3 Camorta i. India
153 A5 Campana, Isla i. Chile
122 B2 Campbell S. Africa
54 B2 Campbell, Cape N.Z.
48 F6 Campbell Island N.Z.
128 B2 Campbell River Can.
140 B2 Campbellsville U.S.A.
131 D2 Campbellton Can.
96 B3 Campbeltown U.K.
145 C3 Campeche Mex.
145 C3 Campeche, Bahía de g. Mex.
52 B3 Camperdown Austr.
110 C1 Câmpina Romania
151 E2 Campina Grande Brazil
154 C1 Campinas Brazil
154 C1 Campina Verde Brazil
108 B2 Campobasso Italy
155 C2 Campo Belo Brazil
154 C1 Campo Florido Brazil
152 B3 Campo Gallo Arg.
154 B2 Campo Grande Brazil
151 D2 Campo Maior Brazil
106 B2 Campo Maior Port.
154 B2 Campo Mourão Brazil
155 D2 Campos Brazil
155 C1 Campos Altos Brazil
155 C2 Campos do Jordão Brazil
110 C1 Câmpulung Romania
138 A2 Camp Verde U.S.A.
128 C2 Camrose Can.
129 D2 Camsell Portage Can.
111 C2 Çan Turkey
126 F2 Canada country N. America

139 C1 Canadian U.S.A.
139 D1 Canadian r. U.S.A.
111 C2 Çanakkale Turkey
144 A1 Cananea Mex.
154 C2 Cananéia Brazil
        Canarias, Islas terr. N. Atlantic Ocean see Canary Islands
114 A2 Canary Islands terr. N. Atlantic Ocean
155 C1 Canastra, Serra da mts Brazil
144 B2 Canatlán Mex.
143 D3 Canaveral, Cape U.S.A.
155 E1 Canavieiras Brazil
53 C1 Canberra Austr.
145 D2 Cancún Mex.
111 C3 Çandarlı Turkey
145 C3 Candelaria Mex.
129 D2 Candle Lake Can.
120 A2 Cangamba Angola
106 B1 Cangas del Narcea Spain
152 C4 Canguçu Brazil
70 B2 Cangzhou China
131 D1 Caniapiscau Can.
131 D1 Caniapiscau r. Can.
131 C1 Caniapiscau, Réservoir de resr Can.
108 B3 Canicattì Sicilia Italy
151 E2 Canindé Brazil
144 B2 Cañitas de Felipe Pescador Mex.
80 B1 Çankırı Turkey
128 C2 Canmore Can.
96 A2 Canna i. U.K.
105 D3 Cannes France
99 B2 Cannock U.K.
53 C3 Cann River Austr.
152 C3 Canoas Brazil
129 D2 Canoe Lake Can.
154 B3 Canoinhas Brazil
136 B3 Canon City U.S.A.
129 D2 Canora Can.
53 C2 Canowindra Austr.
106 C1 Cantábrica, Cordillera mts Spain
106 B1 Cantábrico, Mar sea Spain
99 D3 Canterbury U.K.
54 B2 Canterbury Bight b. N.Z.
54 B2 Canterbury Plains N.Z.
63 B2 Cần Thơ Vietnam
151 D2 Canto do Buriti Brazil
        Canton China see Guangzhou
142 C2 Canton MS U.S.A.
140 C2 Canton OH U.S.A.
139 C1 Canyon U.S.A.
134 D1 Canyon Ferry Lake U.S.A.
62 B1 Cao Băng Vietnam
154 C2 Capão Bonito Brazil
155 D2 Caparaó, Serra do mts Brazil
51 D4 Cape Barren Island Austr.
52 A3 Cape Borda Austr.
131 D2 Cape Breton Island Can.
114 B4 Cape Coast Ghana
141 E2 Cape Cod Bay U.S.A.
127 F2 Cape Dorset Can.
143 E2 Cape Fear r. U.S.A.
137 F3 Cape Girardeau U.S.A.
155 D1 Capelinha Brazil
100 B2 Capelle aan de IJssel Neth.
120 A1 Capenda-Camulemba Angola
122 A3 Cape Town S. Africa
112 C5 Cape Verde country N. Atlantic Ocean
51 D1 Cape York Peninsula Austr.
147 C3 Cap-Haïtien Haiti
151 D2 Capim r. Brazil
58 D1 Capitol Hill N. Mariana Is
109 C2 Čapljina Bos.-Herz.

109 B3 Capo d'Orlando Sicilia Italy
108 A2 Capraia, Isola di i. Italy
108 A2 Caprara, Punta pt Sardegna Italy
108 B2 Capri, Isola di i. Italy
120 B2 Caprivi Strip reg. Namibia
150 B2 Caquetá r. Col.
110 B2 Caracal Romania
150 B1 Caracas Venez.
151 D2 Caracol Brazil
155 C2 Caraguatatuba Brazil
153 A4 Carahue Chile
155 D1 Caraí Brazil
155 D2 Carangola Brazil
110 B1 Caransebeș Romania
131 D2 Caraquet Can.
146 B3 Caratasca, Laguna de lag. Hond.
155 D1 Caratinga Brazil
150 B2 Carauari Brazil
107 C2 Caravaca de la Cruz Spain
155 E1 Caravelas Brazil
129 E3 Carberry Can.
144 A2 Carbó Mex.
107 C2 Carbon, Cap c. Alg.
153 B5 Carbón, Laguna del l. Arg.
108 A3 Carbonara, Capo c. Sardegna Italy
136 B3 Carbondale CO U.S.A.
140 B3 Carbondale IL U.S.A.
131 E2 Carbonear Can.
155 D1 Carbonita Brazil
107 C2 Carcaixent Spain
105 C3 Carcassonne France
128 A1 Carcross Can.
145 C3 Cárdenas Mex.
99 B3 Cardiff U.K.
99 A2 Cardigan U.K.
99 A2 Cardigan Bay U.K.
128 C3 Cardston Can.
110 B1 Carei Romania
104 B2 Carentan France
50 B2 Carey, Lake imp. l. Austr.
155 D2 Cariacica Brazil
146 B3 Caribbean Sea N. Atlantic Ocean
141 F1 Caribou U.S.A.
130 B1 Caribou Lake Can.
128 C2 Caribou Mountains Can.
144 B2 Carichic Mex.
100 B3 Carignan France
53 C2 Carinda Austr.
107 C1 Cariñena Spain
130 C2 Carleton Place Can.
123 C2 Carletonville S. Africa
97 C1 Carlingford Lough inlet Ireland/U.K.
98 B1 Carlisle U.K.
141 D2 Carlisle U.S.A.
155 D1 Carlos Chagas Brazil
97 C2 Carlow Ireland
135 C4 Carlsbad CA U.S.A.
138 C2 Carlsbad NM U.S.A.
129 D3 Carlyle Can.
128 A1 Carmacks Can.
99 A3 Carmarthen U.K.
99 A3 Carmarthen Bay U.K.
104 C3 Carmaux France
145 C3 Carmelita Guat.
144 A2 Carmen, Isla i. Mex.
104 B2 Carnac France
122 B3 Carnarvon S. Africa
97 C1 Carndonagh Ireland
50 B2 Carnegie, Lake imp. l. Austr.
96 B2 Carn Eige mt. U.K.
63 A3 Car Nicobar i. India

118 B2 **Carnot** C.A.R.
52 A2 **Carnot, Cape** Austr.
97 C2 **Carnsore Point** Ireland
151 D2 **Carolina** Brazil
48 D2 **Caroline Islands** *is* N. Pacific Ocean
59 D2 **Caroline Islands** N. Pacific Ocean
103 D2 **Carpathian Mountains** Europe
Carpaţii Meridionali *mts* Romania *see* **Transylvanian Alps**
51 C1 **Carpentaria, Gulf of** Austr.
105 D3 **Carpentras** France
97 B3 **Carrantuohill** *mt.* Ireland
105 E3 **Carrara** Italy
97 C2 **Carrickmacross** Ireland
97 C2 **Carrick-on-Shannon** Ireland
97 C2 **Carrick-on-Suir** Ireland
137 D1 **Carrington** U.S.A.
139 D3 **Carrizo Springs** U.S.A.
138 B2 **Carrizozo** U.S.A.
137 E2 **Carroll** U.S.A.
143 C2 **Carrollton** U.S.A.
129 D2 **Carrot River** Can.
135 C3 **Carson City** U.S.A.
150 A1 **Cartagena** Col.
107 C2 **Cartagena** Spain
146 B4 **Cartago** Costa Rica
137 E3 **Carthage** MO U.S.A.
139 E2 **Carthage** TX U.S.A.
131 E1 **Cartwright** Can.
151 E2 **Caruarú** Brazil
114 B1 **Casablanca** Morocco
154 C2 **Casa Branca** Brazil
144 B1 **Casa de Janos** Mex.
138 A2 **Casa Grande** U.S.A.
108 A1 **Casale Monferrato** Italy
109 C2 **Casarano** Italy
134 C2 **Cascade** U.S.A.
134 B2 **Cascade Range** *mts* Can./U.S.A.
125 A5 **Cascais** Port.
154 B2 **Cascavel** Brazil
108 B2 **Caserta** Italy
97 C2 **Cashel** Ireland
53 D1 **Casino** Austr.
107 C1 **Caspe** Spain
136 B2 **Casper** U.S.A.
76 A2 **Caspian Lowland** Kazakh./ Rus. Fed.
81 C1 **Caspian Sea** Asia/Europe
154 C2 **Cássia** Brazil
128 B2 **Cassiar** Can.
128 A2 **Cassiar Mountains** Can.
154 B1 **Cassilândia** Brazil
108 B2 **Cassino** Italy
96 B2 **Cassley** *r.* U.K.
151 D2 **Castanhal** Brazil
152 B4 **Castaño** *r.* Arg.
144 B2 **Castaños** Mex.
104 C3 **Casteljaloux** France
107 C2 **Castellón de la Plana** Spain
106 B2 **Castelo Branco** Port.
108 B3 **Castelvetrano** *Sicilia* Italy
52 B3 **Casterton** Austr.
108 B2 **Castiglione della Pescaia** Italy
97 B2 **Castlebar** Ireland
96 A2 **Castlebay** U.K.
97 C1 **Castleblayney** Ireland
97 C1 **Castlederg** U.K.
96 C3 **Castle Douglas** U.K.
128 C3 **Castlegar** Can.
97 B2 **Castleisland** Ireland
52 B3 **Castlemaine** Austr.
97 B2 **Castlerea** Ireland
53 C2 **Castlereagh** *r.* Austr.
136 C3 **Castle Rock** U.S.A.
129 C2 **Castor** Can.

104 C3 **Castres** France
100 B1 **Castricum** Neth.
147 D3 **Castries** St Lucia
154 C3 **Castro** Brazil
153 A5 **Castro** Chile
106 B2 **Castro Verde** Port.
109 C3 **Castrovillari** Italy
150 A2 **Catacaos** Peru
155 D2 **Cataguases** Brazil
154 C1 **Catalão** Brazil
152 B3 **Catamarca** Arg.
64 B1 **Catanduanes** *i.* Phil.
154 C2 **Catanduva** Brazil
154 B3 **Catanduvas** Brazil
109 C3 **Catania** *Sicilia* Italy
109 C3 **Catanzaro** Italy
64 B1 **Catarman** Phil.
64 B1 **Catbalogan** Phil.
145 C3 **Catemaco** Mex.
147 C2 **Cat Island** Bahamas
130 A1 **Cat Lake** Can.
145 D2 **Catoche, Cabo** *c.* Mex.
141 E2 **Catskill Mountains** U.S.A.
64 B2 **Cauayan** Phil.
150 A1 **Cauca** *r.* Col.
151 E2 **Caucaia** Brazil
81 C1 **Caucasus** *mts* Asia/Europe
100 A2 **Caudry** France
109 C3 **Caulonia** Italy
131 D2 **Causapscal** Can.
105 D3 **Cavaillon** France
151 D3 **Cavalcante** Brazil
97 C2 **Cavan** Ireland
154 B3 **Cavernoso, Serra do** *mts* Brazil
151 D2 **Caxias** Brazil
152 C3 **Caxias do Sul** Brazil
120 A1 **Caxito** Angola
151 C1 **Cayenne** Fr. Guiana
146 B3 **Cayman Islands** *terr.* West Indies
117 C4 **Caynabo** Somalia
120 B2 **Cazombo** Angola
144 B2 **Ceballos** Mex.
64 B1 **Cebu** Phil.
64 B1 **Cebu** *i.* Phil.
108 B2 **Cecina** Italy
137 F2 **Cedar** *r.* U.S.A.
135 D3 **Cedar City** U.S.A.
137 E2 **Cedar Falls** U.S.A.
129 D2 **Cedar Lake** Can.
137 E2 **Cedar Rapids** U.S.A.
144 A2 **Cedros, Isla** *i.* Mex.
51 C3 **Ceduna** Austr.
117 C4 **Ceeldheere** Somalia
117 C3 **Ceerigaabo** Somalia
108 B3 **Cefalù** *Sicilia* Italy
145 B2 **Celaya** Mex.
58 C3 **Celebes** *i.* Indon.
156 B5 **Celebes Sea** Indon./Phil.
145 C2 **Celestún** Mex.
101 E1 **Celle** Ger.
95 B3 **Celtic Sea** Ireland/U.K.
59 D3 **Cenderawasih, Teluk** *b.* Indon.
150 A1 **Central, Cordillera** *mts* Col.
150 A3 **Central, Cordillera** *mts* Peru
64 B1 **Central, Cordillera** *mts* Phil.
118 C2 **Central African Republic** *country* Africa
74 A2 **Central Brahui Range** *mts* Pak.
137 D2 **Central City** U.S.A.
140 B3 **Centralia** *IL.* U.S.A.
134 B1 **Centralia** *WA* U.S.A.
74 A2 **Central Makran Range** *mts* Pak.
59 D3 **Central Range** *mts* P.N.G.
89 E3 **Central Russian Upland** *hills* Rus. Fed.

83 I2 **Central Siberian Plateau** Rus. Fed.
111 B3 **Cephalonia** *i.* Greece
Ceram Sea Indon. *see* **Seram, Laut**
152 B3 **Ceres** Arg.
154 C1 **Ceres** Brazil
122 A3 **Ceres** S. Africa
104 C3 **Céret** France
106 C1 **Cerezo de Abajo** Spain
109 C2 **Cerignola** Italy
110 C2 **Cernavodă** Romania
145 C2 **Ceralvo** Mex.
144 B2 **Cerralvo, Isla** *i.* Mex.
145 B2 **Cerritos** Mex.
154 C2 **Cerro Azul** Brazil
145 C2 **Cerro Azul** Mex.
150 A3 **Cerro de Pasco** Peru
105 D3 **Cervione** *Corse* France
106 B1 **Cervo** Spain
108 B2 **Cesena** Italy
88 C2 **Cēsis** Latvia
102 C2 **České Budějovice** Czech Rep.
101 F3 **Český les** *mts* Czech Rep.
111 C3 **Çeşme** Turkey
53 D2 **Cessnock** Austr.
109 C2 **Cetinje** Montenegro
109 C3 **Cetraro** Italy
106 B2 **Ceuta** N. Africa
105 C3 **Cévennes** *mts* France
Ceylon *country* Asia *see* **Sri Lanka**
79 D2 **Chābahār** Iran
150 A2 **Chachapoyas** Peru
89 D3 **Chachersk** Belarus
63 B2 **Chachoengsao** Thai.
115 D3 **Chad** *country* Africa
69 C1 **Chadaasan** Mongolia
68 C1 **Chadan** Rus. Fed.
123 C1 **Chadibe** Botswana
136 C2 **Chadron** U.S.A.
65 B2 **Chaeryŏng** N. Korea
74 A2 **Chagai** Pak.
77 C3 **Chaghcharān** Afgh.
89 E2 **Chagoda** Rus. Fed.
75 C2 **Chaibasa** India
63 B2 **Chainat** Thai.
63 B2 **Chaiyaphum** Thai.
152 C4 **Chajarí** Arg.
131 D1 **Chakonipau, Lac** *l.* Can.
150 A3 **Chala** Peru
74 A1 **Chalap Dalan** *mts* Afgh.
131 D2 **Chaleur Bay** *inlet* Can.
74 B2 **Chalisgaon** India
111 C3 **Chalki** *i.* Greece
111 B3 **Chalkida** Greece
104 B2 **Challans** France
134 D2 **Challis** U.S.A.
105 C2 **Châlons-en-Champagne** France
105 C2 **Chalon-sur-Saône** France
138 B1 **Chama** U.S.A.
121 C2 **Chama** Zambia
74 A1 **Chaman** Pak.
74 B1 **Chamba** India
137 D2 **Chambal** *r.* India
137 D2 **Chamberlain** U.S.A.
141 D2 **Chambersburg** U.S.A.
105 D2 **Chambéry** France
121 C2 **Chambeshi** Zambia
140 B2 **Champaign** U.S.A.
141 E2 **Champlain, Lake** Can./U.S.A.
145 C3 **Champotón** Mex.
152 A3 **Chañaral** Chile
126 B2 **Chandalar** *r.* U.S.A.
142 C3 **Chandeleur Islands** U.S.A.

Chandigarh

74 B1 **Chandigarh** India
138 A2 **Chandler** U.S.A.
75 B3 **Chandrapur** India
63 B2 **Chang, Ko** r. Thai.
Chang'an China see **Rong'an**
121 C3 **Changane** r. Moz.
121 C2 **Changara** Moz.
65 B1 **Changbai** China
65 B1 **Changbai Shan** mts China/
N. Korea
69 E2 **Changchun** China
71 B3 **Changde** China
65 B2 **Ch'angdo** N. Korea
65 B3 **Changhŭng** S. Korea
Chang Jiang r. China see
Yangtze
65 B3 **Changjin** N. Korea
65 B1 **Changjin-gang** r. N. Korea
71 B3 **Changsha** China
65 B2 **Changsŏng** S. Korea
71 B3 **Changting** China
65 B2 **Ch'angwŏn** S. Korea
70 B2 **Changyuan** China
70 B2 **Changzhi** China
70 B2 **Changzhou** China
111 B3 **Chania** Greece
95 C4 **Channel Islands** English Chan.
135 C4 **Channel Islands** U.S.A.
131 E2 **Channel-Port-aux-Basques**
Can.
63 B2 **Chanthaburi** Thai.
104 C2 **Chantilly** France
137 D3 **Chanute** U.S.A.
82 G3 **Chany, Ozero** salt l.
Rus. Fed.
71 B3 **Chaoyang** China
Chaoyang China see **Huinan**
71 B3 **Chaozhou** China
144 B2 **Chapala, Laguna de** l. Mex.
76 B1 **Chapayevo** Kazakh.
152 C3 **Chapecó** Brazil
143 E1 **Chapel Hill** U.S.A.
130 B2 **Chapleau** Can.
89 E3 **Chaplygin** Rus. Fed.
91 C2 **Chaplynka** Ukr.
145 B2 **Charcas** Mex.
99 B3 **Chard** U.K.
104 B2 **Charente** r. France
77 C3 **Charikar** Afgh.
86 E2 **Charkayuvom** Rus. Fed.
100 B2 **Charleroi** Belgium
141 D3 **Charles, Cape** U.S.A.
137 E2 **Charles City** U.S.A.
140 B3 **Charleston** IL U.S.A.
143 E2 **Charleston** SC U.S.A.
140 C3 **Charleston** WV U.S.A.
135 C3 **Charleston Peak** U.S.A.
51 D2 **Charleville** Austr.
105 C2 **Charleville-Mézières** France
143 D1 **Charlotte** U.S.A.
143 D3 **Charlotte Harbor** b. U.S.A.
141 D3 **Charlottesville** U.S.A.
131 D2 **Charlottetown** Can.
52 B3 **Charlton** Austr.
130 C1 **Charlton Island** Can.
51 D2 **Charters Towers** Austr.
104 C2 **Chartres** France
128 C2 **Chase** Can.
88 C3 **Chashniki** Belarus
54 A3 **Chaslands Mistake** c. N.Z.
65 B1 **Chasŏng** N. Korea
104 B2 **Chassiron, Pointe de** pt
France
104 B2 **Châteaubriant** France
104 C2 **Château-du-Loir** France
104 C2 **Châteaudun** France
104 B2 **Châteaulin** France

105 D3 **Châteauneuf-les-Martigues**
France
104 C2 **Châteauneuf-sur-Loire** France
105 C2 **Château-Thierry** France
100 B2 **Châtelet** Belgium
104 C2 **Châtellerault** France
140 C2 **Chatham** Ont. Can.
49 G5 **Chatham Islands** is N.Z.
105 C2 **Châtillon-sur-Seine** France
143 D2 **Chattahoochee** r. U.S.A.
143 C1 **Chattanooga** U.S.A.
63 B2 **Châu Đốc** Vietnam
62 A1 **Chauk** Myanmar
105 D2 **Chaumont** France
105 C2 **Chauny** France
151 D2 **Chaves** Brazil
106 B1 **Chaves** Port.
130 C1 **Chavigny, Lac** l. Can.
89 D3 **Chavusy** Belarus
89 E2 **Chayevo** Rus. Fed.
86 E3 **Chaykovskiy** Rus. Fed.
102 C2 **Cheb** Czech Rep.
87 D3 **Cheboksary** Rus. Fed.
140 C1 **Cheboygan** U.S.A.
65 B3 **Chech'ŏn** S. Korea
114 B2 **Chegga** Maur.
134 B1 **Chehalis** U.S.A.
65 B3 **Cheju** S. Korea
65 B3 **Cheju-do** i. S. Korea
65 B3 **Cheju-haehyŏp** sea chan.
S. Korea
89 E2 **Chekhov** Rus. Fed.
134 B1 **Chelan, Lake** U.S.A.
103 E1 **Chełm** Pol.
99 D3 **Chelmer** r. U.K.
103 D1 **Chełmno** Pol.
99 D3 **Chelmsford** U.K.
99 B3 **Cheltenham** U.K.
87 F3 **Chelyabinsk** Rus. Fed.
101 F2 **Chemnitz** Ger.
114 B2 **Chenachane** Alg.
70 B1 **Chengde** China
70 A2 **Chengdu** China
71 A3 **Chengguan** China
71 B4 **Chengmai** China
Chengzhou China see
Yingshan
70 A2 **Chengxian** China
Chengyang China see **Juxian**
73 C3 **Chennai** India
71 B3 **Chenzhou** China
99 B3 **Chepstow** U.K.
104 B2 **Cherbourg-Octeville** France
89 E3 **Cheremisinovo** Rus. Fed.
69 C1 **Cheremkhovo** Rus. Fed.
89 E2 **Cherepovets** Rus. Fed.
87 D4 **Cherkasy** Ukr.
91 C1 **Chernihiv** Ukr.
91 D2 **Cherninivka** Ukr.
90 B2 **Chernivtsi** Ukr.
90 B1 **Chernyakhiv** Ukr.
88 B3 **Chernyakhovsk** Rus. Fed.
89 E3 **Chernyanka** Rus. Fed.
83 I2 **Chernyshevskiy** Rus. Fed.
137 D2 **Cherokee** U.S.A.
83 K2 **Cherskogo, Khrebet** mts
Rus. Fed.
91 E2 **Chertkovo** Rus. Fed.
90 A1 **Chervonohrad** Ukr.
88 C3 **Chervyen'** Belarus
89 D3 **Cherykaw** Belarus
141 D3 **Chesapeake Bay** U.S.A.
86 D2 **Cheshskaya Guba** b. Rus. Fed.
98 B2 **Chester** U.K.
140 B3 **Chester** IL U.S.A.

143 D2 **Chester** SC U.S.A.
98 C2 **Chesterfield** U.K.
129 E1 **Chesterfield Inlet** Can.
129 E1 **Chesterfield Inlet** Can.
141 F1 **Chesuncook Lake** U.S.A.
131 D2 **Chéticamp** Can.
145 D3 **Chetumal** Mex.
128 B2 **Chetwynd** Can.
98 B1 **Cheviot Hills** U.K.
136 C2 **Cheyenne** U.S.A.
136 C2 **Cheyenne** r. U.S.A.
136 C3 **Cheyenne Wells** U.S.A.
75 C2 **Chhapra** India
75 B2 **Chhatarpur** India
62 A2 **Chiang Dao** Thai.
62 A2 **Chiang Mai** Thai.
62 A2 **Chiang Rai** Thai.
108 A1 **Chiavenna** Italy
67 C4 **Chiba** Japan
121 C3 **Chiboma** Moz.
130 C2 **Chibougamau** Can.
123 D1 **Chibuto** Moz.
75 D1 **Chibuzhang Co** l. China
140 B2 **Chicago** U.S.A.
128 A2 **Chichagof Island** U.S.A.
99 C3 **Chichester** U.K.
50 A2 **Chichester Range** mts Austr.
139 D1 **Chickasha** U.S.A.
150 A2 **Chiclayo** Peru
153 B5 **Chico** r. Arg.
135 B3 **Chico** U.S.A.
108 B2 **Chicoutimi** Can.
145 C3 **Chietla** Mex.
69 D2 **Chifeng** China
155 D1 **Chifre, Serra do** mts Brazil
145 C3 **Chignahuapán** Mex.
121 C3 **Chigubo** Moz.
144 B2 **Chihuahua** Mex.
88 C2 **Chikhachevo** Rus. Fed.
67 C3 **Chikuma-gawa** r. Japan
128 B2 **Chilanko** r. Can.
74 B1 **Chilas** Pak.
139 C2 **Childress** U.S.A.
153 A4 **Chile** country S. America
152 B3 **Chilecito** Arg.
75 C3 **Chilika Lake** India
121 B2 **Chililabombwe** Zambia
128 B2 **Chilko** r. Can.
128 B2 **Chilko Lake** Can.
153 A4 **Chillán** Chile
137 E3 **Chillicothe** MO U.S.A.
140 C3 **Chillicothe** OH U.S.A.
128 B3 **Chilliwack** Can.
153 A5 **Chiloé, Isla de** i. Chile
145 C3 **Chilpancingo** Mex.
53 C3 **Chiltern** Austr.
71 C3 **Chilung** Taiwan
119 D3 **Chimala** Tanz.
152 B4 **Chimbas** Arg.
150 A2 **Chimborazo** mt. Ecuador
150 A2 **Chimbote** Peru
87 E4 **Chimboy** Uzbek.
Chimkent Kazakh. see
Shymkent
121 C2 **Chimoio** Moz.
77 C3 **Chimtargha, Qullai** mt. Tajik.
68 C2 **China** country Asia
145 C2 **China** Mex.
150 A3 **Chincha Alta** Peru
128 C2 **Chinchaga** r. Can.
145 D3 **Chinchorro, Banco** Mex.
121 C2 **Chinde** Moz.
65 B3 **Chindo** S. Korea
65 B3 **Chin-do** i. S. Korea
68 C2 **Chindu** China
62 A1 **Chindwin** r. Myanmar

65	B2	Chinghwa N. Korea
120	B2	Chingola Zambia
120	A2	Chinguar Angola
65	B2	Chinhae S. Korea
121	C2	Chinhoyi Zimbabwe
74	B1	Chiniot Pak.
144	B2	Chinipas Mex.
65	B2	Chinju S. Korea
118	C2	Chinko r. C.A.R.
138	B1	Chinle U.S.A.
71	B3	Chinmen Taiwan
67	C3	Chino Japan
104	C2	Chinon France
138	A2	Chino Valley U.S.A.
121	C2	Chinsali Zambia
108	B1	Chioggia Italy
111	C3	Chios Greece
111	C3	Chios i. Greece
121	C2	Chipata Zambia
120	A2	Chipindo Angola
121	C3	Chipinge Zimbabwe
73	B3	Chiplun India
99	B3	Chippenham U.K.
99	C3	Chipping Norton U.K.
121	C2	Chirchiq Uzbek.
121	C3	Chiredzi Zimbabwe
138	B2	Chiricahua Peak U.S.A.
146	B4	Chiriquí, Golfo de b. Panama
65	B2	Chiri-san mt. S. Korea
146	B4	Chirripó mt. Costa Rica
121	B2	Chirundu Zimbabwe
130	C1	Chisasibi Can.
137	E1	Chisholm U.S.A.
90	B2	Chişinău Moldova
87	C3	Chistopol' Rus. Fed.
69	D1	Chita Rus. Fed.
120	A2	Chitado Angola
121	C2	Chitambo Zambia
120	B1	Chitato Angola
121	C1	Chitipa Malawi
73	B3	Chitradurga India
74	B1	Chitral Pak.
146	B4	Chitré Panama
75	D2	Chittagong Bangl.
74	B2	Chittaurgarh India
121	C2	Chitungwiza Zimbabwe
120	B2	Chiume Angola
121	C2	Chivhu Zimbabwe
70	B2	Chizhou China
114	C1	Chlef Alg.
107	D2	Chlef, Oued r. Alg.
153	B4	Choele Choel Arg.
144	B2	Choix Mex.
103	D1	Chojnice Pol.
117	B3	Ch'ok'ē Mountains Eth.
117	B3	Ch'ok'ē Terara mt. Eth.
83	K2	Chokurdakh Rus. Fed.
121	C3	Chókwé Moz.
104	B2	Cholet France
102	C1	Chomutov Czech Rep.
83	I2	Chona r. Rus. Fed.
65	B2	Ch'ōnan S. Korea
150	A2	Chone Ecuador
65	B1	Ch'ŏngjin N. Korea
65	B2	Chŏngju N. Korea
65	B2	Chŏngp'yŏng N. Korea
70	A3	Chongqing China
70	A2	Chongqing mun. China
71	A3	Chongzuo China
65	B2	Chŏnju S. Korea
153	A5	Chonos, Archipiélago de los is Chile
154	B3	Chopimzinho Brazil
111	B3	Chora Sfakion Greece
98	B2	Chorley U.K.
91	C2	Chornomors'ke Ukr.
90	B2	Chortkiv Ukr.

65	B2	Ch'ŏrwŏn S. Korea
65	B1	Ch'osan N. Korea
67	D3	Chōshi Japan
103	D1	Choszczno Pol.
114	A2	Choûm Maur.
69	D1	Choybalsan Mongolia
69	D1	Choyr Mongolia
54	B2	Christchurch N.Z.
99	C3	Christchurch U.K.
127	G2	Christian, Cape Can.
123	C2	Christiana S. Africa
54	A2	Christina, Mount N.Z.
153	B5	Chubut r. Arg.
90	B1	Chudniv Ukr.
89	D2	Chudovo Rus. Fed.
		Chudskoye Ozero l. Estonia/ Rus. Fed. see Peipus, Lake
126	B2	Chugach Mountains U.S.A.
67	B4	Chūgoku-sanchi mts Japan
66	B2	Chuguyevka Rus. Fed.
91	D2	Chuhuyiv Ukr.
160	J3	Chukchi Sea Rus. Fed./U.S.A.
83	N2	Chukotskiy Poluostrov pen. Rus. Fed.
135	C4	Chula Vista U.S.A.
82	G3	Chulym Rus. Fed.
152	B3	Chumbicha Arg.
83	K3	Chumikan Rus. Fed.
63	A2	Chumphon Thai.
65	B2	Ch'unch'ŏn S. Korea
		Chungking China see Chongqing
83	H2	Chunya r. Rus. Fed.
150	A3	Chuquibamba Peru
152	B3	Chuquicamata Chile
105	D2	Chur Switz.
62	A1	Churachandpur India
129	E2	Churchill Can.
129	E2	Churchill r. Man. Can.
131	D1	Churchill r. Nfld. and Lab. Can.
129	E2	Churchill, Cape Can.
131	D1	Churchill Falls Can.
129	D2	Churchill Lake Can.
74	B2	Churu India
131	C2	Chute-des-Passes Can.
62	B1	Chuxiong China
90	B2	Ciadîr-Lunga Moldova
61	B2	Ciamis Indon.
60	B2	Cianjur Indon.
154	B2	Cianorte Brazil
103	E1	Ciechanów Pol.
146	C2	Ciego de Ávila Cuba
146	B2	Cienfuegos Cuba
107	C2	Cieza Spain
80	B2	Cigüela r. Spain
144	B3	Cihuatlán Mex.
106	C2	Cíjara, Embalse de resr Spain
61	B2	Cilacap Indon.
139	C1	Cimarron r. U.S.A.
90	B2	Cimişlia Moldova
108	B2	Cimone, Monte mt. Italy
140	C3	Cincinnati U.S.A.
111	C3	Çine Turkey
100	B2	Ciney Belgium
145	C3	Cintalapa Mex.
71	B3	Ciping China
126	B2	Circle AK U.S.A.
136	B1	Circle MT U.S.A.
58	B3	Cirebon Indon.
99	C3	Cirencester U.K.
108	A1	Ciriè Italy
109	C3	Cirò Marina Italy
109	C2	Čitluk Bos.-Herz.
122	A3	Citrusdal S. Africa
145	B2	Ciudad Acuña Mex.
145	B3	Ciudad Altamirano Mex.

150	B1	Ciudad Bolívar Venez.
144	B2	Ciudad Camargo Mex.
144	A2	Ciudad Constitución Mex.
145	C3	Ciudad del Carmen Mex.
144	B2	Ciudad Delicias Mex.
145	C2	Ciudad de Valles Mex.
150	B1	Ciudad Guayana Venez.
138	B3	Ciudad Guerrero Mex.
144	B3	Ciudad Guzmán Mex.
145	C3	Ciudad Hidalgo Mex.
145	C3	Ciudad Ixtepec Mex.
144	B1	Ciudad Juárez Mex.
145	C2	Ciudad Mante Mex.
145	C2	Ciudad Mier Mex.
144	B2	Ciudad Obregón Mex.
106	C2	Ciudad Real Spain
145	C2	Ciudad Río Bravo Mex.
106	B1	Ciudad Rodrigo Spain
145	C2	Ciudad Victoria Mex.
107	D1	Ciutadella Spain
111	C3	Cıvan Dağ mt. Turkey
108	B1	Cividale del Friuli Italy
108	B2	Civitanova Marche Italy
108	B2	Civitavecchia Italy
104	C2	Civray France
111	C3	Çivril Turkey
70	C2	Cixi China
99	D3	Clacton-on-Sea U.K.
128	C2	Claire, Lake Can.
105	C2	Clamecy France
122	A3	Clanwilliam S. Africa
52	A2	Clare Austr.
97	A2	Clare Island Ireland
141	E2	Claremont U.S.A.
97	B2	Claremorris Ireland
54	B2	Clarence N.Z.
131	E2	Clarenville Can.
128	C2	Claresholm Can.
137	D2	Clarinda U.S.A.
123	C3	Clarkebury S. Africa
134	C1	Clark Fork r. U.S.A.
141	D2	Clark Hill Reservoir U.S.A.
140	C3	Clarksburg U.S.A.
142	B2	Clarksdale U.S.A.
142	B1	Clarksville AR U.S.A.
142	C1	Clarksville TN U.S.A.
154	B1	Claro r. Brazil
139	C1	Clayton U.S.A.
97	B3	Clear, Cape Ireland
137	E2	Clear Lake U.S.A.
135	B3	Clear Lake U.S.A.
128	C2	Clearwater Can.
129	C2	Clearwater r. Can.
143	D3	Clearwater U.S.A.
134	C1	Clearwater r. U.S.A.
139	D2	Cleburne U.S.A.
51	D2	Clermont Austr.
105	C2	Clermont-Ferrand France
52	A2	Cleve Austr.
142	B2	Cleveland MS U.S.A.
140	C2	Cleveland OH U.S.A.
143	D1	Cleveland TN U.S.A.
134	D1	Cleveland, Mount U.S.A.
143	D3	Clewiston U.S.A.
97	A2	Clifden Ireland
53	C1	Clifton Austr.
138	B2	Clifton U.S.A.
128	B2	Clinton Can.
137	E2	Clinton IA U.S.A.
137	E3	Clinton MO U.S.A.
139	D1	Clinton OK U.S.A.
96	A2	Clisham h. U.K.
98	B2	Clitheroe U.K.
97	B3	Clonakilty Ireland
51	D2	Cloncurry Austr.
97	C1	Clones Ireland
97	C2	Clonmel Ireland

100 D1 Cloppenburg Ger.
50 A2 Cloud Break Austr.
136 B2 Cloud Peak U.S.A.
139 C2 Clovis U.S.A.
129 D2 Cluff Lake Mine Can.
110 B1 Cluj-Napoca Romania
51 C2 Cluny Austr.
105 D2 Cluses France
54 A3 Clutha r. N.Z.
96 B3 Clyde r. U.K.
96 B3 Clyde, Firth of est. U.K.
96 B3 Clydebank U.K.
127 G2 Clyde River Can.
144 B3 Coalcomán Mex.
135 C3 Coaldale U.S.A.
128 B2 Coal River Can.
150 B2 Coari Brazil
150 B2 Coari r. Brazil
142 B2 Coastal Plain U.S.A.
128 B2 Coast Mountains Can.
135 B2 Coast Ranges mts U.S.A.
96 B3 Coatbridge U.K.
127 F2 Coats Island Can.
55 R2 Coats Land reg. Antarctica
145 C3 Coatzacoalcos Mex.
146 A3 Cobán Guat.
53 C2 Cobar Austr.
97 B3 Cobh Ireland
152 B2 Cobija Bol.
141 D2 Cobourg Can.
50 C1 Cobourg Peninsula Austr.
53 C2 Cobram Austr.
101 E2 Coburg Ger.
152 B2 Cochabamba Bol.
100 C2 Cochem Ger.
     Cochin India see Kochi
128 C2 Cochrane Alta Can.
130 B2 Cochrane Ont. Can.
153 A5 Cochrane Chile
52 B2 Cockburn Austr.
     Cockburn Town Turks and
     Caicos Is see Grand Turk
98 B1 Cockermouth U.K.
122 B3 Cockscomb mt. S. Africa
146 B3 Coco r. Hond./Nic.
144 B2 Cocula Mex.
150 A1 Cocuy, Sierra Nevada del
     mt. Col.
141 E2 Cod, Cape U.S.A.
108 B2 Codigoro Italy
131 D1 Cod Island Can.
151 D2 Codó Brazil
136 B2 Cody U.S.A.
51 D1 Coen Austr.
100 C2 Coesfeld Ger.
134 C1 Coeur d'Alene U.S.A.
123 C3 Coffee Bay S. Africa
137 D3 Coffeyville U.S.A.
53 D2 Coffs Harbour Austr.
104 C2 Cognac France
118 A2 Cogo Equat. Guinea
52 B2 Cohuna Austr.
146 B4 Coiba, Isla de i. Panama
153 A5 Coihaique Chile
73 B3 Coimbatore India
106 B1 Coimbra Port.
52 B3 Colac Austr.
155 D1 Colatina Brazil
136 C3 Colby U.S.A.
99 D3 Colchester U.K.
129 C2 Cold Lake Can.
96 C3 Coldstream U.K.
139 D2 Coleman U.S.A.
52 B3 Coleraine Austr.
97 C1 Coleraine U.K.
123 C3 Colesberg S. Africa
144 B3 Colima Mex.

144 B3 Colima, Nevado de vol. Mex.
96 A2 Coll i. U.K.
53 C1 Collarenebri Austr.
50 B1 Collier Bay Austr.
54 B2 Collingwood N.Z.
97 B1 Collooney Ireland
105 D2 Colmar France
100 C2 Cologne Ger.
154 C2 Colômbia Brazil
150 A1 Colombia country S. America
73 B4 Colombo Sri Lanka
104 C3 Colomiers France
152 C4 Colón Arg.
146 C4 Colón Panama
109 C3 Colonna, Capo c. Italy
96 A2 Colonsay i. U.K.
153 B4 Colorado r. Arg.
138 A2 Colorado r. Mex./U.S.A.
139 D3 Colorado r. U.S.A.
136 B3 Colorado state U.S.A.
135 E3 Colorado Plateau U.S.A.
136 C3 Colorado Springs U.S.A.
144 B2 Colotlán Mex.
136 B1 Colstrip U.S.A.
137 E3 Columbia MO U.S.A.
143 D2 Columbia SC U.S.A.
143 C1 Columbia TN U.S.A.
134 B1 Columbia r. U.S.A.
128 C2 Columbia, Mount Can.
134 D1 Columbia Falls U.S.A.
128 B2 Columbia Mountains Can.
134 C1 Columbia Plateau U.S.A.
143 D2 Columbus GA U.S.A.
140 B3 Columbus IN U.S.A.
142 C2 Columbus MS U.S.A.
137 D2 Columbus NE U.S.A.
138 B2 Columbus NM U.S.A.
140 C3 Columbus OH U.S.A.
134 C1 Colville U.S.A.
126 A2 Colville r. U.S.A.
126 C2 Colville Lake Can.
98 B2 Colwyn Bay U.K.
108 B2 Comacchio Italy
145 C3 Comalcalco Mex.
110 C1 Comănești Romania
130 C1 Comencho, Lac l. Can.
97 C2 Comeragh Mountains hills
     Ireland
75 D2 Comilla Bangl.
108 A2 Comino, Capo c. Sardegna Italy
145 C3 Comitán de Domínguez Mex.
104 C2 Commentry France
139 D2 Commerce U.S.A.
127 F2 Committee Bay Can.
108 A1 Como Italy
153 B5 Comodoro Rivadavia Arg.
121 D2 Comoros country Africa
104 C2 Compiègne France
90 B2 Comrat Moldova
114 A4 Conakry Guinea
155 E1 Conceição da Barra Brazil
151 D2 Conceição do Araguaia Brazil
155 D1 Conceição do Mato Dentro
     Brazil
152 B3 Concepción Arg.
153 A4 Concepción Chile
144 B2 Concepción Mex.
135 B4 Conception, Point U.S.A.
154 C2 Conchas Brazil
138 C1 Conchas Lake U.S.A.
144 B2 Conchos r. Chihuahua Mex.
145 C2 Conchos r. Nuevo León/
     Tamaulipas Mex.
135 B3 Concord CA U.S.A.
141 E2 Concord NH U.S.A.
152 C4 Concordia Arg.

122 A2 Concordia S. Africa
137 D3 Concordia U.S.A.
53 C2 Condobolin Austr.
104 C3 Condom France
134 B1 Condon U.S.A.
108 B1 Conegliano Italy
104 C2 Confolens France
75 C2 Congdü China
118 B3 Congo country Africa
118 B3 Congo r. Congo/Dem. Rep.
     Congo
118 C3 Congo, Democratic Republic
     of the country Africa
129 C2 Conklin Can.
97 B1 Conn, Lough l. Ireland
97 B2 Connaught reg. Ireland
141 E2 Connecticut r. U.S.A.
141 E2 Connecticut state U.S.A.
97 B2 Connemara reg. Ireland
134 D1 Conrad U.S.A.
139 D2 Conroe U.S.A.
155 D2 Conselheiro Lafaiete Brazil
155 D1 Conselheiro Pena Brazil
98 C1 Consett U.K.
63 B2 Côn Sơn, Đao i. Vietnam
110 C2 Constanța Romania
106 B2 Constantina Spain
115 C1 Constantine Alg.
134 D2 Contact U.S.A.
150 A2 Contamana Peru
153 A6 Contreras, Isla i. Chile
126 D2 Contwoyto Lake Can.
142 B1 Conway AR U.S.A.
141 E2 Conway NH U.S.A.
51 C2 Coober Pedy Austr.
     Cook, Mount mt. N.Z. see
     Aoraki
143 D1 Cookeville U.S.A.
49 H4 Cook Islands S. Pacific Ocean
131 E1 Cook's Harbour Can.
97 C1 Cookstown U.K.
54 B2 Cook Strait N.Z.
51 D1 Cooktown Austr.
53 C2 Coolabah Austr.
53 C2 Coolamon Austr.
53 D1 Coolangatta Austr.
50 B3 Coolgardie Austr.
53 C3 Cooma Austr.
52 B2 Coombah Austr.
53 C2 Coonabarabran Austr.
52 A3 Coonalpyn Austr.
53 C2 Coonamble Austr.
52 A1 Cooper Creek watercourse Austr.
134 B2 Coos Bay U.S.A.
53 C2 Cootamundra Austr.
145 C3 Copainalá Mex.
145 C3 Copala Mex.
93 F4 Copenhagen Denmark
109 C2 Copertino Italy
152 A3 Copiapó Chile
140 B1 Copper Harbor U.S.A.
     Coppermine Can. see
     Kugluktuk
126 D2 Coppermine r. Can.
122 B2 Copperton S. Africa
152 A3 Coquimbo Chile
110 B2 Corabia Romania
155 D1 Coração de Jesus Brazil
150 A3 Coracora Peru
53 D1 Coraki Austr.
50 A2 Coral Bay Austr.
127 F2 Coral Harbour Can.
156 D7 Coral Sea S. Pacific Ocean
48 D4 Coral Sea Islands Territory
     Austr.
52 B3 Corangamite, Lake Austr.
99 C2 Corby U.K.

153	A5	Corcovado, Golfo de *sea chan.* Chile
143	D2	Cordele U.S.A.
64	B1	Cordilleras Range *mts* Phil.
152	B4	Córdoba Arg.
145	C3	Córdoba Mex.
106	C2	Córdoba Spain
153	B4	Córdoba, Sierras de *mts* Arg.
111	A3	Corfu *i.* Greece
106	B2	Coria Spain
111	B3	Corinth Greece
142	C2	Corinth U.S.A.
155	D1	Corinto Brazil
97	B3	Cork Ireland
111	C2	Çorlu Turkey
154	B2	Cornélio Procópio Brazil
131	E2	Corner Brook Can.
53	C3	Corner Inlet *b.* Austr.
135	B3	Corning CA U.S.A.
141	D2	Corning NY U.S.A.
		Corn Islands *is* Nic. see Maíz, Islas del
108	B2	Corno Grande *mt.* Italy
130	C2	Cornwall Can.
126	E1	Cornwallis Island Can.
150	B1	Coro Venez.
154	C1	Coromandel Brazil
54	C1	Coromandel Peninsula N.Z.
129	C2	Coronation Can.
126	D2	Coronation Gulf Can.
152	C3	Coronel Oviedo Para.
153	B4	Coronel Suárez Arg.
150	A3	Coropuna, Nudo *mt.* Peru
109	D2	Çorovodë Albania
139	D3	Corpus Christi U.S.A.
152	B2	Corque Bol.
151	D3	Corrente Brazil
154	B1	Correntes Brazil
151	D3	Correntina Brazil
97	B2	Corrib, Lough *l.* Ireland
152	C3	Corrientes Arg.
144	B2	Corrientes, Cabo *c.* Mex.
53	C3	Corryong Austr.
		Corse *i.* France see Corsica
105	D3	Corse, Cap *c.* Corse France
105	D3	Corsica *i.* France
139	D2	Corsicana U.S.A.
105	D3	Corte Corse France
106	B2	Cortegana Spain
136	B3	Cortez U.S.A.
108	B1	Cortina d'Ampezzo Italy
141	D2	Cortland U.S.A.
108	B2	Cortona Italy
106	B2	Coruche Port.
		Çoruh Turkey see Artvin
80	B1	Çorum Turkey
152	C2	Corumbá Brazil
154	C1	Corumbá *r.* Brazil
134	B2	Corvallis U.S.A.
98	B2	Corwen U.K.
144	B2	Cosalá Mex.
145	C3	Cosamaloapan Mex.
109	C3	Cosenza Italy
105	C2	Cosne-Cours-sur-Loire France
107	C2	Costa Blanca *coastal area* Spain
107	D1	Costa Brava *coastal area* Spain
106	B2	Costa del Sol *coastal area* Spain
154	B1	Costa Rica Brazil
146	B3	Costa Rica *country* Central America
144	B2	Costa Rica Mex.
110	B2	Costeşti Romania
64	B2	Cotabato Phil.
114	B4	Côte d'Ivoire *country* Africa

150	A2	Cotopaxi, Volcán *vol.* Ecuador
99	B3	Cotswold Hills U.K.
134	B2	Cottage Grove U.S.A.
102	C1	Cottbus Ger.
104	B2	Coubre, Pointe de la *pt* France
52	A3	Couedic, Cape du Austr.
137	D2	Council Bluffs U.S.A.
88	B2	Courland Lagoon *b.* Lith./Rus. Fed.
128	B3	Courtenay Can.
104	B2	Coutances France
104	B2	Coutras France
100	B2	Couvin Belgium
99	C2	Coventry U.K.
140	C3	Covington U.S.A.
50	B3	Cowan, Lake *imp. l.* Austr.
96	C2	Cowdenbeath U.K.
53	C3	Cowes Austr.
134	B1	Cowlitz *r.* U.S.A.
53	C2	Cowra Austr.
154	B1	Coxim Brazil
75	D2	Cox's Bazar Bangl.
145	B3	Coyuca de Benítez Mex.
75	C1	Cozhê China
145	C2	Cozumel Mex.
145	D2	Cozumel, Isla de *i.* Mex.
123	C3	Cradock S. Africa
136	B2	Craig U.S.A.
102	C2	Crailsheim Ger.
110	B2	Craiova Romania
129	D2	Cranberry Portage Can.
53	C3	Cranbourne Austr.
128	C3	Cranbrook Can.
151	D2	Crateús Brazil
151	E2	Crato Brazil
136	C2	Crawford U.S.A.
140	B2	Crawfordsville U.S.A.
99	C3	Crawley U.K.
134	D1	Crazy Mountains U.S.A.
129	C2	Cree *r.* Can.
144	B2	Creel Mex.
129	D2	Cree Lake Can.
100	B1	Creil Neth.
105	D2	Crema Italy
108	B1	Cremona Italy
108	B2	Cres *i.* Croatia
134	B2	Crescent City U.S.A.
128	C3	Creston Can.
137	E2	Creston U.S.A.
142	C2	Crestview U.S.A.
111	B3	Crete *i.* Greece
107	D1	Creus, Cabo de *c.* Spain
98	B2	Crewe U.K.
96	B2	Crianlarich U.K.
152	D3	Criciúma Brazil
96	C2	Crieff U.K.
108	B1	Crikvenica Croatia
91	C2	Crimea *pen.* Ukr.
101	F2	Crimmitschau Ger.
154	C1	Cristalina Brazil
101	E1	Crivitz Ger.
		Crna Gora *country* Europe see Montenegro
109	D2	Crni Vrh *h.* Serbia
109	C1	Črnomelj Slovenia
97	B2	Croagh Patrick *h.* Ireland
109	C1	Croatia *country* Europe
61	C1	Crocker, Banjaran *mts* Malaysia
139	D2	Crockett U.S.A.
59	C1	Croker Island Austr.
99	D2	Cromer U.K.
54	A3	Cromwell N.Z.
137	D1	Crookston U.S.A.
53	C2	Crookwell Austr.
136	C1	Crosby U.S.A.
143	D3	Cross City U.S.A.

142	B2	Crossett U.S.A.
98	B1	Cross Fell *h.* U.K.
129	E2	Cross Lake Can.
143	C1	Crossville U.S.A.
109	C3	Crotone Italy
99	D3	Crowborough U.K.
142	B2	Crowley U.S.A.
128	C3	Crowsnest Pass Can.
146	C3	Cruz, Cabo *c.* Cuba
152	C3	Cruz Alta Brazil
152	B4	Cruz del Eje Arg.
155	D2	Cruzeiro Brazil
150	A2	Cruzeiro do Sul Brazil
52	A2	Crystal Brook Austr.
139	D3	Crystal City U.S.A.
140	B1	Crystal Falls U.S.A.
103	E2	Csongrád Hungary
120	B2	Cuando *r.* Angola/Zambia
120	A2	Cuangar Angola
118	B3	Cuango *r.* Angola/Dem. Rep. Congo
120	A1	Cuanza *r.* Angola
139	C3	Cuatro Ciénegas Mex.
144	B2	Cuauhtémoc Mex.
145	C3	Cuautla Mex.
146	B2	Cuba *country* West Indies
120	A2	Cubal Angola
120	B2	Cubango *r.* Angola/Namibia
150	A1	Cúcuta Col.
73	B3	Cuddalore India
73	B3	Cuddapah India
106	C1	Cuéllar Spain
120	A2	Cuemba Angola
150	A2	Cuenca Ecuador
107	C1	Cuenca Spain
107	C1	Cuenca, Serranía de *mts* Spain
145	C3	Cuernavaca Mex.
139	D3	Cuero U.S.A.
151	C3	Cuiabá Brazil
151	C3	Cuiabá *r.* Brazil
96	A2	Cuillin Sound *sea chan.* U.K.
120	A1	Cuilo Angola
120	A2	Cuito *r.* Angola
120	A2	Cuito Cuanavale Angola
60	B1	Cukai Malaysia
53	C3	Culcairn Austr.
53	C1	Culgoa *r.* Austr.
144	B2	Culiacán Mex.
64	A1	Culion *i.* Phil.
107	C2	Cullera Spain
142	C2	Cullman U.S.A.
97	C1	Cullybackey U.K.
151	C3	Culuene *r.* Brazil
150	B1	Cumaná Venez.
141	D3	Cumberland U.S.A.
140	B3	Cumberland *r.* U.S.A.
129	D2	Cumberland Lake Can.
127	C4	Cumberland Peninsula Can.
142	C1	Cumberland Plateau U.S.A.
127	G2	Cumberland Sound *sea chan.* Can.
96	C3	Cumbernauld U.K.
135	B3	Cummings U.S.A.
96	B3	Cumnock U.K.
144	B1	Cumpas Mex.
145	C3	Cunduacán Mex.
120	A2	Cunene *r.* Angola
108	A2	Cuneo Italy
53	C1	Cunnamulla Austr.
108	A1	Cuorgnè Italy
96	C2	Cupar U.K.
147	D3	Curaçao *terr.* West Indies
150	A2	Curaray *r.* Ecuador
153	A4	Curicó Chile
154	B3	Curitiba Brazil
52	A2	Curnamona Austr.

51 D3 Currie Austr.
51 E2 Curtis Island Austr.
151 C1 Curuá r. Brazil
60 B2 Curup Indon.
151 B2 Cururupu Brazil
155 D1 Curvelo Brazil
150 A3 Cusco Peru
139 D1 Cushing U.S.A.
134 C1 Cut Bank U.S.A.
75 C2 Cuttack India
101 D1 Cuxhaven Ger.
64 B1 Cuyo Islands Phil.
Cuzco Peru see Cusco
119 C3 Cyangugu Rwanda
111 B3 Cyclades is Greece
129 C3 Cypress Hills Can.
80 B2 Cyprus country Asia
102 C2 Czech Republic country Europe
103 D1 Czersk Pol.
103 D1 Częstochowa Pol.

D

Đa, Sông r. Vietnam see Black River
69 D2 Daban China
114 A3 Dabola Guinea
Dacca Bangl. see Dhaka
102 C2 Dachau Ger.
74 A2 Dadu Pak.
64 B1 Daet Phil.
114 A3 Dagana Senegal
64 B1 Dagupan Phil.
74 B2 Dahanu India
69 D2 Da Hinggan Ling mts China
116 C3 Dahlak Archipelago is Eritrea
100 C2 Dahlem Ger.
78 B3 Dahm, Ramlat des. audi Arabia/Yemen
60 B2 Daik Indon.
106 C2 Daimiel Spain
51 C2 Dajarra Austr.
114 A3 Dakar Senegal
116 A2 Dākhilah, Wāḩāt ad oasis Egypt
Dakhla Oasis Egypt see Dākhilah, Wāḩāt ad
63 A3 Dakoank India
88 C3 Dakol'ka r. Belarus
Đakovica Kosovo see Gjakovë
109 C1 Đakovo Croatia
120 B2 Dala Angola
68 C2 Dalain Hob China
93 G3 Dalälven r. Sweden
111 C3 Dalaman Turkey
111 C3 Dalaman r. Turkey
69 C2 Dalandzadgad Mongolia
63 B2 Đa Lat Vietnam
74 A2 Dalbandin Pak.
96 C3 Dalbeattie U.K.
51 E2 Dalby Austr.
143 C1 Dale Hollow Lake U.S.A.
53 C3 Dalgety Austr.
139 C1 Dalhart U.S.A.
131 D2 Dalhousie Can.
62 B1 Dali China
70 C2 Dalian China
96 C3 Dalkeith U.K.
139 D2 Dallas U.S.A.
128 A2 Dall Island U.S.A.
109 C2 Dalmatia reg. Bos.-Herz./Croatia
66 C2 Dal'negorsk Rus. Fed.
66 B1 Dal'nerechensk Rus. Fed.
114 B4 Daloa Côte d'Ivoire

51 D2 Dalrymple, Mount Austr.
92 □A3 Dalsmynni Iceland
75 C2 Daltenganj India
143 D2 Dalton U.S.A.
60 B1 Daludalu Indon.
92 □B2 Dalvík Iceland
50 C1 Daly r. Austr.
51 C1 Daly Waters Austr.
74 B2 Daman India
80 B2 Damanhūr Egypt
59 C3 Damar i. Indon.
80 B2 Damascus Syria
115 D3 Damaturu Nigeria
76 B3 Damāvand, Qolleh-ye mt. Iran
81 D2 Dāmghān Iran
79 C2 Dammam Saudi Arabia
101 D1 Damme Ger.
75 B2 Damoh India
114 B4 Damongo Ghana
59 C3 Dampir, Selat sea chan. Indon.
75 C2 Damqoq Zangbo r. China
117 C3 Danakil reg. Africa
114 B4 Danané Côte d'Ivoire
63 B2 Đa Năng Vietnam
141 E2 Danbury U.S.A.
65 A1 Dandong China
146 B3 Dangriga Belize
70 B2 Dangshan China
89 F2 Danilov Rus. Fed.
89 E2 Danilovskaya Vozvyshennost' hills Rus. Fed.
70 B2 Danjiangkou China
89 E3 Dankov Rus. Fed.
146 B3 Danlí Hond.
101 E1 Dannenberg (Elbe) Ger.
54 C2 Dannevirke N.Z.
62 B2 Dan Sai Thai.
Dantu China see Zhenjiang
110 A1 Danube r. Europe
110 C1 Danube Delta Romania/Ukr.
140 B2 Danville IL U.S.A.
140 C3 Danville KY U.S.A.
141 D3 Danville VA U.S.A.
71 A4 Danzhou China
71 B3 Daoxian China
114 C3 Dapaong Togo
64 B2 Dapitan Phil.
68 C2 Da Qaidam China
69 E1 Daqing China
80 B2 Dar'a Syria
79 C2 Dārāb Iran
81 D2 Dārān Iran
75 C2 Darbhanga India
119 D3 Dar es Salaam Tanz.
117 A3 Darfur reg. Sudan
74 B1 Dargai Pak.
54 B1 Dargaville N.Z.
53 C3 Dargo Austr.
69 D1 Darhan Mongolia
150 A1 Darién, Golfo del g. Col.
75 C2 Darjiling India
52 B2 Darling r. Austr.
53 C1 Darling Downs hills Austr.
50 A3 Darling Range hills Austr.
98 C1 Darlington U.K.
53 C2 Darlington Point Austr.
103 D1 Darłowo Pol.
101 D2 Darmstadt Ger.
115 E1 Darnah Libya
52 B2 Darnick Austr.
107 C1 Daroca Spain
99 D3 Dartford U.K.
131 D2 Dartmoor hills U.K.
99 B3 Dartmouth Can.
99 B3 Dartmouth U.K.
59 D3 Daru P.N.G.
50 C1 Darwin Austr.

74 A2 Dasht r. Pak.
76 B2 Daşoguz Turkm.
61 C1 Datadian Indon.
111 C3 Datça Turkey
70 B1 Datong China
64 B2 Datu Piang Phil.
74 B1 Daud Khel Pak.
88 B2 Daugava r. Latvia
88 C2 Daugavpils Latvia
100 C2 Daun Ger.
129 D2 Dauphin Can.
129 E2 Dauphin Lake Can.
73 B3 Davangere India
64 B2 Davao Phil.
64 B2 Davao Gulf Phil.
137 E2 Davenport U.S.A.
99 C2 Daventry U.K.
123 C2 Daveyton S. Africa
64 B2 David Panama
129 D2 Davidson Can.
126 E3 Davidson Lake Can.
136 B2 Davis U.S.A.
131 D1 Davis Inlet (abandoned) Can.
159 F3 Davis Sea Antarctica
160 P3 Davis Strait Can./Greenland
105 D2 Davos Switz.
78 A2 Dawmat al Jandal Saudi Arabia
79 C3 Dawqah Oman
126 B2 Dawson Can.
143 D2 Dawson U.S.A.
128 B2 Dawson Creek Can.
128 B2 Dawsons Landing Can.
68 C2 Dawu China
Dawukou China see Shizuishan
104 B3 Dax France
68 C2 Da Xueshan mts China
80 C2 Dayr az Zawr Syria
143 D3 Dayton U.S.A.
143 D3 Daytona Beach U.S.A.
70 A2 Dazhou China
122 B3 De Aar S. Africa
80 B2 Dead Sea salt l. Asia
71 B3 De'an China
152 B4 Deán Funes Arg.
128 B2 Dease Lake Can.
126 D2 Dease Strait Can.
135 C3 Death Valley depr. U.S.A.
104 C2 Deauville France
61 C1 Debak Sarawak Malaysia
109 D2 Debar Macedonia
103 E2 Debrecen Hungary
117 B3 Debre Markos Eth.
117 B3 Debre Tabor Eth.
117 B4 Debre Zeyit Eth.
142 C2 Decatur AL U.S.A.
140 B3 Decatur IL U.S.A.
73 B3 Deccan plat. India
102 C1 Děčín Czech Rep.
137 E2 Decorah U.S.A.
88 C2 Dedovichi Rus. Fed.
121 C2 Dedza Malawi
98 B2 Dee r. England/Wales U.K.
96 C2 Dee r. Scotland U.K.
53 C1 Deepwater Austr.
131 E2 Deer Lake Can.
134 D1 Deer Lodge U.S.A.
140 C2 Defiance U.S.A.
68 C2 Dêgê China
117 C4 Degeh Bur Eth.
102 C2 Deggendorf Ger.
91 E2 Degtevo Rus. Fed.
75 B1 Dehra Dun India
75 C2 Dehri India
69 E2 Dehui China
100 A2 Deinze Belgium
110 B1 Dej Romania

140 B2 De Kalb U.S.A.
78 A3 Dekemhare Eritrea
118 C3 Dekese Dem. Rep. Congo
135 C3 Delano U.S.A.
135 D3 Delano Peak U.S.A.
123 C2 Delareyville S. Africa
129 D2 Delaronde Lake Can.
140 C2 Delaware U.S.A.
141 D3 Delaware r. U.S.A.
141 D3 Delaware state U.S.A.
141 D3 Delaware Bay U.S.A.
53 C3 Delegate Austr.
106 C1 Delémont Switz.
100 B1 Delft Neth.
100 C1 Delfzijl Neth.
121 D2 Delgado, Cabo c. Moz.
69 C1 Delgerhaan Mongolia
75 B2 Delhi India
60 B2 Deli i. Indon.
126 C2 Déljne Can.
101 F2 Delitzsch Ger.
107 D2 Dellys Alg.
101 D1 Delmenhorst Ger.
109 B1 Delnice Croatia
83 L1 De-Longa, Ostrova is Rus. Fed.
129 D2 Deloraine Can.
111 B3 Delphi tourist site Greece
139 C3 Del Rio U.S.A.
78 A3 Delta CO U.S.A.
135 D3 Delta UT U.S.A.
126 B2 Delta Junction U.S.A.
109 D3 Delvinë Albania
106 C1 Demanda, Sierra de la mts
      Spain
118 C3 Demba Dem. Rep. Congo
117 B4 Dembī Dolo Eth.
89 D2 Demidov Rus. Fed.
138 B2 Deming U.S.A.
111 C3 Demirci Turkey
110 C2 Demirköy Turkey
102 C1 Demmin Ger.
142 C2 Demopolis U.S.A.
60 B2 Dempo, Gunung vol. Indon.
89 D2 Demyansk Rus. Fed.
122 B3 De Naawte S. Africa
100 B1 Den Burg Neth.
100 B2 Dendermonde Belgium
70 A1 Dengkou China
70 B2 Dengzhou China
      Den Haag Neth. see
      The Hague
50 A2 Denham Austr.
100 B1 Den Helder Neth.
52 B3 Deniliquin Austr.
134 C2 Denio U.S.A.
137 D2 Denison IA U.S.A.
139 D2 Denison TX U.S.A.
111 C3 Denizli Turkey
52 D2 Denman Austr.
50 A3 Denmark Austr.
93 E4 Denmark country Europe
160 Q3 Denmark Strait
      Greenland/Iceland
61 C2 Denpasar Indon.
139 D2 Denton U.S.A.
50 A3 D'Entrecasteaux, Point Austr.
136 B3 Denver U.S.A.
75 C2 Deogarh Orissa India
74 B2 Deogarh Rajasthan India
75 C2 Deoghar India
83 K2 Deputatskiy Rus. Fed.
68 C3 Dêqên China
142 B2 De Queen U.S.A.
74 A2 Dera Bugti Pak.
74 B1 Dera Ghazi Khan Pak.
74 B1 Dera Ismail Khan Pak.
87 D4 Derbent Rus. Fed.

50 B1 Derby Austr.
99 C2 Derby U.K.
99 D2 Dereham U.K.
97 B2 Derg, Lough l. Ireland
91 D1 Derhachi Ukr.
142 B2 De Ridder U.S.A.
91 D2 Derkul r. Rus. Fed./Ukr.
      Derry U.K. see Londonderry
75 B1 Dêrub China
116 B3 Derudeb Sudan
122 B3 De Rust S. Africa
109 C2 Derventa Bos.-Herz.
98 C2 Derwent r. U.K.
98 C1 Derwent Water l. U.K.
77 C1 Derzhavinsk Kazakh.
152 B2 Desaguadero r. Bol.
129 D2 Deschambault Lake Can.
134 B1 Deschutes r. U.S.A.
117 B3 Desē Eth.
153 B5 Deseado Arg.
153 B5 Deseado r. Arg.
137 E2 Des Moines U.S.A.
137 E2 Des Moines r. U.S.A.
91 C1 Desna r. Rus. Fed./Ukr.
89 D3 Desnogorsk Rus. Fed.
101 F2 Dessau Ger.
126 B2 Destruction Bay Can.
149 C3 Desventuradas, Islas is
      S. Pacific Ocean
128 C1 Detah Can.
101 D2 Detmold Ger.
140 C2 Detroit U.S.A.
137 D1 Detroit Lakes U.S.A.
100 B1 Deurne Neth.
110 B1 Deva Romania
100 C1 Deventer Neth.
96 C2 Deveron r. U.K.
103 D2 Devět skal h. Czech Rep.
137 D1 Devils Lake U.S.A.
128 A2 Devils Paw mt. U.S.A.
99 C3 Devizes U.K.
74 B2 Devli India
110 C2 Devnya Bulg.
128 C2 Devon r. Can.
126 E1 Devon Island Can.
51 D4 Devonport Austr.
74 B2 Dewas India
137 F3 Dexter U.S.A.
70 A2 Deyang China
59 D3 Deyong, Tanjung pt Indon.
81 C2 Dezfūl Iran
70 B2 Dezhou China
79 C2 Dhahran Saudi Arabia
75 D2 Dhaka Bangl.
78 B3 Dhamār Yemen
75 C2 Dhamtari India
75 C2 Dhanbad India
75 C2 Dhankuta Nepal
62 A1 Dharmanagar India
75 C2 Dharmjaygarh India
73 B3 Dharwad India
74 B2 Dhasa India
78 B3 Dhubāb Yemen
74 B2 Dhule India
144 A1 Diablo, Picacho del mt. Mex.
51 C2 Diamantina watercourse Austr.
155 D1 Diamantina Brazil
151 D3 Diamantina, Chapada plat.
      Brazil
151 C3 Diamantino Brazil
71 B3 Dianbai China
151 D3 Dianópolis Brazil
114 B4 Dianra Côte d'Ivoire
79 C2 Dibā al Ḥiṣn U.A.E.
118 C3 Dibaya Dem. Rep. Congo
62 A1 Dibrugarh India

136 C1 Dickinson U.S.A.
142 C1 Dickson U.S.A.
      Dicle r. Turkey see Tigris
105 D3 Die France
129 D2 Diefenbaker, Lake Can.
114 B3 Diéma Mali
62 B2 Điện Châu Vietnam
101 D1 Diepholz Ger.
104 C2 Dieppe France
115 D3 Diffa Niger
131 D2 Digby Can.
105 D3 Digne-les-Bains France
105 C2 Digoin France
64 B1 Digos Phil.
59 D3 Digul r. Indon.
      Dihang r. China/India see
      Brahmaputra
      Dihang r. China/India see
      Yarlung Zangbo
105 D2 Dijon France
117 D2 Dikhil Djibouti
111 C3 Dikili Turkey
100 A2 Diksmuide Belgium
115 D3 Dikwa Nigeria
117 B4 Dila Eth.
74 A1 Dilārām Afgh.
59 C3 Dili East Timor
101 D2 Dillenburg Ger.
134 D1 Dillon U.S.A.
118 C4 Dilolo Dem. Rep. Congo
62 A1 Dimapur India
72 D2 Dimapur India
72 D2 Dimapur India
      Dimashq Syria see Damascus
52 B3 Dimboola Austr.
110 C2 Dimitrovgrad Bulg.
87 D3 Dimitrovgrad Rus. Fed.
64 B1 Dinagat i. Phil.
104 B2 Dinan France
100 B2 Dinant Belgium
111 D3 Dinar Turkey
81 C2 Dīnār, Kūh-e mt. Iran
73 B3 Dindigul India
123 D1 Dindiza Moz.
101 E2 Dingelstädt Ger.
75 C2 Dinggyê China
97 A2 Dingle Bay Ireland
96 B2 Dingwall U.K.
70 A2 Dingxi China
154 B3 Dionísio Cerqueira Brazil
114 A3 Diourbel Senegal
74 B1 Dir Pak.
51 D1 Direction, Cape Austr.
117 C4 Dirē Dawa Eth.
120 B2 Dirico Angola
115 D1 Dirj Libya
50 A2 Dirk Hartog Island Austr.
53 C1 Dirranbandi Austr.
78 B3 Dirs Saudi Arabia
50 B2 Disappointment, Lake imp. l.
      Austr.
52 B3 Discovery Bay Austr.
143 E1 Dismal Swamp U.S.A.
99 D2 Diss U.K.
108 B3 Dittaino r. Sicilia Italy
74 B2 Diu India
155 D2 Divinópolis Brazil
87 D4 Divnoye Rus. Fed.
114 B4 Divo Côte d'Ivoire
80 B2 Divriği Turkey
140 B2 Dixon U.S.A.
128 A2 Dixon Entrance sea chan.
      Can./U.S.A.
80 C2 Diyarbakır Turkey
74 A2 Diz Pak.
115 D2 Djado Niger
115 D2 Djado, Plateau du Niger

118 B3 Djambala Congo
115 C2 Djanet Alg.
115 C1 Djelfa Alg.
112 C2 Djéma C.A.R.
114 B3 Djenné Mali
114 B3 Djibo Burkina Faso
117 C3 Djibouti *country* Africa
117 C3 Djibouti Djibouti
114 C4 Djougou Benin
92 □C3 Djúpivogur Iceland
91 E1 Dmitriyevka Rus. Fed.
89 E3 Dmitriyev-L'govskiy Rus. Fed.
89 E2 Dmitrov Rus. Fed.
Dnepr *r.* Ukr. *see* Dnieper
91 C2 Dnieper *r.* Ukr.
90 B2 Dniester *r.* Ukr.
Dnipro *r.* Ukr. *see* Dnieper
91 C2 Dniprodzerzhyns'k Ukr.
91 D2 Dnipropetrovs'k Ukr.
91 C2 Dniprorudne Ukr.
Dnister *r.* Ukr. *see* Dniester
88 C2 Dno Rus. Fed.
115 D4 Doba Chad
88 B2 Dobele Latvia
101 F2 Döbeln Ger.
59 C3 Doberai, Jazirah *pen.* Indon.
59 C3 Dobo Indon.
109 C2 Doboj Bos.-Herz.
110 C2 Dobrich Bulg.
89 F3 Dobrinka Rus. Fed.
89 E3 Dobroye Rus. Fed.
89 D3 Dobrush Belarus
155 E1 Doce *r.* Brazil
145 B2 Doctor Arroyo Mex.
144 B2 Doctor Belisario Domínguez Mex.
111 C3 Dodecanese *is* Greece
Dodekanisos *is* Greece *see* Dodecanese
136 C3 Dodge City U.S.A.
119 D3 Dodoma Tanz.
100 C2 Doetinchem Neth.
59 C3 Dofa Indon.
75 C1 Dogai Coring *salt l.* China
128 B2 Dog Creek Can.
67 B3 Dōgo *i.* Japan
115 C3 Dogondoutchi Niger
81 C2 Doğubeyazıt Turkey
79 C2 Doha Qatar
62 A2 Doi Saket Thai.
100 B1 Dokkum Neth.
88 C3 Dokshytsy Belarus
91 D2 Dokuchayevs'k Ukr.
131 C2 Dolbeau-Mistassini Can.
104 B2 Dol-de-Bretagne France
105 D2 Dole France
99 B2 Dolgellau U.K.
89 E3 Dolgorukovo Rus. Fed.
89 E3 Dolgoye Rus. Fed.
Dolisie Congo *see* Loubomo
59 D3 Dolok, Pulau *i.* Indon.
108 B1 Dolomites *mts* Italy
117 C4 Dolo Odo Eth.
126 D2 Dolphin and Union Strait Can.
90 A2 Dolyna Ukr.
102 C2 Domažlice Czech Rep.
93 E3 Dombås Norway
103 D2 Dombóvár Hungary
128 B2 Dome Creek Can.
147 D3 Dominica *country* West Indies
147 C3 Dominican Republic *country* West Indies
89 F2 Domodedovo Rus. Fed.
111 B3 Domokos Greece
61 C2 Dompu Indon.
89 E3 Don *r.* Rus. Fed.
96 C2 Don *r.* U.K.

97 D1 Donaghadee U.K.
52 B3 Donald Austr.
Donau *r.* Austria/Ger. *see* Danube
102 C2 Donauwörth Ger.
106 B2 Don Benito Spain
98 C2 Doncaster U.K.
120 A1 Dondo Angola
121 C2 Dondo Moz.
73 C4 Dondra Head Sri Lanka
97 B1 Donegal Ireland
97 B1 Donegal Bay Ireland
91 D2 Donets'k Ukr.
91 D2 Donets'kyy Kryazh *hills* Rus. Fed./Ukr.
50 A2 Dongara Austr.
62 B1 Dongchuan China
71 A4 Dongfang China
66 B1 Dongfanghong China
58 B3 Donggala Indon.
65 A2 Donggang China
71 B3 Dongguan China
62 B2 Đông Ha Vietnam
Dong Hai *sea* N. Pacific Ocean *see* East China Sea
62 B2 Đông Hơi Vietnam
118 B2 Dongou Congo
71 B3 Dongshan China
70 C2 Dongtai China
71 B3 Dongting Hu *l.* China
Dong Ujimqin Qi China *see* Uliastai
70 B2 Dongying China
54 B1 Donnellys Crossing N.Z.
Donostia Spain *see* San Sebastián
99 B3 Dorchester U.K.
121 A2 Dordabis Namibia
104 B2 Dordogne *r.* France
100 B2 Dordrecht Neth.
123 C3 Dordrecht S. Africa
129 D2 Doré Lake Can.
101 D1 Dorfmark Ger.
114 B3 Dori Burkina Faso
122 A3 Doring *r.* S. Africa
96 B1 Dornoch U.K.
96 B2 Dornoch Firth *est.* U.K.
89 D3 Dorogobuzh Rus. Fed.
110 C1 Dorohoi Romania
68 C1 Döröö Nuur *salt l.* Mongolia
92 G3 Dorotea Sweden
50 A2 Dorre Island Austr.
53 D2 Dorrigo Austr.
100 C2 Dortmund Ger.
100 C2 Dortmund-Ems-Kanal *canal* Ger.
153 B5 Dos Bahías, Cabo *c.* Arg.
101 F1 Dosse *r.* Ger.
115 C3 Dosso Niger
143 C2 Dothan U.S.A.
101 D1 Dötlingen Ger.
105 C1 Douai France
118 A2 Douala Cameroon
104 B2 Douarnenez France
114 B3 Douentza Mali
98 A1 Douglas Isle of Man
122 B2 Douglas S. Africa
128 A2 Douglas AK U.S.A.
138 B2 Douglas AZ U.S.A.
143 D2 Douglas GA U.S.A.
136 B2 Douglas WY U.S.A.
71 C3 Douliu Taiwan
105 C2 Doullens France
154 B1 Dourada, Serra *hills* Brazil
154 B2 Dourados Brazil
154 B2 Dourados, Serra dos *hills* Brazil

106 B1 Douro *r.* Port.
99 D3 Dover U.K.
141 D3 Dover U.S.A.
95 D3 Dover, Strait of France/U.K.
141 F1 Dover-Foxcroft U.S.A.
79 C2 Dowlatābād *Būshehr* Iran
79 C2 Dowlatābād *Kermān* Iran
97 D1 Downpatrick U.K.
77 C3 Dowshī Afgh.
67 B3 Dōzen *is* Japan
130 C2 Dozois, Réservoir *resr* Can.
114 B2 Drâa, Hamada du *plat.* Alg.
154 B2 Dracena Brazil
100 C1 Drachten Neth.
110 B2 Drăgănești-Olt Romania
110 B2 Drăgășani Romania
88 C3 Drahichyn Belarus
123 C2 Drakensberg *mts* Lesotho/S. Africa
123 C2 Drakensberg *mts* S. Africa
158 B8 Drake Passage S. Atlantic Ocean
111 B2 Drama Greece
93 F4 Drammen Norway
109 C1 Drava *r.* Europe
101 D2 Drayton Valley Can.
101 D2 Dreieich Ger.
102 C1 Dresden Ger.
104 C2 Dreux France
100 B1 Driemond Neth.
109 C2 Drina *r.* Bosnia-Herzegovina/Serbia
109 C2 Drniš Croatia
110 B2 Drobeta-Turnu Severin Romania
101 D1 Drochtersen Ger.
97 C2 Drogheda Ireland
90 A2 Drohobych Ukr.
97 C1 Dromore U.K.
74 B1 Drosh Pak.
53 C3 Drouin Austr.
128 C2 Drumheller Can.
140 C1 Drummond Island U.S.A.
131 C2 Drummondville Can.
88 B3 Druskininkai Lith.
91 D2 Druzhkivka Ukr.
88 D2 Druzhnaya Gorka Rus. Fed.
130 A2 Dryden Can.
51 C1 Drysdale *r.* Austr.
78 A2 Dubā Saudi Arabia
79 C2 Dubai U.A.E.
129 C1 Dubawnt Lake Can.
Dubayy U.A.E. *see* Dubai
78 A2 Dubbagh, Jabal ad *mt.* Saudi Arabia
53 C2 Dubbo Austr.
97 C2 Dublin Ireland
143 D2 Dublin U.S.A.
90 B1 Dubno Ukr.
141 D2 Du Bois U.S.A.
114 A4 Dubréka Guinea
109 C2 Dubrovnik Croatia
90 B1 Dubrovytsya Ukr.
89 D3 Dubrowna Belarus
137 E2 Dubuque U.S.A.
129 D2 Duck Bay Can.
101 E2 Duderstadt Ger.
83 I2 Dudinka Rus. Fed.
99 B2 Dudley U.K.
106 B1 Duero *r.* Spain
131 C1 Duffreboy, Lac *l.* Can.
96 C2 Dufftown U.K.
109 C2 Dugi Rat Croatia
100 C2 Duisburg Ger.
123 C3 Dukathole S. Africa
79 C2 Dukhān Qatar
89 D2 Dukhovshchina Rus. Fed.

Dukou China see Panzhihua
88 C2 Dūkštas Lith.
68 C2 Dulan China
152 B4 Dulce r. Arg.
100 C2 Dülmen Ger.
110 C2 Dulovo Bulg.
137 E1 Duluth U.S.A.
64 B2 Dumaguete Phil.
60 B1 Dumai Indon.
64 B1 Dumaran i. Phil.
142 B2 Dumas AR U.S.A.
139 C1 Dumas TX U.S.A.
96 B3 Dumbarton U.K.
103 D2 Ďumbier mt. Slovakia
96 C3 Dumfries U.K.
55 J3 Dumont d'Urville Sea
Antarctica
116 B1 Dumyāṭ Egypt
Duna r. Hungary see Danube
Dunaj r. Slovakia see Danube
103 D2 Dunakeszi Hungary
Dunărea r. Romania see
Danube
103 D2 Dunaújváros Hungary
Dunav r. Yugo. see Danube
90 B2 Dunayivtsi Ukr.
96 C2 Dunbar U.K.
96 C1 Dunbeath U.K.
128 B3 Dunblane U.K.
139 D2 Duncan Can.
96 C1 Duncansby Head U.K.
97 C1 Dundalk Ireland
97 C2 Dundalk Bay Ireland
127 G1 Dundas Greenland
123 D2 Dundee S. Africa
96 C2 Dundee U.K.
97 D1 Dundrum Bay U.K.
54 B3 Dunedin N.Z.
96 C2 Dunfermline U.K.
97 C1 Dungannon U.K.
74 B2 Dungarpur India
97 C2 Dungarvan Ireland
99 D3 Dungeness hd U.K.
97 C1 Dungiven U.K.
53 D2 Dungog Austr.
119 C2 Dungu Dem. Rep. Congo
60 B1 Dungun Malaysia
116 B3 Dungunab Sudan
69 E2 Dunhua China
68 C2 Dunhuang China
Dunkerque France see Dunkirk
104 C1 Dunkirk France
141 D2 Dunkirk U.S.A.
97 C2 Dún Laoghaire Ireland
97 D1 Dunmurry U.K.
60 B3 Dunnet Head U.K.
96 C3 Duns U.K.
99 C3 Dunstable U.K.
110 B2 Dupnitsa Bulg.
136 C1 Dupree U.S.A.
50 B1 Durack r. Austr.
144 B2 Durango Mex.
106 C1 Durango Spain
136 B3 Durango U.S.A.
139 D3 Durant U.S.A.
153 C4 Durazno Uru.
123 D2 Durban S. Africa
104 C3 Durban-Corbières France
122 A3 Durbanville S. Africa
100 B2 Durbuy Belgium
100 C2 Düren Ger.
73 C2 Durg India
98 C1 Durham U.K.
143 E1 Durham U.S.A.
60 B1 Duri Indon.
109 C2 Durmitor mt. Montenegro
96 B1 Durness U.K.

109 C2 Durrës Albania
97 A3 Dursey Island Ireland
111 C3 Dursunbey Turkey
59 D3 D'Urville, Tanjung pt Indon.
54 B2 D'Urville Island N.Z.
71 A3 Dushan China
77 C3 Dushanbe Tajik.
100 C2 Düsseldorf Ger.
71 A3 Duyun China
91 D2 Dvorichna Ukr.
74 A2 Dwarka India
123 C1 Dwarsberg S. Africa
134 C1 Dworshak Reservoir U.S.A.
89 D3 Dyat'kovo Rus. Fed.
96 C2 Dyce U.K.
127 G2 Dyer, Cape Can.
142 C1 Dyersburg U.S.A.
103 D2 Dyje r. Austria/Czech Rep.
103 D1 Dylewska Góra h. Pol.
91 D2 Dymytrov Ukr.
123 C3 Dyoki S. Africa
87 E3 Dyurtyuli Rus. Fed.
69 D2 Dzamīn Üüd Mongolia
120 D2 Dzaoudzi Mayotte
Dzhambul Kazakh. see Taraz
91 C2 Dzhankoy Ukr.
91 D3 Dzhubga Rus. Fed.
83 K3 Dzhugdzhur, Khrebet mts
Rus. Fed.
103 E1 Działdowo Pol.
69 D1 Dzuunmod Mongolia
88 C3 Dzyarzhynsk Belarus
88 C3 Dzyatlavichy Belarus

E

131 E1 Eagle r. Can.
134 C1 Eagle Cap mt. U.S.A.
130 A2 Eagle Lake Can.
134 B2 Eagle Lake U.S.A.
139 C3 Eagle Pass U.S.A.
126 B2 Eagle Plain Can.
130 A1 Ear Falls Can.
99 D3 Easington U.K.
156 C1 East China Sea N. Pacific
Ocean
54 C1 East Coast Bays N.Z.
129 D3 Eastend Can.
123 C3 Eastern Cape prov. S. Africa
116 B2 Eastern Desert Egypt
73 B3 Eastern Ghats mts India
129 E2 Easterville Can.
153 C6 East Falkland i. Falkland Is
100 C1 East Frisian Islands Ger.
96 B3 East Kilbride U.K.
99 C3 Eastleigh U.K.
140 C2 East Liverpool U.S.A.
123 C3 East London S. Africa
130 C1 Eastmain Can.
130 C1 Eastmain r. Can.
143 D2 East St Louis U.S.A.
140 A3 East St Louis U.S.A.
East Sea N. Pacific Ocean see
Japan, Sea of
83 K2 East Siberian Sea Rus. Fed.
59 C3 East Timor country Asia
140 A2 Eau Claire U.S.A.
130 C1 Eau Claire, Lac à l' l. Can.
59 D2 Eauripik atoll Micronesia
145 C3 Ebano Mex.
99 B3 Ebbw Vale U.K.
102 C1 Eberswalde-Finow Ger.
109 C2 Eboli Italy
118 B2 Ebolowa Cameroon
107 D1 Ebro r. Spain

144 A2 Echeverria, Pico mt. Mex.
129 E2 Echoing r. Can.
100 C2 Echternach Lux.
52 B3 Echuca Austr.
106 B2 Écija Spain
102 B1 Eckernförde Ger.
127 F2 Eclipse Sound sea chan. Can.
150 B1 Ecuador country S. America
116 C3 Ed Eritrea
117 A3 Ed Da'ein Sudan
117 B3 Ed Damazin Sudan
116 B3 Ed Damer Sudan
116 B3 Ed Debba Sudan
116 B3 Ed Dueim Sudan
51 D4 Eddystone Point Austr.
100 B1 Ede Neth.
118 B2 Edéa Cameroon
154 C1 Edéia Brazil
53 C3 Eden r. Austr.
98 B1 Eden r. U.K.
123 C2 Edenburg S. Africa
97 C2 Edenderry Ireland
52 B3 Edenhope Austr.
111 B2 Edessa Greece
82 C1 Edgeøya i. Svalbard
139 D3 Edinburg U.S.A.
96 C3 Edinburgh U.K.
110 C2 Edirne Turkey
128 C2 Edmonton Can.
131 D2 Edmundston Can.
111 C3 Edremit Turkey
111 C3 Edremit Körfezi b. Turkey
128 C2 Edson Can.
119 C3 Edward, Lake Dem. Rep.
Congo/Uganda
139 C2 Edwards Plateau TX U.S.A.
100 C1 Eenrum Neth.
48 F4 Éfaté i. Vanuatu
140 B3 Effingham U.S.A.
135 C3 Egan Range mts U.S.A.
103 E2 Eger Hungary
93 E4 Egersund Norway
92 □C2 Egilsstaðir Iceland
80 B2 Eğirdir Turkey
80 B2 Eğirdir Gölü l. Turkey
104 C2 Égletons France
83 M2 Egvekinot Rus. Fed.
116 A2 Egypt country Africa
68 C2 Ehen Hudag China
100 C1 Eibergen Neth.
100 C1 Eifel hills Ger.
96 A2 Eigg i. U.K.
73 B4 Eight Degree Channel
India/Maldives
50 B1 Eighty Mile Beach Austr.
80 B3 Eilat Israel
101 F2 Eilenburg Ger.
101 D2 Einbeck Ger.
100 B2 Eindhoven Neth.
150 B2 Eirunepé Brazil
120 B2 Eiseb watercourse Namibia
101 E2 Eisenach Ger.
102 C1 Eisenhüttenstadt Ger.
103 D2 Eisenstadt Austria
101 E2 Eisleben Lutherstadt Ger.
Eivissa Spain see Ibiza
Eivissa i. Spain see Ibiza
107 C2 Ejea de los Caballeros Spain
121 □D3 Ejeda Madag.
Ejin Qi China see Dalain Hob
93 H4 Ekenäs Fin.
92 J2 Ekostrovskaya Imandra,
Ozero l. Rus. Fed.
93 F4 Eksjö Sweden
122 A3 Eksteenfontein S. Africa
130 B1 Ekwan r. Can.
62 A2 Ela Myanmar

Elandsdoorn

123 C2 Elandsdoorn S. Africa
111 B3 Elassona Greece
80 B2 Elazığ Turkey
108 B2 Elba, Isola d' i. Italy
150 A1 El Banco Col.
64 A1 El Barreal salt l. Mex.
144 B1 El Barreal salt l. Mex.
109 D2 Elbasan Albania
150 B1 El Baúl Venez.
114 C1 El Bayadh Alg.
101 D1 Elbe r. Ger.
136 B3 Elbert, Mount U.S.A.
143 D2 Elberton U.S.A.
104 C2 Elbeuf France
80 B2 Elbistan Turkey
103 D1 Elbląg Pol.
87 D4 El'brus mt. Rus. Fed.
81 C2 Elburz Mountains Iran
150 B1 El Callao Venez.
139 D3 El Campo U.S.A.
135 C4 El Centro U.S.A.
152 B3 El Cerro Bol.
107 C2 Elche-Elx Spain
107 C2 Elda Spain
137 E3 Eldon U.S.A.
144 B2 El Dorado Mex.
142 B2 El Dorado AR U.S.A.
137 D3 El Dorado KS U.S.A.
114 B2 El Eglab plat. Alg.
106 C2 El Ejido Spain
89 E2 Elektrostal' Rus. Fed.
150 A2 El Encanto Col.
146 C2 Eleuthera i. Bahamas
117 A3 El Fasher Sudan
144 B2 El Fuerte Mex.
117 A3 El Geneina Sudan
116 B3 El Geteina Sudan
96 C2 Elgin U.K.
140 B2 Elgin U.S.A.
115 C1 El Goléa Alg.
144 A1 El Golfo de Santa Clara Mex.
119 D2 Elgon, Mount Kenya/Uganda
114 A2 El Hammâmi reg. Maur.
114 A2 El Hierro i. Islas Canarias
145 C2 El Higo Mex.
114 C2 El Homr Alg.
87 D4 Elista Rus. Fed.
141 E2 Elizabeth U.S.A.
143 E1 Elizabeth City U.S.A.
143 D1 Elizabethtown U.S.A.
114 B1 El Jadida Morocco
103 E1 Ełk Pol.
139 D1 Elk City U.S.A.
128 C2 Elkford U.S.A.
140 B2 Elkhart U.S.A.
        El Khartum Sudan see
        Khartoum
110 C2 Elkhovo Bulg.
140 D3 Elkins U.S.A.
128 C3 Elko Can.
134 C2 Elko U.S.A.
129 C2 Elk Point Can.
126 E1 Ellef Ringnes Island Can.
137 D1 Ellendale U.S.A.
134 B1 Ellensburg U.S.A.
54 B2 Ellesmere, Lake N.Z.
127 F1 Ellesmere Island Can.
98 B2 Ellesmere Port U.K.
126 E2 Ellice r. Can.
        Ellice Islands country S. Pacific
        Ocean see Tuvalu
123 C3 Elliotdale S. Africa
96 C2 Ellon U.K.
141 F2 Ellsworth U.S.A.
55 O2 Ellsworth Mountains
        Antarctica
111 C3 Elmalı Turkey

115 C1 El Meghaïer Alg.
141 D2 Elmira U.S.A.
107 C2 El Moral Spain
101 D1 Elmshorn Ger.
117 A3 El Muglad Sudan
64 A1 El Nido Phil.
117 B3 El Obeid Sudan
144 B2 El Oro Mex.
115 C1 El Oued Alg.
138 A2 Eloy U.S.A.
138 B2 El Paso U.S.A.
144 B1 El Porvenir Mex.
107 D1 El Prat de Llobregat Spain
139 D1 El Reno U.S.A.
145 B2 El Salado Mex.
144 B2 El Salto Mex.
146 B3 El Salvador country Central
        America

145 B2 El Salvador Mex.
138 B3 El Sauz Mex.
144 A1 El Socorro Mex.
145 C2 El Temascal Mex.
150 B1 El Tigre Venez.
147 D4 El Tocuyo Venez.
88 C2 Elva Estonia
106 B2 Elvas Port.
93 F3 Elverum Norway
119 E2 El Wak Kenya
99 D2 Ely U.K.
137 E1 Ely MN U.S.A.
135 D3 Ely NV U.S.A.
123 C2 eMalahleni S. Africa
81 D2 Emāmrūd Iran
93 G4 Emån r. Sweden
123 D3 eManzamtoti S. Africa
76 B2 Emba Kazakh.
123 C2 Embalenhle S. Africa
154 C1 Emborcação, Represa de resr
        Brazil
119 D3 Embu Kenya
100 C1 Emden Ger.
51 D2 Emerald Austr.
129 E3 Emerson Can.
111 C3 Emet Turkey
123 D2 eMgwenya S. Africa
115 D3 Emi Koussi mt. Chad
110 C2 Emine, Nos pt Bulg.
80 B2 Emirdağ Turkey
123 D2 eMjindini S. Africa
88 B2 Emmaste Estonia
100 B1 Emmeloord Neth.
100 C2 Emmelshausen Ger.
100 C1 Emmen Neth.
123 D2 eMondlo S. Africa
139 C3 Emory Peak U.S.A.
144 A2 Empalme Mex.
123 D2 Empangeni S. Africa
108 B2 Empoli Italy
137 D3 Emporia KS U.S.A.
141 D3 Emporia VA U.S.A.
        Empty Quarter des. Saudi
        Arabia see Rub' al Khāli
100 C1 Ems r. Ger.
100 C1 Emsdetten Ger.
123 C2 eMzinoni S. Africa
59 D3 Enarotali Indon.
144 B2 Encarnación Mex.
152 C3 Encarnación Para.
155 D1 Encruzilhada Brazil
58 C3 Ende Indon.
126 A2 Endicott Mountains U.S.A.
91 C2 Enerhodar Ukr.
87 D3 Engel's Rus. Fed.
60 B2 Enggano i. Indon.
98 C2 England admin. div. U.K.
130 A1 English r. Can.
95 C4 English Channel France/U.K.

139 D1 Enid U.S.A.
100 B1 Enkhuizen Neth.
93 G4 Enköping Sweden
108 B3 Enna Sicilia Italy
129 D1 Ennadai Lake Can.
117 A3 En Nahud Sudan
115 E3 Ennedi, Massif des Chad
53 C1 Enngonia Austr.
97 B2 Ennis Ireland
139 D2 Ennis U.S.A.
97 C2 Enniscorthy Ireland
97 C1 Enniskillen U.K.
97 B2 Ennistymon Ireland
102 C2 Enns r. Austria
92 H2 Enontekiö Fin.
53 C3 Ensay Austr.
100 C1 Enschede Neth.
144 A1 Ensenada Mex.
70 A2 Enshi China
128 C1 Enterprise Can.
142 C2 Enterprise AL U.S.A.
134 C1 Enterprise OR U.S.A.
152 B3 Entre Ríos Bol.
106 B2 Entroncamento Port.
115 C4 Enugu Nigeria
150 A2 Envira Brazil
135 D3 Ephraim U.S.A.
134 C1 Ephrata U.S.A.
105 D2 Épinal France
99 C3 Epsom U.K.
118 A2 Equatorial Guinea country
        Africa
101 F3 Erbendorf Ger.
100 C3 Erbeskopf h. Ger.
81 C2 Erciş Turkey
65 B1 Erdao Jiang r. China
111 C2 Erdek Turkey
80 B2 Erdemli Turkey
152 C3 Erechim Brazil
69 D1 Ereentsav Mongolia
80 B2 Ereğli Konya Turkey
80 B1 Ereğli Zonguldak Turkey
69 D2 Erenhot China
        Erevan Armenia see Yerevan
101 E2 Erfurt Ger.
80 B2 Ergani Turkey
114 B2 'Erg Chech des. Alg./Mali
111 C2 Ergene r. Turkey
140 C2 Erie U.S.A.
140 C2 Erie, Lake Can./U.S.A.
66 D2 Erimo-misaki c. Japan
116 B3 Eritrea country Africa
101 E3 Erlangen Ger.
50 C2 Erldunda Austr.
123 C2 Ermelo S. Africa
80 B2 Ermenek Turkey
111 B3 Ermoupoli Greece
73 B4 Ernakulam India
73 B3 Erode India
100 B2 Erp Neth.
114 B1 Er Rachidia Morocco
117 B3 Er Rahad Sudan
97 B1 Errigal h. Ireland
97 A1 Erris Head Ireland
109 D2 Ersekë Albania
91 E1 Ertil' Rus. Fed.
101 D2 Erwitte Ger.
102 C1 Erzgebirge mts
        Czech Rep./Ger.
80 B2 Erzincan Turkey
81 C2 Erzurum Turkey
93 E4 Esbjerg Denmark
135 D3 Escalante U.S.A.
144 B2 Escalón Mex.
140 B1 Escanaba U.S.A.
145 C3 Escárcega Mex.
107 C1 Escatrón Spain

100	A2	Escaut *r.* Belgium/France
101	E1	Eschede Ger.
100	B3	Esch-sur-Alzette Lux.
101	E2	Eschwege Ger.
100	C2	Eschweiler Ger.
135	C4	Escondido U.S.A.
144	B2	Escuinapa Mex.
111	C3	Eşen Turkey
81	D2	Esfahān Iran
123	D2	eSikhaleni S. Africa
98	B1	Esk *r.* U.K.
131	D1	Esker Can.
92	□C2	Eskifjörður Iceland
93	G4	Eskilstuna Sweden
		Eskimo Point Can. *see* Arviat
80	B2	Eskişehir Turkey
81	C2	Eslāmābād-e Gharb Iran
111	C3	Esler Dağı *mt.* Turkey
111	C3	Eşme Turkey
150	A1	Esmeraldas Ecuador
79	D2	Espakeh Iran
104	C3	Espalion France
130	B2	Espanola Can.
138	B1	Espanola U.S.A.
50	B3	Esperance Austr.
144	B2	Esperanza Mex.
106	B2	Espichel, Cabo *c.* Port.
155	D1	Espinhaço, Serra do *mts* Brazil
151	D3	Espinosa Brazil
48	F4	Espíritu Santo *i.* Vanuatu
144	A2	Espíritu Santo, Isla *i.* Mex.
93	H3	Espoo Fin.
153	A5	Esquel Arg.
114	B1	Essaouira Morocco
114	A2	Es Semara Western Sahara
100	C2	Essen Ger.
150	C1	Essequibo *r.* Guyana
83	L3	Esso Rus. Fed.
79	C2	Eştahbān Iran
151	E3	Estância Brazil
123	C2	Estcourt S. Africa
107	C1	Estella Spain
106	B2	Estepona Spain
106	C1	Esteras de Medinaceli Spain
129	D2	Esterhazy Can.
152	B3	Esteros Para.
136	B2	Estes Park U.S.A.
129	D3	Estevan Can.
137	E2	Estherville U.S.A.
129	D2	Eston Can.
88	C2	Estonia *country* Europe
106	B1	Estrela, Serra da *mts* Port.
106	B2	Estremoz Port.
52	A1	Etadunna Austr.
104	C2	Étampes France
104	C1	Étaples France
75	B2	Etawah India
123	D2	Ethandakukhanya S. Africa
117	B4	Ethiopia *country* Africa
109	C3	Etna, Mount *vol.* Sicilia Italy
128	A2	Etolin Island U.S.A.
120	A2	Etosha Pan *salt pan* Namibia
100	C3	Ettelbruck Lux.
100	B2	Etten-Leur Neth.
107	C1	Etxarri-Aranatz Spain
99	D3	Eu France
53	C2	Euabalong Austr.
50	B3	Eucla Austr.
143	C2	Eufaula U.S.A.
139	D1	Eufaula Lake *resr* U.S.A.
134	B2	Eugene U.S.A.
144	A2	Eugenia, Punta *pt* Mex.
53	C1	Eulo Austr.
53	C2	Eumungerie Austr.
139	C2	Eunice U.S.A.
80	C2	Euphrates *r.* Asia
134	B2	Eureka *CA* U.S.A.
134	C1	Eureka *MT* U.S.A.
135	C3	Eureka *NV* U.S.A.
52	C2	Euriowie Austr.
53	C2	Euroa Austr.
106	B2	Europa Point Gibraltar
128	B2	Eutsuk Lake Can.
130	C1	Evans, Lac *l.* Can.
53	D1	Evans Head Austr.
127	F2	Evans Strait Can.
136	A2	Evanston U.S.A.
140	B3	Evansville U.S.A.
123	C2	Evaton S. Africa
79	C2	Evaz Iran
83	L2	Evensk Rus. Fed.
50	C2	Everard Range *hills* Austr.
75	C2	Everest, Mount China/Nepal
134	B1	Everett U.S.A.
100	A2	Evergem Belgium
143	D3	Everglades *swamp* U.S.A.
118	B2	Evinayong Equat. Guinea
93	E4	Evje Norway
106	B2	Évora Port.
104	C2	Évreux France
111	C2	Evros *r.* Greece/Turkey
111	B3	Evrotas *r.* Greece
80	B2	Evrychou Cyprus
111	B3	Evvoia *i.* Greece
119	E2	Ewaso Ngiro *r.* Kenya
152	B2	Exaltación Bol.
99	B3	Exe *r.* U.K.
99	B3	Exeter U.K.
99	B3	Exmoor *hills* U.K.
99	B3	Exmouth U.K.
50	A2	Exmouth Gulf Austr.
146	C2	Exuma Cays *is* Bahamas
117	C4	Eyl Somalia
52	A1	Eyre (North), Lake *imp. l.* Austr.
51	C3	Eyre Peninsula Austr.
94	□B1	Eysturoy *i.* Faroe Is
123	D2	Ezakheni S. Africa
123	C2	Ezenzeleni S. Africa
70	B2	Ezhou China
86	E2	Ezhva Rus. Fed.
111	C3	Ezine Turkey

F

138	B2	Fabens U.S.A.
108	B2	Fabriano Italy
115	D3	Fachi Niger
114	C3	Fada-N'Gourma Burkina Faso
108	B2	Faenza Italy
59	C3	Fafanlap Indon.
110	B1	Făgăraş Romania
49	G3	Fagatogo American Samoa
93	E3	Fagernes Norway
93	G4	Fagersta Sweden
153	B6	Fagnano, Lago *l.* Arg./Chile
114	B3	Faguibine, Lac *l.* Mali
92	□B3	Fagurhólsmýri Iceland
126	B2	Fairbanks U.S.A.
137	D2	Fairbury U.S.A.
135	B3	Fairfield U.S.A.
96	□	Fair Isle *i.* U.K.
137	E2	Fairmont *MN* U.S.A.
140	C3	Fairmont *WV* U.S.A.
128	C2	Fairview Can.
59	D2	Fais *i.* Micronesia
74	B1	Faisalabad Pak.
136	C1	Faith U.S.A.
77	D3	Faīzābād Afgh.
75	C2	Faizabad India
59	C3	Fakfak Indon.
65	A1	Faku China
114	A4	Falaba Sierra Leone
139	D3	Falcon Lake Mex./U.S.A.
139	D3	Falfurrias U.S.A.
128	C2	Falher Can.
101	F2	Falkenberg Ger.
93	F4	Falkenberg Sweden
101	F1	Falkensee Ger.
96	C3	Falkirk U.K.
153	C6	Falkland Islands *terr.* S. Atlantic Ocean
93	F4	Falköping Sweden
135	C3	Fallon U.S.A.
141	E2	Fall River U.S.A.
137	D2	Falls City U.S.A.
99	A3	Falmouth U.K.
122	A3	False Bay S. Africa
93	F4	Falster *i.* Denmark
110	C1	Fălticeni Romania
93	G3	Falun Sweden
71	A3	Fangcheng China
71	C3	Fangshan Taiwan
69	E1	Fangzheng China
108	B2	Fano Italy
119	C2	Faradje Dem. Rep. Congo
121	□D3	Farafangana Madag.
116	A2	Farāfirah, Wāḥāt al *oasis* Egypt
76	C3	Farāh Afgh.
114	A3	Faranah Guinea
78	B3	Farasān, Jazā'ir *is* Saudi Arabia
127	J3	Farewell, Cape Greenland
54	B2	Farewell, Cape N.Z.
137	D1	Fargo U.S.A.
77	D2	Farg'ona Uzbek.
137	E2	Faribault U.S.A.
141	E2	Farmington *ME* U.S.A.
138	B1	Farmington *NM* U.S.A.
141	D3	Farmville U.S.A.
99	C3	Farnborough U.K.
128	C2	Farnham, Mount Can.
128	A1	Faro Can.
106	B2	Faro Port.
88	A2	Fårö *i.* Sweden
94	B1	Faroe Islands *terr.* N. Atlantic Ocean
79	C2	Farräshband Iran
139	C2	Farwell U.S.A.
79	C2	Fāryāb Iran
79	C2	Fasā Iran
109	C2	Fasano Italy
90	B1	Fastiv Ukr.
75	C2	Fatehgarh India
75	C2	Fatehpur India
92	G2	Fauske Norway
92	□A3	Faxaflói *b.* Iceland
93	G3	Faxälven *r.* Sweden
115	D3	Faya Chad
142	B1	Fayetteville *AR* U.S.A.
143	E1	Fayetteville *NC* U.S.A.
142	C1	Fayetteville *TN* U.S.A.
74	B1	Fazilka India
114	A2	Fdérik Maur.
143	E2	Fear, Cape U.S.A.
54	C2	Featherston N.Z.
104	C2	Fécamp France
102	C1	Fehmarn *i.* Ger.
101	F1	Fehrbellin Ger.
155	D2	Feia, Lagoa *lag.* Brazil
150	A2	Feijó Brazil
54	C2	Feilding N.Z.
151	E3	Feira de Santana Brazil
107	D2	Felanitx Spain
145	D3	Felipe C. Puerto Mex.
155	D1	Felixlândia Brazil
99	D3	Felixstowe U.K.
101	E2	Felsberg Ger.
108	B1	Feltre Italy
93	F3	Femunden *l.* Norway

Fengcheng

71 B3 Fengcheng *Jiangxi* China
65 A1 Fengcheng *Liaoning* China
62 A1 Fengqing China
70 B2 Fengxian China
Fengxiang China *see* Lincang
71 C3 Fengyuan Taiwan
70 B1 Fengzhen China
105 D3 Feno, Capo di *c. Corse* France
121 □D2 Fenoarivo Atsinanana Madag.
91 C2 Feodosiya Ukr.
108 A3 Fer, Cap de *c.* Alg.
137 D1 Ferizaj Kosovo
129 D2 Fergus Falls U.S.A.
114 B4 Ferkessédougou Côte d'Ivoire
108 B2 Fermo Italy
131 D1 Fermont Can.
106 B1 Fermoselle Spain
97 B2 Fermoy Ireland
143 D2 Fernandina Beach U.S.A.
154 B2 Fernandópolis Brazil
128 C3 Fernie Can.
108 B2 Ferrara Italy
154 B2 Ferreiros Brazil
108 A2 Ferro, Capo *c. Sardegna* Italy
106 B1 Ferrol Spain
100 B1 Ferwert Neth.
116 B1 Fès Morocco
118 B3 Feshi Dem. Rep. Congo
137 E3 Festus U.S.A.
111 C3 Fethiye Turkey
96 □ Fetlar *i.* U.K.
Fez Morocco *see* Fès
121 □D3 Fianarantsoa Madag.
117 B4 Fichê Eth.
109 C2 Fier Albania
96 C2 Fife Ness *pt* U.K.
104 C3 Figeac France
106 B1 Figueira da Foz Port.
107 D1 Figueres France
114 B1 Figuig Morocco
152 B3 Fiji *country* S. Pacific Ocean
Filadélfia Para.
55 Q2 Filchner Ice Shelf Antarctica
98 C1 Filey U.K.
111 B3 Filippiada Greece
93 F4 Filipstad Sweden
96 C2 Findhorn *r.* U.K.
140 C2 Findlay U.S.A.
51 D4 Fingal Austr.
141 D2 Finger Lakes U.S.A.
106 B1 Finisterre, Cape Spain
92 I3 Finland *country* Europe
93 H4 Finland, Gulf of Europe
128 B2 Finlay *r.* Can.
53 C3 Finley Austr.
101 E2 Finne *ridge* Ger.
92 H2 Finnmarksvidda *reg.* Norway
92 G2 Finnsnes Norway
93 G4 Finspång Sweden
96 A2 Fionnphort U.K.
Firat *r.* Turkey *see* Euphrates
Firenze Italy *see* Florence
105 C2 Firminy France
75 B2 Firozabad India
74 B1 Firozpur India
79 C2 Firūzābād Iran
122 A2 Fish *watercourse* Namibia
122 B3 Fish *i.* S. Africa
99 A3 Fishguard U.K.
105 C2 Fismes France
Fisterra, Cabo *c. Spain see* Finisterre, Cape
141 E2 Fitchburg U.S.A.
129 E3 Fitzgerald Can.
50 B1 Fitzroy Crossing Austr.
108 B2 Fivizzano Italy

119 C3 Fizi Dem. Rep. Congo
92 G3 Fjällsjöälven *r.* Sweden
123 C3 Flagstaff S. Africa
138 A1 Flagstaff U.S.A.
130 C1 Flaherty Island Can.
98 C1 Flamborough Head U.K.
101 F1 Fläming *hills* Ger.
136 B2 Flaming Gorge Reservoir U.S.A.
134 D1 Flathead *r.* U.S.A.
134 D1 Flathead Lake U.S.A.
51 D1 Flattery, Cape Austr.
134 B1 Flattery, Cape U.S.A.
98 B2 Fleetwood U.K.
93 E4 Flekkefjord Norway
102 B1 Flensburg Ger.
104 B2 Flers France
51 D1 Flinders *r.* Austr.
50 A3 Flinders Bay Austr.
51 D3 Flinders Island Austr.
52 A2 Flinders Ranges *mts* Austr.
129 D2 Flin Flon Can.
140 C2 Flint U.S.A.
107 D1 Florac France
108 B2 Florence Italy
142 C2 Florence AL U.S.A.
138 A2 Florence AZ U.S.A.
134 B2 Florence OR U.S.A.
143 E2 Florence SC U.S.A.
150 A1 Florencia Col.
146 B3 Flores Guat.
58 C3 Flores *i.* Indon.
58 B3 Flores, Laut *sea* Indon.
Flores Sea Indon. *see* Flores, Laut
151 E2 Floresta Brazil
139 D3 Floresville U.S.A.
151 D2 Floriano Brazil
152 D3 Florianópolis Brazil
153 C4 Floriano Uru.
143 D3 Florida *state* U.S.A.
143 D4 Florida, Straits of N. Atlantic Ocean
143 D4 Florida Keys *is* U.S.A.
111 B2 Florina Greece
93 E3 Florø Norway
129 D2 Foam Lake Can.
109 C2 Foča Bos.-Herz.
110 C1 Focşani Romania
71 B3 Fogang China
109 C2 Foggia Italy
131 E2 Fogo Island Can.
104 C3 Foix France
89 D3 Fokino Rus. Fed.
130 B2 Foleyet Can.
108 B2 Foligno Italy
99 D3 Folkestone U.K.
143 D2 Folkston U.S.A.
108 B2 Follonica Italy
129 D2 Fond-du-Lac Can.
129 D2 Fond du Lac *r.* Can.
140 B2 Fond du Lac U.S.A.
106 B1 Fondevila Spain
108 B2 Fondi Italy
146 B3 Fonseca, Golfo de *b.* Central America
151 D2 Fonte Boa Brazil
104 B2 Fontenay-le-Comte France
92 □C2 Fontur *pt* Iceland
53 C2 Forbes Austr.
101 E3 Forchheim Ger.
93 E3 Førde Norway
51 C1 Forde Bridge Austr.
142 B2 Fordyce U.S.A.
142 C2 Forest U.S.A.
53 C3 Forest Hill Austr.
131 D2 Forestville Can.

96 C2 Forfar U.K.
134 B1 Forks U.S.A.
108 B2 Forlì Italy
107 D2 Formentera *i.* Spain
107 D2 Formentor, Cap de *c.* Spain
155 C2 Formiga Brazil
152 C3 Formosa Arg.
Formosa *country* Asia *see* Taiwan
154 C1 Formosa Brazil
96 C2 Forres U.K.
50 B3 Forrest Austr.
142 B1 Forrest City U.S.A.
51 D1 Forsayth Austr.
93 H3 Forssa Fin.
53 D2 Forster Austr.
136 B1 Forsyth U.S.A.
74 B2 Fort Abbas Pak.
130 B1 Fort Albany Can.
151 E2 Fortaleza Brazil
128 C2 Fort Assiniboine Can.
96 B2 Fort Augustus U.K.
134 D1 Fort Benton U.S.A.
135 B3 Fort Bragg U.S.A.
Fort Chimo Can. *see* Kuujjuaq
129 C2 Fort Chipewyan Can.
136 B2 Fort Collins U.S.A.
147 D3 Fort-de-France Martinique
137 E2 Fort Dodge U.S.A.
130 A2 Fort Frances Can.
Fort Franklin Can. *see* Déline
Fort George Can. *see* Chisasibi
126 C2 Fort Good Hope Can.
96 C2 Forth *r.* U.K.
96 C2 Forth, Firth of *est.* U.K.
152 C3 Fortín Madrejón Para.
143 D3 Fort Lauderdale U.S.A.
128 B1 Fort Liard Can.
129 C2 Fort Mackay Can.
129 C2 Fort McMurray Can.
126 D2 Fort McPherson Can.
136 C2 Fort Morgan U.S.A.
143 D3 Fort Myers U.S.A.
128 B1 Fort Nelson Can.
128 B2 Fort Nelson *r.* Can.
142 C2 Fort Payne U.S.A.
136 B1 Fort Peck U.S.A.
136 B1 Fort Peck Reservoir U.S.A.
143 D3 Fort Pierce U.S.A.
128 C1 Fort Providence Can.
129 D2 Fort Qu'Appelle Can.
128 C1 Fort Resolution Can.
Fort Rupert Can. *see* Waskaganish
128 B2 Fort St James Can.
128 B2 Fort St John Can.
129 C2 Fort Saskatchewan Can.
137 E3 Fort Scott U.S.A.
130 B1 Fort Severn Can.
76 B2 Fort-Shevchenko Kazakh.
128 B1 Fort Simpson Can.
129 C1 Fort Smith Can.
142 B1 Fort Smith U.S.A.
139 C2 Fort Stockton U.S.A.
138 C2 Fort Sumner U.S.A.
128 C2 Fort Vermilion Can.
142 C2 Fort Walton Beach U.S.A.
140 B2 Fort Wayne U.S.A.
96 B2 Fort William U.K.
139 D2 Fort Worth U.S.A.
126 B2 Fort Yukon U.S.A.
71 B3 Foshan China
92 F3 Fosna *pen.* Norway
93 E3 Fosnavåg Norway
92 □B3 Foss Iceland
92 □A2 Fossá Iceland
108 A2 Fossano Italy

53 C3 Foster Austr.
104 B2 Fougères France
96 □ Foula i. U.K.
111 C3 Fournoí i. Greece
114 A3 Fouta Djallon reg. Guinea
54 A3 Foveaux Strait N.Z.
136 C3 Fowler U.S.A.
50 C3 Fowlers Bay Austr.
128 C2 Fox Creek Can.
127 F2 Foxe Basin g. Can.
127 F2 Foxe Channel Can.
127 F2 Foxe Peninsula Can.
54 B2 Fox Glacier N.Z.
128 C2 Fox Lake Can.
128 A1 Fox Mountain Can.
54 C2 Foxton N.Z.
129 D2 Fox Valley Can.
97 C1 Foyle, Lough b. Ireland/U.K.
154 B3 Foz de Areia, Represa de resr Brazil
120 A2 Foz do Cunene Angola
154 B3 Foz do Iguaçu Brazil
107 D1 Fraga Spain
154 C2 Franca Brazil
109 C2 Francavilla Fontana Italy
104 C2 France country Europe
118 B3 Franceville Gabon
137 D2 Francis Case, Lake U.S.A.
155 D1 Francisco Sá Brazil
120 B3 Francistown Botswana
128 B2 François Lake Can.
101 D2 Frankenberg (Eder) Ger.
101 D3 Frankenthal (Pfalz) Ger.
101 E2 Frankenwald mts Ger.
140 C3 Frankfort U.S.A.
101 D2 Frankfurt am Main Ger.
102 C1 Frankfurt an der Oder Ger.
102 C2 Fränkische Alb hills Ger.
101 E3 Fränkische Schweiz reg. Ger.
141 D2 Franklin U.S.A.
126 C2 Franklin Bay Can.
134 C1 Franklin D. Roosevelt Lake U.S.A.
128 B2 Franklin Mountains Can.
126 E2 Franklin Strait Can.
82 E1 Frantsa-Iosifa, Zemlya is Rus. Fed.
54 B2 Franz Josef Glacier N.Z.
Franz Josef Land is Rus. Fed. see Frantsa-Iosifa, Zemlya
108 A3 Frasca, Capo della c. Sardegna Italy
128 B3 Fraser r. B.C. Can.
131 D1 Fraser r. Nfld. and Lab. Can.
122 B3 Fraserburg S. Africa
96 C2 Fraserburgh U.K.
130 B2 Fraserdale Can.
51 E2 Fraser Island Austr.
128 B2 Fraser Lake Can.
153 C4 Fray Bentos Uru.
93 E4 Fredericia Denmark
139 D2 Frederick U.S.A.
139 D2 Fredericksburg TX U.S.A.
141 D3 Fredericksburg VA U.S.A.
128 A2 Frederick Sound sea chan. U.S.A.
131 D2 Fredericton Can.
93 F4 Frederikshavn Denmark
Fredrikshamn Fin. see Hamina
93 F4 Fredrikstad Norway
140 B2 Freeport IL U.S.A.
139 D3 Freeport TX U.S.A.
146 C2 Freeport City Bahamas
139 D3 Freer U.S.A.
123 C2 Free State prov. S. Africa
114 A4 Freetown Sierra Leone
106 B2 Fregenal de la Sierra Spain

104 B2 Fréhel, Cap c. France
102 B2 Freiburg im Breisgau Ger.
102 C2 Freising Ger.
102 C2 Freistadt Austria
105 D3 Fréjus France
50 A3 Fremantle Austr.
137 D2 Fremont NE U.S.A.
140 C2 Fremont OH U.S.A.
151 C1 French Guiana terr. S. America
134 E1 Frenchman r. U.S.A.
49 I4 French Polynesia terr. S. Pacific Ocean
144 B2 Fresnillo Mex.
135 C3 Fresno U.S.A.
107 D2 Freu, Cap des c. Spain
105 D2 Freyming-Merlebach France
114 A3 Fria Guinea
152 B3 Frias Arg.
102 B2 Friedrichshafen Ger.
101 F1 Friesack Ger.
100 C1 Friesoythe Ger.
Frobisher Bay Can. see Iqaluit
127 G2 Frobisher Bay Can.
101 F2 Frohburg Ger.
87 D4 Frolovo Rus. Fed.
52 A2 Frome, Lake imp. l. Austr.
52 A2 Frome Downs Austr.
100 C2 Fröndenberg Ger.
145 C3 Frontera Mex.
144 B1 Fronteras Mex.
108 B2 Frosinone Italy
92 E3 Frøya i. Norway
Frunze Kyrg. see Bishkek
105 D2 Frutigen Switz.
103 D2 Frýdek-Místek Czech Rep.
71 B3 Fu'an China
106 C1 Fuenlabrada Spain
152 C3 Fuerte Olimpo Para.
114 A2 Fuerteventura i. Islas Canarias
64 B1 Fuga i. Phil.
79 C2 Fujairah U.A.E.
67 C3 Fuji Japan
71 B3 Fujian prov. China
67 C3 Fujinomiya Japan
67 C3 Fuji-san vol. Japan
67 C3 Fukui Japan
67 B4 Fukuoka Japan
67 D3 Fukushima Japan
101 D2 Fulda Ger.
101 D2 Fulda r. Ger.
70 A3 Fuling China
137 D3 Fulton U.S.A.
105 C2 Fumay France
114 A1 Funchal Arquipélago da Madeira
106 B1 Fundão Port.
131 D2 Fundy, Bay of g. Can.
70 B2 Funing Jiangsu China
71 A3 Funing Yunnan China
115 C3 Funtua Nigeria
79 C2 Fürgun, Küh-e mt. Iran
89 F2 Furmanov Rus. Fed.
155 D2 Furnas, Represa resr Brazil
51 D4 Furneaux Group is Austr.
100 C1 Fürstenau Ger.
101 E3 Fürth Ger.
66 D3 Furukawa Japan
127 F2 Fury and Hecla Strait Can.
65 A1 Fushun China
65 B1 Fusong China
79 C2 Fuwayriṭ Qatar
70 B2 Fuyang China
69 E1 Fuyu China
68 B1 Fuyun China

71 B3 Fuzhou China
71 B3 Fuzhou China
Fuzhou China see Fuzhou
93 F4 Fyn i. Denmark
F.Y.R.O.M. country Europe see Macedonia

G

117 C4 Gaalkacyo Somalia
120 A2 Gabela Angola
115 D1 Gabès Tunisia
115 D1 Gabès, Golfe de g. Tunisia
118 B3 Gabon country Africa
123 C1 Gaborone Botswana
110 C2 Gabrovo Bulg.
114 A3 Gabú Guinea-Bissau
73 B3 Gadag India
75 C2 Gadchiroli India
101 E1 Gadebusch Ger.
142 C2 Gadsden U.S.A.
110 C2 Găeşti Romania
108 B2 Gaeta Italy
143 D1 Gaffney U.S.A.
115 C1 Gafsa Tunisia
89 E2 Gagarin Rus. Fed.
114 B4 Gagnoa Côte d'Ivoire
131 D1 Gagnon Can.
81 C1 Gagra Georgia
122 A2 Gaiab watercourse Namibia
111 C3 Gaïdouronisi i. Greece
104 C3 Gaillac France
143 D3 Gainesville FL U.S.A.
143 D2 Gainesville GA U.S.A.
139 D2 Gainesville TX U.S.A.
98 C2 Gainsborough U.K.
52 A2 Gairdner, Lake imp. l. Austr.
96 B2 Gairloch U.K.
119 E3 Galana r. Kenya
103 D2 Galanta Slovakia
148 B3 Galapagos Islands Ecuador
96 C3 Galashiels U.K.
110 C1 Galaţi Romania
93 E3 Galdhøpiggen mt. Norway
145 B2 Galeana Mex.
128 C2 Galena Bay Can.
140 A2 Galesburg U.S.A.
122 B2 Galeshewe S. Africa
86 D3 Galich Rus. Fed.
116 B1 Galilee, Sea of l. Israel
142 C1 Gallatin U.S.A.
73 C4 Galle Sri Lanka
150 A1 Gallinas, Punta pt Col.
109 C2 Gallipoli Italy
111 C2 Gallipoli Turkey
92 H2 Gällivare Sweden
138 B1 Gallup U.S.A.
117 C4 Galmudug reg. Somalia
114 A2 Galtat Zemmour Western Sahara
97 B2 Galtymore h. Ireland
139 E3 Galveston U.S.A.
139 E3 Galveston Bay U.S.A.
97 B2 Galway Ireland
97 B2 Galway Bay Ireland
154 C1 Gamá Brazil
123 D3 Gamalakhe S. Africa
Gambia country Africa see The Gambia
114 A3 Gambia, The country Africa
52 A3 Gambier Islands Austr.
131 E2 Gambo Can.
118 B3 Gamboma Congo
128 B1 Gamêtî Can.
138 B1 Ganado U.S.A.

Gäncä

81 C1	Gäncä Azer.	
	Gand Belgium see Ghent	
61 C2	Gandadiwata, Bukit mt. Indon.	
118 C3	Gandajika Dem. Rep. Congo	
131 E2	Gander Can.	
131 E2	Gander r. Can.	
101 D1	Ganderkesee Ger.	
107 D1	Gandesa Spain	
74 B2	Gandhidham India	
74 B2	Gandhinagar India	
74 B2	Gandhi Sagar resr India	
107 D2	Gandia Spain	
	Ganga r. Bangl./India see Ganges	
153 B5	Gangán Arg.	
74 B2	Ganganagar India	
68 C2	Gangca China	
75 C1	Gangdisê Shan mts China	
75 D2	Ganges r. Bangl./India	
105 C3	Ganges France	
75 C2	Ganges, Mouths of the Bangl./India	
75 C2	Gangtok India	
105 C2	Gannat France	
136 B2	Gannett Peak U.S.A.	
122 A3	Gansbaai S. Africa	
70 A1	Gansu prov. China	
71 B3	Ganzhou China	
114 B3	Gao Mali	
97 B1	Gaoth Dobhair Ireland	
114 A3	Gaoual Guinea	
71 C3	Gaoxiong Taiwan	
70 B2	Gaoyou China	
70 B2	Gaoyou Hu l. China	
105 D3	Gap France	
75 C1	Gar China	
76 B2	Garabogaz Turkm.	
76 B2	Garabogazköl Turkm.	
76 B2	Garabogazköl Aýlagy b. Turkm.	
53 C1	Garah Austr.	
151 E2	Garanhuns Brazil	
135 B2	Garberville U.S.A.	
101 D1	Garbsen Ger.	
154 C2	Garça Brazil	
101 E1	Gardelegen Ger.	
136 C3	Garden City U.S.A.	
129 E2	Garden Hill Can.	
77 C3	Gardēz Afgh.	
88 B2	Gargždai Lith.	
123 C3	Gariep Dam dam S. Africa	
122 A3	Garies S. Africa	
119 D3	Garissa Kenya	
102 C2	Garmisch-Partenkirchen Ger.	
52 B2	Garnpung Lake imp. l. Austr.	
104 B3	Garonne r. France	
117 C4	Garoowe Somalia	
74 B1	Garoth India	
118 B2	Garoua Cameroon	
96 B2	Garry r. U.K.	
126 E2	Garry Lake Can.	
119 E3	Garsen Kenya	
61 B2	Garut Indon.	
140 B2	Gary U.S.A.	
145 B2	Garza García Mex.	
68 C2	Garzê China	
104 B2	Gascony, Gulf of France	
50 A2	Gascoyne r. Austr.	
115 D3	Gashua Nigeria	
131 D2	Gaspé Can.	
131 D2	Gaspésie, Péninsule de la pen. Can.	
143 E1	Gaston, Lake U.S.A.	
143 D1	Gastonia U.S.A.	
107 C2	Gata, Cabo de c. Spain	
88 D2	Gatchina Rus. Fed.	
98 C1	Gateshead U.K.	
139 D2	Gatesville U.S.A.	
130 C2	Gatineau r. Can.	
53 D1	Gatton Austr.	
129 E2	Gauer Lake Can.	
93 E4	Gausta mt. Norway	
123 C2	Gauteng prov. S. Africa	
79 C2	Gävbandi Iran	
111 B3	Gavdos i. Greece	
93 G3	Gävle Sweden	
89 F2	Gavrilov Posad Rus. Fed.	
89 E2	Gavrilov-Yam Rus. Fed.	
62 A1	Gawai Myanmar	
52 A2	Gawler Austr.	
52 A2	Gawler Ranges hills Austr.	
75 C2	Gaya India	
114 C3	Gaya Niger	
140 C1	Gaylord U.S.A.	
86 F2	Gayny Rus. Fed.	
80 B2	Gaza terr. Asia	
80 B2	Gaziantep Turkey	
76 C2	Gazojak Turkm.	
114 B4	Gbarnga Liberia	
103 D1	Gdańsk Pol.	
88 A3	Gdańsk, Gulf of Pol./Rus. Fed.	
88 C2	Gdov Rus. Fed.	
103 D1	Gdynia Pol.	
116 B3	Gedaref Sudan	
101 D2	Gedern Ger.	
111 C3	Gediz r. Turkey	
102 C1	Gedser Denmark	
100 B2	Geel Belgium	
52 B3	Geelong Austr.	
101 E1	Geesthacht Ger.	
75 C1	Gê'gyai China	
129 D2	Geikie r. Can.	
93 E3	Geilo Norway	
62 B1	Gejiu China	
108 B3	Gela Sicilia Italy	
91 D3	Gelendzhik Rus. Fed.	
	Gelibolu Turkey see Gallipoli	
100 C2	Gelsenkirchen Ger.	
118 B2	Gemena Dem. Rep. Congo	
111 C2	Gemlik Turkey	
117 C4	Genalē Wenz r. Eth.	
81 D3	Genāveh Iran	
153 B4	General Acha Arg.	
153 B4	General Alvear Arg.	
153 C4	General Belgrano Arg.	
144 B2	General Cepeda Mex.	
153 B4	General Pico Arg.	
153 B4	General Roca Arg.	
64 B2	General Santos Phil.	
141 D2	Genesee r. U.S.A.	
141 D2	Geneseo U.S.A.	
105 D2	Geneva Switz.	
141 D2	Geneva U.S.A.	
105 D2	Geneva, Lake France/Switz.	
	Genève Switz. see Geneva	
106 B2	Genil r. Spain	
100 B2	Genk Belgium	
108 A2	Genoa Italy	
	Genova Italy see Genoa	
101 F1	Genthin Ger.	
50 A3	Geographe Bay Austr.	
131 D1	George r. Can.	
122 B3	George S. Africa	
143 D3	George, Lake FL U.S.A.	
141 E2	George, Lake NY U.S.A.	
114 A3	Georgetown Gambia	
151 C1	Georgetown Guyana	
60 B1	George Town Malaysia	
143 E2	Georgetown SC U.S.A.	
139 D2	Georgetown TX U.S.A.	
55 I2	George V Land reg. Antarctica	
81 C1	Georgia country Asia	
143 D2	Georgia state U.S.A.	
130 B2	Georgian Bay Can.	
51 C2	Georgina watercourse Austr.	
77 E2	Georgiyevka Kazakh.	
87 D4	Georgiyevsk Rus. Fed.	
101 F2	Gera Ger.	
151 D3	Geral de Goiás, Serra hills Brazil	
54 B2	Geraldine N.Z.	
50 A2	Geraldton Austr.	
80 B1	Gerede Turkey	
135 C3	Gerlach U.S.A.	
103 E2	Gerlachovský štít mt. Slovakia	
102 C1	Germany country Europe	
100 C2	Geseke Ger.	
101 E3	Geretshofen Ger.	
101 D2	Gersfeld (Rhön) Ger.	
75 C1	Gêrzê China	
141 D3	Gettysburg PA U.S.A.	
136 D1	Gettysburg SD U.S.A.	
109 D2	Gevgelija Macedonia	
111 C3	Geyikli Turkey	
122 B2	Ghaap Plateau S. Africa	
115 C1	Ghadāmis Libya	
75 C2	Ghaghara r. India	
114 B4	Ghana country Africa	
120 B3	Ghanzi Botswana	
115 C1	Ghardaïa Alg.	
115 D1	Gharyān Libya	
75 C2	Ghatal India	
75 B2	Ghaziabad India	
75 C2	Ghazipur India	
77 C3	Ghaznī Afgh.	
	Ghent Belgium	
100 A2	Ghent Belgium	
110 B1	Gherla Romania	
105 D3	Ghisonaccia Corse France	
74 B2	Ghotaru India	
74 A2	Ghotki Pak.	
91 E3	Giaginskaya Rus. Fed.	
97 C1	Giant's Causeway lava field U.K.	
61 C2	Gianyar Indon.	
109 C3	Giarre Sicilia Italy	
108 A1	Giaveno Italy	
122 A2	Gibeon Namibia	
106 B2	Gibraltar Gibraltar	
106 B2	Gibraltar, Strait of Morocco/Spain	
50 B2	Gibson Desert Austr.	
68 C1	Gichgeniyn Nuruu mts Mongolia	
117 B4	Gidolē Eth.	
104 C2	Gien France	
101 D2	Gießen Ger.	
101 E1	Gifhorn Ger.	
128 C2	Gift Lake Can.	
67 C3	Gifu Japan	
96 B3	Gigha i. U.K.	
106 B1	Gijón Spain	
138 A2	Gila r. U.S.A.	
138 A2	Gila Bend U.S.A.	
51 D1	Gilbert r. Austr.	
49 F2	Gilbert Islands is Kiribati	
134 D1	Gildford U.S.A.	
53 C2	Gilgandra Austr.	
74 B1	Gilgit Pak.	
74 B1	Gilgit r. Pak.	
53 C2	Gilgunnia Austr.	
129 E2	Gillam Can.	
136 B2	Gillette U.S.A.	
99 D3	Gillingham U.K.	
129 E2	Gimli Can.	
117 C4	Ginir Eth.	
109 C2	Ginosa Italy	
53 C3	Gippsland reg. Austr.	
74 A2	Girdar Dhor r. Pak.	
80 B1	Giresun Turkey	
74 A1	Girishk Afgh.	
107 D1	Girona Spain	
96 B3	Girvan U.K.	

54 C1 Gisborne N.Z.
93 F4 Gislaved Sweden
119 C3 Gitarama Rwanda
108 B2 Giulianova Italy
110 C2 Giurgiu Romania
110 C1 Giuvala, Pasul *pass* Romania
105 C2 Givors France
123 D1 Giyani S. Africa
54 A3 Giza Egypt
109 D2 Gjakovë Kosovo
109 D2 Gjilan Kosovo
109 D2 Gjirokastër Albania
126 E2 Gjoa Haven Can.
93 F3 Gjøvik Norway
131 E2 Glace Bay Can.
134 B1 Glacier Peak *vol.* U.S.A.
51 E2 Gladstone Austr.
92 □A2 Gláma *mts* Iceland
100 C3 Glan *r.* Ger.
97 B2 Glanaruddery Mountains *hills*
       Ireland
96 B3 Glasgow U.K.
140 B3 Glasgow KY U.S.A.
136 B1 Glasgow MT U.S.A.
99 B3 Glastonbury U.K.
101 F2 Glauchau Ger.
86 E3 Glazov Rus. Fed.
89 E3 Glazunovka Rus. Fed.
96 B2 Glen Coe *val.* U.K.
138 A2 Glendale U.S.A.
53 D2 Glen Davis Austr.
136 C1 Glendive U.S.A.
52 B3 Glenelg *r.* Austr.
53 D1 Glen Innes Austr.
126 B2 Glennallen U.S.A.
96 C2 Glenrothes U.K.
141 E2 Glens Falls U.S.A.
96 C2 Glen Shee *val.* U.K.
97 B1 Glenties Ireland
138 B2 Glenwood U.S.A.
136 B3 Glenwood Springs U.S.A.
103 D1 Gliwice Pol.
138 A2 Globe U.S.A.
103 D1 Głogów Pol.
92 F2 Glomfjord Norway
93 F4 Glomma *r.* Norway
53 D2 Gloucester Austr.
99 B3 Gloucester U.K.
101 F1 Glöwen Ger.
77 E1 Glubokoye Kazakh.
101 D1 Glückstadt Ger.
102 C2 Gmünd Austria
102 C2 Gmunden Austria
101 D1 Gnarrenburg Ger.
103 D1 Gniezno Pol.
75 D2 Goalpara India
96 B3 Goat Fell *h.* U.K.
117 C4 Goba Eth.
120 A3 Gobabis Namibia
153 A5 Gobernador Gregores Arg.
69 D2 Gobi *des.* China/Mongolia
100 C2 Goch Ger.
122 A1 Gochas Namibia
74 B3 Godavari *r.* India
73 C3 Godavari, Mouths of the India
130 B2 Goderich Can.
74 B2 Godhra India
129 E2 Gods *r.* Can.
129 E2 Gods Lake Can.
       Godthåb Greenland see Nuuk
       Godwin-Austen, Mount
       China/Pakistan see K2
130 C2 Goéland, Lac au *l.* Can.
131 D1 Goélands, Lac aux *l.* Can.
100 A2 Goes Neth.
154 C1 Goiandira Brazil

154 C1 Goiânia Brazil
154 B1 Goiás Brazil
154 B2 Goio-Erê Brazil
111 C2 Gökçeada *i.* Turkey
111 C3 Gökçedağ Turkey
121 B2 Gokwe Zimbabwe
93 E3 Gol Norway
62 A1 Golaghat India
111 C2 Gölcük Turkey
103 E1 Gołdap Pol.
101 F1 Goldberg Ger.
53 D1 Gold Coast Austr.
114 B4 Gold Coast Ghana
128 C2 Golden Can.
54 C2 Golden Bay N.Z.
128 B3 Golden Hinde *mt.* Can.
97 B2 Golden Vale *lowland* Ireland
135 C3 Goldfield U.S.A.
128 B3 Gold River Can.
143 E1 Goldsboro U.S.A.
135 C4 Goleta U.S.A.
68 C2 Golmud China
81 D2 Golpāyegān Iran
96 C2 Golspie U.K.
119 C3 Goma Dem. Rep. Congo
75 C2 Gomati *r.* India
115 D3 Gombe Nigeria
115 D3 Gombi Nigeria
       Gomel' Belarus *see* Homyel'
144 B2 Gómez Palacio Mex.
147 C3 Gonaïves Haiti
147 C3 Gonâve, Île de la *i.* Haiti
81 D2 Gonbad-e Kāvūs Iran
117 B3 Gonder Eth.
75 C2 Gondia India
111 C2 Gönen Turkey
115 D4 Gongola *r.* Nigeria
53 C2 Gongolgon Austr.
75 D1 Gongtang China
145 C2 Gonzáles Mex.
139 D3 Gonzales U.S.A.
122 A3 Good Hope, Cape of S. Africa
134 D2 Gooding U.S.A.
136 C3 Goodland U.S.A.
53 C1 Goodooga Austr.
98 C2 Goole U.K.
53 C2 Goolgowi Austr.
52 A3 Goolwa Austr.
53 D1 Goondiwindi Austr.
134 B2 Goose Lake U.S.A.
102 B2 Göppingen Ger.
75 C2 Gorakhpur India
109 C2 Goražde Bos.-Herz.
111 C3 Gördes Turkey
89 D3 Gordeyevka Rus. Fed.
51 D1 Gordon, Lake Austr.
116 A3 Goré Chad
117 B4 Goré Eth.
54 A3 Gore N.Z.
97 C2 Gorey Ireland
81 D2 Gorgān Iran
81 C1 Gori Georgia
108 B1 Gorizia Italy
       Gor'kiy Rus. Fed. *see*
       Nizhniy Novgorod
103 E2 Gorlice Pol.
103 C1 Görlitz Ger.
109 D2 Gornji Milanovac Serbia
109 C2 Gornji Vakuf Bos.-Herz.
77 E1 Gorno-Altaysk Rus. Fed.
110 C2 Gornotrakiyska Nizina *lowland*
       Bulg.
77 E1 Gornyak Rus. Fed.
59 D3 Goroka P.N.G.
114 B3 Gorom Gorom Burkina Faso
59 C2 Gorontalo Indon.
89 E3 Gorshechnoye Rus. Fed.

97 B2 Gorumna Island Ireland
91 D3 Goryachiy Klyuch Rus. Fed.
103 D1 Gorzów Wielkopolski Pol.
53 D2 Gosford Austr.
66 D2 Goshogawara Japan
101 E2 Goslar Ger.
109 C2 Gospić Croatia
99 C3 Gosport U.K.
109 D2 Gostivar Macedonia
       Göteborg Sweden *see*
       Gothenburg
101 E2 Gotha Ger.
93 F4 Gothenburg Sweden
136 C2 Gothenburg U.S.A.
93 G4 Gotland *i.* Sweden
111 B2 Gotse Delchev Bulg.
93 G4 Gotska Sandön *i.* Sweden
67 B4 Gōtsu Japan
101 D2 Göttingen Ger.
128 B2 Gott Peak Can.
100 B1 Gouda Neth.
114 A3 Goudiri Senegal
115 D3 Goudoumaria Niger
130 C2 Gouin, Réservoir *resr* Can.
53 C2 Goulburn Austr.
53 B3 Goulburn *r.* N.S.W. Austr.
53 B3 Goulburn *r.* Vic. Austr.
114 B3 Goundam Mali
107 D2 Gouraya Alg.
104 C3 Gourdon France
115 D3 Gouré Niger
122 B3 Gourits *r.* S. Africa
114 B3 Gourma-Rharous Mali
53 C3 Gourock Range *mts* Austr.
155 D1 Governador Valadares Brazil
143 E3 Governor's Harbour Bahamas
68 C2 Goví Altayn Nuruu *mts*
       Mongolia
75 C2 Govind Ballash Pant Sagar
       resr India
99 A3 Gower *pen.* U.K.
152 C3 Goya Arg.
81 C1 Göyçay Azer.
75 C1 Gozha Co *salt l.* China
122 A3 Graaff-Reinet S. Africa
101 E1 Grabow Ger.
109 C2 Gračac Croatia
87 E3 Grachevka Rus. Fed.
101 F2 Gräfenhainichen Ger.
53 D1 Grafton Austr.
137 D1 Grafton U.S.A.
139 D2 Graham U.S.A.
128 A2 Graham Island Can.
55 P3 Graham Land *pen.* Antarctica
123 C3 Grahamstown S. Africa
151 E2 Grajaú Brazil
111 B2 Grammos *mt.* Greece
96 B2 Grampian Mountains U.K.
146 B3 Granada Nic.
106 C2 Granada Spain
141 E1 Granby Can.
114 A2 Gran Canaria *i.* Islas Canarias
152 B3 Gran Chaco *reg.* Arg./Para.
136 C1 Grand *r.* U.S.A.
146 C2 Grand Bahama *i.* Bahamas
131 E2 Grand Bank Can.
158 C2 Grand Banks of
       Newfoundland N. Atlantic
       Ocean
138 A1 Grand Canyon U.S.A.
138 A1 Grand Canyon *gorge* U.S.A.
146 B3 Grand Cayman *i.* Cayman Is
129 C2 Grand Centre Can.
134 C1 Grand Coulee U.S.A.
152 B2 Grande *r.* Bol.
154 B2 Grande *r.* Brazil
153 B6 Grande, Bahía *b.* Arg.

Grande, Ilha

155 D2 Grande, Ilha *i.* Brazil
128 C2 Grande Cache Can.
128 C2 Grande Prairie Can.
114 B1 Grand Erg Occidental *des.* Alg.
115 C2 Grand Erg Oriental *des.* Alg.
131 D2 Grande-Rivière Can.
152 B4 Grandes, Salinas *salt flat* Arg.
131 E2 Grand Falls N.B. Can.
131 E2 Grand Falls–Windsor *Nfld. and Lab.* Can.
128 C3 Grand Forks Can.
137 D1 Grand Forks U.S.A.
128 C1 Grandin, Lac *l.* Can.
137 D2 Grand Island U.S.A.
142 B3 Grand Isle U.S.A.
136 B3 Grand Junction U.S.A.
114 B4 Grand-Lahou Côte d'Ivoire
131 D2 Grand Lake N.B. Can.
131 E2 Grand Lake *Nfld. and Lab.* Can.
137 E1 Grand Marais U.S.A.
106 B2 Grândola Port.
129 E2 Grand Rapids Can.
137 E2 Grand Rapids MI U.S.A.
137 E1 Grand Rapids MN U.S.A.
136 A2 Grand Teton *mt.* U.S.A.
147 C2 Grand Turk Turks and Caicos Is
134 C1 Grangeville U.S.A.
128 B2 Granisle Can.
134 C1 Granite Peak U.S.A.
108 B3 Granitola, Capo *c. Sicilia* Italy
93 F4 Gränna Sweden
101 F1 Gransee Ger.
99 C2 Grantham U.K.
96 C2 Grantown-on-Spey U.K.
138 B1 Grants U.S.A.
134 C1 Grants Pass U.S.A.
104 B2 Granville France
129 D2 Granville Lake Can.
151 D1 Grão Mogol Brazil
123 D1 Graskop S. Africa
105 D3 Grasse France
107 D1 Graus Spain
92 F2 Gravdal Norway
129 D3 Gravelbourg Can.
130 C2 Gravenhurst Can.
53 D1 Gravesend Austr.
99 D3 Gravesend U.K.
105 D2 Gray France
103 D2 Graz Austria
146 C2 Great Abaco *i.* Bahamas
50 B3 Great Australian Bight *g.* Austr.
54 C1 Great Barrier Island N.Z.
51 D1 Great Barrier Reef Austr.
135 C3 Great Basin U.S.A.
126 D2 Great Bear Lake Can.
93 F4 Great Belt *sea chan.* Denmark
137 D3 Great Bend U.S.A.
63 A2 Great Coco Island Cocos Is
53 B3 Great Dividing Range *mts* Austr.
146 B2 Greater Antilles *is* Caribbean Sea
58 A3 Greater Sunda Islands *is* Indon.
60 A3 Greater Sunda Islands *is* Indon.
61 A3 Greater Sunda Islands *is* Indon.
134 D1 Great Falls U.S.A.
123 C3 Great Fish *r.* S. Africa
123 C3 Great Fish Point S. Africa
147 C2 Great Inagua *i.* Bahamas
122 B3 Great Karoo *plat.* S. Africa
123 C3 Great Kei *r.* S. Africa

99 B2 Great Malvern U.K.
122 A2 Great Namaqualand *reg.* Namibia
63 A3 Great Nicobar *i.* India
99 D2 Great Ouse *r.* U.K.
119 D3 Great Rift Valley Africa
119 D3 Great Ruaha *r.* Tanz.
134 D2 Great Salt Lake U.S.A.
135 D2 Great Salt Lake Desert U.S.A.
116 A2 Great Sand Sea *des.* Egypt/Libya
50 B2 Great Sandy Desert Austr.
128 C1 Great Slave Lake Can.
143 D1 Great Smoky Mountains U.S.A.
50 B2 Great Victoria Desert Austr.
70 B1 Great Wall *tourist site* China
99 D2 Great Yarmouth U.K.
106 B1 Gredos, Sierra de *mts* Spain
111 B3 Greece *country* Europe
136 C2 Greeley U.S.A.
82 F1 Greem-Bell, Ostrov *i.* Rus. Fed.
140 B3 Green *r.* KY U.S.A.
136 B3 Green *r.* WY U.S.A.
140 B2 Green Bay U.S.A.
140 B1 Green Bay U.S.A.
140 C3 Greenbrier *r.* U.S.A.
140 B3 Greencastle U.S.A.
143 D1 Greeneville U.S.A.
141 E2 Greenfield U.S.A.
129 D2 Green Lake Can.
127 I2 Greenland *terr.* N. America
160 R2 Greenland Sea Greenland/Svalbard
96 B3 Greenock U.K.
135 D3 Green River UT U.S.A.
136 B2 Green River WY U.S.A.
140 B3 Greensburg IN U.S.A.
141 D2 Greensburg PA U.S.A.
143 E2 Green Swamp U.S.A.
138 A2 Green Valley U.S.A.
114 B4 Greenville Liberia
142 C2 Greenville AL U.S.A.
142 B2 Greenville MS U.S.A.
143 E1 Greenville NC U.S.A.
143 D2 Greenville SC U.S.A.
139 D2 Greenville TX U.S.A.
53 D2 Greenwell Point Austr.
143 D2 Greenwood U.S.A.
50 B2 Gregory, Lake *imp. l.* Austr.
51 D1 Gregory Range *hills* Austr.
102 C1 Greifswald Ger.
101 F2 Greiz Ger.
93 F4 Grenaa Denmark
142 C2 Grenada U.S.A.
147 D3 Grenada *country* West Indies
104 C3 Grenade France
53 C2 Grenfell Austr.
129 D2 Grenfell Can.
105 D2 Grenoble France
51 D1 Grenville, Cape Austr.
134 B1 Gresham U.S.A.
100 C1 Greven Ger.
111 B3 Grevena Greece
100 C2 Grevenbroich Ger.
101 E1 Grevesmühlen Ger.
136 B2 Greybull U.S.A.
128 A1 Grey Hunter Peak Can.
131 E1 Grey Islands Can.
54 B2 Greymouth N.Z.
52 B1 Grey Range *hills* Austr.
97 C2 Greystones Ireland
143 D2 Griffin U.S.A.
53 D2 Griffith Austr.
101 F2 Grimma Ger.
102 C1 Grimmen Ger.
98 C2 Grimsby U.K.

128 C2 Grimshaw Can.
92 □B2 Grímsstaðir Iceland
93 E4 Grimstad Norway
137 D2 Grinnell U.S.A.
123 C3 Griqualand East *reg.* S. Africa
122 B2 Griqualand West *reg.* S. Africa
127 F1 Grise Fiord Can.
96 C1 Gritley U.K.
123 C2 Groblersdal S. Africa
122 B2 Groblershoop S. Africa
Grodno Belarus *see* Hrodna
104 B2 Groix, Île de *i.* France
100 C1 Gronau (Westfalen) Ger.
92 F3 Grong Norway
100 C1 Groningen Neth.
122 B2 Grootdrink S. Africa
51 C1 Groote Eylandt *i.* Austr.
120 A2 Grootfontein Namibia
122 A2 Groot Karas Berg *plat.* Namibia
122 B3 Groot Swartberge *mts* S. Africa
123 C3 Groot Winterberg *mts* S. Africa
101 D2 Großenlüder Ger.
102 C2 Großer Rachel *mt.* Ger.
103 C2 Grosser Speikkogel *mt.* Austria
108 B2 Grosseto Italy
101 D3 Groß-Gerau Ger.
102 C2 Großglockner *mt.* Austria
100 C1 Groß-Hesepe Ger.
101 E2 Großröhra Ger.
122 A1 Gross Ums Namibia
131 E1 Groswater Bay Can.
130 B2 Groundhog *r.* Can.
49 I4 Groupe Actéon *is* Fr. Polynesia
135 B3 Grover Beach U.S.A.
141 E2 Groveton U.S.A.
87 D4 Groznyy Rus. Fed.
109 C1 Grubišno Polje Croatia
103 D1 Grudziądz Pol.
122 A2 Grünau Namibia
92 □A3 Grundarfjörður Iceland
89 E3 Gryazi Rus. Fed.
89 F2 Gryazovets Rus. Fed.
103 D1 Gryfice Pol.
102 C1 Gryfino Pol.
146 C2 Guacanayabo, Golfo de *b.* Cuba
144 B2 Guadalajara Mex.
106 C1 Guadalajara *prov.* Spain
49 E3 Guadalcanal *i.* Solomon Is
107 C1 Guadalope *r.* Spain
106 B2 Guadalquivir *r.* Spain
132 B4 Guadalupe *i.* Mex.
106 B2 Guadalupe, Sierra de *mts* Spain
138 C2 Guadalupe Peak U.S.A.
144 B2 Guadalupe Victoria Mex.
144 B2 Guadalupe y Calvo Mex.
106 C1 Guadarrama, Sierra de *mts* Spain
147 D3 Guadeloupe *terr.* West Indies
106 B2 Guadiana *r.* Port./Spain
106 C2 Guadix Spain
154 B2 Guaíra Brazil
147 C3 Guajira, Península de la *pen.* Col.
150 A2 Gualaceo Ecuador
59 D2 Guam *terr.* N. Pacific Ocean
144 B2 Guamúchil Mex.
144 B2 Guanacevi Mex.
151 D3 Guanambi Brazil
150 B1 Guanare Venez.
146 B2 Guane Cuba
70 A2 Guang'an China
71 B3 Guangchang China
71 B3 Guangdong *prov.* China
71 A3 Guangxi Zhuangzu Zizhiqu *aut. reg.* China

70	A2	Guangyuan China
71	B3	Guangzhou China
155	D1	Guanhães Brazil
147	D4	Guanipa r. Venez.
71	A3	Guanling China
65	A1	Guanshui China
		Guansuo China see Guanling
147	C2	Guantánamo Cuba
150	B3	Guaporé r. Bol./Brazil
154	B3	Guarapuava Brazil
154	C3	Guaraqueçaba Brazil
155	C2	Guaratinguetá Brazil
106	B1	Guarda Port.
154	C1	Guarda Mor Brazil
106	C1	Guardo Spain
155	C2	Guarujá Brazil
144	B2	Guasave Mex.
146	A3	Guatemala country
		Central America
146	A3	Guatemala City Guat.
150	B3	Guaviare r. Col.
155	C2	Guaxupé Brazil
150	A2	Guayaquil Ecuador
150	B3	Guayaramerín Bol.
144	A2	Guaymas Mex.
68	C2	Guazhou China
117	B3	Guba Eth.
86	E1	Guba Dolgaya Rus. Fed.
89	E3	Gubkin Rus. Fed.
115	C1	Guelma Alg.
114	A2	Guelmim Morocco
130	B2	Guelph Can.
145	C2	Guémez Mex.
104	C2	Guéret France
95	C4	Guernsey terr. Channel Is
144	A2	Guerrero Negro Mex.
131	D1	Guers, Lac l. Can.
118	B2	Guider Cameroon
108	B2	Guidonia-Montecelio Italy
71	A3	Guigang China
100	A3	Guignicourt France
123	D1	Guija Moz.
99	C3	Guildford U.K.
71	B3	Guilin China
130	C1	Guillaume-Delisle, Lac l. Can.
106	B1	Guimarães Port.
114	A3	Guinea country Africa
113	F6	Guinea, Gulf of Africa
114	A3	Guinea-Bissau country Africa
104	B2	Guingamp France
154	B1	Guirapa France
154	B1	Guiratinga Brazil
150	B1	Güiria Venez.
100	A3	Guise France
64	B1	Guiuan Phil.
71	A3	Guiyang China
71	A3	Guizhou prov. China
74	B2	Gujarat India
74	B1	Gujranwala Pak.
74	B1	Gujrat Pak.
91	D2	Gukovo Rus. Fed.
53	C2	Gulargambone Austr.
73	B3	Gulbarga India
88	C2	Gulbene Latvia
79	C2	Gulf, the Asia
111	B3	Gulf of Corinth sea chan.
		Greece
142	C2	Gulfport U.S.A.
69	E1	Gulian China
77	C2	Guliston Uzbek.
		Gulja China see Yining
129	D2	Gull Lake Can.
111	C3	Güllük Turkey
119	D2	Gulu Uganda
120	B2	Gumare Botswana
76	B3	Gumdag Turkm.
75	C2	Gumla India
100	C2	Gummersbach Ger.

74	B2	Guna India
53	C3	Gundagai Austr.
111	C3	Güney Turkey
118	B3	Gungu Dem. Rep. Congo
129	E2	Gunisao r. Can.
53	D2	Gunnedah Austr.
136	B3	Gunnison CO U.S.A.
135	D3	Gunnison UT U.S.A.
136	B3	Gunnison r. U.S.A.
73	B3	Guntakal India
60	A1	Gunungsitoli Indon.
60	A1	Gunungtua Indon.
102	C2	Günzburg Ger.
102	C2	Gunzenhausen Ger.
70	B2	Guojiaba China
74	B2	Gurgaon India
151	D2	Gurgueia r. Brazil
150	B1	Guri, Embalse de resr Venez.
154	C1	Gurinhatã Brazil
151	D2	Gurupi r. Brazil
74	B2	Guru Sikhar mt. India
		Gur'yev Kazakh. see Atyrau
115	C3	Gusau Nigeria
65	A2	Gushan China
70	B2	Gushi China
83	I3	Gusinoozersk Rus. Fed.
89	F2	Gus'-Khrustal'nyy Rus. Fed.
108	A3	Guspini Sardegna Italy
128	A2	Gustavus U.S.A.
101	F1	Güstrow Ger.
101	D2	Gütersloh Ger.
121	C2	Gutu Mupandawana
		Zimbabwe
75	D2	Guwahati India
150	C1	Guyana country S. America
		Guyi China see Sanjiang
139	C1	Guymon U.S.A.
53	D2	Guyra Austr.
70	B2	Guyuan China
144	B1	Guzmán Mex.
74	A2	Gwadar Pak.
128	A2	Gwaii Haanas Can.
75	B2	Gwalior India
121	B3	Gwanda Zimbabwe
117	D3	Gwardafuy, Gees c. Somalia
97	B1	Gweebarra Bay Ireland
121	B2	Gweru Zimbabwe
115	D3	Gwoza Nigeria
53	D2	Gwydir r. Austr.
75	C1	Gyangzê China
75	C1	Gyaring Co l. China
68	C2	Gyaring Hu l. China
86	G1	Gydan Peninsula Rus. Fed.
		Gydanskiy Poluostrov pen.
		Rus. Fed. see Gydan Peninsula
		Gyêgu China see Yushu
51	E2	Gympie Austr.
103	D2	Gyöngyös Hungary
103	D2	Győr Hungary
129	E2	Gypsumville Can.
103	D2	Gyula Hungary
81	C1	Gyumri Armenia

H

88	B2	Haapsalu Estonia
100	B1	Haarlem Neth.
101	C2	Haarstrang ridge Ger.
54	A2	Haast N.Z.
78	B3	Habbān Yemen
81	C2	Habbānīyah, Hawr al l. Iraq
67	C4	Hachijō-jima i. Japan
66	D2	Hachinohe Japan
81	C1	Hacıqabul Azer.
121	C3	Hacufera Moz.

79	C2	Ḥadd, Ra's al pt Oman
96	C3	Haddington U.K.
115	C3	Hadejia Nigeria
93	E4	Haderslev Denmark
91	C1	Hadyach Ukr.
65	B2	Haeju N. Korea
65	B2	Haeju-man b. N. Korea
65	B3	Haenam S. Korea
78	B2	Ḥafar al Bāṭin Saudi Arabia
62	A1	Haflong India
92	☐A3	Hafnarfjörður Iceland
78	A3	Hagar Nish Plateau
		Eritrea/Sudan
48	D2	Hagåtña Guam
100	D2	Hagen Ger.
101	E1	Hagenow Ger.
128	B2	Hagensborg Can.
141	D3	Hagerstown U.S.A.
93	F3	Hagfors Sweden
67	B4	Hagi Japan
62	B1	Ha Giang Vietnam
97	B2	Hag's Head Ireland
104	B2	Hague, Cap de la c. France
119	D3	Hai Tanz.
128	A2	Haida Gwaii Can.
62	B1	Hai Dương Vietnam
80	B2	Haifa Israel
71	B3	Haifeng China
71	B3	Haikou China
78	B2	Ḥā'il Saudi Arabia
92	H2	Hailuoto i. Fin.
71	A4	Hainan prov. China
69	D3	Hainan Dao i. China
128	A2	Haines U.S.A.
128	A1	Haines Junction Can.
101	E2	Hainich ridge Ger.
101	E2	Hainleite ridge Ger.
62	B1	Hai Phong Vietnam
147	D3	Haiti country West Indies
116	B3	Haiya Sudan
103	E2	Hajdúböszörmény Hungary
78	B3	Ḥajjah Yemen
79	C2	Ḥājjīābād Iran
62	A1	Haka Myanmar
81	C2	Hakkâri Turkey
66	D2	Hakodate Japan
		Ḥalab Syria see Aleppo
78	B2	Ḥalabān Saudi Arabia
81	C2	Ḥalabja Iraq
116	B2	Halaib Sudan
79	C3	Ḥalānīyāt, Juzur al is Oman
78	A2	Ḥālat 'Ammār Saudi Arabia
101	E2	Halberstadt Ger.
64	B1	Halcon, Mount Phil.
93	F4	Halden Norway
101	E1	Haldensleben Ger.
75	B2	Haldwani India
79	C2	Hāleh Iran
54	A3	Halfmoon Bay N.Z.
131	D2	Halifax Can.
98	C2	Halifax U.K.
141	D3	Halifax U.S.A.
65	B3	Halla-san mt. S. Korea
127	F2	Hall Beach Can.
100	B2	Halle Belgium
101	E2	Halle (Saale) Ger.
102	C2	Hallein Austria
137	D1	Hallock U.S.A.
127	G2	Hall Peninsula Can.
50	B1	Halls Creek Austr.
59	C2	Halmahera i. Indon.
93	F4	Halmstad Sweden
62	B1	Ha Long Vietnam
67	B4	Hamada Japan
81	C2	Hamadān Iran
80	B2	Ḥamāh Syria
67	C4	Hamamatsu Japan

93 F3	Hamar Norway	
116 B2	Ḥamāṭah, Jabal mt. Egypt	
73 C4	Hambantota Sri Lanka	
101 D1	Hamburg Ger.	
78 A2	Ḥamḍ, Wādī al watercourse Saudi Arabia	
78 B3	Ḥamḍah Saudi Arabia	
93 H3	Hämeenlinna Fin.	
101 D1	Hameln Ger.	
50 A2	Hamersley Range mts Austr.	
65 B2	Hamhŭng N. Korea	
68 C2	Hami China	
116 B2	Hamid Sudan	
52 B3	Hamilton Austr.	
130 C2	Hamilton Can.	
54 C1	Hamilton N.Z.	
96 B3	Hamilton U.K.	
142 C2	Hamilton AL U.S.A.	
134 D1	Hamilton MT U.S.A.	
140 C3	Hamilton OH U.S.A.	
93 I3	Hamina Fin.	
100 C2	Hamm Ger.	
81 C2	Ḥammār, Hawr al imp. l. Iraq	
101 D2	Hammelburg Ger.	
92 G3	Hammerdal Sweden	
92 H1	Hammerfest Norway	
142 B2	Hammond U.S.A.	
141 E3	Hammonton U.S.A.	
115 D2	Ḥamrā', Al Ḥamādah al plat. Libya	
78 A2	Ḥanak Saudi Arabia	
66 D3	Hanamaki Japan	
101 D2	Hanau Ger.	
69 D2	Hanbogd Mongolia	
70 B2	Hancheng China	
140 B1	Hancock U.S.A.	
70 B2	Handan China	
135 C3	Hanford U.S.A.	
68 C1	Hangayn Nuruu mts Mongolia	
	Hanggin Houqi China see Xamba	
	Hángö Fin. see Hanko	
70 C2	Hangzhou China	
70 C2	Hangzhou Wan b. China	
	Hanjia China see Pengshui	
	Hanjiang China see Yangzhou	
93 H4	Hanko Fin.	
135 D3	Hanksville U.S.A.	
54 C2	Hanmer Springs N.Z.	
129 C2	Hanna Can.	
137 E3	Hannibal U.S.A.	
101 D1	Hannover Ger.	
101 D2	Hannoversch Münden Ger.	
93 F4	Hanöbukten b. Sweden	
62 B1	Ha Nôi Vietnam	
	Hanoi Vietnam see Ha Nôi	
130 B2	Hanover Can.	
122 B3	Hanover S. Africa	
93 E4	Hanstholm Denmark	
88 C3	Hantsavichy Belarus	
75 C2	Hanumana India	
74 B2	Hanumangarh India	
70 A2	Hanzhong China	
92 H2	Haparanda Sweden	
100 B2	Hapert Neth.	
131 D1	Happy Valley-Goose Bay Can.	
78 A2	Ḥaql Saudi Arabia	
78 B3	Ḥaraḍh Saudi Arabia	
88 C2	Haradok Belarus	
78 B3	Ḥarajā Saudi Arabia	
121 C2	Harare Zimbabwe	
79 C3	Ḥarāsīs, Jiddat al des. Oman	
69 D1	Har-Ayrag Mongolia	
69 E1	Harbin China	
131 E2	Harbour Breton Can.	
74 B2	Harda India	
	Hardangerfjorden sea chan. Norway	
100 C1	Hardenberg Neth.	
100 B1	Harderwijk Neth.	
122 A3	Hardeveld mts S. Africa	
134 E1	Hardin U.S.A.	
128 C1	Hardisty Lake Can.	
100 C1	Haren (Ems) Ger.	
117 C4	Härer Eth.	
117 C4	Hargeysa Somalia	
110 C1	Harghita-Mădăraş, Vârful mt. Romania	
68 C2	Har Hu l. China	
74 B1	Haripur Pak.	
74 A1	Hari Rūd r. Afgh./Iran	
100 B1	Harlingen Neth.	
139 D3	Harlingen U.S.A.	
99 D3	Harlow U.K.	
134 E1	Harlowton U.S.A.	
134 C2	Harney Basin U.S.A.	
134 C2	Harney Lake U.S.A.	
93 G3	Härnösand Sweden	
69 E1	Har Nur China	
68 C1	Har Nuur l. Mongolia	
114 B4	Harper Liberia	
101 D1	Harpstedt Ger.	
130 C1	Harricana, Rivière d' r. Can.	
53 D2	Harrington Austr.	
131 E1	Harrington Harbour Can.	
96 A2	Harris, Sound of sea chan. U.K.	
140 B3	Harrisburg IL U.S.A.	
141 D2	Harrisburg PA U.S.A.	
123 C2	Harrismith S. Africa	
142 B1	Harrison U.S.A.	
131 E1	Harrison, Cape Can.	
126 A2	Harrison Bay U.S.A.	
141 D3	Harrisonburg U.S.A.	
137 E3	Harrisonville U.S.A.	
98 C2	Harrogate U.K.	
110 C2	Hârşova Romania	
92 G2	Harstad Norway	
122 B2	Hartbees watercourse S. Africa	
103 D2	Hartberg Austria	
141 E2	Hartford U.S.A.	
99 A3	Hartland Point U.K.	
98 C1	Hartlepool U.K.	
128 B2	Hartley Bay Can.	
123 B2	Harts r. S. Africa	
143 D2	Hartwell Reservoir U.S.A.	
68 C1	Har Us Nuur l. Mongolia	
136 C1	Harvey U.S.A.	
99 D3	Harwich U.K.	
101 E2	Harz hills Ger.	
73 B3	Hassan India	
100 B2	Hasselt Belgium	
115 C1	Hassi Messaoud Alg.	
93 F4	Hässleholm Sweden	
100 B2	Hastière-Lavaux Belgium	
53 D2	Hastings Austr.	
54 C1	Hastings N.Z.	
99 D3	Hastings U.K.	
137 E2	Hastings MN U.S.A.	
137 D2	Hastings NE U.S.A.	
	Hatay Turkey see Antakya	
129 D2	Hatchet Lake Can.	
52 B2	Hatfield Austr.	
68 C1	Hatgal Mongolia	
62 B2	Ha Tinh Vietnam	
143 E1	Hatteras, Cape U.S.A.	
142 C2	Hattiesburg U.S.A.	
100 C2	Hattingen Ger.	
63 B3	Hat Yai Thai.	
117 C4	Haud reg. Eth.	
93 E4	Haugesund Norway	
93 E4	Haukeligrend Norway	
92 I2	Haukipudas Fin.	
54 C1	Hauraki Gulf N.Z.	
114 B1	Haut Atlas mts Morocco	
131 D2	Hauterive Can.	
114 B1	Hauts Plateaux Alg.	
146 B2	Havana Cuba	
99 C3	Havant U.K.	
101 E1	Havel r. Ger.	
101 F1	Havelberg Ger.	
54 C1	Havelock N.Z.	
54 C1	Havelock North N.Z.	
99 A3	Haverfordwest U.K.	
103 D2	Havlíčkův Brod Czech Rep.	
92 H1	Havøysund Norway	
111 C3	Havran Turkey	
134 E1	Havre U.S.A.	
131 D2	Havre-Aubert Can.	
131 D1	Havre-St-Pierre Can.	
124 E5	Hawai'i i. U.S.A.	
124 E5	Hawai'ian Islands N. Pacific Ocean	
98 B2	Hawarden U.K.	
54 A2	Hawea, Lake N.Z.	
54 B1	Hawera N.Z.	
98 B1	Hawes U.K.	
96 C3	Hawick U.K.	
54 C1	Hawke Bay N.Z.	
52 A2	Hawker Austr.	
52 B1	Hawkers Gate Austr.	
135 C3	Hawthorne U.S.A.	
52 B2	Hay Austr.	
54 C1	Hay r. Can.	
134 C1	Hayden U.S.A.	
129 E2	Hayes r. Man. Can.	
126 E2	Hayes r. Nunavut Can.	
79 C3	Haymā' Oman	
77 C2	Hayotboshi tog'i mt. Uzbek.	
111 C2	Hayrabolu Turkey	
128 C1	Hay River Can.	
137 D3	Hays U.S.A.	
90 B2	Haysyn Ukr.	
99 C3	Hayward's Heath U.K.	
81 D2	Hazar Turkm.	
74 A1	Hazārah Jāt reg. Afgh.	
140 C3	Hazard U.S.A.	
75 C2	Hazaribagh India	
75 C2	Hazaribagh Range mts India	
128 B2	Hazelton Can.	
141 D2	Hazleton U.S.A.	
53 C3	Healesville Austr.	
130 B2	Hearst Can.	
70 B2	Hebei prov. China	
53 C1	Hebel Austr.	
142 B1	Heber Springs U.S.A.	
131 D1	Hebron Can.	
128 A2	Hecate Strait Can.	
71 A3	Hechi China	
93 F3	Hede Sweden	
100 B1	Heerenveen Neth.	
100 B1	Heerhugowaard Neth.	
100 B2	Heerlen Neth.	
	Hefa Israel see Haifa	
70 B2	Hefei China	
70 B3	Hefeng China	
69 E1	Hegang China	
102 B1	Heide Ger.	
122 A1	Heide Namibia	
122 B2	Heidelberg S. Africa	
122 B3	Heidelberg S. Africa	
101 D3	Heilbronn Ger.	
69 E1	Heilong Jiang r. China	
93 I3	Heinola Fin.	
92 F3	Helagsfjället mt. Sweden	
142 B2	Helena AR U.S.A.	
134 D1	Helena MT U.S.A.	
96 B2	Helensburgh U.K.	
102 B1	Helgoland i. Ger.	

102 B1 Helgoländer Bucht *g.* Ger.
Helixi China *see* Ningguo
92 □A3 Hella Iceland
100 B2 Helvoetsluis Neth.
107 C2 Hellín Spain
76 C3 Helmand *r.* Afgh.
121 E1 Helmbrechts Ger.
122 A2 Helmeringhausen Namibia
100 B2 Helmond Neth.
96 C1 Helmsdale U.K.
96 C1 Helmsdale *r.* U.K.
81 E1 Helmstedt Ger.
65 B1 Helong China
93 F4 Helsingborg Sweden
Helsingfors Fin. *see* Helsinki
93 F4 Helsingør Denmark
93 H3 Helsinki Fin.
97 C3 Helvick Head Ireland
99 C3 Hemel Hempstead U.K.
99 D1 Hemmoor Ger.
92 F2 Hemnesberget Norway
70 B2 Henan *prov.* China
140 B3 Henderson *KY* U.S.A.
143 E1 Henderson *NC* U.S.A.
135 D3 Henderson *NV* U.S.A.
139 E2 Henderson *TX* U.S.A.
143 D1 Hendersonville U.S.A.
99 C3 Hendon U.K.
62 A1 Hengduan Shan *mts* China
100 C2 Hengelo Neth.
Hengnan China *see* Hengyang
70 B2 Hengshui China
71 B3 Hengxian China
71 B3 Hengyang China
Hengzhou China *see* Hengxian
91 C2 Heniches'k Ukr.
100 C2 Hennef (Sieg) Ger.
130 B1 Henrietta Maria, Cape Can.
139 D1 Henryetta U.S.A.
127 G2 Henry Kater, Cape Can.
100 A3 Henstedt-Ulzburg Ger.
120 A3 Hentiesbaai Namibia
71 A3 Hepu China
76 C3 Herät Afgh.
101 D2 Herbert Can.
101 D2 Herbstein Ger.
99 B2 Hereford U.K.
139 C2 Hereford U.S.A.
101 D1 Herford Ger.
100 C2 Herkenbosch Neth.
96 □ Herma Ness *hd* U.K.
122 A3 Hermanus S. Africa
53 C2 Hermidale Austr.
134 C1 Hermiston U.S.A.
59 D3 Hermit Islands P.N.G.
144 A2 Hermosillo Mex.
154 B3 Hernandarias Para.
100 C2 Herne Ger.
93 E4 Herning Denmark
99 C3 Hertford U.K.
123 C2 Hertzogville S. Africa
51 F2 Hervey Bay Austr.
101 F2 Herzberg Ger.
101 E3 Herzogenaurach Ger.
71 A3 Heshan China
128 A1 Hess *r.* Can.
101 D2 Hessisch Lichtenau Ger.
136 C1 Hettinger U.S.A.
101 E2 Hettstedt Ger.
98 B1 Hexham U.K.
71 B3 Heyuan China
52 B3 Heywood Austr.
70 B2 Heze China
71 B3 Hezhou China
137 D3 Hiawatha U.S.A.
137 E1 Hibbing U.S.A.

54 C1 Hicks Bay N.Z.
66 D2 Hidaka-sanmyaku *mts* Japan
145 C2 Hidalgo Mex.
144 B2 Hidalgo del Parral Mex.
154 C1 Hidrolândia Brazil
High Atlas *mts* Morocco *see* Haut Atlas
134 B2 High Desert U.S.A.
128 C2 High Level Can.
143 E1 High Point U.S.A.
128 C2 High Prairie Can.
128 C2 High River Can.
129 D2 Highrock Lake Can.
99 C3 High Wycombe U.K.
88 B2 Hiiumaa *i.* Estonia
78 A2 Hijaz *reg.* Saudi Arabia
54 C1 Hikurangi *mt.* N.Z.
101 E2 Hildburghausen Ger.
101 E2 Hilders Ger.
101 D1 Hildesheim Ger.
81 C2 Hillah Iraq
100 C2 Hillesheim Ger.
140 C3 Hillsboro *OH* U.S.A.
139 D1 Hillsboro *TX* U.S.A.
53 C2 Hillston Austr.
143 D2 Hilton Head Island U.S.A.
100 B1 Hilversum Neth.
68 B2 Himalaya *mts* Asia
67 B4 Himeji Japan
123 C2 Himeville S. Africa
51 D1 Hinchinbrook Island Austr.
74 A1 Hindu Kush *mts* Afgh./Pak.
143 D2 Hinesville U.S.A.
75 B2 Hinganghat India
81 C2 Hınıs Turkey
92 G2 Hinnøya *i.* Norway
106 B2 Hinojosa del Duque Spain
62 A2 Hinthada Myanmar
128 C2 Hinton Can.
75 C2 Hirakud Reservoir India
66 D2 Hirosaki Japan
67 B4 Hiroshima Japan
101 E3 Hirschaid Ger.
101 E2 Hirschberg Ger.
105 C2 Hirson France
93 E4 Hirtshals Denmark
74 B2 Hisar India
147 C2 Hispaniola *i.* Caribbean Sea
81 C2 Hīt Iraq
67 D3 Hitachi Japan
67 D3 Hitachinaka Japan
92 E3 Hitra *i.* Norway
49 I3 Hiva Oa *i.* Fr. Polynesia
93 G4 Hjälmaren *l.* Sweden
129 D1 Hjalmar Lake Can.
93 F4 Hjørring Denmark
123 D2 Hlabisa S. Africa
92 □B2 Hlíð Iceland
91 C2 Hlobyne Ukr.
123 C2 Hlohlowane S. Africa
123 C2 Hlotse Lesotho
91 C1 Hlukhiv Ukr.
88 C2 Hlybokaye Belarus
114 C4 Ho Ghana
62 B2 Hoa Binh Vietnam
122 A1 Hoachanas Namibia
51 D4 Hobart Austr.
139 D1 Hobart U.S.A.
139 C2 Hobbs U.S.A.
93 E4 Hobro Denmark
117 C4 Hobyo Somalia
63 B2 Ho Chi Minh City Vietnam
114 B3 Hôd *reg.* Maur.
78 B3 Hodeidah Yemen
103 E2 Hódmezővásárhely Hungary
Hoek van Holland Neth. *see* Hook of Holland

65 B2 Hoeyang N. Korea
101 E2 Hof Ger.
101 E2 Hofheim in Unterfranken Ger.
92 □B3 Höfn *Austurland* Iceland
92 □A2 Höfn *Vestfirðir* Iceland
92 □B3 Hofsjökull Iceland
67 B4 Hōfu Japan
93 G4 Högsby Sweden
101 D2 Hohe Rhön *mts* Ger.
100 C2 Hohe Venn *moorland* Belgium
70 B1 Hohhot China
75 C1 Hoh Xil Shan *mts* China
63 B2 Hôi An Vietnam
62 A1 Hojai India
54 B2 Hokitika N.Z.
66 D2 Hokkaidō *i.* Japan
128 B2 Holberg Can.
138 A2 Holbrook U.S.A.
137 D2 Holdrege U.S.A.
146 C2 Holguín Cuba
92 □B2 Hóll Iceland
Holland *country* Europe *see* Netherlands
140 B2 Holland U.S.A.
100 B1 Hollum Neth.
142 C2 Holly Springs U.S.A.
134 C4 Hollywood *CA* U.S.A.
143 D3 Hollywood *FL* U.S.A.
92 F2 Holm Norway
92 H3 Holmsund Sweden
122 A2 Holoog Namibia
93 E4 Holstebro Denmark
143 D1 Holston *r.* U.S.A.
98 A2 Holyhead U.K.
98 C1 Holy Island *England* U.K.
98 A2 Holy Island *Wales* U.K.
136 C2 Holyoke U.S.A.
101 D2 Holzminden Ger.
62 A1 Homalin Myanmar
101 D2 Homberg (Efze) Ger.
114 B3 Hombori Mali
127 G2 Home Bay Can.
143 D3 Homestead U.S.A.
92 F3 Hommelvik Norway
80 B2 Homs Syria
89 D3 Homyel' Belarus
122 A3 Hondeklipbaai S. Africa
145 D3 Hondo *r.* Belize/Mex.
139 D3 Hondo U.S.A.
146 B3 Honduras *country* Central America
93 F3 Hønefoss Norway
135 B2 Honey Lake U.S.A.
104 C2 Honfleur France
70 B2 Honghu China
71 A3 Hongjiang China
69 D3 Hong Kong China
71 B3 Hong Kong China
65 B1 Hongwŏn N. Korea
70 B2 Hongze Hu *l.* China
49 E3 Honiara Solomon Is
66 D3 Honjō Japan
92 I1 Honningsvåg Norway
67 C3 Honshū *i.* Japan
134 B1 Hood, Mount *vol.* U.S.A.
50 A3 Hood Point Austr.
134 B1 Hood River U.S.A.
100 C1 Hoogeveen Neth.
100 C1 Hoogezand-Sappemeer Neth.
100 C1 Hoog-Keppel Neth.
100 B2 Hook of Holland Neth.
128 A2 Hoonah U.S.A.
100 B1 Hoorn Neth.
128 B3 Hope Can.
142 B2 Hope U.S.A.
83 N2 Hope, Point U.S.A.
131 D1 Hopedale Can.

Hope Mountains

131	D1	Hope Mountains Can.
52	D3	Hopetoun Austr.
122	B2	Hopetown S. Africa
141	D3	Hopewell U.S.A.
130	C1	Hopewell Islands Can.
50	A2	Hopkins, Lake *imp.* l. Austr.
140	B3	Hopkinsville U.S.A.
134	B1	Hoquiam U.S.A.
81	C1	Horasan Turkey
93	F4	Hörby Sweden
89	D3	Horki Belarus
91	D2	Horlivka Ukr.
79	D2	Hormak Iran
79	C2	Hormuz, Strait of Iran/Oman
103	D2	Horn Austria
92	□A2	Horn *c.* Iceland
153	B6	Horn, Cape Chile
141	D2	Hornell U.S.A.
130	B2	Hornepayne Can.
98	C2	Hornsea U.K.
90	B2	Horodenka Ukr.
91	C1	Horodnya Ukr.
90	B2	Horodok *Khmel'nyts'ka Oblast'* Ukr.
90	A2	Horodok *L'vivs'ka Oblast'* Ukr.
90	A1	Horokhiv Ukr.
		Horqin Youyi Qianqi China *see* Ulanhot
131	E1	Horse Islands Can.
52	B3	Horsham Austr.
126	C2	Horton *r.* Can.
117	B4	Hosa'ina Eth.
74	A2	Hoshab Pak.
74	B1	Hoshiarpur India
77	E3	Hotan China
122	B2	Hotazel S. Africa
142	B2	Hot Springs *AR* U.S.A.
136	C2	Hot Springs *SD* U.S.A.
128	C1	Hottah Lake Can.
62	C1	Houayxay Laos
100	B2	Houffalize Belgium
70	B2	Houma China
142	B3	Houma U.S.A.
128	B2	Houston Can.
139	D3	Houston U.S.A.
122	B3	Houwater S. Africa
68	C1	Hovd Mongolia
99	C3	Hove U.K.
68	C1	Hövsgöl Nuur *l.* Mongolia
116	A3	Howar, Wadi *watercourse* Sudan
53	C3	Howe, Cape Austr.
49	G2	Howland Island N. Pacific Ocean
53	C3	Howlong Austr.
101	D2	Höxter Ger.
96	C1	Hoy *i.* U.K.
93	E3	Høyanger Norway
102	C1	Hoyerswerda Ger.
62	A2	Hpapun Myanmar
103	D1	Hradec Králové Czech Rep.
109	C2	Hrasnica Bos.-Herz.
91	C1	Hrebinka Ukr.
88	B3	Hrodna Belarus
62	A1	Hsi-hseng Myanmar
62	A1	Hsipaw Myanmar
70	A2	Huachi China
150	A3	Huacho Peru
69	D2	Huade China
65	B1	Huadian China
70	B2	Huaibei China
71	A3	Huaihua China
70	B2	Huainan China
70	B2	Huaiyang China
145	C3	Huajuápan de León Mex.
59	C3	Huaki Indon.
71	C3	Hualian Taiwan
150	A2	Huallaga *r.* Peru
120	A2	Huambo Angola
150	A3	Huancayo Peru
		Huangcaoba China *see* Xingyi
70	B2	Huangchuan China
		Huang Hai *sea* N. Pacific Ocean *see* Yellow Sea
		Huang He *r.* China *see* Yellow River
71	A4	Huangliu China
70	B3	Huangshan China
70	B2	Huangshi China
70	A2	Huangtu Gaoyuan *plat.* China
71	C3	Huangyan China
65	B1	Huanren China
150	A2	Huánuco Peru
152	B2	Huanuni Bol.
150	A2	Huaráz Peru
150	A3	Huarmey Peru
152	A3	Huasco Chile
152	A3	Huasco *r.* Chile
144	B2	Huatabampo Mex.
145	C3	Huatusco Mex.
71	A3	Huayuan China
		Hubballi India *see* Hubli
70	B2	Hubei *prov.* China
73	B3	Hubli India
100	C2	Hückelhoven Ger.
98	C2	Hucknall U.K.
98	C2	Huddersfield U.K.
93	G3	Hudiksvall Sweden
141	E2	Hudson *r.* U.S.A.
129	D2	Hudson Bay Can.
127	F3	Hudson Bay *sea* Can.
128	B2	Hudson's Hope Can.
127	G2	Hudson Strait Can.
63	B2	Huê Vietnam
146	A3	Huehuetenango Guat.
144	B2	Huehueto, Cerro *mt.* Mex.
145	C2	Huejutla Mex.
106	B2	Huelva Spain
107	C2	Huércal-Overa Spain
107	C1	Huesca Spain
106	C2	Huéscar Spain
50	A2	Hughes (abandoned) Austr.
139	D2	Hugo U.S.A.
122	B2	Huhudi S. Africa
122	A2	Huib-Hoch Plateau Namibia
71	B3	Huichang China
65	B1	Huich'ŏn N. Korea
120	A2	Huila, Planalto da Angola
71	B3	Huilai China
62	B1	Huili China
65	B1	Huinan China
93	H3	Huittinen Fin.
145	C3	Huixtla Mex.
		Huiyang China *see* Huizhou
62	B1	Huize China
71	B3	Huizhou China
78	B2	Hujr Saudi Arabia
122	B1	Hukuntsi Botswana
78	B2	Hulayfah Saudi Arabia
66	B1	Hulin China
130	C2	Hull Can.
		Hulun China *see* Hulun Buir
69	D1	Hulun Buir China
69	D1	Hulun Nur *l.* China
91	D2	Hulyaypole Ukr.
69	E1	Huma China
150	B2	Humaitá Brazil
122	B3	Humansdorp S. Africa
98	C2	Humber *est.* U.K.
126	D3	Humboldt Can.
142	C1	Humboldt U.S.A.
135	C2	Humboldt *r.* U.S.A.
103	E2	Humenné Slovakia
53	C3	Hume Reservoir Austr.
138	A1	Humphreys Peak U.S.A.
92	□A2	Húnaflói *b.* Iceland
71	B3	Hunan *prov.* China
65	C1	Hunchun China
110	B1	Hunedoara Romania
101	D2	Hünfeld Ger.
103	D2	Hungary *country* Europe
52	B1	Hungerford Austr.
65	B2	Hüngnam N. Korea
65	A1	Hun He *r.* China
99	D2	Hunstanton U.K.
101	D1	Hunte *r.* Ger.
51	D4	Hunter Islands Austr.
99	C2	Huntingdon U.K.
140	B2	Huntington *IN* U.S.A.
140	C3	Huntington *WV* U.S.A.
54	C1	Huntly N.Z.
96	C2	Huntly U.K.
130	C2	Huntsville Can.
142	C2	Huntsville *AL* U.S.A.
139	D2	Huntsville *TX* U.S.A.
59	D3	Huon Peninsula P.N.G.
70	B2	Huozhou China
137	D2	Huron U.S.A.
140	C2	Huron, Lake Can./U.S.A.
135	D3	Hurricane U.S.A.
92	□B2	Húsavík Iceland
110	C1	Huşi Romania
126	A2	Huslia U.S.A.
78	B3	Ḩuṣn Āl 'Abr Yemen
102	B1	Husum Ger.
69	C1	Hutag-Öndör Mongolia
60	A1	Hutanopan Indon.
137	D3	Hutchinson U.S.A.
70	C2	Huzhou China
92	□C3	Hvalnes Iceland
92	□B3	Hvannadalshnúkur *vol.* Iceland
109	C2	Hvar *i.* Croatia
120	B2	Hwange Zimbabwe
136	C2	Hyannis U.S.A.
68	C1	Hyargas Nuur *salt l.* Mongolia
50	A3	Hyden Austr.
73	B3	Hyderabad India
74	A2	Hyderabad Pak.
105	D3	Hyères France
105	D3	Hyères, Îles d' *is* France
65	B1	Hyesan N. Korea
128	B2	Hyland Post Can.
67	B3	Hyōno-sen *mt.* Japan
99	D3	Hythe U.K.
93	H3	Hyvinkää Fin.

I

150	B2	Iaco *r.* Brazil
110	C2	Ialomiţa *r.* Romania
110	C1	Ianca Romania
110	C1	Iaşi Romania
64	A1	Iba Phil.
115	C4	Ibadan Nigeria
150	A1	Ibagué Col.
150	A1	Ibarra Ecuador
78	B3	Ibb Yemen
100	C1	Ibbenbüren Ger.
115	C4	Ibi Nigeria
155	C1	Ibiá Brazil
155	D1	Ibiraçu Brazil
107	D2	Ibiza Spain
107	D2	Ibiza *i.* Spain
151	D3	Ibotirama Brazil
79	C2	Ibrā' Oman
79	C2	Ibrī Oman
150	A3	Ica Peru
92	□B2	Iceland *country* Europe
66	D3	Ichinoseki Japan

91 C1 Ichnya Ukr.
65 B2 Ich'ŏn N. Korea
139 E2 Idabel U.S.A.
134 D2 Idaho state U.S.A.
134 D1 Idaho Falls U.S.A.
100 C3 Idar-Oberstein Ger.
116 B3 Idfu Egypt
115 D2 Idhān Murzuq des. Libya
118 B4 Idiofa Dem. Rep. Congo
80 B2 Idlib Syria
154 B2 Iepê Brazil
100 A2 Ieper Belgium
119 D3 Ifakara Tanz.
□D3 Ifanadiana Madag.
115 C4 Ife Nigeria
114 C1 Ifôghas, Adrar des hills Mali
61 C1 Igan Sarawak Malaysia
152 B2 Igarapava Brazil
82 G2 Igarka Rus. Fed.
74 B3 Igatpuri India
81 C2 Iğdır Turkey
108 A3 Iglesias Sardegna Italy
127 F2 Igloolik Can.
Igluligaarjuk Can. see
Chesterfield Inlet
130 A2 Ignace Can.
88 C2 Ignalina Lith.
110 C2 İğneada Turkey
111 A4 Igoumenitsa Greece
86 E3 Igra Rus. Fed.
86 F2 Igrim Rus. Fed.
154 B3 Iguaçu r. Brazil
154 B3 Iguaçu Falls Arg./Brazil
145 C3 Iguala Mex.
107 D1 Igualada Spain
154 B2 Iguatemi Brazil
154 B2 Iguatemi r. Brazil
151 E2 Iguatu Brazil
118 A3 Iguéla Gabon
119 D3 Igunga Tanz.
□D3 Ihosy Madag.
92 I3 Iisalmi Fin.
115 C4 Ijebu-Ode Nigeria
100 B1 IJmuiden Neth.
100 B1 IJssel r. Neth.
100 B1 IJsselmeer l. Neth.
123 C2 Ikageng S. Africa
111 C3 Ikaria i. Greece
118 C4 Ikela Dem. Rep. Congo
110 B2 Ikhtiman Bulg.
67 A4 Iki-shima i. Japan
□D3 Ikongo Madag.
65 B3 Iksan S. Korea
64 B1 Ilagan Phil.
81 C2 Īlām Iran
75 C2 Ilam Nepal
103 D1 Iława Pol.
79 C2 Ilazārān, Kūh-e mt. Iran
129 D2 Île-à-la-Crosse Can.
129 D2 Île-à-la-Crosse, Lac l. Can.
118 C3 Ilebo Dem. Rep. Congo
124 H6 Île Clipperton terr. N. Pacific
Ocean
119 D2 Ilemi Triangle terr. Kenya
119 D2 Ileret Kenya
113 K11 Îles Crozet is Indian Ocean
49 I3 Îles du Désappointement is
Fr. Polynesia
49 I4 Îles Gambier is Fr. Polynesia
99 D3 Ilford U.K.
99 A3 Ilfracombe U.K.
155 D2 Ilha Grande, Baía da b. Brazil
154 B2 Ilha Grande, Represa resr
Brazil
154 B2 Ilha Solteíra, Represa resr
Brazil
106 B1 Ílhavo Port.
151 E3 Ilhéus Brazil
64 B2 Iligan Phil.
152 A4 Illapel Chile
90 C2 Illichivs'k Ukr.
140 A3 Illinois r. U.S.A.
140 B3 Illinois state U.S.A.
90 B2 Illintsi Ukr.
115 C2 Illizi Alg.
89 D2 Il'men', Ozero l. Rus. Fed.
101 E2 Ilmenau Ger.
150 A3 Ilo Peru
64 B1 Iloilo Phil.
101 E2 Ilomantsi Fin.
115 C4 Ilorin Nigeria
53 D1 Iluka Austr.
127 H2 Ilulissat Greenland
67 A4 Imari Japan
117 C4 Imī Eth.
108 B2 Imola Italy
151 D2 Imperatriz Brazil
136 C2 Imperial U.S.A.
118 B2 Impfondo Congo
62 A1 Imphal India
111 C2 İmroz Turkey
150 B3 Inambari r. Peru
115 C2 In Aménas Alg.
59 C3 Inanwatan Indon.
92 I2 Inari Fin.
92 I2 Inari, Järvi l. Fin.
67 D3 Inawashiro-ko l. Japan
80 B1 İnce Burun pt Turkey
65 B2 Inch'ŏn S. Korea
123 D2 Incomati r. Moz.
78 A3 Inda Silasē Eth.
144 B2 Indé Mex.
135 C3 Independence CA U.S.A.
137 E2 Independence IA U.S.A.
137 D3 Independence KS U.S.A.
137 E3 Independence MO U.S.A.
134 C2 Independence Mountains
U.S.A.
76 B2 Inderbor Kazakh.
72 B2 India country Asia
141 D2 Indiana U.S.A.
140 B2 Indiana state U.S.A.
140 B3 Indianapolis U.S.A.
129 D2 Indian Head Can.
159 Indian Ocean World
137 E2 Indianola IA U.S.A.
142 B2 Indianola MS U.S.A.
135 C3 Indian Springs U.S.A.
86 D2 Indiga Rus. Fed.
83 K2 Indigirka r. Rus. Fed.
109 D1 Inđija Serbia
135 C4 Indio U.S.A.
58 B3 Indonesia country Asia
74 B2 Indore India
61 B2 Indramayu, Tanjung pt Indon.
104 C2 Indre r. France
74 A2 Indus r. China/Pak.
74 A2 Indus, Mouths of the Pak.
80 B1 İnebolu Turkey
111 C2 İnegöl Turkey
144 B3 Infiernillo, Presa resr Mex.
53 D1 Inglewood Austr.
102 C2 Ingolstadt Ger.
75 C2 Ingraj Bazar India
123 D2 Inhaca Moz.
123 D2 Inhambane Moz.
97 A2 Inishbofin i. Ireland
97 B2 Inishmore i. Ireland
97 C1 Inishowen pen. Ireland
54 B2 Inland Kaikoura Range mts
N.Z.
102 C2 Inn r. Europe
127 G1 Innaanganeq c. Greenland
96 B2 Inner Sound sea chan. U.K.
51 D1 Innisfail Austr.
102 C2 Innsbruck Austria
154 B1 Inocência Brazil
118 B3 Inongo Dem. Rep. Congo
103 D1 Inowrocław Pol.
114 C2 In Salah Alg.
62 A1 Insein Myanmar
86 F2 Inta Rus. Fed.
137 E1 International Falls U.S.A.
130 C1 Inukjuak Can.
126 C2 Inuvik Can.
96 B2 Inveraray U.K.
54 A3 Invercargill N.Z.
53 D1 Inverell Austr.
96 B2 Invergordon U.K.
128 C2 Invermere Can.
131 D2 Inverness Can.
96 B2 Inverness U.K.
96 C2 Inverurie U.K.
52 A3 Investigator Strait Austr.
77 E1 Inya Rus. Fed.
119 D3 Inyonga Tanz.
87 D3 Inza Rus. Fed.
111 B3 Ioannina Greece
137 D3 Iola U.S.A.
96 A2 Iona i. U.K.
111 B3 Ionian Islands Greece
109 C3 Ionian Sea Greece/Italy
Ionioi Nisoi is Greece see
Ionian Islands
111 C3 Ios i. Greece
137 E2 Iowa state U.S.A.
137 E2 Iowa City U.S.A.
154 C1 Ipameri Brazil
155 D1 Ipatinga Brazil
81 C1 Ipatovo Rus. Fed.
123 C2 Ipelegeng S. Africa
150 A1 Ipiales Col.
155 D1 Ipiranga Brazil
60 B1 Ipoh Malaysia
154 B1 Iporá Brazil
118 C2 Ippy C.A.R.
111 C2 İpsala Turkey
53 D1 Ipswich Austr.
99 D2 Ipswich U.K.
127 G2 Iqaluit Can.
152 A3 Iquique Chile
150 A2 Iquitos Peru
Irakleio Greece see Iraklion
111 C3 Iraklion Greece
76 B3 Iran country Asia
61 C1 Iran, Pegunungan mts Indon.
79 D2 Īrānshahr Iran
144 B2 Irapuato Mex.
81 C2 Iraq country Asia
154 B3 Irati Brazil
80 B2 Irbid Jordan
86 F3 Irbit Rus. Fed.
151 D3 Irecê Brazil
97 C2 Ireland country Europe
118 C3 Irema Dem. Rep. Congo
114 B3 Irîgui reg. Mali/Maur.
119 D3 Iringa Tanz.
151 C2 Iriri r. Brazil
95 B3 Irish Sea Ireland/U.K.
69 C1 Irkutsk Rus. Fed.
52 A2 Iron Knob Austr.
140 B1 Iron Mountain U.S.A.
140 A1 Ironwood U.S.A.
64 B1 Irosin Phil.
67 C4 Irō-zaki pt Japan
90 C1 Irpin' Ukr.
62 A2 Irrawaddy r. Myanmar
63 A2 Irrawaddy, Mouths of the
Myanmar
86 F2 Irtysh r. Kazakh./Rus. Fed.

107 C1 Irun Spain
96 B3 Irvine U.K.
64 B2 Isabela Phil.
146 B3 Isabela, Cordillera mts Nic.
92 □A2 Ísafjörður Iceland
67 B4 Isahaya Japan
105 E2 Isar r. Ger.
96 □ Isbister U.K.
108 B2 Ischia, Isola d' i. Italy
67 C4 Ise Japan
118 C2 Isengi Dem. Rep. Congo
100 C2 Iserlohn Ger.
101 D1 Isernhagen Ger.
67 C4 Ise-wan b. Japan
114 C4 Iseyin Nigeria
Isfahan Iran see Eşfahān
66 D2 Ishikari-wan b. Japan
66 D3 Ishinomaki Japan
67 D3 Ishioka Japan
140 B1 Ishpeming U.S.A.
111 C2 Işıklar Dağı mts Turkey
111 C3 Işıklı Turkey
123 D2 Isipingo S. Africa
119 C2 Isiro Dem. Rep. Congo
80 B2 İskenderun Turkey
82 G3 Iskitim Rus. Fed.
110 B2 Iskür r. Bulg.
128 A2 Iskut r. Can.
74 B1 Islamabad Pak.
52 A2 Island Lagoon imp. l. Austr.
129 C2 Island Lake Can.
54 B1 Islands, Bay of N.Z.
96 A3 Islay i. U.K.
77 D3 Ismoili Somoní, Qullai mt. Tajik.
109 C3 Isola di Capo Rizzuto Italy
110 C2 Isperikh Bulg.
80 B2 Israel country Asia
105 C2 Issoire France
111 C2 İstanbul Turkey
İstanbul Boğazı str. Turkey see Bosporus
111 B3 Istiaia Greece
105 C3 Istres France
108 B1 Istria pen. Croatia
151 D3 Itaberaba Brazil
155 D1 Itabira Brazil
155 D2 Itabirito Brazil
151 E3 Itabuna Brazil
150 C2 Itacoatiara Brazil
154 B3 Itaguajé Brazil
154 C2 Itaí Brazil
154 B3 Itaipu, Represa de resr Brazil
151 C2 Itaituba Brazil
152 B3 Itajaí Brazil
155 C2 Itajubá Brazil
108 B2 Italy country Europe
155 D1 Itamarandiba Brazil
155 D1 Itambacuri Brazil
155 D1 Itambé, Pico de mt. Brazil
62 A1 Itanagar India
154 C2 Itanhaém Brazil
155 D1 Itanhém Brazil
155 D1 Itaobím Brazil
154 C1 Itapajipe Brazil
155 E1 Itapebi Brazil
151 D2 Itapecuru Mirim Brazil
155 E2 Itapemirim Brazil
155 D2 Itaperuna Brazil
155 D1 Itapetinga Brazil
154 C2 Itapetininga Brazil
154 C2 Itapeva Brazil
151 E3 Itapicuru r. Brazil
154 C1 Itapuranga Brazil
154 C2 Itararé Brazil
75 B2 Itarsi India
154 B1 Itarumã Brazil

155 D2 Itaúna Brazil
71 C3 Itbayat i. Phil.
141 D2 Ithaca U.S.A.
101 D1 Ith Hils ridge Ger.
118 C2 Itimbiri r. Dem. Rep. Congo
155 D1 Itinga Brazil
154 B1 Itiquira Brazil
154 A1 Itiquira r. Brazil
67 C4 Itō Japan
154 C2 Itu Brazil
150 A2 Itui r. Brazil
154 C1 Ituiutaba Brazil
119 C3 Itula Dem. Rep. Congo
154 C1 Itumbiara Brazil
154 B1 Iturama Brazil
101 D1 Itzehoe Ger.
83 N2 Iul'tin Rus. Fed.
154 B2 Ivaí r. Brazil
92 I2 Ivalo Fin.
88 C3 Ivanava Belarus
52 B2 Ivanhoe Austr.
90 B1 Ivankiv Ukr.
90 A2 Ivano-Frankivs'k Ukr.
89 F2 Ivanovo Rus. Fed.
88 C3 Ivatsevichy Belarus
111 C2 Ivaylovgrad Bulg.
86 F2 Ivdel' Rus. Fed.
154 B2 Ivinheima Brazil
154 B2 Ivinheima r. Brazil
127 H2 Ivittuut Greenland
Ivory Coast country Africa see Côte d'Ivoire
108 A1 Ivrea Italy
111 C3 İvrindi Turkey
127 F2 Ivujivik Can.
67 D3 Iwaki Japan
67 B4 Iwakuni Japan
66 D2 Iwamizawa Japan
66 D2 Iwanai Japan
88 C3 Iwye Belarus
123 D3 Ixopo S. Africa
144 B2 Ixtlán Mex.
145 D2 Izamal Mex.
81 C1 Izberbash Rus. Fed.
86 E3 Izhevsk Rus. Fed.
86 E2 Izhma Rus. Fed.
89 E3 Izmalkovo Rus. Fed.
90 B2 Izmayil Ukr.
111 C3 İzmir Turkey
111 C2 İznik Gölü l. Turkey
152 B2 Izozog, Bañados del swamp Bol.
67 B3 Izumo Japan
90 B1 Izyaslav Ukr.
91 D2 Izyum Ukr.

J

Jabal, Bahr el r. S. Sudan/Uganda see White Nile
106 C2 Jabalón r. Spain
75 B2 Jabalpur India
50 C1 Jabiru Austr.
109 C2 Jablanica Bos.-Herz.
151 E2 Jaboatão dos Guararapes Brazil
154 C2 Jaboticabal Brazil
107 C1 Jaca Spain
145 C2 Jacala Mex.
151 C2 Jacareacanga Brazil
155 C2 Jacareí Brazil
155 D1 Jacinto Brazil
141 E1 Jackman U.S.A.
142 C2 Jackson AL U.S.A.
140 C2 Jackson MI U.S.A.

142 B2 Jackson MS U.S.A.
142 C1 Jackson TN U.S.A.
136 A2 Jackson WY U.S.A.
54 A2 Jackson Head N.Z.
142 B2 Jacksonville AR U.S.A.
143 D2 Jacksonville FL U.S.A.
140 A3 Jacksonville IL U.S.A.
143 E2 Jacksonville NC U.S.A.
139 D2 Jacksonville TX U.S.A.
147 C3 Jacmel Haiti
74 A2 Jacobabad Pak.
151 D3 Jacobina Brazil
131 D2 Jacques-Cartier, Mont mt. Can.
151 D2 Jacundá Brazil
154 C2 Jacupiranga Brazil
109 C2 Jadovnik mt. Bos.-Herz.
150 A2 Jaén Peru
106 C2 Jaén Spain
52 A3 Jaffa, Cape Austr.
73 B4 Jaffna Sri Lanka
73 C3 Jagdalpur India
123 C2 Jagersfontein S. Africa
79 C2 Jaghin Iran
154 C2 Jaguariaíva Brazil
79 C2 Jahrom Iran
74 B2 Jaipur India
74 B2 Jaisalmer India
75 C2 Jajarkot Nepal
109 C2 Jajce Bos.-Herz.
60 B2 Jakarta Indon.
128 A1 Jakes Corner Can.
92 G2 Jäkkvik Sweden
92 H3 Jakobstad Fin.
77 D3 Jalālābād Afgh.
77 D2 Jalal-Abad Kyrg.
74 B1 Jalandhar India
Jalapa Mex. see Xalapa
154 B2 Jales Brazil
74 B2 Jalgaon India
115 D4 Jalingo Nigeria
74 B3 Jalna India
144 B2 Jalpa Mex.
75 C2 Jalpaiguri India
145 C2 Jalpan Mex.
115 E2 Jālū Libya
146 C3 Jamaica country West Indies
146 C3 Jamaica Channel Haiti/Jamaica
75 C2 Jamalpur Bangl.
60 B2 Jambi Indon.
137 D2 James r. N. Dakota/S. Dakota U.S.A.
141 D3 James r. VA U.S.A.
130 B1 James Bay Can.
52 A2 Jamestown Austr.
137 D1 Jamestown ND U.S.A.
141 D2 Jamestown NY U.S.A.
74 B1 Jammu India
74 B2 Jamnagar India
93 I3 Jämsä Fin.
75 C2 Jamshedpur India
75 C2 Jamuna r. Bangl.
75 C2 Janakpur Nepal
155 D1 Janaúba Brazil
81 D2 Jandaq Iran
140 B2 Janesville U.S.A.
84 F1 Jan Mayen terr. Arctic Ocean
81 D1 Jañña Turkm.
122 B3 Jansenville S. Africa
155 D1 Januária Brazil
74 B2 Jaora India
67 C3 Japan country Asia
156 C3 Japan, Sea of N. Pacific Ocean
150 B2 Japurá r. Brazil
154 C1 Jaraguá Brazil
154 B2 Jaraguari Brazil

70 A2 Jarantai China
152 C3 Jardim Brazil
103 D1 Jarocin Pol.
103 E1 Jarosław Pol.
92 F3 Järpen Sweden
150 B3 Jarú Brazil
Jarud China see Lubei
49 H3 Jarvis Island
S. Pacific Ocean
79 C2 Jāsk Iran
103 E2 Jasło Pol.
128 C2 Jasper Can.
140 B3 Jasper IN U.S.A.
139 E2 Jasper TX U.S.A.
103 D2 Jastrzębie-Zdrój Pol.
103 D2 Jászberény Hungary
154 B1 Jataí Brazil
74 A2 Jati Pak.
154 C2 Jaú Brazil
150 B2 Jaú r. Brazil
145 C2 Jaumave Mex.
75 C2 Jaunpur India
154 B1 Jauru Brazil
61 B2 Java i. Indon.
Java Sea Indon. see Jawa, Laut
Jawa i. Indon. see Java
Jawa, Laut sea Indon.
159 D4 Jawhar Somalia
117 C4 Jawor Pol.
103 D1 Jawor Pol.
103 D1 Jaworzno Pol.
59 D3 Jaya, Puncak mt. Indon.
59 D3 Jayapura Indon.
79 C2 Jaz Mūrīān, Hāmūn-e imp. l.
Iran
128 B1 Jean Marie River Can.
131 D1 Jeannin, Lac l. Can.
116 A3 Jebel Abyad Plateau Sudan
96 C3 Jedburgh U.K.
78 A2 Jeddah Saudi Arabia
101 E1 Jeetze r. Ger.
135 C3 Jefferson, Mount U.S.A.
137 E3 Jefferson City U.S.A.
88 C2 Jēkabpils Latvia
103 D1 Jelenia Góra Pol.
88 B2 Jelgava Latvia
88 B2 Jelgava Latvia
101 E2 Jena Ger.
Jengish Chokusu mt. China/
Kyrg. see Pobeda Peak
80 B2 Jenin West Bank
142 B2 Jennings U.S.A.
131 D1 Jens Munk Island Can.
155 D1 Jequié Brazil
155 D1 Jequitaí Brazil
155 E1 Jequitinhonha Brazil
155 E1 Jequitinhonha r. Brazil
147 C3 Jérémie Haiti
144 B2 Jerez Mex.
106 B2 Jerez de la Frontera Spain
109 C2 Jergucat Albania
115 C1 Jerid, Chott el salt l.
Tunisia
134 D2 Jerome U.S.A.
95 C4 Jersey terr. Channel Is
151 D2 Jerumenha Brazil
80 B2 Jerusalem Israel/West Bank
53 D3 Jervis Bay Territory admin. div.
Austr.
108 B1 Jesenice Slovenia
108 B2 Jesi Italy
101 F2 Jessen Ger.
75 C2 Jessore Bangl.
143 D2 Jesup U.S.A.
145 C3 Jesús Carranza Mex.
109 C2 Jezercë, Maja mt. Albania
74 B2 Jhalawar India
74 B1 Jhang Pak.
75 B2 Jhansi India

75 C2 Jharsuguda India
74 B1 Jhelum Pak.
70 C2 Jiading China
69 E1 Jiamusi China
71 B3 Ji'an Jiangxi China
65 B1 Ji'an Jilin China
62 A1 Jianchuan China
Jiandaoyu China see Guojiang
70 B2 Jiangsu prov. China
71 B3 Jiangxi prov. China
70 B3 Jianli China
70 B3 Jianqiao China
71 B3 Jianyang Fujian China
70 A2 Jianyang Sichuan China
103 C2 Jiaozhou China
70 B2 Jiaozuo China
70 C2 Jiaxing China
71 C3 Jiayi Taiwan
68 C2 Jiayuguan China
Jiddah Saudi Arabia see Jeddah
92 G2 Jiehkkevárri mt. Norway
70 B3 Jiexiu China
68 C2 Jigzhi China
103 D2 Jihlava Czech Rep.
117 C4 Jijiga Eth.
116 A2 Jilf al Kabir, Hadabat al plat.
Egypt
117 C3 Jilib Somalia
69 E2 Jilin China
65 B1 Jilin prov. China
65 A1 Jilin Hada Ling mts China
117 B4 Jīma Eth.
144 B2 Jiménez Chihuahua Mex.
145 C2 Jiménez Tamaulipas Mex.
70 B2 Jinan China
70 B2 Jincheng China
53 C3 Jindabyne Austr.
103 D2 Jindřichův Hradec Czech Rep.
71 B3 Jingdezhen China
70 B2 Jinghang Yunhe canal China
Jinghang Yunhe canal China
see Jinghang Yunhe
62 B1 Jinghong China
70 B2 Jingmen China
70 A2 Jingning China
70 A2 Jingtai China
71 A3 Jingxi China
65 B1 Jingyu China
70 A2 Jingyuan China
70 B2 Jingzhou China
70 B2 Jingzhou China
71 B3 Jinhua China
Jining Shandong China
119 D2 Jinja Uganda
117 B4 Jinka Eth.
146 B3 Jinotepe Nic.
71 A3 Jinping China
Jinsha Jiang r. China see
Yangtze
70 B3 Jinshi China
70 C1 Jinzhou China
70 C1 Jinzhou China
150 B2 Jiparaná r. Brazil
75 C1 Jirang China
79 C2 Jiroft Iran
71 A3 Jishou China
110 B3 Jiu r. Romania
70 A2 Jiuding Shan mt. China
70 B3 Jiujiang China
66 B1 Jixi China
58 B3 Jīzān Saudi Arabia
77 C2 Jizzax Uzbek.
151 E2 João Pessoa Brazil
155 C1 João Pinheiro Brazil
74 B2 Jodhpur India
92 I3 Joensuu Fin.

67 C3 Jōetsu Japan
121 C3 Jofane Moz.
88 C2 Jõgeva Estonia
123 C2 Johannesburg S. Africa
134 C2 John Day U.S.A.
134 B1 John Day r. U.S.A.
128 C2 John D'Or Prairie Can.
143 E1 John H. Kerr Reservoir U.S.A.
96 C1 John o' Groats U.K.
143 D1 Johnson City U.S.A.
128 A1 Johnson's Crossing Can.
49 H1 Johnston Atoll N. Pacific
Ocean
96 B3 Johnstone U.K.
141 D2 Johnstown U.S.A.
60 B1 Johor Bahru Malaysia
88 C2 Jõhvi Estonia
154 C3 Joinville Brazil
105 D2 Joinville France
92 G2 Jokkmokk Sweden
92 □B2 Jökulsá á Fjöllum r. Iceland
140 B2 Joliet U.S.A.
130 C2 Joliette Can.
64 B2 Jolo Phil.
64 B2 Jolo i. Phil.
61 C2 Jombang Indon.
75 C2 Jomsom Nepal
88 B2 Jonava Lith.
142 B1 Jonesboro AR U.S.A.
142 B2 Jonesboro LA U.S.A.
127 I1 Jones Sound sea chan. Can.
93 F4 Jönköping Sweden
131 C2 Jonquière Can.
145 C3 Jonuta Mex.
137 E3 Joplin U.S.A.
80 B2 Jordan country Asia
80 B2 Jordan r. Asia
136 B1 Jordan r. U.S.A.
134 C2 Jordan Valley U.S.A.
74 B2 Jorhat India
93 E4 Jørpeland Norway
115 C4 Jos Nigeria
145 C3 José Cardel Mex.
131 D1 Joseph, Lac l. Can.
50 B1 Joseph Bonaparte Gulf Austr.
115 C4 Jos Plateau Nigeria
93 E3 Jotunheimen mts Norway
122 B3 Joubertina S. Africa
123 C2 Jouberton S. Africa
93 I3 Joutseno Fin.
134 B1 Juan de Fuca Strait
Can./U.S.A.
Juanshui China see
Tongcheng
145 B2 Juárez Mex.
151 D2 Juazeiro Brazil
151 E2 Juazeiro do Norte Brazil
117 B4 Juba S. Sudan
117 C5 Jubba r. Somalia
78 B2 Jubbah Saudi Arabia
145 C3 Juchitán Mex.
102 C2 Judenburg Austria
101 D2 Jühnde Ger.
146 B3 Juigalpa Nic.
100 C1 Juist i. Ger.
155 D2 Juiz de Fora Brazil
150 A3 Juliaca Peru
75 C2 Jumla Nepal
74 B2 Junagadh India
139 D2 Junction U.S.A.
137 D3 Junction City U.S.A.
154 C2 Jundiaí Brazil
128 A2 Juneau U.S.A.
53 C2 Junee Austr.
105 D2 Jungfrau mt. Switz.
141 D2 Juniata r. U.S.A.
92 G3 Junsele Sweden

Juntura

134	C2	**Juntura** U.S.A.
154	C2	**Juquiá** Brazil
117	A4	**Jur** r. S. Sudan
105	D2	**Jura** mts France/Switz.
96	B2	**Jura** i. U.K.
96	B3	**Jura, Sound of** sea chan. U.K.
88	B2	**Jurbarkas** Lith.
88	B2	**Jūrmala** Latvia
150	B2	**Juruá** r. Brazil
150	C2	**Juruena** r. Brazil
150	B2	**Jutaí** r. Brazil
101	F2	**Jüterbog** Ger.
146	B2	**Juventud, Isla de la** i. Cuba
70	B2	**Juxian** China
79	C2	**Jūyom** Iran
122	B1	**Jwaneng** Botswana
93	I3	**Jyväskylä** Fin.

K

74	B1	**K2** mt. China/Pakistan
119	C3	**Kabalo** Dem. Rep. Congo
119	C3	**Kabare** Dem. Rep. Congo
130	B2	**Kabinakagami Lake** Can.
118	C3	**Kabinda** Dem. Rep. Congo
118	B2	**Kabo** C.A.R.
120	B2	**Kabompo** Zambia
119	C3	**Kabongo** Dem. Rep. Congo
77	B3	**Kābul** Afgh.
64	B2	**Kaburuang** i. Indon.
121	B2	**Kabwe** Zambia
74	A2	**Kachchh, Gulf of** India
74	B2	**Kachchh, Rann of** marsh India
83	I3	**Kachug** Rus. Fed.
81	C1	**Kaçkar Dağı** mt. Turkey
		Kadapa India see **Cuddapah**
111	C2	**Kadıköy** Turkey
114	B3	**Kadiolo** Mali
73	B3	**Kadmat** atoll India
121	B2	**Kadoma** Zimbabwe
63	A2	**Kadonkani** Myanmar
117	A3	**Kadugli** Sudan
115	C3	**Kaduna** Nigeria
89	E2	**Kaduy** Rus. Fed.
86	E2	**Kadzherom** Rus. Fed.
114	A3	**Kaédi** Maur.
118	B1	**Kaélé** Cameroon
65	B2	**Kaesŏng** N. Korea
114	A3	**Kaffrine** Senegal
121	B2	**Kafue** Zambia
120	B2	**Kafue** r. Zambia
118	B2	**Kaga Bandoro** C.A.R.
91	E2	**Kagal'nitskaya** Rus. Fed.
67	B4	**Kagoshima** Japan
90	C2	**Kaharlyk** Ukr.
61	C2	**Kahayan** r. Indon.
118	B3	**Kahemba** Dem. Rep. Congo
101	E2	**Kahla** Ger.
79	C2	**Kahnūj** Iran
93	H2	**Kahperusvaarat** mts Fin.
80	B2	**Kahramanmaraş** Turkey
79	C2	**Kahūrak** Iran
59	C3	**Kai, Kepulauan** is Indon.
115	C4	**Kaiama** Nigeria
54	B2	**Kaiapoi** N.Z.
59	C3	**Kai Besar** i. Indon.
70	B2	**Kaifeng** China
		Kaihua China see **Wenshan**
122	B2	**Kaiingveld** reg. S. Africa
59	C3	**Kai Kecil** i. Indon.
54	B2	**Kaikoura** N.Z.
114	A4	**Kailahun** Sierra Leone
71	A3	**Kaili** China
59	C3	**Kaimana** Indon.
54	C1	**Kaimanawa Mountains** N.Z.

67	C4	**Kainan** Japan
115	C3	**Kainji Reservoir** Nigeria
54	B1	**Kaipara Harbour** N.Z.
74	B2	**Kairana** India
115	D1	**Kairouan** Tunisia
54	B1	**Kaitaia** N.Z.
54	C1	**Kaitawa** N.Z.
		Kaitong China see **Tongyu**
59	C3	**Kaiwatu** Indon.
65	A1	**Kaiyuan** Liaoning China
62	B1	**Kaiyuan** Yunnan China
92	I3	**Kajaani** Fin.
51	D2	**Kajabbi** Austr.
122	B2	**Kakamas** S. Africa
119	D2	**Kakamega** Kenya
91	C2	**Kakhovka** Ukr.
91	C2	**Kakhovs'ke Vodoskhovyshche** resr Ukr.
73	C3	**Kakinada** India
128	C1	**Kakisa** Can.
119	C3	**Kakoswa** Dem. Rep. Congo
126	B2	**Kaktovik** U.S.A.
		Kalaallit Nunaat terr. N. America see **Greenland**
59	C3	**Kalabahi** Indon.
120	B2	**Kalabo** Zambia
91	E1	**Kalach** Rus. Fed.
119	D2	**Kalacha Dida** Kenya
62	A1	**Kaladan** r. India/Myanmar
120	B3	**Kalahari Desert** Africa
92	H3	**Kalajoki** Fin.
111	B2	**Kalamaria** Greece
111	B3	**Kalamata** Greece
140	B2	**Kalamazoo** U.S.A.
111	B3	**Kalampaka** Greece
91	C2	**Kalanchak** Ukr.
115	E1	**Kalanshiyū ar Ramlī al Kabīr, Sarīr** des. Libya
63	B2	**Kalasin** Thai.
79	C2	**Kalāt** Iran
74	A2	**Kalat** Pak.
50	A2	**Kalbarri** Austr.
		Kalburgi India see **Gulbarga**
111	C3	**Kale** Turkey
80	B1	**Kalecik** Turkey
118	C3	**Kalema** Dem. Rep. Congo
119	C3	**Kalemie** Dem. Rep. Congo
62	A1	**Kalemyo** Myanmar
		Kalgan China see **Zhangjiakou**
50	B3	**Kalgoorlie** Austr.
109	C2	**Kali** Croatia
110	C2	**Kaliakra, Nos** pt Bulg.
119	C3	**Kalima** Dem. Rep. Congo
61	C2	**Kalimantan** reg. Indon.
88	B3	**Kaliningrad** Rus. Fed.
91	D2	**Kalininskaya** Rus. Fed.
88	C3	**Kalinkavichy** Belarus
134	D1	**Kalispell** U.S.A.
103	D1	**Kalisz** Pol.
91	E2	**Kalitva** r. Rus. Fed.
92	H2	**Kalix** Sweden
92	H2	**Kalixälven** r. Sweden
111	C3	**Kalkan** Turkey
120	A3	**Kalkfeld** Namibia
92	I3	**Kallavesi** l. Fin.
92	F3	**Kallsjön** l. Sweden
93	G4	**Kalmar** Sweden
93	G4	**Kalmarsund** sea chan. Sweden
120	B2	**Kalomo** Zambia
128	B2	**Kalone Peak** Can.
75	B1	**Kalpa** India
73	B3	**Kalpeni** atoll India
75	B2	**Kalpi** India
101	D1	**Kaltenkirchen** Ger.
89	E3	**Kaluga** Rus. Fed.
93	F4	**Kalundborg** Denmark
90	A2	**Kalush** Ukr.

89	E2	**Kalyazin** Rus. Fed.
111	C3	**Kalymnos** i. Greece
119	C3	**Kama** Dem. Rep. Congo
62	A2	**Kama** Myanmar
86	E3	**Kama** r. Rus. Fed.
66	D3	**Kamaishi** Japan
80	B2	**Kaman** Turkey
120	A2	**Kamanjab** Namibia
78	B3	**Kamarān** i. Yemen
74	A2	**Kamarod** Pak.
50	B3	**Kambalda** Austr.
119	C4	**Kambove** Dem. Rep. Congo
183	L3	**Kamchatka Peninsula** Rus. Fed.
110	C2	**Kamchiya** r. Bulg.
110	B2	**Kamenitsa** mt. Bulg.
108	B2	**Kamenjak, Rt** pt Croatia
91	D1	**Kamenka** Rus. Fed.
91	E2	**Kamenolomni** Rus. Fed.
83	M2	**Kamenskoye** Rus. Fed.
91	E2	**Kamensk-Shakhtinskiy** Rus. Fed.
86	F3	**Kamensk-Ural'skiy** Rus. Fed.
122	A3	**Kamiesberge** mts S. Africa
122	A3	**Kamieskroon** S. Africa
129	D1	**Kamilukuak Lake** Can.
119	C3	**Kamina** Dem. Rep. Congo
129	E1	**Kaminak Lake** Can.
90	A1	**Kamin'-Kashyrs'kyy** Ukr.
128	B2	**Kamloops** Can.
118	C3	**Kamonia** Dem. Rep. Congo
119	D2	**Kampala** Uganda
60	B1	**Kampar** r. Indon.
60	B1	**Kampar** Malaysia
100	B1	**Kampen** Neth.
119	C3	**Kampene** Dem. Rep. Congo
63	A2	**Kamphaeng Phet** Thai.
63	B2	**Kâmpóng Cham** Cambodia
63	B2	**Kâmpóng Chhnăng** Cambodia
		Kâmpóng Saôm Cambodia see **Sihanoukville**
63	B2	**Kâmpóng Spœ** Cambodia
63	B2	**Kâmpôt** Cambodia
129	D2	**Kamsack** Can.
86	E3	**Kamskoye Vodokhranilishche** resr Rus. Fed.
117	C4	**Kamsuuma** Somalia
90	B2	**Kam"yanets'-Podil's'kyy** Ukr.
90	A1	**Kam"yanka-Buz'ka** Ukr.
88	B3	**Kamyanyets** Belarus
91	D2	**Kamyshevatskaya** Rus. Fed.
87	D3	**Kamyshin** Rus. Fed.
135	D3	**Kanab** U.S.A.
118	C3	**Kananga** Dem. Rep. Congo
87	D3	**Kanash** Rus. Fed.
140	C3	**Kanawha** r. U.S.A.
67	C3	**Kanazawa** Japan
62	A1	**Kanbalu** Myanmar
63	A2	**Kanchanaburi** Thai.
73	B3	**Kanchipuram** India
77	C3	**Kandahār** Afgh.
86	C2	**Kandalaksha** Rus. Fed.
61	C2	**Kandangan** Indon.
74	A2	**Kandh Kot** Pak.
114	C3	**Kandi** Benin
74	B2	**Kandla** India
53	C2	**Kandos** Austr.
121	□D2	**Kandreho** Madag.
73	C4	**Kandy** Sri Lanka
76	B2	**Kandyagash** Kazakh.
127	G1	**Kane Bassin** b. Greenland
91	D2	**Kanevskaya** Rus. Fed.
122	B1	**Kang** Botswana
127	H2	**Kangaatsiaq** Greenland
114	B3	**Kangaba** Mali
80	B2	**Kangal** Turkey
79	C2	**Kangān** Iran

60 B1 **Kangar** Malaysia
52 A3 **Kangaroo Island** Austr.
75 C2 **Kangchenjunga** mt.
India/Nepal
65 B2 **Kangdong** N. Korea
61 C2 **Kangean, Kepulauan** is Indon.
127 I2 **Kangeq** c. Greenland
127 H2 **Kangerlussuaq** inlet Greenland
127 I2 **Kangerlussuaq** inlet Greenland
127 H2 **Kangersuatsiaq** Greenland
65 B1 **Kanggye** N. Korea
131 D1 **Kangiqsualujjuaq** Can.
127 G2 **Kangiqsujuaq** Can.
127 G2 **Kangirsuk** Can.
72 B2 **Kangmar** China
65 A1 **Kangping** China
72 D2 **Kangto** mt. China/India
62 A1 **Kani** Myanmar
86 D2 **Kanin, Poluostrov** pen.
Rus. Fed.
86 D2 **Kanin Nos** Rus. Fed.
91 C2 **Kaniv** Ukr.
93 H3 **Kankaanpää** Fin.
140 C2 **Kankakee** U.S.A.
114 B3 **Kankan** Guinea
75 C2 **Kanker** India
Kannur India see **Kannur**
73 B3 **Kannur** India
115 C3 **Kano** Nigeria
122 B3 **Kanonpunt** pt S. Africa
67 B4 **Kanoya** Japan
75 C2 **Kanpur** India
136 C3 **Kansas** r. U.S.A.
137 D3 **Kansas** state U.S.A.
137 E3 **Kansas City** U.S.A.
83 H3 **Kansk** Rus. Fed.
114 B3 **Kantchari** Burkina Faso
91 D2 **Kantemirovka** Rus. Fed.
97 B2 **Kanturk** Ireland
123 D2 **Kanyamazane** S. Africa
123 C1 **Kanye** Botswana
120 A2 **Kaokoveld** plat. Namibia
114 A3 **Kaolack** Senegal
121 B2 **Kaoma** Zambia
118 C3 **Kapanga** Dem. Rep. Congo
100 B2 **Kapellen** Belgium
121 B2 **Kapiri Mposhi** Zambia
127 H2 **Kapisillit** Greenland
130 B1 **Kapiskau** r. Can.
61 C1 **Kapit** Sarawak Malaysia
63 A3 **Kapoe** Thai.
117 B4 **Kapoeta** S. Sudan
103 D2 **Kaposvár** Hungary
77 D2 **Kapshagay** Kazakh.
77 D2 **Kapshagay,**
Vodokhranilishche resr
Kazakh.
61 B2 **Kapuas** r. Indon.
52 A2 **Kapunda** Austr.
130 B2 **Kapuskasing** Can.
103 D2 **Kapuvár** Hungary
88 C3 **Kapyl'** Belarus
114 C4 **Kara** Togo
111 C3 **Kara Ada** i. Turkey
76 C1 **Karabalyk** Kazakh.
80 B1 **Karabük** Turkey
76 C2 **Karabutak** Kazakh.
110 C2 **Karacaköy** Turkey
89 D3 **Karachev** Rus. Fed.
74 A2 **Karachi** Pak.
Kara Deniz sea Asia/Europe
see **Black Sea**
77 D2 **Karagandy** Kazakh.
77 D2 **Karagayly** Kazakh.
83 L3 **Karaginskiy Zaliv** b. Rus. Fed.
81 D2 **Karaj** Iran

64 B2 **Karakelong** i. Indon.
77 D2 **Kara-Köl** Kyrg.
77 D2 **Karakol** Kyrg.
74 B1 **Karakoram Range** mts Asia
Karakum, Peski des. Kazakh.
see **Karakum Desert**
76 B2 **Karakum Desert** Kazakh.
76 C3 **Karakum Desert** Turkm.
Karakumy, Peski des. Turkm.
see **Karakum Desert**
80 B2 **Karaman** Turkey
77 E2 **Karamay** China
54 B2 **Karamea** N.Z.
54 B2 **Karamea Bight** b. N.Z.
80 B2 **Karapınar** Turkey
122 A2 **Karasburg** Namibia
86 F1 **Kara Sea** Rus. Fed.
92 I1 **Karasjok** Norway
82 G3 **Karasuk** Rus. Fed.
77 D2 **Karatau** Kazakh.
77 C2 **Karatau, Khrebet** mts Kazakh.
86 F2 **Karatayka** Rus. Fed.
67 A4 **Karatsu** Japan
60 B2 **Karawang** Indon.
81 C2 **Karbalā'** Iraq
103 E2 **Karcag** Hungary
111 B3 **Karditsa** Greece
88 B2 **Kärdla** Estonia
122 B3 **Kareeberge** mts S. Africa
75 B2 **Kareli** India
74 B1 **Kargil** India
121 B2 **Kariba** Zimbabwe
121 B2 **Kariba, Lake** resr
Zambia/Zimbabwe
61 B2 **Karimata, Pulau-pulau** is
Indon.
61 B2 **Karimata, Selat** str. Indon.
73 B3 **Karimnagar** India
61 C2 **Karimunjawa, Pulau-pulau** is
Indon.
91 C2 **Karkinits'ka Zatoka** g. Ukr.
91 D2 **Karlivka** Ukr.
109 C1 **Karlovac** Croatia
102 C1 **Karlovy Vary** Czech Rep.
93 F4 **Karlshamn** Sweden
93 G4 **Karlskrona** Sweden
102 B2 **Karlsruhe** Ger.
93 F4 **Karlstad** Sweden
101 D3 **Karlstadt** Ger.
89 D3 **Karma** Belarus
93 E4 **Karmøy** i. Norway
75 D2 **Karnafuli Reservoir** Bangl.
74 B2 **Karnal** India
110 C2 **Karnobat** Bulg.
74 A2 **Karodi** Pak.
121 B2 **Karoi** Zimbabwe
121 C1 **Karonga** Malawi
116 B3 **Karora** Eritrea
111 C3 **Karpathos** i. Greece
111 B3 **Karpenisi** Greece
86 D2 **Karpogory** Rus. Fed.
50 A2 **Karratha** Austr.
81 C1 **Kars** Turkey
88 C2 **Kārsava** Latvia
86 E2 **Karskiye Vorota, Proliv** str.
Rus. Fed.
Karskoye More sea Rus. Fed.
see **Kara Sea**
101 E1 **Karstädt** Ger.
111 D3 **Kartal** Turkey
87 F3 **Kartaly** Rus. Fed.
73 B3 **Karwar** India
83 I3 **Karymskoye** Rus. Fed.
111 B3 **Karystos** Greece
80 A2 **Kaş** Turkey
130 B1 **Kasabonika Lake** Can.
118 C4 **Kasaji** Dem. Rep. Congo

121 C2 **Kasama** Zambia
120 B2 **Kasane** Botswana
118 B3 **Kasangulu** Dem. Rep. Congo
73 B3 **Kasaragod** India
129 D1 **Kasba Lake** Can.
120 B2 **Kasempa** Zambia
119 C4 **Kasenga** Dem. Rep. Congo
119 C3 **Kasese** Dem. Rep. Congo
119 D2 **Kasese** Uganda
81 D2 **Kāshān** Iran
Kashgar China see **Kashi**
77 D3 **Kashi** China
67 D3 **Kashima-nada** b. Japan
89 E2 **Kashin** Rus. Fed.
89 E3 **Kashira** Rus. Fed.
67 C3 **Kashiwazaki** Japan
67 C3 **Kashiwazaki** Japan
76 B3 **Kashmar** Iran
74 B1 **Kashmir** reg. Asia
74 A2 **Kashmore** Pak.
119 C3 **Kashyukulu** Dem. Rep. Congo
87 D3 **Kasimov** Rus. Fed.
93 H3 **Kaskinen** Fin.
119 C3 **Kasongo** Dem. Rep. Congo
118 B3 **Kasongo-Lunda** Dem. Rep.
Congo
111 C3 **Kasos** i. Greece
Kaspiyskoye More l.
Asia/Europe see **Caspian Sea**
116 B3 **Kassala** Sudan
101 D2 **Kassel** Ger.
80 B1 **Kastamonu** Turkey
111 B2 **Kastoria** Greece
89 D3 **Katsyukovichy** Belarus
119 D3 **Kasulu** Tanz.
121 C2 **Kasungu** Malawi
141 F1 **Katahdin, Mount** U.S.A.
118 C3 **Katako-Kombe** Dem. Rep.
Congo
50 A3 **Katanning** Austr.
63 A3 **Katchall** i. India
111 B2 **Katerini** Greece
128 A2 **Kate's Needle** mt. Can./U.S.A.
121 C2 **Katete** Zambia
62 A1 **Katha** Myanmar
50 C1 **Katherine** r. Austr.
74 B2 **Kathiawar** pen. India
75 C2 **Kathmandu** Nepal
122 B2 **Kathu** S. Africa
74 B1 **Kathua** India
114 B3 **Kati** Mali
75 C2 **Katihar** India
54 C1 **Katikati** N.Z.
123 C3 **Katikati** S. Africa
120 B2 **Katima Mulilo** Namibia
123 C2 **Katlehong** S. Africa
111 B3 **Kato Achaïa** Greece
53 D2 **Katoomba** Austr.
103 D1 **Katowice** Pol.
78 A2 **Kātrīnā, Jabal** mt. Egypt
93 G4 **Katrineholm** Sweden
115 C3 **Katsina** Nigeria
115 C4 **Katsina-Ala** Nigeria
77 C3 **Kattaqo'rg'on** Uzbek.
93 F4 **Kattegat** str. Denmark/Sweden
100 B1 **Katwijk aan Zee** Neth.
124 E5 **Kaua'i** i. U.S.A.
93 H3 **Kauhajoki** Fin.
88 B3 **Kaunas** Lith.
115 C3 **Kaura-Namoda** Nigeria
92 H2 **Kautokeino** Norway
111 B3 **Kavala** Greece
66 C2 **Kavalerovo** Rus. Fed.
73 C3 **Kavali** India
73 B3 **Kavaratti** atoll India
110 C2 **Kavarna** Bulg.
81 D2 **Kavīr, Dasht-e** des. Iran

Kawagoe

67 C3 Kawagoe Japan
54 B1 Kawakawa N.Z.
67 C3 Kawanishi Japan
130 C2 Kawartha Lakes Can.
54 C1 Kawasaki Japan
54 C1 Kawerau N.Z.
63 A2 Kawkareik Myanmar
62 A1 Kawlin Myanmar
63 A2 Kawmapyin Myanmar
63 A2 Kawthaung Myanmar
77 B3 Kaxgar He r. China
114 B3 Kaya Burkina Faso
61 C1 Kayan r. Indon.
136 B2 Kaycee U.S.A.
138 A1 Kayenta U.S.A.
114 A3 Kayes Mali
77 D2 Kaynar Kazakh.
80 B2 Kayseri Turkey
73 D1 Kazakhskiy Zaliv b. Kazakh.
76 C2 Kazakhstan country Asia
87 D1 Kazan' Rus. Fed.
80 A1 Kazanlük Bulg.
76 A2 Kazbek mt. Georgia/Rus. Fed.
81 D3 Kāzerūn Iran
103 E2 Kazincbarcika Hungary
86 F2 Kazym-Mys Rus. Fed.
111 B3 Kea i. Greece
97 C1 Keady U.K.
137 D2 Kearney U.S.A.
138 A2 Kearny U.S.A.
116 A3 Kebkabiya Sudan
92 G2 Kebnekaise mt. Sweden
117 C4 K'ebri Dehar Eth.
61 B2 Kebumen Indon.
128 B2 Kechika r. Can.
103 D2 Kecskemét Hungary
88 B2 Kėdainiai Lith.
114 A3 Kédougou Senegal
103 D1 Kędzierzyn-Koźle Pol.
128 B1 Keele r. Can.
128 A1 Keele Peak Can.
           Keeling Taiwan see Chilung
141 E2 Keene U.S.A.
122 A2 Keetmanshoop Namibia
129 E3 Keewatin Can.
           Kefallonia i. Greece see
           Cephalonia
59 C3 Kefamenanu Indon.
92 □A3 Keflavík Iceland
77 D2 Kegen Kazakh.
128 C2 Keg River Can.
62 A1 Kehsi Mansam Myanmar
98 C2 Keighley U.K.
88 B2 Keila Estonia
122 B2 Keimoes S. Africa
92 I3 Keitele l. Fin.
52 B3 Keith Austr.
103 E2 Kékes mt. Hungary
91 J2 Kelesuayv, Gora h. Rus. Fed.
102 C2 Kelheim Ger.
80 B1 Kelkit r. Turkey
128 B1 Keller Lake Can.
134 C1 Kellogg U.S.A.
92 I2 Kelloselkä Fin.
97 C2 Kells Ireland
88 B2 Kelmė Lith.
115 D4 Kélo Chad
128 C3 Kelowna Can.
96 C3 Kelso U.K.
134 B1 Kelso U.S.A.
60 B1 Keluang Malaysia
129 D2 Kelvington Can.
86 C2 Kem' Rus. Fed.
128 B2 Kemano (abandoned) Can.
111 C3 Kemer Turkey
82 G3 Kemerovo Rus. Fed.
92 H2 Kemi Fin.

92 I2 Kemijärvi Fin.
92 I2 Kemijoki r. Fin.
136 A2 Kemmerer U.S.A.
92 I3 Kempele Fin.
53 D2 Kempsey Austr.
130 C2 Kempt, Lac l. Can.
102 C2 Kempten (Allgäu) Ger.
123 C2 Kempton Park S. Africa
61 C2 Kemujan i. Indon.
129 D2 Kenaston Can.
98 B1 Kendal U.K.
59 C3 Kendari Indon.
61 C2 Kendawangan Indon.
115 D3 Kendégué Chad
114 A4 Kenema Sierra Leone
118 B3 Kenge Dem. Rep. Congo
62 A1 Kengtung Myanmar
122 B2 Kenhardt S. Africa
114 B1 Kenitra Morocco
97 B3 Kenmare Ireland
136 C1 Kenmare U.S.A.
97 A3 Kenmare River inlet Ireland
100 C3 Kenn Ger.
137 E3 Kennett U.S.A.
134 C1 Kennewick U.S.A.
129 E3 Kenora Can.
140 B2 Kenosha U.S.A.
138 C2 Kent U.S.A.
77 C2 Kentau Kazakh.
140 B3 Kentucky r. U.S.A.
140 C3 Kentucky state U.S.A.
140 B3 Kentucky Lake U.S.A.
119 D2 Kenya country Africa
119 D3 Kenya, Mount Kenya
137 E2 Keokuk U.S.A.
75 C2 Keonjhar India
111 C3 Kepsut Turkey
52 B3 Kerang Austr.
91 D2 Kerch Ukr.
59 D3 Kerema P.N.G.
128 C3 Keremeos Can.
116 B3 Keren Eritrea
81 C2 Kerend Iran
           Kerepakupai Merú Venez. see
           Angel Falls
159 C7 Kerguelen Plateau Indian
           Ocean
119 D3 Kericho Kenya
54 B1 Kerikeri N.Z.
60 B2 Kerinci, Gunung vol. Indon.
111 A3 Kerkyra Greece
           Kerkyra i. Greece see Corfu
116 B3 Kerma Sudan
49 G4 Kermadec Islands S. Pacific
           Ocean
79 C1 Kermān Iran
81 C2 Kermānshāh Iran
139 C2 Kermit U.S.A.
135 C3 Kern r. U.S.A.
100 C2 Kerpen Ger.
129 D2 Kerrobert Can.
139 D2 Kerrville U.S.A.
           Keryneia Cyprus see Kyrenia
130 B1 Kesagami Lake Can.
111 C2 Keşan Turkey
66 D3 Kesennuma Japan
74 B2 Keshod India
100 C2 Kessel Neth.
98 B1 Keswick U.K.
103 D2 Keszthely Hungary
82 G3 Ket' r. Rus. Fed.
61 C2 Ketapang Indon.
128 A2 Ketchikan U.S.A.
134 D2 Ketchum U.S.A.
99 C2 Kettering U.K.
93 H3 Keuruu Fin.
100 C2 Kevelaer Ger.

140 B2 Kewanee U.S.A.
140 B1 Keweenaw Bay U.S.A.
140 B1 Keweenaw Peninsula U.S.A.
143 D3 Key Largo U.S.A.
141 D3 Keyser U.S.A.
143 D4 Key West U.S.A.
123 C2 Kgotsong S. Africa
69 E1 Khabarovsk Rus. Fed.
80 B1 Khadyzhensk Rus. Fed.
62 A1 Khagrachari Bangl.
74 A2 Khairpur Pak.
122 B1 Khakhea Botswana
68 C1 Khamar-Daban, Khrebet mts
           Rus. Fed.
74 B2 Khambhat India
73 B3 Khambhat, Gulf of India
74 B2 Khamgaon India
78 B3 Khamir Yemen
78 B3 Khamis Mushayt Saudi Arabia
77 C3 Khānābād Afgh.
74 B2 Khandwa India
83 K2 Khandyga Rus. Fed.
74 B1 Khanewal Pak.
66 B2 Khanka, Lake China/Rus. Fed.
74 B2 Khanpur Pak.
77 D2 Khantau Kazakh.
83 H2 Khantayskoye, Ozero l.
           Rus. Fed.
86 F2 Khanty-Mansiysk Rus. Fed.
63 A2 Khao Chum Thong Thai.
63 A2 Khao Laem, Ang Kep Nam
           Thai.
87 D4 Kharabali Rus. Fed.
75 C2 Kharagpur India
79 C2 Khārān r. Iran
116 B2 Khārijah, Wāḥāt al oasis Egypt
91 D2 Kharkiv Ukr.
           Khar'kov Ukr. see Kharkiv
110 C2 Kharmanli Bulg.
86 D3 Kharovsk Rus. Fed.
116 B3 Khartoum Sudan
87 D4 Khasavyurt Rus. Fed.
79 D2 Khāsh Iran
78 A3 Khashm el Girba Sudan
78 A3 Khashm el Girba Dam Sudan
74 D2 Khasi Hills India
110 C2 Khaskovo Bulg.
123 C3 Khayamnandi S. Africa
78 A2 Khaybar Saudi Arabia
122 A3 Khayelitsha S. Africa
107 D2 Khemis Miliana Alg.
63 B2 Khemmarat Thai.
115 C1 Khenchela Alg.
81 D3 Kherāmeh Iran
91 C2 Kherson Ukr.
83 H2 Kheta r. Rus. Fed.
91 C2 Khilok Rus. Fed.
89 E2 Khimki Rus. Fed.
74 A2 Khipro Pak.
90 B2 Khlevnoye Rus. Fed.
90 B2 Khmel'nyts'kyy Ukr.
89 E3 Khokhol'skiy Rus. Fed.
74 B2 Khokhropar Pak.
89 D2 Kholm Rus. Fed.
89 D2 Kholm-Zhirkovskiy Rus. Fed.
79 C2 Khonj Iran
63 B2 Khon Kaen Thai.
62 A1 Khonsa India
86 C2 Khonuu Rus. Fed.
86 E2 Khorey-Ver Rus. Fed.
69 D1 Khorinsk Rus. Fed.
91 C1 Khorol Ukr.
81 C2 Khorramābād Iran
81 C2 Khorramshahr Iran
74 A1 Khorugh Tajik.
74 A1 Khōst Afgh.
62 A1 Khreum Myanmar

76 B1 **Khromtau** Kazakh.
90 B2 **Khrystynivka** Ukr.
77 C2 **Khŭjand** Tajik.
63 B2 **Khu Khan** Thai.
78 A2 **Khulays** Saudi Arabia
75 C2 **Khulna** Bangl.
79 B2 **Khurays** Saudi Arabia
74 B1 **Khushab** Pak.
90 A2 **Khust** Ukr.
123 C2 **Khutsong** S. Africa
74 D2 **Khuzdar** Pak.
81 D2 **Khvānsār** Iran
81 C2 **Khvormūj** Iran
81 C2 **Khvoy** Iran
89 D2 **Khvoynaya** Rus. Fed.
77 D3 **Khyber Pass** Afgh./Pak.
53 D2 **Kiama** Austr.
119 D3 **Kiambi** Dem. Rep. Congo
119 D3 **Kibiti** Tanz.
109 D2 **Kičevo** Macedonia
114 C3 **Kidal** Mali
87 D2 **Kidderminster** U.K.
114 A3 **Kidira** Senegal
47 C5 **Kidnappers, Cape** N.Z.
102 C1 **Kiel** Ger.
103 E1 **Kielce** Pol.
98 B1 **Kielder Water** U.K.
90 C1 **Kiev** Ukr.
114 A3 **Kiffa** Maur.
119 D3 **Kigali** Rwanda
119 C3 **Kigoma** Tanz.
88 D2 **Kihnu** i. Estonia
92 I2 **Kiiminki** Fin.
67 B4 **Kii-suidō** sea chan. Japan
109 D1 **Kikinda** Serbia
119 C3 **Kikondja** Dem. Rep. Congo
59 D3 **Kikori** P.N.G.
59 D3 **Kikori** r. P.N.G.
118 B3 **Kikwit** Dem. Rep. Congo
65 B1 **Kilchu** N. Korea
119 C3 **Kilembe** Dem. Rep. Congo
139 E2 **Kilgore** U.S.A.
119 D3 **Kilimanjaro** vol. Tanz.
80 B2 **Kilis** Turkey
91 D3 **Kiliya** Ukr.
97 B2 **Kilkee** Ireland
97 D1 **Kilkeel** U.K.
97 C2 **Kilkenny** Ireland
111 B2 **Kilkís** Greece
97 B1 **Killala Bay** Ireland
97 B2 **Killaloe** Ireland
129 C2 **Killam** Can.
97 B2 **Killarney** Ireland
139 D2 **Killeen** U.S.A.
96 B2 **Killin** U.K.
97 C1 **Killybegs** Ireland
96 B3 **Kilmarnock** U.K.
53 C3 **Kilmore** Austr.
119 D3 **Kilosa** Tanz.
97 B2 **Kilrush** Ireland
119 C3 **Kilwa** Dem. Rep. Congo
119 D3 **Kilwa Masoko** Tanz.
119 D3 **Kimambi** Tanz.
52 A2 **Kimba** Austr.
136 C2 **Kimball** U.S.A.
128 C3 **Kimberley** Can.
122 B2 **Kimberley** S. Africa
50 B1 **Kimberley Plateau** Austr.
65 B1 **Kimch'aek** N. Korea
65 B2 **Kimch'ŏn** S. Korea
127 G2 **Kimmirut** Can.
89 E3 **Kimovsk** Rus. Fed.
118 B3 **Kimpese** Dem. Rep. Congo
89 E2 **Kimry** Rus. Fed.
61 C1 **Kinabalu, Gunung** mt. Sabah Malaysia
128 C2 **Kinbasket Lake** Can.

130 B2 **Kincardine** Can.
62 A1 **Kinchang** Myanmar
119 C3 **Kinda** Dem. Rep. Congo
98 C2 **Kinder Scout** h. U.K.
129 D2 **Kindersley** Can.
114 A3 **Kindia** Guinea
119 C3 **Kindu** Dem. Rep. Congo
86 D3 **Kineshma** Rus. Fed.
51 E2 **Kingaroy** Austr.
135 B3 **King City** U.S.A.
130 C1 **King George Islands** Can.
88 C2 **Kingisepp** Rus. Fed.
51 D3 **King Island** Austr.
50 B1 **King Leopold Ranges** hills Austr.
138 A1 **Kingman** U.S.A.
135 B3 **Kings** r. U.S.A.
52 A3 **Kingscote** Austr.
99 D2 **King's Lynn** U.K.
48 F3 **Kingsmill Group** is Kiribati
50 B1 **King Sound** b. Austr.
134 D2 **Kings Peak** U.S.A.
143 D1 **Kingsport** U.S.A.
130 C2 **Kingston** Can.
146 C3 **Kingston** Jamaica
141 E2 **Kingston** U.S.A.
52 A3 **Kingston South East** Austr.
98 C2 **Kingston upon Hull** U.K.
147 D3 **Kingstown** St Vincent
139 D3 **Kingsville** U.S.A.
99 B3 **Kingswood** U.K.
96 B2 **Kingussie** U.K.
126 F2 **King William Island** Can.
123 C3 **King William's Town** S. Africa
67 D3 **Kinka-san** i. Japan
93 F4 **Kinna** Sweden
97 B3 **Kinsale** Ireland
118 B3 **Kinshasa** Dem. Rep. Congo
143 E1 **Kinston** U.S.A.
88 B2 **Kintai** Lith.
114 B4 **Kintampo** Ghana
96 B3 **Kintyre** pen. U.K.
62 A1 **Kin-U** Myanmar
130 C2 **Kipawa, Lac** l. Can.
83 I3 **Kipensk** Rus. Fed.
89 E3 **Kireyevsk** Rus. Fed.
  Kirghizia country Asia see Kyrgyzstan
49 G3 **Kiribati** country Pacific Ocean
80 B2 **Kırıkkale** Turkey
89 E2 **Kirillov** Rus. Fed.
  Kirin China see Jilin
  Kirinyaga mt. Kenya see Kenya, Mount
89 D2 **Kirishi** Rus. Fed.
49 H2 **Kiritimati** atoll Kiribati
111 C2 **Kırkağaç** Turkey
96 C2 **Kirkcaldy** U.K.
96 B3 **Kirkcudbright** U.K.
92 J2 **Kirkenes** Norway
130 B2 **Kirkland Lake** Can.
137 D2 **Kirksville** U.S.A.
81 C2 **Kirkūk** Iraq
96 C1 **Kirkwall** U.K.
89 D3 **Kirov** Kaluzhskaya Oblast' Rus. Fed.
86 D3 **Kirov** Rus. Fed.
86 E3 **Kirovo-Chepetsk** Rus. Fed.
91 C1 **Kirovohrad** Ukr.
86 C2 **Kirovsk** Rus. Fed.
91 D2 **Kirovs'ke** Ukr.
74 A2 **Kirthar Range** mts Pak.
92 H2 **Kiruna** Sweden
67 C3 **Kiryū** Japan

89 E2 **Kirzhach** Rus. Fed.
119 C2 **Kisangani** Dem. Rep. Congo
118 B3 **Kisantu** Dem. Rep. Congo
60 A1 **Kisaran** Indon.
82 G3 **Kiselevsk** Rus. Fed.
75 C2 **Kishanganj** India
115 C4 **Kishi** Nigeria
  Kishinev Moldova see Chişinău
77 D1 **Kishkenekol'** Kazakh.
74 B1 **Kishtwar** India
119 D3 **Kisii** Kenya
103 D2 **Kiskunfélegyháza** Hungary
103 D2 **Kiskunhalas** Hungary
89 D3 **Kislovodsk** Rus. Fed.
117 C5 **Kismaayo** Somalia
119 C3 **Kisoro** Uganda
111 B3 **Kissamos** Greece
114 A4 **Kissidougou** Guinea
143 D3 **Kissimmee** U.S.A.
143 D3 **Kissimmee, Lake** U.S.A.
129 D2 **Kississing Lake** Can.
119 D3 **Kisumu** Kenya
114 B3 **Kita** Mali
66 D3 **Kitakami** Japan
66 D3 **Kitakami-gawa** r. Japan
67 B4 **Kita-Kyūshū** Japan
119 D2 **Kitale** Kenya
66 D2 **Kitami** Japan
130 C2 **Kitchener** Can.
93 J3 **Kitee** Fin.
119 D2 **Kitgum** Uganda
128 B2 **Kitimat** Can.
118 B3 **Kitona** Dem. Rep. Congo
119 D3 **Kitunda** Tanz.
128 B2 **Kitwanga** Can.
121 B2 **Kitwe** Zambia
101 E3 **Kitzingen** Ger.
92 I3 **Kiuruvesi** Fin.
119 C3 **Kivu, Lac** Dem. Rep. Congo/Rwanda
110 C2 **Kıyıköy** Turkey
86 E3 **Kizel** Rus. Fed.
111 C3 **Kızılca Dağ** mt. Turkey
81 C1 **Kizlyar** Rus. Fed.
92 I1 **Kjøllefjord** Norway
92 G2 **Kjøpsvik** Norway
102 C1 **Kladno** Czech Rep.
102 C2 **Klagenfurt** Austria
88 B2 **Klaipėda** Lith.
94 □ **Klaksvík** Faroe Is
134 B2 **Klamath** r. U.S.A.
134 B2 **Klamath Falls** U.S.A.
134 B2 **Klamath Mountains** U.S.A.
60 B1 **Klang** Malaysia
102 C2 **Klatovy** Czech Rep.
122 A3 **Klawer** S. Africa
128 A2 **Klawock** U.S.A.
128 B2 **Kleena Kleene** Can.
122 B2 **Kleinbegin** S. Africa
122 A2 **Kleinsee** S. Africa
123 C2 **Klerksdorp** S. Africa
89 D3 **Kletnya** Rus. Fed.
100 C2 **Kleve** Ger.
89 D3 **Klimavichy** Belarus
89 D3 **Klimovo** Rus. Fed.
89 E2 **Klimovsk** Rus. Fed.
89 E2 **Klin** Rus. Fed.
101 F2 **Klínovec** mt. Czech Rep.
93 G4 **Klintehamn** Sweden
89 D3 **Klintsy** Rus. Fed.
109 C2 **Ključ** Bos.-Herz.
103 D1 **Kłodzko** Pol.
100 C1 **Kloosterhaar** Neth.
103 D2 **Klosterneuburg** Austria
101 E1 **Klötze (Altmark)** Ger.
103 D1 **Kluczbork** Pol.
128 A2 **Klukwan** U.S.A.

Klyetsk

88 C3 **Klyetsk** Belarus
98 C1 **Knaresborough** U.K.
93 F3 **Knästen** h. Sweden
129 E2 **Knee Lake** Can.
101 E1 **Knesebeck** Ger.
101 E3 **Knetzgau** Ger.
109 C2 **Knin** Croatia
103 C2 **Knittelfeld** Austria
109 D2 **Knjaževac** Serbia
100 A2 **Knokke-Heist** Belgium
143 D1 **Knoxville** U.S.A.
122 B3 **Knysna** S. Africa
76 B1 **Kobda** Kazakh.
67 C4 **Kōbe** Japan
    København Denmark *see* **Copenhagen**
100 C2 **Koblenz** Ger.
59 C3 **Kobroör** i. Indon.
88 B3 **Kobryn** Belarus
109 D2 **Kočani** Macedonia
111 C2 **Kocasu** r. Turkey
75 C2 **Koch Bihar** India
73 B4 **Kochi** India
67 B4 **Kōchi** Japan
87 D4 **Kochubey** Rus. Fed.
75 C2 **Kodarma** India
117 B4 **Kodok** S. Sudan
90 B2 **Kodyma** Ukr.
111 C2 **Kodzhaele** mt. Bulg./Greece
65 A2 **Koës** Namibia
122 C2 **Koffiefontein** S. Africa
114 B4 **Koforidua** Ghana
67 C3 **Kōfu** Japan
131 D1 **Kogaluk** r. Can.
117 B5 **Kogelo** Kenya
74 B1 **Kohat** Pak.
62 A1 **Kohima** India
88 C2 **Kohtla-Järve** Estonia
92 H3 **Kokkola** Fin.
140 B2 **Kokomo** U.S.A.
77 E2 **Kokpekty** Kazakh.
77 C1 **Kokshetau** Kazakh.
131 D1 **Koksoak** r. Can.
123 C3 **Kokstad** S. Africa
    Koktokay China *see* **Fuyun**
58 C3 **Kolaka** Indon.
86 C2 **Kola Peninsula** Rus. Fed.
92 H2 **Kolari** Fin.
114 A3 **Kolda** Senegal
93 E4 **Kolding** Denmark
107 D2 **Koléa** Alg.
86 D2 **Kolguyev, Ostrov** i. Rus. Fed.
73 B3 **Kolhapur** India
88 B2 **Kolkasrags** pt Latvia
75 C2 **Kolkata** India
    Kollam India *see* **Kollam**
73 B4 **Kollam** India
    Köln Ger. *see* **Cologne**
103 D1 **Kołobrzeg** Pol.
114 B3 **Kolokani** Mali
89 E2 **Kolomna** Rus. Fed.
90 B2 **Kolomyya** Ukr.
122 B2 **Kolonkwaneng** Botswana
82 G3 **Kolpashevo** Rus. Fed.
89 E3 **Kolpino** Rus. Fed.
    Kol'skiy Poluostrov pen. Rus. Fed. *see* **Kola Peninsula**
78 B3 **Koluli** Eritrea
119 C4 **Kolwezi** Dem. Rep. Congo
83 L2 **Kolyma** r. Rus. Fed.
83 L2 **Kolymskaya Nizmennost'** lowland Rus. Fed.
83 M2 **Kolymskiy, Khrebet** mts Rus. Fed.
83 M3 **Komaki** Japan
83 M3 **Komandorskiye Ostrova** is Rus. Fed.

103 D2 **Komárno** Slovakia
123 D2 **Komati** r. S. Africa/Swaziland
67 C3 **Komatsu** Japan
119 C3 **Kombe** Dem. Rep. Congo
90 C2 **Kominternivs'ke** Ukr.
109 C2 **Komiža** Croatia
103 D2 **Komló** Hungary
118 B3 **Komono** Congo
111 C2 **Komotini** Greece
122 B3 **Komsberg** mts S. Africa
83 H1 **Komsomolets, Ostrov** i. Rus. Fed.
89 F2 **Komsomol'sk** Rus. Fed.
91 C2 **Komsomol's'k** Ukr.
87 D4 **Komsomol'skiy** Rus. Fed.
69 E1 **Komsomol'sk-na-Amure** Rus. Fed.
89 E2 **Konakovo** Rus. Fed.
75 C3 **Kondagaon** India
86 F2 **Kondinskoye** Rus. Fed.
119 D3 **Kondoa** Tanz.
86 C2 **Kondopoga** Rus. Fed.
89 E3 **Kondrovo** Rus. Fed.
127 I2 **Kong Christian IX Land** reg. Greenland
127 I2 **Kong Frederik VI Kyst** coastal area Greenland
65 B2 **Kongju** S. Korea
119 C3 **Kongolo** Dem. Rep. Congo
93 E4 **Kongsberg** Norway
93 F3 **Kongsvinger** Norway
77 D3 **Kongur Shan** mt. China
100 C2 **Königswinter** Ger.
103 D1 **Konin** Pol.
109 C2 **Konjic** Bos.-Herz.
122 A2 **Konkiep** watercourse Namibia
91 C1 **Konotop** Ukr.
102 B2 **Konstanz** Ger.
115 C3 **Kontagora** Nigeria
63 B2 **Kon Tum** Vietnam
63 B2 **Kon Tum, Cao Nguyên** plat. Vietnam
80 B2 **Konya** Turkey
100 C3 **Konz** Ger.
86 E3 **Konzhakovskiy Kamen', Gora** mt. Rus. Fed.
134 C1 **Kooskia** U.S.A.
128 C3 **Kootenay Lake** Can.
122 B3 **Kootjieskolk** S. Africa
92 □B2 **Kópasker** Iceland
108 B1 **Koper** Slovenia
93 G4 **Kopparberg** Sweden
109 C1 **Koprivnica** Croatia
89 F3 **Korablino** Rus. Fed.
73 C3 **Koraput** India
101 D2 **Korbach** Ger.
109 D2 **Korçë** Albania
109 C2 **Korčula** Croatia
109 C2 **Korčula** i. Croatia
70 C2 **Korea Bay** g. China/N. Korea
65 B3 **Korea Strait** Japan/S. Korea
91 D2 **Korenovsk** Rus. Fed.
90 B1 **Korets'** Ukr.
111 C2 **Körfez** Turkey
114 B4 **Korhogo** Côte d'Ivoire
    Korinthos Greece *see* **Corinth**
103 D2 **Köris-hegy** h. Hungary
109 D2 **Koritnik** mt. Albania/Kosovo
67 D3 **Kōriyama** Japan
80 B2 **Korkuteli** Turkey
68 B2 **Korla** China
103 D2 **Körmend** Hungary
114 B3 **Koro** Mali
131 D1 **Koroc** r. Can.
91 D1 **Korocha** Rus. Fed.
119 D3 **Korogwe** Tanz.
59 C2 **Koror** Palau

90 B1 **Korosten'** Ukr.
90 B1 **Korostyshiv** Ukr.
115 D3 **Koro Toro** Chad
91 C2 **Korsun'-Shevchenkivs'kyy** Ukr.
103 E1 **Korsze** Pol.
100 A2 **Kortrijk** Belgium
83 L3 **Koryakskaya, Sopka** vol. Rus. Fed.
83 M2 **Koryakskoye Nagor'ye** mts Rus. Fed.
89 D2 **Koryazhma** Rus. Fed.
65 B2 **Koryŏng** S. Korea
91 C1 **Koryukivka** Ukr.
111 C3 **Kos** Greece
111 C3 **Kos** i. Greece
65 B2 **Kosan** N. Korea
103 D1 **Kościan** Pol.
53 C3 **Kosciuszko, Mount** Austr.
68 B1 **Kosh-Agach** Rus. Fed.
103 E2 **Košice** Slovakia
92 H2 **Koskullskulle** Sweden
65 B2 **Kosŏng** N. Korea
109 D2 **Kosovo** country Europe
    Kosovska Mitrovica Kosovo *see* **Mitrovicë**
48 E2 **Kosrae** atoll Micronesia
114 B4 **Kossou, Lac de** l. Côte d'Ivoire
76 C1 **Kostanay** Kazakh.
110 B2 **Kostenets** Bulg.
123 C2 **Koster** S. Africa
117 B3 **Kosti** Sudan
86 C2 **Kostomuksha** Rus. Fed.
90 B1 **Kostopil'** Ukr.
89 F2 **Kostroma** Rus. Fed.
89 F2 **Kostroma** r. Rus. Fed.
102 C1 **Kostrzyn** Pol.
103 D1 **Koszalin** Pol.
103 D2 **Kőszeg** Hungary
74 B2 **Kota** India
60 B2 **Kotaagung** Indon.
61 C2 **Kotabaru** Indon.
61 C1 **Kota Belud** Sabah Malaysia
60 B1 **Kota Bharu** Malaysia
60 B2 **Kotabumi** Indon.
61 C1 **Kota Kinabalu** Sabah Malaysia
61 C1 **Kota Samarahan** Sarawak Malaysia
86 D3 **Kotel'nich** Rus. Fed.
87 D4 **Kotel'nikovo** Rus. Fed.
83 K1 **Kotel'nyy, Ostrov** i. Rus. Fed.
101 E2 **Köthen (Anhalt)** Ger.
93 I3 **Kotka** Fin.
86 D3 **Kotlas** Rus. Fed.
109 C2 **Kotor Varoš** Bos.-Herz.
87 D3 **Kotovo** Rus. Fed.
91 E1 **Kotovsk** Rus. Fed.
90 B2 **Kotovs'k** Ukr.
100 A2 **Koudekerke** Neth.
114 B3 **Koudougou** Burkina Faso
122 B3 **Kougaberge** mts S. Africa
118 B3 **Koulamoutou** Gabon
114 B3 **Koulikoro** Mali
114 A3 **Koundâra** Guinea
151 C1 **Kourou** Fr. Guiana
114 B3 **Kouroussa** Guinea
115 D3 **Kousséri** Cameroon
114 B3 **Koutiala** Mali
93 I3 **Kouvola** Fin.
92 J2 **Kovdor** Rus. Fed.
90 A1 **Kovel'** Ukr.
89 F2 **Kovrov** Rus. Fed.
54 B2 **Kowhitirangi** N.Z.
    Koyamutthoor India *see* **Coimbatore**
111 C3 **Köyceğiz** Turkey
86 D2 **Koyda** Rus. Fed.

126 A2 Koyukuk *r.* U.S.A.
111 B2 Kozani Greece
89 E3 Kozelets' Ukr.
73 B3 Kozhikode India
90 B2 Kozyatyn Ukr.
63 A3 Krabi Thai.
63 A3 Kra Buri Thai.
63 A4 Krâchéh Cambodia
93 E4 Kragerø Norway
100 B1 Kraggenburg Neth.
109 D2 Kragujevac Serbia
60 B2 Krakatau *i.* Indon.
103 D1 Kraków Pol.
91 D2 Kramators'k Ukr.
93 G3 Kramfors Sweden
111 B3 Kranidi Greece
86 E1 Krasino Rus. Fed.
88 C2 Krāslava Latvia
101 F2 Kraslice Czech Rep.
89 D3 Krasnapollye Belarus
87 D3 Krasnaya Gora Rus. Fed.
89 D3 Krasnoarmeysk Rus. Fed.
91 D2 Krasnoarmiys'k Ukr.
86 D2 Krasnoborsk Rus. Fed.
91 D2 Krasnodar Rus. Fed.
91 D2 Krasnodarskoye
       Vodokhranilishche *resr*
       Rus. Fed.
91 D2 Krasnodon Ukr.
88 C2 Krasnogorodsk Rus. Fed.
91 D2 Krasnohrad Ukr.
91 D2 Krasnohvardiys'ke Ukr.
86 E3 Krasnokamsk Rus. Fed.
89 D2 Krasnomayskiy Rus. Fed.
91 C2 Krasnoperekops'k Ukr.
87 D3 Krasnoslobodsk Rus. Fed.
86 E3 Krasnoufimsk Rus. Fed.
83 H3 Krasnoyarsk Rus. Fed.
89 F2 Krasnoye-na-Volge Rus. Fed.
89 D3 Krasnyy Rus. Fed.
89 E3 Krasnyy Kholm Rus. Fed.
91 D2 Krasnyy Luch Ukr.
91 E2 Krasnyy Sulin Rus. Fed.
90 B2 Krasyliv Ukr.
100 C2 Krefeld Ger.
91 C2 Kremenchuk Ukr.
91 C2 Kremenchuts'ke
       Vodoskhovyshche *resr* Ukr.
103 D2 Křemešník *h.* Czech Rep.
91 D2 Kreminna Ukr.
103 D2 Krems an der Donau Austria
89 D2 Kresttsy Rus. Fed.
88 B2 Kretinga Lith.
100 C2 Kreuzau Ger.
100 C2 Kreuztal Ger.
118 A2 Kribi Cameroon
111 B3 Krikellos Greece
66 D1 Kril'on, Mys *c.* Rus. Fed.
73 C3 Krishna *r.* India
73 C3 Krishna, Mouths of the India
75 C2 Krishnanagar India
93 E4 Kristiansand Norway
93 F4 Kristianstad Sweden
92 E3 Kristiansund Norway
93 F4 Kristinehamn Sweden
111 C3 Kriti *i.* Greece *see* Crete
111 C3 Kritiko Pelagos *sea* Greece
       Krivoy Rog Ukr. *see* Kryvyy Rih
109 C1 Križevci Croatia
108 B1 Krk *i.* Croatia
92 F3 Krokom Sweden
91 C2 Krolevets' Ukr.
101 E2 Kronach Ger.
63 B2 Krŏng Kaôh Kŏng Cambodia
127 I2 Kronprins Frederik Bjerge
       nunataks Greenland

123 C2 Kroonstad S. Africa
87 D4 Kropotkin Rus. Fed.
103 E2 Krosno Pol.
103 D1 Krotoszyn Pol.
60 B2 Krui Indon.
109 C2 Krujë Albania
111 C2 Krumovgrad Bulg.
       Krung Thep Thai. *see* Bangkok
88 C3 Krupki Belarus
109 D2 Kruševac Serbia
101 F2 Krušné hory *mts* Czech Rep.
128 A2 Kruzof Island U.S.A.
88 D2 Krychaw Belarus
91 D3 Krymsk Rus. Fed.
91 C2 Kryvyy Rih Ukr.
114 B2 Ksabi Alg.
107 D2 Ksar el Boukhari Alg.
114 B1 Ksar el Kebir Morocco
89 E3 Kshenskiy Rus. Fed.
78 B2 Kü', Jabal al *h.* Saudi Arabia
61 C1 Kuala Belait Brunei
60 B1 Kuala Kerai Malaysia
60 B1 Kuala Lipis Malaysia
60 B1 Kuala Lumpur Malaysia
61 C2 Kuala Terengganu Malaysia
60 B1 Kualatungal Indon.
61 C2 Kuamut *Sabah* Malaysia
85 A1 Kuandian China
60 B1 Kuantan Malaysia
91 D2 Kuban' *r.* Rus. Fed.
89 E2 Kubenskoye, Ozero *l.* Rus. Fed.
110 C2 Kubrat Bulg.
61 C1 Kubuang Indon.
61 C1 Kuching *Sarawak* Malaysia
109 C2 Kuçovë Albania
61 C1 Kudat *Sabah* Malaysia
61 C2 Kudus Indon.
102 C2 Kufstein Austria
127 F2 Kugaaruk Can.
126 D2 Kugluktuk Can.
92 I3 Kuhmo Fin.
79 C2 Kührān, Kūh-e *mt.* Iran
       Kuitin China *see* Kuytun
120 A2 Kuito Angola
92 I2 Kuivaniemi Fin.
65 B2 Kujang N. Korea
109 D2 Kukës Albania
111 C3 Kula Turkey
75 D2 Kula Kangri *mt.* Bhutan/China
76 B2 Kulandy Kazakh.
88 B2 Kuldīga Latvia
122 B1 Kule Botswana
101 E2 Kulmbach Ger.
77 C3 Kŭlob Tajik.
76 B2 Kul'sary Kazakh.
71 H1 Kulunda Rus. Fed.
114 B4 Kulusuk Greenland
67 C3 Kumagaya Japan
67 B4 Kumamoto Japan
109 D2 Kumanovo Macedonia
114 B4 Kumasi Ghana
118 A2 Kumba Cameroon
78 A2 Kumdah Saudi Arabia
87 E3 Kumertau Rus. Fed.
65 B2 Kumi S. Korea
93 G4 Kumla Sweden
115 D3 Kumo Nigeria
62 A1 Kumon Range *mts* Myanmar
       Kumul China *see* Hami
66 D2 Kunashir, Ostrov *i.* Rus. Fed.
120 A2 Kunene *r.* Angola/Namibia
77 D2 Kungei Alatau *mts* Kazakh./
       Kyrg.
93 F4 Kungsbacka Sweden
118 B2 Kungu Dem. Rep. Congo

86 E3 Kungur Rus. Fed.
62 A1 Kunhing Myanmar
77 D3 Kunlun Shan *mts* China
62 B1 Kunming China
65 B2 Kunsan S. Korea
50 B1 Kununurra Austr.
92 I3 Kuopio Fin.
109 C1 Kupa *r.* Croatia/Slovenia
59 C3 Kupang Indon.
88 B2 Kupiškis Lith.
111 C2 Küplü Turkey
128 A2 Kupreanof Island U.S.A.
91 D2 Kup"yans'k Ukr.
77 E2 Kuqa China
67 B4 Kurashiki Japan
67 B3 Kurayoshi Japan
89 E3 Kurchatov Rus. Fed.
110 C2 Kürdzhali Bulg.
67 B4 Kure Japan
88 B2 Kuressaare Estonia
86 F3 Kurgan Rus. Fed.
93 H3 Kurikka Fin.
156 C1 Kuril Trench N. Pacific Ocean
89 E3 Kurkino Rus. Fed.
117 B3 Kurmuk Sudan
73 B3 Kurnool India
67 D3 Kuroiso Japan
53 D2 Kurri Kurri Austr.
89 E3 Kursk Rus. Fed.
122 B2 Kuruman S. Africa
122 B2 Kuruman *watercourse* S. Africa
67 B4 Kurume Japan
83 I3 Kurumkan Rus. Fed.
73 C4 Kurunegala Sri Lanka
111 C3 Kuşadası Turkey
111 C3 Kuşadası Körfezi *b.* Turkey
111 C2 Kuş Gölü *l.* Turkey
91 D2 Kushchevskaya Rus. Fed.
66 D2 Kushiro Japan
75 C2 Kushtia Bangl.
76 C1 Kusmuryn Kazakh.
66 D2 Kussharo-ko *l.* Japan
111 C3 Kütahya Turkey
81 C1 Kutaisi Georgia
109 C1 Kutjevo Croatia
103 D1 Kutno Pol.
118 B3 Kutu Dem. Rep. Congo
126 D2 Kuujjua *r.* Can.
131 D1 Kuujjuaq Can.
130 C1 Kuujjuarapik Can.
92 I2 Kuusamo Fin.
120 A2 Kuvango Angola
89 D2 Kuvshinovo Rus. Fed.
78 B2 Kuwait *country* Asia
79 B2 Kuwait Kuwait
       Kuybyshev Rus. Fed. *see*
       Samara
91 D2 Kuybysheve Ukr.
87 D3 Kuybyshevskoye
       Vodokhranilishche *resr*
       Rus. Fed.
77 E2 Kuytun China
111 C3 Kuyucak Turkey
87 D3 Kuznetsk Rus. Fed.
90 B1 Kuznetsovs'k Ukr.
92 H1 Kvalsund Norway
123 D2 KwaDukuza S. Africa
123 D2 KwaMashu S. Africa
65 B2 Kwangju S. Korea
65 B1 Kwanmo-bong *mt.* N. Korea
123 C3 KwaNobuhle S. Africa
123 C3 KwaNonzame S. Africa
123 C3 Kwatinidubu S. Africa
123 C2 KwaZamokuhle S. Africa
123 D2 KwaZulu-Natal *prov.* S. Africa
121 B2 Kwekwe Zimbabwe
118 B3 Kwenge *r.* Dem. Rep. Congo

103 D1 Kwidzyn Pol.
118 B3 Kwilu r. Angola/Dem. Rep. Congo
59 C3 Kwoka mt. Indon.
53 C3 Kyabram Austr.
62 A2 Kyaikto Myanmar
69 D1 Kyakhta Rus. Fed.
52 A2 Kyancutta Austr.
62 A1 Kyaukpadaung Myanmar
62 A2 Kyaukpyu Myanmar
88 B3 Kybartai Lith.
62 A2 Kyebogyi Myanmar
62 A2 Kyeintali Myanmar
74 B1 Kyelang India
Kyiv Ukr. see Kiev
90 C1 Kyiv'ske Vodoskhovyshche resr Ukr.
Kyklades is Greece see Cyclades
129 C2 Kyle Can.
96 B2 Kyle of Lochalsh U.K.
100 C3 Kyll r. Ger.
111 B3 Kyllini mt. Greece
111 B3 Kymi Greece
52 B3 Kyneton Austr.
119 C2 Kyoga, Lake Uganda
53 D1 Kyogle Austr.
65 B2 Kyŏnggi-man b. S. Korea
65 B2 Kyŏngju S. Korea
67 C4 Kyōto Japan
111 B3 Kyparissia Greece
111 B3 Kyra Panagia i. Greece
80 B2 Kyrenia Cyprus
77 D2 Kyrgyzstan country Asia
101 F1 Kyritz Ger.
92 H3 Kyrönjoki r. Fin.
86 E2 Kyrta Rus. Fed.
86 D2 Kyssa Rus. Fed.
111 B3 Kythira i. Greece
111 B3 Kythnos i. Greece
128 B2 Kyuquot Can.
67 B4 Kyūshū i. Japan
110 B2 Kyustendil Bulg.
92 H3 Kyyjärvi Fin.
68 C1 Kyzyl Rus. Fed.
76 C2 Kyzylkum Desert Kazakh./Uzbek.
77 C2 Kyzylorda Kazakh.

L

145 C3 La Angostura, Presa de resr Mex.
117 C4 Laascaanood Somalia
150 B1 La Asunción Venez.
114 A2 Laâyoune Western Sahara
87 D4 Laba r. Rus. Fed.
144 B2 La Babia Mex.
146 B3 La Bahía, Islas de is Hond.
152 B3 La Banda Arg.
104 B2 La Baule-Escoublac France
114 A3 Labé Guinea
128 A1 Laberge, Lake Can.
129 C2 La Biche, Lac l. Can.
87 D4 Labinsk Rus. Fed.
64 B1 Labo Phil.
104 B3 Labouheyre France
131 C1 Labrador reg. Can.
131 C1 Labrador City Can.
158 C1 Labrador Sea Can./Greenland
150 B2 Lábrea Brazil
61 C1 Labuan Malaysia
60 B1 Labuanbilik Indon.
59 C3 Labuna Indon.
63 A2 Labutta Myanmar
86 F2 Labytnangi Rus. Fed.

109 C2 Laç Albania
105 C2 La Capelle France
73 B3 Laccadive Islands India
129 E2 Lac du Bonnet Can.
146 B3 La Ceiba Hond.
53 B2 Lachlan r. Austr.
141 E1 Lachute Can.
105 D3 La Ciotat France
129 C2 Lac la Biche Can.
La la Martre Can. see Whatì
141 E1 Lac-Mégantic Can.
128 C2 Lacombe Can.
146 B4 La Concepción Panama
145 C3 La Concordia Mex.
108 A3 Laconi Sardegna Italy
141 E2 Laconia U.S.A.
128 C2 La Crete Can.
140 A2 La Crosse U.S.A.
144 B2 La Cruz Mex.
144 B2 La Cuesta Mex.
75 B1 Ladakh Range mts India/Pak.
122 B3 Ladismith S. Africa
79 D2 Lādīz Iran
86 C2 Ladoga, Lake Rus. Fed.
Ladozhskoye Ozero l. Rus. Fed. see Ladoga, Lake
128 B3 Ladysmith Can.
123 C2 Ladysmith S. Africa
59 D3 Lae P.N.G.
152 B3 La Esmeralda Bol.
93 F4 Læsø i. Denmark
143 C2 La Fayette U.S.A.
140 B2 Lafayette IN U.S.A.
142 B2 Lafayette LA U.S.A.
115 C4 Lafia Nigeria
104 B2 La Flèche France
143 D1 La Follette U.S.A.
131 C1 Laforge Can.
79 C2 Lāft Iran
108 A3 La Galite i. Tunisia
81 C1 Lagan' Rus. Fed.
118 B2 Lagdo, Lac de l. Cameroon
115 C1 Laghouat Alg.
155 D1 Lagoa Santa Brazil
114 A2 La Gomera i. Islas Canarias
114 C4 Lagos Nigeria
106 B2 Lagos Port.
134 C1 La Grande U.S.A.
130 C1 La Grande 3, Réservoir resr Can.
131 C1 La Grande 4, Réservoir resr Can.
50 B1 La Grange Austr.
143 C2 La Grange U.S.A.
150 B1 La Gran Sabana plat. Venez.
152 D3 Laguna Brazil
144 A2 Laguna, Picacho de la mt. Mex.
150 A2 Lagunas Peru
61 C1 La Habana Cuba see Havana
60 B2 Lahad Datu Sabah Malaysia
78 B3 Lahat Indon.
81 C2 Laḥij Yemen
81 C2 Lāhījān Iran
100 C2 Lahnstein Ger.
74 B1 Lahore Pak.
74 A2 Lahri Pak.
93 I3 Lahti Fin.
115 D4 Laï Chad
53 D1 Laidley Austr.
104 C2 L'Aigle France
111 B3 Laimos, Akrotirio pt Greece
122 B3 Laingsburg S. Africa
92 H2 Lainioälven r. Sweden
96 B1 Lairg U.K.
108 B1 Laives Italy
70 B2 Laiwu China
70 C2 Laiyang China

70 B2 Laizhou China
70 B2 Laizhou Wan b. China
50 C1 Lajamanu Austr.
152 C3 Lajes Brazil
144 B2 La Junta Mex.
136 C3 La Junta U.S.A.
121 C2 Lake Cabora Bassa resr Moz.
53 C2 Lake Cargelligo Austr.
53 D2 Lake Cathie Austr.
142 B2 Lake Charles U.S.A.
143 D2 Lake City FL U.S.A.
143 E2 Lake City SC U.S.A.
108 A1 Lake Como Italy
128 B3 Lake Cowichan Can.
108 B1 Lake Garda Italy
138 A2 Lake Havasu City U.S.A.
143 D3 Lakeland U.S.A.
128 C2 Lake Louise Can.
134 B1 Lake Oswego U.S.A.
54 A2 Lake Paringa N.Z.
142 B2 Lake Providence U.S.A.
54 B2 Lake Pukaki N.Z.
53 C3 Lakes Entrance Austr.
134 B2 Lakeview U.S.A.
136 B3 Lakewood CO U.S.A.
141 E2 Lakewood NJ U.S.A.
143 D3 Lake Worth U.S.A.
74 A2 Lakhpat India
74 B1 Lakki Marwat Pak.
111 B3 Lakonikos Kolpos b. Greece
92 H1 Lakselv Norway
107 C1 L'Alcora Spain
145 C3 La Libertad Guat.
106 B1 Lalín Spain
75 B2 Lalitpur India
129 D2 La Loche Can.
100 B2 La Louvière Belgium
108 A2 La Maddalena Sardegna Italy
61 C1 Lamag Sabah Malaysia
La Manche str. France/U.K. see English Channel
136 C3 Lamar U.S.A.
79 C2 Lamerd Iran
108 A3 La Marmora, Punta mt. Sardegna Italy
128 C1 La Martre, Lac l. Can.
118 B3 Lambaréné Gabon
122 A3 Lambert's Bay S. Africa
92 □A2 Lambeyri Iceland
106 B1 Lamego Port.
150 A3 La Merced Peru
52 B3 Lameroo Austr.
139 C2 Lamesa U.S.A.
111 B3 Lamia Greece
137 E2 Lamoni U.S.A.
62 A2 Lampang Thai.
139 D2 Lampasas U.S.A.
145 B2 Lampazos Mex.
99 A2 Lampeter U.K.
62 A2 Lamphun Thai.
119 E3 Lamu Kenya
62 A2 Lan, Loi mt. Myanmar/Thai.
96 C3 Lanark U.K.
63 A2 Lanbi Kyun i. Myanmar
Lancang Jiang r. China see Mekong
98 B1 Lancaster U.K.
135 C4 Lancaster CA U.S.A.
140 C3 Lancaster OH U.S.A.
141 D2 Lancaster PA U.S.A.
143 D2 Lancaster SC U.S.A.
127 F2 Lancaster Sound str. Can.
Lanchow China see Lanzhou
102 C2 Landeck Austria
136 B2 Lander U.S.A.
99 A3 Land's End pt U.K.
102 C2 Landshut Ger.

93 F4 Landskrona Sweden
143 C2 Lanett U.S.A.
122 B2 Langberg mts S. Africa
137 D1 Langdon U.S.A.
93 F4 Langeland i. Denmark
101 D1 Langen Ger.
100 C1 Langeoog Ger.
100 C1 Langeoog i. Ger.
101 D2 Langgöns Ger.
129 D2 Langham Can.
92 □A3 Langjökull Iceland
105 C3 Langogne France
104 B3 Langon France
105 D2 Langres France
60 A1 Langsa Indon.
62 B1 Lang Son Vietnam
101 D1 Langwedel Ger.
129 D2 Lanigan Can.
153 A4 Lanín, Volcán vol.
       Arg./Chile
81 C2 Länkäran Azer.
104 B2 Lannion France
140 C2 Lansing U.S.A.
71 B3 Lanxi China
117 B4 Lanya S. Sudan
114 A2 Lanzarote i. Islas Canarias
70 A2 Lanzhou China
62 B1 Laoag City Phil.
62 B1 Lao Cai Vietnam
70 B2 Laohekou China
68 C2 Laojunmiao China
65 B1 Laoling China
65 B1 Lao Ling mts China
68 C2 Lao Mangnai China
105 C2 Laon France
62 B2 Laos country Asia
65 B1 Laotougou China
154 C3 Lapa Brazil
114 A2 La Palma i. Islas Canarias
146 C4 La Palma Panama
150 B1 La Paragua Venez.
152 B2 La Paz Bol.
144 A2 La Paz Mex.
66 D1 La Pedrera Col.
       La Pérouse Strait Japan/
       Rus. Fed.
145 C2 La Pesca Mex.
144 B2 La Piedad Mex.
153 C4 La Plata Arg.
153 C4 La Plata, Río de sea chan.
       Arg./Uru.
106 B1 La Pola Spain
93 I3 Lappeenranta Fin.
92 G2 Lappland reg. Europe
111 C2 Lâpseki Turkey
83 J1 Laptev Sea Rus. Fed.
       Laptevykh, More sea Rus. Fed.
       see Laptev Sea
92 H3 Lapua Fin.
152 B3 La Quiaca Arg.
79 C2 Lār Iran
114 B1 Larache Morocco
136 B2 Laramie U.S.A.
136 B2 Laramie Mountains U.S.A.
154 B3 Laranjeiras do Sul Brazil
59 C3 Larantuka Indon.
59 C3 Larat i. Indon.
107 D2 Larba Alg.
106 C1 Laredo Spain
139 D3 Laredo U.S.A.
96 B3 Largs U.K.
53 La Rioja Arg.
111 B3 Larisa Greece
74 A2 Larkana Pak.
80 B2 Larnaca Cyprus
97 D1 Larne U.K.
100 B2 La Roche-en-Ardenne
       Belgium

104 B2 La Rochelle France
104 B2 La Roche-sur-Yon France
107 C2 La Roda Spain
147 D3 La Romana Dom. Rep.
129 D2 La Ronge Can.
129 D2 La Ronge, Lac l. Can.
50 C1 Larrimah Austr.
55 P3 Larsen Ice Shelf Antarctica
93 F4 Larvik Norway
130 C2 La Sarre Can.
138 B2 Las Cruces U.S.A.
153 C4 Las Flores Arg.
153 B4 Las Heras Arg.
62 A1 Lashio Myanmar
74 A1 Lashkar Gāh Afgh.
109 C3 La Sila reg. Italy
152 B3 Las Lomitas Arg.
144 B2 Las Nieves Mex.
114 A2 Las Palmas de Gran Canaria
       Islas Canarias
108 A2 La Spezia Italy
153 B5 Las Piedras Arg.
129 D2 Last Mountain Lake Can.
152 B3 Las Tórtolas, Cerro mt. Arg./
       Chile
118 B3 Lastoursville Gabon
109 C2 Lastovo i. Croatia
144 A2 Las Tres Vírgenes, Volcán vol.
       Mex.
146 C2 Las Tunas Cuba
144 B2 Las Varas Chihuahua Mex.
144 B2 Las Varas Nayarit Mex.
138 B1 Las Vegas NM U.S.A.
135 C3 Las Vegas NV U.S.A.
131 E1 La Tabatière Can.
80 B2 Latakia Syria
104 B3 La Teste-de-Buch France
108 B2 Latina Italy
147 D3 La Tortuga, Isla i. Venez.
64 B1 La Trinidad Phil.
89 E2 Latskoye Rus. Fed.
131 C2 La Tuque Can.
88 B2 Latvia country Europe
102 C1 Lauchhammer Ger.
106 C1 Laudio Spain
101 E3 Lauf an der Pegnitz Ger.
105 D2 Laufen Switz.
51 D4 Launceston Austr.
99 A3 Launceston U.K.
62 A1 Launggyaung Myanmar
51 D1 Laura Austr.
142 C2 Laurel MS U.S.A.
134 E1 Laurel MT U.S.A.
109 C2 Lauria Italy
143 E2 Laurinburg U.S.A.
105 D2 Lausanne Switz.
61 C2 Laut i. Indon.
61 C2 Laut Bali sea Indon.
101 D2 Lautersbach (Hessen) Ger.
61 C2 Laut Kecil, Kepulauan is
       Indon.
100 C1 Lauwersmeer l. Neth.
104 B2 Laval France
107 C2 La Vall d'Uixó Spain
50 B2 Laverton Austr.
155 D2 Lavras Brazil
123 D2 Lavumisa Swaziland
61 C1 Lawas Sarawak Malaysia
62 A1 Lawksawk Myanmar
114 B3 Lawra Ghana
137 D3 Lawrence U.S.A.
142 C1 Lawrenceburg U.S.A.
139 D2 Lawton U.S.A.
78 A2 Lawz, Jabal al mt.
       Saudi Arabia
93 F4 Laxå Sweden
74 B1 Layyah Pak.

109 D2 Lazarevac Serbia
144 A1 Lázaro Cárdenas Baja
       California Mex.
144 B3 Lázaro Cárdenas Michoacán
       Mex.
88 B3 Lazdijai Lith.
136 C2 Lead U.S.A.
129 D2 Leader Can.
136 B3 Leadville U.S.A.
       Leaf Bay Can. see Tasiujaq
129 D2 Leaf Rapids Can.
97 B2 Leane, Lough l. Ireland
137 E3 Leavenworth U.S.A.
80 B2 Lebanon country Asia
137 E3 Lebanon MO U.S.A.
141 E2 Lebanon NH U.S.A.
134 B2 Lebanon OR U.S.A.
141 D2 Lebanon PA U.S.A.
89 E3 Lebedyan' Rus. Fed.
91 C1 Lebedyn Ukr.
104 C2 Le Blanc France
103 D1 Lębork Pol.
123 C1 Lebowakgomo S. Africa
106 B2 Lebrija Spain
153 A4 Lebu Chile
104 C3 Le Bugue France
109 C2 Lecce Italy
108 A1 Lecco Italy
102 C2 Lech r. Austria/Ger.
111 B3 Lechaina Greece
71 B3 Lechang China
102 B1 Leck Ger.
104 C3 Lectoure France
106 B1 Ledesma Spain
104 C2 Le Dorat France
128 C2 Leduc Can.
137 E1 Leech Lake U.S.A.
98 C2 Leeds U.K.
98 B2 Leek U.K.
100 C1 Leer (Ostfriesland) Ger.
143 D3 Leesburg U.S.A.
142 B2 Leesville U.S.A.
53 C2 Leeton Austr.
122 B3 Leeu-Gamka S. Africa
100 B1 Leeuwarden Neth.
50 A3 Leeuwin, Cape Austr.
147 D3 Leeward Islands Caribbean
       Sea
111 B3 Lefkada Greece
111 B3 Lefkada i. Greece
       Lefkosia Cyprus see
       Nicosia
64 B1 Legazpi Phil.
108 B1 Legnago Italy
103 D1 Legnica Pol.
75 B1 Leh India
104 C2 Le Havre France
122 B1 Lehututu Botswana
109 D2 Leibnitz Austria
99 C2 Leicester U.K.
51 C1 Leichhardt r. Austr.
100 B1 Leiden Neth.
100 A2 Leie r. Belgium
52 A2 Leigh Creek Austr.
93 E3 Leikanger Norway
101 D1 Leine r. Ger.
97 C2 Leinster reg. Ireland
101 F2 Leipzig Ger.
92 F2 Leiranger Norway
106 B2 Leiria Port.
93 E4 Leirvik Norway
97 C2 Leixlip Ireland
71 B3 Leiyang China
71 B3 Leizhou China
71 A3 Leizhou Bandao pen. China
118 B3 Lékana Congo
100 B1 Lelystad Neth.

Le Maire, Estrecho de

153 B6 **Le Maire, Estrecho de**
         sea chan. Arg.
         Léman, Lac *l.* France/Switz. *see*
         Geneva, Lake
104 C2 **Le Mans** France
137 D2 **Le Mars** U.S.A.
154 C2 **Leme** Brazil
         Lemesos Cyprus
         see Limassol
101 D1 **Lemförde** Ger.
127 G2 **Lemieux Islands** Can.
136 C1 **Lemmon** U.S.A.
135 C3 **Lemoore** U.S.A.
131 D1 **Le Moyne, Lac** *l.* Can.
62 A1 **Lemro** *r.* Myanmar
109 C2 **Le Murge** *hills* Italy
83 J2 **Lena** *r.* Rus. Fed.
100 C1 **Lengerich** Ger.
71 B3 **Lengshuijiang** China
91 D2 **Lenine** Ukr.
         Leningrad Rus. Fed. *see*
         St Petersburg
91 D2 **Leningradskaya** Rus. Fed.
77 D3 **Lenin Peak** Kyrg./Tajik.
         Leninsk Kazakh.
         see Baykonyr
89 E3 **Leninskiy** Rus. Fed.
100 A2 **Lens** Belgium
104 C1 **Lens** France
83 I2 **Lensk** Rus. Fed.
103 D2 **Lenti** Hungary
114 B3 **Lentini** *Sicilia* Italy
114 B3 **Léo** Burkina Faso
103 D2 **Leoben** Austria
99 B2 **Leominster** U.K.
144 B2 **León** Mex.
146 B3 **León** Nic.
106 B1 **León** Spain
122 A1 **Leonardville** Namibia
50 B2 **Leonora** Austr.
155 D2 **Leopoldina** Brazil
123 C1 **Lephalale** S. Africa
123 C1 **Lephepe** Botswana
123 C1 **Lephoi** S. Africa
71 B3 **Leping** China
105 C2 **Le Puy-en-Velay** France
150 A2 **Lérida** Col.
106 C1 **Lerma** Spain
111 C3 **Leros** *i.* Greece
130 C1 **Le Roy, Lac** *l.* Can.
93 F4 **Lerum** Sweden
96 □ **Lerwick** U.K.
111 C3 **Lesbos** *i.* Greece
147 C3 **Les Cayes** Haiti
69 C3 **Leshan** China
86 D2 **Leshukonskoye** Rus. Fed.
109 D2 **Leskovac** Serbia
104 B2 **Lesneven** France
89 E2 **Lesnoye** Rus. Fed.
83 H3 **Lesosibirsk** Rus. Fed.
123 C2 **Lesotho** *country* Africa
66 B1 **Lesozavodsk** Rus. Fed.
104 B2 **Les Sables-d'Olonne** France
147 D3 **Lesser Antilles** *is* Caribbean
         Sea
81 C1 **Lesser Caucasus** *mts* Asia
128 C2 **Lesser Slave Lake** Can.
58 B3 **Lesser Sunda Islands** *is* Indon.
105 C3 **Les Vans** France
         Lesvos *i.* Greece *see* Lesbos
103 D1 **Leszno** Pol.
99 C3 **Letchworth Garden City** U.K.
128 C3 **Lethbridge** Can.
150 C1 **Lethem** Guyana
59 C3 **Leti, Kepulauan** *is* Indon.
150 B2 **Leticia** Col.
123 C1 **Letlhakeng** Botswana

104 C1 **Le Touquet-Paris-Plage**
         France
99 D3 **Le Tréport** France
63 A2 **Letsok-aw Kyun** *i.* Myanmar
123 C2 **Letsopa** S. Africa
97 C1 **Letterkenny** Ireland
105 C3 **Leucate, Étang de** *l.* France
60 A1 **Leuser, Gunung** *mt.* Indon.
100 B2 **Leuven** Belgium
92 F3 **Levanger** Norway
139 C2 **Levelland** U.S.A.
50 B1 **Lévêque, Cape** Austr.
100 C2 **Leverkusen** Ger.
103 D2 **Levice** Slovakia
54 C2 **Levin** N.Z.
131 C2 **Lévis** Can.
89 E3 **Lev Tolstoy** Rus. Fed.
99 D3 **Lewes** U.K.
96 A1 **Lewis, Isle of** *i.* U.K.
140 C3 **Lewisburg** U.S.A.
134 D1 **Lewis Range** *mts* U.S.A.
134 C1 **Lewiston** *ID* U.S.A.
141 E2 **Lewiston** *ME* U.S.A.
134 E1 **Lewistown** U.S.A.
140 C3 **Lexington** *KY* U.S.A.
137 D2 **Lexington** *NE* U.S.A.
141 D3 **Lexington** *VA* U.S.A.
64 B1 **Leyte** *i.* Phil.
109 C2 **Lezhë** Albania
89 F2 **Lezhnevo** Rus. Fed.
89 E3 **L'gov** Rus. Fed.
75 C2 **Lhagoi Kangri** *mt.* China
68 C2 **Lharigarbo** China
75 D2 **Lhasa** China
75 C2 **Lhazê** China
60 A1 **Lhokseumawe** Indon.
111 B3 **Liakoura** *mt.* Greece
67 B3 **Liancourt Rocks** *i.* N. Pacific
         Ocean
71 B3 **Lianhua** China
71 B3 **Lianjiang** China
70 C1 **Lianshan** China
70 B2 **Lianyungang** China
71 B3 **Lianzhou** China
70 B2 **Liaocheng** China
70 C1 **Liaodong Bandao** *pen.* China
70 C1 **Liaodong Wan** *b.* China
65 A1 **Liao He** *r.* China
70 C1 **Liaoning** *prov.* China
65 A1 **Liaoyang** China
65 B1 **Liaoyuan** China
128 B1 **Liard** *r.* Can.
134 C1 **Libby** U.S.A.
118 B2 **Libenge** Dem. Rep. Congo
136 C3 **Liberal** U.S.A.
103 D1 **Liberec** Czech Rep.
114 B4 **Liberia** *country* Africa
146 B3 **Liberia** Costa Rica
150 B1 **Libertad** Venez.
100 B3 **Libin** Belgium
118 A2 **Libourne** France
118 A2 **Libreville** Gabon
115 D2 **Libya** *country* Africa
115 E2 **Libyan Desert** Egypt/Libya
116 A1 **Libyan Plateau** Egypt/Libya
108 B3 **Licata** *Sicilia* Italy
         Licheng China *see* Lipu
121 C2 **Lichinga** Moz.
101 E2 **Lichte** Ger.
123 C2 **Lichtenburg** S. Africa
101 E2 **Lichtenfels** Ger.
88 C3 **Lida** Belarus
93 F4 **Lidköping** Sweden
50 C2 **Liebig, Mount** Austr.
105 D2 **Liechtenstein** *country* Europe
100 B2 **Liège** Belgium
92 J3 **Lieksa** Fin.

119 C2 **Lienart** Dem. Rep. Congo
63 B2 **Liên Nghia** Vietnam
102 C2 **Lienz** Austria
88 B2 **Liepāja** Latvia
102 C2 **Liezen** Austria
97 C2 **Liffey** *r.* Ireland
97 C1 **Lifford** Ireland
53 C1 **Lightning Ridge** Austr.
121 C2 **Ligonha** *r.* Moz.
105 D3 **Ligurian Sea** France/Italy
119 C4 **Likasi** Dem. Rep. Congo
128 B2 **Likely** Can.
89 E2 **Likhoslavl'** Rus. Fed.
61 B1 **Liku** Indon.
105 D3 **L'Île-Rousse** *Corse* France
71 B3 **Liling** China
93 F4 **Lilla Edet** Sweden
100 B2 **Lille** Belgium
105 C1 **Lille** France
         Lille Bælt *sea chan.* Denmark
         see Little Belt
93 F3 **Lillehammer** Norway
93 F4 **Lillestrøm** Norway
128 B2 **Lillooet** Can.
121 C2 **Lilongwe** Malawi
64 B2 **Liloy** Phil.
150 A3 **Lima** Peru
140 C2 **Lima** U.S.A.
80 B2 **Limassol** Cyprus
97 C1 **Limavady** U.K.
54 A1 **Limay** *r.* Arg.
101 F2 **Limbach-Oberfrohna** Ger.
88 B2 **Limbaži** Latvia
118 A2 **Limbe** Cameroon
100 D2 **Limburg an der Lahn** Ger.
122 B2 **Lime Acres** S. Africa
154 C2 **Limeira** Brazil
97 B2 **Limerick** Ireland
93 E4 **Limfjorden** *sea chan.* Denmark
111 C3 **Limnos** *i.* Greece
104 C2 **Limoges** France
136 C3 **Limon** U.S.A.
104 C3 **Limoux** France
123 C1 **Limpopo** *prov.* S. Africa
121 C3 **Limpopo** *r.* S. Africa/
         Zimbabwe
64 A1 **Linapacan** *i.* Phil.
153 A4 **Linares** Chile
145 C2 **Linares** Mex.
106 C2 **Linares** Spain
62 B1 **Lincang** China
98 C2 **Lincoln** U.K.
140 B2 **Lincoln** *IL* U.S.A.
141 F1 **Lincoln** *ME* U.S.A.
137 D2 **Lincoln** *NE* U.S.A.
151 C1 **Linden** Guyana
142 C1 **Linden** U.S.A.
119 C2 **Lindi** *r.* Dem. Rep. Congo
119 D3 **Lindi** Tanz.
         Lindisfarne *i.* U.K. *see*
         Holy Island
80 A2 **Lindos** Greece
141 D2 **Lindsay** Can.
49 H2 **Line Islands** Kiribati
70 B2 **Linfen** China
64 B1 **Lingayen** Phil.
70 B2 **Lingbao** China
123 C3 **Lingelethu** S. Africa
123 C3 **Lingelihle** S. Africa
100 C1 **Lingen (Ems)** Ger.
60 B2 **Lingga, Kepulauan** *is* Indon.
71 A3 **Lingshan** China
71 A4 **Lingshui** China
114 A3 **Linguère** Senegal
63 B2 **Linh, Ngok** *mt.* Vietnam
155 D1 **Linhares** Brazil
93 G4 **Linköping** Sweden

66 B1 Linkou China
70 B2 Linqing China
154 C2 Lins Brazil
136 C1 Linton U.S.A.
69 D2 Linxi China
69 C2 Linxia China
70 B2 Linyi Shandong China
70 B2 Linyi Shandong China
70 B2 Linying China
102 C2 Linz Austria
105 C3 Lion, Golfe du g. France
109 B3 Lipari Italy
108 B3 Lipari, Isole is Italy
89 E3 Lipetsk Rus. Fed.
110 B1 Lipova Romania
101 D2 Lippstadt Ger.
71 B3 Lipu China
76 C1 Lisakovsk Kazakh.
118 C2 Lisala Dem. Rep. Congo
         Lisboa Port. see Lisbon
106 B2 Lisbon Port.
97 C1 Lisburn U.K.
97 B2 Liscannor Bay Ireland
104 C2 Lisieux France
99 A3 Liskard U.K.
89 E3 Liski Rus. Fed.
53 D1 Lismore Austr.
97 C1 Lisnaskea U.K.
97 B2 Listowel Ireland
71 A3 Litang Guangxi China
68 C2 Litang Sichuan China
140 B3 Litchfield IL U.S.A.
137 E1 Litchfield MN U.S.A.
53 D2 Lithgow Austr.
111 B3 Lithino, Akrotirio pt Greece
88 B2 Lithuania country Europe
102 C1 Litoměřice Czech Rep.
146 C2 Little Abaco i. Bahamas
73 D3 Little Andaman i. India
93 E4 Little Belt sea chan. Denmark
137 E1 Little Falls U.S.A.
139 C2 Littlefield U.S.A.
99 C3 Littlehampton U.K.
122 A2 Little Karas Berg plat.
         Namibia
122 B3 Little Karoo plat. S. Africa
96 A2 Little Minch sea chan. U.K.
136 C1 Little Missouri r. U.S.A.
63 A3 Little Nicobar i. India
142 B2 Little Rock U.S.A.
141 E2 Littleton U.S.A.
70 B2 Liujiachang China
71 A3 Liupanshui China
71 A3 Liuzhou China
111 B3 Livadeia Greece
88 C2 Līvāni Latvia
51 B1 Liveringa Austr.
138 C2 Livermore, Mount U.S.A.
131 D2 Liverpool Can.
98 B2 Liverpool U.K.
127 F2 Liverpool, Cape Can.
53 C2 Liverpool Range mts Austr.
134 D1 Livingston MT U.S.A.
139 E2 Livingston TX U.S.A.
139 D2 Livingston, Lake U.S.A.
120 B2 Livingstone Zambia
109 C2 Livno Bos.-Herz.
89 E3 Livny Rus. Fed.
140 C2 Livonia U.S.A.
108 B2 Livorno Italy
119 D3 Liwale Tanz.
71 B3 Liyang China
99 A4 Lizard Point U.K.
108 B1 Ljubljana Slovenia
93 G3 Ljungan r. Sweden
93 F4 Ljungby Sweden
93 G3 Ljusdal Sweden

93 G3 Ljusnan r. Sweden
99 B3 Llandeilo U.K.
99 B3 Llandovery U.K.
99 B2 Llandrindod Wells U.K.
98 B2 Llandudno U.K.
99 A3 Llanelli U.K.
98 A2 Llangefni U.K.
139 C2 Llano Estacado plain U.S.A.
150 B1 Llanos plain Col./Venez.
107 D1 Lleida Spain
99 A2 Lleyn Peninsula U.K.
107 C2 Lliria Spain
128 B2 Lloyd George, Mount Can.
129 D2 Lloyd Lake Can.
129 C2 Lloydminster Can.
152 B3 Llullaillaco, Volcán vol. Chile
123 C2 Lobatse Botswana
120 A2 Lobito Angola
101 F1 Loburg Ger.
96 B2 Lochaber reg. U.K.
104 C2 Loches France
96 B2 Lochgilphead U.K.
96 B1 Lochinver U.K.
96 A2 Lochmaddy U.K.
96 C2 Lochnagar mt. U.K.
52 A2 Lock Austr.
96 C3 Lockerbie U.K.
139 D3 Lockhart U.S.A.
141 D2 Lock Haven U.S.A.
141 D2 Lockport U.S.A.
63 B2 Lộc Ninh Vietnam
105 C3 Lodève France
86 C2 Lodeynoye Pole Rus. Fed.
92 F2 Løding Norway
119 D2 Lodwar Kenya
103 D1 Łódź Pol.
92 F2 Loei Thai.
122 A3 Loeriesfontein S. Africa
92 F2 Lofoten is Norway
134 D2 Logan U.S.A.
126 B2 Logan, Mount Can.
140 B2 Logansport U.S.A.
108 B1 Logatec Slovenia
106 C1 Logroño Spain
101 D1 Löhne Ger.
101 D1 Lohne (Oldenburg) Ger.
62 A2 Loikaw Myanmar
104 B2 Loire r. France
150 A2 Loja Ecuador
106 C2 Loja Spain
92 I2 Lokan tekojärvi resr Fin.
74 B1 Lokar Afgh.
100 B2 Lokeren Belgium
122 B1 Lokgwabe Botswana
119 D2 Lokichar Kenya
119 D2 Lokichokio Kenya
89 D2 Loknya Rus. Fed.
115 C4 Lokoja Nigeria
89 D3 Lokot' Rus. Fed.
88 C2 Loksa Estonia
127 G2 Loks Land i. Can.
93 F4 Lolland i. Denmark
119 D3 Lollondo Tanz.
122 B3 Lolwane S. Africa
110 B2 Lom Bulg.
93 E3 Lom Norway
119 C2 Lomami r. Dem. Rep. Congo
153 C4 Lomas de Zamora Arg.
61 C2 Lombok i. Indon.
61 C2 Lombok, Selat sea chan. Indon.
114 C4 Lomé Togo
118 C3 Lomela r. Dem. Rep. Congo
100 B2 Lommel Belgium
96 B2 Lomond, Loch l. U.K.
88 C2 Lomonosov Rus. Fed.
135 B4 Lompoc U.S.A.
63 B2 Lom Sak Thai.

103 E1 Łomża Pol.
130 B2 London Can.
99 C3 London U.K.
140 C3 London U.S.A.
97 C1 Londonderry U.K.
50 B1 Londonderry, Cape Austr.
154 B2 Londrina Brazil
83 M2 Longa, Proliv sea chan.
         Rus. Fed.
61 C1 Long Akah Sarawak Malaysia
143 E2 Long Bay U.S.A.
135 C4 Long Beach U.S.A.
97 C2 Longford Ireland
61 C2 Longiram Indon.
147 C2 Long Island Bahamas
131 C1 Long Island Can.
59 D3 Long Island P.N.G.
141 E2 Long Island U.S.A.
130 B2 Longlac Can.
130 B2 Long Lake Can.
136 B2 Longmont U.S.A.
70 A2 Longnan China
140 C2 Long Point Can.
71 B3 Longquan China
131 E2 Long Range Mountains Can.
51 D2 Longreach Austr.
70 C2 Long Stratton U.K.
98 B1 Longtown U.K.
105 D2 Longuyon France
139 E2 Longview TX U.S.A.
134 B1 Longview WA U.S.A.
70 A2 Longxi China
71 B3 Longxi Shan mt. China
63 B2 Long Xuyên Vietnam
71 B3 Longyan China
82 C1 Longyearbyen Svalbard
102 B2 Lons-le-Saunier France
143 E2 Lookout, Cape U.S.A.
97 B2 Loop Head Ireland
63 B2 Lop Buri Thai.
64 B1 Lopez Phil.
68 C2 Lop Nur salt flat China
118 B2 Lopori r. Dem. Rep. Congo
74 A2 Lora, Hämūn-i- dry lake
         Afgh./Pak.
106 B2 Lora del Río Spain
140 C2 Lorain U.S.A.
74 A1 Loralai Pak.
107 C2 Lorca Spain
48 E5 Lord Howe Island Austr.
138 B2 Lordsburg U.S.A.
155 C2 Lorena Brazil
152 B2 Loreto Bol.
144 A2 Loreto Mex.
104 B2 Lorient France
96 B2 Lorn, Firth of est. U.K.
52 B3 Lorne Austr.
138 B1 Los Alamos U.S.A.
139 D3 Los Aldamas Mex.
153 A4 Los Ángeles Chile
135 C4 Los Angeles U.S.A.
135 B3 Los Banos U.S.A.
152 B3 Los Blancos Arg.
91 E1 Losevo Rus. Fed.
108 B2 Lošinj i. Croatia
144 B2 Los Mochis Mex.
118 B2 Losombo Dem. Rep. Congo
147 D3 Los Roques, Islas is Venez.
96 C2 Lossiemouth U.K.
150 B1 Los Teques Venez.
152 A4 Los Vilos Chile
104 C3 Lot r. France
96 C1 Loth U.K.
119 D2 Lotikipi Plain Kenya/Sudan
118 C3 Loto Dem. Rep. Congo
89 E2 Lotoshino Rus. Fed.
62 B1 Louangnamtha Laos

Louangphabang

62	B2	**Louangphabang** Laos
118	B3	**Loubomo** Congo
104	B2	**Loudéac** France
71	B3	**Loudi** China
118	B3	**Loudima** Congo
114	A3	**Louga** Senegal
99	C2	**Loughborough** U.K.
97	C2	**Loughrea** Ireland
105	D2	**Louhans** France
97	C2	**Louisburgh** Ireland
142	B2	**Louisiana** *state* U.S.A.
140	B3	**Louisville** *KY* U.S.A.
142	C2	**Louisville** *MS* U.S.A.
86	C2	**Loukhi** Rus. Fed.
130	C1	**Loups Marins, Lacs des** *lakes* Can.
104	B3	**Lourdes** France
151	C1	**Lourenço** Brazil
106	C1	**Lousã** Port.
53	C2	**Louth** Austr.
98	C2	**Louth** U.K.
		Louvain Belgium *see* **Leuven**
89	D2	**Lovat'** *r.* Rus. Fed.
110	B2	**Lovech** Bulg.
136	B2	**Loveland** U.S.A.
135	C2	**Lovelock** U.S.A.
139	C2	**Lovington** U.S.A.
119	C3	**Lowa** Dem. Rep. Congo
141	E2	**Lowell** U.S.A.
128	C3	**Lower Arrow Lake** Can.
54	B2	**Lower Hutt** N.Z.
97	C1	**Lower Lough Erne** *l.* U.K.
128	B2	**Lower Post** Can.
99	D2	**Lowestoft** U.K.
103	D1	**Łowicz** Pol.
141	D2	**Lowville** U.S.A.
52	B2	**Loxton** Austr.
		Loyang China *see* **Luoyang**
48	F4	**Loyauté, Îles** *is* New Caledonia
89	D3	**Loyew** Belarus
92	F2	**Løypskardtinden** *mt.* Norway
109	C2	**Loznica** Serbia
91	D2	**Lozova** Ukr.
120	B2	**Luacano** Angola
70	B2	**Lu'an** China
120	A1	**Luanda** Angola
121	C2	**Luangwa** *r.* Zambia
121	B2	**Luanshya** Zambia
106	B1	**Luarca** Spain
120	B2	**Luau** Angola
103	E1	**Lubaczów** Pol.
120	A2	**Lubango** Angola
119	C3	**Lubao** Dem. Rep. Congo
103	E1	**Lubartów** Pol.
101	D1	**Lübbecke** Ger.
139	C2	**Lubbock** U.S.A.
101	E1	**Lübeck** Ger.
69	E2	**Lubei** China
77	E3	**Lubenka** Kazakh.
103	D1	**Lubin** Pol.
103	E1	**Lublin** Pol.
91	C1	**Lubny** Ukr.
61	C1	**Lubok Antu** *Sarawak* Malaysia
101	E1	**Lübow** Ger.
101	E1	**Lübtheen** Ger.
119	C3	**Lubudi** Dem. Rep. Congo
60	B2	**Lubuklinggau** Indon.
119	C4	**Lubumbashi** Dem. Rep. Congo
120	B2	**Lubungu** Zambia
119	C3	**Lubutu** Dem. Rep. Congo
120	A1	**Lucala** Angola
97	C2	**Lucan** Ireland
120	B1	**Lucapa** Angola
96	B3	**Luce Bay** U.K.
154	B2	**Lucélia** Brazil
64	B1	**Lucena** Phil.
106	C2	**Lucena** Spain
103	D2	**Lučenec** Slovakia
109	C2	**Lucera** Italy
105	D2	**Lucerne** Switz.
101	E1	**Lüchow** Ger.
120	A2	**Lucira** Angola
101	F1	**Luckenwalde** Ger.
122	B2	**Luckhoff** S. Africa
75	C2	**Lucknow** India
120	B2	**Lucusse** Angola
		Lüda China *see* **Dalian**
100	C2	**Lüdenscheid** Ger.
101	E1	**Lüder** Ger.
120	A3	**Lüderitz** Namibia
74	B1	**Ludhiana** India
140	B2	**Ludington** U.S.A.
99	B2	**Ludlow** U.K.
135	C4	**Ludlow** U.S.A.
110	C2	**Ludogorie** *reg.* Bulg.
93	G3	**Ludvika** Sweden
102	B2	**Ludwigsburg** Ger.
101	F1	**Ludwigsfelde** Ger.
101	D3	**Ludwigshafen am Rhein** Ger.
101	E1	**Ludwigslust** Ger.
88	C2	**Ludza** Latvia
118	C3	**Luebo** Dem. Rep. Congo
120	A2	**Luena** Angola
70	A2	**Lüeyang** China
71	B3	**Lufeng** China
139	E2	**Lufkin** U.S.A.
88	C2	**Luga** Rus. Fed.
88	C2	**Luga** *r.* Rus. Fed.
105	D2	**Lugano** Switz.
121	C2	**Lugenda** *r.* Moz.
97	C2	**Lugnaquilla** *h.* Ireland
106	B1	**Lugo** Spain
110	B1	**Lugoj** Romania
91	D2	**Luhans'k** Ukr.
119	D3	**Luhombero** Tanz.
90	B1	**Luhyny** Ukr.
120	B2	**Luiana** Angola
118	C3	**Luilaka** *r.* Dem. Rep. Congo
105	D2	**Luino** Italy
92	I2	**Luiro** *r.* Fin.
118	C3	**Luiza** Dem. Rep. Congo
70	B2	**Lujiang** China
109	C2	**Lukavac** Bos.-Herz.
118	B3	**Lukenie** *r.* Dem. Rep. Congo
138	A2	**Lukeville** U.S.A.
89	E3	**Lukhovitsy** Rus. Fed.
103	E1	**Łuków** Pol.
120	B2	**Lukulu** Zambia
92	H2	**Luleå** Sweden
92	H2	**Luleälven** *r.* Sweden
110	C2	**Lüleburgaz** Turkey
70	B2	**Lüliang Shan** *mts* China
61	C2	**Lumajang** Indon.
75	C1	**Lumajangdong Co** *salt l.* China
120	B2	**Lumbala Kaquengue** Angola
120	B2	**Lumbala N'guimbo** Angola
143	E2	**Lumberton** U.S.A.
61	C1	**Lumbis** Indon.
106	B1	**Lumbrales** Spain
63	B2	**Lumphăt** Cambodia
129	D2	**Lumsden** Can.
54	A3	**Lumsden** N.Z.
93	F4	**Lund** Sweden
121	C2	**Lundazi** Zambia
99	A3	**Lundy** *i.* U.K.
101	E1	**Lüneburg** Ger.
101	E1	**Lüneburger Heide** *reg.* Ger.
100	C2	**Lünen** Ger.
105	D2	**Lunéville** France
120	B2	**Lunga** *r.* Zambia
114	A4	**Lungi** Sierra Leone
62	A1	**Lunglei** India
120	B2	**Lungwebungu** *r.* Zambia
74	B2	**Luni** *r.* India
88	C3	**Luninyets** Belarus
114	A4	**Lunsar** Sierra Leone
77	E2	**Luntai** China
71	A3	**Luodian** China
71	B3	**Luoding** China
70	B2	**Luohe** China
70	B2	**Luoyang** China
121	B2	**Lupane** Zimbabwe
110	B1	**Lupeni** Romania
121	C2	**Lupilichi** Moz.
101	F2	**Luppa** Ger.
121	D2	**Lúrio** Moz.
121	D2	**Lurio** *r.* Moz.
121	B2	**Lusaka** Zambia
118	C3	**Lusambo** Dem. Rep. Congo
109	C2	**Lushnjë** Albania
136	C2	**Lusk** U.S.A.
76	B3	**Lüt, Kavir-e** *des.* Iran
99	C3	**Luton** U.K.
61	C1	**Lutong** *Sarawak* Malaysia
129	C1	**Łutselk'e** Can.
90	B1	**Luts'k** Ukr.
122	B2	**Lutzputs** S. Africa
122	A3	**Lutzville** S. Africa
117	C4	**Luuq** Somalia
137	D2	**Luverne** U.S.A.
119	C3	**Luvua** *r.* Dem. Rep. Congo
123	D1	**Luvuvhu** *r.* S. Africa
119	D2	**Luwero** Uganda
59	C3	**Luwuk** Indon.
100	C3	**Luxembourg** *country* Europe
100	C3	**Luxembourg** Lux.
105	D2	**Luxeuil-les-Bains** France
123	C2	**Luxolweni** S. Africa
116	B2	**Luxor** Egypt
100	B2	**Luyksgestel** Neth.
86	D2	**Luza** Rus. Fed.
		Luzern Switz. *see* **Lucerne**
71	A3	**Luzhou** China
154	C1	**Luziânia** Brazil
151	D2	**Luzilândia** Brazil
64	B1	**Luzon** *i.* Phil.
71	C3	**Luzon Strait** Phil./Taiwan
90	A2	**L'viv** Ukr.
		L'vov Ukr. *see* **L'viv**
88	C3	**Lyakhavichy** Belarus
92	G3	**Lycksele** Sweden
88	C3	**Lyel'chytsy** Belarus
88	C2	**Lyepyel'** Belarus
99	B3	**Lyme Bay** U.K.
141	D3	**Lynchburg** U.S.A.
129	D2	**Lynn Lake** Can.
129	D1	**Lynx Lake** Can.
105	C2	**Lyon** France
89	D2	**Lyozna** Belarus
86	E3	**Lys'va** Rus. Fed.
91	D2	**Lysychans'k** Ukr.
98	B2	**Lytham St Anne's** U.K.
88	C3	**Lyuban'** Belarus
89	E2	**Lyubertsy** Rus. Fed.
90	B1	**Lyubeshiv** Ukr.
89	F2	**Lyubim** Rus. Fed.
91	D2	**Lyubotyn** Ukr.
89	D2	**Lyubytino** Rus. Fed.
89	D3	**Lyudinovo** Rus. Fed.

M

80	B2	**Ma'ān** Jordan
88	C2	**Maardu** Estonia
100	B2	**Maas** *r.* Neth.
100	B2	**Maaseik** Belgium
64	B1	**Maasin** Phil.

100 B2 Maastricht Neth.
121 C3 Mabalane Moz.
150 C1 Mabaruma Guyana
121 C3 Mabote Moz.
122 B2 Mabule Botswana
122 B1 Mabutsane Botswana
155 D2 Macaé Brazil
121 C2 Macaloge Moz.
126 E2 MacAlpine Lake Can.
71 B3 Macao aut. reg. China
151 E1 Macapá Brazil
150 A2 Macará Ecuador
155 D1 Macarani Brazil
123 D1 Macarretane Moz.
151 E2 Macau Brazil
98 B2 Macclesfield U.K.
50 C1 Macdonald, Lake imp. l. Austr.
50 C2 Macdonnell Ranges mts Austr.
130 A1 MacDowell Lake Can.
106 B1 Macedo de Cavaleiros Port.
52 B3 Macedon mt. Austr.
109 D2 Macedonia country Europe
151 E2 Maceió Brazil
108 B2 Macerata Italy
52 A2 Macfarlane, Lake salt l. Austr.
97 B3 Macgillycuddy's Reeks mts Ireland
74 A2 Mach Pak.
155 C2 Machado Brazil
121 C2 Machaila Moz.
119 D3 Machakos Kenya
150 A2 Machala Ecuador
68 C2 Machali China
121 C3 Machanga Moz.
70 B2 Macheng China
141 F2 Machias U.S.A.
150 A1 Machiques Venez.
150 A3 Machu Picchu tourist site Peru
123 D2 Macia Moz.
110 C1 Măcin Romania
114 B3 Macina Mali
53 D1 Macintyre r. Austr.
51 D2 Mackay Austr.
50 B2 Mackay, Lake imp. l. Austr.
129 C1 MacKay Lake Can.
128 B2 Mackenzie r. Can.
128 A1 Mackenzie r. Can.
126 B2 Mackenzie Bay Can.
126 D1 Mackenzie King Island Can.
128 A1 Mackenzie Mountains Can.
129 C2 Macklin Can.
53 D2 Macksville Austr.
53 D1 Maclean Austr.
50 A2 MacLeod, Lake dry lake Austr.
140 A2 Macomb U.S.A.
108 A2 Macomer Sardegna Italy
105 C2 Mâcon France
143 D2 Macon GA U.S.A.
137 E3 Macon MO U.S.A.
53 C2 Macquarie r. Austr.
48 E6 Macquarie Island S. Pacific Ocean
53 C2 Macquarie Marshes Austr.
97 B3 Macroom Ireland
52 A1 Macumba watercourse Austr.
145 C3 Macuspana Mex.
144 B2 Macuzari, Presa resr Mex.
123 D2 Madadeni S. Africa
121 □D3 Madagascar country Africa
115 D2 Madama Niger
111 B2 Madan Bulg.
59 D3 Madang P.N.G.
150 C2 Madeira r. Brazil
114 A1 Madeira terr. N. Atlantic Ocean
131 D2 Madeleine, Îles de la is Can.
144 B2 Madera Mex.

135 B3 Madera U.S.A.
73 B3 Madgaon India
118 B3 Madingou Congo
140 B3 Madison IN U.S.A.
137 D2 Madison SD U.S.A.
140 B2 Madison WI U.S.A.
140 C3 Madison WV U.S.A.
134 D1 Madison r. U.S.A.
140 B3 Madisonville U.S.A.
61 C2 Madiun Indon.
119 D2 Mado Gashi Kenya
88 C2 Madona Latvia
78 A2 Madrakah Saudi Arabia
    Madras India see Chennai
134 B2 Madras U.S.A.
145 C2 Madre, Laguna lag. Mex.
145 B3 Madre del Sur, Sierra mts Mex.
144 B2 Madre Occidental, Sierra mts Mex.
145 B2 Madre Oriental, Sierra mts Mex.
106 C1 Madrid Spain
106 C2 Madridejos Spain
61 C2 Madura i. Indon.
61 C2 Madura, Selat sea chan. Indon.
73 B4 Madurai India
67 C3 Maebashi Japan
62 A2 Mae Hong Son Thai.
62 A1 Mae Sai Thai.
62 A2 Mae Sariang Thai.
62 A2 Mae Suai Thai.
123 C2 Mafeteng Lesotho
119 D3 Mafia Island Tanz.
119 D3 Mafinga Tanz.
154 C3 Mafra Brazil
83 L3 Magadan Rus. Fed.
147 C4 Magangué Col.
144 A1 Magdalena Mex.
138 B2 Magdalena U.S.A.
144 A2 Magdalena, Bahia b. Mex.
101 E1 Magdeburg Ger.
153 A6 Magellan, Strait of Chile
97 C1 Magherafelt U.K.
87 E3 Magnitogorsk Rus. Fed.
142 B2 Magnolia U.S.A.
131 D1 Magpie, Lac l. Can.
114 A3 Magta' Lahjar Maur.
151 D2 Maguarinho, Cabo c. Brazil
123 D2 Magude Moz.
62 A1 Magwe Myanmar
81 C2 Mahābād Iran
74 B2 Mahajan India
121 □D2 Mahajanga Madag.
61 C2 Mahakam r. Indon.
123 C1 Mahalapye Botswana
121 □D2 Mahalevona Madag.
75 C2 Mahanadi r. India
121 □D2 Mahanoro Madag.
63 B2 Maha Sarakham Thai.
121 □D2 Mahavavy r. Madag.
78 B2 Mahd adh Dhahab Saudi Arabia
150 C1 Mahdia Guyana
113 K7 Mahé i. Seychelles
74 B2 Mahesana India
74 B2 Mahi r. India
54 C1 Mahia Peninsula N.Z.
120 B3 Mahikeng S. Africa
123 C2 Mahikeng S. Africa
89 D3 Mahilyow Belarus
74 B2 Mahuva India
110 C2 Mahya Dağı mt. Turkey
74 A1 Maidan Shahr Afgh.
129 D2 Maidstone Can.
99 D3 Maidstone U.K.
115 D3 Maiduguri Nigeria

75 C2 Mailani India
76 C3 Maïmanah Afgh.
101 D2 Main r. Ger.
118 B3 Mai-Ndombe, Lac l. Dem. Rep. Congo
101 E3 Main-Donau-Kanal canal Ger.
141 F1 Maine state U.S.A.
62 A1 Maingkwan Myanmar
96 C1 Mainland i. Scotland U.K.
96 □ Mainland i. Scotland U.K.
121 □D2 Maintirano Madag.
101 D2 Mainz Ger.
150 B1 Maiquetía Venez.
53 D2 Maitland N.S.W. Austr.
52 A2 Maitland S.A. Austr.
146 B3 Maíz, Islas del is Nic.
67 C3 Maizuru Japan
61 C2 Majene Indon.
107 D2 Majorca i. Spain
48 F2 Majuro atoll Marshall Is
123 C2 Majwemasweu S. Africa
118 B3 Makabana Congo
58 B3 Makale Indon.
77 E2 Makanshy Kazakh.
109 C2 Makarska Croatia
58 B3 Makassar Indon.
61 C2 Makassar, Selat str. Indon.
    Makassar Strait Indon. see Makassar, Selat
76 B2 Makat Kazakh.
123 D2 Makatini Flats lowland S. Africa
114 A4 Makeni Sierra Leone
120 B3 Makgadikgadi depr. Botswana
87 D4 Makhachkala Rus. Fed.
123 C1 Makhado S. Africa
76 B2 Makhambet Kazakh.
119 D3 Makindu Kenya
77 D1 Makinsk Kazakh.
91 D2 Makiyivka Ukr.
    Makkah Saudi Arabia see Mecca
131 E1 Makkovik Can.
103 E2 Makó Hungary
118 B2 Makokou Gabon
119 D3 Makongolosi Tanz.
122 B2 Makopong Botswana
79 D2 Makran reg. Iran/Pak.
74 A2 Makran Coast Range mts Pak.
89 E2 Maksatikha Rus. Fed.
81 C2 Mākū Iran
62 A1 Makum India
67 B4 Makurazaki Japan
115 C4 Makurdi Nigeria
92 G2 Malå Sweden
146 B4 Mala, Punta pt Panama
118 A2 Malabo Equat. Guinea
60 A1 Malacca, Strait of Indon./ Malaysia
134 D2 Malad City U.S.A.
88 C3 Maladzyechna Belarus
106 C2 Málaga Spain
97 E3 Málainn Mhóir Ireland
48 E3 Malaita i. Solomon Is
117 B4 Malakal S. Sudan
48 F4 Malakula i. Vanuatu
61 C2 Malang Indon.
120 A1 Malanje Angola
93 G4 Mälaren i. Sweden
153 B4 Malargüe Arg.
80 B2 Malatya Turkey
121 C2 Malawi country Africa
    Malawi, Lake Africa see Nyasa, Lake
89 D2 Malaya Vishera Rus. Fed.
64 B2 Malaybalay Phil.
81 C2 Malāyer Iran

Malaysia

60 B1 **Malaysia** *country* Asia
81 B2 **Malazgirt** Turkey
103 D1 **Malbork** Pol.
101 F1 **Malchin** Ger.
100 A2 **Maldegem** Belgium
49 H3 **Malden Island** Kiribati
56 G6 **Maldives** *country* Indian Ocean
153 C4 **Maldonado** Uru.
56 G6 **Male** Maldives
111 B3 **Maleas, Akrotirio** *pt* Greece
103 D2 **Malé Karpaty** *hills* Slovakia
134 C2 **Malheur Lake** U.S.A.
114 B3 **Mali** *country* Africa
114 A3 **Mali** Guinea
58 C3 **Malili** Indon.
119 E3 **Malindi** Kenya
97 C1 **Malin Head** Ireland
111 C2 **Malkara** Turkey
88 C3 **Mal'kavichy** Belarus
110 C2 **Malko Tŭrnovo** Bulg.
53 C1 **Mallacoota** Austr.
53 C3 **Mallacoota Inlet** *b.* Austr.
96 B2 **Mallaig** U.K.
129 E1 **Mallery Lake** Can.
  Mallorca *i.* Spain *see* **Majorca**
97 B2 **Mallow** Ireland
92 H2 **Malmberget** Sweden
100 C2 **Malmédy** Belgium
122 A3 **Malmesbury** S. Africa
93 F4 **Malmö** Sweden
62 B1 **Malong** China
118 C4 **Malonga** Dem. Rep. Congo
93 E3 **Måløy** Norway
89 E2 **Maloyaroslavets** Rus. Fed.
89 E2 **Maloye Borisovo** Rus. Fed.
85 H5 **Malta** *country* Europe
88 C2 **Malta** Latvia
134 E1 **Malta** U.S.A.
122 A1 **Maltahöhe** Namibia
98 C1 **Malton** U.K.
  Maluku *is* Indon. *see* **Moluccas**
59 C3 **Maluku, Laut** *sea* Indon.
93 F3 **Malung** Sweden
123 C2 **Maluti Mountains** Lesotho
73 B3 **Malvan** India
142 B2 **Malvern** U.S.A.
90 B1 **Malyn** Ukr.
83 L2 **Malyy Anyuy** *r.* Rus. Fed.
83 K2 **Malyy Lyakhovskiy, Ostrov** *i.* Rus. Fed.
123 C2 **Mamafubedu** S. Africa
119 C2 **Mambasa** Dem. Rep. Congo
118 B2 **Mambéré** *r.* C.A.R.
123 C2 **Mamelodi** S. Africa
148 B3 **Mamoré** *r.* Bol./Brazil
114 A3 **Mamou** Guinea
61 C2 **Mamuju** Indon.
114 B4 **Man** Côte d'Ivoire
98 A1 **Man, Isle of** *i.* Irish Sea
150 B2 **Manacapuru** Brazil
107 D2 **Manacor** Spain
59 C2 **Manado** Indon.
146 B3 **Managua** Nic.
121 □D3 **Manakara** Madag.
78 B3 **Manākhah** Yemen
79 C2 **Manama** Bahrain
59 D3 **Manam Island** P.N.G.
121 □D2 **Mananara** *r.* Madag.
121 □D2 **Mananara Avaratra** Madag.
121 □D3 **Mananjary** Madag.
114 A3 **Manantali, Lac de** *l.* Mali
77 E2 **Manas Hu** *l.* China
59 C3 **Manatuto** East Timor
62 A2 **Man-aung Kyun** *i.* Myanmar
150 B2 **Manaus** Brazil

80 B2 **Manavgat** Turkey
98 B2 **Manchester** U.K.
141 E2 **Manchester** U.S.A.
121 □D3 **Mandabe** Madag.
93 E4 **Mandal** Norway
59 D3 **Mandala, Puncak** *mt.* Indon.
62 A1 **Mandalay** Myanmar
69 D2 **Mandalgovĭ** Mongolia
136 C1 **Mandan** U.S.A.
118 B1 **Mandara Mountains** Cameroon/Nigeria
108 A3 **Mandas** *Sardegna* Italy
100 C2 **Manderscheid** Ger.
74 B1 **Mandi** India
114 B3 **Mandiana** Guinea
75 C2 **Mandla** India
121 □D2 **Mandritsara** Madag.
74 B2 **Mandsaur** India
50 A3 **Mandurah** Austr.
73 B3 **Mandya** India
108 B1 **Manerbio** Italy
90 B1 **Manevychi** Ukr.
109 C2 **Manfredonia** Italy
114 B3 **Manga** Burkina Faso
118 B3 **Mangai** Dem. Rep. Congo
54 C1 **Mangakino** N.Z.
110 B1 **Mangalia** Romania
73 B3 **Mangalore** India
123 C2 **Mangaung** S. Africa
61 B2 **Manggar** Indon.
76 B2 **Mangistau** Kazakh.
121 C2 **Mangochi** Malawi
59 C3 **Mangole** *i.* Indon.
154 B3 **Mangueirinha** Brazil
69 E1 **Mangui** China
137 D3 **Manhattan** U.S.A.
121 C3 **Manhica** Moz.
155 D2 **Manhuaçu** Brazil
121 □D2 **Mania** *r.* Madag.
108 B1 **Maniago** Italy
150 C2 **Manicoré** Brazil
131 D2 **Manicouagan** *r.* Can.
131 D1 **Manicouagan, Petit Lac** *l.* Can.
131 D1 **Manicouagan, Réservoir** *resr* Can.
79 B2 **Manifah** Saudi Arabia
64 B1 **Manila** Phil.
53 D3 **Manilla** Austr.
111 C3 **Manisa** Turkey
140 B2 **Manistee** U.S.A.
129 E2 **Manitoba** *prov.* Can.
129 E2 **Manitoba, Lake** Can.
140 B1 **Manitou Islands** U.S.A.
130 B2 **Manitoulin Island** Can.
130 C2 **Manitowoc** U.S.A.
130 C2 **Maniwaki** Can.
150 A1 **Manizales** Col.
137 E2 **Mankato** U.S.A.
114 B4 **Mankono** Côte d'Ivoire
129 D3 **Mankota** Can.
73 C4 **Mankulam** Sri Lanka
74 B2 **Manmad** India
73 B4 **Mannar, Gulf of** India/Sri Lanka
101 D3 **Mannheim** Ger.
128 C2 **Manning** Can.
52 A2 **Mannum** Austr.
129 C2 **Mannville** Can.
59 C3 **Manokwari** Indon.
119 C3 **Manono** Dem. Rep. Congo
105 D3 **Manosque** France
131 C1 **Manouane, Lac** *l.* Can.
107 D1 **Manresa** Spain
121 B2 **Mansa** Zambia
127 F2 **Mansel Island** Can.
92 I2 **Mansel'kya** *ridge* Fin./Rus. Fed.

53 C3 **Mansfield** Austr.
98 C2 **Mansfield** U.K.
142 B2 **Mansfield** *LA* U.S.A.
140 C2 **Mansfield** *OH* U.S.A.
141 D2 **Mansfield** *PA* U.S.A.
150 A2 **Manta** Ecuador
143 E1 **Manteo** U.S.A.
104 C2 **Mantes-la-Jolie** France
155 C2 **Mantiqueira, Serra de** *mts* Brazil
  Mantova Italy *see* **Mantua**
108 B1 **Mantua** Italy
151 C2 **Manuelzinho** Brazil
59 C3 **Manui** *i.* Indon.
54 B1 **Manukau** N.Z.
142 B2 **Many** U.S.A.
119 D3 **Manyoni** Tanz.
106 C2 **Manzanares** Spain
144 B3 **Manzanillo** Mex.
69 D1 **Manzhouli** China
123 D2 **Manzini** Swaziland
115 D3 **Mao** Chad
107 D2 **Maó** Spain
59 D3 **Maoke, Pegunungan** *mts* Indon.
123 C2 **Maokeng** S. Africa
65 A1 **Maokui Shan** *mt.* China
71 B3 **Maoming** China
121 C3 **Mapai** Moz.
75 C1 **Mapam Yumco** *l.* China
145 C3 **Mapastepec** Mex.
144 B2 **Mapimí** Mex.
144 B2 **Mapimí, Bolsón de** *des.* Mex.
121 C3 **Mapinhane** Moz.
129 D3 **Maple Creek** Can.
121 C3 **Maputo** Moz.
123 D2 **Maputo** *r.* Moz./S. Africa
120 A1 **Maquela do Zombo** Angola
153 B5 **Maquinchao** Arg.
137 E2 **Maquoketa** U.S.A.
148 B2 **Maraã** Brazil
151 D2 **Marabá** Brazil
151 C1 **Maracá, Ilha de** *i.* Brazil
150 A1 **Maracaibo** Venez.
150 A1 **Maracaibo, Lake** Venez.
152 C3 **Maracaju, Serra de** *hills* Brazil
154 A2 **Maracaju, Serra de** *hills* Brazil
150 B1 **Maracay** Venez.
115 D2 **Marādah** Libya
115 C3 **Maradi** Niger
81 C2 **Marāgheh** Iran
151 D2 **Marajó, Baía de** *est.* Brazil
151 C1 **Marajó, Ilha de** *i.* Brazil
79 C2 **Marāki** Iran
119 D2 **Maralal** Kenya
50 C3 **Maralinga** Austr.
81 C2 **Marand** Iran
150 A2 **Marañón** *r.* Peru
130 B2 **Marathon** Can.
143 D4 **Marathon** U.S.A.
106 C2 **Marbella** Spain
50 A2 **Marble Bar** Austr.
123 C1 **Marble Hall** S. Africa
123 D3 **Marburg** S. Africa
101 D2 **Marburg an der Lahn** Ger.
99 D2 **March** U.K.
100 B2 **Marche-en-Famenne** Belgium
106 B2 **Marchena** Spain
152 B4 **Mar Chiquita, Laguna** *l.* Arg.
141 E2 **Marcy, Mount** U.S.A.
74 B1 **Mardan** Pak.
153 C4 **Mar del Plata** Arg.
81 C2 **Mardin** Turkey
96 B2 **Maree, Loch** *l.* U.K.
108 B3 **Marettimo, Isola** *i.* *Sicilia* Italy
89 D2 **Marevo** Rus. Fed.
138 C2 **Marfa** U.S.A.

50 A3   Margaret River Austr.
147 D3   Margarita, Isla de i. Venez.
123 D3   Margate S. Africa
99 D3   Margate U.K.
119 C2   Margherita Peak Dem. Rep. Congo/Uganda
76 C3   Mārgō, Dasht-e des. Afgh.
91 C2   Marhanets' Ukr.
62 A1   Mari Myanmar
152 B3   María Elena Chile
156 C5   Mariana Trench N. Pacific Ocean
142 B2   Marianna AR U.S.A.
143 C2   Marianna FL U.S.A.
102 C2   Mariánské Lázně Czech Rep.
144 B2   Marías, Islas is Mex.
78 B3   Ma'rib Yemen
109 C1   Maribor Slovenia
117 A4   Maridi watercourse S. Sudan
55 M2   Marie Byrd Land reg. Antarctica
147 D3   Marie-Galante i. Guadeloupe
93 G3   Mariehamn Fin.
122 A1   Marienthal Namibia
93 F4   Mariestad Sweden
143 D2   Marietta GA U.S.A.
140 C3   Marietta OH U.S.A.
105 D3   Marignane France
83 K3   Marii, Mys pt Rus. Fed.
88 B3   Marijampolė Lith.
154 C2   Marília Brazil
106 B1   Marín Spain
109 C3   Marina di Gioiosa Ionica Italy
88 C3   Mar"ina Horka Belarus
140 B1   Marinette U.S.A.
154 B2   Maringá Brazil
106 B2   Marinha Grande Port.
140 B2   Marion IN U.S.A.
140 C2   Marion OH U.S.A.
143 E2   Marion SC U.S.A.
140 C3   Marion VA U.S.A.
143 D2   Marion, Lake U.S.A.
52 A3   Marion Bay Austr.
152 B3   Mariscal José Félix Estigarribia Para.
110 C2   Maritsa r. Bulg.
91 D2   Mariupol' Ukr.
117 C4   Marka Somalia
123 C1   Marken S. Africa
100 B1   Markermeer l. Neth.
83 I2   Markha r. Rus. Fed.
91 D2   Markivka Ukr.
142 B2   Marksville U.S.A.
101 D3   Marktheidenfeld Ger.
101 F2   Marktredwitz Ger.
100 C2   Marl Ger.
100 A3   Marle France
105 D3   Marlin U.S.A.
104 C3   Marmande France
111 C2   Marmara, Sea of g. Turkey
      Marmara Denizi g. Turkey see Marmara, Sea of
111 C3   Marmaris Turkey
104 C2   Marne-la-Vallée France
101 E2   Maroldsweisach Ger.
121 □D2   Maroantsetra Madag.
121 □D2   Maromokotro mt. Madag.
121 C2   Marondera Zimbabwe
151 C1   Maroni r. Fr. Guiana
118 B1   Maroua Cameroon
121 □D2   Marovoay Madag.
49 I3   Marquesas Islands is Fr. Polynesia
140 B1   Marquette U.S.A.
117 A3   Marra, Jebel mt. Sudan
117 A3   Marra, Jebel plat. Sudan

123 D2   Marracuene Moz.
114 B1   Marrakech Morocco
52 A1   Marree Austr.
121 C2   Marromeu Moz.
121 C2   Marrupa Moz.
116 B2   Marsá al 'Alam Egypt
115 E1   Marsá al Burayqah Libya
119 D2   Marsabit Kenya
108 B3   Marsala Sicilia Italy
116 A1   Marsá Maṭrūḥ Egypt
101 D2   Marsberg Ger.
108 B2   Marsciano Italy
53 C2   Marsden Austr.
105 D3   Marseille France
137 D2   Marshall MO U.S.A.
137 E3   Marshall MO U.S.A.
139 E2   Marshall TX U.S.A.
48 F2   Marshall Islands country N. Pacific Ocean
140 A2   Marshalltown U.S.A.
143 E3   Marsh Harbour Bahamas
142 B3   Marsh Island U.S.A.
88 A2   Märsta Sweden
61 C2   Martapura Kalimantan Selatan Indon.
60 B2   Martapura Sumatera Selatan Indon.
141 E2   Martha's Vineyard i. U.S.A.
105 D2   Martigny Switz.
103 D2   Martin Slovakia
136 C2   Martin U.S.A.
145 C2   Martínez Mex.
147 D3   Martinique terr. West Indies
141 D3   Martinsburg U.S.A.
140 D3   Martinsville U.S.A.
76 B1   Martok Kazakh.
54 C2   Marton N.Z.
107 D1   Martorell Spain
106 C2   Martos Spain
105 C3   Marvejols France
76 C3   Mary Turkm.
51 E2   Maryborough Austr.
122 B2   Marydale S. Africa
141 D3   Maryland state U.S.A.
137 D3   Marysville U.S.A.
137 E2   Maryville MO U.S.A.
143 D1   Maryville TN U.S.A.
119 D3   Masai Steppe plain Tanz.
119 D3   Masaka Uganda
65 B2   Masan S. Korea
119 D4   Masasi Tanz.
64 B1   Masbate Phil.
64 B1   Masbate i. Phil.
123 C2   Maseru Lesotho
76 B3   Mashhad Iran
123 D2   Mashishing S. Africa
74 A2   Mashkel, Hamun-i- salt flat Pak.
123 C3   Masibambane S. Africa
79 C3   Masīlah, Wādī al watercourse Yemen
123 C2   Masilo S. Africa
119 D2   Masindi Uganda
79 C3   Maşīrah, Jazīrat i. Oman
79 C3   Maşīrah, Khalīj b. Oman
81 C2   Masjed-e Soleymān Iran
97 B2   Mask, Lough l. Ireland
121 □E2   Masoala, Tanjona c. Madag.
137 E2   Mason City U.S.A.
      Masqaṭ Oman see Muscat
108 B2   Massa Italy
141 E2   Massachusetts state U.S.A.
141 E2   Massachusetts Bay U.S.A.
121 C3   Massangena Moz.
120 A1   Massango Angola
116 B3   Massawa Eritrea

141 E2   Massena U.S.A.
128 A2   Masset Can.
105 C2   Massif Central mts France
140 C2   Massillon U.S.A.
121 C3   Massinga Moz.
123 D1   Massingir Moz.
78 A2   Mastābah Saudi Arabia
54 C2   Masterton N.Z.
74 A2   Mastung Pak.
78 A2   Mastūrah Saudi Arabia
88 B3   Masty Belarus
67 B4   Masuda Japan
      Masuku Gabon see Franceville
121 C3   Masvingo Zimbabwe
69 D1   Matad Mongolia
118 B3   Matadi Dem. Rep. Congo
146 B3   Matagalpa Nic.
130 C2   Matagami Can.
130 C2   Matagami, Lac l. Can.
139 D3   Matagorda Island U.S.A.
120 A2   Matala Angola
114 A3   Matam Senegal
144 B2   Matamoros Coahuila Mex.
145 C2   Matamoros Tamaulipas Mex.
119 D3   Matandu r. Tanz.
131 D2   Matane Can.
146 B2   Matanzas Cuba
73 C4   Matara Sri Lanka
61 C2   Mataram Indon.
50 C1   Mataranka Austr.
107 D1   Mataró Spain
123 C3   Matatiele S. Africa
54 A3   Mataura N.Z.
49 G3   Matā'utu Wallis and Futuna Is
54 C1   Matawai N.Z.
152 B2   Mategua Bol.
145 B2   Matehuala Mex.
109 C2   Matera Italy
139 D3   Mathis U.S.A.
75 B2   Mathura India
64 B2   Mati Phil.
98 C2   Matlock U.K.
150 C3   Mato Grosso Brazil
154 B1   Mato Grosso, Planalto do plat. Brazil
123 D2   Matola Moz.
      Matou China see Pingguo
67 B3   Matsue Japan
66 D2   Matsumae Japan
67 C4   Matsumoto Japan
67 B4   Matsuyama Japan
130 B1   Mattagami r. Can.
105 D2   Matterhorn mt. Italy/Switz.
134 C2   Matterhorn mt. U.S.A.
140 B3   Mattoon U.S.A.
150 B1   Maturín Venez.
123 C2   Matwabeng S. Africa
100 A2   Maubeuge France
104 C3   Maubourguet France
124 E5   Maui i. U.S.A.
140 C2   Maumee r. U.S.A.
120 B2   Maun Botswana
62 A1   Maungdaw Myanmar
50 □   Maurice, Lake imp. l. Austr.
114 A3   Mauritania country Africa
113 K9   Mauritius country Indian Ocean
78 B2   Māwān, Khashm mt. Saudi Arabia
118 B3   Mawanga Dem. Rep. Congo
71 B3   Mawei China
62 A1   Mawkmai Myanmar
62 A1   Mawlaik Myanmar
63 A2   Mawlamyaing Myanmar
78 B2   Mawqaq Saudi Arabia
78 B3   Mawza Yemen

Maxia, Punta

108 A3   **Maxia, Punta** *mt. Sardegna* Italy
83 J2   **Maya** *r.* Rus. Fed.
147 C2   **Mayaguana** *i.* Bahamas
96 B3   **Maybole** U.K.
104 B2   **Mayenne** France
104 B2   **Mayenne** *r.* France
128 C2   **Mayerthorpe** Can.
140 B3   **Mayfield** U.S.A.
87 D4   **Maykop** Rus. Fed.
126 B2   **Mayo** Can.
118 B3   **Mayoko** Congo
121 D2   **Mayotte** *terr.* Africa
83 J3   **Mayskiy** Rus. Fed.
140 C3   **Maysville** U.S.A.
118 B3   **Mayumba** Gabon
137 D1   **Mayville** U.S.A.
151 C2   **Mazagão** Brazil
104 C3   **Mazamet** France
77 D3   **Mazar** China
108 B3   **Mazara del Vallo** *Sicilia* Italy
77 C3   **Mazār-e Sharīf** Afgh.
144 A2   **Mazatán** Mex.
146 A3   **Mazatenango** Guat.
144 B2   **Mazatlán** Mex.
88 B2   **Mažeikiai** Lith.
88 B2   **Mazirbe** Latvia
71 C3   **Mazu Dao** *i.* Taiwan
121 B3   **Mazunga** Zimbabwe
88 C3   **Mazyr** Belarus
123 D2   **Mbabane** Swaziland
118 B2   **Mbaïki** C.A.R.
121 C1   **Mbala** Zambia
119 D2   **Mbale** Uganda
118 B2   **Mbalmayo** Cameroon
118 B3   **Mbandaka** Dem. Rep. Congo
118 A2   **Mbanga** Cameroon
120 A1   **M'banza Congo** Angola
119 D3   **Mbeya** Tanz.
119 D4   **Mbinga** Tanz.
123 D2   **Mbombela** S. Africa
118 B2   **Mbomo** Congo
118 B2   **Mbouda** Cameroon
114 A3   **Mbour** Senegal
114 A3   **Mbout** Maur.
118 C3   **Mbuji-Mayi** Dem. Rep. Congo
119 D3   **Mbuyuni** Tanz.
139 D2   **McAlester** U.S.A.
139 D3   **McAllen** U.S.A.
128 B2   **McBride** Can.
134 C2   **McCall** U.S.A.
126 E2   **McClintock Channel** Can.
126 D2   **McClure Strait** Can.
142 B2   **McComb** U.S.A.
136 C2   **McConaughy, Lake** U.S.A.
136 C2   **McCook** U.S.A.
134 C2   **McDermitt** U.S.A.
134 D1   **McDonald Peak** U.S.A.
134 D1   **McGuire, Mount** U.S.A.
128 C2   **McLennan** Can.
128 B2   **McLeod Lake** Can.
134 B1   **McMinnville** OR U.S.A.
142 C1   **McMinnville** TN U.S.A.
137 D3   **McPherson** U.S.A.
123 C3   **Mdantsane** S. Africa
135 D3   **Mead, Lake** *resr* U.S.A.
129 D2   **Meadow Lake** Can.
140 C2   **Meadville** U.S.A.
66 D2   **Meaken-dake** *vol.* Japan
106 B1   **Mealhada** Port.
131 E1   **Mealy Mountains** Can.
128 C2   **Meander River** Can.
78 A2   **Mecca** Saudi Arabia
100 B2   **Mechelen** Belgium
100 B2   **Mechelen** Neth.
100 C2   **Mechernich** Ger.
100 C2   **Meckenheim** Ger.

106 B1   **Meda** Port.
60 A1   **Medan** Indon.
153 B5   **Medanosa, Punta** *pt* Arg.
73 C4   **Medawachchiya** Sri Lanka
107 D2   **Médéa** Alg.
150 A1   **Medellín** Col.
115 D1   **Medenine** Tunisia
134 B2   **Medford** U.S.A.
110 C2   **Medgidia** Romania
110 B1   **Mediaş** Romania
136 B2   **Medicine Bow Mountains** U.S.A.
136 B2   **Medicine Bow Peak** U.S.A.
129 C2   **Medicine Hat** Can.
137 D3   **Medicine Lodge** U.S.A.
155 D1   **Medina** Brazil
78 A2   **Medina** Saudi Arabia
106 C1   **Medinaceli** Spain
106 C1   **Medina del Campo** Spain
106 B1   **Medina de Rioseco** Spain
84 G5   **Mediterranean Sea** World
87 E3   **Medley** Can.
87 E3   **Mednogorsk** Rus. Fed.
83 L2   **Medvezh'i, Ostrova** *is* Rus. Fed.
86 C2   **Medvezh'yegorsk** Rus. Fed.
50 A2   **Meekatharra** Austr.
136 B2   **Meeker** U.S.A.
75 B2   **Meerut** India
100 A2   **Meetkerke** Belgium
111 B3   **Megalopoli** Greece
75 C2   **Meghasani** *mt.* India
80 A2   **Megisti** *i.* Greece
92 I1   **Mehamn** Norway
50 A2   **Meharry, Mount** Austr.
79 C2   **Mehrān** *watercourse* Iran
74 B1   **Mehtar Lām** Afgh.
154 C1   **Meia Ponte** *r.* Brazil
118 B2   **Meiganga** Cameroon
65 B1   **Meihekou** China
    Meijiang China *see* **Ningdu**
62 A1   **Meiktila** Myanmar
101 E2   **Meiningen** Ger.
102 C1   **Meißen** Ger.
71 B3   **Meizhou** China
152 B3   **Mejicana** *mt.* Arg.
152 A3   **Mejillones** Chile
117 B3   **Mek'elē** Eth.
114 C2   **Mekerrhane, Sebkha** *salt pan* Alg.
114 B1   **Meknès** Morocco
63 B2   **Mekong** *r.* Asia
63 B3   **Mekong, Mouths of the** Vietnam
60 B1   **Melaka** Malaysia
53 B3   **Melbourne** Austr.
143 D3   **Melbourne** U.S.A.
108 A2   **Mele, Capo** *c.* Italy
131 C1   **Mélèzes, Rivière aux** *r.* Can.
115 D3   **Melfi** Chad
109 C2   **Melfi** Italy
129 D2   **Melfort** Can.
92 F3   **Melhus** Norway
106 B1   **Melide** Spain
114 B1   **Melilla** N. Africa
91 D2   **Melitopol'** Ukr.
101 D1   **Melle** Ger.
93 F4   **Mellerud** Sweden
101 E2   **Mellrichstadt** Ger.
100 D1   **Mellum** *i.* Ger.
152 C4   **Melo** Uru.
115 C1   **Melrhir, Chott** *salt l.* Alg.
99 C2   **Melton Mowbray** U.K.
104 C2   **Melun** France
129 D2   **Melville** Can.
51 D1   **Melville, Cape** Austr.
131 E1   **Melville, Lake** Can.

50 C1   **Melville Island** Austr.
126 D1   **Melville Island** Can.
127 F2   **Melville Peninsula** Can.
102 C2   **Memmingen** Ger.
61 B1   **Mempawah** Indon.
80 B3   **Memphis** *tourist site* Egypt
142 B1   **Memphis** TN U.S.A.
139 C2   **Memphis** TX U.S.A.
91 C1   **Mena** Ukr.
142 B2   **Mena** U.S.A.
114 C3   **Ménaka** Mali
    Mènam Khong *r.* Laos/Thai. *see* **Mekong**
105 C3   **Mende** France
116 B3   **Mendebo** Eritrea
145 C2   **Méndez** Mex.
119 D2   **Mendi** Eth.
59 D3   **Mendi** P.N.G.
99 B3   **Mendip Hills** U.K.
153 B4   **Mendoza** Arg.
111 C3   **Menemen** Turkey
60 B2   **Menggala** Indon.
62 B1   **Mengzi** China
131 D1   **Menihek** Can.
52 B2   **Menindee** Austr.
52 B2   **Menindee Lake** Austr.
52 A3   **Meningie** Austr.
104 C2   **Mennecy** France
140 B1   **Menominee** U.S.A.
120 A2   **Menongue** Angola
    Menorca *i.* Spain *see* **Minorca**
60 A1   **Mentawai, Kepulauan** *is* Indon.
50 B2   **Mentok** Indon.
50 B2   **Menzies** Austr.
100 C1   **Meppel** Neth.
100 C1   **Meppen** Ger.
123 D1   **Mepuze** Moz.
123 C2   **Meqheleng** S. Africa
108 B1   **Merano** Italy
59 D3   **Merauke** Indon.
52 B2   **Merbein** Austr.
135 B3   **Merced** U.S.A.
152 C3   **Mercedes** Arg.
127 G2   **Mercy, Cape** Can.
139 C1   **Meredith, Lake** U.S.A.
90 B2   **Merefa** Ukr.
116 A3   **Merga Oasis** Sudan
63 A2   **Mergui Archipelago** *is* Myanmar
110 C2   **Meriç** *r.* Greece/Turkey
145 D2   **Mérida** Mex.
106 B2   **Mérida** Spain
150 A1   **Mérida** Venez.
142 C2   **Meridian** U.S.A.
53 C3   **Merimbula** Austr.
116 B3   **Merowe** Sudan
50 A3   **Merredin** Austr.
96 B3   **Merrick** *h.* U.K.
140 B1   **Merrill** U.S.A.
140 B2   **Merrillville** U.S.A.
128 B2   **Merritt** Can.
53 C2   **Merrygoen** Austr.
116 C3   **Mersa Fatma** Eritrea
100 C3   **Mersch** Lux.
101 E2   **Merseburg (Saale)** Ger.
98 B2   **Mersey** *r.* U.K.
80 B2   **Mersin** Turkey
60 B1   **Mersing** Malaysia
99 D3   **Mers-les-Bains** France
74 B2   **Merta** India
99 B3   **Merthyr Tydfil** U.K.
106 B2   **Mértola** Port.
76 B2   **Mertvyy Kultuk, Sor** *dry lake* Kazakh.
119 D3   **Meru** *vol.* Tanz.
100 C3   **Merzig** Ger.
138 A2   **Mesa** U.S.A.

109	C2	Mesagne Italy
101	D2	Meschede Ger.
89	E3	Meshchovsk Rus. Fed.
91	E2	Meshkovskaya Rus. Fed.
111	B2	Mesimeri Greece
111	B3	Mesolongi Greece
121	D2	Messalo r. Moz.
109	C3	Messina Sicilia Italy
109	C3	Messina, Strait of Italy
111	B3	Messiniakos Kolpos g. Greece
110	B2	Mesta r. Bulg.
150	B1	Meta r. Col./Venez.
127	G2	Meta Incognita Peninsula Can.
152	B3	Metán Arg.
111	B3	Methoni Greece
109	C2	Metković Croatia
60	B2	Metro Indon.
117	B4	Metu Eth.
105	D2	Metz France
100	B2	Meuse r. Belgium/France
139	D2	Mexia U.S.A.
144	A1	Mexicali Mex.
144	B2	Mexico country Central America
137	E3	Mexico U.S.A.
125	I5	Mexico, Gulf of Mex./U.S.A.
145	C3	Mexico City Mex.
101	F1	Meyenburg Ger.
86	D2	Mezen' Rus. Fed.
86	D2	Mezen' r. Rus. Fed.
86	E1	Mezhdusharskiy, Ostrov i. Rus. Fed.
103	E2	Mezőtúr Hungary
144	B2	Mezquitic Mex.
88	C2	Mežvidi Latvia
121	C2	Mfuwe Zambia
123	D2	Mhlume Swaziland
74	B2	Mhow India
145	C3	Miahuatlán Mex.
106	B2	Miajadas Spain
143	D3	Miami FL U.S.A.
139	E1	Miami OK U.S.A.
143	D3	Miami Beach U.S.A.
81	C2	Miāndowāb Iran
121	□D2	Miandrivazo Madag.
81	C2	Miāneh Iran
74	B1	Mianwali Pak.
70	A2	Mianyang China
121	□D2	Miarinarivo Madag.
87	F3	Miass Rus. Fed.
128	C2	Mica Creek Can.
103	E2	Michalovce Slovakia
140	B1	Michigan state U.S.A.
140	B2	Michigan, Lake U.S.A.
140	B2	Michigan City U.S.A.
130	B2	Michipicoten Island Can.
130	B2	Michipicoten River Can.
89	F3	Michurinsk Rus. Fed.
48	D2	Micronesia, Federated States of country N. Pacific Ocean
100	A2	Middelburg Neth.
123	C3	Middelburg E. Cape S. Africa
123	C2	Middelburg Mpumalanga S. Africa
100	B2	Middelharnis Neth.
134	B3	Middle Alkali Lake U.S.A.
73	D3	Middle Andaman i. India
136	D2	Middle Loup r. U.S.A.
140	C3	Middlesboro U.S.A.
98	C1	Middlesbrough U.K.
141	E2	Middletown NY U.S.A.
140	C3	Middletown OH U.S.A.
78	B3	Midi Yemen
130	C2	Midland Can.
140	C2	Midland MI U.S.A.
139	C2	Midland TX U.S.A.
97	B3	Midleton Ireland
94	B1	Miðvágur Faroe Is
109	D2	Midzhur mt. Bulg./S.M.
103	E1	Mielec Pol.
110	C1	Miercurea-Ciuc Romania
106	B1	Mieres del Camín Spain
101	E1	Mieste Ger.
145	C3	Miguel Alemán, Presa resr Mex.
144	B2	Miguel Auza Mex.
144	B2	Miguel Hidalgo, Presa resr Mex.
63	A2	Migyaunglaung Myanmar
89	E3	Mikhaylov Rus. Fed.
		Mikhaylovgrad Bulg. see Montana
66	B2	Mikhaylovka Rus. Fed.
77	D1	Mikhaylovskoye Rus. Fed.
93	I3	Mikkeli Fin.
86	E2	Mikun' Rus. Fed.
67	C3	Mikuni-sanmyaku mts Japan
108	A1	Milan Italy
121	C2	Milange Moz.
		Milano Italy see Milan
111	C3	Milas Turkey
137	D1	Milbank U.S.A.
99	D2	Mildenhall U.K.
52	B2	Mildura Austr.
62	B1	Mile China
136	B1	Miles City U.S.A.
141	D3	Milford DE U.S.A.
135	D3	Milford UT U.S.A.
99	A3	Milford Haven U.K.
54	A2	Milford Sound N.Z.
107	D2	Miliana Alg.
116	B3	Milk, Wadi el watercourse Sudan
83	L3	Mil'kovo Rus. Fed.
129	C3	Milk River Can.
105	C3	Millau France
143	D2	Milledgeville U.S.A.
137	E1	Mille Lacs lakes U.S.A.
130	A2	Mille Lacs, Lac des l. Can.
137	D2	Miller U.S.A.
91	E2	Millerovo Rus. Fed.
52	A2	Millers Creek Austr.
52	B3	Millicent Austr.
141	F1	Millinocket U.S.A.
53	D1	Millmerran Austr.
98	B1	Millom U.K.
128	C1	Mills Lake Can.
111	B3	Milos i. Greece
89	E3	Miloslavskoye Rus. Fed.
91	E2	Milove Ukr.
52	B1	Milparinka Austr.
54	A3	Milton N.Z.
99	C2	Milton Keynes U.K.
140	B2	Milwaukee U.S.A.
104	B3	Mimizan France
118	B3	Mimongo Gabon
79	C2	Mīnāb Iran
58	C2	Minahasa, Semenanjung pen. Indon.
79	C2	Mina Jebel Ali U.A.E.
60	B1	Minas Indon.
153	C4	Minas Uru.
155	D1	Minas Novas Brazil
145	C3	Minatitlán Mex.
62	A1	Minbu Myanmar
64	B2	Mindanao i. Phil.
101	D1	Minden Ger.
142	B2	Minden LA U.S.A.
137	D2	Minden NE U.S.A.
64	A1	Mindoro i. Phil.
64	A1	Mindoro Strait Phil.
118	B3	Mindouli Congo
99	B3	Minehead U.K.
154	B1	Mineiros Brazil
139	D2	Mineral Wells U.S.A.
77	E3	Minfeng China
119	C4	Minga Dem. Rep. Congo
81	C1	Mingäçevir Azer.
131	D1	Mingan Can.
52	B2	Mingary Austr.
70	B2	Mingguang China
62	A1	Mingin Myanmar
106	B2	Minglanilla Spain
119	D4	Mingoyo Tanz.
69	E1	Mingshui China
71	B3	Mingxi China
73	B4	Minicoy atoll India
50	A2	Minilya Austr.
131	D1	Minipi Lake Can.
130	A1	Miniss Lake Can.
114	A3	Minna Nigeria
137	E2	Minneapolis U.S.A.
129	E2	Minnedosa Can.
137	E2	Minnesota r. U.S.A.
137	E1	Minnesota state U.S.A.
106	B1	Miño r. Port./Spain
107	D1	Minorca i. Spain
136	C1	Minot U.S.A.
88	C3	Minsk Belarus
103	E1	Mińsk Mazowiecki Pol.
131	D2	Minto Can.
130	C1	Minto, Lac l. Can.
70	A2	Minxian China
155	D1	Mirabela Brazil
155	D1	Miralta Brazil
131	D2	Miramichi N.B. Can.
111	C3	Mirampellou, Kolpos b. Greece
152	B3	Miranda Brazil
152	C2	Miranda r. Brazil
106	C1	Miranda de Ebro Spain
106	B1	Mirandela Port.
154	B2	Mirandópolis Brazil
79	C2	Mirbāţ Oman
61	C1	Miri Sarawak Malaysia
153	C4	Mirim, Lagoa l. Brazil/Uru.
79	D2	Mīrjāveh Iran
83	I2	Mirnyy Rus. Fed.
101	F1	Mirow Ger.
74	A2	Mirpur Khas Pak.
111	B3	Mirtoö Pelagos sea Greece
65	B2	Miryang S. Korea
75	C2	Mirzapur India
66	B1	Mishan China
146	B3	Miskitos, Cayos is Nic.
103	E2	Miskolc Hungary
59	C3	Misoöl i. Indon.
115	D1	Mişrātah Libya
130	B1	Missinaibi r. Can.
130	B2	Missinaibi Lake Can.
128	B3	Mission Can.
130	B1	Missisa Lake Can.
142	C3	Mississippi r. U.S.A.
142	C3	Mississippi state U.S.A.
142	C3	Mississippi Delta U.S.A.
134	D1	Missoula U.S.A.
137	E3	Missouri r. U.S.A.
137	E3	Missouri state U.S.A.
131	C2	Mistassibi r. Can.
130	C1	Mistassini, Lac l. Can.
131	D1	Mistastin Lake Can.
103	D2	Mistelbach Austria
131	D1	Mistinibi, Lac l. Can.
130	C1	Mistissini Can.
51	D2	Mitchell Austr.
51	D1	Mitchell r. Austr.
137	D2	Mitchell U.S.A.
97	B2	Mitchelstown Ireland
74	A2	Mithi Pak.
67	D3	Mito Japan
119	D3	Mitole Tanz.

109	D2	Mitrovicë Kosovo
53	D2	Mittagong Austr.
101	E2	Mittelhausen Ger.
101	D1	Mittellandkanal *canal* Ger.
101	F3	Mitterteich Ger.
150	A1	Mitú Col.
119	C3	Mitumba, Chaîne des *mts* Dem. Rep. Congo
119	C3	Mitumba, Monts *mts* Dem. Rep. Congo
118	B2	Mitzic Gabon
78	B2	Miyah, Wādī al *watercourse* Saudi Arabia
67	C4	Miyake-jima *i.* Japan
66	D3	Miyako Japan
67	B4	Miyakonojō Japan
76	B2	Miyaly Kazakh.
		Miyang China *see* Mile
67	B4	Miyazaki Japan
115	D1	Mizdah Libya
97	B3	Mizen Head Ireland
90	A2	Mizhhir''ya Ukr.
93	G4	Mjölby Sweden
93	F3	Mjøsa *l.* Norway
119	D3	Mkomazi Tanz.
103	C1	Mladá Boleslav Czech Rep.
109	D2	Mladenovac Serbia
103	E1	Mława Pol.
123	C3	Mlungisi S. Africa
90	B1	Mlyniv Ukr.
123	C2	Mmabatho S. Africa
123	C2	Mmathethe Botswana
135	E3	Moab U.S.A.
123	D2	Moamba Moz.
119	C3	Moba Dem. Rep. Congo
118	C2	Mobayi-Mbongo Dem. Rep. Congo
137	E3	Moberly U.S.A.
142	C2	Mobile U.S.A.
142	C2	Mobile Bay U.S.A.
136	C1	Mobridge U.S.A.
121	D2	Moçambique Moz.
62	B1	Môc Châu Vietnam
78	B3	Mocha Yemen
123	C1	Mochudi Botswana
121	D2	Mocímboa da Praia Moz.
150	A1	Mocoa Col.
154	C2	Mococa Brazil
144	B2	Mocorito Mex.
144	B1	Moctezuma *Chihuahua* Mex.
145	B2	Moctezuma *San Luis Potosí* Mex.
144	B2	Moctezuma *Sonora* Mex.
121	C2	Mocuba Moz.
105	D2	Modane France
122	B2	Modder *r.* S. Africa
108	B2	Modena Italy
135	B3	Modesto U.S.A.
123	C1	Modimolle S. Africa
123	C1	Modjadjiskloof S. Africa
53	C3	Moe Austr.
100	C2	Moers Ger.
96	C3	Moffat U.K.
117	C4	Mogadishu Somalia
123	C1	Mogalakwena *r.* S. Africa
62	A1	Mogaung Myanmar
		Mogilev Belarus *see* **Mahilyow**
		Mogi-Mirim Brazil
83	I3	Mogocha Rus. Fed.
62	A1	Mogok Myanmar
103	D2	Mohács Hungary
123	C3	Mohale's Hoek Lesotho
74	B1	Mohali India
107	D2	Mohammadia Alg.
141	F1	Mohawk *r.* U.S.A.
119	D3	Mohoro Tanz.
90	B2	Mohyliv-Podil's'kyy Ukr.

110	C1	Moineşti Romania
92	F2	Mo i Rana Norway
104	C3	Moissac France
135	C3	Mojave U.S.A.
135	C3	Mojave Desert U.S.A.
62	B1	Mojiang China
155	C2	Moji das Cruzes Brazil
154	C2	Moji-Guaçu *r.* Brazil
54	B1	Mokau N.Z.
123	C2	Mokhotlong Lesotho
123	C1	Mokopane S. Africa
65	B3	Mokp'o S. Korea
145	C2	Molango Mex.
		Moldavia *country* Europe *see* Moldova
92	E3	Molde Norway
90	B2	Moldova *country* Europe
110	B1	Moldoveanu, Vârful *mt.* Romania
90	B2	Moldovei Centrale, Podişul *plat.* Moldova
123	C1	Molepolole Botswana
88	C2	Moletai Lith.
109	C2	Molfetta Italy
107	C1	Molina de Aragón Spain
150	A3	Mollendo Peru
53	C2	Molong Austr.
122	B2	Molopo *watercourse* Botswana/S. Africa
118	B2	Moloundou Cameroon
59	C3	Moluccas *is* Indon.
		Molucca Sea Indon. *see* Maluku, Laut
52	B2	Momba Austr.
119	D3	Mombasa Kenya
154	B1	Mombuca, Serra da *hills* Brazil
93	F4	Møn *i.* Denmark
105	D3	Monaco *country* Europe
96	B2	Monadhliath Mountains U.K.
97	C1	Monaghan Ireland
89	D3	Monastyrshchina Rus. Fed.
90	B2	Monastyryshche Ukr.
66	D2	Monbetsu Japan
108	A1	Moncalieri Italy
107	C1	Moncayo *mt.* Spain
86	C2	Monchegorsk Rus. Fed.
100	C2	Mönchengladbach Ger.
144	B2	Monclova Mex.
131	D2	Moncton Can.
106	B1	Mondego *r.* Port.
108	A2	Mondovì Italy
111	B3	Monemvasia Greece
66	D1	Moneron, Ostrov *i.* Rus. Fed.
137	E3	Monett U.S.A.
108	B1	Monfalcone Italy
106	B1	Monforte de Lemos Spain
62	B1	Mông Cai Vietnam
62	B1	Mong Lin Myanmar
68	C1	Mongolia *country* Asia
62	A1	Mong Pawk Myanmar
62	A1	Mong Ping Myanmar
120	B2	Mongu Zambia
135	C3	Monitor Range *mts* U.S.A.
114	C4	Mono *r.* Benin/Togo
135	C3	Mono Lake U.S.A.
109	C2	Monopoli Italy
107	C1	Monreal del Campo Spain
142	B2	Monroe *LA* U.S.A.
140	B2	Monroe *WI* U.S.A.
142	C2	Monroeville U.S.A.
114	A4	Monrovia Liberia
100	A2	Mons Belgium
122	B3	Montagu S. Africa
109	C3	Montalto *mt.* Italy
110	B2	Montana Bulg.
134	E1	Montana *state* U.S.A.
104	C2	Montargis France

104	C3	Montauban France
141	E2	Montauk Point U.S.A.
123	C2	Mont-aux-Sources *mt.* Lesotho
105	C2	Montbard France
105	C2	Montbrison France
100	B3	Montcornet France
104	B3	Mont-de-Marsan France
104	C2	Montdidier France
151	C2	Monte Alegre Brazil
105	D3	Monte-Carlo Monaco
152	C4	Monte Caseros Arg.
146	C3	Montego Bay Jamaica
105	C3	Montélimar France
109	C2	Montella Italy
145	C2	Montemorelos Mex.
104	B2	Montendre France
109	C2	Montenegro *country* Europe
121	C2	Montepuez Moz.
108	B2	Montepulciano Italy
135	B3	Monterey U.S.A.
135	B3	Monterey Bay U.S.A.
150	A1	Montería Col.
152	B2	Montero Bol.
145	B2	Monterrey Mex.
109	C2	Montesano sulla Marcellana Italy
109	C2	Monte Sant'Angelo Italy
151	E3	Monte Santo Brazil
108	A2	Monte Santu, Capo di *c.* Sardegna Italy
155	D1	Montes Claros Brazil
153	C4	Montevideo Uru.
137	D2	Montevideo U.S.A.
136	B3	Monte Vista U.S.A.
142	C2	Montgomery U.S.A.
105	D2	Monthey Switz.
142	B2	Monticello *AR* U.S.A.
135	E3	Monticello *UT* U.S.A.
104	C2	Montignac France
105	D2	Montigny-le-Roi France
106	C2	Montilla Spain
131	D2	Mont-Joli Can.
104	C2	Mont-Laurier Can.
104	C2	Montluçon France
131	C2	Montmagny Can.
104	C2	Montmorillon France
51	E2	Monto Austr.
134	D2	Montpelier *ID* U.S.A.
141	E2	Montpelier *VT* U.S.A.
105	C3	Montpellier France
130	C2	Montréal Can.
129	D2	Montreal Lake Can.
129	D2	Montreal Lake Can.
99	D3	Montreuil France
105	D2	Montreux Switz.
96	C2	Montrose U.K.
136	B3	Montrose U.S.A.
147	D3	Montserrat *terr.* West Indies
62	A1	Monywa Myanmar
108	A1	Monza Italy
107	C1	Monzón Spain
123	C1	Mookane Botswana
123	C1	Mookgophong S. Africa
53	D1	Moonie Austr.
53	C1	Moonie *r.* Austr.
52	A2	Moonta Austr.
50	A2	Moore, Lake *imp. l.* Austr.
137	D1	Moorhead U.S.A.
53	C3	Mooroopna Austr.
122	A3	Moorreesburg S. Africa
130	B1	Moose *r.* Can.
130	B1	Moose Factory Can.
141	F1	Moosehead Lake U.S.A.
129	D2	Moose Jaw Can.
137	E1	Moose Lake U.S.A.
129	D2	Moosomin Can.
130	B1	Moosonee Can.

52	B2	Mootwingee Austr.
123	C1	Mopane S. Africa
114	B3	Mopti Mali
150	A3	Moquegua Peru
93	F3	Mora Sweden
137	E1	Mora U.S.A.
75	B2	Moradabad India
103	D2	Morava r. Europe
96	B2	Moray Firth b. U.K.
100	C3	Morbach Ger.
74	B2	Morbi India
128	B2	Morcenx France
69	E1	Mordaga China
129	E3	Morden Can.
91	E1	Mordovo Rus. Fed.
98	B1	Morecambe U.K.
98	B1	Morecambe Bay U.K.
53	C1	Moree Austr.
59	D3	Morehead P.N.G.
140	C3	Morehead U.S.A.
143	E2	Morehead City U.S.A.
145	B3	Morelia Mex.
107	C1	Morella Spain
106	B2	Morena, Sierra mts Spain
110	C2	Moreni Romania
128	A2	Moresby, Mount Can.
142	B3	Morgan City U.S.A.
143	D1	Morganton U.S.A.
140	D3	Morgantown U.S.A.
105	D2	Morges Switz.
77	C3	Morghāb, Daryā-ye r. Afgh.
66	D2	Mori Japan
128	B2	Morice Lake Can.
66	D3	Morioka Japan
53	D2	Morisset Austr.
104	B2	Morlaix France
51	C1	Mornington Island Austr.
59	D3	Morobe P.N.G.
114	B1	Morocco country Africa
119	D3	Morogoro Tanz.
64	B2	Moro Gulf Phil.
122	B2	Morokweng S. Africa
121	□D3	Morombe Madag.
68	C1	Mörön Mongolia
121	□D3	Morondava Madag.
121	D2	Moroni Comoros
59	C2	Morotai i. Indon.
119	D2	Moroto Uganda
98	C1	Morpeth U.K.
86	F2	Morrasale Rus. Fed.
154	C1	Morrinhos Brazil
129	E3	Morris Can.
137	D1	Morris U.S.A.
143	D1	Morristown U.S.A.
87	D3	Morshansk Rus. Fed.
154	B1	Mortes, Rio das r. Brazil
52	B3	Mortlake Austr.
53	D3	Moruya Austr.
96	B2	Morvern reg. U.K.
53	C3	Morwell Austr.
102	B2	Mosbach Ger.
89	E2	Moscow Rus. Fed.
134	C1	Moscow U.S.A.
100	C2	Mosel r. Ger.
105	D2	Moselle r. France
134	C1	Moses Lake U.S.A.
92	□A3	Mosfellsbær Iceland
54	B3	Mosgiel N.Z.
89	D2	Moshenskoye Rus. Fed.
119	D3	Moshi Tanz.
92	F2	Mosjøen Norway
		Moskva Rus. Fed. see
		Moscow
103	D2	Mosonmagyaróvár Hungary
146	B3	Mosquitos, Costa de coastal
		area Nic.

146	B4	Mosquitos, Golfo de los b. Panama
93	F4	Moss Norway
122	B3	Mossel Bay S. Africa
122	B3	Mossel Bay S. Africa
118	B3	Mossendjo Congo
52	B2	Mossgiel Austr.
51	D1	Mossman Austr.
151	E2	Mossoró Brazil
53	D2	Moss Vale Austr.
102	C1	Most Czech Rep.
114	C1	Mostaganem Alg.
109	C2	Mostar Bos.-Herz.
152	C4	Mostardas Brazil
81	C2	Mosul Iraq
93	G4	Motala Sweden
96	C3	Motherwell U.K.
107	C2	Motilla del Palancar Spain
122	B1	Motokwe Botswana
106	C2	Motril Spain
110	B2	Motru Romania
63	A2	Mottama, Gulf of Myanmar
145	D2	Motul Mex.
111	C3	Moudros Greece
118	B3	Mouila Gabon
52	B3	Moulamein Austr.
105	C2	Moulins France
143	D2	Moultrie U.S.A.
143	E2	Moultrie, Lake U.S.A.
140	B3	Mound City U.S.A.
115	D4	Moundou Chad
137	E3	Mountain Grove U.S.A.
142	B1	Mountain Home AR U.S.A.
134	C2	Mountain Home ID U.S.A.
143	D1	Mount Airy U.S.A.
52	A3	Mount Barker Austr.
121	C2	Mount Beauty Austr.
123	C2	Mount Darwin Zimbabwe
141	F2	Mount Desert Island U.S.A.
123	C3	Mount Fletcher S. Africa
123	C3	Mount Frere S. Africa
52	B3	Mount Gambier Austr.
59	D3	Mount Hagen P.N.G.
53	C2	Mount Hope Austr.
51	C2	Mount Isa Austr.
50	A2	Mount Magnet Austr.
52	B2	Mount Manara Austr.
54	C1	Mount Maunganui N.Z.
111	B3	Mount Olympus Greece
137	E2	Mount Pleasant IA U.S.A.
140	C2	Mount Pleasant MI U.S.A.
139	E2	Mount Pleasant TX U.S.A.
99	A3	Mount's Bay U.K.
134	B2	Mount Shasta U.S.A.
140	B3	Mount Vernon IL U.S.A.
140	C3	Mount Vernon OH U.S.A.
134	B1	Mount Vernon WA U.S.A.
51	D2	Moura Austr.
115	E3	Mourdi, Dépression du depr. Chad
97	C1	Mourne Mountains hills U.K.
100	A2	Mouscron Belgium
115	D3	Moussoro Chad
58	C2	Moutong Indon.
115	C2	Mouydir, Monts du plat. Alg.
100	B3	Mouzon France
97	B1	Moy r. Ireland
117	B4	Moyale Eth.
123	C3	Moyeni Lesotho
76	B2	Mo'ynoq Uzbek.
77	D2	Moyynty Kazakh.
113	I9	Mozambique country Africa
113	I9	Mozambique Channel Africa
89	E2	Mozhaysk Rus. Fed.
119	D3	Mpanda Tanz.
121	C2	Mpika Zambia
121	C1	Mporokoso Zambia

123	C2	Mpumalanga prov. S. Africa
62	A1	Mrauk-U Myanmar
88	C2	Mshinskaya Rus. Fed.
107	D2	M'Sila Alg.
89	D2	Msta r. Rus. Fed.
89	D2	Mstinskiy Most Rus. Fed.
89	D3	Mstsislaw Belarus
123	C3	Mthatha S. Africa
89	E3	Mtsensk Rus. Fed.
119	E4	Mtwara Tanz.
118	B3	Muanda Dem. Rep. Congo
63	B2	Muang Không Laos
62	B1	Muang Ngoy Laos
62	B2	Muang Pakbeng Laos
62	B1	Muang Sing Laos
62	B2	Muang Vangviang Laos
60	B1	Muar Malaysia
60	B2	Muarabungo Indon.
60	B2	Muaradua Indon.
61	C2	Muaralaung Indon.
60	A2	Muarasiberut Indon.
60	B2	Muaratembesi Indon.
61	C2	Muarateweh Indon.
119	D2	Mubende Uganda
115	D3	Mubi Nigeria
120	B2	Muconda Angola
155	E1	Mucuri Brazil
155	E1	Mucuri r. Brazil
66	A2	Mudanjiang China
66	A1	Mudan Jiang r. China
111	C2	Mudanya Turkey
101	E1	Muden (Örtze) Ger.
53	C2	Mudgee Austr.
63	A2	Mudon Myanmar
80	B1	Mudurnu Turkey
121	C2	Mueda Moz.
121	B2	Mufulira Zambia
120	B2	Mufumbwe Zambia
111	C3	Muğla Turkey
116	B3	Muhammad Qol Sudan
101	F2	Mühlberg Ger.
101	E2	Mühlhausen (Thüringen) Ger.
121	C2	Muite Moz.
65	B2	Muju S. Korea
90	A2	Mukacheve Ukr.
61	C1	Mukah Sarawak Malaysia
79	B3	Mukalla Yemen
63	A2	Mukdahan Thai.
50	A3	Mukinbudin Austr.
60	B2	Mukomuko Indon.
121	C2	Mulanje, Mount Malawi
101	F2	Mulde r. Ger.
144	A2	Mulegé Mex.
139	C2	Muleshoe U.S.A.
106	C2	Mulhacén mt. Spain
100	C2	Mülheim an der Ruhr Ger.
105	D2	Mulhouse France
66	B2	Muling China
66	B1	Muling He r. China
96	B2	Mull i. U.K.
53	C2	Mullaley Austr.
136	C2	Mullen U.S.A.
61	C1	Muller, Pegunungan mts Indon.
50	A2	Mullewa Austr.
97	C2	Mullingar Ireland
96	B3	Mull of Galloway c. U.K.
96	B3	Mull of Kintyre hd U.K.
96	A3	Mull of Oa hd U.K.
120	B2	Mulobezi Zambia
74	B1	Multan Pak.
73	B3	Mumbai India
120	B2	Mumbwa Zambia
145	D2	Muna Mex.
101	E2	Münchberg Ger.
		München Ger. see Munich
140	B2	Muncie U.S.A.

Mundrabilla

50	B3	Mundrabilla Austr.
119	C2	Mungbere Dem. Rep. Congo
75	C2	Munger India
52	A1	Mungeranie Austr.
53	C1	Mungindi Austr.
102	C2	Munich Ger.
155	D2	Muniz Freire Brazil
101	E1	Münster Niedersachsen Ger.
100	C2	Münster Nordrhein-Westfalen Ger.
97	B2	Munster reg. Ireland
100	C2	Münsterland reg. Ger.
62	B1	Mương Nhe Vietnam
92	H2	Muonio Fin.
92	H2	Muonioälven r. Fin./Sweden
		Muqdisho Somalia see Mogadishu
103	D2	Mur r. Austria
119	C3	Muramvya Burundi
119	D3	Murang'a Kenya
81	B2	Murat r. Turkey
111	C2	Muratlı Turkey
50	A2	Murchison watercourse Austr.
107	C2	Murcia Spain
111	C2	Mürefte Turkey
110	B1	Mureşul r. Romania
104	C3	Muret France
142	C1	Murfreesboro U.S.A.
77	D3	Murghob Tajik.
155	D2	Muriaé Brazil
120	B1	Muriege Angola
101	F1	Müritz l. Ger.
86	C2	Murmansk Rus. Fed.
87	D3	Murom Rus. Fed.
66	D2	Muroran Japan
106	B1	Muros Spain
67	B4	Muroto Japan
67	B4	Muroto-zaki pt Japan
143	D1	Murphy U.S.A.
53	C1	Murra Murra Austr.
52	A3	Murray r. Austr.
128	B2	Murray r. Can.
140	B3	Murray U.S.A.
143	D2	Murray, Lake U.S.A.
52	A3	Murray, Lake Austr.
122	B3	Murraysburg S. Africa
52	B3	Murrayville Austr.
52	B2	Murrumbidgee r. Austr.
121	C2	Murrupula Moz.
53	D2	Murrurundi Austr.
109	C1	Murska Sobota Slovenia
54	C1	Murupara N.Z.
49	I4	Mururoa atoll Fr. Polynesia
75	C2	Murwara India
53	D1	Murwillumbah Austr.
115	D2	Murzūq Libya
81	C2	Muş Turkey
110	B2	Musala mt. Bulg.
65	B1	Musan N. Korea
78	B3	Musaymīr Yemen
79	C2	Muscat Oman
137	E2	Muscatine U.S.A.
50	C2	Musgrave Ranges mts Austr.
118	B3	Mushie Dem. Rep. Congo
60	B2	Musi r. Indon.
123	D1	Musina S. Africa
140	B2	Muskegon U.S.A.
139	D1	Muskogee U.S.A.
128	B2	Muskwa r. Can.
74	A1	Muslimbagh Pak.
78	A3	Musmar Sudan
119	D3	Musoma Tanz.
96	C3	Musselburgh U.K.
88	B2	Mustjala Estonia
53	D2	Muswellbrook Austr.
116	A2	Mūţ Egypt
121	C2	Mutare Zimbabwe

66	D2	Mutsu Japan
121	C2	Mutuali Moz.
92	I2	Muurola Fin.
70	A2	Mu Us Shadi des. China
120	A1	Muxaluando Angola
86	C2	Muyezerskiy Rus. Fed.
119	D3	Muyinga Burundi
74	B1	Muzaffargarh Pak.
75	C2	Muzaffarpur India
144	B2	Múzquiz Mex.
75	C1	Muz Shan mt. China
119	C3	Mwanza Dem. Rep. Congo
119	D3	Mwanza Tanz.
118	C3	Mweka Dem. Rep. Congo
121	B2	Mwenda Zambia
118	C3	Mwene-Ditu Dem. Rep. Congo
121	C3	Mwenezi Zimbabwe
119	C3	Mweru, Lake Dem. Rep. Congo/Zambia
118	C3	Mwimba Dem. Rep. Congo
120	B2	Mwinilunga Zambia
88	C3	Myadzyel Belarus
62	A2	Myanaung Myanmar
62	A1	Myanmar country Asia
63	A2	Myaungmya Myanmar
63	A2	Myeik Myanmar
		Myeik Kyunzu is Myanmar see Mergui Archipelago
62	A1	Myingyan Myanmar
62	A1	Myitkyina Myanmar
91	C2	Mykolayiv Ukr.
111	C3	Mykonos Greece
111	C3	Mykonos i. Greece
86	E2	Myla Rus. Fed.
75	D2	Mymensingh Bangl.
65	B1	Myŏnggan N. Korea
88	C2	Myory Belarus
92	□B3	Mýrdalsjökull Iceland
91	C2	Myrhorod Ukr.
90	C2	Myronivka Ukr.
143	E2	Myrtle Beach U.S.A.
53	C3	Myrtleford Austr.
134	B2	Myrtle Point U.S.A.
89	E2	Myshkin Rus. Fed.
103	C1	Myślibórz Pol.
73	B3	Mysore India
83	N2	Mys Shmidta Rus. Fed.
		Mysuru India see Mysore
63	B2	My Tho Vietnam
111	C3	Mytilini Greece
89	E3	Mytishchi Rus. Fed.
123	C3	Mzamomhle S. Africa
121	C2	Mzimba Malawi
121	C2	Mzuzu Malawi

N

97	C2	Naas Ireland
122	A2	Nababeep S. Africa
87	E3	Naberezhnyye Chelny Rus. Fed.
59	D3	Nabire Indon.
80	B2	Nāblus West Bank
121	D2	Nacala Moz.
63	A2	Nachuge India
139	E2	Nacogdoches U.S.A.
144	B1	Nacozari de García Mex.
74	B2	Nadiad India
90	A2	Nadvirna Ukr.
86	C2	Nadvoitsy Rus. Fed.
86	G2	Nadym Rus. Fed.
93	F4	Næstved Denmark
111	B3	Nafpaktos Greece
111	B3	Nafplio Greece

115	D1	Nafūsah, Jabal hills Libya
78	B2	Nafy Saudi Arabia
64	B1	Naga Phil.
130	B1	Nagagami r. Can.
67	C3	Nagano Japan
67	C3	Nagaoka Japan
75	D2	Nagaon India
74	B1	Nagar India
74	B2	Nagar Parkar Pak.
67	A4	Nagasaki Japan
67	B4	Nagato Japan
74	B2	Nagaur India
73	B4	Nagercoil India
74	A2	Nagha Kalat Pak.
75	B2	Nagina India
67	C3	Nagoya Japan
75	B2	Nagpur India
68	C2	Nagqu China
103	D2	Nagyatád Hungary
103	D2	Nagykanizsa Hungary
128	B1	Nahanni Butte Can.
76	A3	Nahāvand Iran
101	E1	Nahrendorf Ger.
153	A5	Nahuel Huapí, Lago l. Arg.
131	E1	Nain Can.
81	D2	Nā'īn Iran
96	C2	Nairn U.K.
119	D3	Nairobi Kenya
119	D3	Naivasha Kenya
81	D2	Najafābād Iran
78	B2	Najd reg. Saudi Arabia
106	C1	Nájera Spain
65	C1	Najin N. Korea
78	B3	Najrān Saudi Arabia
		Nakambé r. Burkina/Ghana see White Volta
67	C3	Nakatsugawa Japan
78	A3	Nakfa Eritrea
66	B2	Nakhodka Rus. Fed.
63	B2	Nakhon Pathom Thai.
63	B2	Nakhon Ratchasima Thai.
63	B2	Nakhon Sawan Thai.
63	A3	Nakhon Si Thammarat Thai.
130	B1	Nakina Can.
121	C1	Nakonde Zambia
93	F4	Nakskov Denmark
119	D3	Nakuru Kenya
128	C2	Nakusp Can.
75	D2	Nalbari India
87	D4	Nal'chik Rus. Fed.
115	D1	Nālūt Libya
123	C2	Namahadi S. Africa
77	D2	Namangan Uzbek.
122	A2	Namaqualand reg. S. Africa
51	E2	Nambour Austr.
53	D2	Nambucca Heads Austr.
75	D1	Nam Co salt l. China
62	B1	Nam Đinh Vietnam
120	A3	Namib Desert Namibia
120	A2	Namibe Angola
120	A3	Namibia country Africa
72	D2	Namjagbarwa Feng mt. China
59	C3	Namlea Indon.
53	C2	Namoi r. Austr.
134	C2	Nampa U.S.A.
114	B3	Nampala Mali
65	B2	Namp'o N. Korea
121	C2	Nampula Moz.
62	A1	Namrup India
62	A1	Namsang Myanmar
92	F3	Namsos Norway
62	A1	Nam Tok Thai.
83	J2	Namtsy Rus. Fed.
62	A1	Namtu Myanmar
100	B2	Namur Belgium
120	B2	Namwala Zambia
65	B2	Namwŏn S. Korea

62 A1 **Namya Ra** Myanmar
62 B2 **Nan** Thai.
128 B3 **Nanaimo** Can.
71 B3 **Nan'an** China
122 A1 **Nananib Plateau** Namibia
67 C3 **Nanao** Japan
71 B3 **Nanchang** *Jiangxi* China
71 B3 **Nanchang** *Jiangxi* China
70 A2 **Nanchong** China
63 A3 **Nancowry** i. India
105 D2 **Nancy** France
75 C1 **Nanda Devi** *mt.* India
71 A3 **Nandan** China
73 B3 **Nanded** India
74 B2 **Nandurbar** India
73 B3 **Nandyal** India
71 B3 **Nanfeng** China
118 B2 **Nanga Eboko** Cameroon
61 C2 **Nangahpinoh** Indon.
74 B1 **Nanga Parbat** *mt.* Pak.
61 C2 **Nangatayap** Indon.
70 A2 **Nangong** China
119 D3 **Nangulangwa** Tanz.
70 C2 **Nanhui** China
70 B2 **Nanjing** China
Nanking China *see* **Nanjing**
120 A2 **Nankova** Angola
71 B3 **Nan Ling** *mts* China
71 A3 **Nanning** China
127 H2 **Nanortalik** Greenland
71 A3 **Nanpan Jiang** r. China
75 C2 **Nanpara** India
71 B3 **Nanping** China
Nansei-shotō *is* Japan *see* **Ryukyu Islands**
104 B2 **Nantes** France
70 C2 **Nantong** China
141 F2 **Nantucket Island** U.S.A.
155 C3 **Nanuque** Brazil
64 B2 **Nanusa, Kepulauan** *is* Indon.
71 B3 **Nanxiong** China
70 B2 **Nanyang** China
70 B2 **Nanzhang** China
107 D2 **Nao, Cabo de la** c. Spain
131 C1 **Naococane, Lac** l. Can.
135 B3 **Napa** U.S.A.
126 D2 **Napaktulik Lake** Can.
127 H2 **Napasoq** Greenland
54 C1 **Napier** N.Z.
108 B2 **Naples** Italy
143 D3 **Naples** U.S.A.
150 A2 **Napo** r. Ecuador/Peru
Napoli Italy *see* **Naples**
114 B3 **Nara** Mali
93 I4 **Narach** Belarus
52 B3 **Naracoorte** Austr.
145 C2 **Naranjos** Mex.
63 B3 **Narathiwat** Thai.
105 C3 **Narbonne** France
63 A2 **Narcondam Island** India
127 G1 **Nares Strait** Can./Greenland
122 A1 **Narib** Namibia
87 D4 **Narimanov** Rus. Fed.
67 D3 **Narita** Japan
74 B2 **Narmada** r. India
74 B2 **Narnaul** India
108 B2 **Narni** Italy
90 B1 **Narodychi** Ukr.
89 E2 **Naro-Fominsk** Rus. Fed.
53 D3 **Narooma** Austr.
88 C3 **Narowlya** Belarus
53 C2 **Narrabri** Austr.
53 C2 **Narrandera** Austr.
53 C2 **Narromine** Austr.
88 C2 **Narva** Estonia
88 C2 **Narva Bay** Estonia/Rus. Fed.

92 G2 **Narvik** Norway
88 C2 **Narvskoye Vodokhranilishche** *resr* Estonia/Rus. Fed.
86 E2 **Nar'yan-Mar** Rus. Fed.
77 D2 **Naryn** Kyrg.
74 B2 **Nashik** India
141 E2 **Nashua** U.S.A.
142 C1 **Nashville** U.S.A.
49 I5 **Nasinu** Fiji
117 B4 **Nasir** S. Sudan
128 B2 **Nass** r. Can.
146 C2 **Nassau** Bahamas
116 B2 **Nasser, Lake** *resr* Egypt
93 F4 **Nässjö** Sweden
130 C1 **Nastapoca** r. Can.
130 C1 **Nastapoka Islands** Can.
120 B3 **Nata** Botswana
151 E2 **Natal** Brazil
131 D1 **Natashquan** Can.
131 D1 **Natashquan** r. Can.
142 B2 **Natchez** U.S.A.
142 B2 **Natchitoches** U.S.A.
53 C3 **Nathalia** Austr.
107 D1 **Nati, Punta** *pt* Spain
114 C3 **Natitingou** Benin
151 D1 **Natividade** Brazil
67 D3 **Natori** Japan
131 D1 **Natuashish** Can.
61 B1 **Natuna, Kepulauan** *is* Indon.
61 B1 **Natuna Besar** i. Indon.
120 A3 **Nauchas** Namibia
101 F1 **Nauen** Ger.
88 B2 **Naujoji Akmenė** Lith.
74 A2 **Naukot** Pak.
101 E2 **Naumburg (Saale)** Ger.
48 F3 **Nauru** *country* S. Pacific Ocean
145 C2 **Nautla** Mex.
88 C3 **Navahrudak** Belarus
106 B2 **Navalmoral de la Mata** Spain
106 B2 **Navalvillar de Pela** Spain
97 C2 **Navan** Ireland
88 C2 **Navapolatsk** Belarus
83 M2 **Navarin, Mys** c. Rus. Fed.
153 B6 **Navarino, Isla** i. Chile
96 B1 **Naver** r. U.K.
73 B3 **Navi Mumbai** India
89 D3 **Navlya** Rus. Fed.
110 C2 **Năvodari** Romania
77 C2 **Navoiy** Uzbek.
144 B2 **Navojoa** Mex.
144 B2 **Navolato** Mex.
74 A2 **Nawabshah** Pak.
62 A1 **Nawnghkio** Myanmar
62 A1 **Nawngleng** Myanmar
81 C2 **Naxçivan** Azer.
111 C3 **Naxos** i. Greece
144 B2 **Nayar** Mex.
66 D2 **Nayoro** Japan
144 B2 **Nazas** Mex.
144 B2 **Nazas** r. Mex.
150 A3 **Nazca** Peru
80 B2 **Nazerat** Israel
111 C3 **Nazilli** Turkey
117 B4 **Nazrēt** Eth.
79 C2 **Nazwá** Oman
121 B2 **Nchelenge** Zambia
122 B1 **Ncojane** Botswana
120 A1 **N'dalatando** Angola
118 C2 **Ndélé** C.A.R.
118 B3 **Ndendé** Gabon
115 D3 **Ndjamena** Chad
121 B2 **Ndola** Zambia
97 C1 **Neagh, Lough** l. U.K.
50 C1 **Neale, Lake** *imp.* l. Austr.
111 B3 **Nea Roda** Greece
99 B3 **Neath** U.K.
53 C1 **Nebine Creek** r. Austr.

150 B1 **Neblina, Pico da** *mt.* Brazil
89 D2 **Nebolchi** Rus. Fed.
136 C2 **Nebraska** *state* U.S.A.
137 D2 **Nebraska City** U.S.A.
108 B3 **Nebrodi, Monti** *mts Sicilia* Italy
153 C4 **Necochea** Arg.
131 C1 **Nedlouc, Lac** l. Can.
135 D4 **Needles** U.S.A.
74 B2 **Neemuch** India
129 E2 **Neepawa** Can.
87 E3 **Neftekamsk** Rus. Fed.
82 F2 **Nefteyugansk** Rus. Fed.
120 A1 **Negage** Angola
117 B4 **Negēlē** Eth.
150 A2 **Negra, Punta** *pt* Peru
63 A2 **Negrais, Cape** Myanmar
153 B5 **Negro** r. Arg.
150 C2 **Negro** r. S. America
152 C4 **Negro** r. Uru.
106 B2 **Negro, Cabo** c. Morocco
64 B2 **Negros** i. Phil.
69 E1 **Nehe** China
70 A3 **Neijiang** China
129 D2 **Neilburg** Can.
150 A1 **Neiva** Col.
129 E2 **Nejanilini Lake** Can.
117 B4 **Nek'emtē** Eth.
89 F2 **Nekrasovskoye** Rus. Fed.
89 D2 **Nelidovo** Rus. Fed.
73 B3 **Nellore** India
128 C3 **Nelson** Can.
129 E2 **Nelson** r. Can.
54 B2 **Nelson** N.Z.
52 B3 **Nelson, Cape** Austr.
53 D2 **Nelson Bay** Austr.
129 E2 **Nelson House** Can.
134 E1 **Nelson Reservoir** U.S.A.
114 B3 **Néma** Maur.
88 B2 **Neman** Rus. Fed.
104 C2 **Nemours** France
66 D2 **Nemuro** Japan
90 B2 **Nemyriv** Ukr.
97 B2 **Nenagh** Ireland
99 D2 **Nene** r. U.K.
69 E1 **Nenjiang** China
137 E3 **Neosho** U.S.A.
75 C2 **Nepal** *country* Asia
75 C2 **Nepalganj** Nepal
135 D3 **Nephi** U.S.A.
97 B1 **Nephin** h. Ireland
97 B1 **Nephin Beg Range** *hills* Ireland
131 D1 **Nepisiguit** r. Can.
119 C2 **Nepoko** r. Dem. Rep. Congo
104 C3 **Nérac** France
71 C3 **Nerang** Austr.
69 D1 **Nerchinsk** Rus. Fed.
89 F2 **Nerekhta** Rus. Fed.
109 C2 **Neretva** r. Bos.-Herz./Croatia
120 B2 **Neriquinha** Angola
88 B3 **Neris** r. Lith.
89 E2 **Nerl'** r. Rus. Fed.
86 F2 **Nerokhi** Rus. Fed.
154 C1 **Nerópolis** Brazil
83 J3 **Neryungri** Rus. Fed.
92 □C2 **Neskaupstaður** Iceland
96 B2 **Ness, Loch** l. U.K.
136 D3 **Ness City** U.S.A.
111 B2 **Nestos** r. Greece
100 B1 **Netherlands** *country* Europe
Netherlands Antilles *terr.* West Indies *see* **Aruba, Bonaire, Curaçao, Saba, Sint Eustatius, Sint Maarten**
127 G2 **Nettilling Lake** Can.
101 F1 **Neubrandenburg** Ger.

Neuchâtel

105 D2 **Neuchâtel** Switz.
100 C2 **Neuerburg** Ger.
100 B3 **Neufchâteau** Belgium
105 D2 **Neufchâteau** France
104 C2 **Neufchâtel-en-Bray** France
101 E2 **Neuhof** Ger.
102 B1 **Neumünster** Ger.
102 B2 **Neunkirchen** Ger.
153 B4 **Neuquén** Arg.
153 B4 **Neuquén** r. Arg.
101 F1 **Neuruppin** Ger.
100 C2 **Neuss** Ger.
101 D1 **Neustadt am Rübenberge** Ger.
101 E3 **Neustadt an der Aisch** Ger.
101 F1 **Neustrelitz** Ger.
101 E2 **Neuwied** Ger.
137 E3 **Nevada** U.S.A.
135 C3 **Nevada** state U.S.A.
106 C2 **Nevada, Sierra** mts Spain
135 B2 **Nevada, Sierra** mts U.S.A.
88 C2 **Nevel'** Rus. Fed.
105 C2 **Nevers** France
53 C2 **Nevertire** Austr.
109 C2 **Nevesinje** Bos.-Herz.
87 D4 **Nevinnomyssk** Rus. Fed.
128 B2 **New Aiyansh** Can.
140 B3 **New Albany** U.S.A.
151 C1 **New Amsterdam** Guyana
141 E2 **Newark** NJ U.S.A.
140 C2 **Newark** OH U.S.A.
98 C2 **Newark-on-Trent** U.K.
141 E2 **New Bedford** U.S.A.
143 E1 **New Bern** U.S.A.
143 D2 **Newberry** U.S.A.
139 E2 **New Boston** U.S.A.
139 D3 **New Braunfels** U.S.A.
97 C2 **Newbridge** Ireland
48 E3 **New Britain** i. P.N.G.
131 D2 **New Brunswick** prov. Can.
99 C3 **Newbury** U.K.
64 A1 **New Busuanga** Phil.
48 E4 **New Caledonia** terr. S. Pacific Ocean
53 D2 **Newcastle** Austr.
123 C2 **Newcastle** S. Africa
97 D1 **Newcastle** U.K.
140 C2 **New Castle** U.S.A.
136 C2 **Newcastle** U.S.A.
98 B2 **Newcastle-under-Lyme** U.K.
98 C1 **Newcastle upon Tyne** U.K.
97 C2 **Newcastle West** Ireland
74 B2 **New Delhi** India
128 C3 **New Denver** Can.
53 D2 **New England Range** mts Austr.
131 E2 **Newfoundland** i. Can.
131 E1 **Newfoundland and Labrador** prov. Can.
131 D2 **New Glasgow** Can.
59 D3 **New Guinea** i. Indon./P.N.G.
141 E2 **New Hampshire** state U.S.A.
141 E2 **New Haven** U.S.A.
128 B2 **New Hazelton** Can.
New Hebrides country S. Pacific Ocean see **Vanuatu**
142 B2 **New Iberia** U.S.A.
48 E3 **New Ireland** i. P.N.G.
141 E2 **New Jersey** state U.S.A.
130 C2 **New Liskeard** Can.
50 A2 **Newman** Austr.
138 B2 **New Mexico** state U.S.A.
142 B3 **New Orleans** U.S.A.
140 C2 **New Philadelphia** U.S.A.
54 B1 **New Plymouth** N.Z.
99 C3 **Newport** England U.K.
99 B3 **Newport** Wales U.K.
142 B1 **Newport** AR U.S.A.

134 B2 **Newport** OR U.S.A.
141 E2 **Newport** RI U.S.A.
141 E2 **Newport** VT U.S.A.
134 C1 **Newport** WA U.S.A.
143 E1 **Newport News** U.S.A.
143 E3 **New Providence** i. Bahamas
99 A3 **Newquay** U.K.
142 B2 **New Roads** U.S.A.
97 C2 **New Ross** Ireland
97 C1 **Newry** U.K.
83 K1 **New Siberia Islands** Rus. Fed.
52 B2 **New South Wales** state Austr.
137 E2 **Newton** IA U.S.A.
137 D3 **Newton** KS U.S.A.
99 B3 **Newton Abbot** U.K.
96 B3 **Newton Stewart** U.K.
97 B2 **Newtown** Ireland
99 B2 **Newtown** U.K.
136 C1 **New Town** U.S.A.
97 D1 **Newtownabbey** U.K.
97 D1 **Newtownards** U.K.
96 C3 **Newtown St Boswells** U.K.
97 C1 **Newtownstewart** U.K.
137 E2 **New Ulm** U.S.A.
141 E2 **New York** U.S.A.
141 D2 **New York** state U.S.A.
54 B2 **New Zealand** country Oceania
79 C2 **Neyrīz** Iran
76 B3 **Neyshābūr** Iran
145 C3 **Nezahualcóyotl** Mex.
145 C3 **Nezahualcóyotl, Presa** resr Mex.
61 B1 **Ngabang** Indon.
75 C2 **Ngamring** China
75 C1 **Ngangla Ringco** salt l. China
77 E3 **Nganglong Kangri** mt. China
75 C1 **Nganglong Kangri** mts China
75 C1 **Ngangzê Co** salt l. China
62 A2 **Ngao** Thai.
118 B2 **Ngaoundéré** Cameroon
54 C1 **Ngaruawahia** N.Z.
62 A2 **Ngathaingyyaung** Myanmar
121 D2 **Ngazidja** i. Comoros
63 B2 **Ngo** Congo
115 D4 **Ngol Bembo** Nigeria
68 C2 **Ngoring Hu** l. China
115 D3 **Ngourti** Niger
115 D3 **Nguigmi** Niger
59 D2 **Ngulu** atoll Micronesia
115 D3 **Nguru** Nigeria
123 D2 **Ngwelezana** S. Africa
121 C2 **Nhamalabué** Moz.
63 B2 **Nha Trang** Vietnam
52 B3 **Nhill** Austr.
123 D2 **Nhlangano** Swaziland
51 C1 **Nhulunbuy** Austr.
141 D2 **Niagara Falls** Can.
114 C3 **Niamey** Niger
119 C2 **Niangara** Dem. Rep. Congo
114 B3 **Niangay, Lac** l. Mali
60 A1 **Nias** i. Indon.
146 B3 **Nicaragua** country Central America
146 B3 **Nicaragua, Lake** Nic.
105 D3 **Nice** France
73 D4 **Nicobar Islands** India
80 B2 **Nicosia** Cyprus
146 B4 **Nicoya, Golfo de** b. Costa Rica
88 B2 **Nida** Lith.
103 E1 **Nidzica** Pol.
102 B2 **Niebüll** Ger.
101 D2 **Niederaula** Ger.
118 B2 **Niefang** Equat. Guinea
101 F1 **Niemegk** Ger.
101 D1 **Nienburg (Weser)** Ger.

100 B1 **Nieuwe-Niedorp** Neth.
151 C1 **Nieuw Nickerie** Suriname
122 A3 **Nieuwoudtville** S. Africa
100 A2 **Nieuwpoort** Belgium
80 B2 **Niğde** Turkey
115 C3 **Niger** country Africa
115 C4 **Niger** r. Africa
115 C4 **Niger, Mouths of the** Nigeria
115 C4 **Nigeria** country Africa
130 B2 **Nighthawk Lake** Can.
111 B2 **Nigrita** Greece
67 C3 **Niigata** Japan
67 B4 **Niihama** Japan
67 C4 **Nii-jima** i. Japan
67 C3 **Niitsu** Japan
100 B2 **Nijmegen** Neth.
100 C1 **Nijverdal** Neth.
92 J2 **Nikel'** Rus. Fed.
83 M3 **Nikol'skoye** Rus. Fed.
91 C2 **Nikopol'** Ukr.
80 B1 **Niksar** Turkey
79 D2 **Nikshahr** Iran
109 C2 **Nikšić** Montenegro
116 B1 **Nile** r. Africa
140 B2 **Niles** U.S.A.
74 A1 **Nīlī** Afgh.
105 C3 **Nîmes** France
53 C3 **Nimmitabel** Austr.
117 B4 **Nimule** Sudan
53 C1 **Nindigully** Austr.
73 B4 **Nine Degree Channel** India
52 B3 **Ninety Mile Beach** Austr.
54 B1 **Ninety Mile Beach** N.Z.
70 C2 **Ningbo** China
71 B3 **Ningde** China
70 B2 **Ningguo** China
71 C3 **Ninghai** China
Ningjiang China see **Songyuan**
68 C2 **Ningjing Shan** mts China
70 A2 **Ningxia Huizu Zizhiqu** aut. reg. China
70 B2 **Ningyang** China
62 B1 **Ninh Binh** Vietnam
63 B2 **Ninh Hoa** Vietnam
66 D2 **Ninohe** Japan
137 D2 **Niobrara** r. U.S.A.
114 B3 **Niono** Mali
104 B2 **Niort** France
129 D2 **Nipawin** Can.
130 B2 **Nipigon** Can.
130 B2 **Nipigon, Lake** Can.
131 D1 **Nipishish Lake** Can.
130 C2 **Nipissing, Lake** Can.
135 C3 **Nipton** U.S.A.
151 D3 **Niquelândia** Brazil
73 B3 **Nirmal** India
109 D2 **Nišava** r. Serbia
108 B3 **Niscemi** Sicilia Italy
67 B4 **Nishino-omote** Japan
155 D2 **Niterói** Brazil
96 C3 **Nith** r. U.K.
103 D2 **Nitra** Slovakia
49 G4 **Niue** terr. S. Pacific Ocean
92 H3 **Nivala** Fin.
100 B2 **Nivelles** Belgium
73 B3 **Nizamabad** India
87 D3 **Nizhnekamsk** Rus. Fed.
83 H3 **Nizhneudinsk** Rus. Fed.
82 G2 **Nizhnevartovsk** Rus. Fed.
89 F3 **Nizhniy Kislyay** Rus. Fed.
89 E3 **Nizhniy Lomov** Rus. Fed.
87 D3 **Nizhniy Novgorod** Rus. Fed.
86 E2 **Nizhniy Odes** Rus. Fed.
86 E3 **Nizhniy Tagil** Rus. Fed.

83 G2 Nizhnyaya Tunguska r. Rus. Fed.
91 C1 Nizhyn Ukr.
119 D3 Njinjo Tanz.
119 D3 Njombe Tanz.
121 C2 Nkhotakota Malawi
118 A2 Nkongsamba Cameroon
123 C3 Nkululeko S. Africa
123 C3 Nkwenkwezi S. Africa
67 B4 Nobeoka Japan
52 B1 Noccundra Austr.
144 A1 Nogales Mex.
138 A2 Nogales U.S.A.
104 C2 Nogent-le-Rotrou France
89 E2 Noginsk Rus. Fed.
74 B2 Nohar India
100 C3 Nohfelden Ger.
104 B2 Noirmoutier, Île de i. France
104 B2 Noirmoutier-en-l'Île France
67 C4 Nojima-zaki c. Japan
74 B2 Nokha India
93 H3 Nokia Fin.
74 B2 Nok Kundi Pak.
118 B2 Nola C.A.R.
86 D3 Nolinsk Rus. Fed.
123 C3 Nomonde S. Africa
123 D2 Nondweni S. Africa
62 B2 Nong Khai Thai.
52 A2 Nonning Austr.
144 B2 Nonoava Mex.
65 B2 Nonsan S. Korea
63 B2 Nonthaburi Thai.
122 B3 Nonzwakazi S. Africa
77 C3 Norak Tajik.
141 D1 Noranda Can.
82 C1 Nordaustlandet i. Svalbard
128 C2 Nordegg Can.
100 C1 Norden Ger.
83 H1 Nordenshel'da, Arkhipelag is Rus. Fed.
100 C1 Norderney Ger.
100 C1 Norderney i. Ger.
101 E1 Norderstedt Ger.
93 E3 Nordfjordeid Norway
101 E2 Nordhausen Ger.
101 D1 Nordholz Ger.
100 C1 Nordhorn Ger.
Nordkapp c. Norway see North Cape
92 F3 Nordli Norway
102 C2 Nördlingen Ger.
92 G3 Nordmaling Sweden
94 B1 Norðoyar is Faroe Is
97 C2 Nore r. Ireland
137 D2 Norfolk NE U.S.A.
141 D3 Norfolk VA U.S.A.
48 F4 Norfolk Island terr. S. Pacific Ocean
93 E3 Norheimsund Norway
82 G2 Noril'sk Rus. Fed.
75 C2 Norkyung China
139 D1 Norman U.S.A.
Normandes, Îles is English Chan. see Channel Islands
51 D1 Normanton Austr.
93 G4 Norrköping Sweden
93 G4 Norrtälje Sweden
50 B3 Norseman Austr.
92 G3 Norsjö Sweden
92 H2 Northallerton U.K.
50 A2 Northampton Austr.
99 C2 Northampton U.K.
73 D3 North Andaman i. India
129 D2 North Battleford Can.
130 C2 North Bay Can.
130 C1 North Belcher Islands Can.
96 C2 North Berwick U.K.

92 I1 North Cape Norway
54 B1 North Cape N.Z.
130 A1 North Caribou Lake Can.
143 E1 North Carolina state U.S.A.
130 B2 North Channel lake channel Can.
96 A3 North Channel U.K.
128 B3 North Cowichan Can.
136 C1 North Dakota state U.S.A.
99 C3 North Downs hills U.K.
143 E3 Northeast Providence Channel Bahamas
101 D2 Northeim Ger.
122 A2 Northern Cape prov. S. Africa
129 E2 Northern Indian Lake Can.
141 D1 Northern Ireland prov. U.K.
48 D1 Northern Mariana Islands terr. N. Pacific Ocean
50 C1 Northern Territory admin. div. Austr.
96 C2 North Esk r. U.K.
137 E2 Northfield U.S.A.
99 D3 North Foreland c. U.K.
54 B1 North Island N.Z.
129 E2 North Knife Lake Can.
65 B1 North Korea country Asia
62 A1 North Lakhimpur India
128 B1 North Nahanni r. Can.
136 C2 North Platte U.S.A.
136 C2 North Platte r. U.S.A.
96 C1 North Ronaldsay i. U.K.
94 D2 North Sea Europe
130 A1 North Spirit Lake Can.
53 D2 North Stradbroke Island Austr.
54 B1 North Taranaki Bight b. N.Z.
130 C1 North Twin Island Can.
98 B1 North Tyne r. U.K.
96 A2 North Uist i. U.K.
131 D2 Northumberland Strait Can.
122 C2 North West prov. S. Africa
50 A2 North West Cape Austr.
143 E3 Northwest Providence Channel Bahamas
131 E1 North West River Can.
128 B1 Northwest Territories admin. div. Can.
98 C1 North York Moors moorland U.K.
140 C3 Norton U.S.A.
121 C3 Norton Zimbabwe
140 C2 Norwalk U.S.A.
93 F3 Norway country Europe
129 E2 Norway House Can.
160 A3 Norwegian Sea N. Atlantic Ocean
99 D2 Norwich U.K.
141 E2 Norwich CT U.S.A.
141 D2 Norwich NY U.S.A.
66 D2 Noshiro Japan
91 C1 Nosivka Ukr.
122 B2 Nosop watercourse Africa
86 E2 Nosovaya Rus. Fed.
79 C2 Noşratābād Iran
Nossob watercourse Africa see Nosop
103 D1 Noteć r. Pol.
93 E4 Notodden Norway
67 C3 Noto-hantō pen. Japan
131 D2 Notre-Dame, Monts mts Can.
131 D2 Notre Dame Bay Can.
99 C2 Nottingham U.K.
114 A2 Nouâdhibou Maur.
114 A3 Nouakchott Maur.
114 A3 Nouâmghâr Maur.
48 F4 Nouméa New Caledonia

114 B3 Nouna Burkina Faso
154 B2 Nova Esperança Brazil
155 D2 Nova Friburgo Brazil
109 C1 Nova Gradiška Croatia
154 C2 Nova Granada Brazil
155 D2 Nova Iguaçu Brazil
91 C2 Nova Kakhovka Ukr.
155 D1 Nova Lima Brazil
154 B2 Nova Londrina Brazil
91 C2 Nova Odesa Ukr.
131 D2 Nova Scotia prov. Can.
155 D1 Nova Venécia Brazil
83 K1 Novaya Sibir', Ostrov i. Rus. Fed.
86 E1 Novaya Zemlya is Rus. Fed.
103 D2 Nové Zámky Slovakia
91 C1 Novhorod-Sivers'kyy Ukr.
110 B2 Novi Iskŭr Bulg.
108 A2 Novi Ligure Italy
109 D2 Novi Pazar Serbia
109 C1 Novi Sad Serbia
87 D3 Novoanninskiy Rus. Fed.
150 B2 Novo Aripuanã Brazil
91 C2 Novoazovs'k Ukr.
91 E2 Novocherkassk Rus. Fed.
86 D2 Novodvinsk Rus. Fed.
152 C3 Novo Hamburgo Brazil
154 C2 Novo Horizonte Brazil
90 B1 Novohrad-Volyns'kyy Ukr.
103 D2 Novo mesto Slovenia
91 D3 Novomikhaylovskiy Rus. Fed.
89 E3 Novomoskovsk Rus. Fed.
91 D2 Novomoskovs'k Ukr.
91 C2 Novomyrhorod Ukr.
91 C2 Novooleksiyivka Ukr.
150 B1 Novo Paraíso Brazil
91 D3 Novopskov Ukr.
91 D3 Novorossiysk Rus. Fed.
88 C2 Novorzhev Rus. Fed.
87 E3 Novosergiyevka Rus. Fed.
91 D2 Novoshakhtinsk Rus. Fed.
82 G3 Novosibirsk Rus. Fed.
Novosibirskiye Ostrova is Rus. Fed. see New Siberia Islands
89 E3 Novosil' Rus. Fed.
89 D2 Novosokol'niki Rus. Fed.
91 D1 Novotroyits'ke Ukr.
90 A1 Novovolyns'k Ukr.
89 D3 Novozybkov Rus. Fed.
103 D2 Nový Jičín Czech Rep.
86 E2 Novyy Bor Rus. Fed.
91 D1 Novyy Oskol Rus. Fed.
86 G2 Novyy Port Rus. Fed.
82 G2 Novyy Urengoy Rus. Fed.
69 E1 Novyy Urgal Rus. Fed.
103 D1 Nowogard Pol.
53 D2 Nowra Austr.
81 D2 Nowshahr Iran
74 B1 Nowshera Pak.
103 E2 Nowy Sącz Pol.
103 E2 Nowy Targ Pol.
87 G2 Noyabr'sk Rus. Fed.
105 C2 Noyon France
68 C2 Noyon Mongolia
121 C2 Nsanje Malawi
118 B3 Ntandembele Dem. Rep. Congo
111 B3 Ntoro, Kavo pt Greece
119 D3 Ntungamo Uganda
79 C2 Nu'aym reg. Oman
116 B2 Nubian Desert Sudan
129 E1 Nueltin Lake Can.
153 A5 Nueva Lubecka Arg.
145 B2 Nueva Rosita Mex.
144 B1 Nuevo Casas Grandes Mex.
144 B2 Nuevo Ideal Mex.

Nuevo Laredo

145	C2	Nuevo Laredo Mex.
117	C4	Nugaal *watercourse* Somalia
117	C4	Nugaaleed, Dooxo *val.* Somalia
105	C2	Nuits-St-Georges France
		Nu Jiang *r.* China/Myanmar see Salween
49	G4	Nuku'alofa Tonga
49	I3	Nuku Hiva *i.* Fr. Polynesia
76	B2	Nukus Uzbek.
50	B2	Nullagine Austr.
50	B3	Nullarbor Plain Austr.
115	D4	Numan Nigeria
67	C3	Numazu Japan
93	E3	Numedal *val.* Norway
59	C3	Numfoor *i.* Indon.
53	C3	Numurkah Austr.
		Nunap Isua *c.* Greenland see Farewell, Cape
127	G3	Nunavik *reg.* Can.
129	E1	Nunavut *admin. div.* Can.
99	C2	Nuneaton U.K.
106	B1	Nuñomoral Spain
108	A2	Nuoro *Sardegna* Italy
78	B2	Nuqrah Saudi Arabia
101	E3	Nuremberg Ger.
52	A2	Nuriootpa Austr.
92	I3	Nurmes Fin.
		Nürnberg Ger. *see* Nuremberg
62	A1	Nu Shan *mts* China
74	A2	Nushki Pak.
127	H2	Nuuk Greenland
127	H2	Nuussuaq Greenland
127	H2	Nuussuaq *pen.* Greenland
78	A2	Nuwaybi' al Muzaynah Egypt
122	B3	Nuweveldberge *mts* S. Africa
86	F2	Nyagan' Rus. Fed.
75	D1	Nyainqêntanglha Feng *mt.* China
75	D2	Nyainqêntanglha Shan *mts* China
117	A3	Nyala Sudan
86	D2	Nyandoma Rus. Fed.
118	B3	Nyanga *r.* Gabon
121	C2	Nyanga Zimbabwe
		Nyang'oma Kenya *see* Kogelo
121	C1	Nyasa, Lake Africa
93	F4	Nyborg Denmark
92	I1	Nyborg Norway
93	G4	Nybro Sweden
119	D3	Nyeri Kenya
68	C3	Nyingchi China
103	E2	Nyíregyháza Hungary
93	F4	Nykøbing Denmark
93	G4	Nyköping Sweden
53	C2	Nymagee Austr.
93	G4	Nynäshamn Sweden
53	C2	Nyngan Austr.
88	B3	Nyoman *r.* Belarus/Lith.
105	D3	Nyons France
86	E2	Nyrob Rus. Fed.
134	C2	Nyssa U.S.A.
119	C3	Nyunzu Dem. Rep. Congo
91	C2	Nyzhn'ohirs'kyy Ukr.
119	D3	Nzega Tanz.
114	B4	Nzérékoré Guinea
120	A1	N'zeto Angola

O

136	C2	Oahe, Lake U.S.A.
124	E5	O'ahu *i.* U.S.A.
52	B2	Oakbank Austr.
142	B2	Oakdale U.S.A.
53	D1	Oakey Austr.
134	B1	Oak Harbor U.S.A.
140	C3	Oak Hill U.S.A.
135	B3	Oakland U.S.A.
52	B2	Oakover *r.* Austr.
134	B2	Oakridge U.S.A.
143	D1	Oak Ridge U.S.A.
54	B3	Oamaru N.Z.
64	B1	Oas Phil.
145	C3	Oaxaca Mex.
86	F2	Ob' *r.* Rus. Fed.
118	B2	Obala Cameroon
96	B2	Oban U.K.
106	B1	O Barco Spain
53	C2	Oberon Austr.
101	F3	Oberpfälzer Wald *mts* Ger.
101	F3	Oberviechtach Ger.
59	C3	Obi *i.* Indon.
151	C2	Óbidos Brazil
66	D2	Obihiro Japan
69	E1	Obluch'ye Rus. Fed.
89	E2	Obninsk Rus. Fed.
119	C2	Obo C.A.R.
117	C3	Obock Djibouti
118	B3	Obouya Congo
89	E3	Oboyan' Rus. Fed.
144	B2	Obregón, Presa *resr* Mex.
109	D2	Obrenovac Serbia
87	E3	Obshchiy Syrt *hills* Kazakh./Rus. Fed.
86	G2	Obskaya Guba *sea chan.* Rus. Fed.
114	B4	Obuasi Ghana
90	C1	Obukhiv Ukr.
87	M2	Ob''yachevo Rus. Fed.
143	D3	Ocala U.S.A.
144	B2	Ocampo Mex.
106	C2	Ocaña Spain
150	A1	Occidental, Cordillera *mts* Col.
150	A3	Occidental, Cordillera *mts* Peru
141	D3	Ocean City U.S.A.
128	B2	Ocean Falls Can.
135	C4	Oceanside U.S.A.
91	C2	Ochakiv Ukr.
86	E3	Ocher Rus. Fed.
101	E3	Ochsenfurt Ger.
143	D2	Oconee *r.* U.S.A.
145	C3	Ocosingo Mex.
58	C3	Ocussi *enclave* East Timor
116	B2	Oda, Jebel *mt.* Sudan
66	D2	Ōdate Japan
67	C3	Odawara Japan
93	E3	Odda Norway
106	B2	Odemira Port.
111	C3	Ödemiş Turkey
93	F4	Odense Denmark
101	D3	Odenwald *reg.* Ger.
102	C1	Oderbucht *b.* Ger.
		Odesa Ukr. *see* Odessa
90	C2	Odessa Ukr.
139	C2	Odessa U.S.A.
114	B4	Odienné Côte d'Ivoire
103	D2	Odra *r.* Ger./Pol.
151	D2	Oeiras Brazil
100	D2	Oelde Ger.
136	C2	Oelrichs U.S.A.
101	F2	Oelsnitz Ger.
100	B1	Oenkerk Neth.
109	C2	Ofanto *r.* Italy
101	D2	Offenbach am Main Ger.
102	B2	Offenburg Ger.
117	C4	Ogadēn *reg.* Eth.
66	C3	Oga-hantō *pen.* Japan
67	C3	Ōgaki Japan
136	C2	Ogallala U.S.A.
115	C4	Ogbomosho Nigeria
134	D2	Ogden U.S.A.
141	D2	Ogdensburg U.S.A.
126	B2	Ogilvie *r.* Can.
126	B2	Ogilvie Mountains Can.
143	D2	Oglethorpe, Mount U.S.A.
130	B1	Ogoki *r.* Can.
130	B1	Ogoki Reservoir Can.
88	B2	Ogre Latvia
109	C1	Ogulin Croatia
140	B3	Ohio *r.* U.S.A.
140	C2	Ohio *state* U.S.A.
101	E2	Ohrdruf Ger.
109	D2	Ohrid Macedonia
151	C1	Oiapoque Brazil
141	D2	Oil City U.S.A.
100	A3	Oise *r.* France
67	B4	Ōita Japan
144	B2	Ojinaga Mex.
152	B3	Ojos del Salado, Nevado *mt.* Arg./Chile
89	F2	Oka *r.* Rus. Fed.
120	A3	Okahandja Namibia
120	A3	Okakarara Namibia
128	C3	Okanagan Falls Can.
128	C3	Okanagan Lake Can.
134	C1	Okanogan U.S.A.
134	C1	Okanogan *r.* U.S.A.
74	B1	Okara Pak.
120	B2	Okavango *r.* Africa
120	B2	Okavango Delta *swamp* Botswana
67	C3	Okaya Japan
67	B4	Okayama Japan
67	C4	Okazaki Japan
143	D3	Okeechobee, Lake U.S.A.
143	D2	Okefenokee Swamp U.S.A.
99	A3	Okehampton U.K.
74	A2	Okha India
83	K3	Okha Rus. Fed.
75	C2	Okhaldhunga Nepal
83	K3	Okhota *r.* Rus. Fed.
83	K3	Okhotsk Rus. Fed.
156	C2	Okhotsk, Sea of Japan/Rus. Fed.
91	C1	Okhtyrka Ukr.
69	E3	Okinawa *i.* Japan
67	B3	Oki-shotō *is* Japan
139	D1	Oklahoma *state* U.S.A.
139	D1	Oklahoma City U.S.A.
139	D1	Okmulgee U.S.A.
78	A2	Oko, Wadi *watercourse* Sudan
118	B3	Okondja Gabon
128	C2	Okotoks Can.
89	D3	Okovskiy Les *for.* Rus. Fed.
118	B3	Okoyo Congo
92	H1	Øksfjord Norway
62	A2	Oktwin Myanmar
86	D2	Oktyabr'skiy Arkhangel'skaya Oblast' Rus. Fed.
83	L3	Oktyabr'skiy Kamchatskiy Kray Rus. Fed.
87	E3	Oktyabr'skiy Respublika Bashkortostan Rus. Fed.
86	F2	Oktyabr'skoye Rus. Fed.
83	H1	Oktyabr'skoy Revolyutsii, Ostrov *i.* Rus. Fed.
89	D2	Okulovka Rus. Fed.
66	C2	Okushiri-tō *i.* Japan
92	☐A3	Ólafsvík Iceland
93	G4	Öland *i.* Sweden
52	B2	Olary Austr.
153	B4	Olavarría Arg.
103	D1	Oława Pol.
108	A2	Olbia *Sardegna* Italy
126	B2	Old Crow Can.
101	D1	Oldenburg Ger.
102	C1	Oldenburg in Holstein Ger.

100	C1	Oldenzaal Neth.
97	B3	Old Head of Kinsale Ireland
128	C2	Olds U.S.A.
129	D2	Old Wives Lake Can.
141	D2	Olean U.S.A.
103	E1	Olecko Pol.
83	J2	Olekminsk Rus. Fed.
91	C2	Oleksandriya Ukr.
86	C2	Olenegorsk Rus. Fed.
83	I2	Olenek Rus. Fed.
83	I2	Olenek r. Rus. Fed.
89	D2	Olenino Rus. Fed.
90	B1	Olevs'k Ukr.
106	B2	Olhão Port.
122	A2	Olifants watercourse Namibia
123	D1	Olifants S. Africa
123	D1	Olifants r. Northern S. Africa
122	A3	Olifants r. W. Cape S. Africa
122	B2	Olifantshoek S. Africa
154	C2	Olímpia Brazil
151	E2	Olinda Brazil
123	C1	Oliphants Drift Botswana
107	C2	Oliva Spain
155	D2	Oliveira Brazil
106	B2	Olivenza Spain
152	B3	Ollagüe Chile
150	A2	Olmos Peru
140	B3	Olney U.S.A.
103	D2	Olomouc Czech Rep.
64	B1	Olongapo Phil.
104	B3	Oloron-Ste-Marie France
107	D1	Olot Spain
69	D1	Olovyannaya Rus. Fed.
83	L2	Oloy r. Rus. Fed.
100	C2	Olpe Ger.
103	E1	Olsztyn Pol.
110	B2	Olt r. Romania
81	C1	Oltu Turkey
111	B3	Olympia tourist site Greece
134	B1	Olympia U.S.A.
134	B1	Olympus, Mount U.S.A.
83	M3	Olyutorskiy, Mys c. Rus. Fed.
97	C1	Omagh U.K.
137	D2	Omaha U.S.A.
79	C2	Oman country Asia
79	C2	Oman, Gulf of Asia
120	A3	Omaruru Namibia
120	B2	Omatako watercourse Namibia
116	B3	Omdurman Sudan
53	C3	Omeo Austr.
145	C3	Ometepec Mex.
78	A2	Om Hajēr Eritrea
128	B2	Omineca Mountains Can.
67	C3	Ōmiya Japan
100	C1	Ommen Neth.
83	L2	Omolon r. Rus. Fed.
100	B3	Omont France
82	F3	Omsk Rus. Fed.
83	L2	Omsukchan Rus. Fed.
110	C1	Omu, Vârful mt. Romania
67	A4	Ōmura Japan
141	D3	Onancock U.S.A.
140	C1	Onaping Lake Can.
131	D2	Onatchiway, Lac l. Can.
120	A2	Oncócua Angola
122	B3	Onderstedorings S. Africa
120	A2	Ondjiva Angola
86	C2	Onega Rus. Fed.
86	C2	Onega r. Rus. Fed.
141	D2	Oneida Lake U.S.A.
137	D2	O'Neill U.S.A.
141	D2	Oneonta U.S.A.
110	C1	Oneşti Romania
		Onezhskoye, Ozero l. Rus. Fed. see Onezhskoye Ozero
86	C2	Onezhskoye Ozero l. Rus. Fed.
122	B2	Ongers watercourse S. Africa
65	B2	Ongjin N. Korea
73	C3	Ongole India
121	□D3	Onilahy r. Madag.
115	C4	Onitsha Nigeria
122	A2	Onseepkans S. Africa
50	A2	Onslow Austr.
143	E2	Onslow Bay U.S.A.
130	A1	Ontario prov. Can.
134	C2	Ontario U.S.A.
141	D2	Ontario, Lake Can./U.S.A.
51	C2	Oodnadatta Austr.
		Oostende Belgium see Ostend
100	B2	Oosterhout Neth.
100	B1	Oosterschelde est. Neth.
100	B1	Oost-Vlieland Neth.
128	B2	Ootsa Lake Can.
128	B2	Ootsa Lake l. Can.
118	C3	Opala Dem. Rep. Congo
130	C1	Opataca, Lac l. Can.
103	D2	Opava Czech Rep.
143	C2	Opelika U.S.A.
142	B2	Opelousas U.S.A.
130	C1	Opinaca, Réservoir resr Can.
131	D1	Opiscotéo, Lac l. Can.
88	C2	Opochka Rus. Fed.
144	A2	Opodepe Mex.
103	D1	Opole Pol.
106	B1	Oporto Port.
54	C1	Opotiki N.Z.
93	E3	Oppdal Norway
54	B1	Opunake N.Z.
120	A2	Opuwo Namibia
110	B1	Oradea Romania
		Orahovac Kosovo see Rahovec
114	B1	Oran Alg.
152	B3	Orán Arg.
65	B1	Ŏrang N. Korea
53	C2	Orange Austr.
105	C3	Orange France
122	A2	Orange r. Namibia/S. Africa
139	E2	Orange U.S.A.
143	D2	Orangeburg U.S.A.
140	C2	Orangeville Can.
101	F1	Oranienburg Ger.
122	A2	Oranjemund Namibia
120	B3	Orapa Botswana
110	B1	Orăştie Romania
108	B2	Orbetello Italy
53	C3	Orbost Austr.
50	B1	Ord, Mount h. Austr.
106	B1	Ordes Spain
70	B2	Ordos China
80	B1	Ordu Turkey
		Ordzhonikidze Rus. Fed. see Vladikavkaz
91	C2	Ordzhonikidze Ukr.
93	G4	Örebro Sweden
134	B2	Oregon state U.S.A.
134	B1	Oregon City U.S.A.
87	C3	Orekhovo-Zuyevo Rus. Fed.
89	E3	Orel Rus. Fed.
83	K3	Orel', Ozero l. Rus. Fed.
135	D2	Orem U.S.A.
111	C3	Ören Turkey
87	E3	Orenburg Rus. Fed.
54	A3	Orepuki N.Z.
93	F4	Øresund str. Denmark/Sweden
99	D2	Orford Ness hd U.K.
111	C3	Orhaneli Turkey
111	C2	Orhangazi Turkey
83	I3	Orhon Gol r. Mongolia
152	B2	Oriental, Cordillera mts Bol.
150	A1	Oriental, Cordillera mts Col.
150	A3	Oriental, Cordillera mts Peru
107	C2	Orihuela Spain
91	D2	Orikhiv Ukr.
130	C2	Orillia Can.
150	B1	Orinoco r. Col./Venez.
150	B1	Orinoco, Delta del Venez.
93	H4	Orissaare Estonia
108	A3	Oristano Sardegna Italy
93	I3	Orivesi l. Fin.
151	C2	Oriximiná Brazil
145	C3	Orizaba Mex.
145	C3	Orizaba, Pico de vol. Mex.
92	E3	Orkanger Norway
93	F4	Orkelljunga Sweden
92	E3	Orkla r. Norway
96	C1	Orkney Islands U.K.
154	C2	Orlândia Brazil
143	D3	Orlando U.S.A.
104	C2	Orléans France
74	A2	Ormara Pak.
64	B1	Ormoc Phil.
98	B2	Ormskirk U.K.
92	G3	Örnsköldsvik Sweden
114	B3	Orodara Burkina Faso
134	C1	Orofino U.S.A.
		Oroqen Zizhiqi China see Alihe
64	B2	Oroquieta Phil.
108	A2	Orosei Sardegna Italy
108	A2	Orosei, Golfo di b. Sardegna Italy
103	E2	Orosháza Hungary
135	B3	Oroville U.S.A.
52	A2	Orroroo Austr.
89	D3	Orsha Belarus
87	E3	Orsk Rus. Fed.
93	E3	Ørsta Norway
106	B1	Ortegal, Cabo c. Spain
104	B3	Orthez France
106	B1	Ortigueira Spain
137	D1	Ortonville U.S.A.
83	J2	Orulgan, Khrebet mts Rus. Fed.
		Orūmīyeh, Daryācheh-ye salt l. Iran see Urmia, Lake
152	B2	Oruro Bol.
108	B2	Orvieto Italy
146	B4	Osa, Península de pen. Costa Rica
137	E3	Osage r. U.S.A.
67	C4	Ōsaka Japan
101	E1	Oschersleben (Bode) Ger.
108	A2	Oschiri Sardegna Italy
89	E3	Osetr r. Rus. Fed.
77	D2	Osh Kyrg.
120	A2	Oshakati Namibia
130	C2	Oshawa Can.
66	C2	Ō-shima i. Japan
67	C4	Ō-shima i. Japan
140	B2	Oshkosh U.S.A.
81	C2	Oshnoviyeh Iran
115	C4	Oshogbo Nigeria
118	B3	Oshwe Dem. Rep. Congo
109	C1	Osijek Croatia
128	C2	Osilinka r. Can.
108	B2	Osimo Italy
123	D2	oSizweni S. Africa
137	E2	Oskaloosa U.S.A.
93	G4	Oskarshamn Sweden
89	E3	Oskol r. Rus. Fed.
93	F4	Oslo Norway
93	F4	Oslofjorden sea chan. Norway
80	B1	Osmancık Turkey
111	C2	Osmaneli Turkey
80	B2	Osmaniye Turkey
88	C2	Os'mino Rus. Fed.
100	D1	Osnabrück Ger.
153	A5	Osorno Chile
106	C1	Osorno Spain
128	C3	Osoyoos Can.

Oss

100	B2	Oss Neth.
51	D4	Ossa, Mount Austr.
83	L3	Ossora Rus. Fed.
89	D2	Ostashkov Rus. Fed.
101	D1	Oste r. Ger.
100	A2	Ostend Belgium
101	E1	Osterburg (Altmark) Ger.
93	F3	Österdalälven r. Sweden
101	D1	Osterholz-Scharmbeck Ger.
101	E2	Osterode am Harz Ger.
92	F3	Östersund Sweden
		Ostfriesische Inseln is Ger. see East Frisian Islands
100	C1	Ostfriesland reg. Ger.
93	G3	Östhammar Sweden
103	D2	Ostrava Czech Rep.
103	D1	Ostróda Pol.
89	E3	Ostrogozhsk Rus. Fed.
103	E1	Ostrołęka Pol.
101	F2	Ostrov Czech Rep.
88	C2	Ostrov Rus. Fed.
103	E1	Ostrowiec Świętokrzyski Pol.
103	E1	Ostrów Mazowiecka Pol.
103	D1	Ostrów Wielkopolski Pol.
110	B2	Osŭm r. Bulg.
67	B4	Ōsumi-kaikyō sea chan. Japan
67	B4	Ōsumi-shotō is Japan
106	B2	Osuna Spain
141	D2	Oswego U.S.A.
99	B2	Oswestry U.K.
67	C3	Ōta Japan
54	B3	Otago Peninsula N.Z.
54	C2	Otaki N.Z.
66	D2	Otaru Japan
120	A2	Otavi Namibia
134	C1	Othello U.S.A.
120	A3	Otjiwarongo Namibia
117	B3	Otoro, Jebel mt. Sudan
93	E4	Otra r. Norway
109	C2	Otranto, Strait of Albania/Italy
67	C3	Ōtsu Japan
93	E3	Otta Norway
130	C2	Ottawa Can.
130	C2	Ottawa r. Can.
140	B2	Ottawa IL U.S.A.
137	D3	Ottawa KS U.S.A.
130	B1	Otter Rapids Can.
100	B2	Ottignies Belgium
137	E2	Ottumwa U.S.A.
150	A2	Otuzco Peru
52	B3	Otway, Cape Austr.
142	B2	Ouachita r. U.S.A.
142	B2	Ouachita, Lake U.S.A.
142	B2	Ouachita Mountains U.S.A.
118	C2	Ouadda C.A.R.
115	D3	Ouaddaï reg. Chad
114	B3	Ouagadougou Burkina Faso
114	B3	Ouahigouya Burkina Faso
114	B3	Oualâta Maur.
118	C2	Ouanda-Djalié C.A.R.
114	B2	Ouarâne reg. Maur.
115	C1	Ouargla Alg.
114	B1	Ouarzazate Morocco
100	A2	Oudenaarde Belgium
122	B3	Oudtshoorn S. Africa
107	C2	Oued Tlélat Alg.
104	A2	Ouessant, Île d' i. France
118	B2	Ouesso Congo
114	B1	Oujda Morocco
107	D2	Ouled Farès Alg.
92	I2	Oulu Fin.
92	I3	Oulujärvi l. Fin.
108	A1	Oulx Italy
115	E3	Oum-Chalouba Chad
115	D3	Oum-Hadjer Chad

115	E3	Ounianga Kébir Chad
100	B2	Oupeye Belgium
106	B1	Ourense Spain
154	C2	Ourinhos Brazil
155	D2	Ouro Preto Brazil
100	B2	Ourthe r. Belgium
98	C2	Ouse r. U.K.
131	D2	Outardes, Rivière aux r. Can.
131	D1	Outardes Quatre, Réservoir resr Can.
96	A2	Outer Hebrides is U.K.
120	A3	Outjo Namibia
129	D2	Outlook Can.
92	I3	Outokumpu Fin.
52	B3	Ouyen Austr.
106	B1	Ovar Port.
92	H2	Överkalix Sweden
135	D3	Overton U.S.A.
92	H2	Övertorneå Sweden
106	B1	Oviedo Spain
93	E3	Øvre Årdal Norway
93	F3	Øvre Rendal Norway
90	B1	Ovruch Ukr.
118	B3	Owando Congo
67	C4	Owase Japan
137	E2	Owatonna U.S.A.
140	B3	Owensboro U.S.A.
135	C3	Owens Lake U.S.A.
130	B2	Owen Sound Can.
115	C4	Owerri Nigeria
140	C2	Owosso U.S.A.
134	C2	Owyhee U.S.A.
134	C2	Owyhee r. U.S.A.
54	B2	Oxford N.Z.
99	C3	Oxford U.K.
142	C2	Oxford U.S.A.
129	E2	Oxford Lake Can.
135	C4	Oxnard U.S.A.
97	B1	Ox Mountains hills Ireland
135	C4	Oxnard U.S.A.
67	C3	Oyama Japan
118	B2	Oyem Gabon
129	C2	Oyen Can.
105	D2	Oyonnax France
64	B2	Ozamis Phil.
142	C2	Ozark U.S.A.
137	E3	Ozark Plateau U.S.A.
137	E3	Ozarks, Lake of the U.S.A.
83	L3	Ozernovskiy Rus. Fed.
88	B3	Ozersk Rus. Fed.
89	E3	Ozery Rus. Fed.
87	D3	Ozinki Rus. Fed.

P

127	H2	Paamiut Greenland
122	A3	Paarl S. Africa
103	D1	Pabianice Pol.
75	C2	Pabna Bangl.
74	A2	Pab Range mts Pak.
109	C3	Pachino Sicilia Italy
145	C2	Pachuca Mex.
156		Pacific Ocean World
103	D1	Paczków Pol.
60	B2	Padang Indon.
60	B1	Padang Endau Malaysia
60	B2	Padangpanjang Indon.
60	A1	Padangsidimpuan Indon.
101	D2	Paderborn Ger.
		Padova Italy see Padua
139	D3	Padre Island U.S.A.
52	B3	Padthaway Austr.
108	B1	Padua Italy
140	B3	Paducah KY U.S.A.

139	C2	Paducah TX U.S.A.
65	B1	Paegam N. Korea
65	A2	Paengnyŏng-do i. S. Korea
54	C1	Paeroa N.Z.
		Pafos Cyprus see Paphos
109	C2	Pag Croatia
64	B2	Pagadian Phil.
60	B2	Pagai Selatan i. Indon.
60	B2	Pagai Utara i. Indon.
59	D1	Pagan i. N. Mariana Is
61	C2	Pagatan Indon.
138	A1	Page U.S.A.
88	B2	Pagėgiai Lith.
136	B3	Pagosa Springs U.S.A.
88	C2	Paide Estonia
93	I3	Päijänne l. Fin.
75	C2	Paikū Co l. China
138	A1	Painted Desert U.S.A.
96	B3	Paisley U.K.
92	H2	Pajala Sweden
150	B1	Pakaraima Mountains S. America
150	C1	Pakaraima Mountains S. America
74	A2	Pakistan country Asia
62	A1	Pakokku Myanmar
88	B2	Pakruojis Lith.
103	D2	Paks Hungary
130	A1	Pakwash Lake Can.
62	B2	Pakxan Laos
63	B2	Pakxé Laos
115	D4	Pala Chad
60	B2	Palabuhanratu, Teluk b. Indon.
111	C3	Palaikastro Greece
111	B3	Palaiochora Greece
122	B1	Palamakoloi Botswana
107	D1	Palamós Spain
83	L3	Palana Rus. Fed.
64	B1	Palanan Phil.
61	C2	Palangkaraya Indon.
74	B2	Palanpur India
120	B3	Palapye Botswana
83	L2	Palatka Rus. Fed.
143	D3	Palatka U.S.A.
59	C2	Palau country N. Pacific Ocean
63	A2	Palaw Myanmar
64	A2	Palawan i. Phil.
93	H4	Paldiski Estonia
60	B2	Palembang Indon.
106	C1	Palencia Spain
145	C3	Palenque Mex.
108	B3	Palermo Sicilia Italy
139	D2	Palestine U.S.A.
62	A1	Paletwa Myanmar
74	B2	Pali India
48	E2	Palikir Micronesia
109	C2	Palinuro, Capo c. Italy
111	B3	Paliouri, Akrotirio pt Greece
100	B3	Paliseul Belgium
92	I3	Paljakka h. Fin.
73	B4	Palk Strait India/Sri Lanka
54	C2	Palliser, Cape N.Z.
49	I3	Palliser, Îles is Fr. Polynesia
106	B2	Palma del Río Spain
107	D2	Palma de Mallorca Spain
154	B3	Palmas Brazil
151	D3	Palmas Brazil
114	B4	Palmas, Cape Liberia
154	C3	Palmeira Brazil
151	D2	Palmeirais Brazil
55	P2	Palmer Land reg. Antarctica
54	C2	Palmerston North N.Z.
109	C2	Palmi Italy
145	C2	Palmillas Mex.
150	A1	Palmira Col.

224

135 C4	**Palm Springs** U.S.A.	
49 H2	**Palmyra Atoll** N. Pacific Ocean	
117 B3	**Paloich** S. Sudan	
145 D2	**Palomares** Mex.	
107 C2	**Palos, Cabo de** c. Spain	
92 I3	**Paltamo** Fin.	
58 B3	**Palu** Indon.	
83 M2	**Palyavaam** r. Rus. Fed.	
104 C3	**Pamiers** France	
77 D3	**Pamir** mts Asia	
143 E1	**Pamlico Sound** sea chan. U.S.A.	
152 B2	**Pampa Grande** Bol.	
153 B4	**Pampas** reg. Arg.	
150 A1	**Pamplona** Col.	
107 C1	**Pamplona** Spain	
111 D2	**Pamukova** Turkey	
60 B2	**Panaitan** i. Indon.	
63 H4	**Panaji** India	
146 B4	**Panama** country Central America	
146 C4	**Panamá, Canal de** Panama	
146 C4	**Panama, Gulf of** Panama	
146 C4	**Panama City** Panama	
142 C2	**Panama City** U.S.A.	
135 C3	**Panamint Range** mts U.S.A.	
61 B1	**Panarik** Indon.	
61 A1	**Panay** i. Phil.	
109 D2	**Pančevo** Serbia	
61 B1	**Pandan** Phil.	
75 C2	**Pandaria** India	
73 B3	**Pandharpur** India	
88 B2	**Panevėžys** Lith.	
61 C2	**Pangkalanbuun** Indon.	
60 A1	**Pangkalansusu** Indon.	
60 B2	**Pangkalpinang** Indon.	
127 G2	**Pangnirtung** Can.	
86 G2	**Pangody** Rus. Fed.	
89 F3	**Panino** Rus. Fed.	
74 B2	**Panipat** India	
74 A2	**Panjgur** Pak.	
65 C1	**Pan Ling** mts China	
75 C2	**Panna** India	
50 A2	**Pannawonica** Austr.	
154 B2	**Panorama** Brazil	
65 B1	**Panshi** China	
145 C2	**Pánuco** Mex.	
62 B1	**Panzhihua** China	
109 C3	**Paola** Italy	
63 C2	**Paôy Pêt** Cambodia	
103 D2	**Pápa** Hungary	
54 B1	**Papakura** N.Z.	
145 C2	**Papantla** Mex.	
49 I4	**Papeete** Fr. Polynesia	
100 C1	**Papenburg** Ger.	
80 B2	**Paphos** Cyprus	
59 D3	**Papua, Gulf of** P.N.G.	
59 D3	**Papua New Guinea** country Oceania	
50 A2	**Paraburdoo** Austr.	
154 C1	**Paracatu** Brazil	
155 C1	**Paracatu** r. Brazil	
52 A2	**Parachilna** Austr.	
109 C2	**Paraćin** Serbia	
155 D1	**Pará de Minas** Brazil	
135 B3	**Paradise** U.S.A.	
142 B1	**Paragould** U.S.A.	
151 C3	**Paraguai** r. Brazil	
152 C3	**Paraguay** r. Arg./Para.	
152 C3	**Paraguay** country S. America	
155 D2	**Paraíba do Sul** r. Brazil	
154 B1	**Paraíso** Brazil	
145 C3	**Paraíso** Mex.	
114 C4	**Parakou** Benin	
151 C1	**Paramaribo** Suriname	
83 L3	**Paramushir, Ostrov** i. Rus. Fed.	
152 B4	**Paraná** Arg.	
154 A3	**Paraná** r. S. America	
154 C3	**Paranaguá** Brazil	
154 B1	**Paranaíba** Brazil	
154 B2	**Paranaíba** r. Brazil	
154 B2	**Paranapanema** r. Brazil	
154 B2	**Paranapiacaba, Serra** mts Brazil	
154 B2	**Paranavaí** Brazil	
54 B2	**Paraparaumu** N.Z.	
155 D2	**Parati** Brazil	
154 B1	**Paraúna** Brazil	
105 C2	**Paray-le-Monial** France	
73 B3	**Parbhani** India	
101 E1	**Parchim** Ger.	
155 C1	**Pardo** r. Bahia Brazil	
154 B2	**Pardo** r. Mato Grosso do Sul Brazil	
154 B2	**Pardo** r. São Paulo Brazil	
103 D1	**Pardubice** Czech Rep.	
150 B3	**Parecis, Serra dos** hills Brazil	
130 C2	**Parent, Lac** l. Can.	
58 B3	**Parepare** Indon.	
89 D2	**Parfino** Rus. Fed.	
111 B3	**Parga** Greece	
109 C3	**Parghelia** Italy	
147 D3	**Paria, Gulf of** Trin. and Tob./Venez.	
150 B1	**Parima, Serra** mts Brazil	
151 C2	**Parintins** Brazil	
104 C2	**Paris** France	
142 C1	**Paris** TN U.S.A.	
139 D2	**Paris** TX U.S.A.	
93 H3	**Parkano** Fin.	
138 A2	**Parker** U.S.A.	
140 C3	**Parkersburg** U.S.A.	
53 C2	**Parkes** Austr.	
140 A1	**Park Falls** U.S.A.	
137 D1	**Park Rapids** U.S.A.	
108 B2	**Parma** Italy	
151 D2	**Parnaíba** Brazil	
151 D2	**Parnaíba** r. Brazil	
54 B2	**Parnassus** N.Z.	
111 B3	**Parnonas** mts Greece	
88 B2	**Pärnu** Estonia	
65 B2	**P'aro-ho** l. S. Korea	
52 B2	**Paroo** watercourse Austr.	
111 C3	**Paros** i. Greece	
144 B2	**Parras** Mex.	
126 C2	**Parry, Cape** Can.	
126 D1	**Parry Islands** Can.	
130 B2	**Parry Sound** Can.	
137 D3	**Parsons** U.S.A.	
101 D2	**Partenstein** Ger.	
104 B2	**Parthenay** France	
97 B2	**Partry Mountains** hills Ireland	
151 C2	**Paru** r. Brazil	
135 C4	**Pasadena** U.S.A.	
59 A2	**Pasawng** Myanmar	
142 C2	**Pascagoula** U.S.A.	
110 C1	**Paşcani** Romania	
134 C1	**Pasco** U.S.A.	
102 C1	**Pasewalk** Ger.	
129 D2	**Pasfield Lake** Can.	
64 B1	**Pasig** Phil.	
60 B1	**Pasir Putih** Malaysia	
74 A2	**Pasni** Pak.	
153 A5	**Paso Río Mayo** Arg.	
135 B3	**Paso Robles** U.S.A.	
155 C2	**Passa Tempo** Brazil	
102 C2	**Passau** Ger.	
152 C3	**Passo Fundo** Brazil	
155 C2	**Passos** Brazil	
88 C2	**Pastavy** Belarus	
150 A2	**Pastaza** r. Peru	
150 A1	**Pasto** Col.	
61 C2	**Pasuruan** Indon.	
88 B2	**Pasvalys** Lith.	
153 A6	**Patagonia** reg. Arg.	
75 C2	**Patan** Nepal	
54 B1	**Patea** N.Z.	
141 E2	**Paterson** U.S.A.	
	Pathein Myanmar see Bassein	
136 B2	**Pathfinder Reservoir** U.S.A.	
61 C2	**Pati** Indon.	
62 B1	**Patkai Bum** mts India/Myanmar	
111 C3	**Patmos** i. Greece	
75 C2	**Patna** India	
81 C2	**Patnos** Turkey	
154 B3	**Pato Branco** Brazil	
152 C4	**Patos, Lagoa dos** l. Brazil	
155 C2	**Patos de Minas** Brazil	
152 B4	**Patquía** Arg.	
111 B3	**Patras** Greece	
75 C2	**Patratu** India	
154 C1	**Patrocínio** Brazil	
63 B3	**Pattani** Thai.	
63 B2	**Pattaya** Thai.	
128 B2	**Pattullo, Mount** Can.	
129 D2	**Patuanak** Can.	
144 B3	**Pátzcuaro** Mex.	
104 B3	**Pau** France	
104 B3	**Pauillac** France	
62 A1	**Pauk** Myanmar	
151 E2	**Paulistana** Brazil	
151 E2	**Paulo Afonso** Brazil	
123 D2	**Paulpietersburg** S. Africa	
139 D2	**Pauls Valley** U.S.A.	
62 A2	**Paungde** Myanmar	
155 D1	**Pavão** Brazil	
108 A1	**Pavia** Italy	
88 B2	**Pāvilosta** Latvia	
110 C2	**Pavlikeni** Bulg.	
77 D1	**Pavlodar** Kazakh.	
91 D2	**Pavlohrad** Ukr.	
91 E1	**Pavlovsk** Rus. Fed.	
91 D2	**Pavlovskaya** Rus. Fed.	
60 B2	**Payakumbuh** Indon.	
134 C2	**Payette** U.S.A.	
134 C2	**Payette** r. U.S.A.	
86 F2	**Pay-Khoy, Khrebet** hills Rus. Fed.	
152 C4	**Paysandú** Uru.	
81 C1	**Pazar** Turkey	
110 B2	**Pazardzhik** Bulg.	
111 C3	**Pazarköy** Turkey	
108 B1	**Pazin** Croatia	
63 A2	**Pe** Myanmar	
128 C2	**Peace** r. Can.	
128 C2	**Peace River** Can.	
135 E3	**Peale, Mount** U.S.A.	
139 C2	**Pearl** r. U.S.A.	
139 D3	**Pearsall** U.S.A.	
121 C2	**Pebane** Moz.	
	Peć Kosovo see Pejë	
155 D1	**Peçanha** Brazil	
86 E2	**Pechora** Rus. Fed.	
88 C2	**Pechory** Rus. Fed.	
139 C2	**Pecos** U.S.A.	
139 C3	**Pecos** r. U.S.A.	
103 D2	**Pécs** Hungary	
155 D1	**Pedra Azul** Brazil	
154 C2	**Pedregulho** Brazil	
151 E2	**Pedreiras** Brazil	
73 C4	**Pedro, Point** Sri Lanka	
151 D2	**Pedro Afonso** Brazil	
154 B1	**Pedro Gomes** Brazil	
152 C3	**Pedro Juan Caballero** Para.	
96 C3	**Peebles** U.K.	
143 E1	**Pee Dee** r. U.S.A.	
126 C2	**Peel** r. Can.	
98 A1	**Peel** Isle of Man	

Peerless Lake

128 C2 Peerless Lake Can.
54 B2 Pegasus Bay N.Z.
101 E3 Pegnitz Ger.
62 A2 Pegu Myanmar
62 A2 Pegu Yoma mts Myanmar
153 B4 Pehuajó Arg.
101 E1 Peine Ger.
88 C2 Peipus, Lake Estonia/Rus. Fed.
154 B2 Peixe r. Brazil
109 D2 Pejë Kosovo
61 B2 Pekalongan Indon.
60 B1 Pekan Malaysia
60 B1 Pekanbaru Indon.
Peking China see Beijing
130 B2 Pelee Island Can.
59 C3 Peleng i. Indon.
92 I2 Pelkosenniemi Fin.
122 A2 Pella S. Africa
59 D3 Pelleluhu Islands P.N.G.
92 H2 Pello Fin.
128 A1 Pelly r. Can.
128 A1 Pelly Mountains Can.
152 C4 Pelotas Brazil
152 C3 Pelotas, Rio das r. Brazil
61 B1 Pemangkat Indon.
60 A1 Pematangsiantar Indon.
121 D2 Pemba Moz.
120 B2 Pemba Zambia
119 D3 Pemba Island Tanz.
128 B2 Pemberton Can.
137 D3 Pembina r. Can./U.S.A.
130 C2 Pembroke Can.
99 A3 Pembroke U.K.
145 C2 Peña Nevada, Cerro mt. Mex.
154 B2 Penápolis Brazil
106 B1 Peñaranda de Bracamonte Spain
107 C1 Peñarroya mt. Spain
106 B2 Peñarroya-Pueblonuevo Spain
106 B1 Peñas, Cabo de c. Spain
153 A5 Penas, Golfo de g. Chile
134 C1 Pendleton U.S.A.
128 B2 Pendleton Bay Can.
134 C1 Pend Oreille Lake U.S.A.
74 B3 Penganga r. India
123 D1 Penge S. Africa
70 C2 Penglai China
71 A3 Pengshui China
106 B2 Peniche Port.
98 B3 Penicuik U.K.
108 B2 Penne Italy
98 B3 Pennines hills U.K.
141 D2 Pennsylvania state U.S.A.
127 G2 Penny Icecap Can.
141 F2 Penobscot r. U.S.A.
52 B3 Penola Austr.
50 C3 Penong Austr.
49 H3 Penrhyn atoll Cook Is
98 B1 Penrith U.K.
142 C2 Pensacola U.S.A.
55 Q1 Pensacola Mountains Antarctica
61 C1 Pensiangan Sabah Malaysia
128 C3 Penticton Can.
96 C1 Pentland Firth sea chan. U.K.
99 B2 Penygadair h. U.K.
87 D3 Penza Rus. Fed.
99 A3 Penzance U.K.
140 C3 Peoria U.S.A.
107 C1 Perales del Alfambra Spain
51 E2 Percy Isles Austr.
86 F2 Peregrebnoye Rus. Fed.
150 A1 Pereira Col.
154 B2 Pereira Barreto Brazil
90 A2 Peremyshl' Ukr.
89 E2 Pereslavl'-Zalesskiy Rus. Fed.

91 C1 Pereyaslav-Khmel'nyts'kyy Ukr.
153 B4 Pergamino Arg.
92 H3 Perhonjoki r. Fin.
131 C1 Péribonka, Lac l. Can.
152 B3 Perico Arg.
144 B2 Pericos Mex.
104 C2 Périgueux France
147 C4 Perijá, Sierra de mts Venez.
153 A5 Perito Moreno Arg.
101 E1 Perleberg Ger.
86 F3 Perm' Rus. Fed.
52 A2 Pernatty Lagoon imp. l. Austr.
105 C2 Péronne France
145 C3 Perote Mex.
104 C3 Perpignan France
99 A3 Perranporth U.K.
143 D2 Perry FL U.S.A.
143 D2 Perry GA U.S.A.
137 E2 Perry IA U.S.A.
139 C1 Perryton U.S.A.
137 F3 Perryville U.S.A.
99 B2 Pershore U.K.
91 D2 Pershotravens'k Ukr.
Persian Gulf Asia see The Gulf
50 A3 Perth Austr.
96 C2 Perth U.K.
105 D2 Pertuis France
108 A2 Pertusato, Capo c. Corse France
150 A2 Peru country S. America
157 H4 Peru-Chile Trench S. Pacific Ocean
108 B2 Perugia Italy
154 C2 Peruíbe Brazil
100 A2 Péruwelz Belgium
90 C2 Pervomays'k Ukr.
91 C2 Pervomays'ke Ukr.
89 F3 Pervomayskiy Rus. Fed.
91 D2 Pervomays'kyy Ukr.
108 B2 Pesaro Italy
108 B2 Pescara Italy
108 B2 Pescara r. Italy
74 B1 Peshawar Pak.
109 D2 Peshkopi Albania
109 C1 Pesnica Slovenia
89 E2 Pestovo Rus. Fed.
144 B3 Petatlán Mex.
140 B2 Petenwell Lake U.S.A.
52 A2 Peterborough Austr.
130 C2 Peterborough Can.
99 C2 Peterborough U.K.
96 C2 Peterhead U.K.
50 B2 Petermann Ranges mts Austr.
129 D2 Peter Pond Lake Can.
128 A2 Petersburg AK U.S.A.
141 D3 Petersburg VA U.S.A.
101 D1 Petershagen Ger.
131 E1 Petit Mécatina r. Can.
145 D2 Peto Mex.
140 C1 Petoskey U.S.A.
80 B2 Petra tourist site Jordan
66 B2 Petra Velikogo, Zaliv b. Rus. Fed.
111 B2 Petrich Bulg.
151 D2 Petrolina Brazil
83 L3 Petropavlovsk-Kamchatskiy Rus. Fed.
77 C1 Petropavlovskoye Kazakh.
110 B1 Petroşani Romania
89 F3 Petrovskoye Rus. Fed.
86 C2 Petrozavodsk Rus. Fed.
123 C2 Petrusburg S. Africa
123 C2 Petrus Steyn S. Africa
122 B3 Petrusville S. Africa
89 E2 Petushki Rus. Fed.
60 A1 Peureula Indon.

83 M2 Pevek Rus. Fed.
102 B2 Pforzheim Ger.
102 C2 Pfunds Austria
101 D3 Pfungstadt Ger.
123 C2 Phahameng S. Africa
123 D1 Phalaborwa S. Africa
74 B2 Phalodi India
63 B2 Phang Hoei, San Khao mts Thai.
63 A3 Phangnga Thai.
62 B1 Phăng Xi Păng mt. Vietnam
63 B2 Phan Rang-Thap Cham Vietnam
63 B2 Phan Thiêt Vietnam
63 B3 Phatthalung Thai.
62 A2 Phayao Thai.
129 D2 Phelps Lake Can.
143 C2 Phenix City U.S.A.
63 A2 Phet Buri Thai.
63 B2 Phichit Thai.
141 D3 Philadelphia U.S.A.
136 C2 Philip U.S.A.
100 B2 Philippeville Belgium
100 A2 Philippine Neth.
64 B1 Philippines country Asia
64 B1 Philippine Sea N. Pacific Ocean
126 B2 Philip Smith Mountains U.S.A.
122 B3 Philipstown S. Africa
53 C3 Phillip Island Austr.
137 D3 Phillipsburg U.S.A.
123 C2 Phiritona S. Africa
63 B2 Phitsanulok Thai.
63 B2 Phnom Penh Cambodia
138 A2 Phoenix U.S.A.
49 G3 Phoenix Islands Kiribati
63 B2 Phon Thai.
62 B1 Phôngsali Laos
62 B2 Phônsavan Laos
63 B2 Phrae Thai.
63 A3 Phuket Thai.
62 A2 Phumĭphon, Khuan Thai.
63 B2 Phumĭ Sâmraông Cambodia
123 C2 Phuthaditjhaba S. Africa
62 A2 Phyu Myanmar
108 A1 Piacenza Italy
110 C1 Piatra Neamţ Romania
151 D2 Piauí r. Brazil
108 B1 Piave r. Italy
117 B4 Pibor r. S. Sudan
117 B4 Pibor Post S. Sudan
142 C2 Picayune U.S.A.
152 B3 Pichanal Arg.
144 A2 Pichilingue Mex.
98 C1 Pickering U.K.
130 A1 Pickle Lake Can.
151 D2 Picos Brazil
153 B5 Pico Truncado Arg.
53 D2 Picton Austr.
150 B3 Piedras, Río de las r. Peru
145 C3 Piedras Negras Guat.
145 B2 Piedras Negras Mex.
93 I3 Pieksämäki Fin.
92 I3 Pielinen l. Fin.
136 C2 Pierre U.S.A.
105 C2 Pierrelatte France
123 D2 Pietermaritzburg S. Africa
110 B1 Pietrosa mt. Romania
123 C3 Pigeon Lake Can.
153 B4 Pigüé Arg.
92 I3 Pihtipudas Fin.
145 C3 Pijijiapan Mex.
136 C3 Pikes Peak U.S.A.
122 A3 Piketberg S. Africa
140 C3 Pikeville U.S.A.

103 D1 Piła Pol.
153 C4 Pilar Arg.
152 C3 Pilar Para.
53 C2 Pilliga Austr.
154 C1 Pilões, Serra dos mts Brazil
150 B3 Pimenta Bueno Brazil
153 C4 Pinamar Arg.
80 B2 Pınarbaşı Turkey
146 B2 Pinar del Río Cuba
103 E1 Pińczów Pol.
151 D2 Pindaré r. Brazil
        Pindaré mts Greece see Pindus
        Mountains
111 B2 Pindus Mountains Greece
141 D2 Pine Bluff U.S.A.
50 C1 Pine Creek Austr.
136 B2 Pinedale U.S.A.
86 D2 Pinega Rus. Fed.
129 D2 Pinehouse Lake Can.
111 B3 Pineios r. Greece
128 C1 Pine Point (abandoned) Can.
136 C2 Pine Ridge U.S.A.
123 D2 Pinetown S. Africa
70 B2 Pingdingshan China
71 A3 Pingguo China
71 B3 Pingjiang China
70 A2 Pingliang China
71 C3 P'ingtung Taiwan
71 A3 Pingxiang Guangxi China
71 B3 Pingxiang Jiangxi China
70 B2 Pingyin China
151 D2 Pinheiro Brazil
101 D1 Pinneberg Ger.
145 C3 Pinotepa Nacional Mex.
88 C3 Pinsk Belarus
135 D3 Pioche U.S.A.
119 C3 Piodi Dem. Rep. Congo
103 E1 Pionki Pol.
103 D1 Piotrków Trybunalski Pol.
137 D2 Pipestone U.S.A.
131 C2 Pipmuacan, Réservoir resr
        Can.
154 B2 Piquiri r. Brazil
154 C1 Piracanjuba Brazil
154 C2 Piracicaba Brazil
155 D1 Piracicaba r. Brazil
154 C2 Piraçununga Brazil
111 B3 Piraeus Greece
154 C2 Piraí do Sul Brazil
154 B1 Pirajuí Brazil
154 B1 Piranhas Brazil
151 E2 Piranhas r. Brazil
155 D1 Pirapora Brazil
154 C1 Pires do Rio Brazil
151 D2 Piripiri Brazil
59 C2 Piru Indon.
108 B2 Pisa Italy
152 A2 Pisagua Chile
150 A3 Pisco Peru
102 C2 Písek Czech Rep.
79 D2 Pīshīn Iran
145 D2 Pisté Mex.
109 C2 Pisticci Italy
108 B2 Pistoia Italy
106 C1 Pisuerga r. Spain
134 B2 Pit r. U.S.A.
154 B2 Pitanga Brazil
155 D1 Pitangui Brazil
49 J4 Pitcairn Island i. Pitcairn Is
92 H2 Piteå Sweden
92 H2 Piteälven r. Sweden
110 B2 Pitești Romania
75 C2 Pithoragarh India
96 C2 Pitlochry U.K.
128 B2 Pitt Island Can.
137 E3 Pittsburg U.S.A.
141 D2 Pittsburgh U.S.A.

141 E2 Pittsfield U.S.A.
53 D1 Pittsworth Austr.
155 C2 Piumhi Brazil
150 A2 Piura Peru
90 C2 Pivdennyy Buh r. Ukr.
131 E2 Placentia Can.
135 B3 Placerville U.S.A.
146 C2 Placetas Cuba
139 C2 Plainview U.S.A.
154 C1 Planaltina Brazil
142 B2 Plaquemine U.S.A.
106 B1 Plasencia Spain
147 C4 Plato Col.
137 D2 Platte r. U.S.A.
141 E2 Plattsburgh U.S.A.
101 F1 Plau Ger.
101 F2 Plauen Ger.
101 F1 Plauer See l. Ger.
89 E3 Plavsk Rus. Fed.
129 E2 Playgreen Lake Can.
63 B2 Plây Ku Vietnam
153 B4 Plaza Huincul Arg.
139 D3 Pleasanton U.S.A.
54 B2 Pleasant Point N.Z.
104 C2 Pleaux France
130 B1 Pledger Lake Can.
54 C1 Plenty, Bay of g. N.Z.
136 C1 Plentywood U.S.A.
86 D2 Plesetsk Rus. Fed.
131 C1 Plétipi, Lac l. Can.
100 C2 Plettenberg Ger.
122 B3 Plettenberg Bay S. Africa
110 B2 Pleven Bulg.
109 C2 Pljevlja Montenegro
109 C2 Ploče Croatia
103 D1 Płock Pol.
109 C2 Pločno mt. Bos.-Herz.
104 B2 Ploemeur France
110 C2 Ploiești Romania
89 F2 Ploskoye Rus. Fed.
104 B2 Plouzané France
110 B2 Plovdiv Bulg.
88 B2 Plungė Lith.
88 C3 Plyeshchanitsy Belarus
99 A3 Plymouth U.K.
140 B2 Plymouth U.S.A.
147 D3 Plymouth (abandoned)
        Montserrat
88 C2 Plyussa Rus. Fed.
102 C2 Plzeň Czech Rep.
114 B3 Pô Burkina Faso
108 B1 Po r. Italy
77 E2 Pobeda Peak China/Kyrg.
142 B1 Pocahontas U.S.A.
134 D2 Pocatello U.S.A.
90 B1 Pochayiv Ukr.
89 D3 Pochep Rus. Fed.
89 D3 Pochinok Rus. Fed.
145 C3 Pochutla Mex.
141 D3 Pocomoke City U.S.A.
154 C1 Poços de Caldas Brazil
89 D2 Poddor'ye Rus. Fed.
91 D1 Podgorenskiy Rus. Fed.
109 C2 Podgorica Montenegro
82 G3 Podgornoye Rus. Fed.
83 H2 Podkamennaya Tunguska r.
        Rus. Fed.
89 E2 Podol'sk Rus. Fed.
109 D2 Podujevë Kosovo
        Podujevo Kosovo see Podujevë
122 A2 Pofadder S. Africa
89 D3 Pogar Rus. Fed.
109 D2 Pogradec Albania
65 B2 P'ohang S. Korea
48 E2 Pohnpei atoll Micronesia
110 B2 Poiana Mare Romania
118 C3 Poie Dem. Rep. Congo

118 B3 Pointe-Noire Congo
126 D2 Point Lake Can.
140 C3 Point Pleasant U.S.A.
104 C2 Poitiers France
74 B2 Pokaran India
75 C2 Pokhara Nepal
83 J2 Pokrovsk Rus. Fed.
91 D2 Pokrovskoye Rus. Fed.
138 A1 Polacca U.S.A.
103 D1 Poland country Europe
88 C2 Polatsk Belarus
61 C2 Polewali Indon.
118 B2 Poli Cameroon
102 C1 Police Pol.
109 C2 Policoro Italy
105 C2 Poligny France
64 B1 Polillo Islands Phil.
90 B1 Polis'ke Ukr.
103 D1 Polkowice Pol.
109 C3 Pollino, Monte mt. Italy
91 D2 Polohy Ukr.
123 C1 Polokwane S. Africa
123 C1 Polokwane r. S. Africa
90 B1 Polonne Ukr.
134 D1 Polson U.S.A.
91 C2 Poltava Ukr.
66 B2 Poltavka Rus. Fed.
91 D2 Poltavskaya Rus. Fed.
88 C2 Põlva Estonia
111 B2 Polygyros Greece
102 C1 Pomeranian Bay Ger./Pol.
108 B2 Pomezia Italy
92 I2 Pomokaira reg. Fin.
110 C2 Pomorie Bulg.
        Pomorska, Zatoka b. Ger./Pol.
        see Pomeranian Bay
155 D1 Pompéu Brazil
139 D1 Ponca City U.S.A.
147 D3 Ponce Puerto Rico
127 F2 Pond Inlet Can.
106 B1 Ponferrada Spain
117 A4 Pongo watercourse
        S. Sudan
123 D2 Pongola r. S. Africa
128 C2 Ponoka Can.
84 D5 Ponta Delgada Arquipélago
        dos Açores
154 B3 Ponta Grossa Brazil
154 C1 Pontalina Brazil
105 D2 Pont-à-Mousson France
105 D2 Pontarlier France
102 C2 Pontcharra France
142 B2 Pontchartrain, Lake U.S.A.
106 B2 Ponte de Sor Port.
129 D3 Ponteix Can.
150 D3 Pontes-e-Lacerda Brazil
106 B1 Pontevedra Spain
140 B2 Pontiac IL U.S.A.
140 C2 Pontiac MI U.S.A.
61 B2 Pontianak Indon.
104 B2 Pontivy France
151 C1 Pontoetoe Suriname
129 E2 Ponton r. Can.
99 B3 Pontypool U.K.
108 B2 Ponziane, Isole is Italy
99 C3 Poole U.K.
        Poona India see Pune
52 B2 Pooncarie Austr.
152 B2 Poopó, Lago de l. Bol.
150 A1 Popayán Col.
83 I2 Popigay r. Rus. Fed.
52 B2 Popiltah Austr.
129 E2 Poplar r. Can.
137 E3 Poplar Bluff U.S.A.
118 B3 Popokabaka Dem. Rep. Congo
110 C2 Popovo Bulg.

103	E2	Poprad Slovakia
151	D3	Porangatu Brazil
74	A2	Porbandar India
126	B2	Porcupine r. Can./U.S.A.
108	B1	Poreč Croatia
54	A2	Porirua N.Z.
88	C2	Porkhov Rus. Fed.
104	B2	Pornic France
83	K3	Poronaysk Rus. Fed.
111	B3	Poros Greece
93	E4	Porsgrunn Norway
97	C1	Portadown U.K.
97	D1	Portaferry U.K.
140	B2	Portage U.S.A.
129	E3	Portage la Prairie Can.
128	B3	Port Alberni Can.
106	B2	Portalegre Port.
139	C2	Portales U.S.A.
128	A2	Port Alexander U.S.A.
128	B2	Port Alice Can.
134	B1	Port Angeles U.S.A.
51	D4	Port Arthur Austr.
139	E3	Port Arthur U.S.A.
96	A3	Port Askaig U.K.
52	A2	Port Augusta Austr.
147	C3	Port-au-Prince Haiti
131	E1	Port aux Choix Can.
73	D3	Port Blair India
52	B3	Port Campbell Austr.
54	B3	Port Chalmers N.Z.
143	D3	Port Charlotte U.S.A.
147	C3	Port-de-Paix Haiti
128	A2	Port Edward Can.
155	D1	Porteirinha Brazil
151	C2	Portel Brazil
130	B2	Port Elgin Can.
123	C3	Port Elizabeth S. Africa
96	A3	Port Ellen U.K.
98	A1	Port Erin Isle of Man
122	A3	Porterville S. Africa
135	C3	Porterville U.S.A.
52	B3	Port Fairy Austr.
54	C1	Port Fitzroy N.Z.
118	A3	Port-Gentil Gabon
115	C4	Port Harcourt Nigeria
128	B2	Port Hardy Can.
		Port Harrison Can. see Inukjuak
131	D2	Port Hawkesbury Can.
50	A2	Port Hedland Austr.
99	A2	Porthmadog U.K.
131	E1	Port Hope Simpson Can.
140	C2	Port Huron U.S.A.
106	B2	Portimão Port.
53	C2	Portland N.S.W. Austr.
52	B3	Portland Vic. Austr.
141	E2	Portland ME U.S.A.
134	B1	Portland OR U.S.A.
128	A2	Portland Canal inlet Can.
97	C2	Portlaoise Ireland
139	D3	Port Lavaca U.S.A.
52	A2	Port Lincoln Austr.
114	A4	Port Loko Sierra Leone
113	K9	Port Louis Mauritius
53	D2	Port Macquarie Austr.
128	B2	Port McNeill Can.
131	D2	Port-Menier Can.
59	D3	Port Moresby P.N.G.
122	A2	Port Nolloth S. Africa
		Port-Nouveau-Québec Can. see Kangiqsualujjuaq
		Porto Port. see Oporto
150	B2	Porto Acre Brazil
152	C4	Porto Alegre Brazil
151	C3	Porto Artur Brazil
151	C3	Porto dos Gaúchos Óbidos Brazil
150	C3	Porto Esperidião Brazil
108	B2	Portoferraio Italy
96	A1	Port of Ness U.K.
151	D2	Porto Franco Brazil
147	D3	Port of Spain Trin. and Tob.
108	B1	Portogruaro Italy
108	B2	Portomaggiore Italy
154	B2	Porto Mendes Brazil
152	C3	Porto Murtinho Brazil
151	D3	Porto Nacional Brazil
114	C4	Porto-Novo Benin
154	B2	Porto Primavera, Represa resr Brazil
151	C2	Porto Santana Brazil
155	E1	Porto Seguro Brazil
108	B2	Porto Tolle Italy
108	A2	Porto Torres Sardegna Italy
105	D3	Porto-Vecchio Corse France
150	B2	Porto Velho Brazil
150	A2	Portoviejo Ecuador
52	B3	Port Phillip Bay Austr.
52	A2	Port Pirie Austr.
96	A2	Portree U.K.
128	B3	Port Renfrew Can.
97	C1	Portrush U.K.
116	B1	Port Said Egypt
143	C3	Port St Joe U.S.A.
123	C3	Port St Johns S. Africa
123	D3	Port Shepstone S. Africa
99	C3	Portsmouth U.K.
141	E2	Portsmouth NH U.S.A.
140	C3	Portsmouth OH U.S.A.
141	D3	Portsmouth VA U.S.A.
97	C1	Portstewart U.K.
116	B3	Port Sudan Sudan
142	C3	Port Sulphur U.S.A.
99	B3	Port Talbot U.K.
106	B2	Portugal country Europe
97	B2	Portumna Ireland
105	C3	Port-Vendres France
48	F4	Port Vila Vanuatu
93	I3	Porvoo Fin.
65	B2	Poryŏng S. Korea
152	C3	Posadas Arg.
89	E2	Poshekhon'ye Rus. Fed.
92	I2	Posio Fin.
58	C3	Poso Indon.
151	D3	Posse Brazil
101	E2	Pößneck Ger.
139	C2	Post U.S.A.
		Poste-de-la-Baleine Can. see Kuujjuarapik
122	B2	Postmasburg S. Africa
109	C2	Posušje Bos.-Herz.
139	E1	Poteau U.S.A.
109	C2	Potenza Italy
151	D2	Poti r. Brazil
81	C1	Poti Georgia
115	D3	Potiskum Nigeria
141	D3	Potomac, South Branch r. U.S.A.
152	B2	Potosí Bol.
64	B1	Pototan Phil.
138	C3	Potrero del Llano Mex.
101	F1	Potsdam Ger.
141	E2	Potsdam U.S.A.
141	D2	Pottstown U.S.A.
141	D2	Pottsville U.S.A.
131	E2	Pouch Cove Can.
141	E2	Poughkeepsie U.S.A.
98	B2	Poulton-le-Fylde U.K.
155	C2	Pouso Alegre Brazil
63	B2	Poŭthisăt Cambodia
103	D2	Považská Bystrica Slovakia
109	C2	Povlen mt. Serbia
106	B1	Póvoa de Varzim Port.
136	B2	Powell U.S.A.
135	D3	Powell, Lake resr U.S.A.
128	B3	Powell River Can.
154	B1	Poxoréu Brazil
		Poyang China see Poyang
71	B3	Poyang China
71	B3	Poyang Hu l. China
109	D2	Požarevac Serbia
145	C2	Poza Rica Mex.
109	C1	Požega Croatia
109	D2	Požega Serbia
79	D2	Pozm Tiāb Iran
103	D1	Poznań Pol.
106	C2	Pozoblanco Spain
108	B2	Pozzuoli Italy
60	B2	Prabumulih Indon.
63	A2	Prachatice Czech Rep.
63	A2	Prachuap Khiri Khan Thai.
155	E1	Prado Brazil
102	C1	Prague Czech Rep.
		Praha Czech Rep. see Prague
112	C5	Praia Cape Verde
139	C2	Prairie Dog Town Fork r. U.S.A.
140	A2	Prairie du Chien U.S.A.
60	A1	Prapat Indon.
154	C1	Prata Brazil
105	E3	Prato Italy
137	D3	Pratt U.S.A.
61	C2	Praya Indon.
63	B2	Preăh Vihéar Cambodia
89	F2	Prechistoye Rus. Fed.
129	D2	Preeceville Can.
88	C2	Preiļi Latvia
53	C2	Premer Austr.
105	C2	Prémery France
101	F1	Premnitz Ger.
102	C1	Prenzlau Ger.
63	A3	Preparis Island Cocos Is
63	A2	Preparis North Channel Cocos Is
63	A2	Preparis South Channel Cocos Is
103	D2	Přerov Czech Rep.
138	A2	Prescott U.S.A.
109	D2	Preševo Serbia
152	B3	Presidencia Roque Sáenz Peña Arg.
151	D2	Presidente Dutra Brazil
154	B2	Presidente Epitácio Brazil
64	B2	Presidente Manuel A Roxas Zamboanga del Norte Phil.
154	B2	Presidente Prudente Brazil
138	C3	Presidio U.S.A.
103	E2	Prešov Slovakia
141	F1	Presque Isle U.S.A.
101	F2	Pressel Ger.
98	B2	Preston U.K.
134	D2	Preston U.S.A.
96	B3	Prestwick U.K.
155	C1	Preto r. Brazil
123	C2	Pretoria S. Africa
111	B3	Preveza Greece
63	B2	Prey Vêng Cambodia
109	C2	Priboj Serbia
135	D3	Price U.S.A.
88	B3	Prienai Lith.
122	B2	Prieska S. Africa
103	D2	Prievidza Slovakia
109	C2	Prijedor Bos.-Herz.
		Prikaspiyskaya Nizmennost' lowland Kazakh./Rus. Fed. see Caspian Lowland
109	D2	Prilep Macedonia
91	D2	Primorsko-Akhtarsk Rus. Fed.
129	D2	Primrose Lake Can.
129	D2	Prince Albert Can.
122	B3	Prince Albert S. Africa

126 D2 Prince Albert Peninsula Can.
122 B3 Prince Albert Road S. Africa
126 C2 Prince Alfred, Cape Can.
122 A3 Prince Alfred Hamlet S. Africa
127 F2 Prince Charles Island Can.
55 E2 Prince Charles Mountains
        Antarctica
131 D2 Prince Edward Island prov.
        Can.
113 I11 Prince Edward Islands Indian
        Ocean
128 B2 Prince George Can.
126 C2 Prince of Wales Island Can.
128 A2 Prince of Wales Island U.S.A.
126 D2 Prince of Wales Strait Can.
126 D1 Prince Patrick Island Can.
126 E2 Prince Regent Inlet sea chan.
        Can.
128 A2 Prince Rupert Can.
51 D1 Princess Charlotte Bay Austr.
128 B2 Princess Royal Island Can.
128 B3 Princeton Can.
134 B2 Prineville U.S.A.
90 B1 Pripet r. Belarus/Ukr.
90 A1 Pripet Marshes Belarus/Ukr.
109 D2 Prishtinë Kosovo
        Priština Kosovo see Prishtinë
101 F1 Pritzwalk Ger.
109 C2 Privlaka Croatia
89 F2 Privolzhsk Rus. Fed.
109 D2 Prizren Kosovo
151 C1 Professor van Blommestein
        Meer resr Suriname
145 D2 Progreso Mex.
81 C1 Prokhladnyy Rus. Fed.
109 D2 Prokuplje Serbia
87 D4 Proletarskoye
        Vodokhranilishche l. Rus. Fed.
126 C3 Prophet r. Can.
128 B2 Prophet River Can.
59 E3 Proserpine Austr.
89 E3 Protvino Rus. Fed.
110 C2 Provadiya Bulg.
141 E2 Providence U.S.A.
146 B3 Providencia, Isla de i.
        Caribbean Sea
83 N2 Provideniya Rus. Fed.
135 D2 Provo U.S.A.
129 C2 Provost Can.
154 B3 Prudentópolis Brazil
126 B2 Prudhoe Bay U.S.A.
100 C2 Prüm Ger.
105 D3 Prunelli-di-Fiumorbo Corse
        France
103 E1 Pruszków Pol.
110 C1 Prut r. Europe
91 C1 Pryluky Ukr.
91 D2 Prymors'k Ukr.
139 D1 Pryor U.S.A.
        Prypyats' r. Belarus see Pripet
103 E2 Przemyśl Pol.
111 C3 Psara i. Greece
81 C1 Psebay Rus. Fed.
91 D3 Pshekha r. Rus. Fed.
88 C2 Pskov Rus. Fed.
88 C2 Pskov, Lake Estonia/Rus. Fed.
111 B2 Ptolemaïda Greece
109 C1 Ptuj Slovenia
150 A2 Pucallpa Peru
71 B3 Pucheng China
103 D1 Puck Pol.
92 I2 Pudasjärvi Fin.
86 C2 Pudozh Rus. Fed.
        Puducheri India see
        Puducherry
73 B3 Puducherry India

145 C3 Puebla Mex.
136 C3 Pueblo U.S.A.
153 B4 Puelén Arg.
106 C2 Puente Genil Spain
153 A5 Puerto Aisén Chile
152 B2 Puerto Alegre Bol.
145 C3 Puerto Ángel Mex.
146 B4 Puerto Armuelles Panama
150 B1 Puerto Ayacucho Venez.
146 B3 Puerto Cabezas Nic.
150 B1 Puerto Carreño Col.
153 A5 Puerto Cisnes Chile
144 A2 Puerto Cortés Mex.
145 C3 Puerto Escondido Mex.
152 B2 Puerto Frey Bol.
150 B1 Puerto Inírida Col.
152 C2 Puerto Isabel Bol.
150 A2 Puerto Leguizamo Col.
144 A2 Puerto Libertad Mex.
146 B3 Puerto Limón Costa Rica
106 C2 Puertollano Spain
153 B5 Puerto Madryn Arg.
150 A3 Puerto Maldonado Peru
153 A5 Puerto Montt Chile
153 A6 Puerto Natales Chile
150 B1 Puerto Nuevo Col.
144 A1 Puerto Peñasco Mex.
152 C3 Puerto Pinasco Para.
147 C3 Puerto Plata Dom. Rep.
150 A2 Puerto Portillo Peru
64 A2 Puerto Princesa Phil.
147 D3 Puerto Rico terr. West Indies
158 B3 Puerto Rico Trench
        Caribbean Sea
146 A3 Puerto San José Guat.
153 B6 Puerto Santa Cruz Arg.
144 B2 Puerto Vallarta Mex.
87 D3 Pugachev Rus. Fed.
74 B2 Pugal India
54 B2 Pukaki, Lake N.Z.
129 D2 Pukatawagan Can.
65 B1 Pukchin N. Korea
65 B1 Pukch'ŏng N. Korea
54 B1 Pukekohe N.Z.
65 B1 Puksubaek-san mt. N. Korea
108 B2 Pula Croatia
108 A3 Pula Sardegna Italy
152 B3 Pulacayo Bol.
77 C3 Pul-e Khumri Afgh.
92 I3 Pulkkila Fin.
134 C1 Pullman U.S.A.
64 B1 Pulog, Mount Phil.
150 A2 Puná, Isla i. Ecuador
54 B2 Punakaiki N.Z.
123 D1 Punda Maria S. Africa
73 B3 Pune India
65 B1 P'ungsan N. Korea
121 C2 Púnguè r. Moz.
153 B4 Punta Alta Arg.
153 A6 Punta Arenas Chile
146 B3 Puntarenas Costa Rica
117 C4 Puntland reg. Somalia
150 A1 Punto Fijo Venez.
92 I3 Puolanka Fin.
82 G2 Pur r. Rus. Fed.
75 C3 Puri India
100 B1 Purmerend Neth.
75 C2 Purnia India
150 B2 Purus r. Brazil/Peru
61 B2 Purwakarta Indon.
65 B1 Puryŏng N. Korea
65 B2 Pusan S. Korea
88 C2 Pushkinskiye Gory
        Rus. Fed.
88 C2 Pustoshka Rus. Fed.
62 A1 Putao Myanmar

71 B3 Putian China
        Puting China see De'an
61 C2 Puting, Tanjung pt Indon.
101 F1 Putlitz Ger.
58 A2 Putrajaya Malaysia
102 C1 Puttgarden Ger.
150 A2 Putumayo r. Col.
61 C1 Putusibau Indon.
91 C1 Putyvl' Ukr.
127 F2 Puvirnituq Can.
70 B2 Puyang China
104 C3 Puylaurens France
99 A2 Pwllheli U.K.
63 A2 Pyapon Myanmar
82 G2 Pyasina r. Rus. Fed.
87 D4 Pyatigorsk Rus. Fed.
91 C2 P'yatykhatky Ukr.
62 A2 Pyè Myanmar
88 C3 Pyetrykaw Belarus
93 H3 Pyhäjärvi l. Fin.
92 H3 Pyhäjoki r. Fin.
92 I3 Pyhäsalmi Fin.
62 A2 Pyinmana Myanmar
65 B2 Pyŏksŏng N. Korea
65 B2 P'yŏnggang N. Korea
65 B2 P'yŏngsan N. Korea
65 B2 P'yŏngyang N. Korea
135 C2 Pyramid Lake U.S.A.
80 B3 Pyramids of Giza tourist site
        Egypt
107 D2 Pyrenees mts Europe
111 B3 Pyrgos Greece
91 C1 Pyryatyn Ukr.
103 C1 Pyrzyce Pol.
88 C2 Pytalovo Rus. Fed.
111 B3 Pyxaria mt. Greece

Q

        Qaanaaq Greenland see Thule
123 C3 Qacha's Nek Lesotho
68 C2 Qaidam Pendi basin China
74 A1 Qalāt Afgh.
78 B2 Qal'at Bīshah Saudi Arabia
129 E1 Qamanirjuaq Lake Can.
        Qamanittuaq Can. see
        Baker Lake
79 C3 Qamar, Ghubbat al b. Yemen
78 B3 Qam Ḩadīl Saudi Arabia
77 C3 Qarshi Uzbek.
78 B2 Qaryat al Ulyā Saudi Arabia
127 H2 Qasigiannguit Greenland
79 D2 Qaşr-e Qand Iran
81 C2 Qaşr-e Shīrīn Iran
127 H2 Qassimiut Greenland
78 B3 Qa'tabah Yemen
79 C2 Qatar country Asia
116 A2 Qattara Depression Egypt
81 C1 Qazax Azer.
81 C2 Qazvīn Iran
127 H2 Qeqertarsuaq i. Greenland
127 H2 Qeqertarsuatsiaat Greenland
127 H2 Qeqertarsuup Tunua b.
        Greenland
79 C2 Qeshm Iran
70 A3 Qianjiang Chongqing China
70 B2 Qianjiang Hubei China
65 A1 Qian Shan mts China
70 C2 Qidong China
68 B2 Qiemo China
71 A3 Qijiang China
127 G2 Qijiaojing China
127 G2 Qikiqtarjuaq Can.
74 A2 Qila Ladgasht Pak.
68 C2 Qilian Shan mts China

127	I2	Qillak i. Greenland
70	B3	Qimen China
127	G1	Qimusseriarsuaq b. Greenland
116	B2	Qina Egypt
70	C2	Qingdao China
68	C2	Qinghai Hu salt l. China
68	C2	Qinghai Nanshan mts China
70	A2	Qingyang Gansu China
71	B3	Qingyuan Guangdong China
65	A1	Qingyuan Liaoning China
		Qingzang Gaoyuan plat. China see Tibet, Plateau of
70	B2	Qingzhou China
70	B2	Qinhuangdao China
70	A2	Qin Ling mts China
		Qinting China see Lianhua
70	B2	Qinyang China
71	A3	Qinzhou China
71	B4	Qionghai China
68	C2	Qionglai Shan mts China
71	B4	Qiongshan China
69	E1	Qiqihar China
79	C2	Qir Iran
66	B1	Qitaihe China
71	B4	Qixian China
		Qogir Feng mt. China/Pakistan see K2
81	D2	Qom Iran
		Qomolangma Feng mt. China/Nepal see Everest, Mount
76	B3	Qo'ng'irot Uzbek.
		Qoqek China see Tacheng
77	D2	Qo'qon Uzbek.
76	B2	Qoraqalpog'iston Uzbek.
100	C1	Quakenbrück Ger.
63	B2	Quang Ngai Vietnam
63	B2	Quang Tri Vietnam
71	B3	Quanzhou Fujian China
71	B3	Quanzhou Guangxi China
108	A3	Quartu Sant'Elena Sardegna Italy
138	A2	Quartzsite U.S.A.
81	C1	Quba Azer.
53	C3	Queanbeyan Austr.
131	C2	Québec Can.
130	C1	Québec prov. Can.
101	E2	Quedlinburg Ger.
128	A2	Queen Charlotte Can.
128	B2	Queen Charlotte Sound sea chan. Can.
128	B2	Queen Charlotte Strait Can.
126	D1	Queen Elizabeth Islands Can.
126	E2	Queen Maud Gulf Can.
55	B2	Queen Maud Land reg. Antarctica
55	N1	Queen Maud Mountains Antarctica
52	B1	Queensland state Austr.
51	D4	Queenstown Austr.
54	A3	Queenstown N.Z.
123	C3	Queenstown S. Africa
121	C2	Quelimane Moz.
138	B2	Quemado U.S.A.
154	B2	Querência do Norte Brazil
145	B2	Querétaro Mex.
101	E2	Querfurt Ger.
128	B2	Quesnel Can.
128	B2	Quesnel Lake Can.
74	A1	Quetta Pak.
64	A1	Quezon Phil.
64	B1	Quezon City Phil.
120	A2	Quibala Angola
150	A1	Quibdó Col.
104	B2	Quiberon France
104	C3	Quillan France
153	C4	Quilmes Arg.
51	D2	Quilpie Austr.
153	A4	Quilpué Chile
120	A1	Quimbele Angola
152	B3	Quimili Arg.
104	B2	Quimper France
104	B2	Quimperlé France
137	E3	Quincy Il. U.S.A.
141	E2	Quincy MA U.S.A.
107	C1	Quinto Spain
121	D2	Quionga Moz.
53	D2	Quirindi Austr.
121	C3	Quissico Moz.
120	A2	Quitapa Angola
150	A2	Quito Ecuador
151	E2	Quixadá Brazil
71	A3	Qujing China
79	C2	Qurayat Oman
77	C3	Qŭrghonteppa Tajik.
63	B2	Quy Nhon Vietnam
71	B3	Quzhou China

R

103	D2	Raab r. Austria
92	H3	Raahe Fin.
100	C1	Raalte Neth.
61	C2	Raas i. Indon.
61	C2	Raba Indon.
114	B1	Rabat Morocco
48	E3	Rabaul P.N.G.
78	A2	Rābigh Saudi Arabia
131	E2	Race, Cape Can.
142	B3	Raceland U.S.A.
63	B3	Rach Gia Vietnam
140	B2	Racine U.S.A.
78	B3	Radā' Yemen
110	C1	Rădăuți Romania
140	B3	Radcliff U.S.A.
74	B2	Radhanpur India
130	C1	Radisson Can.
103	E1	Radom Pol.
103	D1	Radomsko Pol.
90	B1	Radomyshl' Ukr.
109	D2	Radoviš Macedonia
88	B2	Radviliškis Lith.
78	A2	Radwá, Jabal mt. Saudi Arabia
90	B1	Radyvyliv Ukr.
75	C2	Rae Bareli India
100	C2	Raeren Belgium
54	C1	Raetihi N.Z.
152	B4	Rafaela Arg.
118	C2	Rafaï C.A.R.
78	B2	Rafḥā' Saudi Arabia
79	C1	Rafsanjān Iran
64	B2	Ragang, Mount vol. Phil.
109	B3	Ragusa Sicilia Italy
59	C3	Raha Indon.
88	D3	Rahachow Belarus
74	B2	Rahimyar Khan Pak.
109	D2	Rahovec Kosovo
73	B3	Raichur India
75	C2	Raigarh India
128	C2	Rainbow Lake Can.
134	B1	Rainier, Mount vol. U.S.A.
130	A2	Rainy Lake Can./U.S.A.
129	E3	Rainy River Can.
75	C2	Raipur India
93	H3	Raisio Fin.
73	C3	Rajahmundry India
61	C1	Rajang r. Sarawak Malaysia
74	B2	Rajanpur Pak.
73	B4	Rajapalayam India
74	B2	Rajasthan Canal India
74	B2	Rajgarh India
74	B2	Rajkot India
74	B2	Rajpur India
75	C2	Rajshahi Bangl.
54	B2	Rakaia r. N.Z.
90	A2	Rakhiv Ukr.
91	D1	Rakitnoye Rus. Fed.
88	C2	Rakke Estonia
88	C2	Rakvere Estonia
143	E1	Raleigh U.S.A.
48	F2	Ralik Chain is Marshall Is
74	B2	Ramgarh India
81	C2	Rāmhormoz Iran
		Ramlat Rabyānah des. Libya see Rebiana Sand Sea
110	C1	Râmnicu Sărat Romania
110	B1	Râmnicu Vâlcea Romania
89	E3	Ramon' Rus. Fed.
123	C1	Ramotswa Botswana
75	B2	Rampur India
62	A2	Ramree Island Myanmar
98	A1	Ramsey Isle of Man
99	D3	Ramsgate U.K.
75	C2	Ranaghat India
61	C1	Ranau Sabah Malaysia
153	A4	Rancagua Chile
75	C2	Ranchi India
93	F4	Randers Denmark
54	B2	Rangiora N.Z.
54	C1	Rangitaiki r. N.Z.
62	A2	Rangoon Myanmar
75	C2	Rangpur Bangl.
129	E1	Rankin Inlet Can.
53	C2	Rankin's Springs Austr.
96	B2	Rannoch Moor moorland U.K.
63	A3	Ranong Thai.
59	C3	Ransiki Indon.
61	C2	Rantaupanjang Indon.
60	A1	Rantauprapat Indon.
92	I2	Ranua Fin.
78	B2	Ranyah, Wādī watercourse Saudi Arabia
49	I4	Rapa i. Fr. Polynesia
136	C2	Rapid City U.S.A.
88	B2	Rapla Estonia
74	A2	Rapur India
49	H4	Rarotonga i. Cook Is
153	B5	Rasa, Punta pt Arg.
79	C2	Ra's al Khaymah U.A.E.
117	B3	Ras Dejen mt. Eth.
88	B2	Raseiniai Lith.
81	C2	Rasht Iran
74	A2	Ras Koh mt. Pak.
88	C2	Rasony Belarus
87	D3	Rasskazovo Rus. Fed.
79	C2	Ras Tannūrah Saudi Arabia
101	D1	Rastede Ger.
93	F3	Rätan Sweden
74	B2	Ratangarh India
63	A2	Rat Buri Thai.
62	A1	Rathedaung Myanmar
101	F1	Rathenow Ger.
97	B1	Rathlin Island U.K.
74	B2	Ratlam India
73	B3	Ratnagiri India
73	C4	Ratnapura Sri Lanka
90	A1	Ratne Ukr.
138	C1	Raton U.S.A.
96	D2	Rattray Head U.K.
101	E1	Ratzeburg Ger.
92	□B2	Raufarhöfn Iceland
54	C1	Raukumara Range mts N.Z.
93	H3	Rauma Fin.
61	C2	Raung, Gunung vol. Indon.
75	C2	Raurkela India
134	D1	Ravalli U.S.A.
81	C2	Ravānsar Iran

108 B2 **Ravenna** Italy
102 B2 **Ravensburg** Ger.
74 B1 **Ravi** r. Pak.
74 B1 **Rawalpindi** Pak.
103 D1 **Rawicz** Pol.
50 B3 **Rawlinna** Austr.
136 B2 **Rawlins** U.S.A.
153 B5 **Rawson** Arg.
73 C2 **Rayagada** India
69 E1 **Raychikhinsk** Rus. Fed.
78 B2 **Raydah** Yemen
87 E3 **Rayevskiy** Rus. Fed.
134 B1 **Raymond** U.S.A.
53 D2 **Raymond Terrace** Austr.
139 D3 **Raymondville** U.S.A.
145 C2 **Rayón** Mex.
63 B2 **Rayong** Thai.
78 A2 **Rayyis** Saudi Arabia
104 B2 **Raz, Pointe du** pt France
81 C2 **Razāzah, Buhayrat ar** l. Iraq
110 C2 **Razgrad** Bulg.
110 B2 **Razim, Lacul** lag. Romania
110 B2 **Razlog** Bulg.
104 B2 **Ré, Île de** i. France
99 C3 **Reading** U.K.
141 D2 **Reading** U.S.A.
115 E2 **Rebiana Sand Sea** des. Libya
66 D1 **Rebun-tō** i. Japan
50 B3 **Recherche, Archipelago of the** is Austr.
89 D3 **Rechytsa** Belarus
151 E2 **Recife** Brazil
123 C3 **Recife, Cape** S. Africa
100 C2 **Recklinghausen** Ger.
152 C3 **Reconquista** Arg.
142 B2 **Red** r. U.S.A.
131 E1 **Red Bay** Can.
135 B2 **Red Bluff** U.S.A.
98 C2 **Redcar** U.K.
129 C2 **Redcliff** Can.
52 B2 **Red Cliffs** Austr.
128 C2 **Red Deer** Can.
128 C2 **Red Deer** r. Can.
129 D2 **Red Deer Lake** Can.
134 B2 **Redding** U.S.A.
99 C2 **Redditch** U.K.
137 D2 **Redfield** U.S.A.
130 A1 **Red Lake** Can.
137 E1 **Red Lakes** U.S.A.
134 E1 **Red Lodge** U.S.A.
134 B2 **Redmond** U.S.A.
137 D2 **Red Oak** U.S.A.
106 B2 **Redondo** Port.
126 B3 **Red Sea** Africa/Asia
128 B1 **Redstone** r. Can.
100 B1 **Reduzum** Neth.
137 D2 **Red Wing** U.S.A.
137 D2 **Redwood Falls** U.S.A.
97 C2 **Ree, Lough** l. Ireland
54 B2 **Reefton** N.Z.
102 C2 **Regen** Ger.
155 E1 **Regência** Brazil
102 C2 **Regensburg** Ger.
114 C2 **Reggane** Alg.
109 C3 **Reggio di Calabria** Italy
108 B2 **Reggio nell'Emilia** Italy
110 B1 **Reghin** Romania
129 D2 **Regina** Can.
122 A1 **Rehoboth** Namibia
101 F2 **Reichenbach** Ger.
143 E1 **Reidsville** U.S.A.
99 C3 **Reigate** U.K.
105 C2 **Reims** France
101 E1 **Reinbek** Ger.
129 D2 **Reindeer** r. Can.
129 E2 **Reindeer Island** Can.

129 D2 **Reindeer Lake** Can.
92 F2 **Reine** Norway
100 C3 **Reinsfeld** Ger.
123 C3 **Reitz** S. Africa
122 B2 **Reivilo** S. Africa
129 D1 **Reliance** Can.
107 D2 **Relizane** Alg.
79 C2 **Remeshk** Iran
105 D2 **Remiremont** France
100 C2 **Remscheid** Ger.
102 B1 **Rendsburg** Ger.
141 D1 **Renfrew** Can.
60 B2 **Rengat** Indon.
90 B2 **Reni** Ukr.
52 B2 **Renmark** Austr.
100 C2 **Rennerod** Ger.
104 B2 **Rennes** France
129 D1 **Rennie Lake** Can.
108 B2 **Reno** r. Italy
135 C3 **Reno** U.S.A.
70 A3 **Renshou** China
140 B2 **Rensselaer** U.S.A.
75 C2 **Renukut** India
54 B2 **Renwick** N.Z.
58 C3 **Reo** Indon.
136 D3 **Republican** r. U.S.A.
127 F2 **Repulse Bay** Can.
150 A2 **Requena** Ecuador
107 C2 **Requena** Spain
154 B2 **Reserva** Brazil
152 C3 **Resistencia** Arg.
110 B1 **Reşiţa** Romania
126 E2 **Resolute** Can.
127 G2 **Resolution Island** Can.
105 C2 **Rethel** France
111 B3 **Rethymno** Greece
113 K9 **Réunion** terr. Indian Ocean
107 D1 **Reus** Spain
102 B2 **Reutlingen** Ger.
128 C2 **Revelstoke** Can.
144 A3 **Revillagigedo, Islas** is Mex.
128 A2 **Revillagigedo Island** U.S.A.
75 C2 **Rewa** India
134 D2 **Rexburg** U.S.A.
92 □A3 **Reykjanestá** pt Iceland
92 □A3 **Reykjavík** Iceland
145 C2 **Reynosa** Mex.
88 C2 **Rēzekne** Latvia
Rhein r. Ger. see Rhine
100 C1 **Rheine** Ger.
101 F1 **Rheinsberg** Ger.
Rhin r. France see Rhine
100 C1 **Rhine** r. Europe
140 B1 **Rhinelander** U.S.A.
101 F1 **Rhinluch** marsh Ger.
101 F1 **Rhinow** Ger.
141 E2 **Rhode Island** state U.S.A.
111 C3 **Rhodes** Greece
111 C3 **Rhodes** i. Greece
111 B2 **Rhodope Mountains** Bulg./ Greece
105 C2 **Rhône** r. France/Switz.
Rhuthun U.K. see Ruthin
98 B2 **Rhyl** U.K.
154 C1 **Rianápolis** Brazil
60 B1 **Riau, Kepulauan** is Indon.
106 B1 **Ribadeo** Spain
106 B1 **Ribadesella** Spain
154 B2 **Ribas do Rio Pardo** Brazil
121 C2 **Ribáuè** Moz.
98 B2 **Ribble** r. U.K.
154 C2 **Ribeira** r. Brazil
154 C2 **Ribeirão Preto** Brazil
104 C2 **Ribérac** France
152 B2 **Riberalta** Bol.
90 B2 **Ribniţa** Moldova
102 C1 **Ribnitz-Damgarten** Ger.

140 A1 **Rice Lake** U.S.A.
123 D2 **Richards Bay** S. Africa
126 B2 **Richardson Mountains** Can.
135 D3 **Richfield** U.S.A.
134 C1 **Richland** U.S.A.
140 A2 **Richland Center** U.S.A.
53 D2 **Richmond** N.S.W. Austr.
51 D2 **Richmond** Qld Austr.
54 B2 **Richmond** N.Z.
122 B3 **Richmond** S. Africa
98 C1 **Richmond** U.K.
140 C3 **Richmond** IN U.S.A.
140 C3 **Richmond** KY U.S.A.
141 D3 **Richmond** VA U.S.A.
130 C2 **Rideau Lakes** Can.
135 C3 **Ridgecrest** U.S.A.
102 C1 **Riesa** Ger.
100 D1 **Rieste** Ger.
123 B2 **Riet** r. S. Africa
101 D2 **Rietberg** Ger.
108 B2 **Rieti** Italy
136 B3 **Rifle** U.S.A.
88 B2 **Riga** Latvia
88 B2 **Riga, Gulf of** Estonia/Latvia
79 C2 **Rīgān** Iran
134 D2 **Rigby** U.S.A.
131 E1 **Rigolet** Can.
93 H3 **Riihimäki** Fin.
108 B1 **Rijeka** Croatia
134 C2 **Riley** U.S.A.
78 B2 **Rimah, Wādī al** watercourse Saudi Arabia
103 D2 **Rimavská Sobota** Slovakia
128 C2 **Rimbey** Can.
108 B2 **Rimini** Italy
131 D2 **Rimouski** Can.
93 F3 **Ringebu** Norway
93 E4 **Ringkøbing** Denmark
92 G2 **Ringvassøya** i. Norway
101 D1 **Rinteln** Ger.
150 A2 **Riobamba** Ecuador
151 D3 **Rio Branco** Brazil
154 C3 **Rio Branco do Sul** Brazil
154 B2 **Rio Brilhante** Brazil
154 C2 **Rio Claro** Brazil
153 B4 **Río Colorado** Arg.
153 B4 **Río Cuarto** Arg.
155 D2 **Rio de Janeiro** Brazil
153 B5 **Río Gallegos** Arg.
153 B6 **Río Grande** Arg.
152 C4 **Rio Grande** Brazil
144 B2 **Río Grande** Mex.
139 D3 **Rio Grande** r. Mex./U.S.A.
139 D3 **Rio Grande City** U.S.A.
150 A1 **Ríohacha** Col.
150 A2 **Rioja** Peru
145 D2 **Río Lagartos** Mex.
105 C2 **Riom** France
152 B2 **Río Mulatos** Bol.
154 C3 **Rio Negro** Brazil
155 D1 **Rio Pardo de Minas** Brazil
138 B1 **Rio Rancho** U.S.A.
150 A2 **Río Tigre** Ecuador
154 B1 **Rio Verde** Brazil
145 C2 **Rio Verde** Mex.
154 B1 **Rio Verde de Mato Grosso** Brazil
90 C1 **Ripky** Ukr.
98 C2 **Ripley** U.S.A.
107 D1 **Ripoll** Spain
98 C1 **Ripon** U.K.
66 D1 **Rishiri-tō** i. Japan
93 E4 **Risør** Norway
122 B2 **Ritchie** S. Africa
63 A2 **Ritchie's Archipelago** is India
134 C1 **Ritzville** U.S.A.
152 B3 **Rivadavia** Arg.

108	B1	Riva del Garda Italy
146	B3	Rivas Nic.
152	C4	Rivera Uru.
129	D2	Riverhurst Can.
52	B2	Riverina reg. Austr.
122	B3	Riversdale S. Africa
135	C4	Riverside U.S.A.
136	B2	Riverton U.S.A.
131	D2	Riverview Can.
104	C3	Rivesaltes France
131	D2	Rivière-du-Loup Can.
90	B1	Rivne Ukr.
54	B2	Riwaka N.Z.
78	B2	Riyadh Saudi Arabia
81	C1	Rize Turkey
70	B2	Rizhao China
105	C2	Roanne France
141	D3	Roanoke U.S.A.
143	E1	Roanoke r. U.S.A.
143	E1	Roanoke Rapids U.S.A.
52	A3	Robe Austr.
101	F1	Röbel Ger.
130	C1	Robert-Bourassa, Réservoir resr Can.
92	H3	Robertsfors Sweden
122	A3	Robertson S. Africa
114	A4	Robertsport Liberia
131	C2	Roberval Can.
50	A2	Robinson Ranges hills Austr.
52	B2	Robinvale Austr.
129	D2	Roblin Can.
128	C2	Robson, Mount Can.
108	B3	Rocca Busambra mt. Sicilia Italy
153	C4	Rocha Uru.
98	B2	Rochdale U.K.
154	B1	Rochedo Brazil
100	B3	Rochefort Belgium
104	B2	Rochefort France
137	E2	Rochester MN U.S.A.
141	E2	Rochester NH U.S.A.
141	D2	Rochester NY U.S.A.
140	B2	Rockford U.S.A.
51	E2	Rockhampton Austr.
143	D2	Rock Hill U.S.A.
50	A3	Rockingham Austr.
140	A2	Rock Island U.S.A.
136	B1	Rock Springs MT U.S.A.
139	C3	Rocksprings U.S.A.
136	B2	Rock Springs WY U.S.A.
136	C3	Rocky Ford U.S.A.
143	E1	Rocky Mount U.S.A.
128	C2	Rocky Mountain House Can.
124	G3	Rocky Mountains Can./U.S.A.
100	B3	Rocroi France
102	C1	Rødbyhavn Denmark
131	E1	Roddickton Can.
104	C3	Rodez France
89	F2	Rodniki Rus. Fed.
		Rodos Greece see Rhodes
		Rodos i. Greece see Rhodes
50	A2	Roebourne Austr.
50	B1	Roebuck Bay Austr.
123	C1	Roedtan S. Africa
100	B2	Roermond Neth.
100	A2	Roeselare Belgium
127	F2	Roes Welcome Sound sea chan. Can.
142	B1	Rogers U.S.A.
122	B3	Roggeveldberge esc. S. Africa
92	G2	Rognan Norway
134	B2	Rogue r. U.S.A.
88	B2	Roja Latvia
60	B1	Rokan r. Indon.
88	C2	Rokiškis Lith.
90	B1	Rokytne Ukr.
154	B1	Rolândia Brazil

137	E3	Rolla U.S.A.
51	D2	Roma Austr.
		Roma Italy see Rome
123	C2	Roma Lesotho
139	D3	Roma U.S.A.
143	E2	Romain, Cape U.S.A.
110	C1	Roman Romania
59	C3	Romang, Pulau i. Indon.
110	B1	Romania country Europe
91	C3	Roman-Kosh mt. Ukr.
69	D1	Romanovka Rus. Fed.
104	B2	Rombas France
64	B1	Romblon Phil.
108	B2	Rome Italy
143	C2	Rome GA U.S.A.
141	D2	Rome NY U.S.A.
99	D3	Romford U.K.
105	C2	Romilly-sur-Seine France
91	C1	Romny Ukr.
104	C2	Romorantin-Lanthenay France
99	C3	Romsey U.K.
96	□	Ronas Hill U.K.
151	C3	Roncador, Serra do hills Brazil
106	B2	Ronda Spain
154	B2	Rondon Brazil
154	B1	Rondonópolis Brazil
74	B1	Rondu Pak.
71	A3	Rong'an China
71	A3	Rongjiang China
62	A1	Rongklang Range mts Myanmar
		Rongmei China see Hefeng
93	F4	Rønne Denmark
55	T2	Ronne Ice Shelf Antarctica
101	D1	Ronnenberg Ger.
100	A2	Ronse Belgium
75	B2	Roorkee India
100	B2	Roosendaal Neth.
135	E2	Roosevelt U.S.A.
128	B2	Roosevelt, Mount Can.
55	K2	Roosevelt Island Antarctica
104	B3	Roquefort France
150	B1	Roraima, Mount Guyana
93	F3	Røros Norway
153	B4	Rosario Arg.
144	A1	Rosario Baja California Mex.
144	B2	Rosario Sinaloa Mex.
144	B2	Rosario Sonora Mex.
151	C3	Rosário Oeste Brazil
144	A2	Rosarito Mex.
109	C3	Rosarno Italy
104	B2	Roscoff France
97	B2	Roscommon Ireland
97	C2	Roscrea Ireland
147	D3	Roseau Dominica
137	D1	Roseau U.S.A.
134	B2	Roseburg U.S.A.
139	D3	Rosenberg U.S.A.
101	D1	Rosengarten Ger.
102	C2	Rosenheim Ger.
129	D2	Rosetown Can.
122	A2	Rosh Pinah Namibia
110	C2	Roșiori de Vede Romania
93	F4	Roskilde Denmark
89	D3	Roslavl' Rus. Fed.
109	C3	Rossano Italy
97	B1	Rossan Point Ireland
55	K1	Ross Ice Shelf Antarctica
131	D2	Rossignol, Lake Can.
128	C3	Rossland Can.
97	C2	Rosslare Ireland
114	A3	Rosso Maur.
105	D3	Rosso, Capo c. Corse France
99	B3	Ross-on-Wye U.K.
91	D1	Rossosh' Rus. Fed.
128	A1	Ross River Can.
55	K2	Ross Sea Antarctica

92	F2	Røssvatnet l. Norway
79	C2	Rostāq Iran
129	D2	Rosthern Can.
102	C1	Rostock Ger.
89	E2	Rostov Rus. Fed.
91	D2	Rostov-na-Donu Rus. Fed.
92	H2	Rosvik Sweden
138	C2	Roswell U.S.A.
59	D2	Rota i. N. Mariana Is
59	C3	Rote i. Indon.
101	D1	Rotenburg (Wümme) Ger.
102	C2	Roth Ger.
98	C1	Rothbury U.K.
98	C2	Rotherham U.K.
96	B3	Rothesay U.K.
53	C2	Roto Austr.
105	D3	Rotondo, Monte mt. Corse France
54	C1	Rotorua N.Z.
54	C1	Rotorua, Lake N.Z.
101	E2	Rottenbach Ger.
102	C2	Rottenmann Austria
100	B2	Rotterdam Neth.
102	B2	Rottweil Ger.
49	F3	Rotuma i. Fiji
105	C1	Roubaix France
104	C2	Rouen France
		Roulers Belgium see Roeselare
53	D2	Round Mountain Austr.
131	E2	Round Pond l. Can.
139	D2	Round Rock U.S.A.
134	E1	Roundup U.S.A.
96	C1	Rousay i. U.K.
130	C2	Rouyn-Noranda Can.
92	I2	Rovaniemi Fin.
91	D2	Roven'ki Rus. Fed.
91	D2	Roven'ky Ukr.
108	B1	Rovereto Italy
63	B2	Rôviĕng Tbong Cambodia
108	B1	Rovigo Italy
108	B1	Rovinj Croatia
53	C1	Rowena Austr.
64	B1	Roxas Capiz Phil.
64	B1	Roxas Oriental Mindoro Phil.
64	A1	Roxas Palawan Phil.
52	A2	Roxby Downs Austr.
138	C1	Roy U.S.A.
140	B1	Royale, Isle i. U.S.A.
104	B2	Royan France
99	C2	Royston U.K.
90	C2	Rozdil'na Ukr.
91	C2	Rozdol'ne Ukr.
100	B3	Rozoy-sur-Serre France
87	D3	Rtishchevo Rus. Fed.
54	C1	Ruapehu, Mount vol. N.Z.
54	A3	Ruapuke Island N.Z.
78	B3	Rub' al Khali des. Saudi Arabia
90	B2	Rubizhne Ukr.
77	E1	Rubtsovsk Rus. Fed.
135	C2	Ruby Mountains U.S.A.
66	C2	Rudnaya Pristan' Rus. Fed.
89	D3	Rudnya Rus. Fed.
76	C1	Rudnyy Kazakh.
82	E1	Rudol'fa, Ostrov i. Rus. Fed.
101	E2	Rudolstadt Ger.
119	D3	Rufiji r. Tanz.
153	B4	Rufino Arg.
121	B2	Rufunsa Zambia
70	C2	Rugao China
99	C2	Rugby U.K.
136	C1	Rugby U.S.A.
102	C1	Rügen i. Ger.
101	E2	Ruhla Ger.
88	B2	Ruhnu i. Estonia
100	C2	Ruhr r. Ger.
71	C3	Rui'an China
138	B2	Ruidoso U.S.A.

144 B2 Ruiz Mex.
119 D3 Rukwa, Lake Tanz.
96 A2 Rum i. U.K.
109 C1 Ruma Serbia
78 B2 Rumāh Saudi Arabia
117 A4 Rumbek S. Sudan
105 D2 Rumilly France
50 C1 Rum Jungle Austr.
94 B2 Runanga N.Z.
98 B2 Runcorn U.K.
120 A2 Rundu Namibia
68 B2 Ruoqiang China
130 C1 Rupert r. Can.
130 C1 Rupert Bay Can.
121 C2 Rusape Zimbabwe
110 C2 Ruse Bulg.
77 D3 Rushon Tajik.
136 C2 Rushville U.S.A.
53 C3 Rushworth Austr.
129 D2 Russell Can.
54 B1 Russell N.Z.
142 C2 Russellville AL U.S.A.
142 B1 Russellville AR U.S.A.
140 B3 Russellville KY U.S.A.
101 D2 Rüsselsheim Ger.
82 F2 Russian Federation country Asia/Europe
123 C2 Rustenburg S. Africa
142 B2 Ruston U.S.A.
96 B1 Ruthin U.K.
141 E2 Rutland U.S.A.
119 E4 Ruvuma r. Moz./Tanz.
79 C2 Ruweis U.A.E.
77 C1 Ruzayevka Kazakh.
87 D3 Ruzayevka Rus. Fed.
119 C3 Rwanda country Africa
89 E3 Ryazan' Rus. Fed.
89 F3 Ryazhsk Rus. Fed.
86 C2 Rybachiy, Poluostrov pen. Rus. Fed.
89 E2 Rybinsk Rus. Fed.
89 E2 Rybinskoye Vodokhranilishche resr Rus. Fed.
103 D1 Rybnik Pol.
89 E3 Rybnoye Rus. Fed.
99 D3 Rye U.K.
89 D3 Ryl'sk Rus. Fed.
67 C3 Ryōtsu Japan
69 E3 Ryukyu Islands Japan
103 E1 Rzeszów Pol.
89 D2 Rzhev Rus. Fed.

S

79 C2 Saʻādatābād Iran
101 E2 Saale r. Ger.
101 E2 Saalfeld Ger.
102 B2 Saarbrücken Ger.
88 B2 Saaremaa i. Estonia
92 I2 Saarenkylä Fin.
93 I3 Saarijärvi Fin.
102 B2 Saarlouis Ger.
80 B2 Sabʻ Ābār Syria
107 D1 Sabadell Spain
61 C1 Sabah state Malaysia
61 C2 Sabalana i. Indon.
155 D1 Sabará Brazil
108 B2 Sabaudia Italy
115 D3 Sabha Libya
123 C3 Sabie r. Moz./S. Africa
145 B2 Sabinas Mex.
145 B2 Sabinas Hidalgo Mex.
131 D2 Sable, Cape Can.
143 D3 Sable, Cape U.S.A.

131 E2 Sable Island Can.
106 B1 Sabugal Port.
78 B3 Şabyā Saudi Arabia
76 B3 Sabzevār Iran
120 A2 Sachanga Angola
130 A1 Sachigo Lake Can.
65 B2 Sach'on S. Korea
126 C2 Sachs Harbour Can.
135 B3 Sacramento U.S.A.
138 B2 Sacramento Mountains U.S.A.
135 B2 Sacramento Valley U.S.A.
123 C3 Sada S. Africa
107 C1 Sádaba Spain
78 B3 Şaʻdah Yemen
62 A1 Sadiya India
67 C3 Sadoga-shima i. Japan
107 D2 Sa Dragonera i. Spain
93 F4 Säffle Sweden
138 B2 Safford U.S.A.
99 C3 Saffron Walden U.K.
114 B1 Safi Morocco
86 D2 Safonovo Arkhangel'skaya Oblast' Rus. Fed.
89 D2 Safonovo Smolenskaya Oblast' Rus. Fed.
75 C2 Saga China
67 B4 Saga Japan
62 A1 Sagaing Myanmar
67 C3 Sagamihara Japan
75 C2 Sagar India
140 C2 Saginaw U.S.A.
140 C2 Saginaw Bay U.S.A.
106 B2 Sagres Port.
146 B2 Sagua la Grande Cuba
141 F1 Saguenay r. Can.
107 C2 Sagunto Spain
76 B2 Sagyndyk, Mys pt Kazakh.
106 B1 Sahagún Spain
114 C3 Sahara des. Africa
Saharan Atlas mts Alg. see Atlas Sahariens
75 B2 Saharanpur India
75 C2 Saharsa India
114 B3 Sahel reg. Africa
144 B2 Sahuayo Mex.
78 B2 Şaḩuq reg. Saudi Arabia
Saïda Lebanon see Sidon
75 C2 Saidpur Bangl.
Saigon Vietnam see Ho Chi Minh City
62 A1 Saiha India
69 D2 Saihan Tal China
67 B4 Saiki Japan
93 I3 Saimaa l. Fin.
144 B2 Sain Alto Mex.
96 B3 St Abb's Head U.K.
99 C3 St Albans U.K.
99 B3 St Aldhelm's Head U.K.
96 C2 St Andrews U.K.
131 E1 St Anthony Can.
134 D2 St Anthony U.S.A.
52 B3 St Arnaud Austr.
131 E1 St-Augustin Can.
131 E1 St Augustin r. Can.
143 D3 St Augustine U.S.A.
99 A3 St Austell U.K.
104 C2 St-Avertin France
98 B1 St Bees Head U.K.
105 D3 St-Bonnet-en-Champsaur France
99 A3 St Bride's Bay U.K.
104 B2 St-Brieuc France
130 C2 St Catharines Can.
99 C3 St Catherine's Point U.K.
137 E3 St Charles U.S.A.
140 C2 St Clair, Lake Can./U.S.A.
105 D2 St-Claude France

137 E1 St Cloud U.S.A.
140 A1 St Croix r. U.S.A.
147 D3 St Croix i. Virgin Is (U.S.A.)
105 C2 St-Dizier France
131 D2 Ste-Anne-des-Monts Can.
105 D2 St-Égrève France
126 B2 St Elias Mountains Can.
131 D1 Ste-Marguerite r. Can.
129 E2 Sainte Rose du Lac Can.
104 B2 Saintes France
105 C2 St-Étienne France
108 A2 St-Florent Corse France
105 C2 St-Flour France
136 C3 St Francis U.S.A.
104 C3 St-Gaudens France
53 C1 St George Austr.
135 D3 St George U.S.A.
143 D3 St George Island U.S.A.
131 C2 St-Georges Can.
147 D3 St George's Grenada
97 C3 St George's Channel Ireland/U.K.
105 D2 St Gotthard Pass Switz.
113 E8 St Helena terr. S. Atlantic Ocean
122 A3 St Helena Bay S. Africa
122 A3 St Helena Bay S. Africa
98 B2 St Helens U.K.
134 B1 St Helens, Mount vol. U.S.A.
95 C4 St Helier Channel Is
100 B2 St-Hubert Belgium
141 E1 St-Hyacinthe Can.
140 C1 St Ignace U.S.A.
130 B2 St Ignace Island Can.
99 A3 St Ives U.K.
128 A2 St James, Cape Can.
131 C2 St-Jean, Lac l. Can.
104 B2 St-Jean-d'Angély France
104 B2 St-Jean-de-Monts France
130 C2 St-Jean-sur-Richelieu Can.
141 E1 St-Jérôme Can.
134 C1 St Joe r. U.S.A.
131 D2 Saint John Can.
141 F1 St John r. U.S.A.
147 D3 St John's Antigua
131 E2 St John's Can.
138 B2 St Johns U.S.A.
141 E2 St Johnsbury U.S.A.
137 E3 St Joseph U.S.A.
130 A1 St Joseph, Lake Can.
130 B2 St Joseph Island Can.
104 C2 St-Junien France
94 B2 St Kilda is U.K.
147 D3 St Kitts and Nevis country West Indies
St-Laurent, Golfe du g. Can. see St Lawrence, Gulf of
151 C1 St-Laurent-du-Maroni Fr. Guiana
131 D2 St Lawrence inlet Can.
131 D2 St Lawrence, Gulf of Can.
83 N2 St Lawrence Island U.S.A.
104 B2 St-Lô France
114 A3 St-Louis Senegal
137 E3 St Louis U.S.A.
137 E1 St Louis r. U.S.A.
147 D3 St Lucia country West Indies
123 D2 St Lucia Estuary S. Africa
104 B2 St-Malo France
104 B2 St-Malo, Golfe de g. France
122 A3 St Martin, Cape S. Africa
141 D2 St Marys U.S.A.
130 C2 St-Maurice r. Can.
104 B2 St-Nazaire France
104 C1 St-Omer France
129 C2 St Paul Can.
137 E2 St Paul U.S.A.

137	E2	St Peter U.S.A.
95	C4	St Peter Port Channel Is
89	D2	St Petersburg Rus. Fed.
143	D3	St Petersburg U.S.A.
131	E2	St-Pierre St Pierre and Miquelon
131	E2	St Pierre and Miquelon terr. N. America
104	B2	St-Pierre-d'Oléron France
105	C2	St-Pourçain-sur-Sioule France
131	D2	St Quentin Can.
105	C2	St-Quentin France
131	D2	St-Siméon Can.
129	E2	St Theresa Point Can.
130	B2	St Thomas Can.
105	D3	St-Tropez France
105	D3	St-Tropez, Cap de c. France
52	A3	St Vincent, Gulf Austr.
147	D3	St Vincent and the Grenadines country West Indies
100	C2	St-Vith Belgium
129	D2	St Walburg Can.
104	C2	St-Yrieix-la-Perche France
59	D1	Saipan i. N. Mariana Is
152	B2	Sajama, Nevado mt. Bol.
122	B2	Sak watercourse S. Africa
67	C4	Sakai Japan
67	B4	Sakaide Japan
78	B2	Sakākah Saudi Arabia
136	C1	Sakakawea, Lake U.S.A.
111	D2	Sakarya r. Turkey
66	C3	Sakata Japan
65	B1	Sakchu N. Korea
83	K3	Sakhalin i. Rus. Fed.
123	C2	Sakhile S. Africa
81	C1	Şäki Azer.
88	B3	Sakiai Lith.
69	E3	Sakishima-shotō is Japan
62	B2	Sakon Nakhon Thai.
122	B3	Sakrivier S. Africa
67	D3	Sakura Japan
91	C2	Saky Ukr.
93	G4	Sala Sweden
130	C2	Salaberry-de-Valleyfield Can.
88	B2	Salacgrīva Latvia
109	C2	Sala Consilina Italy
135	C4	Salada, Laguna salt l. Mex.
152	B4	Salado r. Arg.
145	C2	Salado r. Mex.
114	B4	Salaga Ghana
122	B1	Salajwe Botswana
115	D3	Salal Chad
78	A2	Salāla Sudan
79	C3	Şalālah Oman
145	B2	Salamanca Mex.
106	B1	Salamanca Spain
106	B1	Salas Spain
63	B2	Salavan Laos
59	C3	Salawati i. Indon.
104	C2	Sabris France
88	C3	Šalčininkai Lith.
106	C1	Saldaña Spain
122	A3	Saldanha S. Africa
88	B2	Saldus Latvia
53	C3	Sale Austr.
86	F2	Salekhard Rus. Fed.
73	B3	Salem India
137	E3	Salem MO U.S.A.
134	B2	Salem OR U.S.A.
96	B2	Salen U.K.
109	B2	Salerno Italy
98	B2	Salford U.K.
151	E2	Salgado r. Brazil
103	D2	Salgótarján Hungary
151	E2	Salgueiro Brazil
136	B3	Salida U.S.A.

111	C3	Salihli Turkey
88	C3	Salihorsk Belarus
121	C2	Salima Malawi
121	C2	Salimo Moz.
137	D3	Salina U.S.A.
108	B3	Salina, Isola i. Italy
145	C3	Salina Cruz Mex.
155	C1	Salinas Brazil
144	B2	Salinas Mex.
135	B3	Salinas U.S.A.
107	D2	Salines, Cap de ses c. Spain
151	D2	Salinópolis Brazil
99	C3	Salisbury U.K.
141	D3	Salisbury MD U.S.A.
143	D1	Salisbury NC U.S.A.
99	B3	Salisbury Plain U.K.
151	D2	Salitre r. Brazil
92	I2	Salla Fin.
127	F2	Salluit Can.
75	C2	Sallyana Nepal
81	C2	Salmās Iran
134	D1	Salmon U.S.A.
134	C1	Salmon r. U.S.A.
128	C2	Salmon Arm Can.
134	C2	Salmon River Mountains U.S.A.
100	C3	Salmtal Ger.
93	H3	Salo Fin.
87	D4	Sal'sk Rus. Fed.
122	B3	Salt watercourse S. Africa
138	A2	Salt r. U.S.A.
152	B3	Salta Arg.
145	B2	Saltillo Mex.
134	D2	Salt Lake City U.S.A.
154	C2	Salto Brazil
152	C4	Salto Uru.
155	E1	Salto da Divisa Brazil
154	B2	Salto del Guairá Para.
135	C4	Salton Sea salt l. U.S.A.
143	D2	Saluda U.S.A.
108	A2	Saluzzo Italy
151	E3	Salvador Brazil
79	C2	Salwah Saudi Arabia
62	A1	Salween r. China/Myanmar
81	C2	Salyan Azer.
102	C2	Salzburg Austria
101	E1	Salzgitter Ger.
101	D2	Salzkotten Ger.
101	E1	Salzwedel Ger.
144	B1	Samalayuca Mex.
66	D2	Samani Japan
64	B1	Samar i. Phil.
87	E3	Samara Rus. Fed.
61	C2	Samarinda Indon.
77	C3	Samarqand Uzbek.
81	C2	Sämarrä' Iraq
81	C1	Şämaxı Azer.
119	C3	Samba Dem. Rep. Congo
61	C1	Sambaliung mts Indon.
75	C2	Sambalpur India
61	C2	Sambar, Tanjung pt Indon.
61	B1	Sambas Indon.
121	□E2	Sambava Madag.
90	A2	Sambir Ukr.
153	C4	Samborombón, Bahía b. Arg.
65	B2	Samch'ŏk S. Korea
81	C2	Samdi Dag mt. Turkey
119	D3	Same Tanz.
78	B2	Samirah Saudi Arabia
65	B1	Samjiyŏn N. Korea
49	G3	Samoa country S. Pacific Ocean
109	C1	Samobor Croatia
111	C3	Samos i. Greece
111	C2	Samothraki Greece
111	C2	Samothraki i. Greece
61	C2	Sampit Indon.

119	C3	Sampwe Dem. Rep. Congo
139	E2	Sam Rayburn Reservoir U.S.A.
80	B1	Samsun Turkey
81	C1	Samt'redia Georgia
63	B3	Samui, Ko i. Thai.
63	B2	Samut Songkhram Thai.
114	B3	San Mali
78	B3	Şan'ā' Yemen
118	A2	Sanaga r. Cameroon
81	C2	Sanandaj Iran
146	B3	San Andrés, Isla de i. Caribbean Sea
138	B2	San Andres Mountains U.S.A.
145	C3	San Andrés Tuxtla Mex.
139	C2	San Angelo U.S.A.
139	D3	San Antonio U.S.A.
135	C4	San Antonio, Mount U.S.A.
152	B3	San Antonio de los Cobres Arg.
153	B5	San Antonio Oeste Arg.
108	B2	San Benedetto del Tronto Italy
144	A3	San Benedicto, Isla i. Mex.
135	C4	San Bernardino U.S.A.
135	C4	San Bernardino Mountains U.S.A.
143	C3	San Blas, Cape U.S.A.
152	B2	San Borja Bol.
144	B2	San Buenaventura Mex.
64	B1	San Carlos Phil.
147	D4	San Carlos Venez.
153	A5	San Carlos de Bariloche Arg.
147	C4	San Carlos del Zulia Venez.
135	C4	San Clemente Island U.S.A.
104	C2	Sancoins France
150	A1	San Cristóbal Venez.
145	C3	San Cristóbal de las Casas Mex.
146	C2	Sancti Spíritus Cuba
61	C1	Sandakan Sabah Malaysia
93	E3	Sandane Norway
111	B2	Sandanski Bulg.
96	C1	Sanday i. U.K.
139	C2	Sanderson U.S.A.
150	B3	Sandia Peru
135	C4	San Diego U.S.A.
80	B2	Sandıklı Turkey
93	E4	Sandnes Norway
92	F2	Sandnessjøen Norway
118	C3	Sandoa Dem. Rep. Congo
103	E1	Sandomierz Pol.
89	E2	Sadovo Rus. Fed.
94	B1	Sandoy i. Faroe Is
134	C1	Sandpoint U.S.A.
71	B3	Sandu China
94	B1	Sandur Faroe Is
140	C2	Sandusky U.S.A.
122	A3	Sandveld mts S. Africa
93	F4	Sandvika Norway
93	G3	Sandviken Sweden
131	E1	Sandwich Bay Can.
129	D2	Sandy Bay Can.
51	E2	Sandy Cape Austr.
130	A1	Sandy Lake Can.
130	A1	Sandy Lake Can.
144	A1	San Felipe Baja California Mex.
145	B2	San Felipe Guanajuato Mex.
150	B1	San Felipe Venez.
144	A2	San Fernando Baja California Mex.
145	C2	San Fernando Tamaulipas Mex.
64	B1	San Fernando La Union Phil.
64	B1	San Fernando Pampanga Phil.
106	B2	San Fernando Spain
147	D3	San Fernando Trin. and Tob.

150 B1	San Fernando de Apure Venez.	
143 D3	Sanford FL U.S.A.	
141 E2	Sanford ME U.S.A.	
152 B4	San Francisco Arg.	
135 B3	San Francisco U.S.A.	
74 B3	Sangamner India	
83 J2	Sangar Rus. Fed.	
108 A3	San Gavino Monreale Sardegna Italy	
101 E2	Sangerhausen Ger.	
61 C1	Sangihe Indon.	
118 B3	Sangha r. Congo	
109 C3	San Giovanni in Fiore Italy	
64 B2	Sangir i. Indon.	
59 C2	Sangir, Kepulauan is Indon.	
65 B2	Sangju S. Korea	
61 C1	Sangkulirang Indon.	
73 B3	Sangli India	
118 B2	Sangmélima Cameroon	
121 C3	Sango Zimbabwe	
136 B3	Sangre de Cristo Range mts U.S.A.	
75 C2	Sangsang China	
144 A1	San Hipólito, Punta pt Mex.	
144 A2	San Ignacio Mex.	
130 C1	Sanikiluaq Can.	
71 A3	Sanjiang China	
135 B3	San Joaquin r. U.S.A.	
153 B5	San Jorge, Golfo de g. Arg.	
146 B4	San Jose Costa Rica	
64 B1	San Jose Nueva Ecija Phil.	
64 B1	San Jose Occidental Mindoro Phil.	
135 B3	San Jose U.S.A.	
144 A2	San José, Isla i. Mex.	
64 B1	San Jose de Bavicora Mex.	
144 A2	San Jose de Buenavista Phil.	
144 A2	San José de Comondú Mex.	
144 B2	San José del Cabo Mex.	
150 A1	San José del Guaviare Col.	
152 B4	San Juan Arg.	
146 B3	San Juan r. Costa Rica/Nic.	
147 D3	San Juan Puerto Rico	
135 D3	San Juan r. U.S.A.	
145 C3	San Juan Bautista Tuxtepec Mex.	
134 B1	San Juan Islands U.S.A.	
144 B2	San Juanito Mex.	
136 B3	San Juan Mountains U.S.A.	
153 B5	San Julián Arg.	
75 C2	Sankh r. India	
105 D2	Sankt Gallen Switz.	
105 D2	Sankt Moritz Switz.	
	Sankt-Peterburg Rus. Fed. see St Petersburg	
102 C2	Sankt Veit an der Glan Austria	
100 C3	Sankt Wendel Ger.	
80 B2	Şanlıurfa Turkey	
138 B3	San Lorenzo Mex.	
106 B2	Sanlúcar de Barrameda Spain	
153 B4	San Luis Arg.	
145 B2	San Luis de la Paz Mex.	
138 A2	San Luisito Mex.	
135 B3	San Luis Obispo U.S.A.	
145 B2	San Luis Potosí Mex.	
144 A1	San Luis Río Colorado Mex.	
139 D3	San Marcos U.S.A.	
108 B2	San Marino country Europe	
108 B2	San Marino San Marino	
144 B2	San Martín de Bolaños Mex.	
153 A5	San Martín de los Andes Arg.	
153 B5	San Matías, Golfo g. Arg.	
70 B2	Sanmenxia China	
146 B3	San Miguel El Salvador	
152 B3	San Miguel de Tucumán Arg.	
145 C3	San Miguel Sola de Vega Mex.	
71 B3	Sanming China	
153 B4	San Nicolás de los Arroyos Arg.	
135 C4	San Nicolas Island U.S.A.	
123 C2	Sannieshof S. Africa	
103 E2	Sanok Pol.	
64 B1	San Pablo Phil.	
144 B2	San Pablo Balleza Mex.	
152 B3	San Pedro Arg.	
152 B2	San Pedro Bol.	
114 B4	San-Pédro Côte d'Ivoire	
144 A2	San Pedro watercourse U.S.A.	
106 B2	San Pedro, Sierra de mts Spain	
144 B2	San Pedro de las Colonias Mex.	
146 B3	San Pedro Sula Hond.	
108 A3	San Pietro, Isola di i. Sardegna Italy	
144 A1	San Quintín, Cabo c. Mex.	
153 B4	San Rafael Arg.	
108 A2	San Remo Italy	
146 B3	San Salvador El Salvador	
152 B3	San Salvador de Jujuy Arg.	
107 C1	San Sebastián Spain	
109 C2	San Severo Italy	
109 C2	Sanski Most Bos.-Herz.	
152 B2	Santa Ana Bol.	
146 B3	Santa Ana El Salvador	
144 A1	Santa Ana Mex.	
135 C4	Santa Ana U.S.A.	
144 B2	Santa Bárbara Mex.	
135 C4	Santa Barbara U.S.A.	
154 B2	Santa Bárbara, Serra de hills Brazil	
152 B3	Santa Catalina Chile	
150 B1	Santa Clara Col.	
146 C2	Santa Clara Cuba	
135 C4	Santa Clarita U.S.A.	
109 C3	Santa Croce, Capo c. Sicilia Italy	
153 B6	Santa Cruz r. Arg.	
152 B2	Santa Cruz Bol.	
64 B1	Santa Cruz Phil.	
135 B3	Santa Cruz U.S.A.	
145 C3	Santa Cruz Barillas Guat.	
155 E1	Santa Cruz Cabrália Brazil	
107 C2	Santa Cruz de Moya Spain	
114 A2	Santa Cruz de Tenerife Islas Canarias	
135 C4	Santa Cruz Island U.S.A.	
48 F3	Santa Cruz Islands Solomon Is	
152 B4	Santa Fe Arg.	
138 B1	Santa Fe U.S.A.	
154 B1	Santa Helena de Goiás Brazil	
153 B4	Santa Isabel Arg.	
154 B1	Santa Luisa, Serra de hills Brazil	
152 C3	Santa Maria Brazil	
144 B1	Santa María r. Mex.	
135 B4	Santa Maria U.S.A.	
123 D2	Santa María, Cabo de c. Moz.	
106 B2	Santa María, Cabo de c. Port.	
151 D2	Santa Maria das Barreiras Brazil	
109 C3	Santa Maria di Leuca, Capo c. Italy	
150 A1	Santa Marta Col.	
135 C4	Santa Monica U.S.A.	
151 D3	Santana Brazil	
106 C1	Santander Spain	
108 A3	Sant'Antioco Sardegna Italy	
108 A3	Sant'Antioco, Isola di i. Sardegna Italy	
107 D2	Sant Antoni de Portmany Spain	
151 C2	Santarém Brazil	
106 B2	Santarém Port.	
154 B1	Santa Rita do Araguaia Brazil	
153 B4	Santa Rosa Arg.	
152 C3	Santa Rosa Brazil	
135 B3	Santa Rosa CA U.S.A.	
138 C2	Santa Rosa NM U.S.A.	
146 B3	Santa Rosa de Copán Hond.	
135 B4	Santa Rosa Island U.S.A.	
144 A2	Santa Rosalía Mex.	
107 D2	Sant Francesc de Formentera Spain	
152 C3	Santiago Brazil	
153 A4	Santiago Chile	
147 C3	Santiago Dom. Rep.	
144 B2	Santiago Mex.	
146 B4	Santiago Panama	
64 B1	Santiago Phil.	
106 B1	Santiago de Compostela Spain	
144 B2	Santiago Ixcuintla Mex.	
144 B2	Santiago Papasquiaro Mex.	
107 D2	Sant Joan de Labritja Spain	
107 D1	Sant Jordi, Golf de g. Spain	
155 D2	Santo Amaro de Campos Brazil	
155 D3	Santo André Brazil	
152 C3	Santo Ângelo Brazil	
154 B2	Santo Antônio da Platina Brazil	
151 E3	Santo Antônio de Jesus Brazil	
150 B2	Santo Antônio do Içá Brazil	
155 C2	Santo Antônio do Monte Brazil	
147 D3	Santo Domingo Dom. Rep.	
138 B1	Santo Domingo Pueblo U.S.A.	
111 C3	Santorini i. Greece	
155 C2	Santos Brazil	
152 C3	Santo Tomé Arg.	
153 A5	San Valentín, Cerro mt. Chile	
146 B3	San Vicente El Salvador	
144 A1	San Vicente Mex.	
150 A3	San Vicente de Cañete Peru	
108 B2	San Vincenzo Italy	
108 B3	San Vito, Capo c. Sicilia Italy	
71 A4	Sanya China	
155 C2	São Bernardo do Campo Brazil	
152 C3	São Borja Brazil	
154 C2	São Carlos Brazil	
151 C3	São Félix Mato Grosso Brazil	
151 C2	São Félix Pará Brazil	
155 D2	São Fidélis Brazil	
155 D1	São Francisco Brazil	
151 E3	São Francisco r. Brazil	
154 C3	São Francisco, Ilha de i. Brazil	
154 C3	São Francisco do Sul Brazil	
152 C4	São Gabriel Brazil	
155 D2	São Gonçalo Brazil	
155 C1	São Gotardo Brazil	
155 D2	São João da Barra Brazil	
155 C2	São João da Boa Vista Brazil	
106 B1	São João da Madeira Port.	
155 D1	São João do Paraíso Brazil	
155 C2	São João Nepomuceno Brazil	
154 C2	São Joaquim da Barra Brazil	
154 C2	São José do Rio Preto Brazil	
155 C2	São José dos Campos Brazil	
154 C3	São José dos Pinhais Brazil	
155 C2	São Lourenço Brazil	
151 D2	São Luís Brazil	
154 C2	São Manuel Brazil	
154 C1	São Marcos r. Brazil	

São Marcos, Baía de

151 D2 São Marcos, Baía de *b.* Brazil
155 E1 São Mateus Brazil
155 C2 São Paulo Brazil
151 D2 São Raimundo Nonato Brazil
155 C1 São Romão Brazil
155 E3 São Sebastião, Ilha do *i.* Brazil
154 C2 São Sebastião do Paraíso Brazil
154 B1 São Simão Brazil
154 B1 São Simão, Barragem de *resr* Brazil
59 C2 Sao-Siu Indon.
113 F6 São Tomé São Tomé and Príncipe
155 D2 São Tomé, Cabo de *c.* Brazil
113 F6 São Tomé and Príncipe *country* Africa
155 C2 São Vicente Brazil
106 B2 São Vicente, Cabo de *c.* Port.
59 C3 Saparua Indon.
89 F3 Sapozhok Rus. Fed.
66 D2 Sapporo Japan
109 C2 Sapri Italy
81 C2 Saqqez Iran
81 C2 Sarāb Iran
63 B2 Sara Buri Thai.
109 C2 Sarajevo Bos.-Herz.
76 B1 Saraktash Rus. Fed.
141 E2 Saranac Lake U.S.A.
109 D3 Sarandë Albania
64 B2 Sarangani Islands Phil.
87 D3 Saransk Rus. Fed.
87 E3 Sarapul Rus. Fed.
143 D3 Sarasota U.S.A.
90 B2 Sarata Ukr.
136 B2 Saratoga U.S.A.
141 E2 Saratoga Springs U.S.A.
61 C1 Saratok *Sarawak* Malaysia
87 D3 Saratov Rus. Fed.
79 D2 Sarāvān Iran
61 C1 Sarawak *state* Malaysia
110 C1 Saray Turkey
79 D2 Sāreḵ Iran
74 B2 Sardarshahr India
Sardegna *i.* Italy *see* Sardinia
108 A2 Sardinia *i.* Italy
92 G2 Sarektjåkkå *mt.* Sweden
77 C3 Sar-e Pul Afgh.
158 B3 Sargasso Sea N. Atlantic Ocean
74 B1 Sargodha Pak.
115 D4 Sarh Chad
79 D2 Sārī Iran
81 C2 Sārī Iran
111 C3 Sarıgöl Turkey
61 C1 Sarıkamış Turkey
61 C1 Sarikei *Sarawak* Malaysia
51 D2 Sarina Austr.
65 B2 Sariwŏn N. Korea
111 C2 Sarıyer Turkey
78 B2 Sark, Safrā' as *esc.* Saudi Arabia
77 D2 Sarkand Kazakh.
111 C2 Şarköy Turkey
59 C3 Sarmi Indon.
140 C2 Sarnia Can.
90 B1 Sarny Ukr.
60 B2 Sarolangun Indon.
111 B3 Saronikos Kolpos *g.* Greece
111 C2 Saros Körfezi *b.* Turkey
87 D3 Sarov Rus. Fed.
105 D2 Sarrebourg France
106 B1 Sarria Spain
107 C1 Sarrión Spain
105 D3 Sartène *Corse* France
103 D2 Sárvár Hungary

77 D1 Saryarka *plain* Kazakh.
76 B2 Sarykamyshskoye Ozero *salt l.* Turkm./Uzbek.
77 D2 Saryozek Kazakh.
77 D2 Saryshagan Kazakh.
82 F3 Sarysu *watercourse* Kazakh.
77 D3 Sary-Tash Kyrg.
75 C2 Sasaram India
74 A2 Sasebo Japan
129 D2 Saskatchewan *prov.* Can.
129 D2 Saskatchewan *r.* Can.
129 D2 Saskatoon Can.
83 I2 Saskylakh Rus. Fed.
123 C2 Sasolburg S. Africa
87 D3 Sasovo Rus. Fed.
114 B4 Sassandra Côte d'Ivoire
108 A2 Sassari *Sardegna* Italy
102 C1 Sassnitz Ger.
114 A3 Satadougou Mali
123 D1 Satara S. Africa
75 C2 Satna India
74 B2 Satpura Range *mts* India
63 B2 Sattahip Thai.
110 B1 Satu Mare Romania
63 B3 Satun Thai.
144 B2 Saucillo Mex.
93 E4 Sauda Norway
92 □B2 Sauðárkrókur Iceland
78 B2 Saudi Arabia *country* Asia
105 C3 Saugues France
105 C2 Saujon France
130 B2 Sault Sainte Marie Can.
140 C1 Sault Sainte Marie U.S.A.
77 C1 Saumalkol' Kazakh.
59 C3 Saumlakki Indon.
104 B2 Saumur France
120 B1 Saurimo Angola
109 D2 Sava *r.* Europe
49 G3 Savai'i *i.* Samoa
91 E1 Savala *r.* Rus. Fed.
143 D2 Savannah GA U.S.A.
142 C1 Savannah *TN* U.S.A.
143 D2 Savannah *r.* U.S.A.
62 B2 Savannakhét Laos
130 A1 Savant Lake Can.
111 C3 Savaştepe Turkey
89 F2 Savino Rus. Fed.
86 D2 Savinskiy Rus. Fed.
108 A2 Savona Italy
93 I3 Savonlinna Fin.
92 I2 Savukoski Fin.
Savu Sea Indon. *see* Sawu, Laut
74 B2 Sawai Madhopur India
62 A2 Sawankhalok Thai.
136 B3 Sawatch Range *mts* U.S.A.
53 D2 Sawtell Austr.
59 C3 Sawu, Laut *sea* Indon.
79 C3 Saýbüt Yemen
69 D2 Saynshand Mongolia
141 D2 Sayre U.S.A.
144 B3 Sayula *Jalisco* Mex.
145 C3 Sayula *Veracruz* Mex.
128 B2 Sayward Can.
89 E2 Sazonovo Rus. Fed.
114 B2 Sbaa Alg.
98 B1 Scafell Pike *hill* U.K.
109 C3 Scalea Italy
96 C1 Scapa Flow *inlet* U.K.
130 C2 Scarborough Can.
147 D3 Scarborough Trin. and Tob.
98 C1 Scarborough U.K.
64 A1 Scarborough Shoal *sea feature* S. China Sea
96 A2 Scarinish U.K.
Scarpanto *i.* Greece *see* Karpathos

105 D2 Schaffhausen Switz.
100 B1 Schagen Neth.
102 C2 Schärding Austria
100 A2 Scharendijke Neth.
101 D1 Scharhörn *i.* Ger.
101 D1 Scheeßel Ger.
131 D1 Schefferville Can.
135 D3 Schell Creek Range *mts* U.S.A.
141 E2 Schenectady U.S.A.
101 E3 Scheßlitz Ger.
100 C1 Schiermonnikoog *i.* Neth.
108 B1 Schio Italy
101 F2 Schkeuditz Ger.
101 E1 Schladen Ger.
101 E2 Schleiz Ger.
102 B1 Schleswig Ger.
101 D2 Schloss Holte-Stukenbrock Ger.
101 D2 Schlüchtern Ger.
101 E3 Schlüsselfeld Ger.
101 D1 Schmallenberg Ger.
101 D1 Schneverdingen Ger.
101 E1 Schönebeck (Elbe) Ger.
101 E1 Schöningen Ger.
100 B2 Schoonhoven Neth.
59 D3 Schouten Islands P.N.G.
102 B2 Schwäbische Alb *mts* Ger.
102 C2 Schwandorf Ger.
61 C2 Schwaner, Pegunungan *mts* Indon.
101 E1 Schwarzenbek Ger.
101 F2 Schwarzenberg Ger.
122 A2 Schwarzrand *mts* Namibia
Schwarzwald *mts* Ger. *see* Black Forest
102 C2 Schwaz Austria
102 C1 Schwedt an der Oder Ger.
101 E2 Schweinfurt Ger.
101 E1 Schwerin Ger.
101 E1 Schweriner See *l.* Ger.
105 D2 Schwyz Switz.
108 B3 Sciacca *Sicilia* Italy
95 B4 Scilly, Isles of U.K.
140 C3 Scioto *r.* U.S.A.
136 B1 Scobey U.S.A.
53 D2 Scone Austr.
55 R3 Scotia Ridge S. Atlantic Ocean
158 C8 Scotia Sea S. Atlantic Ocean
96 C2 Scotland *admin. div.* U.K.
128 B2 Scott, Cape Can.
123 C3 Scottburgh S. Africa
136 C3 Scott City U.S.A.
136 C2 Scottsbluff U.S.A.
142 C2 Scottsboro U.S.A.
96 B1 Scourie U.K.
141 D2 Scranton U.S.A.
98 C2 Scunthorpe U.K.
105 E2 Scuol Switz.
129 E2 Seal *r.* Can.
122 B3 Seal, Cape S. Africa
52 B3 Sea Lake Austr.
139 D3 Sealy U.S.A.
142 B1 Searcy U.S.A.
98 B1 Seascale U.K.
134 B1 Seattle U.S.A.
141 E2 Sebago Lake U.S.A.
144 A2 Sebastián Vizcaíno, Bahía *b.* Mex.
110 B1 Sebeş Romania
60 B2 Sebesi *i.* Indon.
88 C2 Sebezh Rus. Fed.
80 B1 Şebinkarahisar Turkey
143 D3 Sebring U.S.A.
128 B3 Sechelt Can.
150 A2 Sechura Peru
73 B3 Secunderabad India
137 E3 Sedalia U.S.A.

236

105 C2 Sedan France
54 B2 Seddon N.Z.
138 A2 Sedona U.S.A.
101 E2 Seeburg Ger.
101 E1 Seehausen (Altmark) Ger.
122 A2 Seeheim Namibia
104 C2 Sées France
101 E2 Seesen Ger.
101 E1 Seevetal Ger.
114 A4 Sefadu Sierra Leone
123 C1 Sefare Botswana
76 C3 Sefīd Kūh, Selseleh-ye mts Afgh.
60 B1 Segamat Malaysia
86 C2 Segezha Rus. Fed.
114 B3 Ségou Mali
106 C1 Segovia Spain
115 D2 Séguédine Niger
114 B4 Séguéla Côte d'Ivoire
139 D3 Seguin U.S.A.
107 C2 Segura r. Spain
106 C2 Segura, Sierra de mts Spain
120 B3 Sehithwa Botswana
93 H3 Seinäjoki Fin.
104 C2 Seine r. France
104 B2 Seine, Baie de b. France
103 E1 Sejny Pol.
60 B2 Sekayu Indon.
114 B4 Sekondi Ghana
59 C3 Selaru r. Indon.
61 C2 Selatan, Tanjung pt Indon.
126 A2 Selawik U.S.A.
58 C3 Selayar, Pulau i. Indon.
98 C2 Selby U.K.
120 B3 Selebi-Phikwe Botswana
105 D2 Sélestat France
92 □A3 Selfoss Iceland
114 A3 Sélibabi Maur.
138 A1 Seligman U.S.A.
116 A2 Selima Oasis Sudan
111 C3 Selimiye Turkey
114 B3 Sélingué, Lac de l. Mali
89 D2 Selizharovo Rus. Fed.
93 E4 Seljord Norway
129 E2 Selkirk Can.
96 C3 Selkirk U.K.
128 C2 Selkirk Mountains Can.
142 C2 Selma AL U.S.A.
135 C3 Selma CA U.S.A.
89 D3 Sel'tso Rus. Fed.
150 A2 Selvas reg. Brazil
134 C1 Selway r. U.S.A.
129 D1 Selwyn Lake Can.
128 A1 Selwyn Mountains Can.
51 C2 Selwyn Range hills Austr.
60 B2 Semangka, Teluk b. Indon.
61 C2 Semarang Indon.
61 C1 Sematan Sarawak Malaysia
118 B2 Sembé Congo
81 C2 Şemdinli Turkey
91 C1 Semenivka Ukr.
86 D3 Semenov Rus. Fed.
61 C2 Semeru, Gunung vol. Indon.
77 E1 Semey Kazakh.
89 E3 Semiluki Rus. Fed.
136 B2 Seminoe Reservoir U.S.A.
139 C2 Seminole U.S.A.
143 D2 Seminole, Lake U.S.A.
61 C1 Semitau Indon.
81 D2 Semnān Iran
61 C1 Semporna Sabah Malaysia
105 C2 Semur-en-Auxois France
150 B2 Sena Madureira Brazil
120 B2 Senanga Zambia
67 B4 Sendai Kagoshima Japan
67 D3 Sendai Miyagi Japan
114 A3 Senegal country Africa

114 A3 Sénégal r. Maur./Senegal
102 C1 Senftenberg Ger.
119 D3 Sengerema Tanz.
151 D3 Senhor do Bonfim Brazil
108 B2 Senigallia Italy
109 B2 Senj Croatia
92 G2 Senja i. Norway
122 B2 Senlac S. Africa
104 C2 Senlis France
63 B2 Senmonorom Cambodia
117 B3 Sennar Sudan
104 C2 Senneterre Can.
123 C3 Senqu r. Lesotho
104 C2 Sens France
109 D1 Senta Serbia
128 B2 Sentinel Peak Can.
123 C1 Senwabarwana S. Africa
75 B2 Seoni India
65 B2 Seoul S. Korea
155 D3 Sepetiba, Baía de b. Brazil
59 D3 Sepik r. P.N.G.
61 C1 Sepinang Indon.
131 D3 Sept-Îles Can.
59 C3 Seram i. Indon.
59 C3 Seram, Laut sea Indon.
60 B2 Serang Indon.
109 D2 Serbia country Europe
76 B3 Serdar Turkm.
89 E3 Serebryanyye Prudy Rus. Fed.
60 B1 Seremban Malaysia
119 D3 Serengeti Plain Tanz.
87 D3 Sergach Rus. Fed.
89 E2 Sergiyev Posad Rus. Fed.
74 A1 Serhetabat Turkm.
61 C1 Seria Brunei
61 C1 Serian Sarawak Malaysia
111 B3 Serifos i. Greece
80 B2 Serik Turkey
59 C3 Sermata, Kepulauan is Indon.
86 F3 Serov Rus. Fed.
120 B3 Serowe Botswana
106 B2 Serpa Port.
89 E3 Serpukhov Rus. Fed.
151 D3 Serra da Mesa, Represa resr Brazil
154 B1 Serranópolis Brazil
100 A3 Serre r. France
111 B2 Serres Greece
151 E3 Serrinha Brazil
155 D1 Sêrro Brazil
154 C2 Sertãozinho Brazil
61 C2 Seruyan r. Indon.
68 C2 Sêrxü China
120 A2 Sesfontein Namibia
108 B2 Sessa Aurunca Italy
108 A2 Sestri Levante Italy
105 C3 Sète France
155 D1 Sete Lagoas Brazil
92 G2 Setermoen Norway
93 E4 Setesdal val. Norway
115 C1 Sétif Alg.
67 B4 Seto-naikai sea Japan
114 B1 Settat Morocco
98 B1 Settle U.K.
106 B2 Setúbal Port.
106 B2 Setúbal, Baía de b. Port.
130 A1 Seul, Lac l. Can.
76 A2 Sevan, Lake Armenia
  Sevana Lich l. Armenia see Sevan, Lake
91 C3 Sevastopol' Ukr.
105 C2 Sévérac-le-Château France
130 B1 Severn r. Can.
122 B2 Severn S. Africa
99 B3 Severn r. U.K.
86 D2 Severnaya Dvina r. Rus. Fed.

83 H1 Severnaya Zemlya is Rus. Fed.
86 D2 Severnyy Nenetskiy Avtonomnyy Okrug Rus. Fed.
86 F2 Severnyy Respublika Komi Rus. Fed.
86 E1 Severnyy, Ostrov i. Rus. Fed.
86 C2 Severodvinsk Rus. Fed.
86 C2 Severomorsk Rus. Fed.
91 D3 Severskaya Rus. Fed.
135 D3 Sevier r. U.S.A.
135 D3 Sevier Lake U.S.A.
  Sevilla Spain see Seville
106 B2 Seville Spain
128 A2 Sewell Inlet Can.
128 C2 Sexsmith Can.
144 B2 Sextín r. Mex.
86 G1 Seyakha Rus. Fed.
113 J7 Seychelles country Indian Ocean
92 □C2 Seyðisfjörður Iceland
91 C1 Seym r. Rus. Fed./Ukr.
83 L2 Seymchan Rus. Fed.
53 C3 Seymour Austr.
140 B3 Seymour IN U.S.A.
139 D2 Seymour TX U.S.A.
105 C2 Sézanne France
115 D1 Sfântu Gheorghe Romania
115 D1 Sfax Tunisia
  's-Gravenhage Neth. see The Hague
96 A2 Sgurr Alasdair h. U.K.
70 A2 Shaanxi prov. China
91 D2 Shabel'skoye Rus. Fed.
77 D3 Shache China
55 R1 Shackleton Range mts Antarctica
99 B3 Shaftesbury U.K.
75 C2 Shahdol India
77 C3 Shāh Fōlādī mt. Afgh.
75 B2 Shahjahanpur India
81 D2 Shahr-e Kord Iran
81 D2 Shāhrezā Iran
77 C3 Shahrisabz Uzbek.
89 E2 Shakhovskaya Rus. Fed.
75 B2 Shakhty Rus. Fed.
86 D3 Shakhun'ya Rus. Fed.
66 D2 Shakotan-misaki c. Japan
76 B2 Shalkar Kazakh.
68 C2 Shaluli Shan mts China
129 E2 Shamattawa Can.
139 C1 Shamrock U.S.A.
70 B2 Shancheng China
68 C2 Shandan China
70 B2 Shandong prov. China
70 C2 Shandong Bandao pen. China
121 B2 Shangani r. Zimbabwe
70 C2 Shanghai China
70 C2 Shanghai mun. China
71 B3 Shanghang China
70 B2 Shangluo China
71 B3 Shangrao China
70 B2 Shangshui China
70 C2 Shangyu China
69 E1 Shangzhi China
97 C2 Shannon r. Ireland
97 B2 Shannon, Mouth of the Ireland
71 B3 Shantou China
70 B2 Shanxi prov. China
71 B3 Shaoguan China
71 B3 Shaowu China
70 C2 Shaoxing China
71 B3 Shaoyang China
116 B2 Shaqra' Saudi Arabia
90 B2 Sharhorod Ukr.
79 C2 Sharjah U.A.E.

Sharkawshchyna

88	B3	**Sharkawshchyna** Belarus
50	A2	**Shark Bay** Austr.
78	A2	**Sharm ash Shaykh** Egypt
140	C2	**Sharon** U.S.A.
86	D3	**Shar'ya** Rus. Fed.
121	B3	**Shashe** *r.* Botswana/Zimbabwe
117	B4	**Shashemenē** Eth.
134	B2	**Shasta, Mount** *vol.* U.S.A.
134	B2	**Shasta Lake** U.S.A.
89	E2	**Shatura** Rus. Fed.
129	D3	**Shaunavon** Can.
140	B2	**Shawano** U.S.A.
131	C2	**Shawinigan** Can.
139	D1	**Shawnee** U.S.A.
50	B2	**Shay Gap (abandoned)** Austr.
89	E3	**Shchekino** Rus. Fed.
89	E2	**Shchelkovo** Rus. Fed.
89	E3	**Shchigry** Rus. Fed.
91	C1	**Shchors** Ukr.
88	B3	**Shchuchyn** Belarus
91	D1	**Shebekino** Rus. Fed.
117	C4	**Shebelē Wenz, Wabē** *r.* Ethiopia/Somalia
140	B2	**Sheboygan** U.S.A.
91	D3	**Shebsh** *r.* Rus. Fed.
97	C2	**Sheelin, Lough** *l.* Ireland
98	C2	**Sheffield** U.K.
89	E2	**Sheksna** Rus. Fed.
89	E2	**Sheksninskoye Vodokhranilishche** *resr* Rus. Fed.
83	M2	**Shelagskiy, Mys** *pt* Rus. Fed.
131	D2	**Shelburne** Can.
134	D1	**Shelby** U.S.A.
140	B3	**Shelbyville** *IN* U.S.A.
142	C1	**Shelbyville** *TN* U.S.A.
83	L2	**Shelikhova, Zaliv** *g.* Rus. Fed.
129	D2	**Shellbrook** Can.
134	B1	**Shelton** U.S.A.
137	D2	**Shenandoah** U.S.A.
141	D3	**Shenandoah** *r.* U.S.A.
141	D3	**Shenandoah Mountains** U.S.A.
118	A2	**Shendam** Nigeria
86	D2	**Shenkursk** Rus. Fed.
65	A1	**Shenyang** China
71	B3	**Shenzhen** China
90	B1	**Shepetivka** Ukr.
53	C3	**Shepparton** Austr.
99	D3	**Sheppey, Isle of** *i.* U.K.
131	D2	**Sherbrooke** *N.S.* Can.
131	C2	**Sherbrooke** *Que.* Can.
116	B3	**Shereiq** Sudan
136	B2	**Sheridan** U.S.A.
139	D2	**Sherman** U.S.A.
100	B2	**'s-Hertogenbosch** Neth.
96	□	**Shetland Islands** U.K.
76	B2	**Shetpe** Kazakh.
		Shevchenko Kazakh. *see* Aktau
137	D1	**Sheyenne** *r.* U.S.A.
79	B3	**Shibām** Yemen
66	D2	**Shibetsu** Japan
77	C3	**Shibirghān** Afgh.
71	B3	**Shicheng** China
96	B2	**Shiel, Loch** *l.* U.K.
77	E2	**Shihezi** China
		Shijiao China *see* Fogang
70	B2	**Shijiazhuang** China
74	A2	**Shikarpur** Pak.
67	B4	**Shikoku** *i.* Japan
66	D2	**Shikotsu-ko** *l.* Japan
86	D2	**Shilega** Rus. Fed.
75	C2	**Shiliguri** India
75	D2	**Shillong** India
89	F3	**Shilovo** Rus. Fed.
117	C3	**Shimbiris** *mt.* Somalia

67	C3	**Shimizu** Japan
73	B3	**Shimoga** India
67	B4	**Shimonoseki** Japan
96	B1	**Shin, Loch** *l.* U.K.
67	C4	**Shingū** Japan
123	D1	**Shingwedzi** S. Africa
123	D1	**Shingwedzi** *r.* S. Africa
119	D3	**Shinyanga** Tanz.
67	C4	**Shiono-misaki** *c.* Japan
138	B1	**Shiprock** U.S.A.
71	A3	**Shiqian** China
70	A2	**Shiquan** China
		Shiquanhe China *see* Gar
		Shiquan He *r.* China/Pak. *see* Indus
67	C3	**Shirane-san** *mt.* Japan
81	D3	**Shīrāz** Iran
66	D2	**Shiretoko-misaki** *c.* Japan
66	D2	**Shiriya-zaki** *c.* Japan
74	B2	**Shiv** India
		Shivamogga India *see* Shimoga
75	B2	**Shivpuri** India
70	B2	**Shiyan** China
70	B2	**Shizhong** China
70	A2	**Shizuishan** China
67	C4	**Shizuoka** Japan
89	D3	**Shklow** Belarus
109	C2	**Shkodër** Albania
83	H1	**Shmidta, Ostrov** *i.* Rus. Fed.
135	C3	**Shoshone** U.S.A.
135	C3	**Shoshone Mountains** U.S.A.
123	C1	**Shoshong** Botswana
91	C1	**Shostka** Ukr.
70	B2	**Shouxian** China
138	A2	**Show Low** U.S.A.
91	C2	**Shpola** Ukr.
142	B2	**Shreveport** U.S.A.
99	B2	**Shrewsbury** U.K.
62	A1	**Shuangjiang** China
87	E4	**Shubarkuduk** Kazakh.
116	B1	**Shubrā al Khaymah** Egypt
89	D2	**Shugozero** Rus. Fed.
120	B2	**Shumba** Zimbabwe
110	C2	**Shumen** Bulg.
88	C2	**Shumilina** Belarus
89	D3	**Shumyachi** Rus. Fed.
126	A2	**Shungnak** U.S.A.
78	B3	**Shuqrah** Yemen
89	F2	**Shushkodom** Rus. Fed.
81	C2	**Shushtar** Iran
128	C2	**Shuswap Lake** Can.
89	F2	**Shuya** Rus. Fed.
89	F2	**Shuyskoye** Rus. Fed.
62	A1	**Shwebo** Myanmar
62	A1	**Shwedwin** Myanmar
62	A2	**Shwegyin** Myanmar
77	D2	**Shyganak** Kazakh.
77	C2	**Shymkent** Kazakh.
91	C2	**Shyroke** Ukr.
59	C3	**Sia** Indon.
74	A2	**Siahan Range** *mts* Pak.
74	B1	**Sialkot** Pak.
64	B2	**Siargao** *i.* Phil.
88	B2	**Šiauliai** Lith.
109	C2	**Šibenik** Croatia
83	I2	**Siberia** *reg.* Rus. Fed.
60	A2	**Siberut** *i.* Indon.
74	A2	**Sibi** Pak.
110	B1	**Sibiu** Romania
60	A1	**Sibolga** Indon.
61	C1	**Sibu** *Sarawak* Malaysia
118	B2	**Sibut** C.A.R.
64	B1	**Sibuyan** *i.* Phil.
64	B1	**Sibuyan Sea** Phil.
128	C2	**Sicamous** Can.
63	A3	**Sichon** Thai.

70	A2	**Sichuan** *prov.* China
70	A3	**Sichuan Pendi** *basin* China
105	D3	**Sicié, Cap** *c.* France
		Sicilia *i.* Italy *see* Sicily
108	B3	**Sicilian Channel** Italy/Tunisia
108	B3	**Sicily** *i.* Italy
150	A3	**Sicuani** Peru
111	C3	**Sideros, Akrotirio** *pt* Greece
74	B2	**Sidhpur** India
107	D2	**Sidi Aïssa** Alg.
107	C2	**Sidi Ali** Alg.
114	B1	**Sidi Bel Abbès** Alg.
114	A2	**Sidi Ifni** Morocco
60	A1	**Sidikalang** Indon.
96	C2	**Sidlaw Hills** U.K.
99	B3	**Sidmouth** U.K.
134	B1	**Sidney** Can.
136	C1	**Sidney** *MT* U.S.A.
136	C2	**Sidney** *NE* U.S.A.
140	C2	**Sidney** *OH* U.S.A.
143	D2	**Sidney Lanier, Lake** U.S.A.
80	B2	**Sidon** Lebanon
154	B2	**Sidrolândia** Brazil
103	E1	**Siedlce** Pol.
100	C2	**Sieg** *r.* Ger.
100	D2	**Siegen** Ger.
63	B2	**Siĕmréab** Cambodia
108	B2	**Siena** Italy
103	D1	**Sieradz** Pol.
153	B5	**Sierra Grande** Arg.
114	A4	**Sierra Leone** *country* Africa
144	B2	**Sierra Mojada** Mex.
138	A2	**Sierra Vista** U.S.A.
105	D2	**Sierre** Switz.
111	B3	**Sifnos** *i.* Greece
107	C2	**Sig** Alg.
127	H2	**Sigguup Nunaa** *pen.* Greenland
103	E2	**Sighetu Marmaţiei** Romania
110	B1	**Sighişoara** Romania
60	A1	**Sigli** Indon.
92	□B2	**Siglufjörður** Iceland
102	B2	**Sigmaringen** Ger.
100	B3	**Signy-l'Abbaye** France
106	C1	**Sigüenza** Spain
114	B3	**Siguiri** Guinea
88	B2	**Sigulda** Latvia
63	B2	**Sihanoukville** Cambodia
92	I3	**Siilinjärvi** Fin.
81	C2	**Siirt** Turkey
60	B2	**Sijunjung** Indon.
114	B3	**Sikar** India
114	B3	**Sikasso** Mali
137	F3	**Sikeston** U.S.A.
66	B2	**Sikhote-Alin'** *mts* Rus. Fed.
111	C3	**Sikinos** *i.* Greece
144	B2	**Silao** Mex.
75	D2	**Silchar** India
77	D1	**Siletyteniz, Ozero** *salt l.* Kazakh.
75	C2	**Silgarhi** Nepal
80	B2	**Silifke** Turkey
75	C1	**Siling Co** *salt l.* China
110	C2	**Silistra** Bulg.
80	A1	**Silivri** Turkey
93	F3	**Siljan** *l.* Sweden
93	E4	**Silkeborg** Denmark
88	C2	**Sillamäe** Estonia
142	B1	**Siloam Springs** U.S.A.
123	D2	**Silobela** S. Africa
88	B2	**Šilutė** Lith.
81	C2	**Silvan** Turkey
138	B2	**Silver City** U.S.A.
136	B3	**Silverton** U.S.A.
62	B1	**Simao** China
130	C2	**Simard, Lac** *l.* Can.
111	C3	**Simav** Turkey

111	C3	Simav Dağları mts Turkey
118	C2	Simba Dem. Rep. Congo
141	D2	Simcoe, Lake Can.
60	A1	Simeulue i. Indon.
91	C3	Simferopol' Ukr.
110	B1	Simleu Silvaniei Romania
100	C3	Şimmern (Hunsrück) Ger.
129	D2	Simonhouse Can.
51	C2	Simpson Desert Austr.
93	F4	Simrishamn Sweden
60	A1	Sinabang Indon.
116	B2	Sinai pen. Egypt
71	A3	Sinan China
65	B2	Sinanju N. Korea
62	A1	Sinbo Myanmar
150	A1	Sincelejo Col.
111	C3	Sindırgı Turkey
86	E2	Sindor Rus. Fed.
111	C2	Sinekçi Turkey
106	B2	Sines Port.
106	B2	Sines, Cabo de c. Port.
75	C2	Singahi India
60	B1	Singapore country Asia
61	C2	Singaraja Indon.
119	D3	Singida Tanz.
62	A1	Singkaling Hkamti Myanmar
61	B1	Singkawang Indon.
60	A1	Singkil Indon.
53	D2	Singleton Austr.
62	A1	Singu Myanmar
108	A2	Siniscola Sardegna Italy
109	C2	Sinj Croatia
116	B3	Sinkat Sudan
		Sinkiang Uighur Autonomous Region aut. reg. China see Xinjiang Uygur Zizhiqu
80	B1	Sinop Turkey
65	B1	Sinp'o N. Korea
61	C1	Sintang Indon.
100	B2	Sint Anthonis Neth.
100	A2	Sint-Laureins Belgium
147	D3	Sint Maarten terr. West Indies
100	B2	Sint-Niklaas Belgium
139	D3	Sinton U.S.A.
65	A1	Sinüiju N. Korea
103	D2	Siófok Hungary
105	D2	Sion Switz.
137	D2	Sioux Center U.S.A.
137	D2	Sioux City U.S.A.
137	D2	Sioux Falls U.S.A.
130	A1	Sioux Lookout Can.
65	A1	Siping China
129	E2	Sipiwesk Lake Can.
60	A2	Sipura i. Indon.
93	E4	Sira r. Norway
		Siracusa Italy see Syracuse
51	C1	Sir Edward Pellew Group is Austr.
116	B3	Sirhan, Wādī an watercourse Saudi Arabia
79	C2	Sirik Iran
62	B2	Siri Kit, Khuan Thai.
128	B1	Sir James MacBrien, Mount Can.
79	C2	Sīrjān Iran
81	C2	Şırnak Turkey
74	B2	Sirohi India
74	B2	Sirsa India
115	D1	Sirte Libya
115	D1	Sirte, Gulf of Libya
88	B2	Širvintos Lith.
145	C2	Sisal Mex.
122	B2	Sishen S. Africa
81	C2	Sisian Armenia
129	D2	Sisipuk Lake Can.
63	B2	Sisŏphŏn Cambodia
105	D3	Sisteron France
75	C2	Sitapur India
123	D2	Siteki Swaziland
128	A2	Sitka U.S.A.
100	B2	Sittard Neth.
62	A2	Sittaung r. Myanmar
62	A1	Sittwe Myanmar
61	C2	Situbondo Indon.
80	B2	Sivas Turkey
62	A1	Sivasagar India
111	C3	Sivash Turkey
80	B2	Siverek Turkey
80	B2	Sivrihisar Turkey
116	A2	Siwah Egypt
74	B1	Siwalik Range mts India/Nepal
105	D3	Six-Fours-les-Plages France
70	B2	Sixian China
123	C2	Siyabuswa S. Africa
109	D2	Sjenica Serbia
92	G2	Sjøvegan Norway
91	C2	Skadovs'k Ukr.
93	F4	Skagen Denmark
93	E4	Skagerrak str. Denmark/Norway
134	B1	Skagit r. U.S.A.
128	A2	Skagway U.S.A.
74	B1	Skardu Pak.
103	E1	Skarżysko-Kamienna Pol.
103	D1	Skawina Pol.
128	B2	Skeena r. Can.
128	B2	Skeena Mountains Can.
98	D2	Skegness U.K.
92	H3	Skellefteå Sweden
92	H3	Skellefteälven r. Sweden
97	C2	Skerries Ireland
111	B3	Skiathos i. Greece
97	B3	Skibbereen Ireland
92	□B2	Skiðadalsjökull glacier Iceland
98	B1	Skiddaw h. U.K.
93	E4	Skien Norway
103	E1	Skierniewice Pol.
115	C1	Skikda Alg.
52	B3	Skipton Austr.
98	B2	Skipton U.K.
93	E4	Skive Denmark
92	H1	Skjervøy Norway
111	B3	Skopelos i. Greece
89	E3	Skopin Rus. Fed.
109	D2	Skopje Macedonia
93	F4	Skövde Sweden
141	F2	Skowhegan U.S.A.
88	B2	Skrunda Latvia
128	A1	Skukum, Mount Can.
123	D1	Skukuza S. Africa
88	B2	Skuodas Lith.
96	A2	Skye i. U.K.
111	B3	Skyros Greece
111	B3	Skyros i. Greece
93	F4	Slagelse Denmark
97	C2	Slaney r. Ireland
88	C2	Slantsy Rus. Fed.
109	C1	Slatina Croatia
110	B2	Slatina Romania
129	C1	Slave r. Can.
114	C4	Slave Coast Africa
128	C2	Slave Lake Can.
82	G3	Slavgorod Rus. Fed.
109	C1	Slavonski Brod Croatia
90	B1	Slavuta Ukr.
90	C1	Slavutych Ukr.
91	D2	Slavyansk-na-Kubani Rus. Fed.
89	D3	Slawharad Belarus
103	D1	Sławno Pol.
97	A2	Slea Head Ireland
130	C1	Sleeper Islands Can.
97	D1	Slieve Donard h. U.K.
97	B1	Sligo Ireland
97	B1	Sligo Bay Ireland
93	G4	Slite Sweden
110	C2	Sliven Bulg.
110	C2	Slobozia Romania
128	C3	Slocan Can.
88	C3	Slonim Belarus
100	B1	Sloten Neth.
99	C3	Slough U.K.
103	D2	Slovakia country Europe
108	B1	Slovenia country Europe
91	D2	Slov"yans'k Ukr.
90	B1	Sluch r. Ukr.
103	D1	Słupsk Pol.
88	C3	Slutsk Belarus
97	A2	Slyne Head Ireland
131	D1	Smallwood Reservoir Can.
88	C3	Smalyavichy Belarus
88	C3	Smarhon' Belarus
129	D2	Smeaton Can.
109	D2	Smederevo Serbia
109	D2	Smederevska Palanka Serbia
91	C2	Smila Ukr.
88	C2	Smiltene Latvia
128	B2	Smithers Can.
143	E1	Smithfield U.S.A.
141	D3	Smith Mountain Lake U.S.A.
130	C2	Smiths Falls Can.
137	D3	Smoky Hills U.S.A.
92	E3	Smøla i. Norway
89	D3	Smolensk Rus. Fed.
110	B2	Smolyan Bulg.
130	B2	Smooth Rock Falls Can.
92	□B3	Snæfell mt. Iceland
98	A1	Snaefell h. Isle of Man
132	B2	Snake r. U.S.A.
134	D2	Snake River Plain U.S.A.
100	B1	Sneek Neth.
97	B3	Sneem Ireland
122	B3	Sneeuberge mts S. Africa
108	B1	Snežnik mt. Slovenia
91	C2	Snihurivka Ukr.
93	E3	Snøhetta mt. Norway
129	D1	Snowbird Lake Can.
98	A2	Snowdon mt. U.K.
		Snowdrift Can. see Łutsel'e
129	C1	Snowdrift r. Can.
138	A2	Snowflake U.S.A.
129	D2	Snow Lake Can.
52	A2	Snowtown Austr.
53	C3	Snowy r. Austr.
53	C3	Snowy Mountains Austr.
139	D2	Snyder U.S.A.
121	□D2	Soalala Madag.
117	B4	Sobat r. S. Sudan
89	F2	Sobinka Rus. Fed.
151	D3	Sobradinho, Barragem de resr Brazil
151	D2	Sobral Brazil
92	C2	Sochi Rus. Fed.
65	B2	Sŏch'ŏn S. Korea
49	H4	Society Islands Fr. Polynesia
150	A1	Socorro Col.
138	B2	Socorro U.S.A.
144	A3	Socorro, Isla i. Mex.
56	F6	Socotra i. Yemen
63	B3	Soc Trăng Vietnam
106	C2	Socuéllamos Spain
92	I2	Sodankylä Fin.
134	D2	Soda Springs U.S.A.
93	G3	Söderhamn Sweden
93	G4	Södertälje Sweden
116	A3	Sodiri Sudan
117	B4	Sodo Eth.
93	G3	Södra Kvarken str. Fin./Sweden
100	D2	Soest Ger.

Sofia

110 B2	**Sofia** Bulg.	
	Sofiya Bulg. *see* **Sofia**	
68 C2	**Sog** China	
93 E3	**Sognefjorden** *inlet* Norway	
111 D2	**Söğüt** Turkey	
100 B2	**Soignies** Belgium	
105 C2	**Soissons** France	
90 A1	**Sokal'** Ukr.	
111 C3	**Söke** Turkey	
81 C1	**Sokhumi** Georgia	
114 C4	**Sokodé** Togo	
89 F2	**Sokol** Rus. Fed.	
101 F2	**Sokolov** Czech Rep.	
115 C3	**Sokoto** Nigeria	
115 C3	**Sokoto** *r.* Nigeria	
90 B2	**Sokyryany** Ukr.	
73 B3	**Solapur** India	
135 B3	**Soledad** U.S.A.	
89 F2	**Soligalich** Rus. Fed.	
99 C2	**Solihull** U.K.	
86 E3	**Solikamsk** Rus. Fed.	
87 E3	**Sol'-Iletsk** Rus. Fed.	
100 C2	**Solingen** Ger.	
92 G3	**Sollefteå** Sweden	
93 G4	**Sollentuna** Sweden	
101 D2	**Solling** *hills* Ger.	
89 E2	**Solnechnogorsk** Rus. Fed.	
60 B2	**Solok** Indon.	
48 E3	**Solomon Islands** *country*	
	S. Pacific Ocean	
48 E3	**Solomon Sea** S. Pacific Ocean	
105 D2	**Solothurn** Switz.	
101 D1	**Soltau** Ger.	
89 D2	**Sol'tsy** Rus. Fed.	
96 C3	**Solway Firth** *est.* U.K.	
120 B2	**Solwezi** Zambia	
111 C3	**Soma** Turkey	
117 C4	**Somalia** *country* Africa	
117 A4	**Somaliland** *terr.* Somalia	
120 B1	**Sombo** Angola	
109 C1	**Sombor** Serbia	
144 B2	**Sombrerete** Mex.	
140 C3	**Somerset** U.S.A.	
123 C3	**Somerset East** S. Africa	
126 F2	**Somerset Island** Can.	
122 A3	**Somerset West** S. Africa	
101 E2	**Sömmerda** Ger.	
75 C2	**Son** *r.* India	
65 C1	**Sönbong** N. Korea	
93 E4	**Sønderborg** Denmark	
101 E2	**Sondershausen** Ger.	
	Søndre Strømfjord *inlet*	
	Greenland *see* **Kangerlussuaq**	
62 B1	**Sông Đa, Hô** *resr* Vietnam	
119 D4	**Songea** Tanz.	
65 B1	**Sŏnggan** N. Korea	
65 B1	**Songhua Hu** *resr* China	
	Sŏngjin N. Korea *see*	
	Kimch'aek	
63 B3	**Songkhla** Thai.	
65 B2	**Sŏngnam** S. Korea	
65 B2	**Songnim** N. Korea	
120 A1	**Songo** Angola	
121 C2	**Songo** Moz.	
69 E1	**Songyuan** China	
	Sonid Youqi China *see*	
	Saihan Tal	
89 E2	**Sonkovo** Rus. Fed.	
62 B1	**Sơn La** Vietnam	
74 A2	**Sonmiani** Pak.	
101 E2	**Sonneberg** Ger.	
138 A2	**Sonoita** Mex.	
144 A2	**Sonora** *r.* Mex.	
135 B3	**Sonora** CA U.S.A.	
139 C2	**Sonora** TX U.S.A.	
117 A4	**Sopo** *watercourse* S. Sudan	
103 D2	**Sopron** Hungary	

108 B2	**Sora** Italy	
130 C2	**Sorel** Can.	
51 D2	**Sorell** Austr.	
106 C1	**Soria** Spain	
90 B2	**Soroca** Moldova	
154 C2	**Sorocaba** Brazil	
87 E3	**Sorochinsk** Rus. Fed.	
59 D2	**Sorol** *atoll* Micronesia	
59 C3	**Sorong** Indon.	
119 D2	**Soroti** Uganda	
92 H1	**Sørøya** *i.* Norway	
92 G2	**Sorsele** Sweden	
64 B1	**Sorsogon** Phil.	
86 C2	**Sortavala** Rus. Fed.	
92 G2	**Sortland** Norway	
65 B2	**Sŏsan** S. Korea	
123 C2	**Soshanguve** S. Africa	
89 E3	**Sosna** *r.* Rus. Fed.	
153 B4	**Sosneado** *mt.* Arg.	
86 E2	**Sosnogorsk** Rus. Fed.	
86 D2	**Sosnovka** Rus. Fed.	
88 C2	**Sosnovyy Bor** Rus. Fed.	
103 D1	**Sosnowiec** Pol.	
91 D2	**Sosyka** *r.* Rus. Fed.	
145 C2	**Soto la Marina** Mex.	
118 B2	**Souanké** Congo	
104 C3	**Souillac** France	
	Sôul S. Korea *see* **Seoul**	
104 B2	**Soulac-sur-Mer** France	
104 B3	**Soulom** France	
	Soûr Lebanon *see* **Tyre**	
107 D2	**Sour el Ghozlane** Alg.	
129 D3	**Souris** Man. Can.	
131 D2	**Souris** P.E.I. Can.	
129 E3	**Souris** *r.* Can.	
151 E2	**Sousa** Brazil	
115 D1	**Sousse** Tunisia	
104 B3	**Soustons** France	
122 B3	**South Africa, Republic of**	
	country Africa	
99 C3	**Southampton** U.K.	
127 F2	**Southampton Island** Can.	
73 D3	**South Andaman** *i.* India	
52 A1	**South Australia** *state* Austr.	
130 B2	**South Baymouth** Can.	
140 B2	**South Bend** U.S.A.	
143 D2	**South Carolina** *state* U.S.A.	
156 B4	**South China Sea** N. Pacific	
	Ocean	
136 C2	**South Dakota** *state* U.S.A.	
99 C3	**South Downs** *hills* U.K.	
129 D2	**Southend** Can.	
99 D3	**Southend-on-Sea** U.K.	
54 B2	**Southern Alps** *mts* N.Z.	
50 A3	**Southern Cross** Austr.	
129 E2	**Southern Indian Lake** Can.	
159	**Southern Ocean** World	
143 E1	**Southern Pines** U.S.A.	
96 B3	**Southern Uplands** *hills* U.K.	
149 F6	**South Georgia and the South**	
	Sandwich Islands *terr.*	
	S. Atlantic Ocean	
96 A2	**South Harris** *pen.* U.K.	
129 E1	**South Henik Lake** Can.	
54 B2	**South Island** N.Z.	
65 B2	**South Korea** *country* Asia	
65 B2	**South Korea** *country* Asia	
135 B3	**South Lake Tahoe** U.S.A.	
55 Q4	**South Orkney Islands** S.	
	Atlantic Ocean	
136 C2	**South Platte** *r.* U.S.A.	
98 B2	**Southport** U.K.	
143 E2	**Southport** U.S.A.	
96 C1	**South Ronaldsay** *i.* U.K.	
123 D3	**South Sand Bluff** *pt* S. Africa	
129 D2	**South Saskatchewan** *r.* Can.	
129 E2	**South Seal** *r.* Can.	

55 P3	**South Shetland Islands**	
	Antarctica	
98 C1	**South Shields** U.K.	
117 A4	**South Sudan** *country* Africa	
54 B1	**South Taranaki Bight** *b.* N.Z.	
130 C1	**South Twin Island** Can.	
96 A2	**South Uist** *i.* U.K.	
53 D2	**South West Rocks** Austr.	
99 D2	**Southwold** U.K.	
109 C3	**Soverato** Italy	
88 B2	**Sovetsk** Rus. Fed.	
86 F2	**Sovetskiy** Rus. Fed.	
91 C2	**Sovyets'kyy** Ukr.	
123 C2	**Soweto** S. Africa	
66 D1	**Sōya-misaki** *c.* Japan	
90 C1	**Sozh** *r.* Europe	
110 C2	**Sozopol** Bulg.	
106 C1	**Spain** *country* Europe	
99 C2	**Spalding** U.K.	
135 D2	**Spanish Fork** U.S.A.	
97 B2	**Spanish Point** Ireland	
108 B3	**Sparagio, Monte** *mt.* Sicilia	
	Italy	
135 C3	**Sparks** U.S.A.	
140 A2	**Sparta** U.S.A.	
143 D2	**Spartanburg** U.S.A.	
111 B3	**Sparti** Greece	
109 C3	**Spartivento, Capo** *c.* Italy	
89 D3	**Spas-Demensk** Rus. Fed.	
89 F2	**Spas-Klepiki** Rus. Fed.	
66 B2	**Spassk-Dal'niy** Rus. Fed.	
89 F3	**Spassk-Ryazanskiy** Rus. Fed.	
111 B3	**Spatha, Akrotirio** *pt* Greece	
136 C2	**Spearfish** U.S.A.	
139 C1	**Spearman** U.S.A.	
137 D2	**Spencer** U.S.A.	
52 A2	**Spencer Gulf** *est.* Austr.	
98 C1	**Spennymoor** U.K.	
54 B2	**Spenser Mountains** N.Z.	
101 D2	**Spessart** *reg.* Ger.	
99 C3	**Spey** *r.* U.K.	
102 B2	**Speyer** Ger.	
100 C1	**Spiekeroog** *i.* Ger.	
100 B2	**Spijkenisse** Neth.	
125 C2	**Spirit River** Can.	
103 E2	**Spišská Nová Ves** Slovakia	
82 C1	**Spitsbergen** *i.* Svalbard	
102 C2	**Spittal an der Drau** Austria	
109 C2	**Split** Croatia	
129 E2	**Split Lake** Can.	
129 E2	**Split Lake** Can.	
134 C1	**Spokane** U.S.A.	
140 A1	**Spooner** U.S.A.	
102 C1	**Spree** *r.* Ger.	
122 A2	**Springbok** S. Africa	
131 E2	**Springdale** Can.	
142 B1	**Springdale** U.S.A.	
101 D1	**Springe** Ger.	
138 C1	**Springer** U.S.A.	
138 B2	**Springerville** U.S.A.	
136 C3	**Springfield** CO U.S.A.	
140 B3	**Springfield** IL U.S.A.	
141 E2	**Springfield** MA U.S.A.	
137 E3	**Springfield** MO U.S.A.	
140 C3	**Springfield** OH U.S.A.	
134 B2	**Springfield** OR U.S.A.	
123 C3	**Springfontein** S. Africa	
131 D2	**Springhill** Can.	
143 D3	**Spring Hill** U.S.A.	
54 B2	**Springs Junction** N.Z.	
98 D2	**Spurn Head** U.K.	
128 B3	**Squamish** Can.	
109 C3	**Squillace, Golfo di** *g.* Italy	
	Srbija *country* Europe *see*	
	Serbia	
109 C2	**Srebrenica** Bos.-Herz.	
110 C2	**Sredets** Bulg.	

83 L3 Sredinnyy Khrebet *mts* Rus. Fed.
83 L2 Srednekolymsk Rus. Fed.
Sredne-Russkaya Vozvyshennost' *hills* Rus. Fed. *see* Central Russian Upland
Sredne-Sibirskoye Ploskogor'ye *plat.* Rus. Fed. *see* Central Siberian Plateau
110 B2 Srednogorie Bulg.
69 D1 Sretensk Rus. Fed.
61 C1 Sri Aman *Sarawak* Malaysia
73 B4 Sri Jayewardenepura Kotte Sri Lanka
73 C3 Srikakulam India
73 C4 Sri Lanka *country* Asia
68 A2 Srinagar India
74 B1 Srinagar India
73 B3 Srivardhan India
101 D1 Stade Ger.
101 E1 Stadensen Ger.
100 C1 Stadskanaal Neth.
101 D2 Stadtallendorf Ger.
101 D1 Stadthagen Ger.
101 E2 Staffelstein Ger.
99 B2 Stafford U.K.
99 C3 Staines U.K.
91 D2 Stakhanov Ukr.
Stalingrad Rus. Fed. *see* Volgograd
103 E1 Stalowa Wola Pol.
99 C2 Stamford U.K.
141 E2 Stamford CT U.S.A.
139 D2 Stamford TX U.S.A.
122 A1 Stampriet Namibia
92 F2 Stamsund Norway
123 C2 Standerton S. Africa
140 C2 Standish U.S.A.
153 C6 Stanley Falkland Is
136 C1 Stanley U.K.
83 I3 Stanovoye Nagor'ye *mts* Rus. Fed.
83 J3 Stanovoy Khrebet *mts* Rus. Fed.
53 D1 Stanthorpe Austr.
103 E1 Starachowice Pol.
Stara Planina *mts* Bulg./S.M. *see* Balkan Mountains
89 D2 Staraya Russa Rus. Fed.
89 D2 Staraya Toropa Rus. Fed.
110 C2 Stara Zagora Bulg.
103 D1 Stargard Szczeciński Pol.
142 C2 Starkville U.S.A.
91 D2 Starobil's'k Ukr.
89 D3 Starodub Rus. Fed.
103 D1 Starogard Gdański Pol.
90 B2 Starokostyantyniv Ukr.
91 D2 Starominskaya Rus. Fed.
91 D2 Staroshcherbinovskaya Rus. Fed.
91 D2 Starotitarovskaya Rus. Fed.
89 F3 Staroyur'yevo Rus. Fed.
99 B3 Start Point U.K.
88 C3 Staryya Darohi Belarus
89 E3 Staryy Oskol Rus. Fed.
101 E2 Staßfurt Ger.
141 D2 State College U.S.A.
143 D2 Statesboro U.S.A.
143 D1 Statesville U.S.A.
93 E4 Stavanger Norway
87 D4 Stavropol' Rus. Fed.
87 D4 Stavropol'skaya Vozvyshennost' *hills* Rus. Fed.
52 B3 Stawell Austr.
123 C2 Steadville S. Africa
136 B2 Steamboat Springs U.S.A.
101 E2 Stedten Ger.

128 C2 Steen River Can.
134 C2 Steens Mountain U.S.A.
100 C1 Steenwijk Neth.
126 D2 Stefansson Island Can.
101 E3 Steigerwald *mts* Ger.
129 E3 Steinbach Can.
100 C1 Steinfurt Ger.
120 A3 Steinhausen Namibia
92 F3 Steinkjer Norway
122 A2 Steinkopf S. Africa
122 B2 Stella S. Africa
105 D2 Stenay France
101 E1 Stendal Ger.
131 D1 Stephenville Can.
139 D2 Stephenville U.S.A.
122 B3 Sterling S. Africa
136 C2 Sterling CO U.S.A.
138 B2 Sterling IL U.S.A.
87 E3 Sterlitamak Rus. Fed.
101 E1 Sternberg Ger.
128 C2 Stettler Can.
140 C2 Steubenville U.S.A.
99 C3 Stevenage U.K.
126 B2 Stevenson Lake Can.
128 A2 Stevens Village U.S.A.
128 B2 Stewart Can.
126 B2 Stewart *r.* Can.
54 A3 Stewart Island N.Z.
127 F2 Stewart Lake Can.
102 C2 Steyr Austria
122 B3 Steytlerville S. Africa
128 A1 Stikine *r.* Can.
128 A2 Stikine Plateau Can.
122 B3 Stilbaai S. Africa
139 D1 Stillwater U.S.A.
109 D2 Štip Macedonia
96 C2 Stirling U.K.
92 F3 Stjørdalshalsen Norway
103 D2 Stockerau Austria
93 G4 Stockholm Sweden
98 B2 Stockport U.K.
135 B3 Stockton U.S.A.
98 C1 Stockton-on-Tees U.K.
63 B2 Stœng Trêng Cambodia
96 B1 Stoer, Point of U.K.
98 B2 Stoke-on-Trent U.K.
109 D2 Stol *mt.* Serbia
109 C2 Stolac Bos.-Herz.
100 C2 Stolberg (Rheinland) Ger.
88 C3 Stolin Belarus
101 F2 Stollberg Ger.
101 D1 Stolzenau Ger.
96 C2 Stonehaven U.K.
129 E2 Stonewall Can.
129 D2 Stony Rapids Can.
92 G2 Storavan *l.* Sweden
Store Bælt *sea chan.* Denmark *see* Great Belt
92 F3 Støren Norway
92 F2 Storforshei Norway
126 D2 Storkerson Peninsula Can.
137 D2 Storm Lake U.S.A.
93 E3 Stornosa *mt.* Norway
96 A1 Stornoway U.K.
86 E2 Storozhevsk Rus. Fed.
90 B2 Storozhynets' Ukr.
92 F3 Storsjön *l.* Sweden
92 H2 Storslett Norway
92 G2 Storuman Sweden
99 C2 Stour *r. England* U.K.
99 C3 Stour *r. England* U.K.
130 A1 Stout Lake Can.
88 C3 Stowbtsy Belarus
97 C1 Strabane U.K.
102 C2 Strakonice Czech Rep.
102 C1 Stralsund Ger.

122 A3 Strand S. Africa
93 E3 Stranda Norway
97 D1 Strangford Lough *inlet* U.K.
96 B3 Stranraer U.K.
105 D2 Strasbourg France
140 C2 Stratford Can.
54 B1 Stratford N.Z.
139 C1 Stratford U.S.A.
99 C2 Stratford-upon-Avon U.K.
128 C2 Strathmore Can.
96 C2 Strathspey *val.* U.K.
102 C2 Straubing Ger.
51 C3 Streaky Bay Austr.
140 B2 Streator U.S.A.
110 B2 Strehaia Romania
153 B5 Stroeder Arg.
101 D1 Ströhen Ger.
109 C3 Stromboli, Isola *i.* Italy
96 C1 Stromness U.K.
92 G3 Strömsund Sweden
96 C1 Stronsay *i.* U.K.
53 D2 Stroud Austr.
99 B3 Stroud U.K.
100 C1 Strücklingen (Saterland) Ger.
109 D2 Struga Macedonia
88 C2 Strugi-Krasnyye Rus. Fed.
122 B3 Struis Bay S. Africa
109 D2 Strumica Macedonia
122 B3 Strydenburg S. Africa
111 B2 Strymonas *r.* Greece
90 A2 Stryy Ukr.
128 B2 Stuart Lake Can.
130 A1 Stull Lake Can.
89 E3 Stupino Rus. Fed.
140 B2 Sturgeon Bay U.S.A.
130 C2 Sturgeon Falls Can.
130 A2 Sturgeon Lake Can.
140 B2 Sturgis MI U.S.A.
136 C2 Sturgis SD U.S.A.
50 B1 Sturt Creek *watercourse* Austr.
52 B1 Sturt Stony Desert Austr.
123 C3 Stutterheim S. Africa
102 B2 Stuttgart Ger.
142 B2 Stuttgart U.S.A.
92 □A2 Stykkishólmur Iceland
90 B1 Styr *r.* Belarus/Ukr.
155 D1 Suaçuí Grande *r.* Brazil
116 B3 Suakin Sudan
78 A3 Suara Eritrea
109 C1 Subotica Serbia
110 C1 Suceava Romania
97 B2 Suck *r.* Ireland
152 B2 Sucre Bol.
154 B2 Sucuriú *r.* Brazil
89 E2 Suda Rus. Fed.
91 C3 Sudak Ukr.
117 A3 Sudan *country* Africa
130 B2 Sudbury Can.
117 A4 Sudd *swamp* S. Sudan
89 F2 Sudislavl' Rus. Fed.
89 F2 Sudogda Rus. Fed.
94 B1 Suðuroy *i.* Faroe Is
107 C2 Sueca Spain
116 B2 Suez Egypt
116 B2 Suez, Gulf of Egypt
80 B2 Suez Canal Egypt
141 D3 Suffolk U.S.A.
116 B2 Súhāj Egypt
79 C2 Şuḩār Oman
69 D1 Sühbaatar Mongolia
101 E2 Suhl Ger.
109 C1 Suhopolje Croatia
70 B2 Suide China
66 B2 Suifenhe China
69 E1 Suihua China
70 A2 Suining China
70 B2 Suiping China

70 B2 **Suiyang** China
70 B2 **Suizhou** China
74 B2 **Sujangarh** India
74 B1 **Sujanpur** India
74 A2 **Sujawal** Pak.
60 B2 **Sukabumi** Indon.
61 B2 **Sukadana** Indon.
61 C2 **Sukaraja** Indon.
89 E3 **Sukhinichi** Rus. Fed.
89 F2 **Sukhona** *r.* Rus. Fed.
62 A2 **Sukhothai** Thai.
74 A2 **Sukkur** Pak.
89 E2 **Sukromny** Rus. Fed.
59 C3 **Sula, Kepulauan** *is* Indon.
74 A1 **Sulaiman Range** *mts* Pak.
Sulawesi *i.* Indon. *see* Celebes
150 A2 **Sullana** Peru
137 E3 **Sullivan** U.S.A.
139 D2 **Sulphur Springs** U.S.A.
64 B2 **Sulu Archipelago** *is* Phil.
64 A2 **Sulu Sea** N. Pacific Ocean
101 E3 **Sulzbach-Rosenberg** Ger.
79 C2 **Sumāil** Oman
Sumatera *i.* Indon. *see* Sumatra
60 B1 **Sumatra** *i.* Indon.
58 C3 **Sumba** *i.* Indon.
61 C2 **Sumbawa** *i.* Indon.
61 C2 **Sumbawabesar** Indon.
119 D3 **Sumbawanga** Tanz.
120 A2 **Sumbe** Angola
96 □ **Sumburgh** U.K.
96 □ **Sumburgh Head** U.K.
61 C2 **Sumenep** Indon.
67 D4 **Sumisu-jima** *i.* Japan
131 D2 **Summerside** Can.
140 C3 **Summersville** U.S.A.
128 B2 **Summit Lake** Can.
103 D2 **Šumperk** Czech Rep.
81 C1 **Sumqayıt** Azer.
143 D2 **Sumter** U.S.A.
91 C1 **Sumy** Ukr.
75 D2 **Sunamganj** Bangl.
65 B2 **Sunan** N. Korea
79 C2 **Şunaynah** Oman
52 B3 **Sunbury** Austr.
141 D2 **Sunbury** U.S.A.
65 B2 **Sunch'ŏn** N. Korea
65 B3 **Sunch'ŏn** S. Korea
123 C2 **Sun City** S. Africa
60 B2 **Sunda, Selat** *str.* Indon.
136 C2 **Sundance** U.S.A.
75 C2 **Sundarbans** *coastal area* Bangl./India
98 C1 **Sunderland** U.K.
128 C2 **Sundre** Can.
93 G3 **Sundsvall** Sweden
123 D2 **Sundumbili** S. Africa
60 B2 **Sungailiat** Indon.
60 B2 **Sungaipenuh** Indon.
60 B1 **Sungai Petani** Malaysia
80 B1 **Sungurlu** Turkey
93 E3 **Sunndalsøra** Norway
134 C1 **Sunnyside** U.S.A.
135 B3 **Sunnyvale** U.S.A.
83 I2 **Suntar** Rus. Fed.
74 A2 **Suntsar** Pak.
114 B4 **Sunyani** Ghana
82 D2 **Suoyarvi** Rus. Fed.
138 A2 **Superior** *AZ* U.S.A.
137 D2 **Superior** *NE* U.S.A.
140 A1 **Superior** *WI* U.S.A.
140 B1 **Superior, Lake** Can./U.S.A.
89 D3 **Suponevo** Rus. Fed.
81 C2 **Süq ash Shuyūkh** Iraq
70 B2 **Suqian** China
78 A2 **Süq Suwayq** Saudi Arabia

79 C2 **Şür** Oman
74 A2 **Surab** Pak.
61 C2 **Surabaya** Indon.
61 C2 **Surakarta** Indon.
74 B2 **Surat** India
63 A3 **Surat Thani** Thai.
74 B2 **Suratgarh** India
89 D3 **Surazh** Rus. Fed.
109 D2 **Surdulica** Serbia
74 B2 **Surendranagar** India
82 F2 **Surgut** Rus. Fed.
64 B2 **Surigao** Phil.
63 B2 **Surin** Thai.
151 C1 **Suriname** *country* S. America
Surt Libya *see* Sirte
Surt, Khalīj *g.* Libya *see* Sirte, Gulf of
60 B2 **Surulangun** Indon.
89 F2 **Susanino** Rus. Fed.
135 B2 **Susanville** U.S.A.
80 B1 **Suşehri** Turkey
131 D2 **Sussex** Can.
101 D1 **Süstedt** Ger.
100 C1 **Sustrum** Ger.
83 K2 **Susuman** Rus. Fed.
111 C3 **Susurluk** Turkey
75 B1 **Sutak** India
122 B3 **Sutherland** S. Africa
99 C3 **Sutton Coldfield** U.K.
66 D2 **Suttsu** Japan
49 F4 **Suva** Fiji
89 E3 **Suvorov** Rus. Fed.
103 E1 **Suwałki** Pol.
63 B2 **Suwannaphum** Thai.
143 D3 **Suwannee** *r.* U.S.A.
Suweis, Qanā el *canal* Egypt *see* Suez Canal
65 B2 **Suwŏn** S. Korea
79 C2 **Sūzā** Iran
89 F2 **Suzdal'** Rus. Fed.
70 B2 **Suzhou** *Anhui* China
70 C2 **Suzhou** *Jiangsu* China
67 C3 **Suzu** Japan
67 C3 **Suzu-misaki** *pt* Japan
82 B1 **Svalbard** *terr.* Arctic Ocean
91 D2 **Svatove** Ukr.
63 B2 **Svay Riĕng** Cambodia
93 F3 **Sveg** Sweden
88 C2 **Švenčionys** Lith.
93 F4 **Svendborg** Denmark
Sverdlovsk Rus. Fed. *see* Yekaterinburg
109 D2 **Sveti Nikole** Macedonia
88 B3 **Svetlogorsk** Rus. Fed.
88 B3 **Svetlyy** Rus. Fed.
93 I3 **Svetogorsk** Rus. Fed.
110 C2 **Svilengrad** Bulg.
110 B2 **Svinecea Mare, Vârful** *mt.* Romania
110 C2 **Svishtov** Bulg.
103 D2 **Svitavy** Czech Rep.
91 C2 **Svitlovods'k** Ukr.
69 E1 **Svobodnyy** Rus. Fed.
92 F2 **Svolvær** Norway
88 C3 **Svyetlahorsk** Belarus
143 D2 **Swainsboro** U.S.A.
120 A3 **Swakopmund** Namibia
52 B3 **Swan Hill** Austr.
128 C2 **Swan Hills** Can.
129 E2 **Swan Lake** Can.
129 D2 **Swan River** Can.
53 D2 **Swansea** Austr.
99 B3 **Swansea** U.K.
123 C3 **Swartruggens** S. Africa
Swatow China *see* Shantou
123 D2 **Swaziland** *country* Africa
93 G3 **Sweden** *country* Europe

139 C2 **Sweetwater** U.S.A.
136 B2 **Sweetwater** *r.* U.S.A.
122 B3 **Swellendam** S. Africa
103 D1 **Świdnica** Pol.
103 D1 **Świdwin** Pol.
103 D1 **Świebodzin** Pol.
103 D1 **Świecie** Pol.
129 D2 **Swift Current** Can.
97 C1 **Swilly, Lough** *inlet* Ireland
99 C3 **Swindon** U.K.
102 C1 **Świnoujście** Pol.
105 D2 **Switzerland** *country* Europe
97 C2 **Swords** Ireland
88 C3 **Syanno** Belarus
89 D2 **Sychevka** Rus. Fed.
53 D2 **Sydney** Austr.
131 D2 **Sydney** Can.
131 D2 **Sydney Mines** Can.
91 D2 **Syeverodonets'k** Ukr.
86 F2 **Syktyvkar** Rus. Fed.
142 C2 **Sylacauga** U.S.A.
75 D2 **Sylhet** Bangl.
102 B1 **Sylt** *i.* Ger.
111 C3 **Symi** *i.* Greece
91 D2 **Synel'nykove** Ukr.
109 C3 **Syracuse** *Sicilia* Italy
136 C3 **Syracuse** *KS* U.S.A.
141 D2 **Syracuse** *NY* U.S.A.
77 C2 **Syrdar'ya** *r.* Asia
80 B2 **Syria** *country* Asia
80 B2 **Syrian Desert** Asia
111 B3 **Syros** *i.* Greece
87 D3 **Syzran'** Rus. Fed.
102 C1 **Szczecin** Pol.
103 D1 **Szczecinek** Pol.
103 E1 **Szczytno** Pol.
103 E2 **Szeged** Hungary
103 D2 **Székesfehérvár** Hungary
103 D2 **Szekszárd** Hungary
103 E2 **Szentes** Hungary
103 D2 **Szentgotthárd** Hungary
103 D2 **Szigetvár** Hungary
103 E1 **Szolnok** Hungary
103 D2 **Szombathely** Hungary

T

78 B2 **Ṭābah** Saudi Arabia
76 B3 **Ṭabas** Iran
81 D3 **Tābask, Kūh-e** *mt.* Iran
150 B2 **Tabatinga** Brazil
114 B2 **Tabelbala** Alg.
129 C3 **Taber** Can.
102 C2 **Tábor** Czech Rep.
119 D3 **Tabora** Tanz.
114 B4 **Tabou** Côte d'Ivoire
81 C2 **Tabriz** Iran
78 A2 **Tabūk** Saudi Arabia
77 E2 **Tacheng** China
102 C2 **Tachov** Czech Rep.
64 B1 **Tacloban** Phil.
150 A3 **Tacna** Peru
134 B1 **Tacoma** U.S.A.
152 C4 **Tacuarembó** Uru.
138 B3 **Tacupeto** Mex.
117 C3 **Tadjourah** Djibouti
80 B2 **Tadmur** Syria
129 E2 **Tadoule Lake** Can.
65 B2 **Taegu** S. Korea
65 B2 **Taejŏn** S. Korea
65 B2 **Taejŏng** S. Korea
65 B2 **T'aepaek** S. Korea
69 E1 **Ta'erqi** China
107 C1 **Tafalla** Spain
152 B3 **Tafí Viejo** Arg.

79	D2	Taftān, Kūh-e mt. Iran
91	D2	Taganrog Rus. Fed.
91	D2	Taganrog, Gulf of Rus. Fed./Ukr.
62	A1	Tagaung Myanmar
84	B1	Tagaytay City Phil.
64	B2	Tagbilaran Phil.
64	B1	Tagudin Phil.
64	B2	Tagum Phil.
106	B2	Tagus r. Port./Spain
60	B1	Tahan, Gunung mt. Malaysia
115	C2	Tahat, Mont mt. Alg.
69	C1	Tahe China
49	I4	Tahiti i. Fr. Polynesia
139	E1	Tahlequah U.S.A.
135	B3	Tahoe, Lake U.S.A.
135	B3	Tahoe City U.S.A.
126	D2	Tahoe Lake Can.
115	C3	Tahoua Niger
79	C2	Tahrūd Iran
128	B3	Tahsis Can.
70	B2	Tai'an China
71	C3	Taibei Taiwan
		Taibus Qi China see Baochang
54	C1	Taihape N.Z.
70	C2	Tai Hu l. China
71	C3	Tailem Bend Austr.
71	C3	Tainan Taiwan
155	D1	Taiobeiras Brazil
60	B1	Taiping Malaysia
71	B3	Taishan China
153	A5	Taitao, Península de pen. Chile
71	C3	T'aitung Taiwan
92	I2	Taivalkoski Fin.
92	H2	Taivaskero h. Fin.
71	C3	Taiwan country Asia
71	B3	Taiwan Strait China/Taiwan
70	B2	Taiyuan China
71	C3	Taizhong Taiwan
70	B2	Taizhou Jiangsu China
71	C3	Taizhou Zhejiang China
78	B3	Ta'izz Yemen
75	D2	Tajikistan country Asia
		Taj Mahal tourist site India
		Tajo r. Port. see Tagus
58	A1	Tak Thai.
54	B2	Takaka N.Z.
67	C3	Takamatsu Japan
67	C3	Takaoka Japan
54	B1	Takapuna N.Z.
67	C3	Takasaki Japan
122	B1	Takatokwane Botswana
67	C3	Takayama Japan
67	C3	Takefu Japan
60	A1	Takengon Indon.
63	B2	Takêv Cambodia
63	B2	Ta Khmau Cambodia
66	D2	Takikawa Japan
128	B2	Takla Lake Can.
128	B2	Takla Landing Can.
77	E3	Taklimakan Desert China
		Taklimakan Shamo des. China see Taklimakan Desert
128	A2	Taku r. Can./U.S.A.
63	A3	Takua Pa Thai.
115	C4	Takum Nigeria
88	C3	Talachyn Belarus
74	B1	Talagang Pak.
150	A2	Talara Peru
59	C2	Talaud, Kepulauan is Indon.
106	C2	Talavera de la Reina Spain
153	A4	Talca Chile
153	A4	Talcahuano Chile
84	B1	Taldom Rus. Fed.
77	E2	Taldykorgan Kazakh.
64	B1	Taliabu i. Indon.
64	B1	Talisay Phil.
61	C2	Taliwang Indon.
81	C2	Tall 'Afar Iraq
143	D2	Tallahassee U.S.A.
88	B2	Tallinn Estonia
142	B2	Tallulah U.S.A.
104	B2	Talmont-St-Hilaire France
90	C2	Tal'ne Ukr.
117	B3	Talodi Sudan
91	E1	Talovaya Rus. Fed.
126	E2	Taloyoak Can.
88	B2	Talsi Latvia
152	A3	Taltal Chile
129	C1	Taltson r. Can.
60	A1	Talu Indon.
53	C1	Talwood Austr.
114	B4	Tamale Ghana
115	C2	Tamanrasset Alg.
99	A3	Tamar r. U.K.
145	C2	Tamazunchale Mex.
114	A3	Tambacounda Senegal
61	B1	Tambelan, Kepulauan is Indon.
91	E1	Tambov Rus. Fed.
145	C2	Tamiahua, Laguna de lag. Mex.
143	D3	Tampa U.S.A.
143	D3	Tampa Bay U.S.A.
93	H3	Tampere Fin.
145	C2	Tampico Mex.
69	D1	Tamsagbulag Mongolia
102	C2	Tamsweg Austria
53	D2	Tamworth Austr.
99	C2	Tamworth U.K.
119	E3	Tana r. Kenya
117	B3	Tana, Lake Eth.
92	I1	Tana Bru Norway
61	C2	Tanahgrogot Indon.
58	C3	Tanahjampea i. Indon.
50	C1	Tanami Desert Austr.
126	A2	Tanana U.S.A.
108	A1	Tanaro r. Italy
65	B1	Tanch'ŏn N. Korea
64	B2	Tandag Phil.
110	C2	Ţăndărei Romania
153	C4	Tandil Arg.
74	A2	Tando Adam Pak.
74	A2	Tando Muhammad Khan Pak.
114	B2	Tanezrouft reg. Alg./Mali
119	D3	Tanga Tanz.
119	C3	Tanganyika, Lake Africa
		Tanger Morocco see Tangier
101	E1	Tangermünde Ger.
75	C1	Tanggula Shan mts China
114	B1	Tangier Morocco
75	C1	Tangra Yumco salt l. China
70	B2	Tangshan China
68	C2	Taniantaweng Shan mts China
59	C3	Tanimbar, Kepulauan is Indon.
64	B2	Tanjay Phil.
60	A1	Tanjungbalai Indon.
61	C2	Tanjungpandan Indon.
60	B1	Tanjungpinang Indon.
61	C1	Tanjungredeb Indon.
61	C1	Tanjungselor Indon.
74	B1	Tank Pak.
115	C3	Tanout Niger
75	C2	Tansen Nepal
116	B1	Ţanţā Egypt
119	D3	Tanzania country Africa
69	E1	Taonan China
138	B1	Taos U.S.A.
114	B2	Taoudenni Mali
88	C2	Tapa Estonia
145	C3	Tapachula Mex.
151	C2	Tapajós r. Brazil
60	A1	Tapaktuan Indon.
145	C3	Tapanatepec Mex.
150	B2	Tapauá Brazil
114	B4	Tapeta Liberia
141	D3	Tappahannock U.S.A.
74	B2	Tapti r. India
150	B2	Tapurucuara Brazil
154	A1	Taquari r. Brazil
154	B1	Taquari, Serra do hills Brazil
154	C2	Taquaritinga Brazil
115	D4	Taraba r. Nigeria
		Tarābulus Libya see Tripoli
61	C1	Tarakan Indon.
88	A3	Taran, Mys pt Rus. Fed.
54	B1	Taranaki, Mount vol. N.Z.
106	C1	Tarancón Spain
109	C2	Taranto Italy
109	C2	Taranto, Golfo di g. Italy
150	A2	Tarapoto Peru
91	E2	Tarasovskiy Rus. Fed.
150	A2	Tarauacá Brazil
150	B2	Tarauacá r. Brazil
48	F2	Tarawa atoll Kiribati
77	D2	Taraz Kazakh.
107	C1	Tarazona Spain
77	E2	Tarbagatay, Khrebet mts Kazakh.
96	A2	Tarbert Scotland U.K.
96	B3	Tarbert Scotland U.K.
104	C3	Tarbes France
96	B2	Tarbet U.K.
51	C3	Tarcoola Austr.
53	D2	Taree Austr.
110	C2	Târgoviște Romania
110	B1	Târgu Jiu Romania
110	B1	Târgu Mureș Romania
110	C1	Târgu Neamț Romania
79	C2	Tarīf U.A.E.
152	B3	Tarija Bol.
79	B3	Tarim Yemen
77	E3	Tarim Basin China
77	E2	Tarim He r. China
		Tarim Pendi basin China see Tarim Basin
59	D3	Taritatu r. Indon.
82	G2	Tarko-Sale Rus. Fed.
114	B4	Tarkwa Ghana
64	B1	Tarlac Phil.
68	C2	Tarlag China
92	G2	Tärnaby Sweden
77	C3	Tarnak Rōd r. Afgh.
110	B1	Târnăveni Romania
103	E1	Tarnobrzeg Pol.
103	E1	Tarnów Pol.
75	C1	Taro Co salt l. China
114	B1	Taroudannt Morocco
108	B2	Tarquinia Italy
107	D1	Tarragona Spain
107	D1	Tàrrega Spain
80	B2	Tarsus Turkey
152	B3	Tartagal Arg.
104	B3	Tartas France
88	C2	Tartu Estonia
80	B2	Ţarţūs Syria
155	D1	Tarumirim Brazil
89	E3	Tarusa Rus. Fed.
108	B1	Tarvisio Italy
81	D3	Tashk, Daryācheh-ye l. Iran
		Tashkent Uzbek. see Toshkent
131	D1	Tasiujaq Can.
76	B1	Taskala Kazakh.
77	E2	Taskesken Kazakh.
54	B2	Tasman Bay N.Z.
51	D4	Tasmania state Austr.
54	B2	Tasman Mountains N.Z.
156	D8	Tasman Sea S. Pacific Ocean

Tatabánya

103 D2 Tatabánya Hungary
90 B2 Tatarbunary Ukr.
83 K3 Tatarskiy Proliv str. Rus. Fed.
67 C4 Tateyama Japan
128 C1 Tathlina Lake Can.
78 B3 Tathlith Saudi Arabia
78 B2 Tathlith, Wādī watercourse Saudi Arabia
53 C3 Tathra Austr.
62 A1 Tatkon Myanmar
128 B2 Tatla Lake Can.
103 D2 Tatra Mountains mts Pol./Slovakia
Tatry mts Pol./Slovakia see Tatra Mountains
154 C2 Tatuí Brazil
139 C2 Tatum U.S.A.
81 C2 Tatvan Turkey
151 D2 Taua Brazil
155 C2 Taubaté Brazil
101 D3 Tauberbischofsheim Ger.
54 C1 Taumarunui N.Z.
62 A1 Taunggyi Myanmar
62 A2 Taung-ngu Myanmar
62 A2 Taungup Myanmar
99 B3 Taunton U.K.
100 C2 Taunus hills Ger.
54 C1 Taupo N.Z.
54 C1 Taupo, Lake N.Z.
88 B2 Tauragė Lith.
54 C1 Tauranga N.Z.
80 B2 Taurus Mountains Turkey
111 C3 Tavas Turkey
86 F3 Tavda Rus. Fed.
106 B2 Tavira Port.
99 A3 Tavistock U.K.
63 A2 Tavoy Myanmar
111 C3 Tavşanlı Turkey
99 A3 Taw r. U.K.
140 C2 Tawas City U.S.A.
61 C1 Tawau Sabah Malaysia
64 A2 Tawi-Tawi i. Phil.
145 C3 Taxco Mex.
76 B2 Taxiatosh Uzbek.
77 D3 Taxkorgan China
96 C2 Tay r. U.K.
96 C2 Tay, Firth of est. U.K.
96 B2 Tay, Loch l. U.K.
128 B2 Taylor Can.
139 D2 Taylor U.S.A.
140 B3 Taylorville U.S.A.
78 A2 Taymā' Saudi Arabia
83 H2 Taymura r. Rus. Fed.
83 H2 Taymyr, Ozero l. Rus. Fed.
Taymyr, Poluostrov pen. Rus. Fed. see Taymyr Peninsula
83 G2 Taymyr Peninsula Rus. Fed.
63 B2 Tây Ninh Vietnam
64 A1 Taytay Phil.
82 G2 Taz r. Rus. Fed.
114 B1 Taza Morocco
129 D2 Tazin Lake Can.
86 G2 Tazovskaya Guba sea chan. Rus. Fed.
81 C1 Tbilisi Georgia
91 E2 Tbilisskaya Rus. Fed.
118 B3 Tchibanga Gabon
118 B2 Tcholliré Cameroon
103 D1 Tczew Pol.
144 B2 Teacapán Mex.
54 A3 Te Anau N.Z.
54 A3 Te Anau, Lake N.Z.
145 C3 Teapa Mex.
54 C1 Te Awamutu N.Z.
115 C1 Tébessa Alg.
60 B2 Tebingtinggi Sumatera Selatan Indon.

60 A1 Tebingtinggi Sumatera Utara Indon.
114 B4 Techiman Ghana
144 B3 Tecomán Mex.
144 B2 Tecoripa Mex.
145 B3 Técpan Mex.
144 B2 Tecuala Mex.
110 C1 Tecuci Romania
68 C1 Teeli Rus. Fed.
98 C1 Tees r. U.K.
111 C3 Tefenni Turkey
61 B2 Tegal Indon.
146 B3 Tegucigalpa Hond.
115 C3 Teguidda-n-Tessoumt Niger
114 B4 Téhini Côte d'Ivoire
81 D2 Tehrān Iran
145 C3 Tehuacán Mex.
145 C3 Tehuantepec, Gulf of Mex.
145 C3 Tehuantepec, Istmo de isth. Mex.
99 A2 Teifi r. U.K.
76 C3 Tejen Turkm.
76 C3 Tejen r. Turkm.
Tejo r. Spain see Tagus
145 B3 Tejupilco Mex.
54 B2 Tekapo, Lake N.Z.
145 D2 Tekax Mex.
116 B3 Tekezē Wenz r. Eritrea/Eth.
111 C2 Tekirdağ Turkey
54 C1 Te Kuiti N.Z.
75 C2 Tel r. India
81 C1 Telavi Georgia
80 B2 Tel Aviv-Yafo Israel
145 D2 Telchac Puerto Mex.
128 A2 Telegraph Creek Can.
154 B2 Telêmaco Borba Brazil
99 B2 Telford U.K.
60 A2 Telo Indon.
86 E2 Telpoziz, Gora mt. Rus. Fed.
88 B2 Telšiai Lith.
61 B2 Telukbatang Indon.
60 A1 Telukdalam Indon.
60 B1 Teluk Intan Malaysia
130 C2 Temagami Lake Can.
61 C2 Temanggung Indon.
123 C2 Temba S. Africa
60 B2 Tembilahan Indon.
120 A1 Tembo Aluma Angola
99 B2 Teme r. U.K.
60 B1 Temerluh Malaysia
77 D1 Temirtau Kazakh.
53 C2 Temora Austr.
139 D2 Temple U.S.A.
97 C2 Templemore Ireland
145 C2 Tempoal Mex.
91 D2 Temryuk Rus. Fed.
153 A4 Temuco Chile
54 B2 Temuka N.Z.
145 C2 Tenabo Mex.
73 C3 Tenali India
63 A2 Tenasserim Myanmar
99 A3 Tenby U.K.
117 C3 Tendaho Eth.
105 D3 Tende France
108 A2 Tende, Col de pass France/Italy
73 D4 Ten Degree Channel India
67 D3 Tendō Japan
114 B3 Ténenkou Mali
115 D3 Ténéré, Erg du des. Niger
115 D3 Ténéré du Tafassâsset des. Niger
114 A2 Tenerife i. Islas Canarias
107 D2 Ténès Alg.
61 C2 Tengah, Kepulauan is Indon.
62 A1 Tengchong China
61 C2 Tenggarong Indon.

70 A2 Tengger Shamo des. China
71 B3 Tengxian China
119 C4 Tenke Dem. Rep. Congo
114 B3 Tenkodogo Burkina Faso
51 C1 Tennant Creek Austr.
142 C1 Tennessee r. U.S.A.
142 C1 Tennessee state U.S.A.
145 C3 Tenosique Mex.
53 D1 Tenterfield Austr.
154 B2 Teodoro Sampaio Brazil
155 D1 Teófilo Otoni Brazil
145 C3 Teopisca Mex.
54 B1 Tepache Mex.
54 B1 Te Paki N.Z.
144 B3 Tepalcatepec Mex.
144 B2 Tepatitlán Mex.
144 B2 Tepehuanes Mex.
109 D2 Tepelenë Albania
144 B2 Tepic Mex.
102 C1 Teplice Czech Rep.
89 E3 Teploye Rus. Fed.
144 B2 Tequila Mex.
108 B2 Teramo Italy
89 E3 Terbuny Rus. Fed.
90 B2 Terebovlya Ukr.
87 D4 Terek r. Rus. Fed.
151 D2 Teresina Brazil
155 D2 Teresópolis Brazil
63 A3 Teressa Island India
80 B1 Terme Turkey
108 B3 Termini Imerese Sicilia Italy
145 C3 Términos, Laguna de lag. Mex.
77 C3 Termiz Uzbek.
109 B2 Termoli Italy
59 C2 Ternate Indon.
100 A2 Terneuzen Neth.
108 B2 Terni Italy
90 B2 Ternopil' Ukr.
128 B2 Terrace Can.
130 B2 Terrace Bay Can.
122 B2 Terra Firma S. Africa
140 B3 Terre Haute U.S.A.
131 E2 Terrenceville Can.
100 B1 Terschelling i. Neth.
108 A3 Tertenia Sardegna Italy
107 C1 Teruel Spain
92 H2 Tervola Fin.
109 C2 Tešanj Bos.-Herz.
116 B3 Teseney Eritrea
66 D2 Teshio-gawa r. Japan
128 A1 Teslin Can.
128 A1 Teslin Lake Can.
154 B1 Tesouro Brazil
115 C3 Tessaoua Niger
121 C2 Tete Moz.
90 C1 Teteriv r. Ukr.
101 F1 Teterow Ger.
90 B2 Tetiyiv Ukr.
114 B1 Tétouan Morocco
109 D2 Tetovo Macedonia
152 B3 Teuco r. Arg.
144 B2 Teul de González Ortega Mex.
101 D1 Teutoburger Wald hills Ger.
Tevere r. Italy see Tiber
54 A3 Teviot N.Z.
51 E2 Tewantin Austr.
54 C2 Te Wharau N.Z.
139 E2 Texarkana U.S.A.
53 D1 Texas Austr.
139 D2 Texas state U.S.A.
139 E3 Texas City U.S.A.
100 B1 Texel i. Neth.
139 D2 Texoma, Lake U.S.A.
123 C2 Teyateyaneng Lesotho
89 F2 Teykovo Rus. Fed.
89 F2 Teza r. Rus. Fed.

75 D2 Tezpur India
62 A1 Tezu India
129 E1 Tha-anne r. Can.
123 C2 Thabana-Ntlenyana mt. Lesotho
123 C2 Thaba Putsoa mt. Lesotho
123 C1 Thabazimbi S. Africa
123 C2 Thabong S. Africa
63 A2 Thagyettaw Myanmar
62 B1 Thai Binh Vietnam
63 B2 Thailand country Asia
63 B2 Thailand, Gulf of Asia
62 B1 Thai Nguyên Vietnam
62 B2 Thakhèk Laos
63 A3 Thalang Thai.
74 B1 Thal Desert Pak.
101 E2 Thale (Harz) Ger.
62 B2 Tha Li Thai.
123 C1 Thamaga Botswana
116 C3 Thamar, Jabal mt. Yemen
79 C3 Thamarīt Oman
130 B2 Thames r. Can.
54 C1 Thames N.Z.
99 D3 Thames est. U.K.
99 D3 Thames r. U.K.
63 A2 Thanbyuzayat Myanmar
62 A2 Thandwè Myanmar
62 B2 Thanh Hoa Vietnam
73 B3 Thanjavur India
63 A2 Thanlyin Myanmar
74 A2 Thano Bula Khan Pak.
62 B1 Than Uyên Vietnam
74 A2 Thar Desert India/Pak.
52 B1 Thargomindah Austr.
81 C2 Tharthār, Buhayrat ath l. Iraq
111 B2 Thasos i. Greece
62 B1 Thât Khê Vietnam
62 A2 Thaton Myanmar
74 A2 Thatta Pak.
62 A1 Thaungdut Myanmar
62 A2 Thayawadi Myanmar
62 A2 Thayetmyo Myanmar
62 A1 Thazi Myanmar
146 C2 The Bahamas country West Indies
98 B1 The Cheviot h. U.K.
134 B1 The Dalles U.S.A.
99 C2 The Fens reg. U.K.
114 A3 The Gambia country Africa
The Great Oasis Egypt see Khārijah, Wāhāt al
79 C2 The Gulf Asia
100 B1 The Hague Neth.
129 E1 Thelon r. Can.
101 E2 Themar Ger.
96 A1 The Minch sea chan. U.K.
150 B2 Theodore Roosevelt r. Brazil
129 D2 The Pas Can.
111 B2 Thermaïkos Kolpos g. Greece
136 B2 Thermopolis U.S.A.
53 C3 The Rock Austr.
130 B2 Thessalon Can.
111 B2 Thessaloniki Greece
99 D2 Thetford U.K.
131 C2 Thetford Mines Can.
62 A1 The Triangle mts Myanmar
131 D1 Thévenet, Lac l. Can.
99 D2 The Wash b. U.K.
139 D2 The Woodlands U.S.A.
142 B3 Thibodaux U.S.A.
129 E2 Thicket Portage Can.
137 D1 Thief River Falls U.S.A.
105 C2 Thiers France
73 B4 Thika Kenya
73 B4 Thiladhunmathi Maldives
75 C2 Thimphu Bhutan

105 D2 Thionville France
98 C1 Thirsk U.K.
73 B4 Thiruvananthapuram India
93 E4 Thisted Denmark
129 E1 Thlewiaza r. Can.
62 A2 Thoen Thai.
123 D1 Thohoyandou S. Africa
101 E1 Thomasburg Ger.
97 C2 Thomastown Ireland
143 D2 Thomasville U.S.A.
100 C2 Thommen Belgium
129 E2 Thompson Can.
128 E3 Thompson r. U.S.A.
134 C1 Thompson Falls U.S.A.
128 B2 Thompson Sound Can.
Thoothukudi India see Tuticorin
96 C3 Thornhill U.K.
55 C2 Thorshavnheiane reg. Antarctica
104 B2 Thouars France
128 C2 Three Hills Can.
63 A2 Three Pagodas Pass Myanmar/Thai.
114 B4 Three Points, Cape Ghana
73 B3 Thrissur India
63 B2 Thu Dâu Môt Vietnam
100 B2 Thuin Belgium
127 G1 Thule Greenland
121 B3 Thuli Zimbabwe
130 B2 Thunder Bay Can.
63 A3 Thung Song Thai.
101 E2 Thüringer Becken reg. Ger.
101 E2 Thüringer Wald mts Ger.
102 C1 Thüringer Wald mts Ger.
97 C2 Thurles Ireland
96 C1 Thurso U.K.
96 C1 Thurso r. U.K.
151 D2 Tianguá Brazil
70 B2 Tianjin China
70 B2 Tianjin mun. China
71 A3 Tianlin China
70 B2 Tianmen China
70 A2 Tianshui China
154 B2 Tiagbi r. Brazil
118 B2 Tibati Cameroon
108 B2 Tiber r. Italy
Tiberias, Lake Israel see Galilee, Sea of
115 D2 Tibesti mts Chad
Tibet aut. reg. China see Xizang Zizhiqu
68 B2 Tibet, Plateau of China
Tibet Autonomous Region aut. reg. China see Xizang Zizhiqu
115 D2 Tibisti, Sarir des. Libya
52 B1 Tibooburra Austr.
144 A1 Tiburón, Isla i. Mex.
114 B3 Tîchît Maur.
114 A2 Tîchla Western Sahara
145 D2 Ticul Mex.
114 A3 Tidjikja Maur.
100 B2 Tiel Neth.
65 A1 Tieling China
100 A2 Tielt Belgium
100 B2 Tienen Belgium
68 B2 Tien Shan mts China/Kyrg.
Tientsin China see Tianjin
93 G3 Tierp Sweden
145 C3 Tierra Blanca Mex.
145 C3 Tierra Colorada Mex.
153 B6 Tierra del Fuego, Isla Grande de i. Arg./Chile
154 C2 Tietê Brazil
Tiflis Georgia see Tbilisi
143 D2 Tifton U.S.A.

90 B2 Tighina Moldova
131 D2 Tignish Can.
150 A2 Tigre r. Ecuador/Peru
81 C2 Tigris r. Asia
145 C2 Tijuatlán Mex.
144 A1 Tijuana Mex.
91 E2 Tikhoretsk Rus. Fed.
89 D2 Tikhvin Rus. Fed.
89 D2 Tikhvinskaya Gryada ridge Rus. Fed.
54 C1 Tikokino N.Z.
81 C2 Tikrīt Iraq
83 J2 Tiksi Rus. Fed.
100 B2 Tilburg Neth.
152 B3 Tilcara Arg.
52 B1 Tilcha (abandoned) Austr.
114 C3 Tillabéri Niger
134 B1 Tillamook U.S.A.
63 A3 Tillanchong Island India
111 C3 Tilos i. Greece
52 B2 Tilpa Austr.
86 F2 Til'tim Rus. Fed.
89 E3 Tim Rus. Fed.
86 D2 Timanskiy Kryazh ridge Rus. Fed.
54 B2 Timaru N.Z.
91 D2 Timashevsk Rus. Fed.
114 B3 Timbedgha Maur.
50 C1 Timber Creek Austr.
114 B3 Timbuktu Mali
114 C2 Timimoun Alg.
111 B2 Timiou Prodromou, Akrotirio pt Greece
110 B1 Timiş r. Romania
110 B1 Timişoara Romania
130 B2 Timmins Can.
89 E2 Timokhino Rus. Fed.
151 E2 Timon Brazil
59 C3 Timor i. East Timor/Indonesia
Timor-Leste country Asia see East Timor
58 C3 Timor Sea Austr./Indon.
93 G3 Timrå Sweden
114 B2 Tindouf Alg.
75 C2 Tingri India
93 F4 Tingsryd Sweden
59 D2 Tinian i. N. Mariana Is
152 B3 Tinogasta Arg.
111 C3 Tinos Greece
111 C3 Tinos i. Greece
115 C2 Tinrhert, Hamada de Alg.
62 A1 Tinsukia India
107 D2 Tipasa Alg.
97 B2 Tipperary Ireland
109 C2 Tirana Albania
Tiranë Albania see Tirana
108 B1 Tirano Italy
90 B2 Tiraspol Moldova
111 C3 Tire Turkey
96 A2 Tiree i. U.K.
74 B1 Tirich Mir mt. Pak.
73 B3 Tiruchchirappalli India
73 B4 Tirunelveli India
73 B3 Tirupati India
73 B3 Tiruppattur India
73 B3 Tiruppur India
109 D1 Tisa r. Serbia
129 D2 Tisdale Can.
107 D2 Tissemsilt Alg.
152 B2 Titicaca, Lake Bol./Peru
75 C2 Titlagarh India
110 C2 Titu Romania
113 C3 Titusville U.S.A.
99 B3 Tiverton U.K.
108 B2 Tivoli Italy
79 C2 Ţīwī Oman
145 D2 Tizimín Mex.

Tizi Ouzou

107 D2 Tizi Ouzou Alg.
114 B2 Tiznit Morocco
145 C3 Tlacotalpán Mex.
144 B2 Tlahualilo Mex.
145 C3 Tlapa Mex.
145 C3 Tlaxcala Mex.
145 C3 Tlaxiaco Mex.
114 B1 Tlemcen Alg.
123 C1 Tlokweng Botswana
128 B2 Toad River Can.
121 □D2 Toamasina Madag.
60 A1 Toba, Danau l. Indon.
74 A1 Toba and Kakar Ranges mts Pak.
147 D3 Tobago i. Trin. and Tob.
59 C2 Tobelo Indon.
130 B2 Tobermory Can.
96 A2 Tobermory U.K.
129 D2 Tobin Lake Can.
60 B2 Toboali Indon.
86 F3 Tobol'sk Rus. Fed.
76 C1 Tobyl r. Kazakh./Rus. Fed.
151 D2 Tocantinópolis Brazil
151 D2 Tocantins r. Brazil
143 D2 Toccoa U.S.A.
108 A1 Toce r. Italy
152 A3 Tocopilla Chile
53 C3 Tocumwal Austr.
144 A2 Todos Santos Mex.
128 B3 Tofino Can.
96 □ Toft U.K.
49 G4 Tofua i. Tonga
59 C3 Togian, Kepulauan is Indon.
114 C4 Togo country Africa
74 B2 Tohana India
126 B2 Tok U.S.A.
116 B3 Tokar Sudan
69 E3 Tokara-rettō is Japan
91 E1 Tokarevka Rus. Fed.
49 G3 Tokelau terr. S. Pacific Ocean
91 D2 Tokmak Ukr.
77 D2 Tokmok Kyrg.
54 C1 Tokoroa N.Z.
68 B2 Toksun China
87 B4 Tokushima Japan
67 C3 Tōkyō Japan
121 □D3 Tôlañaro Madag.
154 B2 Toledo Brazil
106 C2 Toledo Spain
140 C2 Toledo U.S.A.
106 C2 Toledo, Montes de mts Spain
142 B2 Toledo Bend Reservoir U.S.A.
121 □D3 Toliara Madag.
58 C2 Tolitoli Indon.
108 B1 Tolmezzo Italy
104 B3 Tolosa Spain
145 C3 Toluca Mex.
87 D3 Tol'yatti Rus. Fed.
140 A2 Tomah U.S.A.
66 D2 Tomakomai Japan
106 B2 Tomar Port.
103 E1 Tomaszów Lubelski Pol.
103 E1 Tomaszów Mazowiecki Pol.
144 B3 Tomatlán Mex.
142 C2 Tombigbee r. U.S.A.
155 D2 Tombos Brazil
Tombouctou Mali see Timbuktu
120 A2 Tombua Angola
123 C1 Tom Burke S. Africa
53 C2 Tomingley Austr.
58 C3 Tomini, Teluk g. Indon.
109 C2 Tomislavgrad Bos.-Herz.
50 A2 Tom Price Austr.
82 G3 Tomsk Rus. Fed.
93 F4 Tomtabacken h. Sweden
145 C3 Tonalá Mex.

150 B2 Tonantins Brazil
59 C2 Tondano Indon.
49 G4 Tonga country S. Pacific Ocean
49 G4 Tongatapu Group is Tonga
71 B3 Tongcheng China
70 A2 Tongchuan China
71 A3 Tongdao China
65 B2 Tongduch'ŏn S. Korea
100 B2 Tongeren Belgium
65 B2 Tonghae S. Korea
62 B1 Tonghai China
65 B1 Tonghua China
65 B2 Tongjosŏn-man b. N. Korea
62 B1 Tongking, Gulf of China/Vietnam
69 E2 Tongliao China
70 B2 Tongling China
52 B2 Tongo Austr.
71 A3 Tongren China
Tongshan China see Xuzhou
Tongtian He r. China see Yangtze
96 B1 Tongue U.K.
65 B3 T'ongyŏng S. Korea
69 E2 Tongyu China
65 A1 Tongyuanpu China
74 B2 Tonk India
63 B2 Tonle Sap l. Cambodia
135 C3 Tonopah U.S.A.
93 F4 Tønsberg Norway
135 D2 Tooele U.S.A.
52 B3 Tooleybuc Austr.
53 D1 Toowoomba Austr.
137 D3 Topeka U.S.A.
144 B2 Topia Mex.
144 B2 Topolobampo Mex.
86 C2 Topozero, Ozero l. Rus. Fed.
134 B1 Toppenish U.S.A.
111 C3 Torbalı Turkey
76 B3 Torbat-e Ḩeydarīyeh Iran
76 C3 Torbat-e Jām Iran
106 C1 Tordesillas Spain
107 C1 Tordesilos Spain
107 D1 Torelló Spain
101 F2 Torgau Ger.
76 C2 Torgay Kazakh.
100 A2 Torhout Belgium
Torino Italy see Turin
154 B1 Torixoréu Brazil
106 B1 Tormes r. Spain
92 H2 Torneälven r. Sweden
127 G3 Torngat Mountains Can.
92 H2 Tornio Fin.
106 B1 Toro Spain
130 C2 Toronto Can.
119 D2 Tororo Uganda
Toros Dağları mts Turkey see Taurus Mountains
99 B3 Torquay U.K.
106 B2 Torrão Port.
106 B1 Torre mt. Port.
107 D1 Torreblanca Spain
106 C1 Torrecerredo mt. Spain
106 B1 Torre de Moncorvo Port.
106 C1 Torrelavega Spain
106 C2 Torremolinos Spain
52 A2 Torrens, Lake imp. l. Austr.
107 C2 Torrent Spain
144 B2 Torreón Mex.
106 B2 Torres Novas Port.
106 B2 Torres Vedras Port.
107 C2 Torrevieja Spain
96 B2 Torridon U.K.
106 C2 Torrijos Spain
141 E2 Torrington CT U.S.A.
136 C2 Torrington WY U.S.A.
107 D1 Torroella de Montgrí Spain

94 B1 Tórshavn Faroe Is
108 A3 Tortolì Sardegna Italy
107 D1 Tortosa Spain
103 D1 Toruń Pol.
97 B1 Tory Island Ireland
89 D2 Torzhok Rus. Fed.
122 B2 Tosca S. Africa
108 B2 Toscano, Arcipelago is Italy
77 C2 Toshkent Uzbek.
89 D2 Tosno Rus. Fed.
152 B3 Tostado Arg.
101 D1 Tostedt Ger.
80 B1 Tosya Turkey
86 D3 Tot'ma Rus. Fed.
67 B3 Tottori Japan
114 B4 Touba Côte d'Ivoire
114 B1 Toubkal, Jebel mt. Morocco
114 B3 Tougan Burkina Faso
115 C1 Touggourt Alg.
105 D2 Toul France
105 D3 Toulon France
104 C3 Toulouse France
100 A2 Tournai Belgium
105 C2 Tournus France
151 E2 Touros Brazil
104 C2 Tours France
115 D2 Toussidé, Pic mt. Chad
122 B3 Touwsrivier S. Africa
66 D2 Towada Japan
134 D1 Townsend U.S.A.
51 D1 Townsville Austr.
77 E2 Toxkan He r. China
66 D2 Tōya-ko l. Japan
67 C3 Toyama Japan
67 C3 Toyota Japan
115 C1 Tozeur Tunisia
81 C1 T'q'varcheli Georgia
Trâblous Lebanon see Tripoli
80 B1 Trabzon Turkey
106 B2 Trafalgar, Cabo de c. Spain
128 C3 Trail Can.
88 B3 Trakai Lith.
97 B2 Tralee Ireland
97 C2 Tramore Ireland
63 A3 Trang Thai.
59 C3 Trangan i. Indon.
55 I2 Transantarctic Mountains Antarctica
90 B2 Transnistria terr. Moldova
110 B1 Transylvanian Alps mts Romania
108 B3 Trapani Sicilia Italy
53 C3 Traralgon Austr.
63 B2 Trat Thai.
102 C2 Traunstein Ger.
140 B2 Traverse City U.S.A.
103 D2 Třebíč Czech Rep.
109 C2 Trebinje Bos.-Herz.
103 E2 Trebišov Slovakia
109 C1 Trebnje Slovenia
153 C4 Treinta y Tres Uru.
153 B5 Trelew Arg.
93 F4 Trelleborg Sweden
130 C2 Tremblant, Mont h. Can.
109 C2 Tremiti, Isole is Italy
134 D2 Tremonton U.S.A.
107 D1 Tremp Spain
103 D2 Trenčín Slovakia
153 B4 Trenque Lauquén Arg.
98 C2 Trent r. U.K.
108 B1 Trento Italy
141 D2 Trenton Can.
137 E2 Trenton MO U.S.A.
141 E2 Trenton NJ U.S.A.
131 E2 Trepassey Can.
153 B4 Tres Arroyos Arg.
155 C2 Três Corações Brazil

154 B2 **Três Lagoas** Brazil
153 A5 **Tres Lagos** Arg.
155 C1 **Três Marias, Represa** *resr* Brazil
155 C2 **Três Pontas** Brazil
153 B5 **Tres Puntas, Cabo** *c.* Arg.
155 D2 **Três Rios** Brazil
101 F1 **Treuenbrietzen** Ger.
108 A1 **Treviglio** Italy
108 B1 **Treviso** Italy
99 A3 **Trevose Head** U.K.
109 C3 **Tricase** Italy
53 C2 **Trida** Austr.
100 C3 **Trier** Ger.
108 B1 **Trieste** Italy
108 B1 **Triglav** *mt.* Slovenia
59 D3 **Trikora, Puncak** *mt.* Indon.
97 C2 **Trim** Ireland
73 C4 **Trincomalee** Sri Lanka
154 C1 **Trindade** Brazil
152 B2 **Trinidad** Bol.
147 D3 **Trinidad** *i.* Trin. and Tob.
136 C3 **Trinidad** U.S.A.
147 D3 **Trinidad and Tobago** *country* West Indies
131 E2 **Trinity Bay** Can.
111 B3 **Tripoli** Greece
80 B2 **Tripoli** Lebanon
115 D1 **Tripoli** Libya
113 D10 **Tristan da Cunha** *i.* S. Atlantic Ocean
108 B2 **Trivento** Italy
103 D2 **Trnava** Slovakia
109 C2 **Trogir** Croatia
109 C2 **Troia** Italy
100 C2 **Troisdorf** Ger.
131 C2 **Trois-Rivières** Can.
86 E2 **Troitsko-Pechorsk** Rus. Fed.
151 C2 **Trombetas** *r.* Brazil
123 C3 **Trompsburg** S. Africa
92 G2 **Tromsø** Norway
92 F3 **Trondheim** Norway
128 C2 **Trout Lake** Can.
128 B1 **Trout Lake** N.W.T. Can.
130 A1 **Trout Lake** Ont. Can.
99 B3 **Trowbridge** U.K.
142 C2 **Troy** AL U.S.A.
141 E2 **Troy** NY U.S.A.
105 C2 **Troyes** France
109 D2 **Trstenik** Serbia
89 D3 **Trubchevsk** Rus. Fed.
106 B1 **Truchas** Spain
79 C2 **Trucial Coast** U.A.E.
146 B3 **Trujillo** Hond.
150 A2 **Trujillo** Peru
106 B2 **Trujillo** Spain
147 C4 **Trujillo** Venez.
142 B1 **Trumann** U.S.A.
131 D2 **Truro** Can.
99 A3 **Truro** U.K.
138 B2 **Truth or Consequences** U.S.A.
103 D1 **Trutnov** Czech Rep.
93 F3 **Trysil** Norway
103 D1 **Trzebiatów** Pol.
68 B1 **Tsagaannuur** Mongolia
121 □D2 **Tsaratanana, Massif du** *mts* Madag.
110 C2 **Tsarevo** Bulg.
122 A2 **Tses** Namibia
122 B1 **Tsetseng** Botswana
68 C1 **Tsetserleg** Mongolia
122 B2 **Tshabong** Botswana
122 B1 **Tshane** Botswana
118 B3 **Tshela** Dem. Rep. Congo
118 C3 **Tshikapa** Dem. Rep. Congo
118 C3 **Tshikapa** *r.* Dem. Rep. Congo
123 D1 **Tshipise** S. Africa

118 C3 **Tshitanzu** Dem. Rep. Congo
118 C3 **Tshuapa** *r.* Dem. Rep. Congo
Tshwane S. Africa *see* **Pretoria**
87 D4 **Tsimlyanskoye Vodokhranilishche** *resr* Rus. Fed.
Tsingtao China *see* **Qingdao**
Tsining China *see* **Ulan Qab**
121 □D2 **Tsiroanomandidy** Madag.
123 C3 **Tsomo** S. Africa
67 C4 **Tsu** Japan
67 D3 **Tsuchiura** Japan
66 D2 **Tsugarū-kaikyō** *str.* Japan
120 A2 **Tsumeb** Namibia
122 A1 **Tsumis Park** Namibia
120 B2 **Tsumkwe** Namibia
67 C3 **Tsuruga** Japan
66 C3 **Tsuruoka** Japan
67 A4 **Tsushima** *is* Japan
Tsushima-kaikyō *str.* Japan/ S. Korea *see* **Korea Strait**
67 B3 **Tsuyama** Japan
123 C2 **Tswelelang** S. Africa
91 C2 **Tsyurupyns'k** Ukr.
Tthenaagoo Can. *see* **Nahanni Butte**
59 C3 **Tual** Indon.
97 B2 **Tuam** Ireland
49 I4 **Tuamotu, Archipel des** is Fr. Polynesia
91 D3 **Tuapse** Rus. Fed.
54 A3 **Tuatapere** N.Z.
96 A1 **Tuath, Loch a'** *b.* U.K.
138 A1 **Tuba City** U.S.A.
61 C2 **Tuban** Indon.
152 D3 **Tubarão** Brazil
102 B2 **Tübingen** Ger.
115 E1 **Tubruq** Libya
49 H4 **Tubuai** Fr. Polynesia
49 I4 **Tubuai** *i.* Fr. Polynesia
144 A1 **Tubutama** Mex.
152 C2 **Tucavaca** Bol.
128 B1 **Tuchitua** Can.
138 A2 **Tucson** U.S.A.
139 C1 **Tucumcari** U.S.A.
150 B1 **Tucupita** Venez.
151 D2 **Tucuruí** Brazil
151 D2 **Tucuruí, Represa de** *resr* Brazil
107 C1 **Tudela** Spain
106 B1 **Tuela** *r.* Port.
62 A1 **Tuensang** India
64 B1 **Tuguegarao** Phil.
106 B1 **Tui** Spain
59 C3 **Tukangbesi, Kepulauan** *is* Indon.
126 C2 **Tuktoyaktuk** Can.
88 B2 **Tukums** Latvia
145 C2 **Tula** Mex.
89 E3 **Tula** Rus. Fed.
145 C2 **Tulancingo** Mex.
135 C3 **Tulare** U.S.A.
138 B2 **Tularosa** U.S.A.
110 C1 **Tulcea** Romania
90 B2 **Tul'chyn** Ukr.
129 E1 **Tulemalu Lake** Can.
139 D2 **Tulia** U.S.A.
142 C1 **Tullahoma** U.S.A.
97 C2 **Tullamore** Ireland
104 C2 **Tulle** France
51 D1 **Tully** Austr.
139 D1 **Tulsa** U.S.A.
150 A1 **Tumaco** Col.
123 C2 **Tumahole** S. Africa
Tumakuru India *see* **Tumkur**
93 G4 **Tumba** Sweden
118 B3 **Tumba, Lac** *l.* Dem. Rep. Congo
53 C3 **Tumbarumba** Austr.
150 A2 **Tumbes** Peru

128 B2 **Tumbler Ridge** Can.
153 A4 **Tumby Bay** Austr.
65 B1 **Tumen** China
150 B1 **Tumereng** Guyana
64 A2 **Tumindao** *i.* Phil.
73 B3 **Tumkur** India
74 A2 **Tump** Pak.
151 C1 **Tumucumaque, Serra** *hills* Brazil
53 C3 **Tumut** Austr.
99 D3 **Tunbridge Wells, Royal** U.K.
80 B2 **Tunceli** Turkey
53 D2 **Tuncurry** Austr.
119 D4 **Tunduru** Tanz.
110 C2 **Tundzha** *r.* Bulg.
128 B1 **Tungsten (abandoned)** Can.
115 D1 **Tunis** Tunisia
115 C1 **Tunisia** *country* Africa
150 A1 **Tunja** Col.
92 F3 **Tunnsjøen** *l.* Norway
Tunxi China *see* **Huangshan**
154 B2 **Tupã** Brazil
154 C1 **Tupaciguara** Brazil
142 C2 **Tupelo** U.S.A.
152 B3 **Tupiza** Bol.
76 B2 **Tupkaragan, Mys** *pt* Kazakh.
83 H2 **Tura** Rus. Fed.
86 F3 **Tura** *r.* Rus. Fed.
78 B2 **Turabah** Saudi Arabia
83 J3 **Turana, Khrebet** *mts* Rus. Fed.
54 C1 **Turangi** N.Z.
76 B2 **Turan Lowland** Asia
78 A1 **Turayf** Saudi Arabia
88 B2 **Turba** Estonia
74 A2 **Turbat** Pak.
150 A1 **Turbo** Col.
110 B1 **Turda** Romania
Turfan China *see* **Turpan**
111 C3 **Turgutlu** Turkey
80 B1 **Turhal** Turkey
107 C2 **Turia** *r.* Spain
108 A1 **Turin** Italy
86 F3 **Turinsk** Rus. Fed.
90 A1 **Turiys'k** Ukr.
119 D2 **Turkana, Lake** *salt l.* Eth./Kenya
80 B2 **Turkey** *country* Asia/Europe
77 C2 **Turkistan** Kazakh.
76 C3 **Türkmenabat** Turkm.
76 B2 **Türkmenbaşy** Turkm.
76 B2 **Turkmenistan** *country* Asia
147 C2 **Turks and Caicos Islands** *terr.* West Indies
93 H3 **Turku** Fin.
135 B3 **Turlock** U.S.A.
54 C2 **Turnagain, Cape** N.Z.
100 B2 **Turnhout** Belgium
129 D2 **Turnor Lake** Can.
110 B2 **Turnu Măgurele** Romania
68 B2 **Turpan** China
77 D2 **Turugart Pass** China/Kyrg.
142 C2 **Tuscaloosa** U.S.A.
142 C2 **Tuskegee** U.S.A.
73 B4 **Tuticorin** India
120 B3 **Tutume** Botswana
49 F3 **Tuvalu** *country* S. Pacific Ocean
78 B2 **Tuwayq, Jabal** *hills* Saudi Arabia
78 B2 **Tuwayq, Jabal** *mts* Saudi Arabia
78 A2 **Tuwwal** Saudi Arabia
144 B2 **Tuxpan** Nayarit Mex.
145 C2 **Tuxpan** Veracruz Mex.
145 C3 **Tuxtla Gutiérrez** Mex.
62 B1 **Tuyên Quang** Vietnam
63 B2 **Tuy Hoa** Vietnam

Tuz, Lake

80 B2 **Tuz, Lake** salt l. Turkey
    Tuz Gölü salt l. Turkey see **Tuz, Lake**
81 C2 **Tuz Khurmātū** Iraq
109 C2 **Tuzla** Bos.-Herz.
91 E2 **Tuzlov** r. Rus. Fed.
89 E2 **Tver'** Rus. Fed.
98 B1 **Tweed** r. U.K.
122 A2 **Twee Rivier** Namibia
135 C4 **Twentynine Palms** U.S.A.
131 E2 **Twillingate** Can.
134 D2 **Twin Falls** U.S.A.
137 E1 **Two Harbors** U.S.A.
129 C2 **Two Hills** Can.
139 D2 **Tyler** U.S.A.
83 J3 **Tynda** Rus. Fed.
93 F3 **Tynset** Norway
80 B2 **Tyre** Lebanon
111 B3 **Tyrnavos** Greece
52 B3 **Tyrrell, Lake** dry lake Austr.
108 B2 **Tyrrhenian Sea** France/Italy
87 E3 **Tyul'gan** Rus. Fed.
86 F3 **Tyumen'** Rus. Fed.
83 J2 **Tyung** r. Rus. Fed.
99 A3 **Tywi** r. U.K.
123 D1 **Tzaneen** S. Africa

U

120 B2 **Uamanda** Angola
150 B2 **Uaupés** Brazil
155 D2 **Ubá** Brazil
155 D1 **Ubaí** Brazil
151 E3 **Ubaitaba** Brazil
118 B3 **Ubangi** r. C.A.R./Dem. Rep. Congo
64 B4 **Ube** Japan
106 C2 **Úbeda** Spain
154 C1 **Uberaba** Brazil
154 C1 **Uberlândia** Brazil
106 B1 **Ubiña, Peña** mt. Spain
123 D2 **Ubombo** S. Africa
82 B2 **Ubon Ratchathani** Thai.
119 C3 **Ubundu** Dem. Rep. Congo
150 A2 **Ucayali** r. Peru
74 B2 **Uch** Pak.
66 D2 **Uchiura-wan** b. Japan
83 J3 **Uchur** r. Rus. Fed.
128 B3 **Ucluelet** Can.
74 B2 **Udaipur** India
91 C1 **Uday** r. Ukr.
93 F4 **Uddevalla** Sweden
92 G2 **Uddjaure** l. Sweden
100 B2 **Uden** Neth.
74 B1 **Udhampur** India
108 B1 **Udine** Italy
89 E2 **Udomlya** Rus. Fed.
82 B2 **Udon Thani** Thai.
73 B3 **Udupi** India
83 K3 **Udyl', Ozero** l. Rus. Fed.
67 C3 **Ueda** Japan
58 C3 **Uekuli** Indon.
118 C2 **Uele** r. Dem. Rep. Congo
101 E1 **Uelzen** Ger.
119 C2 **Uere** r. Dem. Rep. Congo
87 E3 **Ufa** Rus. Fed.
119 D3 **Ugalla** r. Tanz.
119 D2 **Uganda** country Africa
89 E2 **Uglich** Rus. Fed.
89 D2 **Uglovka** Rus. Fed.
89 D3 **Ugra** Rus. Fed.
103 D2 **Uherské Hradiště** Czech Rep.
101 E2 **Uichteritz** Ger.
96 A2 **Uig** U.K.

120 A1 **Uíge** Angola
65 B2 **Üijŏngbu** S. Korea
135 D2 **Uinta Mountains** U.S.A.
120 A3 **Uis Mine** Namibia
65 B2 **Üisŏng** S. Korea
123 C3 **Uitenhage** S. Africa
100 C1 **Uithuizen** Neth.
74 B2 **Ujjain** India
89 F3 **Ukholovo** Rus. Fed.
62 A1 **Ukhrul** India
86 E2 **Ukhta** Rus. Fed.
135 B3 **Ukiah** U.S.A.
127 H2 **Ukkusissat** Greenland
88 B2 **Ukmergė** Lith.
90 C2 **Ukraine** country Europe
68 C1 **Ulaangom** Mongolia
69 D1 **Ulan Bator** Mongolia
    Ulaanbaatar Mongolia see **Ulan Bator**
    Ulan Bator Mongolia
    Ulanhad China see **Chifeng**
69 E1 **Ulanhot** China
87 D4 **Ulan-Khol** Rus. Fed.
70 B1 **Ulan Qab** Nei Mongol China
69 D1 **Ulan-Ude** Rus. Fed.
75 D1 **Ulan Ul Hu** l. China
65 B2 **Ulchin** S. Korea
    Uleåborg Fin. see **Oulu**
88 C2 **Ülenurme** Estonia
69 D1 **Uliastai** China
68 C1 **Uliastay** Mongolia
59 D2 **Ulithi** atoll Micronesia
53 D3 **Ulladulla** Austr.
96 B2 **Ullapool** U.K.
98 B1 **Ullswater** l. U.K.
65 C2 **Ullŭng-do** i. S. Korea
102 B2 **Ulm** Ger.
65 B2 **Ulsan** S. Korea
96 □ **Ulsta** U.K.
97 C1 **Ulster** reg. Ireland/U.K.
52 B3 **Ultima** Austr.
111 C3 **Ulubey** Turkey
111 C2 **Uludağ** mt. Turkey
126 D2 **Ulukhaktok** Can.
123 D2 **Ulundi** S. Africa
77 E2 **Ulungur Hu** l. China
50 C2 **Uluru** h. Austr.
98 B1 **Ulverston** U.K.
87 D3 **Ul'yanovsk** Rus. Fed.
136 C3 **Ulysses** U.S.A.
90 C2 **Uman'** Ukr.
86 C2 **Umba** Rus. Fed.
59 D3 **Umboi** i. P.N.G.
92 H3 **Umeå** Sweden
92 H3 **Umeälven** r. Sweden
127 I2 **Umiiviip Kangertiva** inlet Greenland
126 D2 **Umingmaktok** (abandoned) Can.
123 D2 **Umlazi** S. Africa
117 A3 **Umm Keddada** Sudan
78 A2 **Umm Lajj** Saudi Arabia
117 B3 **Umm Ruwaba** Sudan
115 E1 **Umm Sa'ad** Libya
134 B2 **Umpqua** r. U.S.A.
120 A2 **Umpulo** Angola
154 B2 **Umuarama** Brazil
109 C1 **Una** r. Bos.-Herz./Croatia
155 E1 **Una** Brazil
154 C1 **Unaí** Brazil
78 B2 **'Unayzah** Saudi Arabia
136 C1 **Underwood** U.S.A.
89 D3 **Unecha** Rus. Fed.
53 C2 **Ungarie** Austr.
52 A2 **Ungarra** Austr.
127 G2 **Ungava, Péninsule d'** pen. Can.
127 G3 **Ungava Bay** Can.

90 B2 **Ungheni** Moldova
    Unguja i. Tanz. see **Zanzibar Island**
154 B3 **União da Vitória** Brazil
150 B2 **Unini** r. Brazil
142 C1 **Union City** U.S.A.
122 B3 **Uniondale** S. Africa
141 D3 **Uniontown** U.S.A.
79 C2 **United Arab Emirates** country Asia
95 C3 **United Kingdom** country Europe
132 D3 **United States of America** country N. America
129 D2 **Unity** Can.
96 □ **Unst** i. U.K.
101 E2 **Unstrut** r. Ger.
89 E3 **Upa** r. Rus. Fed.
119 C3 **Upemba, Lac** l. Dem. Rep. Congo
122 B2 **Upington** S. Africa
134 B2 **Upper Alkali Lake** U.S.A.
128 C2 **Upper Arrow Lake** Can.
134 B2 **Upper Klamath Lake** U.S.A.
128 B1 **Upper Liard** Can.
97 C1 **Upper Lough Erne** l. U.K.
93 G4 **Uppsala** Sweden
78 B2 **'Uqlat aş Şuqūr** Saudi Arabia
    Urad Qianqi China see **Xishanzui**
76 B2 **Ural** r. Kazakh./Rus. Fed.
53 D2 **Uralla** Austr.
87 E3 **Ural Mountains** Rus. Fed.
76 B1 **Ural'sk** Kazakh.
    Ural'skiy Khrebet mts Rus. Fed. see **Ural Mountains**
119 D3 **Urambo** Tanz.
53 C3 **Urana** Austr.
129 D2 **Uranium City** Can.
86 F2 **Uray** Rus. Fed.
98 C1 **Ure** r. U.K.
86 D3 **Uren'** Rus. Fed.
144 A2 **Ures** Mex.
76 C2 **Urganch** Uzbek.
100 B1 **Urk** Neth.
111 C3 **Urla** Turkey
81 C2 **Urmia, Lake** salt l. Iran
    Uroševac Kosovo see **Ferizaj**
144 B2 **Uruáchic** Mex.
151 D3 **Uruaçu** Brazil
144 B3 **Uruapan** Mex.
150 A3 **Urubamba** r. Peru
151 C2 **Urucara** Brazil
151 D2 **Uruçuí** Brazil
151 C2 **Urucurituba** Brazil
152 C3 **Uruguaiana** Brazil
153 C4 **Uruguay** country S. America
    Urumchi China see **Ürümqi**
68 B2 **Ürümqi** China
53 D2 **Urunga** Austr.
110 C2 **Urziceni** Romania
67 B4 **Usa** Japan
82 E2 **Usa** r. Rus. Fed.
111 C3 **Uşak** Turkey
82 G1 **Ushakova, Ostrov** i. Rus. Fed.
77 E2 **Usharal** Kazakh.
77 D2 **Ushtobe** Kazakh.
153 B6 **Ushuaia** Arg.
86 E2 **Usinsk** Rus. Fed.
88 C3 **Uskhodni** Belarus
89 E3 **Usman'** Rus. Fed.
86 D2 **Usogorsk** Rus. Fed.
104 C2 **Ussel** France
66 B2 **Ussuriysk** Rus. Fed.
108 B3 **Ustica, Isola di** i. Sicilia Italy
83 H3 **Ust'-Ilimsk** Rus. Fed.
86 E2 **Ust'-Ilych** Rus. Fed.

103 D1 Ustka Pol.
83 L3 Ust'-Kamchatsk Rus. Fed.
77 C2 Ust'-Kamenogorsk Kazakh.
86 F2 Ust'-Kara Rus. Fed.
86 E2 Ust'-Kulom Rus. Fed.
83 I3 Ust'-Kut Rus. Fed.
91 D2 Ust'-Labinsk Rus. Fed.
88 C2 Ust'-Luga Rus. Fed.
86 E2 Ust'-Nem Rus. Fed.
83 K2 Ust'-Nera Rus. Fed.
83 K2 Ust'-Omchug Rus. Fed.
83 H3 Ust'-Ordynskiy Rus. Fed.
86 E2 Ust'-Tsil'ma Rus. Fed.
86 D2 Ust'-Ura Rus. Fed.
76 B2 Ustyurt Plateau Kazakh./
 Uzbek.
89 E2 Ustyuzhna Rus. Fed.
89 D2 Usvyaty Rus. Fed.
135 D3 Utah state U.S.A.
135 D2 Utah Lake U.S.A.
93 I4 Utena Lith.
123 D2 uThukela r. S. Africa
141 D2 Utica U.S.A.
107 C2 Utiel Spain
128 C2 Utikuma Lake Can.
100 B1 Utrecht Neth.
106 B2 Utrera Spain
92 I2 Utsjoki Fin.
67 C3 Utsunomiya Japan
87 D4 Utta Rus. Fed.
62 B2 Uttaradit Thai.
 Uummannaq Greenland see
 Dundas
127 H2 Uummannaq Fjord inlet
 Greenland
93 H3 Uusikaupunki Fin.
139 D3 Uvalde U.S.A.
119 D3 Uvinza Tanz.
68 C1 Uvs Nuur salt l. Mongolia
67 B4 Uwajima Japan
78 A2 'Uwayriḍ, Ḥarrat al lava field
 Saudi Arabia
116 A2 Uweinat, Jebel mt. Sudan
83 H3 Uyar Rus. Fed.
115 C4 Uyo Nigeria
152 B3 Uyuni, Salar de salt flat Bol.
76 C2 Uzbekistan country Asia
104 C2 Uzerche France
105 C3 Uzès France
90 C1 Uzh r. Ukr.
90 A2 Uzhhorod Ukr.
109 C2 Užice Serbia
89 E3 Uzlovaya Rus. Fed.
111 C3 Üzümlü Turkey
111 C2 Uzunköprü Turkey

V

123 B2 Vaal r. S. Africa
123 C2 Vaal Dam S. Africa
123 C1 Vaalwater S. Africa
92 H3 Vaasa Fin.
103 D2 Vác Hungary
152 C3 Vacaria Brazil
154 B2 Vacaria, Serra hills Brazil
135 B3 Vacaville U.S.A.
74 B2 Vadodara India
92 I1 Vadsø Norway
105 D2 Vaduz Liechtenstein
94 B1 Vágar i. Faroe Is
94 B1 Vágur Faroe Is
103 D2 Vah r. Slovakia
49 F3 Vaiaku Tuvalu
88 B2 Vaida Estonia
136 B3 Vail U.S.A.

79 C2 Vakīlābād Iran
108 B1 Valdagno Italy
89 D2 Valday Rus. Fed.
89 D2 Valdayskaya Vozvyshennost'
 hills Rus. Fed.
106 B2 Valdecañas, Embalse de resr
 Spain
93 G4 Valdemarsvik Sweden
106 C2 Valdepeñas Spain
153 B5 Valdés, Península pen. Arg.
153 A4 Valdivia Chile
130 C2 Val-d'Or Can.
143 D2 Valdosta U.S.A.
128 C2 Valemount Can.
105 C3 Valence France
107 C2 Valencia Spain
150 B1 Valencia Venez.
107 D2 Valencia, Golfo de g. Spain
100 A2 Valenciennes France
136 C2 Valentine U.S.A.
64 B1 Valenzuela Phil.
150 A1 Valera Venez.
109 C2 Valjevo Serbia
88 C2 Valka Latvia
93 H3 Valkeakoski Fin.
100 B2 Valkenswaard Neth.
91 D2 Valky Ukr.
55 D2 Valkyrie Dome Antarctica
145 D2 Valladolid Mex.
106 C1 Valladolid Spain
93 E4 Valle Norway
145 C2 Vallecillos Mex.
150 B1 Valle de la Pascua Venez.
150 A1 Valledupar Col.
144 B2 Valle Hermoso Mex.
135 B3 Vallejo U.S.A.
152 A3 Vallenar Chile
85 H1 Valletta Malta
137 D1 Valley City U.S.A.
134 B2 Valley Falls U.S.A.
127 C2 Valleyview Can.
107 D1 Valls Spain
129 D3 Val Marie Can.
88 C2 Valmiera Latvia
88 C3 Valozhyn Belarus
154 B2 Valparaíso Brazil
153 A4 Valparaíso Chile
105 C3 Valréas France
59 D3 Vals, Tanjung c. Indon.
74 B2 Valsad India
122 B2 Valspan S. Africa
91 D1 Valuyki Rus. Fed.
106 B2 Valverde del Camino Spain
81 C2 Van Turkey
81 C2 Van, Lake salt l. Turkey
141 F1 Van Buren U.S.A.
128 B3 Vancouver Can.
134 B1 Vancouver U.S.A.
128 B3 Vancouver Island Can.
140 B3 Vandalia U.S.A.
123 C2 Vanderbijlpark S. Africa
128 B2 Vanderhoof Can.
88 C2 Vändra Estonia
93 F4 Vänern l. Sweden
93 F4 Vänersborg Sweden
121 □D3 Vangaindrano Madag.
 Van Gölü salt l. Turkey see
 Van, Lake
138 C2 Van Horn U.S.A.
59 D3 Vanimo P.N.G.
83 K3 Vanino Rus. Fed.
104 B2 Vannes France
59 D3 Van Rees, Pegunungan mts
 Indon.
122 A3 Vanrhynsdorp S. Africa
93 H3 Vantaa Fin.
49 F4 Vanua Levu i. Fiji

48 E3 Vanuatu country S. Pacific
 Ocean
140 C2 Van Wert U.S.A.
122 B3 Van Wyksvlei S. Africa
122 B2 Van Zylsrus S. Africa
75 C2 Varanasi India
92 I1 Varangerfjorden sea chan.
 Norway
92 I1 Varangerhalvøya pen. Norway
109 C1 Varaždin Croatia
93 F4 Varberg Sweden
109 D2 Vardar r. Macedonia
93 E4 Varde Denmark
92 J1 Vardø Norway
100 B1 Varel Ger.
88 B3 Varėna Lith.
108 A1 Varese Italy
155 C2 Varginha Brazil
93 I3 Varkaus Fin.
110 C2 Varna Bulg.
93 F4 Värnamo Sweden
155 D1 Várzea da Palma Brazil
86 C2 Varzino Rus. Fed.
 Vasa Fin. see Vaasa
88 C2 Vasknarva Estonia
110 C1 Vaslui Romania
93 G4 Västerås Sweden
93 G3 Västerdalälven r. Sweden
88 A2 Västerhaninge Sweden
93 G4 Västervik Sweden
108 B2 Vasto Italy
90 C1 Vasyl'kiv Ukr.
104 C2 Vatan France
108 B2 Vatican City Europe
92 □B3 Vatnajökull Iceland
110 C1 Vatra Dornei Romania
93 F4 Vättern l. Sweden
138 B2 Vaughn U.S.A.
105 C3 Vauvert France
49 G4 Vava'u Group is Tonga
83 F3 Vawkavysk Belarus
93 F4 Växjö Sweden
86 E1 Vaygach, Ostrov i. Rus. Fed.
101 D1 Vechta Ger.
110 C2 Vedea r. Romania
100 C1 Veendam Neth.
100 B1 Veenendaal Neth.
129 C2 Vegreville Can.
106 B2 Vejer de la Frontera Spain
93 E4 Vejle Denmark
109 D2 Velbŭzhdki Prokhod pass
 Bulg./Macedonia
100 B2 Veldhoven Neth.
109 B2 Velebit mts Croatia
100 C2 Velen Ger.
109 C1 Velenje Slovenia
109 D2 Veles Macedonia
106 C2 Vélez-Málaga Spain
155 D1 Velhas r. Brazil
109 D2 Velika Plana Serbia
88 C2 Velikaya r. Rus. Fed.
89 D2 Velikiye Luki Rus. Fed.
89 D2 Velikiy Novgorod Rus. Fed.
86 D2 Velikiy Ustyug Rus. Fed.
110 C2 Veliko Tŭrnovo Bulg.
108 B2 Veli Lošinj Croatia
89 D2 Velizh Rus. Fed.
86 F2 Vel'sk Rus. Fed.
101 F1 Velten Ger.
91 D1 Velykyy Burluk Ukr.
108 B2 Venafro Italy
154 C2 Venceslau Bráz Brazil
104 C2 Vendôme France
89 E3 Venev Rus. Fed.
 Venezia Italy see Venice
150 B1 Venezuela country S. America
150 A1 Venezuela, Golfo de g. Venez.

Venice

108 B1 **Venice** Italy
143 D3 **Venice** U.S.A.
108 B1 **Venice, Gulf of** Europe
100 C2 **Venlo** Neth.
100 B2 **Venray** Neth.
88 B2 **Venta** r. Latvia/Lith.
88 B2 **Venta** Lith.
123 C3 **Venterstad** S. Africa
99 C3 **Ventnor** U.K.
88 B2 **Ventspils** Latvia
135 C4 **Ventura** U.S.A.
139 C3 **Venustiano Carranza, Presa** resr Mex.
107 C2 **Vera** Spain
145 C3 **Veracruz** Mex.
74 B2 **Veraval** India
108 A1 **Verbania** Italy
108 A1 **Vercelli** Italy
105 D3 **Vercors** reg. France
92 F3 **Verdalsøra** Norway
154 B1 **Verde** r. Goiás Brazil
154 B2 **Verde** r. Mato Grosso do Sul Brazil
144 B2 **Verde** r. Mex.
138 A2 **Verde** r. Mex.
155 D1 **Verde Grande** r. Brazil
101 D1 **Verden (Aller)** Ger.
154 B1 **Verdinho, Serra do** mts Brazil
108 A2 **Verdon** r. France
105 D2 **Verdun** France
123 C2 **Vereeniging** S. Africa
106 B1 **Verín** Spain
91 D3 **Verkhnebakanskiy** Rus. Fed.
92 J2 **Verkhnetulomskiy** Rus. Fed.
91 E1 **Verkhniy Mamon** Rus. Fed.
89 E3 **Verkhov'ye** Rus. Fed.
90 A2 **Verkhovyna** Ukr.
83 J2 **Verkhoyanskiy Khrebet** mts Rus. Fed.
129 C2 **Vermilion** Can.
137 D2 **Vermillion** U.S.A.
130 A2 **Vermillion Bay** Can.
141 E2 **Vermont** state U.S.A.
135 E2 **Vernal** U.S.A.
128 C2 **Vernon** Can.
139 D2 **Vernon** U.S.A.
143 D3 **Vero Beach** U.S.A.
111 B2 **Veroia** Greece
108 B1 **Verona** Italy
104 C2 **Versailles** France
104 B2 **Vertou** France
123 D2 **Verulam** S. Africa
100 B2 **Verviers** Belgium
105 C2 **Vervins** France
105 D3 **Vescovato** Corse France
89 E3 **Veselaya, Gora** mt. Rus. Fed.
91 C2 **Vesele** Ukr.
105 D2 **Vesoul** France
92 F2 **Vesterålen** is Norway
92 F2 **Vestfjorden** sea chan. Norway
94 B1 **Vestmanna** Faroe Is
93 E3 **Vestnes** Norway
108 B2 **Vesuvius** vol. Italy
89 E2 **Ves'yegonsk** Rus. Fed.
93 G4 **Vetlanda** Sweden
86 D3 **Vetluga** Rus. Fed.
100 A2 **Veurne** Belgium
105 D2 **Vevey** Switz.
91 D1 **Veydelevka** Rus. Fed.
80 B1 **Vezirköprü** Turkey
151 D2 **Viana** Brazil
106 B1 **Viana do Castelo** Port.
      Viangchan Laos see Vientiane
62 B1 **Viangphoukha** Laos
111 C3 **Viannos** Greece
154 C1 **Vianópolis** Brazil
108 B2 **Viareggio** Italy

93 E4 **Viborg** Denmark
109 C3 **Vibo Valentia** Italy
107 D1 **Vic** Spain
144 A1 **Vicente Guerrero** Mex.
108 B1 **Vicenza** Italy
105 C2 **Vichy** France
142 B2 **Vicksburg** U.S.A.
155 D2 **Viçosa** Brazil
52 A3 **Victor Harbor** Austr.
50 C1 **Victoria** r. Austr.
52 B3 **Victoria** state Austr.
128 B3 **Victoria** Can.
153 A4 **Victoria** Chile
113 K7 **Victoria** Seychelles
139 D3 **Victoria, Lake** Africa
119 D3 **Victoria, Lake** Africa
52 B2 **Victoria, Lake** Austr.
62 A1 **Victoria, Mount** Myanmar
59 D3 **Victoria, Mount** P.N.G.
120 B2 **Victoria Falls** Zambia/ Zimbabwe
126 D2 **Victoria Island** Can.
50 C1 **Victoria River Downs** Austr.
122 B3 **Victoria West** S. Africa
135 C4 **Victorville** U.S.A.
110 C2 **Videle** Romania
92 □A2 **Víðidalsá** Iceland
153 B5 **Viedma** Arg.
153 A5 **Viedma, Lago** l. Arg.
100 B2 **Vielsalm** Belgium
101 E2 **Vienenburg** Ger.
103 D2 **Vienna** Austria
105 C2 **Vienne** France
104 C2 **Vienne** r. France
62 B2 **Vientiane** Laos
100 C2 **Viersen** Ger.
104 C2 **Vierzon** France
144 B2 **Viesca** Mex.
109 C2 **Vieste** Italy
62 B2 **Vietnam** country Asia
62 B1 **Việt Tri** Vietnam
64 B1 **Vigan** Phil.
108 A1 **Vigevano** Italy
106 B1 **Vigo** Spain
73 C3 **Vijayawada** India
92 □B3 **Vík** Iceland
129 C2 **Viking** Can.
106 B2 **Vila Franca de Xira** Port.
106 B1 **Vilagarcía de Arousa** Spain
106 B1 **Vilalba** Spain
106 B1 **Vila Nova de Gaia** Port.
107 D1 **Vilanova i la Geltrú** Spain
106 B1 **Vila Real** Port.
106 B1 **Vilar Formoso** Port.
155 D2 **Vila Velha** Brazil
150 A3 **Vilcabamba, Cordillera** mts Peru
92 G3 **Vilhelmina** Sweden
150 B3 **Vilhena** Brazil
88 C2 **Viljandi** Estonia
88 B3 **Vilkaviškis** Lith.
83 H1 **Vil'kitskogo, Proliv** str. Rus. Fed.
144 B1 **Villa Ahumada** Mex.
106 B1 **Villablino** Spain
102 C2 **Villach** Austria
144 B2 **Villa de Cos** Mex.
152 B4 **Villa Dolores** Arg.
145 C3 **Villa Flores** Mex.
145 C2 **Villagrán** Mex.
145 C3 **Villahermosa** Mex.
144 A2 **Villa Insurgentes** Mex.
152 B4 **Villa María** Arg.
152 B3 **Villa Montes** Bol.
144 B2 **Villanueva** Mex.
106 B2 **Villanueva de la Serena** Spain

106 C2 **Villanueva de los Infantes** Spain
152 C3 **Villa Ocampo** Arg.
108 A3 **Villaputzu** Sardegna Italy
152 C3 **Villarrica** Para.
106 C2 **Villarrobledo** Spain
152 B3 **Villa Unión** Arg.
144 B2 **Villa Unión** Durango Mex.
144 B2 **Villa Unión** Sinaloa Mex.
150 A1 **Villavicencio** Col.
152 B3 **Villazon** Bol.
107 C2 **Villena** Spain
104 C3 **Villeneuve-sur-Lot** France
142 B2 **Ville Platte** U.S.A.
105 C2 **Villeurbanne** France
102 B2 **Villingen** Ger.
88 C3 **Vilnius** Lith.
91 C2 **Vil'nohirs'k** Ukr.
91 D2 **Vil'nyans'k** Ukr.
100 B2 **Vilvoorde** Belgium
88 C3 **Vilyeyka** Belarus
83 J2 **Vilyuy** r. Rus. Fed.
93 G4 **Vimmerby** Sweden
153 A4 **Viña del Mar** Chile
107 D1 **Vinarós** Spain
140 B3 **Vincennes** U.S.A.
55 G3 **Vincennes Bay** Antarctica
141 D3 **Vineland** U.S.A.
62 B2 **Vinh** Vietnam
63 B2 **Vinh Long** Vietnam
139 D1 **Vinita** U.S.A.
90 B2 **Vinnytsya** Ukr.
55 O2 **Vinson Massif** mt. Antarctica
93 E3 **Vinstra** Norway
108 B1 **Vipiteno** Italy
64 B1 **Virac** Phil.
129 D3 **Virden** Can.
104 B2 **Vire** France
120 A2 **Virei** Angola
155 D1 **Virgem da Lapa** Brazil
138 A1 **Virgin** r. U.S.A.
123 C2 **Virginia** S. Africa
137 E1 **Virginia** U.S.A.
141 D3 **Virginia** state U.S.A.
141 D3 **Virginia Beach** U.S.A.
135 C3 **Virginia City** U.S.A.
147 D3 **Virgin Islands (U.K.)** terr. West Indies
147 D3 **Virgin Islands (U.S.A.)** terr. West Indies
63 B2 **Virôchey** Cambodia
109 C1 **Virovitica** Croatia
100 B3 **Virton** Belgium
88 B2 **Virtsu** Estonia
109 C2 **Vis** i. Croatia
88 C2 **Visaginas** Lith.
135 C3 **Visalia** U.S.A.
74 B2 **Visavadar** India
64 B1 **Visayan Sea** Phil.
93 G4 **Visby** Sweden
126 D2 **Viscount Melville Sound** sea chan. Can.
151 D2 **Viseu** Brazil
106 B1 **Viseu** Port.
73 C3 **Vishakhapatnam** India
88 C2 **Viški** Latvia
109 C2 **Visoko** Bos.-Herz.
103 D1 **Vistula** r. Pol.
108 B2 **Viterbo** Italy
49 F4 **Viti Levu** i. Fiji
83 I3 **Vitim** r. Rus. Fed.
155 D2 **Vitória** Brazil
151 D3 **Vitória da Conquista** Brazil
106 C1 **Vitoria-Gasteiz** Spain
104 B2 **Vitré** France
105 C2 **Vitry-le-François** France
89 D2 **Vitsyebsk** Belarus

105 D2 Vittel France
108 B3 Vittoria *Sicilia* Italy
108 B1 Vittorio Veneto Italy
106 B1 Viveiro Spain
144 A2 Vizcaíno, Sierra *mts* Mex.
110 C2 Vize Turkey
73 C3 Vizianagaram India
100 B2 Vlaardingen Neth.
87 D4 Vladikavkaz Rus. Fed.
89 F2 Vladimir Rus. Fed.
66 B2 Vladivostok Rus. Fed.
109 D2 Vlasotince Serbia
100 B1 Vlieland *i.* Neth.
100 A2 Vlissingen Neth.
109 C3 Vlorë Albania
100 C2 Vöcklabruck Austria
101 D2 Vogelsberg *hills* Ger.
119 D3 Voi Kenya
105 D2 Voiron France
131 D1 Voisey's Bay Can.
109 C1 Vojvodina *prov.* Serbia
92 J3 Voknavolok Rus. Fed.
          Volcano Bay Japan *see*
          Uchiura-wan
89 E2 Volga Rus. Fed.
89 F2 Volga *r.* Rus. Fed.
87 D4 Volgodonsk Rus. Fed.
87 D4 Volgograd Rus. Fed.
89 D2 Volkhov Rus. Fed.
89 D1 Volkhov *r.* Rus. Fed.
101 E2 Volkstedt Ger.
91 D2 Volnovakha Ukr.
90 B2 Volochys'k Ukr.
91 D2 Volodars'ke Ukr.
90 B1 Volodars'k-Volyns'kyy Ukr.
90 B1 Volodymyrets' Ukr.
90 A1 Volodymyr-Volyns'kyy Ukr.
89 E2 Vologda Rus. Fed.
89 E2 Volokolamsk Rus. Fed.
89 D1 Volokonovka Rus. Fed.
111 B3 Volos Greece
88 C2 Volosovo Rus. Fed.
89 D2 Volot Rus. Fed.
89 F2 Volovo Rus. Fed.
87 D3 Vol'sk Rus. Fed.
114 C4 Volta, Lake *resr* Ghana
155 D4 Volta Redonda Brazil
87 D4 Volzhskiy Rus. Fed.
92 □C2 Vopnafjörður Iceland
88 C3 Voranava Belarus
86 F2 Vorkuta Rus. Fed.
88 B2 Vormsi *i.* Estonia
89 E3 Voronezh Rus. Fed.
89 E3 Voronezh *r.* Rus. Fed.
91 E1 Vorontsovka Rus. Fed.
91 C2 Vorskla *r.* Rus. Fed.
88 C2 Võrtsjärv *l.* Estonia
88 C2 Võru Estonia
122 B3 Vosburg S. Africa
105 D2 Vosges *mts* France
89 F2 Voskresensk Rus. Fed.
93 E3 Voss Norway
81 H3 Vostochnyy Sayan *mts* Rus. Fed.
86 E3 Votkinsk Rus. Fed.
154 C2 Votuporanga Brazil
100 B3 Vouziers France
92 J2 Voynitsa Rus. Fed.
91 C2 Voznesens'k Ukr.
93 E4 Vrådal Norway
66 B2 Vrangel' Rus. Fed.
          Vrangelya, Ostrov *i.* Rus. Fed.
          see Wrangel Island
109 D2 Vranje Serbia
110 C2 Vratnik *pass* Bulg.
110 B3 Vratsa Bulg.
109 C1 Vrbas *r.* Bos.-Herz.
109 C1 Vrbas Serbia

122 A3 Vredenburg S. Africa
122 A3 Vredendal S. Africa
100 B3 Vresse Belgium
109 D1 Vršac Serbia
122 B3 Vryburg S. Africa
123 D2 Vryheid S. Africa
89 D1 Vsevolozhsk Rus. Fed.
          Vučitrn Kosovo *see* Vushtrri
109 C1 Vukovar Croatia
86 E2 Vuktyl Rus. Fed.
123 C2 Vukuzakhe S. Africa
109 B3 Vulcano, Isola *i.* Italy
63 B2 Vung Tau Vietnam
109 D2 Vushtrri Kosovo
74 B2 Vyara India
          Vyatka Rus. Fed. *see* Kirov
89 D2 Vyaz'ma Rus. Fed.
93 I3 Vyborg Rus. Fed.
88 C2 Vyerkhnyadzvinsk Belarus
87 D3 Vyksa Rus. Fed.
90 B2 Vylkove Ukr.
90 A2 Vynohradiv Ukr.
89 D2 Vypolzovo Rus. Fed.
89 D2 Vyritsa Rus. Fed.
91 D2 Vyselki Rus. Fed.
90 C1 Vyshhorod Ukr.
89 D2 Vyshniy-Volochek Rus. Fed.
103 D2 Vyškov Czech Rep.
86 C2 Vytegra Rus. Fed.

W

114 B3 Wa Ghana
100 B2 Waal *r.* Neth.
100 B2 Waalwijk Neth.
128 C2 Wabasca *r.* Can.
128 C2 Wabasca-Desmarais Can.
140 B3 Wabash *r.* U.S.A.
117 C4 Wabē Gestro Wenz *r.* Eth.
129 E2 Wabowden Can.
143 D2 Waccasassa Bay U.S.A.
101 D2 Wächtersbach Ger.
139 D2 Waco U.S.A.
115 D2 Waddān Libya
          Waddeneilanden *is* Neth. *see*
          West Frisian Islands
100 B1 Waddenzee *sea chan.* Neth.
128 B2 Waddington, Mount Can.
100 B1 Waddinxveen Neth.
129 D2 Wadena Can.
137 D1 Wadena U.S.A.
74 A2 Wadh Pak.
116 B2 Wadi Halfa Sudan
116 B3 Wad Medani Sudan
70 C2 Wafangdian China
100 B2 Wageningen Neth.
127 F2 Wager Bay Can.
53 C2 Wagga Wagga Austr.
137 D2 Wahoo U.S.A.
137 D1 Wahpeton U.S.A.
54 B2 Waiau *r.* N.Z.
59 C3 Waigeo *i.* Indon.
58 B3 Waikabubak Indon.
52 A2 Waikerie Austr.
54 B2 Waimate N.Z.
75 B3 Wainganga *r.* India
58 C3 Waingapu Indon.
129 C2 Wainwright Can.
54 C1 Waiouru N.Z.
54 B2 Waipara N.Z.
54 C1 Waipawa N.Z.
54 B2 Wairau *r.* N.Z.
54 C1 Wairoa N.Z.
54 B2 Waitaki *r.* N.Z.
54 B1 Waitara N.Z.

54 B1 Waiuku N.Z.
119 E2 Wajir Kenya
67 C3 Wakasa-wan *b.* Japan
54 A3 Wakatipu, Lake N.Z.
129 D2 Wakaw Can.
67 C4 Wakayama Japan
136 D3 WaKeeney U.S.A.
54 B2 Wakefield N.Z.
98 C2 Wakefield U.K.
48 F1 Wake Island N. Pacific Ocean
66 D1 Wakkanai Japan
123 D2 Wakkerstroom S. Africa
103 D1 Wałbrzych Pol.
53 D2 Walcha Austr.
100 C1 Walchum Ger.
103 D1 Wałcz Pol.
99 B2 Wales *admin. div.* U.K.
51 C3 Walgett Austr.
119 C3 Walikale Dem. Rep. Congo
135 C3 Walker Lake U.S.A.
52 A2 Wallaroo Austr.
98 B2 Wallasey U.K.
134 C1 Walla Walla U.S.A.
101 D3 Walldürn Ger.
53 C2 Wallendbeen Austr.
49 G3 Wallis and Futuna Islands
          terr. S. Pacific Ocean
96 □ Walls U.K.
98 B1 Walney, Isle of *i.* U.K.
99 C2 Walsall U.K.
136 C3 Walsenburg U.S.A.
101 D1 Walsrode Ger.
143 D2 Walterboro U.S.A.
120 A3 Walvis Bay Namibia
119 C2 Wamba Dem. Rep. Congo
52 B1 Wanaaring Austr.
54 A2 Wanaka N.Z.
54 A2 Wanaka, Lake N.Z.
54 B2 Wanapitei Lake Can.
154 B3 Wanda Arg.
66 B1 Wanda Shan *mts* China
62 A1 Wanding China
54 C1 Wanganui N.Z.
53 C3 Wangaratta Austr.
65 B1 Wangqing China
62 A1 Wan Hsa-la Myanmar
71 B4 Wanning China
99 C3 Wantage U.K.
70 A2 Wanyuan China
70 A2 Wanzhou China
73 B3 Warangal India
101 D2 Warburg Ger.
50 B2 Warburton Austr.
52 A1 Warburton *watercourse* Austr.
75 B2 Wardha India
96 C1 Ward Hill U.K.
128 B2 Ware Can.
101 F1 Waren Ger.
100 C1 Warendorf Ger.
53 D1 Warialda Austr.
122 A2 Warmbad Namibia
135 C3 Warm Springs U.S.A.
134 C2 Warner Lakes U.S.A.
143 D2 Warner Robins U.S.A.
152 B2 Warnes Bol.
52 B3 Warracknabeal Austr.
53 C2 Warrego *r.* Austr.
53 C2 Warren Austr.
142 B2 Warren AR U.S.A.
140 C2 Warren OH U.S.A.
141 D2 Warren PA U.S.A.
97 C1 Warrenpoint U.K.
137 E3 Warrensburg U.S.A.
122 B2 Warrenton S. Africa
115 C4 Warri Nigeria
98 B2 Warrington U.K.

52 B3 Warrnambool Austr.
103 E1 Warsaw Pol.
        Warszawa Pol. see Warsaw
103 C1 Warta r. Pol.
53 D1 Warwick Austr.
99 C2 Warwick U.K.
135 C3 Wasco U.S.A.
136 C1 Washburn U.S.A.
141 D3 Washington DC U.S.A.
137 E2 Washington IA U.S.A.
140 B3 Washington IN U.S.A.
137 E3 Washington MO U.S.A.
143 E1 Washington NC U.S.A.
140 C2 Washington PA U.S.A.
134 B1 Washington state U.S.A.
141 E2 Washington, Mount U.S.A.
140 C3 Washington Court House
        U.S.A.
74 A2 Washuk Pak.
130 C1 Waskaganish Can.
129 E2 Waskaiowaka Lake Can.
122 A2 Wasser Namibia
130 C2 Waswanipi, Lac l. Can.
58 C3 Watampone Indon.
141 E2 Waterbury U.S.A.
130 D2 Waterbury Lake Can.
97 C2 Waterford Ireland
97 C2 Waterford Harbour Ireland
137 E2 Waterloo U.S.A.
123 C1 Waterpoort S. Africa
141 D2 Watertown NY U.S.A.
137 D2 Watertown SD U.S.A.
140 B2 Watertown WI U.S.A.
141 F2 Waterville U.S.A.
99 C3 Watford U.K.
136 C1 Watford City U.S.A.
129 D2 Wathaman r. Can.
139 D1 Watonga U.S.A.
129 D2 Watrous Can.
119 C2 Watsa Dem. Rep. Congo
140 B2 Watseka U.S.A.
118 C3 Watsi Kengo Dem. Rep.
        Congo
128 B1 Watson Lake Can.
135 B3 Watsonville U.S.A.
59 C3 Watubela, Kepulauan is Indon.
59 D3 Wau P.N.G.
117 A4 Wau S. Sudan
53 D2 Wauchope Austr.
140 B2 Waukegan U.S.A.
139 D2 Waurika U.S.A.
140 B2 Wausau U.S.A.
99 D2 Waveney r. U.K.
137 E2 Waverly U.S.A.
143 D2 Waycross U.S.A.
138 C2 Wayne U.S.A.
143 D2 Waynesboro GA U.S.A.
141 D3 Waynesboro VA U.S.A.
143 D1 Waynesville U.S.A.
74 B1 Wazirabad Pak.
98 C1 Wear r. U.K.
139 D2 Weatherford U.S.A.
134 B2 Weaverville U.S.A.
130 B1 Webequie Can.
117 C4 Webi Shabeelle r. Somalia
137 D1 Webster U.S.A.
137 E2 Webster City U.S.A.
55 Q2 Weddell Sea Antarctica
100 B2 Weert Neth.
53 C2 Wee Waa Austr.
100 C2 Wegberg Ger.
103 E1 Wegorzewo Pol.
101 F3 Weiden in der Oberpfalz
        Ger.
70 B2 Weifang China
70 C2 Weihai China
53 C1 Weilmoringle Austr.

101 E2 Weimar Ger.
70 A2 Weinan China
51 D1 Weipa Austr.
53 C1 Weir r. Austr.
140 C2 Weirton U.S.A.
62 B1 Weishan China
101 E2 Weißenfels Ger.
102 C2 Weißkugel mt. Austria/Italy
103 D1 Wejherowo Pol.
128 C1 Wekweètì Can.
140 C3 Welch U.S.A.
117 B3 Weldiya Eth.
123 C2 Welkom S. Africa
99 C2 Welland r. U.K.
51 C1 Wellesley Islands Austr.
53 C2 Wellington Austr.
54 B2 Wellington N.Z.
122 A3 Wellington S. Africa
137 D3 Wellington U.S.A.
153 A5 Wellington, Isla i. Chile
53 C3 Wellington, Lake Austr.
128 B2 Wells Can.
99 B3 Wells U.K.
134 D2 Wells U.S.A.
50 B2 Wells, Lake imp. l. Austr.
54 B1 Wellsford N.Z.
98 D2 Wells-next-the-Sea U.K.
102 C2 Wels Austria
99 B2 Welshpool U.K.
123 C2 Wembesi S. Africa
130 C1 Wemindji Can.
134 B1 Wenatchee U.S.A.
71 B4 Wenchang China
114 B4 Wenchi Ghana
70 C2 Wendeng China
101 E1 Wendisch Evern Ger.
117 B4 Wendo Eth.
134 D2 Wendover U.S.A.
71 B3 Wengyuan China
71 A3 Wenling China
71 A3 Wenshan China
52 B2 Wentworth Austr.
71 C3 Wenzhou China
123 C2 Wepener S. Africa
122 B2 Werda Botswana
101 F2 Werdau Ger.
101 F1 Werder Ger.
101 F3 Wernberg-Köblitz Ger.
101 E2 Wernigerode Ger.
101 D2 Werra r. Ger.
53 D2 Werris Creek Austr.
101 D3 Wertheim Ger.
100 C2 Wesel Ger.
101 E1 Wesendorf Ger.
101 D1 Weser r. Ger.
101 D1 Weser sea chan. Ger.
51 C1 Wessel, Cape Austr.
51 C1 Wessel Islands Austr.
123 C2 Wesselton S. Africa
80 B2 West Bank terr. Asia
140 B2 West Bend U.S.A.
99 C2 West Bromwich U.K.
100 C1 Westerburg Ger.
100 C1 Westerholt Ger.
50 B2 Western Australia state Austr.
122 B3 Western Cape prov. S. Africa
116 A2 Western Desert Egypt
73 B3 Western Ghats mts India
114 A2 Western Sahara terr. Africa
100 A2 Westerschelde est. Neth.
100 C1 Westerstede Ger.
100 C2 Westerwald hills Ger.
153 B6 West Falkland i. Falkland Is
140 B3 West Frankfort U.S.A.
100 B1 West Frisian Islands is Neth.
147 D2 West Indies is Caribbean Sea
96 A1 West Loch Roag b. U.K.

128 C2 Westlock Can.
100 B2 Westmalle Belgium
142 B1 West Memphis U.S.A.
140 C3 Weston U.S.A.
99 B3 Weston-super-Mare U.K.
143 D3 West Palm Beach U.S.A.
137 E3 West Plains U.S.A.
137 D2 West Point U.S.A.
97 B2 Westport Ireland
54 B2 Westport N.Z.
96 C1 Westray i. U.K.
100 B1 West-Terschelling Neth.
140 C3 West Virginia state U.S.A.
53 C2 West Wyalong Austr.
134 D2 West Yellowstone U.S.A.
59 C3 Wetar i. Indon.
128 C2 Wetaskiwin Can.
101 D2 Wetzlar Ger.
59 C3 Wewak P.N.G.
97 C2 Wexford Ireland
129 D2 Weyakwin Can.
129 D3 Weyburn Can.
101 D1 Weyhe Ger.
99 B3 Weymouth U.K.
54 C1 Whakatane N.Z.
129 E1 Whale Cove Can.
96 □ Whalsay i. U.K.
54 C1 Whangarei N.Z.
98 C2 Wharfe r. U.K.
139 D3 Wharton U.S.A.
128 C1 Whatì Can.
136 B2 Wheatland U.S.A.
138 B1 Wheeler Peak NM U.S.A.
135 D3 Wheeler Peak NV U.S.A.
140 C2 Wheeling U.S.A.
98 B1 Whernside h. U.K.
128 B2 Whistler Can.
98 C1 Whitby U.K.
142 B2 Whitby r. U.S.A.
50 B2 White, Lake imp. l. Austr.
131 E2 White Bay Can.
52 B2 White Butte mt. U.S.A.
52 B2 White Cliffs Austr.
128 C2 Whitecourt Can.
134 D1 Whitefish U.S.A.
98 B1 Whitehaven U.K.
97 D1 Whitehead U.K.
128 A1 Whitehorse Can.
142 B3 White Lake U.S.A.
135 C3 White Mountain Peak U.S.A.
116 B3 White Nile r. Africa
86 C2 White Sea Rus. Fed.
134 D1 White Sulphur Springs U.S.A.
143 E2 Whiteville U.S.A.
114 B3 White Volta r. Burkina/Ghana
138 B2 Whitewater Baldy mt.
        U.S.A.
130 B1 Whitewater Lake Can.
129 D2 Whitewood Can.
96 B3 Whithorn U.K.
54 C1 Whitianga N.Z.
135 C3 Whitney, Mount U.S.A.
51 D2 Whitsunday Island Austr.
52 A2 Whyalla Austr.
100 A2 Wichelen Belgium
137 D3 Wichita U.S.A.
139 D2 Wichita Falls U.S.A.
96 C1 Wick U.K.
138 A2 Wickenburg U.S.A.
97 C2 Wicklow Ireland
97 D2 Wicklow Head Ireland
97 C2 Wicklow Mountains Ireland
98 B2 Widnes U.K.
101 D1 Wiehengebirge hills Ger.
100 C2 Wiehl Ger.
103 D1 Wieluń Pol.

	Wien Austria *see* Vienna
103 D2	Wiener Neustadt Austria
100 B1	Wieringerwerf Neth.
100 D2	Wiesbaden Ger.
100 C1	Wiesmoor Ger.
103 D1	Wieżyca *h.* Pol.
99 C3	Wight, Isle of *i.* U.K.
96 B3	Wigtown U.K.
100 B2	Wijchen Neth.
52 B2	Wilcannia Austr.
123 C3	Wild Coast S. Africa
123 C2	Wilge *r.* S. Africa
141 D2	Wilhelmshaven Ger.
55 H3	Wilkes-Barre U.S.A.
	Wilkes Land *reg.* Antarctica
129 D2	Wilkie Can.
138 B2	Willcox U.S.A.
100 B2	Willebroek Belgium
147 D3	Willemstad Curaçao
52 B3	William, Mount Austr.
52 A1	William Creek Austr.
138 A1	Williams U.S.A.
141 D3	Williamsburg U.S.A.
128 B2	Williams Lake Can.
140 C3	Williamson U.S.A.
141 D2	Williamsport U.S.A.
143 E1	Williamston U.S.A.
122 B3	Williston S. Africa
136 C1	Williston U.S.A.
128 B2	Williston Lake Can.
135 B3	Willits U.S.A.
137 D1	Willmar U.S.A.
122 B3	Willowmore S. Africa
123 C3	Willowvale S. Africa
50 B2	Wills, Lake *imp. l.* Austr.
52 A3	Willunga Austr.
52 A2	Wilmington Austr.
141 D3	Wilmington *DE* U.S.A.
143 E2	Wilmington *NC* U.S.A.
100 D2	Wilnsdorf Ger.
143 E1	Wilson U.S.A.
53 C3	Wilson's Promontory *pen.* Austr.
100 B3	Wiltz Lux.
50 B2	Wiluna Austr.
99 C3	Winchester U.K.
140 C3	Winchester *KY* U.S.A.
141 D3	Winchester *VA* U.S.A.
98 B1	Windermere *l.* U.K.
120 A3	Windhoek Namibia
137 D2	Windom U.S.A.
51 D2	Windorah Austr.
136 B2	Wind River Range *mts* U.S.A.
53 D2	Windsor Austr.
130 B2	Windsor Can.
147 D3	Windsor U.K.
	Windward Islands Caribbean Sea
147 C3	Windward Passage Cuba/Haiti
137 D3	Winfield U.S.A.
100 A2	Wingene Belgium
53 D2	Wingham Austr.
130 B1	Winisk *r.* Can.
130 B1	Winisk (abandoned) Can.
130 B1	Winisk Lake Can.
63 A1	Winkana Myanmar
129 E3	Winkler Can.
114 B4	Winneba Ghana
140 B2	Winnebago, Lake U.S.A.
134 C2	Winnemucca U.S.A.
136 C2	Winner U.S.A.
142 B2	Winnfield U.S.A.
137 E1	Winnibigoshish, Lake U.S.A.
129 E3	Winnipeg Can.
129 E2	Winnipeg *r.* Can.
129 E2	Winnipeg, Lake Can.
129 D2	Winnipegosis Can.
141 E2	Winnipesaukee, Lake U.S.A.
142 B2	Winnsboro U.S.A.
137 E2	Winona *MN* U.S.A.
142 C2	Winona *MS* U.S.A.
100 C1	Winschoten Neth.
101 D1	Winsen (Aller) Ger.
101 E1	Winsen (Luhe) Ger.
138 A1	Winslow U.S.A.
143 D1	Winston-Salem U.S.A.
101 D2	Winterberg Ger.
143 D3	Winter Haven U.S.A.
100 C2	Winterswijk Neth.
105 D2	Winterthur Switz.
51 D2	Winton Austr.
54 A3	Winton N.Z.
52 A2	Wirrabara Austr.
99 D2	Wisbech U.K.
140 A2	Wisconsin *r.* U.S.A.
140 B2	Wisconsin *state* U.S.A.
140 B2	Wisconsin Rapids U.S.A.
	Wisła *r.* Pol. *see* Vistula
101 E1	Wismar Ger.
98 D2	Withernsea U.K.
100 B1	Witmarsum Neth.
99 C3	Witney U.K.
123 D2	Witrivier S. Africa
101 F2	Wittenberg, Lutherstadt Ger.
101 E1	Wittenberge Ger.
101 E1	Wittenburg Ger.
101 E1	Wittingen Ger.
100 C3	Wittlich Ger.
100 C1	Wittmund Ger.
101 F1	Wittstock Ger.
120 A3	Witvlei Namibia
101 D2	Witzenhausen Ger.
103 D1	Władysławowo Pol.
103 D1	Włocławek Pol.
53 C3	Wodonga Austr.
59 C3	Wokam *i.* Indon.
99 C3	Woking U.K.
101 F2	Wolfen Ger.
101 E1	Wolfenbüttel Ger.
101 D2	Wolfhagen Ger.
136 B1	Wolf Point U.S.A.
101 E1	Wolfsburg Ger.
100 C3	Wolfstein Ger.
131 D2	Wolfville Can.
102 C1	Wolgast Ger.
102 C1	Wolin Pol.
129 D2	Wollaston Lake Can.
129 D2	Wollaston Lake Can.
126 D2	Wollaston Peninsula Can.
53 D2	Wollongong Austr.
101 E2	Wolmirsleben Ger.
101 E1	Wolmirstedt Ger.
100 C1	Wolvega Neth.
99 B3	Wolverhampton U.K.
65 B2	Wŏnju S. Korea
128 B2	Wonowon Can.
65 B2	Wŏnsan N. Korea
53 C3	Wonthaggi Austr.
52 A2	Woocalla Austr.
51 C1	Woodah, Isle *i.* Austr.
99 D2	Woodbridge U.K.
136 B3	Woodland Park U.S.A.
50 C2	Woodroffe, Mount Austr.
51 C1	Woods, Lake *imp. l.* Austr.
129 E3	Woods, Lake of the Can./U.S.A.
53 C3	Woods Point Austr.
131 D2	Woodstock N.B. Can.
140 C2	Woodstock *Ont.* Can.
54 C2	Woodville N.Z.
139 D1	Woodward U.S.A.
53 D2	Woolgoolga Austr.
52 A2	Woomera Austr.
140 C2	Wooster U.S.A.
99 C3	Wootton Basset, Royal U.K.
122 A3	Worcester S. Africa
99 B2	Worcester U.K.
141 E2	Worcester U.S.A.
102 C2	Wörgl Austria
98 B1	Workington U.K.
98 C2	Worksop U.K.
136 B2	Worland U.S.A.
101 D3	Worms Ger.
99 C3	Worthing U.K.
137 D2	Worthington U.S.A.
58 C3	Wotu Indon.
59 C3	Wowoni *i.* Indon.
83 N2	Wrangel Island Rus. Fed.
128 A2	Wrangell U.S.A.
96 B1	Wrath, Cape U.K.
136 C2	Wray U.S.A.
122 A2	Wreck Point S. Africa
98 B2	Wrexham U.K.
136 B2	Wright U.S.A.
63 A2	Wrightmyo India
128 B1	Wrigley Can.
103 D1	Wrocław Pol.
103 D1	Września Pol.
70 A2	Wu'an China
70 A2	Wuhai China
70 B2	Wuhan China
70 B2	Wuhu China
	Wujin China *see* Changzhou
115 C4	Wukari Nigeria
62 B1	Wuliang Shan *mts* China
59 C3	Wuliaru *i.* Indon.
71 A3	Wumeng Shan *mts* China
130 B1	Wunnummin Lake Can.
101 F2	Wunsiedel Ger.
101 D1	Wunstorf Ger.
62 A1	Wuntho Myanmar
100 C2	Wuppertal Ger.
122 A3	Wuppertal S. Africa
101 E2	Wurzbach Ger.
101 D3	Würzburg Ger.
101 F2	Wurzen Ger.
68 C2	Wuwei China
70 A2	Wuxi *Chongqing* China
70 C2	Wuxi *Jiangsu* China
	Wuxing China *see* Huzhou
71 A3	Wuxuan China
	Wuyang China *see* Zhenyuan
69 E1	Wuyiling China
71 B3	Wuyishan China
71 B3	Wuyi Shan *mts* China
70 A1	Wuyuan China
71 A4	Wuzhishan China
70 A2	Wuzhong China
71 B3	Wuzhou China
53 C2	Wyangala Reservoir Austr.
52 B3	Wycheproof Austr.
99 B3	Wye *r.* U.K.
50 B1	Wyndham Austr.
142 B1	Wynne U.S.A.
129 D2	Wynyard Can.
136 B2	Wyoming *state* U.S.A.
103 E1	Wyszków Pol.
140 C3	Wytheville U.S.A.

X

117 D3	Xaafuun Somalia
62 B2	Xaignabouli Laos
121 C3	Xai-Xai Moz.
145 C3	Xalapa Mex.
70 A1	Xamba China
62 A1	Xamgyi'nyilha China
62 B1	Xam Nua Laos
120 A2	Xangongo Angola
81 C2	Xankändi Azer.
111 B2	Xanthi Greece

Xapuri

150 B3 Xapuri Brazil
107 C2 Xàtiva Spain
 Xiaguan China see Dali
71 B3 Xiamen China
70 A2 Xi'an China
70 A3 Xianfeng China
 Xiangjiang China see Huichang
71 B3 Xiangtan China
70 B2 Xiangyang China
70 B2 Xiantao China
70 A2 Xianyang China
70 B2 Xiaogan China
69 E1 Xiao Hinggan Ling mts China
70 C2 Xiaoshan China
62 B1 Xichang China
145 C2 Xicohténcatl Mex.
71 A3 Xifeng Guizhou China
75 C2 Xigazê China
83 I4 Xilinhot China
72 C2 Xincai China
68 C2 Xinghai China
70 B2 Xinghua China
71 B3 Xingning China
70 B2 Xingping China
70 B2 Xingtai China
151 C2 Xingu r. Brazil
71 A3 Xingyi China
71 B3 Xinhua China
68 C2 Xining China
 Xinjiang Uygur Autonomous Region aut. reg. China see Xinjiang Uygur Zizhiqu
75 C1 Xinjiang Uygur Zizhiqu aut. reg. China
 Xinjing China see Jingxi
65 A1 Xinmin China
71 B3 Xinning China
71 B3 Xintai China
70 B2 Xinxiang China
70 B2 Xinyang China
70 B2 Xinyi China
71 C3 Xinying Taiwan
71 B3 Xinyu China
69 D2 Xinzhou Shanxi China
70 B2 Xinzhou Shanxi China
71 C3 Xinzhu Taiwan
106 B1 Xinzo de Limia Spain
 Xiongshan China see Zhenghe
68 C2 Xiqing Shan mts China
151 D3 Xique Xique Brazil
70 A1 Xishanzui China
71 A3 Xiushan China
71 B3 Xiuying China
70 B2 Xixia China
 Xixón Spain see Gijón
68 B2 Xizang Zizhiqu aut. reg. China
76 B2 Xo'jayli Uzbek.
70 B2 Xuancheng China
71 A3 Xuanwei China
70 B2 Xuchang China
 Xucheng China see Xuwen
117 C4 Xuddur Somalia
 Xujiang China see Guangchang
71 B3 Xun Jiang r. China
107 C2 Xúquer, Riu r. Spain
71 B3 Xuwen China
71 A3 Xuyong China
70 B2 Xuzhou China

Y

117 B4 Yabēlo Eth.
69 D1 Yablonovyy Khrebet mts Rus. Fed.
143 D1 Yadkin r. U.S.A.
75 C3 Yadong China
89 E2 Yagnitsa Rus. Fed.
118 B3 Yagoua Cameroon
128 C3 Yahk Can.
144 B2 Yahualica Mex.
80 B2 Yahyalı Turkey
67 C4 Yaizu Japan
134 B1 Yakima U.S.A.
114 B3 Yako Burkina Faso
66 D2 Yakumo Japan
126 B3 Yakutat U.S.A.
83 J2 Yakutsk Rus. Fed.
91 D2 Yakymivka Ukr.
63 B3 Yala Thai.
53 C3 Yallourn Austr.
111 C2 Yalova Turkey
91 C3 Yalta Ukr.
65 A1 Yalu Jiang r. China/N. Korea
67 D3 Yamagata Japan
67 B4 Yamaguchi Japan
 Yamal, Poluostrov pen. Rus. Fed. see Yamal Peninsula
86 F1 Yamal Peninsula Rus. Fed.
53 D1 Yamba Austr.
117 A4 Yambio S. Sudan
110 C2 Yambol Bulg.
86 G2 Yamburg Rus. Fed.
62 A1 Yamethin Myanmar
114 B4 Yamoussoukro Côte d'Ivoire
90 B2 Yampil' Ukr.
75 C2 Yamuna r. India
75 D2 Yamzho Yumco l. China
83 K2 Yana r. Rus. Fed.
70 A2 Yan'an China
150 A3 Yanaoca Peru
78 A2 Yanbu' al Bahr Saudi Arabia
70 C2 Yancheng China
50 A3 Yanchep Austr.
70 B2 Yangcheng China
71 B3 Yangchun China
65 B2 Yangdok N. Korea
71 B3 Yangjiang China
 Yangôn Myanmar see Rangoon
70 B2 Yangquan China
71 B3 Yangshuo China
70 C3 Yangtze r. China
69 E2 Yangtze, Mouth of the China
70 B2 Yangzhou China
83 K2 Yano-Indigirskaya Nizmennost' lowland Rus. Fed.
83 K2 Yanskiy Zaliv g. Rus. Fed.
53 C1 Yantabulla Austr.
70 C2 Yantai China
118 B2 Yaoundé Cameroon
59 D2 Yap i. Micronesia
59 D3 Yapen i. Indon.
59 D3 Yapen, Selat sea chan. Indon.
144 A2 Yaqui r. Mex.
51 D2 Yaraka Austr.
86 D3 Yaransk Rus. Fed.
48 F2 Yaren Nauru
78 B3 Yarim Yemen
77 D3 Yarkant He r. China
75 D2 Yarlung Zangbo r. China
131 D2 Yarmouth Can.
86 F2 Yarono Rus. Fed.
89 E2 Yaroslavl' Rus. Fed.
66 B2 Yaroslavskiy Rus. Fed.

53 C3 Yarram Austr.
89 D2 Yartsevo Rus. Fed.
89 E3 Yasnogorsk Rus. Fed.
63 B2 Yasothon Thai.
53 C2 Yass Austr.
111 C3 Yatağan Turkey
129 E1 Yathkyed Lake Can.
67 B4 Yatsushiro Japan
150 B2 Yavari r. Brazil/Peru
75 B2 Yavatmal India
90 A2 Yavoriv Ukr.
67 B4 Yawatahama Japan
81 D2 Yazd Iran
142 B2 Yazoo City U.S.A.
111 B3 Ydra i. Greece
63 A2 Ye Myanmar
77 D3 Yecheng China
144 B2 Yécora Mex.
89 E3 Yefremov Rus. Fed.
89 E2 Yegor'yevsk Rus. Fed.
117 B4 Yei S. Sudan
86 F3 Yekaterinburg Rus. Fed.
77 D1 Yekibastuz Kazakh.
89 E3 Yelets Rus. Fed.
114 A3 Yélimané Mali
96 □ Yell i. U.K.
128 C1 Yellowknife Can.
70 B2 Yellow River r. China
69 E2 Yellow Sea N. Pacific Ocean
136 C1 Yellowstone r. U.S.A.
136 A2 Yellowstone Lake U.S.A.
88 C3 Yel'sk Belarus
78 B3 Yemen country Asia
86 E2 Yemva Rus. Fed.
91 D2 Yenakiyeve Ukr.
62 A1 Yenangyaung Myanmar
62 B1 Yên Bai Vietnam
114 B4 Yendi Ghana
111 C3 Yenice Turkey
111 C3 Yenifoça Turkey
62 C1 Yenisey r. Rus. Fed.
53 C2 Yeoval Austr.
99 B3 Yeovil U.K.
51 E2 Yeppoon Austr.
83 I2 Yerbogachen Rus. Fed.
81 C1 Yerevan Armenia
77 D1 Yereymentau Kazakh.
87 D3 Yershov Rus. Fed.
 Yertis r. Kazakh./Rus. Fed. see Irtysh
65 B2 Yesan S. Korea
77 C1 Yesil' Kazakh.
77 D1 Yesil' r. Kazakh./Rus. Fed.
111 C3 Yeşilova Turkey
99 A3 Yes Tor h. U.K.
53 D1 Yetman Austr.
62 A1 Ye-U Myanmar
104 B2 Yeu, Île d' i. France
91 C2 Yevpatoriya Ukr.
91 D2 Yeya r. Rus. Fed.
91 D2 Yeysk Rus. Fed.
88 C2 Yezyaryshcha Belarus
71 A3 Yibin China
71 A3 Yichang China
69 E1 Yichun Heilong. China
71 B3 Yichun Jiangxi China
110 C2 Yıldız Dağları mts Turkey
80 B2 Yıldızeli Turkey
70 A2 Yinchuan China
65 A3 Yingchengzi China
71 B3 Yingde China
70 C1 Yingkou China
70 B2 Yingshan Hubei China
70 A2 Yingshan Sichuan China
71 B3 Yingtan China
77 E2 Yining China
117 B4 Yirga Alem Eth.